Collins
Spanish
School
Dictionary

Collins
gem

HarperCollins Publishers
Westerhill Road
Bishopbriggs
Glasgow
G64 2QT
Great Britain

First Edition 2006

Reprint 10 9 8 7 6 5 4

© HarperCollins Publishers
2006

ISBN 978-0-00-720888-3

Collins Gem® and Bank of
English® are registered
trademarks of HarperCollins
Publishers Limited

www.collins.co.uk

A catalogue record for this
book is available from the
British Library

Typeset by Thomas Callan
Supplement typeset by
Davidson Pre-Press, Glasgow

Printed in Italy by
Legoprint S.p.A.

Acknowledgements

We would like to thank those
authors and publishers who
kindly gave permission for
copyright material to be used
in the Collins Word Web. We
would also like to thank Time
Newspapers Ltd for providing
valuable data.

MANAGING EDITOR
Michela Clari

EDITORS
Maree Airlie
Cordelia Lilly
Julie Muleba
Marianne Noble

SERIES EDITOR
Lorna Knight

CONTENTS

Acknowledgements
Syllabus lists and exam papers were carefully studied when compiling this dictionary. We are grateful to all those teachers and students who have contributed to the development of the Collins Spanish School Dictionary by advising us on how to tailor it to their needs.

William Collins' dream of knowledge for all began with the publication of his first book in 1819. A self-educated mill worker, he not only enriched millions of lives, but also founded a flourishing publishing house. Today, staying true to this spirit, Collins books are packed with inspiration, innovation, and practical expertise. They place you at the centre of a world of possibility and give you exactly what you need to explore it.

Language is the key to this exploration, and at the heart of Collins Dictionaries is language as it is really used. New words, phrases, and meanings spring up every day, and all of them are captured and analysed by the Collins Word Web. Constantly updated, and with over 2.5 billion entries, this living language resource is unique to our dictionaries.

Words are tools for life. And a Collins Dictionary makes them work for you.

Collins. Do more.

USING THIS DICTIONARY

The *Collins Spanish School Dictionary* is designed specifically for anyone starting to learn Spanish, and has been carefully researched with teachers and students. It is very straightforward, with an accessible layout that is easy on the eye, guiding students quickly to the right translation. It also offers essential help on Spanish culture.

This section gives useful tips on how to use the *Collins Spanish School Dictionary* effectively.

▷ Make sure you look in the right side of the dictionary
There are two sides in a bilingual dictionary. Here, the Spanish-English side comes first, and the second part is English-Spanish. At the top of each page there is a reminder of which side of the dictionary you have open. The middle pages of the book have a blue border so you can see where one side finishes and the other one starts.

▷ Finding the word you want
To help you find a word more quickly, use the alphabet tabs down the side of the page, then look at the words in blue at the top of pages. They show the first and last words on the two pages where the dictionary is open.

▷ Make sure you use the right part of speech
Some entries are split into several parts of speech. For example 'glue' can either be a noun ("Can I borrow your glue?") or a verb ("Glue this into your exercise book"). Parts of speech within an entry are separated by a black triangle ▶ and are given on a new line. They are given in their abbreviated form (*n* for noun, *adj* for adjective, etc). For the full list of abbreviations, look at page viii.

    glue *n* pegamento *m*
     ▶ *vb* pegar

▷ Choosing the right translation

The main translation of a word is underlined and is shown after the part of speech. If there is more than one main translation for a word, each one is numbered. You may also sometimes find bracketed words in *italics* which give you some context. They help you to choose the translation you want.

> **pool** n ❶ (*pond*) estanque m
> ❷ (*swimming pool*) piscina f
> ❸ (*game*) billar m americano

Often you will see phrases in *italics*, preceded by a white triangle ▷. These are examples of the word being used in context. Examples in **bold type** are phrases which are particularly common and important. Sometimes these phrases have a completely different translation.

> **bolsa** nf ❶ bag ▷ *una bolsa de plástico* a plastic bag; ▷ *una bolsa de viaje* a travel bag ❷ (*in Mexico*) handbag; **la Bolsa** the Stock Exchange

Once you have found the right translation, remember that you may need to adapt the Spanish word you have found. You may need to make a noun plural, or make an adjective feminine or plural. Remember that the feminine form is given for nouns and irregular adjectives, and that irregular plural forms are given also.

> **lawyer** n abogado m, abogada f
> **garden** n jardín m (pl jardines)
> **bossy** adj mandón (f mandona)
> (mpl mandones)

You may also need to adapt the verb. Verbs are given in the infinitive form, but you may want to use them in the present, past or future tense. To do this, use the verb tables in the last section of the dictionary. Verbs on the Spanish-English side are usually followed by a number in square brackets. This number corresponds to a page number in the verb tables at the back of the dictionary.

In the following example, cambiar follows the same pattern as hablar, shown on page 26 in the verb tables.

cambiar [26] *vb* ❶ to change

▷ Find out more

In the *Collins Spanish School Dictionary*, you will find lots of extra information about the Spanish language. These usage notes help you understand how the language works and draw your attention to false friends (words which look similar but have a different meaning).

malo *adj*

▌ **malo** is shortened to **mal**
▌ before masculine singular nouns.

❶ bad ▷ *un mal día* a bad day

librería *nf* ❶ bookshop

❷ bookshelf

▌ Be careful! **librería** does not mean
▌ **library**.

You can also find out more about life in Spain and Spanish-speaking countries by reading the cultural notes.

Nochevieja *nf* New Year's Eve

▌ At midnight on New Year's Eve
▌ in Spain it is traditional to eat
▌ **las uvas de la suerte** (twelve
▌ good-luck grapes) to the chimes
▌ of Madrid's **Puerta del Sol** clock,
▌ which are broadcast live.

▷ Remember!

Never take the first translation you see without looking at the others. Always look to see if there is more than one translation, or more than one part of speech.

ABBREVIATIONS USED IN THIS DICTIONARY

abbr	abbreviation
adj	adjective
adv	adverb
art	article
conj	conjunction
def art	definite article
excl	exclamation
f	feminine
indef art	indefinite article
inv	invariable form, the same for *m*, *f* and *pl*
LatAm	Latin America
m	masculine
n	noun
neut	neuter
nf	feminine noun
nm	masculine noun
nmf	masculine or feminine noun
nm/f	masculine or feminine noun
npl	plural noun
num	number
pl	plural
prep	preposition
pron	pronoun
sg	singular
Sp	Spain
vb	verb

SYMBOLS

▷	example
▶	new part of speech
❷	new meaning
[29]	verb table number (see Verb Tables section at the back of the dictionary)

TIME

¿Qué hora es? What time is it?	¿A qué hora? What time?
 Es la una	 a medianoche
 Es la una y diez	 al mediodía
 Es la una y cuarto	 a la una (de la tarde)
 Es la una y media	 a las nueve (de la noche)
 Son las dos menos veinte	 las 11:15 *or* las once quince
 Son las dos menos cuarto	 las 20:45 *or* las veinte cuarenta y cinco

DATES

▷ Days of the Week

lunes	Monday
martes	Tuesday
miércoles	Wednesday
jueves	Thursday
viernes	Friday
sábado	Saturday
domingo	Sunday

▷ Months of the Year

enero	January	**julio**	July
febrero	February	**agosto**	August
marzo	March	**septiembre**	September
abril	April	**octubre**	October
mayo	May	**noviembre**	November
junio	June	**diciembre**	December

▷ ¿Cuándo?
en febrero
el uno de diciembre
de 2006
en dos mil seis

▷ When?
in February
on the first of December
2006
in two thousand and six

▷ ¿Qué día es hoy?
Es...
lunes, veintiséis de mayo

▷ What day is it?
It's...
Monday, 26th May *or*
Monday, the twenty-sixth of May

NUMBERS

▷ **Cardinal numbers**

1	uno	22	veintidós
2	dos	30	treinta
3	tres	31	treinta y uno
4	cuatro	40	cuarenta
5	cinco	41	cuarenta y uno
6	seis	50	cincuenta
7	siete	60	sesenta
8	ocho	70	setenta
9	nueve	80	ochenta
10	diez	90	noventa
11	once	100	cien
12	doce	101	ciento uno
13	trece	200	doscientos
14	catorce	201	doscientos uno
15	quince	500	quinientos
16	dieciséis	700	setecientos
17	diecisiete	900	novecientos
18	dieciocho	1000	mil
19	diecinueve	1001	mil uno
20	veinte	1,000,000	un millón
21	veintiuno		

▷ **Fractions etc**

1/2	un medio	0.5	cero coma cinco
1/3	un tercio	10%	diez por ciento
1/4	un cuarto	100%	cien por cien
1/5	un quinto		

NUMBERS

▷ Ordinal numbers

1st	primero
2nd	segundo
3rd	tercero
4th	cuarto
5th	quinto
6th	sexto
7th	séptimo
8th	octavo
9th	noveno
10th	décimo
11th	decimoprimero
12th	decimosegundo
13th	decimotercero
14th	decimocuarto
15th	decimoquinto
16th	decimosexto
17th	decimoséptimo
18th	decimoctavo
19th	decimonoveno
20th	vigésimo
21st	vigésimo primero
30th	trigésimo
100th	centésimo
101st	centésimo primero
1000th	milésimo

a *prep*

■ **a + el = al**.

❶ **to** ▷ *Fueron a Madrid.* They went to Madrid. ▷ *Se lo di a Ana.* I gave it to Ana. ▷ *Voy a verle.* I'm going to see him. ▷ *Me obligaban a comer.* They forced me to eat.; **Gira a la derecha.** Turn right.; **Me voy a casa.** I'm going home.; **Me caí al río.** I fell into the river.; **Se subieron al tejado.** They climbed onto the roof.; **Se lo compré a él.** I bought it from him.; **¡A comer!** Lunch is ready!; **Está a 15 km de aquí.** It's 15 km from here.

■ Personal **a** (**a** used between a verb and its direct object when this is a noun referring to a person) isn't translated into English.

▷ *Vi a Juan.* I saw Juan. ▷ *Llamé al médico.* I called the doctor.

■ **a** before an indirect object is sometimes not translated into English.

▷ *Le enseñé a Pablo el libro que me dejaste.* I showed Pablo the book you lent me. ❸ **at** ▷ *a las 10 a 10* o'clock ▷ *a medianoche* at midnight ▷ *a los 24 años* at the age of 24 ▷ *Íbamos a más de 90 km por hora.* We were going at over 90 km an hour.; **Marta llegó a la oficina.** Marta arrived at the office.; **Estamos a 9 de julio.** It's the 9th of July.; **Los huevos están a 1,50 euros la docena.** Eggs are 1.50 euros a dozen.; **una vez a la semana** once a week; **Al verlo, lo reconocí inmediatamente.** When I saw him, I recognized him immediately.; **Nos cruzamos al salir.** We bumped into each other as we were going out.

abadía *nf* **abbey**

abajo *adv* ❶ **below** ▷ *desde abajo* from below; **Mete las cervezas abajo del todo.** Put the beers at the bottom.; **El estante de abajo.** The bottom shelf.; **la parte de abajo del contenedor** the bottom of the container ❷ **downstairs** ▷ *Hay una fiesta en el piso de abajo.* There's a party in the flat downstairs.; **aquí abajo** down here; **allí abajo** down there; **más abajo** further down; **ir calle abajo** to go down the street; **Todos los bolsos son de 50 euros para**

abajo. All the bags are 50 euros or under.; **abajo de** (in Latin America) under

abandonado adj **un pueblo abandonado** a deserted village

abandonar [26] vb ❶ to leave ▷ *Decidieron abandonar el país.* They decided to leave the country. ❷ to abandon ❸ to give up (plan, idea)

abanico nm fan

abarrotado adj packed ▷ *abarrotado de gente* packed with people

abarrotería nf (in Mexico) grocer's

abarrotes nmpl (in Mexico, Chile) groceries

abastecer [13] vb **abastecer de algo a alguien** to supply somebody with something; **abastecerse de** to stock up with

abdomen (pl abdómenes) nm stomach

abdominales nmpl sit-ups

abecedario nm alphabet

abeja nf bee

abeto nm fir

abierto vb see **abrir**

▶ adj ❶ open ▷ *¿Están abiertas las tiendas?* Are the shops open? ❷ on ▷ *No dejes el gas abierto.* Don't leave the gas on.

abogado, -a nm/f lawyer

abolir vb to abolish

abollar [26] vb to dent; **abollarse** to get dented

abombarse [26] vb (in Latin America) to go bad

abonar [26] vb ❶ to pay ❷ to

fertilize; **abonarse a** (1) to take out a subscription to (2) to join

abono nm ❶ fertilizer ❷ season ticket

abortar [26] vb ❶ to have an abortion ❷ to miscarry

aborto nm ❶ abortion ❷ miscarriage

abrasar [26] vb to burn; **abrasarse** to be burned

abrazar [14] vb to hug ▷ *Al verme me abrazó.* He hugged me when he saw me.; **abrazarse** to hug ▷ *Se abrazaron y se besaron.* They hugged and kissed.

abrazo nm hug ▷ *¡Dame un abrazo!* Give me a hug!; **"un abrazo"** "with best wishes"; **"un fuerte abrazo"** "love from"

abrebotellas (pl abrebotellas) nm bottle opener

abrelatas (pl abrelatas) nm tin opener

abreviatura nf abbreviation

abridor nm ❶ bottle opener ❷ tin opener

abrigar [38] vb to be warm (clothing); **Ponte algo que te abrigue.** Put something warm on.; **Abriga bien al niño, que hace frío.** Wrap the little one up well, it's cold.; **abrigarse** to wrap up well

abrigo nm coat; **ropa de abrigo** warm clothing

abril nm

Months start with a small letter in Spanish.

April

abrir [1] vb ➊ to open ▷ *Las tiendas abren a las diez.* The shops open at ten o'clock. ▷ *Abre la ventana.* Open the window. ➋ to turn on (*tap, gas*); **abrirse** to open (*door*)

abrocharse [26] vb to do up; **Abróchense los cinturones.** Please fasten your seatbelts.

absoluto adj absolute ▷ *Nos dio garantía absoluta.* He gave us an absolute guarantee.; **La operación fue un éxito absoluto.** The operation was a complete success.; **¿Te molesta que fume? - En absoluto.** Do you mind if I smoke? - Not at all.; **nada en absoluto** nothing at all

absorber [9] vb to absorb

abstemio adj teetotal

abstención (*pl* abstenciones) nf abstention

abstenerse [54] vb to abstain

abstracto adj abstract

absurdo adj absurd

abuela nf grandmother ▷ *mi abuela* my grandmother; **¿Dónde está la abuela?** Where's Gran?

abuelo nm grandfather ▷ *mi abuelo* my grandfather; **¿Dónde está el abuelo?** Where's Grandad?; **mis abuelos** my grandparents

abultado adj bulky

abultar [26] vb to be bulky; **Tus cosas apenas abultan.** Your things hardly take up any space at all.

abundante adj plenty of ▷ *Habrá comida y bebida abundante.* There'll be plenty of food and drink.

aburrido adj ➊ bored ▷ *Estaba aburrida y me marché.* I was bored so I left. ➋ boring ▷ *una película muy aburrida* a very boring film

aburrimiento nm ¡Qué aburrimiento! What a bore this is!; **Estoy muerto de aburrimiento.** I'm bored stiff.

aburrirse [59] vb to get bored

abusar [26] vb abusar de alguien (1) to take advantage of somebody (2) to abuse somebody; **Está bien beber de vez en cuando pero sin abusar.** Drinking every so often is fine as long as you don't overdo it.; **No conviene abusar del aceite en las comidas.** You shouldn't use too much oil in food.

abuso nm abuse ▷ *el abuso de las drogas* drug abuse; **Lo que han hecho me parece un abuso.** I think what they've done is outrageous.

acá adv here; **Hay que ponerlo más acá.** You'll have to bring it nearer.

acabar [26] vb to finish; **Ayer acabé de pintar la valla.** I finished painting the fence yesterday.; **acabar con** (1) to put an end to (2) to finish up; **Acabo de ver a tu padre.** I've just seen your father. ▷ *Acababa de entrar cuando sonó el teléfono.* I'd just come in when the phone rang.; **acabarse** to run out ▷ *Se me acabó el tabaco.* I ran out of cigarettes.

academia nf school ▷ *una academia de idiomas* a language school

académico adj academic ▷ el curso académico the academic year

acampada nf ir de acampada to go camping

acampar [26] vb to camp

acantilado nm cliff

acariciar [26] vb ① to stroke ② to caress

acaso adv por si acaso just in case; **No necesito nada; si acaso, un poco de leche.** I don't need anything; well maybe a little milk.; **Si acaso lo vieras, dile que me llame.** If you should see him, tell him to call me.

acatarrarse [26] vb to catch a cold

acceder [9] vb acceder a (1) to agree to (2) to gain access to

accesible adj ① accessible ② approachable

acceso nm access; **las pruebas de acceso a la universidad** university entrance exams

accesorio nm accessory

accidentado adj ① rough ② eventful

accidente nm accident ▷ Han tenido un accidente. They've had an accident.

acción (pl acciones) nf ① action; **entrar en acción** to go into action ② share (in company)

accionista nmf shareholder

aceite nm oil; **el aceite de girasol** sunflower oil; **el aceite de oliva** olive oil

aceitoso adj oily

aceituna nf olive ▷ aceitunas rellenas stuffed olives

acelerador nm accelerator

acelerar [26] vb to accelerate; **¡Acelera, que no llegamos!** Speed up or we'll never get there!; **acelerar el paso** to walk faster

acelgas nfpl spinach beet

acento nm ① accent ② stress

acentuarse [2] vb to have an accent ▷ No se acentúa. It doesn't have an accent.

aceptable adj acceptable

aceptar [26] vb to accept; **aceptar hacer algo** to agree to do something

acequia nf irrigation channel

acera nf pavement

acerca adv acerca de about ▷ un documental acerca de la fauna africana a documentary about African wildlife

acercar [49] vb to pass ▷ ¿Me acercas los alicates? Could you pass me the pliers?; **Acerca la silla.** Bring your chair over here.; ¿Acerco más la cama a la ventana? Shall I move the bed nearer the window?; **Nos acercaron al aeropuerto.** They gave us a lift to the airport.; **acercarse** (1) to come closer ▷ Acércate, que te veo. Come closer so that I can see you. (2) to go over ▷ Me acerqué a la ventana. I went over to the window.; **Ya se acerca la Navidad.** Christmas is getting near.

acero nm steel ▷ acero inoxidable

stainless steel

acertar [**40**] *vb* ❶ **to get…right**
▷ *He acertado todas las respuestas.*
I got all the answers right.; **No acerté.** I got it wrong.; **Creo que hemos acertado con estas cortinas.** I think these curtains were a good choice. ❷ **to guess** (correctly); **Acerté en el blanco.** I hit the target.

ácido *adj, nm* acid

acierto *vb see* **acertar**
▶ *nm* ❶ **right answer** ❷ **good idea** ▷ *Fue un acierto ir de vacaciones a la playa.* It was a good idea to have a holiday at the seaside.

aclarar [**26**] *vb* ❶ **to rinse** (washing) ❷ **to clear up** (doubts, matter); **Con tantos números no me aclaro.** With all these numbers I can't get my head round it.

acné *nm* acne

acobardarse [**26**] *vb* **No se acobarda por nada.** He isn't frightened by anything.

acogedor, a *adj* cosy ▷ *un cuarto muy acogedor* a very cosy room

acoger [**8**] *vb* ❶ **to receive**; **Me acogieron muy bien en Estados Unidos.** I was made very welcome in the United States. ❷ **to take in** (guest, refugee)

acogida *nf* reception ▷ *una fría acogida* a cold reception; **una calurosa acogida** a warm welcome; **tener buena acogida** to be well received

acomodado *adj* well-off

acomodador *nm* usher

acomodadora *nf* usherette

acompañar [**26**] *vb* ❶ **to come with** ❷ **to go with** ▷ *Me pidió que la acompañara a la estación.* She asked me to go to the station with her.; **¿Quieres que te acompañe a casa?** Would you like me to see you home?; **Me acompañó hasta que llegó el autobús.** He kept me company until the bus came.

aconsejar [**26**] *vb* ❶ **to advise**; **aconsejar a alguien que haga algo** to advise somebody to do something; **Te aconsejo que lo hagas.** I'd advise you to do it. ❷ **to recommend**

acontecimiento *nm* event

acordar [**12**] *vb* **to agree on**; **acordar hacer algo** to agree to do something

acordarse [**12**] *vb* **to remember**
▷ *No me acuerdo.* I can't remember.; **acordarse de** to remember ▷ *¿Te acuerdas de mí?* Do you remember me? ▷ *Acuérdate de cerrar la puerta con llave.* Remember to lock the door.; **acordarse de haber hecho algo** to remember doing something

acordeón (*pl* acordeones) *nm* accordion

acortar [**26**] *vb* **to shorten**

acostado *adj* **estar acostado** to be in bed

acostarse [**12**] *vb* ❶ **to lie down** ❷ **to go to bed**; **acostarse con alguien** to go to bed with somebody

acostumbrarse [**26**] *vb*

acostumbrarse a algo to get used to something; **acostumbrarse a hacer algo** to get used to doing something

acróbata nmf acrobat

actitud nf attitude

actividad nf activity

activo adj active

acto nm ❶ act ❷ ceremony; **acto seguido** immediately afterwards; **en el acto** instantly; **Te arreglan tus zapatos en el acto.** They repair your shoes while you wait.

actor nm actor

actriz (pl **actrices**) nf actress

actuación (pl **actuaciones**) nf performance

actual adj ❶ present ❷ current; **uno de los mejores pintores del arte actual** one of the greatest painters of today

> Be careful! **actual** does not mean actual.

actualidad nf **un repaso a la actualidad nacional** a round-up of the national news; **un tema de gran actualidad** a very topical issue; **en la actualidad** (1) currently (2) nowadays

actualmente adv ❶ nowadays ❷ currently

> Be careful! **actualmente** does not mean actually.

actuar [2] vb ❶ to act; **No actuó en esa película.** He wasn't in that film.; **Hay que actuar con cautela.** We'll have to be cautious. ❷ to perform

acuarela nf watercolour

acuario nm aquarium

Acuario nm Aquarius (sign); **Soy acuario.** I'm Aquarius.

acuático adj **esquí acuático** water skiing; **aves acuáticas** waterfowl

acudir [59] vb ❶ to go ▷ Acudió a un amigo en busca de consejo. He went to a friend for advice.; **No tengo a quien acudir.** I have no one to turn to.; **acudir a una cita** to keep an appointment ❷ to come ▷ El perro acude cuando lo llamo. The dog comes when I call.

acuerdo vb see **acordar**
  ▶ nm agreement ▷ llegar a un acuerdo to reach an agreement; **estar de acuerdo con alguien** to agree with somebody; **ponerse de acuerdo** to agree ▷ Al final no nos pusimos de acuerdo. In the end we couldn't agree.; **¡De acuerdo!** All right!

acupuntura nf acupuncture

acurrucarse [26] vb to curl up

acusar [26] vb ❶ to accuse ❷ to charge

acústico adj acoustic ▷ una guitarra acústica an acoustic guitar

adaptar [26] vb to adapt; **adaptarse** to adapt

adecuado adj ❶ suitable ▷ No es la ropa más adecuada para ir de boda. They aren't the most suitable clothes to wear to a wedding. ❷ right ▷ el hombre adecuado para el puesto the right man for the job

a: de J.C. abbr (= antes de Jesucristo) B.C. (= before Christ)

adelantado adj ❶ advanced
▷ Suecia es un país muy adelantado.
Sweden is a very advanced
country.; **los niños más
adelantados de la clase** the
children who are doing best in
the class ❷ fast ▷ Este reloj va
adelantado. This watch is fast.;
pagar por adelantado to pay in
advance

adelantar [26] vb ❶ to bring...
forward ▷ Tuvimos que adelantar
la boda. We had to bring the
wedding forward. ❷ to overtake
▷ Adelanta ese camión cuando
puedas. Overtake that lorry when
you can. ❸ to put...forward ▷ El
domingo hay que adelantar los relojes
una hora. On Sunday we'll have to
put the clocks forward an hour.;
Así no adelantas nada. You won't
get anywhere that way.; **Tu reloj
adelanta.** Your watch gains.

adelantarse vb to go on ahead;
adelantarse a alguien to get
ahead of somebody

adelante adv forward; **Se
inclinó hacia adelante.** He leant
forward.; **¿Nos vamos adelante
para ver mejor?** Shall we sit near
the front to get a better view?;
más adelante (1) further on
(2) later; **adelante de** (in Latin
America) in front of; **Hay que
seguir adelante.** We must go
on.; **de ahora en adelante** from
now on
▶ excl ❶ come on! ❷ come in!

adelanto nm advance

adelgazar [14] vb to lose weight
▷ ¡Cómo has adelgazado! What
a lot of weight you've lost!; **He
adelgazado cinco kilos.** I've lost
five kilos.

además adv ❶ what's more
▷ El baño es demasiado pequeño
y, además, no tiene ventana. The
bathroom's too small; what's
more it hasn't got a window.
❷ besides ▷ Además, no tienes
nada que perder. Besides, you've
got nothing to lose. ❸ also ▷ Es
profesor y además carpintero. He's
a teacher and also a carpenter.;
además de as well as

adentro adv inside; **adentro de** (in
Latin America) inside

adhesivo adj sticky ▷ cinta
adhesiva sticky tape
▶ nm sticker

adicción (pl adicciones) nf
addiction

adición (pl adiciones) nf (in River
Plate) bill

adicto, -a nm/f addict ▷ un adicto a
las drogas a drug addict
▶ adj addicted ▷ Es adicto a la
cafeína. He is addicted to caffeine.

adinerado adj wealthy

adiós excl ❶ goodbye!; **decir
adiós a alguien** to say goodbye to
somebody ❷ hello! (on passing)

aditivo nm additive

adivinanza nf guess

adivinar [26] vb to guess ▷ Adivina
quién viene. Guess who's coming.;
adivinar el futuro to see into
the future

a
b
c
d
e
f
g
h
i
j
k
l
m
n
o
p
q
r
s
t
u
v
w
x
y
z

adjetivo nm adjective

adjunto adj ❶ enclosed
❷ attached ▷ deputy ▷ el director
adjunto the deputy head

administración (pl
administraciones) nf
administration; **administración
pública** civil service

**administrador de Web,
administradora de Web** nm/f
webmaster

administrativo, -a nm/f clerk
▸ adj administrative

admiración nf ❶ admiration
❷ amazement ▷ para admiración
de todos to everyone's amazement;
signo de admiración exclamation
mark

admirar [26] vb to admire

admitir [59] vb ❶ to admit
▷ Admite que estabas equivocado.
Admit you were wrong. ❷ to
accept; **Espero que me admitan
a la universidad.** I hope I'll get a
place at university. ❸ to allow
in ▷ Aquí no admiten perros. Dogs
aren't allowed in here.

adolescente nmf teenager

adonde conj where; **la ciudad
adonde nos dirigimos** the city
we're going to

adónde adv where

adopción (pl adopciones) nf
adoption

adoptar [26] vb to adopt

adoptivo adj ❶ adopted; **un
hijo adoptivo** an adopted
child ❷ adoptive; **mis padres
adoptivos** my adoptive parents

adorar [26] vb ❶ to adore ❷ to
worship

adornar [26] vb to decorate

adorno nm ❶ ornament
❷ decoration ▷ Es sólo de adorno.
It's only for decoration.

adosado adj **un chalet adosado** a
semi-detached house

adquirir [3] vb to acquire; **adquirir
velocidad** to gain speed; **adquirir
fama** to achieve fame; **adquirir
una vivienda** to purchase a
property; **adquirir importancia**
to become important

adrede adv on purpose

ADSL nm broadband

aduana nf customs

aduanero, -a nm/f customs
officer

adulto, -a nm/f adult

adverbio nm adverb

adversario, -a nm/f opponent

advertencia nf warning

advertir [52] vb ❶ to warn ▷ Ya te
advertí que no intervinieras. I warned
you not to get involved.; **advertir
a alguien de algo** to warn
somebody about something; **Te
advierto que no va a ser nada
fácil.** I warn you that it won't be at
all easy. ❷ to notice ▷ No advertí
nada extraño en su comportamiento.
I didn't notice anything strange
about his behaviour.

aéreo adj air; **por vía aérea** by air
mail; **una fotografía aérea** an
aerial photograph

aerobic nm aerobics

aeromozo, -a nm/f (in Latin

America) flight attendant

aeropuerto nm airport

aerosol nm aerosol

afán (pl afanes) nm ❶ desire ❸ effort; Trabajan con mucho afán. They put a lot of effort into their work.

afectado adj upset

afectar [26] vb to affect ▷ Esto a ti no te afecta. This doesn't affect you.; **Me afectó mucho la noticia.** The news upset me terribly.

afectivo adj emotional ▷ problemas afectivos emotional problems

afecto nm affection; tener afecto a alguien to be fond of somebody

afectuoso adj affectionate; "Un saludo afectuoso" "With best wishes"

afeitar [26] vb to shave; afeitarse to shave; Me afeité la barba. I shaved off my beard.

Afganistán nm Afghanistan

afiche nm (in Latin America) poster

afición (pl aficiones) nf ❶ hobby ▷ Mi afición es la filatelia. My hobby is stamp collecting. ▷ por afición as a hobby; Tengo mucha afición por el ciclismo. I'm very keen on cycling. ❷ fans ▷ la afición del Athletic the Athletic fans

aficionado, -a nm/f ❶ enthusiast ▷ los aficionados al bricolaje DIY enthusiasts ❷ lover ▷ los aficionados al teatro theatre lovers ❸ amateur ▷ un partido para aficionados a game for amateurs

▶ adj ❶ keen ▷ Es muy aficionada a la pintura. She's very keen on painting. ❷ amateur ▷ un equipo de fútbol aficionado an amateur football team

aficionarse [26] vb aficionarse a algo (1) to become interested in something (2) to take up something

afilado adj sharp

afilar [26] vb to sharpen

afiliarse [26] vb afiliarse a algo to join something

afinar [26] vb to tune ▷ afinar un violín to tune a violin

afirmar [26] vb afirmar que … to say that …; Afirma haberla visto aquella noche. He says that he saw her that night.

afirmativo adj affirmative

aflojar [26] vb to loosen; Tengo que aflojarme la corbata. I must loosen my tie.; aflojarse to come loose

afónico adj Estoy afónico. I've lost my voice.

afortunadamente adv fortunately

afortunado adj lucky ▷ Es un tipo afortunado. He's a lucky guy.

África nf Africa

africano, -a nm/f, adj African

afrontar [26] vb to face up to

afuera adv outside ▷ Vámonos afuera. Let's go outside.; afuera de (in Latin America) outside

afueras nfpl outskirts ▷ en las afueras de Barcelona on the outskirts of Barcelona

a
b
c
d
e
f
g
h
i
j
k
l
m
n
o
p
q
r
s
t
u
v
w
x
y
z

agacharse [26] vb ❶ to crouch down ❷ to bend down

agarradera nf (in Latin America) handle

agarrado adj stingy

agarrar [26] vb ❶ to grab ▷ Agarró al niño por el hombro. He grabbed the child by the shoulder. ❷ to hold ▷ Agarra bien la sartén. Hold the frying pan firmly. ❸ to catch ▷ Ya han agarrado al ladrón. They've already caught the thief. ❹ (in Latin America) to take ▷ Agarré otro pedazo de pastel. I took another piece of cake.; **agarrarse** to hold on

agencia nf agency; **una agencia inmobiliaria** an estate agent's; **una agencia de viajes** a travel agent's

agenda nf ❶ diary ❷ address book

▌Be careful! **agenda** does not mean **agenda**.

agente nmf agent; **un agente de bolsa** a stockbroker; **un agente de seguros** an insurance broker; **un agente de policía** a police officer

ágil adj agile

agitado adj hectic (life)

agitar [26] vb ❶ to stir (tea, coffee) ❷ to shake ▷ Agítese antes de usar. Shake before use. ❸ to wave ▷ La gente agitaba los pañuelos. People were waving their handkerchiefs.

aglomerarse [26] vb **La gente se aglomeraba a la entrada.** People were crowding around the entrance.

agobiante adj ❶ stifling

❷ overwhelming ❸ exhausting

agobiar [26] vb **Le agobian sus problemas.** His problems are getting on top of him.; **agobiarse** to worry

agosto nm

▌Months start with a small letter in Spanish.

August

agotado adj ❶ exhausted ▷ Estoy agotado. I'm exhausted. ❷ sold out ▷ Ese modelo en concreto está agotado. That particular model is sold out.

agotador, a adj exhausting

agotar [26] vb ❶ to use up ❷ to tire out; **agotarse** to run out; **Se agotaron todas las entradas.** The tickets sold out.

agradable adj nice

agradar [26] vb **Esto no me agrada.** I don't like this.

agradecer [13] vb agradecer algo a alguien to thank somebody for something; **Te agradezco tu interés.** Thank you for your interest.; **Le agradecería me enviara ...** I should be grateful if you would send me ...

agradecido adj **estar agradecido a alguien por algo** to be grateful to somebody for something

agrado nm **No fue de mi agrado.** It was not to my liking.

agredir [59] vb to attack

agresión (pl agresiones) nf ❶ aggression ❷ attack

agresivo adj aggressive

agrícola adj agricultural

agricultor, a nm/f farmer

agricultura nf farming

agridulce adj sweet-and-sour

agrio adj sour

agrupación (pl **agrupaciones**) nf group

agrupar [26] vb ① to group ② to bring together; **Los ecologistas se han agrupado en varios partidos.** The ecologists have formed several parties.; **Se agruparon en torno a su jefe.** They gathered round their boss.

agua nf water; **agua corriente** running water; **agua potable** drinking water; **agua dulce** fresh water; **agua salada** salt water; **agua de colonia** cologne; **agua oxigenada** peroxide

aguacate nm avocado

aguafiestas (pl **aguafiestas**) nmf spoilsport

aguanieve nf sleet

aguantar [26] vb ① to stand ▷ No aguanto la ópera. I can't stand opera. ② to take ▷ La estantería no va a aguantar el peso. The shelf won't take the weight. ▷ ¡No aguanto más! I can't take any more! ③ to hold ▷ Aguántame el martillo un momento. Can you hold the hammer for me for a moment? ▷ Aguanta la respiración. Hold your breath. ④ to last ▷ Este abrigo ya no aguanta otro invierno. This coat won't last another winter.; **No pude aguantar la risa.** I couldn't help laughing.; **Últimamente estás que no hay quien te**

aguante. You've been unbearable lately.; **¿Puedes aguantarte hasta que lleguemos a casa?** Can you hold out until we get home?; **Si no puede venir, que se aguante.** If he can't come, he'll just have to get on with it.

aguante nm tener aguante (1) to be patient (2) to have stamina

aguardar [26] vb to wait for

agudo adj ① sharp (hearing, pain) ② high-pitched (sound, voice) ③ acute (illness) ④ witty (comment)

aguijón (pl **aguijones**) nm sting

águila nf eagle

aguja nf ① needle (for sewing) ② hand (of clock)

agujero nm ① hole; hacer un agujero to make a hole ② pocket

agujeta nf (in Mexico) shoe lace

agujetas nfpl tener agujetas to be stiff

ahí adv there ▷ ¡Ahí están! There they are!; **Ahí está el problema.** That's the problem.; **ahí arriba** up there; **Están ahí dentro.** They're in there.; **de ahí que** that's why; **por ahí (1)** over there **(2)** somewhere ▷ Nos iremos por ahí a celebrarlo. We'll go out somewhere to celebrate.; **¿Las tijeras? Andarán por ahí.** The scissors? They must be somewhere around. **(3)** thereabouts

ahogarse [38] vb ① to drown ② to suffocate ③ to get out of breath

ahora adv now ▷ ¿Dónde vamos

ahora? Where are we going now?; **Ahora te lo digo.** I'll tell you in a moment.; **ahora mismo** right now; **Ahora mismo voy.** I'm just coming.; **de ahora en adelante** from now on; **hasta ahora (1)** so far **(2)** till now; **¡Hasta ahora!** See you shortly!; **por ahora** for the moment

ahorcar [49] vb to hang; **ahorcarse** to hang oneself

ahorita adv (in Latin America) now

ahorrar [26] vb to save

ahorros nmpl savings

ahumado adj smoked

aire nm ❶ air; **aire acondicionado** air conditioning; **tomar el aire** to get some fresh air ❷ wind ▷ El aire se le llevó el sombrero. The wind blew his hat off.; **Hace mucho aire.** It's very windy.; **al aire libre (1)** outdoors ▷ Comimos al aire libre. We had lunch outdoors. **(2)** outdoor ▷ una fiesta al aire libre an outdoor party

aislado adj isolated ▷ Es un caso aislado. It's an isolated case.; **El pueblo estaba aislado por la nieve.** The village was cut off by the snow.

ajedrez (pl ajedreces) nm ❶ chess ▷ jugar al ajedrez to play chess ❷ chess set

ajeno adj **No respeta la opinión ajena.** He doesn't respect other people's opinions.; **por razones ajenas a nuestra voluntad** for reasons beyond our control

ajetreado adj busy (day)

ají nm (in River Plate) chili sauce

ajo nm garlic

ajustado adj tight

ajustar [26] vb ❶ to adjust ❷ to tighten ❸ to fit

al prep see **a**

ala nf ❶ wing ❷ brim

alabar [26] vb to praise

alambrada nf fence ▷ una alambrada eléctrica an electric fence

alambre nm wire; **el alambre de púas** barbed wire

álamo nm poplar

alargador nm extension lead

alargar [38] vb ❶ to lengthen ▷ Hay que alargar un poco las mangas. We'll have to lengthen the sleeves a little. ❷ to extend ▷ Decidieron alargar las vacaciones. They decided to extend their holidays. ❸ to stretch out ▷ Alargué el brazo para apagar la luz. I stretched out my arm to turn out the light. ❹ to pass ▷ ¿Me alargas la llave inglesa? Will you pass me the wrench?; **alargarse (1)** to get longer ▷ Ya van alargándose los días. The days are getting longer. **(2)** to go on ▷ La fiesta se alargó hasta el amanecer. The party went on into the early hours.

alarma nf alarm; **dar la voz de alarma** to raise the alarm; **alarma de incendios** fire alarm

alba nf dawn; **al alba** at dawn

albañil nmf ❶ builder ❷ bricklayer

albaricoque nm apricot

alberca nf (in Latin America) swimming pool

albergue nm ❶ hostel; **un albergue juvenil** a youth hostel ❷ refuge

albóndigas nfpl meatballs

albornoz (pl albornoces) nm bathrobe

alboroto nm racket ▷ ¡Vaya alboroto que estaban montando los niños! What a racket the kids were making!

álbum (pl álbumes) nm album

alcachofa nf artichoke

alcalde, -esa nm/f mayor (post holder)

alcance nm ❶ range ▷ misiles de largo alcance long-range missiles ❷ scale ▷ Se desconoce el alcance de la catástrofe. The scale of the disaster isn't yet known.; **Está al alcance de todos.** It's within everybody's reach.

alcantarilla nf ❶ sewer ❷ drain

alcanzar [14] vb ❶ to catch up with ▷ La alcancé cuando salía por la puerta. I caught up with her just as she was going out of the door. ❷ to reach ▷ alcanzar la cima de la montaña to reach the top of the mountain; **alcanzar la fama** to become famous ❸ to pass ▷ ¿Me alcanzas las tijeras? Can you pass me the scissors?; **Con dos botellas alcanzará para todos.** Two bottles will be enough for all of us.

alcaucil nm (in River Plate) artichoke

alcoba nf bedroom

Be careful! **alcoba** does not mean **alcove**.

alcohol nm alcohol; **cerveza sin alcohol** non-alcoholic beer

alcohólico adj alcoholic

aldea nf village

aldeano, -a nm/f villager

alegrar [26] vb to cheer up; **Me alegra que hayas venido.** I'm glad you've come.; **alegrarse** to be glad; **alegrarse de algo** to be glad about something; **Me alegro de oír que estás bien.** I'm glad to hear that you're well.; **alegrarse por alguien** to be happy for somebody

alegre adj cheerful; **Estoy muy alegre.** I'm feeling very happy.

alegría nf Sentí una gran alegría. I was really happy.; ¡Qué alegría! How lovely!

alejarse [26] vb to move away ▷ Aléjate un poco del fuego. Move a bit further away from the fire.; **El barco se iba alejando de la costa.** The boat was getting further and further away from the coast.

alemán, -ana (mpl alemanes) nm/f, adj German
▶ nm German (language) ▷ ¿Habla alemán? Do you speak German?

Alemania nf Germany

alentador, a adj encouraging

alergia nf allergy; **la alergia al polen** hay fever

alerta adj, nf alert; **dar la alerta** to give the alert; **estar alerta** to be alert

aleta nf ❶ flipper (for diving) ❷ fin (of fish) ❸ wing (of car)

alfabeto nm alphabet

alfarería nf pottery

alfarero, -a nm/f potter

alféizar nm sill

alfil nm bishop

alfiler nm pin

alfombra nf ❶ rug ❷ carpet

alfombrilla nf mat

algas nfpl seaweed

algo pron ❶ something ▷ *Algo se está quemando.* Something's burning. ▷ *¿Quieres algo de comer?* Would you like something to eat? ▷ *¿Te pasa algo?* Is something the matter?; **Aún queda algo de café.** There's still some coffee left. ❷ anything ▷ *¿Algo más?* Anything else? ▷ *¿Has visto algo que te guste?* Have you seen anything you like?; **algo así como** a bit like; **o algo así** or something of the sort; **Por algo será.** There must be a reason for it. ▶ adv rather

algodón (pl algodones) nm cotton ▷ *ropa de algodón* cotton clothes; **Me puse algodones en los oídos.** I put cotton wool in my ears.

alguien pron ❶ somebody ▷ *Alguien llama a la puerta.* There's somebody at the door. ❷ anybody ▷ *¿Conoces a alguien aquí?* Do you know anybody here?

algún, -una (mpl algunos) adj ❶ some ▷ *Algún día iré.* I'll go there some day. ❷ any ▷ *¿Compraste algún cuadro?* Did you buy any

pictures?; **¿Quieres alguna cosa más?** Was there anything else?; **algún que otro ...** the odd ... ▷ *He leído algún que otro libro sobre el tema.* I've read the odd book on the subject.

alguno, -a pron ❶ somebody ▷ *Siempre hay alguno que se queja.* There's always somebody who complains.; **Algunos piensan que no ocurrió así.** Some people think that that wasn't how it happened. ❷ one ▷ *Tiene que haber sido alguno de ellos.* It must have been one of them. ▷ *Tiene que estar en alguna de estas cajas.* It must be in one of these boxes. ❸ some ▷ *Son tantas maletas que alguna siempre se pierde.* There are so many suitcases that some inevitably get lost.; **Sólo conozco a algunos de los vecinos.** I only know some of the neighbours. ❹ any ▷ *Necesito una aspirina. ¿Te queda alguna?* I need an aspirin. Have you got any left? ▷ *Si alguno quiere irse que se vaya.* If any of them want to leave, fine. ▷ *¿Lo sabe alguno de vosotros?* Do any of you know?

aliado, -a nm/f ally

alianza nf ❶ alliance ▷ *formar una alianza* to form an alliance ❷ wedding ring

aliarse [22] vb **aliarse con alguien** to form an alliance with somebody

alicates nmpl pliers

aliento nm breath ▷ *Tengo mal aliento.* I've got bad breath.;

Llegué sin aliento. I arrived out of breath.

aligerar [26] *vb* to make...lighter; **¡Aligera o llegaremos tarde!** Hurry up or we'll be late!

alimentación *nf* diet ▷ **Hay que cuidar la alimentación.** You need to be sensible about your diet.; **una tienda de alimentación** a grocer's shop

alimentar [26] *vb* to feed ▷ **alimentar a un niño** to feed a child; **Esto no alimenta.** That's not very nutritious.; **alimentarse de algo** to live on something

alimento *nm* food; **alimentos congelados** frozen food; **Las legumbres tienen mucho alimento.** Pulses are very nutritious.

alineación (*pl* **alineaciones**) *nf* line-up

aliñar [26] *vb* to season

aliño *nm* dressing

aliviar [26] *vb* to make...better

alivio *nm* relief; **¡Qué alivio!** What a relief!

allá *adv* there ▷ **allá arriba** up there; **más allá** further on; **Échate un poco más allá.** Move over that way a bit.; **más allá de** beyond; **¡Allá tú!** That's up to you!; **el más allá** the next world

allanar [26] *vb* to level

allí *adv* there ▷ **Allí está.** There it is.; **Allí viene tu hermana.** Here comes your sister.; **allí abajo** down there; **allí mismo** right there; **Marta es de por allí.** Marta

comes from somewhere around there.

alma *nf* soul; **Lo siento en el alma.** I'm really sorry.

almacén (*pl* **almacenes**) *nm* warehouse; **unos grandes almacenes** a department store

almacenar [26] *vb* to store

almeja *nf* clam

almendra *nf* almond

almíbar *nm* syrup; **en almíbar** in syrup

almirante *nm* admiral

almohada *nf* pillow

almohadilla *nf* cushion

almorzar [4] *vb* to have lunch; **¿Qué has almorzado?** What did you have for lunch?

almuerzo *vb see* **almorzar**
  ▶ *nm* lunch

aló *excl* (*in Latin America*) hello!

alocado *adj* crazy ▷ **una decisión alocada** a crazy decision; **una chica un poco alocada** a rather silly girl

alojamiento *nm* accommodation

alojarse [26] *vb* to stay

alpargata *nf* espadrille

Alpes *nmpl* **los Alpes** the Alps

alpinismo *nm* mountaineering

alpinista *mf* mountaineer

alquilar [26] *vb* ❶ to rent
  ▷ **Alquilaremos un apartamento en la playa.** We'll rent an apartment near the beach. ❷ to let ▷ **Alquilan habitaciones a estudiantes.** They let rooms to students.; **"se alquila"** "to let" ❸ to hire ▷ **Alquilamos un coche.** We hired a car.

alquiler *nm* rent ▷ **pagar el alquiler**

to pay the rent; **un piso de alquiler** a rented flat; **un coche de alquiler** a hire car; **alquiler de automóviles** car hire

alrededor *adv* **alrededor de**
(1) around ▷ *El satélite gira alrededor de la Tierra.* The satellite goes around the Earth. ▷ *A su alrededor todos gritaban.* Everybody around him was shouting. **(2)** about ▷ *Deben de ser alrededor de las dos.* It must be about two o'clock.

alrededores *nmpl* **Ocurrió en los alrededores de Madrid.** It happened near Madrid.; **Hay muchas tiendas en los alrededores del museo.** There are a lot of shops in the area around the museum.

alta *nf* **dar de alta a alguien** to discharge somebody; **darse de alta** to join

altar *nm* altar

altavoz (*pl* **altavoces**) *nm* loudspeaker

alterar [26] *vb* to change ▷ *Alteraron el orden.* They changed the order.; **alterar el orden público** to cause a breach of the peace; **alterarse** to get upset

alternar [26] *vb* **alternar algo con algo** to alternate something with something; **Alterna con gente del teatro.** He mixes with people from the theatre.

alternativa *nf* alternative; **No tenemos otra alternativa.** We have no alternative.

alterno *adj* alternate ▷ *en días alternos* on alternate days

altibajos *nmpl* ups and downs

altitud *nf* altitude

alto *adj* ❶ tall ▷ *Es un chico muy alto.* He's a very tall boy. ▷ *un edificio muy alto* a very tall building ❷ high ▷ *la montaña más alta del mundo* the highest mountain in the world ▷ *Sacó notas altas en todos los exámenes.* He got high marks in all his exams. ❸ loud ▷ *La música está demasiado alta.* The music's too loud.; **a altas horas de la noche** in the middle of the night; **Celebraron la victoria por todo lo alto.** They celebrated the victory in style.; **alta fidelidad** hi-fi; **una familia de clase alta** an upper-class family
▶ *adv* high; **Pepe habla muy alto.** Pepe has got a very loud voice.; **¡Más alto, por favor!** Speak up, please!; **Pon el volumen más alto.** Turn the volume up.
▶ *nm* **La pared tiene dos metros de alto.** The wall is two metres high.; **en lo alto de** at the top of; **hacer un alto** to stop; **pasar algo por alto** to overlook something; **el alto el fuego** ceasefire
▶ *excl* stop!

altoparlante *nm* (*in Latin America*) loudspeaker

altura *nf* height; **La pared tiene dos metros de altura.** The wall's two metres high.; **cuando llegues a la altura del hospital** when you reach the hospital; **a estas alturas** at this stage

alubias nfpl beans

alucinar [26] vb to be amazed
▷ Alucino con las cosas que haces. I'm amazed at the things you do.

alud nm avalanche

aludir [59] vb **aludir a** to mention; **No se dio por aludida.** She didn't take the hint.

aluminio nm aluminium

alumno, -a nm/f pupil

alusión (pl alusiones) nf hacer alusión a to refer to

alverja nf (in Latin America) pea

alza nf rise ▷ un alza de los precios a rise in prices

alzar [14] vb to raise; **alzarse** to rise

ama nf **ama de casa** housewife; **ama de llaves** housekeeper; see also **amo**

amable adj kind ▷ Es usted muy amable. You're very kind.

amamantar [26] vb **①** to breast-feed **②** to suckle

amanecer [13] vb **①** to get light ▷ Amanece a las siete. It gets light at seven. **②** to wake up ▷ El niño amaneció con fiebre. The boy woke up with a temperature.
▷ nm dawn

amante nmf lover; **amantes del cine** cinema lovers

amapola nf poppy

amar [26] vb to love

amargado adj bitter; **estar amargado por algo** to be bitter about something

amargar [38] vb to spoil; **amargar la vida a alguien** to make somebody's life a misery; **amargarse** to get upset

amargo adj bitter

amarillo adj, nm yellow

amarrar [26] vb **①** to moor **②** to tie up **③** (in Latin America) to do up

amateur (pl amateurs) adj, nmf amateur

Amazonas nm **el Amazonas** the Amazon

ámbar nm amber

ambición (pl ambiciones) nf ambition

ambicioso adj ambitious

ambientador nm air freshener

ambiente nm atmosphere ▷ Se respira un ambiente tenso. There's a tense atmosphere.; **Había un ambiente muy cargado en la habitación.** It was very stuffy in the room.; **Necesito cambiar de ambiente.** I need a change of scene.; **el medio ambiente** the environment

ambiguo adj ambiguous

ámbito nm scope

ambos, -as pron both ▷ Vinieron ambos. They both came. ▷ Ambos tenéis los ojos azules. You've both got blue eyes.

ambulancia nf ambulance

ambulatorio nm out-patients' department

amén excl amen

amenace vb see **amenazar**

amenaza nf threat

amenazar [14] vb to threaten; **Le amenazó con decírselo al profesor.** He threatened to tell the teacher.

ameno adj ❶ enjoyable
❷ pleasant

América nf the Americas;
América Central Central America;
América Latina Latin America;
América del Sur South America;
el español de América Latin
American Spanish

americana nf jacket; see also
americano

americano, -a nm/f, adj
American; see also **americana**

ametralladora nf machine gun

amígdalas nfpl tonsils

amigo, -a nm/f friend; **hacerse
amigos** to become friends; **ser
muy amigos** to be good friends

amistad nf friendship; **hacer
amistad con alguien** to make
friends with somebody; **las
amistades** friends

amistoso adj friendly

amo, -a nm/f owner ▷ **el amo del
perro** the dog's owner; see also **ama**

amontonar [26] vb to pile up;
Se me amontona el trabajo. My
work's piling up.

amor nm love; **hacer el amor** to
make love; **amor propio** self-
esteem

amoratado adj ❶ blue ❷ black
and blue

amortiguar vb ❶ to cushion
❷ to muffle

ampliar [22] vb ❶ to expand ❷ to
enlarge ❸ to extend

amplificador nm amplifier

amplio adj ❶ wide ▷ **una calle**
muy amplia a very wide street
❷ spacious ▷ **una habitación
amplia** a spacious room ❸ loose
▷ **ropa amplia** loose clothing

ampolla nf blister

amputar [26] vb to amputate

amueblar [26] vb to furnish; **un
piso sin amueblar** an unfurnished
flat

analfabeto adj illiterate

analgésico nm painkiller

análisis (pl **análisis**) nm
❶ analysis ❷ test ▷ **un análisis de
sangre** a blood test

analizar [14] vb to analyse

anarquía nf anarchy

anatomía nf anatomy

ancho adj ❶ wide ▷ **una calle ancha**
a wide street ❷ loose ▷ **Le gusta
llevar ropa ancha.** He likes to wear
loose clothing.; **Me está ancho
el vestido.** The dress is too big for
me.; **Es ancho de espaldas.** He's
broad-shouldered.
▶ nm width ▷ **el ancho de la tela** the
width of the cloth; **¿Cuánto mide
de ancho?** How wide is it?; **Mide
tres metros de ancho.** It's three
metres wide.

anchoa nf anchovy

anchura nf width; **¿Qué anchura
tiene?** How wide is it?; **Tiene tres
metros de anchura.** It's three
metres wide.

anciano, -a nm/f **un anciano**
an elderly man; **una anciana** an
elderly woman; **los ancianos**
the elderly
▶ adj elderly

ancla nf anchor

anda excl ❶ well I never! ❷ come on; **¡Anda ya!** You're not serious!

Andalucía nf Andalusia

andaluz, a (mpl **andaluces**) adj, nm/f Andalusian

andamio nm scaffolding

andar [5] vb ❶ to walk; **Iremos andando a la estación.** We'll walk to the station. ❷ to be ▷ Últimamente ando muy liado. I've been very busy lately.; **andar mal de dinero** to be short of money; **Anda por los cuarenta.** He's about forty. ❸ to go (clock, car); **¡No andes ahí!** Keep away from there!; **Ándate con cuidado.** Take care.

andén (pl **andenes**) nm platform

Andes nmpl **los Andes** the Andes

anduve vb see **andar**

anécdota nf anecdote

anemia nf anaemia

anestesia nf anaesthetic; **poner anestesia a alguien** to give somebody an anaesthetic

anfiteatro nm ❶ amphitheatre ❷ lecture theatre

ángel nm angel

anginas nfpl **tener anginas** to have tonsillitis

ángulo nm angle

anillo nm ring; **un anillo de boda** a wedding ring

animado adj ❸ cheerful ▷ Últimamente parece que está más animada. She has seemed more cheerful lately. ❷ lively ▷ Fue una fiesta muy animada. It was a very lively party.; **dibujos animados** cartoons

animador, a nm/f ❶ entertainments manager ❷ animator

animal nm animal; **los animales domésticos** pets

animar [26] vb ❶ to cheer up (person) ❷ to cheer on (team) ❸ to liven up (party); **animar a alguien a que haga algo** to encourage somebody to do something; **animarse** to cheer up; **animarse a hacer algo** to make up one's mind to do something

ánimo nm **Está muy mal de ánimo.** He's in very low spirits.; **dar ánimos a alguien** (1) to cheer somebody up (2) to give somebody moral support; **tener ánimos para hacer algo** to feel like doing something

▶ excl cheer up! ▷ ¡Ánimo, chaval, que no es el fin del mundo! Cheer up mate, it's not the end of the world!

anís (pl **anises**) nm anisette

aniversario nm anniversary ▷ su aniversario de boda their wedding anniversary

anoche adv last night; **antes de anoche** the night before last

anochecer [13] vb to get dark ▶ nm nightfall; **al anochecer** at nightfall

anónimo adj anonymous ▶ nm anonymous note

anorak (pl **anoraks**) nm anorak

anormal adj odd ▷ Yo no noté nada anormal en su comportamiento. I didn't notice anything odd about his behaviour.; **¡Soy anormal!** What a fool I am!

anotar [26] vb ❶ to take a note of ❷ to score

ansiedad nf anxiety

ansioso adj **estar ansioso por hacer algo** to be eager to do something

Antártico nm **el Antártico** the Antarctic

ante prep ❶ before ▷ Le da vergüenza aparecer ante tanta gente. She's shy about appearing before so many people. ❷ in the face of ▷ Mantuvo la calma ante el peligro. He remained calm in the face of danger.
▶ nm suede

anteanoche adv the night before last

anteayer adv the day before yesterday

antecedentes nmpl **antecedentes penales** criminal record

antelación nf **hacer una reserva con antelación** to make an advance booking; **Deben avisarte con un mes de antelación.** They must give you a month's notice.

antemano adv **de antemano** in advance

antena nf aerial; **una antena parabólica** a satellite dish

anteojos nmpl (in Latin America) glasses; **los anteojos de sol** sunglasses

antepasados nmpl ancestors

anterior (f anterior) adj ❶ before ▷ La semana anterior llovió mucho. It rained a lot the week before. ▷ Su boda fue anterior a la nuestra. Their wedding was before ours. ❷ front ▷ las extremidades anteriores the front limbs

anteriormente adv previously

antes adv ❶ before ▷ Esta película ya la he visto antes. I've seen this film before. ▷ Él estaba aquí antes que yo. He was here before me. ▷ la noche antes the night before; **El supermercado está justo antes del semáforo.** The supermarket is just before the lights.; **antes de** before ▷ antes de ir al teatro before going to the theatre ▷ antes de que te vayas before you go ❷ first ▷ Nosotros llegamos antes. We arrived first.; **Antes no había tanto desempleo.** There didn't use to be so much unemployment.; **cuanto antes mejor** the sooner the better; **lo antes posible** as soon as possible; **antes de nada** first and foremost; **Antes que verle prefiero esperar aquí.** I'd rather wait here than see him.

antibiótico nm antibiotic

anticipado adj early ▷ convocar elecciones anticipadas to call early elections; **por anticipado** in advance ▷ pagar por anticipado to pay in advance

anticipar [26] vb ❶ to foresee ❸ to bring...forward (event) ❶ to pay...in advance; **anticiparse**

a alguien to get in before somebody; **Se anticipó a su tiempo.** He was ahead of his time.

anticipo nm advance ▷ pedir un anticipo to ask for an advance; **ser un anticipo de algo** to be a foretaste of something

anticonceptivo adj, nm contraceptive

anticuado adj outdated

anticuario, -a nm/f antique dealer
▶ nm antique shop

antifaz (pl antifaces) nm mask

antiguamente adv ❶ in the past ❷ formerly

antigüedad nf **Es un monumento de gran antigüedad.** It's a very old monument.; **en la antigüedad** in ancient times; **las antigüedades** antiques; **una tienda de antigüedades** an antique shop

antiguo adj ❶ old ▷ Este reloj es muy antiguo. This clock is very old. ❷ ancient ▷ Estudia historia antigua. He studies ancient history. ❸ former ▷ el antiguo secretario general del partido the former general secretary of the party

Antillas nfpl the West Indies

antipático adj unfriendly

antiséptico adj, nm antiseptic

antojarse [26] vb to feel like; **Siempre hace lo que se le antoja.** He always does what he feels like.; **Se me ha antojado un helado.** I fancy an ice-cream.

antorcha nf torch

antropología nf anthropology

anual adj annual

anular [26] vb ❶ to call off ▷ Anularon el partido por la lluvia. The match was called off owing to the rain. ❷ to disallow (goal) ❸ to overturn (sentence)
▶ nm ring finger

anunciar [26] vb ❶ to advertise ❷ to announce

anuncio nm ❶ advertisement; **anuncios por palabras** small ads ❷ announcement

anzuelo nm hook

añadidura nf **por añadidura** in addition

añadir [59] vb to add

añicos nmpl **hacer algo añicos** to smash something to pieces; **hacerse añicos** to smash to pieces

año nm year ▷ Estuve allí el año pasado. I was there last year.; **el año que viene** next year; **el año escolar** the school year; **¡Feliz Año Nuevo!** Happy New Year!; **los años 90** the 90s; **¿Cuántos años tiene?** How old is he?; **Tiene 15 años.** He's 15.

apagado adj switched off ▷ La tele estaba apagada. The TV was switched off.

apagar [38] vb ❶ to switch off ❷ to put out; **apagar el fuego** to put the fire out

apagón (pl apagones) nm power cut

apañado adj resourceful

apañarse [26] vb to manage

▷ ¿Podrás hacerlo solo? - Ya me apañaré. Can you do it on your own? - I'll manage.; **apañarse con algo** to make do with something

aparador nm ❶ sideboard ❷ (in Mexico) shop window

aparato nm **No sé manejar este aparato.** I don't know how to operate this.; **un aparato de televisión** a television; **los aparatos de gimnasia** the apparatus; **Fabrican aparatos electrónicos.** They make electronic equipment.; **un aparato electrodoméstico** an electrical appliance

aparcamiento nm ❶ car park ❷ parking space

aparcar[49] vb to park; **"prohibido aparcar"** "no parking"

aparecer[13] vb ❶ to appear ❷ to turn up

aparentar[26] vb to appear; **Aparenta más edad de la que tiene.** He looks older than he is.

aparente adj apparent

aparentemente adv apparently

apariencia nf **Tiene la apariencia de un profesor de universidad.** He looks like a university lecturer.; **guardar las apariencias** to keep up appearances

apartado adj isolated
▶ nm section; **apartado de correos** PO box

apartamento nm apartment

apartar[26] vb ❶ to remove ▷ Lo apartaron del equipo. They removed him from the team. ❷ to move

out of the way ▷ Aparta todas las sillas. Move all the chairs out of the way.; **¡Aparta!** Stand back!
❶ to set aside; **apartarse** to stand back

aparte adv ❶ separately ❷ on one side; **La ropa que no valga ponla aparte.** Put the clothes that aren't any use on one side.; **aparte de** apart from; **punto y aparte** full stop, new paragraph

apasionante adj exciting

apasionar[26] vb **Le apasiona el fútbol.** He's crazy about football.

apdo. abbr (= apartado de correos) PO box (= Post Office box)

apearse[26] vb **apearse de** to get off

apego nm **tener apego a algo** to be attached to something

apellidarse[26] vb **Se apellida Pérez.** His surname is Pérez.

apellido nm surname

- In the Spanish-speaking world, most people have two surnames, the first being their father's first surname and the second being their mother's first surname. So if Juan Mata Pérez marries María Valle García, any children will have Mata Valle as their surnames. Although she would keep her own surname, their mother could also be referred to as la señora de Mata.

apenado adj ❶ sad ❷ (in Latin America) embarrassed

apenas adv, conj ❶ hardly

❷ hardly ever ❸ barely ❹ as soon as

apendicitis nf appendicitis

aperitivo nm aperitif

apertura nf opening ▷ el acto de apertura the opening ceremony

apestar [26] vb to stink; **apestar a** to stink of

apetecer [13] vb ¿Te apetece una tortilla? Do you fancy an omelette?; **No, gracias, ahora no me apetece.** No, thanks, I don't feel like it just now.

apetito nm appetite ▷ Eso te va a quitar el apetito. You won't have any appetite left.; **No tengo apetito.** I'm not hungry.

apetitoso adj ❶ tasty ❷ tempting

apio nm celery

aplastante adj overwhelming

aplastar [26] vb to squash

aplaudir [59] vb to clap

aplauso nm applause; **Los aplausos duraron varios minutos.** The applause lasted for several minutes.

aplazar [14] vb to postpone

aplicación (pl **aplicaciones**) nf application

aplicado adj hard-working

aplicar [49] vb to apply

apoderarse [26] vb **apoderarse de un lugar** to take over a place; **Se apoderaron de las joyas.** They went off with the jewels.

apodo nm nickname

apogeo nm height ▷ en el apogeo de su poder at the height of his power;

La fiesta estaba en su apogeo. The party was in full swing.

aportar [26] vb to provide

aposta adv on purpose

apostar [12] vb to bet; **apostar por algo** to bet on something; ¿Qué te apuestas a que ...? What's the betting that ...?

apóstrofo nm apostrophe

apoyar [26] vb ❶ to lean ▷ Apoya el espejo contra la pared. Lean the mirror against the wall. ❷ to rest ▷ Apoya la espalda en este cojín. Rest your back against this cushion. ❸ to support ▷ Todos mis compañeros me apoyan. All my colleagues support me.; **apoyarse** to lean

apoyo nm support

apreciar [26] vb **apreciar a alguien** to be fond of somebody; **Aprecio mucho mi tiempo libre.** I really value my free time.

aprecio nm **tener aprecio a alguien** to be fond of somebody

aprender [9] vb to learn; **aprender a hacer algo** to learn to do something; **aprender algo de memoria** to learn something by heart

aprendiz, a (mpl **aprendices**) nm/f trainee ▷ Es aprendiz de mecánico. He's a trainee mechanic.; **estar de aprendiz** to be doing an apprenticeship

aprendizaje nm ❶ learning ▷ dificultades de aprendizaje learning difficulties ❷ apprenticeship

a
b
c
d
e
f
g
h
i
j
k
l
m
n
o
p
q
r
s
t
u
v
w
x
y
z

aprensivo adj overanxious

apresurado adj hasty

apresurarse [26] vb **No nos apresuremos.** Let's not be hasty.; **Me apresuré a sugerir que ...** I hastily suggested that ...

apretado adj ❶ tight ❷ cramped

apretar [40] vb ❶ to tighten ❷ to press; **apretar el gatillo** to press the trigger; **Me aprietan los zapatos.** My shoes are too tight.; **Aprietaos un poco para que me siente yo también.** Move up a bit so I can sit down too.

aprieto nm **estar en un aprieto** to be in a tight spot

aprisa adv fast; **¡Aprisa!** Hurry up!

aprobar [12] vb ❶ to pass ▷ **aprobar un examen** to pass an exam; **Han aprobado una ley antitabaco.** They've passed an anti-smoking law.; **aprobar por los pelos** to scrape through ❷ to approve ▷ **No aprovecha el tiempo.** He doesn't make good use of his time. ❷ to use; **aprovecho la ocasión para decirles ...** I'd like to take this opportunity to tell you ...; **Aprovecharé ahora que estoy solo para llamarle.** I'll call him now while I'm on my own.; **¡Que aproveche!** Enjoy your meal!; **aprovecharse de** to take advantage of

aproximadamente adv about

aproximado adj approximate

aproximarse [26] vb to approach

apruebo vb see **aprobar**

aptitud nf ❶ suitability ❷ aptitude

apto adj **ser apto para algo** to be suitable for something

apuesta nf bet ▷ **Hicimos una apuesta.** We had a bet.

apuesto vb see **apostar**

apuntar [26] vb ❶ to write down ▷ **Apúntalo o se te olvidará.** Write it down or you'll forget. ❷ to point; **Me apuntó con el dedo.** He pointed at me.; **Luis me apuntó en el examen.** Luis gave me the answers in the exam.; **apuntarse** to put one's name down; **apuntarse a un curso** to enrol on a course; **¡Yo me apunto!** Count me in!

> Be careful! **apuntar** does not mean **appoint**.

apuntes nmpl notes; **tomar apuntes** to take notes

apuñalar [26] vb to stab

apurado adj ❶ difficult (situation) ❷ in a hurry; **Si estás apurado de dinero, dímelo.** If you're short of money, tell me.; **estar apurado** to feel embarrassed

apurar [26] vb to finish up ▷ **Apura la cerveza que nos vamos.** Finish up your beer and let's go.; **apurarse** (1) to hurry up (2) to worry

apuro nm fix ▷ **El dinero de la herencia los sacó del apuro.** The money they inherited got them out of the fix they were in.; **Pasé muchos apuros para salir del**

agua. I had a lot of trouble getting out of the water.; **Me da mucho apuro no llevar ningún regalo.** I feel very embarrassed about not taking a present.; **estar en apuros** to be in trouble

aquel, aquella adj that ▷ Me gusta más aquella mesa. I prefer that table.

aquél (f **aquélla**) pron that one ▷ Éste no, aquél. Not this one, that one.; **Aquél no era el que yo quería.** That wasn't the one I wanted.

aquello pron **aquello que hay allí** that thing over there; **Me fui; aquello era insoportable.** I left. It was just unbearable.; **¿Qué fue de aquello del viaje alrededor del mundo?** What ever happened to that round-the-world trip idea?

aquellos, -as adj pl those ▷ ¿Ves aquellas montañas? Can you see those mountains?

aquéllos, -as pron pl those ones ▷ Aquéllos de allí son mejores. Those ones over there are better.; **Aquéllos no eran los que vimos ayer.** Those aren't the ones we saw yesterday.

aquí adv **①** here; **aquí abajo** down here; **aquí arriba** up here; **aquí mismo** right here; **por aquí** (1) around here (2) this way **②** now; **de aquí en adelante** from now on; **de aquí a siete días** a week from now; **hasta aquí** (1) to here (2) up to now

árabe nmf, adj Arab

▶ nm Arabic (language)

Arabia nf **Arabia Saudí** Saudi Arabia

arado nm plough

araña nf spider

arañar [26] vb to scratch

arañazo nm scratch

arar [26] vb to plough

árbitro, -a nm/f referee

árbol nm tree; **el árbol de Navidad** the Christmas tree; **un árbol genealógico** a family tree

arbusto ① bush ② shrub

arca nf chest; **el Arca de Noé** Noah's Ark

arcadas nfpl **Me dieron arcadas con el olor.** The smell made me retch.

arcén (pl **arcenes**) nm hard shoulder

archivador nm ① filing cabinet ② file

archivar [26] vb to file

archivo nm ① archive ② file; **los archivos policiales** police files; **un archivo adjunto** an attachment; **un archivo de seguridad** a backup file

arcilla nf clay

arco nm ① arch ② bow (for arrows, violin); **el arco iris** the rainbow

arder [9] vb to burn; **¡La sopa está ardiendo!** The soup's boiling hot!

ardilla nf squirrel

ardor nm passion; **con ardor** passionately; **tener ardor de estómago** to have heartburn

área nf ① area; **en distintas áreas**

del país in different parts of the country; **un área de descanso** a lay-by; **un área de servicios** a service area ❷ penalty area

arena nf sand; **arenas movedizas** quicksand

arenque nm herring; **arenques ahumados** kippers

Argelia nf Algeria

argelino, -a nm/f, adj Algerian

Argentina nf Argentina

argentino, -a nm/f, adj Argentinian

argolla nf ring

argot (pl argots) nm ❶ slang ❷ jargon

argumento nm ❶ argument ❷ plot

árido adj arid

Aries nm Aries (sign); **Soy aries.** I'm Aries.

aristócrata nmf aristocrat

arma nf ❶ weapon; **un fabricante de armas** an arms manufacturer ❷ gun ▷ **Nos apuntaba con un arma.** He pointed a gun at us.; **un arma de fuego** a firearm

armada nf navy

armadura nf armour; **una armadura medieval** a medieval suit of armour

armamento nm arms (weapons)

armar [26] vb ❶ to arm ❷ to assemble (flatpack furniture) ❸ to make ▷ **Los vecinos de arriba arman mucho jaleo.** Our upstairs neighbours make a lot of noise.; **Si no aceptan voy a armar un escándalo.** If they don't agree I'm going to kick up a fuss.; **armarse un lío** to get in a muddle; **armarse de paciencia** to be patient; **armarse de valor** to summon up one's courage; **Se armó la gorda.** All hell broke loose.

armario nm ❶ cupboard; **un armario de cocina** a kitchen cupboard ❷ wardrobe

armazón (pl armazones) nm frame

armonía nf harmony

armónica nf mouth organ

aro nm ❶ ring ▷ **los aros olímpicos** the Olympic rings ❷ hoop

aroma nm aroma

aromaterapia nf aromatherapy

arpa nf harp

arqueología nf archaeology

arqueólogo, -a nm/f archaeologist

arquero, -a nm/f (in Latin America) goalkeeper

arquitecto, -a nm/f architect

arquitectura nf architecture

arrancar [49] vb ❶ to pull up (plant); **El viento arrancó varios árboles.** Several trees were uprooted by the wind. ❷ to pull out (nail, thorn) ❸ to tear out (page, sheet) ❹ to pull off (label, plaster) ❺ to snatch ▷ **Me lo arrancaron de las manos.** They snatched it from me.; **Arranca y vámonos.** Start the engine and let's get going.; **arrancarle información a alguien** to drag information out of somebody

arrasar [26] vb ❶ to sweep away

❷ to destroy; **Los socialistas arrasaron en las elecciones.** The socialists swept the board in the elections.

arrastrar [26] vb ❶ to drag ❷ to sweep along ❸ to trail on the ground; **arrastrarse** to crawl

arrebatar [26] vb snatch ▷ *Me lo arrebató de las manos.* He snatched it from me.

arrecife nm reef; **los arrecifes de coral** coral reefs

arreglar [26] vb ❶ to fix (appliance, object) ❷ to do up (house, room) ❸ to sort out (problem); **Deja tu cuarto arreglado antes de salir.** Leave your room tidy before you go out.; **arreglarse** (1) to get ready (2) to work out (3) to manage; **arreglarse el pelo** to do one's hair; **arreglárselas para hacer algo** to manage to do something

arreglo nm ❶ repair; **Esta tele no tiene arreglo.** The TV's beyond repair.; **Este problema no tiene arreglo.** There's no solution to this problem. ❷ compromise ▷ *Llegamos a un arreglo.* We reached a compromise.; **con arreglo a** in accordance with

arrepentirse [52] vb arrepentirse **de algo** to regret something; **arrepentirse de haber hecho algo** to regret doing something

arrestar [26] vb to arrest

arresto nm arrest ▷ *un arresto domiciliario* a house arrest

arriba adv ❶ above ▷ *Visto desde arriba parece más pequeño.* Seen

from above it looks smaller.; **Pon esos libros arriba del todo.** Put those books on top.; **la parte de arriba del biquini** the bikini top; **allí arriba** up there; **más arriba** further up; **ir calle arriba** to go up the street; **Tenemos bolsos de 20 euros para arriba.** We've got bags from 20 euros upwards.; **arriba de** (1) (in Latin America) on top of (2) (in Latin America) above; **mirar a alguien de arriba abajo** to look somebody up and down ❷ upstairs ▷ *Arriba están los dormitorios.* The bedrooms are upstairs. ▷ *los vecinos de arriba* our upstairs neighbours

arriesgado adj risky

arriesgar [38] vb to risk ▷ *Carlos arriesgó su vida para salvar a su perro.* Carlos risked his life to save his dog.; **arriesgarse** to take a risk; **arriesgarse a hacer algo** to risk doing something

arrimar [26] vb to bring...closer ▷ *Arrima tu silla a la mía.* Bring your chair closer to mine.; **Vamos a arrimar la mesa a la pared.** Let's put the table by the wall.; **arrimarse** to get close ▷ *Al aparcar procura arrimarte a la acera.* Try to get close to the pavement when parking.; **Arrímate a mí.** Come closer.

arroba nf at (sign) (in email address)

arrodillarse [26] vb to kneel down

arrogante adj arrogant

arrojar [26] vb to throw; **"Prohibido arrojar basuras"** "No dumping"

arropar [26] vb ❶ to tuck in ▷ Voy a arropar al niño. I'll go and tuck the little one in. ❷ to wrap up ▷ Arrópala bien. Wrap her up well.; **arrópate bien** (1) tuck yourself up warmly (2) wrap up well

arroyo nm stream

arroz (pl arroces) nm rice; **arroz blanco** white rice; **arroz con leche** rice pudding

arruga nf ❶ wrinkle (in skin) ❷ crease (in paper, clothing)

arrugarse [38] vb ❶ to get wrinkled (skin) ❷ to get creased (paper, clothing) ▷ Procura que no se arrugue el sobre. Try not to let the envelope get creased.

arruinar [26] vb to ruin; **arruinarse** to be ruined

arte (pl artes) nm ❶ art; **el arte abstracto** abstract art; **el arte dramático** drama ❷ flair ▷ Tiene arte para la cocina. She has a flair for cooking.; **por arte de magia** by magic

artefacto nm device ▷ un artefacto explosivo an explosive device

arteria nf artery

artesana nf craftswoman

artesanía nf la artesanía local local crafts; **objetos de artesanía** hand-crafted goods

artesano nm craftsman

ártico adj arctic

articulación (pl articulaciones) nf joint

artículo nm article ▷ el artículo determinado the definite article

▷ el artículo indeterminado the indefinite article; **artículos de lujo** luxury goods; **artículos de escritorio** stationery; **artículos de tocador** toiletries

artificial adj artificial

artista nmf ❶ artist (painter, sculptor) ❷ actor (in theatre, cinema)

arveja nf (in Latin America) pea

arzobispo nm archbishop

as nm ace ▷ el as de picas the ace of spades; **ser un as de la cocina** be a wizard at cooking

asa nf handle

asado adj roast ▷ pollo asado roast chicken
  ▶ nm ❶ roast ❷ (in Latin America) barbecue

asaltar [26] vb ❶ to storm ❷ to raid ❸ to mug

asalto nm ❶ raid ▷ un asalto a una gasolinera a raid on a petrol station; **durante el asalto al parlamento** during the storming of parliament ❷ round (in boxing)

asamblea nf ❶ meeting ❷ assembly

asar [26] vb to roast; **asar algo a la parrilla** to grill something; **Me aso de calor.** I'm boiling.; **Aquí se asa uno.** It's boiling in here.

ascender [21] vb ❶ to rise ▷ El globo comenzó a ascender. The balloon began to rise. ❷ to be promoted; **ascender a primera división** to go up to the first division

ascenso nm promotion

ascensor nm lift

asciendo vb see **ascender**

asco nm **El ajo me da asco.** I think garlic's revolting.; **¡Puaj! ¡Qué asco!** Yuk! How revolting!; **La casa está hecha un asco.** The house is filthy.

asegurar [26] vb **①** to insure **②** to assure; **No he sido yo. Te lo aseguro.** It wasn't me, I assure you.; **Ella asegura que no lo conoce.** She insists she doesn't know him. **③** to fasten securely; **asegurarse de** to make sure

aseo nm **el cuarto de aseo** the toilet; **el aseo personal** personal hygiene; **los aseos** the toilets

asequible adj **①** affordable **②** achievable

asesinar [26] vb to murder

asesinato nm murder

asesino, -a nm/f murderer

asesor, a nm/f consultant; **asesor de imagen** public relations consultant; **asesor fiscal** tax advisor

asfalto nm tarmac

asfixia nf suffocation

asfixiarse [26] vb to suffocate

así adv **①** like this **②** like that; **un tomate así de grande** a tomato this big; **Así es la vida.** That's life.; **así, así** so-so; **así es** that's right; **¿No es así?** Isn't that so?; **así que ... so ...; ... o así ...** or thereabouts; **y así sucesivamente** and so on

Asia nf Asia

asiático, -a nm/f, adj Asian

asiento nm seat; **el asiento delantero** the front seat; **el asiento trasero** the back seat

asignatura nf subject; **Tiene dos asignaturas pendientes.** He's got two subjects to retake.

asilo nm **①** home; **un asilo de ancianos** an old people's home; **un asilo de pobres** a home for the poor **②** asylum ▷ **asilo político** political asylum

asimilar [26] vb to assimilate; **El cambio es grande y cuesta asimilarlo.** It's a big change and it takes getting used to.

asistencia nf **asistencia médica** (1) medical attention (2) medical care; **asistencia técnica** technical support

asistenta nf cleaner

asistente nmf assistant; **asistente social** social worker; **los asistentes al acto** those present at the ceremony

asistir [59] vb **①** to go ▷ **No asistieron a la ceremonia.** They didn't go to the ceremony. **②** to treat ▷ **Le asistió un médico que había de guardia.** He was treated by a duty doctor.

asma nf asthma

asociación (pl **asociaciones**) nf association

asociar [26] vb to associate; **asociarse** to go into partnership

asolearse [26] vb (in Latin America) to sunbathe

asomar [26] vb **Te asoma el pañuelo por el bolsillo.** Your handkerchief's sticking out of your pocket.; **No asomes la cabeza por la ventanilla.** Don't lean out of the window.; **Me asomé a la terraza a ver quién gritaba.** I went out onto the balcony to see who was shouting.; **Asómate a la ventana.** Look out of the window.

asombrar [26] vb to amaze ▷ **Me asombra que no lo sepas.** I'm amazed you don't know.; **asombrarse** to be amazed ▷ **Se asombró de lo tarde que era.** He was amazed at how late it was.

asombro nm amazement

asombroso adj amazing

aspecto nm ❶ appearance; **tener buen aspecto (1)** to look well (person) **(2)** to look good (food) ❷ aspect

áspero adj ❶ rough ❷ harsh

aspiradora nf vacuum cleaner

aspirar [26] vb ❶ to breathe in; **aspirar a hacer algo** to hope to do something ❷ (in Latin America) to hoover

aspirina nf aspirin

asqueroso adj ❶ disgusting (food, smell) ❷ filthy (kitchen, hands) ▷ **Esta cocina está asquerosa.** This kitchen is filthy. ❸ horrible ▷ **Esta gente es asquerosa.** They're horrible people.

astilla nf splinter

astro nm star

astrología nf astrology

astronauta nmf astronaut

astronomía nf astronomy

astuto adj clever

asumir [59] vb to accept; **Asumo toda la responsabilidad.** I take full responsibility.; **No estoy dispuesta a asumir ese riesgo.** I'm not prepared to take that risk.

asunto nm matter ▷ **Es un asunto muy delicado.** It's a very delicate matter.; **el ministro de asuntos exteriores** the minister for foreign affairs; **No me gusta que se metan en mis asuntos.** I don't like anyone meddling in my affairs.; **¡Eso no es asunto tuyo!** That's none of your business!

asustar [26] vb ❶ to frighten ❸ to startle; **asustarse** to get frightened; **No te asustes.** Don't be frightened.

atacar [49] vb to attack

atado nm (in River Plate); **un atado de cigarrillos** a packet of cigarettes

atajo nm short cut

ataque nm attack ▷ **un ataque contra alguien** an attack on somebody; **un ataque cardíaco** a heart attack; **Le dio un ataque de risa.** He burst out laughing.; **un ataque de nervios** a fit of panic

atar [26] vb to tie; **Átate los cordones.** Tie your shoelaces up.

atardecer [12] vb to get dark ▷ **Está atardeciendo.** It's getting dark.
▶ nm dusk ▷ **al atardecer** at dusk

atareado adj busy

atasco nm traffic jam

ataúd nm coffin

Atenas nf Athens

atención (pl atenciones) nf Hay
que poner más atención. You
should pay more attention.;
Escucha con atención. He listens
attentively.; **Me llamó la atención
lo grande que era la casa.** I was
struck by how big the house was.;
**El director del colegio le llamó la
atención.** The headmaster gave
him a talking-to.; **Estás llamando
la atención con ese sombrero.**
You're attracting attention in
that hat.
▸ excl Attention!; **¡Atención, por
favor!** May I have your attention
please?; **"¡Atención!" "**Caution!"

atender [21] vb ❶ to serve (in
a bar, shop) ▷ ¿Le atienden? Are
you being served? ❷ to attend
to (in a bank, office) ▷ Tengo que
atender a un par de clientes. I've
got a couple of clients to attend
to. ❸ to look after ▷ atender a
los enfermos to look after the sick
❹ to pay attention to; **atender
los consejos de alguien** to listen
to somebody's advice

atentado nm un atentado
terrorista a terrorist attack; **un
atentado suicida** a suicide attack

atentamente adv ❶ Yours
sincerely ❷ Yours faithfully

atento adj thoughtful ▷ Es un chico
muy atento. He's a very thoughtful
boy.; **Estaban atentos a las
explicaciones del instructor.**
They were listening attentively to
the instructor's explanations.

aterrizaje nm landing; **un**

aterrizaje forzoso an emergency
landing

aterrizar [14] vb to land

atestado adj packed ▷ El local
estaba atestado de gente. The place
was packed with people.

atiborrarse [26] vb to stuff oneself

ático nm top-floor flat; **un ático de
lujo** a luxury penthouse

atiende vb see **atender**

atlántico adj Atlantic; **el océano
Atlántico** the Atlantic Ocean

atlas (pl atlas) nm atlas

atleta nmf athlete

atletismo nm athletics

atmósfera nf atmosphere

atolondrado adj scatterbrained

atómico adj atomic

átomo nm the atom

atónito adj amazed; **quedarse
atónito** to be amazed

atracador, a nm/f ❶ robber
❷ mugger

atracar [49] vb ❶ to hold up
▷ atracar un banco to hold up a
bank ❷ to mug ▷ La atracaron en
la plaza. She was mugged in the
square.

atracción (pl atracciones) nf
attraction; **sentir atracción por**
to be attracted to

atraco nm ❶ hold-up ❷ mugging

atractivo adj attractive
▸ nm attraction

atraer [55] vb to attract; **Esa chica
me atrae mucho.** I find that girl
very attractive.; **No me atrae
mucho lo del viaje a Turquía.**
That Turkey trip doesn't appeal to

me much.

atrapar [26] vb to catch

atrás adv ❶ back ▷ Yo me quedé atrás porque iba muy cansado. I stayed behind because I was very tired.; **El coche de atrás va a adelantarnos.** The car behind is going to overtake us.; **años atrás** years ago ❷ back ▷ mirar hacia atrás to look back; **ir para atrás** to go backwards ❸ in the back ▷ Los niños viajan siempre atrás. The children always travel in the back.; **la parte de atrás** the back; **el asiento de atrás** the back seat

atrasado adj ❶ backward ▷ Es un país muy atrasado. It's a very backward country. ❷ back ▷ números atrasados de una revista back numbers of a magazine; **pagos atrasados** outstanding payments ❸ behind ▷ Va bastante atrasado en la escuela. He's rather behind at school.; **Tengo mucho trabajo atrasado.** I'm very behind with my work.; **El reloj está atrasado.** The clock's slow. ❹ (in Latin America) late ▷ Siempre llega atrasada al trabajo. She's always late for work.

atrasar [26] vb ❶ to delay ▷ Tuvimos que atrasar nuestra salida. We had to delay our departure. ❷ to put back ▷ Acordaos de atrasar una hora vuestros relojes. Remember to put your watches back an hour.; **atrasarse** to be late ▷ El tren se atrasó. The train was late.

atravesar [40] vb ❶ to cross

▷ Atravesamos el río. We crossed the river. ❷ to go through ▷ Atravesamos un mal momento. We're going through a bad patch.

atravieso vb see **atravesar**

atreverse [9] vb to dare ▷ No me atreví a decírselo. I didn't dare tell him.; **No me atrevo.** I daren't.; **La gente no se atreve a salir de noche.** People are afraid to go out at night.

atrevido adj ❶ daring ▷ un escote muy atrevido a very daring neckline ❷ cheeky ▷ No seas tan atrevido con el jefe. Don't be so cheeky to the boss.

atropellar [26] vb to run over

ATS abbr (= Ayudante Técnico Sanitario) Registered Nurse

atún (pl atunes) nm tuna

audaz (pl audaces) adj daring

audiencia nf audience

audiovisual adj audiovisual

auditorio nm ❶ auditorium ❷ audience

aula nf classroom

aumentar [26] vb to increase; **aumentar de peso** to put on weight

aumento nm increase; **Los precios van en aumento.** Prices are going up.

aun adv even ▷ Aun sentado me duele la pierna. Even when I'm sitting down, my leg hurts.; **aun así** even so; **aun cuando** even if

aún adv ❶ still ▷ ¿Aún te duele? Is it still hurting? ▷ Y aún no me has devuelto el libro. You still haven't

given me the book back. ❷ **yet**
▷ ¿No ha venido aún? Hasn't he got
here yet? ❸ **even** ▷ La película es
aún más aburrida de lo que creía.
The film's even more boring than I
thought it would be.

aunque conj ❶ **although** ▷ Me
gusta el francés, aunque prefiero el
alemán. I like French, although I
prefer German. ❷ **though** ▷ Estoy
pensando en ir, aunque no sé cuándo.
I'm thinking of going, though I
don't know when. ❸ **even
though** ▷ Seguí andando, aunque
me dolía mucho la pierna. I went on
walking, even though my leg was
hurting badly. ❹ **even if** ▷ Pienso
irme, aunque tenga que salir por la
ventana. I shall leave, even if I have
to climb out of the window.; **No
te lo daré, aunque protestes.**
I won't give it to you however
much you complain.

auricular nm receiver (of
telephone); **los auriculares**
headphones

ausencia nf absence

ausente adj absent

Australia nf Australia

australiano, -a nm/f, adj
Australian

Austria nf Austria

austriaco, -a nm/f, adj Austrian

auténtico adj ❶ **real** ▷ Es de cuero
auténtico. It's real leather. ▷ Es
un auténtico campeón. He's a real
champion. ❷ **genuine** ▷ El cuadro
era auténtico. The painting was
genuine.

auto nm car

autobiografía nf autobiography

autobús (pl autobuses) nm bus;
en autobús by bus; **un autobús
de línea** a coach

autocar nm coach

autoedición nf desktop
publishing

autoescuela nf driving school

autógrafo nm autograph

automático adj automatic

automóvil nm car

automovilista nmf motorist

autonomía nf ❶ autonomy
❷ autonomous region

autonómico adj regional

autónomo adj ❶ autonomous
▷ Las comunidades autónomas the
autonomous regions ❷ self-
employed ▷ Ser autónomo tiene sus
ventajas. Being self-employed has
its advantages.

autopista nf motorway;
autopista de peaje toll motorway

autor, a nm/f author; **el autor del
cuadro** the painter; **los presuntos
autores del crimen** the suspected
killers

autorizado adj authorized

autorizar [14] vb to authorize; **Eso
no te autoriza a tratarlo así.** That
doesn't give you the right to treat
him this way.

autoservicio nm ❶ supermarket
❷ self-service restaurant

autostop nm hitch-hiking; **hacer
autostop** to hitch-hike

autostopista nmf hitch-hiker

autovía nf dual carriageway

auxilio nm help ▷ una llamada de auxilio a call for help; **los primeros auxilios** first aid
▶ excl help!

avanzar[14] vb to make progress; **¿Qué tal avanza el proyecto?** How's the project coming on?

avaro adj miserly

Avda. abbr (= Avenida) Ave. (=Avenue)

AVE abbr (= Alta Velocidad Española) high-speed train

ave nf bird; **un ave de rapiña** a bird of prey; **aves de corral** poultry

avellana nf hazelnut

avena nf oats

avenida nf avenue

aventajar[26] vb ▷ **El Salamanca aventaja en tres puntos al Córdoba.** Salamanca has a three-point lead over Córdoba.

aventar[40] vb (in Mexico) to throw

aventón (pl aventones) nm (in Mexico) lift ▷ Le di un aventón. I gave him a lift.

aventura nf ❶ adventure ❷ affair

avergonzar[14] vb to embarrass; **Me avergüenzan estas situaciones.** I find this sort of situation embarrassing.; **No me avergüenza nuestra relación.** I'm not ashamed of our relationship.; **avergonzarse de algo** to be ashamed of something ▷ No hay de qué avergonzarse. There's nothing to be ashamed of.; **Me avergüenzo de haberme portado**

tan mal. I'm ashamed of myself for behaving so badly.

avería nf **El coche tiene una avería.** The car has broken down.

averiarse[22] vb to break down

averiguar vb to find out

avestruz (pl avestruces) nm ostrich

aviación (pl aviaciones) nf ❶ aviation ❷ air force

aviento vb see **aventar**

avión (pl aviones) nm plane; **ir en avión** to fly

avioneta nf light aircraft

avisar[26] vb ❶ to warn ❷ to let…know ▷ Avísanos si hay alguna novedad. Let us know if there's any news. ❸ to call ▷ avisar al médico to call the doctor

aviso nm ❶ warning ▷ El árbitro le dio un aviso. The referee gave him a warning. ❷ notice ▷ Había un aviso en la puerta. There was a notice on the door.; **hasta nuevo aviso** until further notice

avispa nf wasp

ay excl ❶ ow! ▷ ¡Ay! ¡Me has pisado! Ow! You've trodden on my toe! ❷ oh no! ▷ ¡Ay! ¡Creo que nos han engañado! Oh no! I think they've cheated us!

ayer adv yesterday; **antes de ayer** the day before yesterday; **ayer por la mañana** yesterday morning; **ayer por la tarde (1)** yesterday afternoon **(2)** yesterday evening; **ayer por la noche** last night

ayuda nf help; **la ayuda humanitaria** humanitarian aid

ayudante *nmf* assistant

ayudar[**26**] *vb* to help ▷ *¿Me ayudas con los ejercicios?* Can you help me with these exercises?; **ayudar a alguien a hacer algo** to help somebody do something

ayuntamiento *nm* ❶ council ▷ *El ayuntamiento recauda sus propios impuestos.* The council collects its own taxes. ❷ town hall ❸ city hall

azafata *nf* air-hostess; **una azafata de congresos** a conference hostess

azar *nm* chance ▷ *Nos encontramos por azar.* We met by chance.; **al azar** at random ▷ *Escoge uno al azar.* Pick one at random.

azotar[**26**] *vb* to whip

azotea *nf* roof

azteca *nmf, adj* Aztec

azúcar *nm* sugar; **azúcar moreno** brown sugar; **un caramelo sin azúcar** a sugar-free sweet

azul *adj, nm* blue ▷ *una puerta azul* a blue door ▷ *Yo iba de azul.* I was dressed in blue.; **azul celeste** sky blue; **azul marino** navy blue

azulejo *nm* tile

babero *nm* bib

baca *nf* roof rack

bacalao *nm* cod

bache *nm* ❶ pothole ❷ bump

Bachillerato *nm*

- The **Bachillerato** is a two-year
- secondary school course
- leading to university.

bacteria *nf* bacterium

bafle *nm* loudspeaker

bahía *nf* bay

bailar[**26**] *vb* to dance

bailarín, -ina (*mpl* **bailarines**) *nm/f* dancer

baile *nm* dance

baja *nf* **darse de baja** to leave ▷ *Se dieron de baja en el club.* They left the club.; **estar de baja** to be on sick leave

bajada *nf* fall; **Me caí en la bajada**

de la montaña. I fell going down the mountain.; **la bajada hasta la playa** the road down to the beach

bajar [26] vb ❶ to go down ▷ Bajó la escalera muy despacio. He went down the stairs very slowly. ❷ to come down ▷ Los coches han bajado de precio. Cars have come down in price. ❸ to take down ▷ ¿Has bajado la basura? Have you taken the rubbish down? ❹ to bring down ▷ ¿Me bajas el abrigo? Hace frío aquí fuera. Could you bring my coat down, it's cold out here. ❺ to get down ▷ ¿Me bajas la maleta del armario? Could you get my case down from the wardrobe? ❻ to put down ▷ Los comercios han bajado los precios. Businesses have put their prices down. ❼ to turn down ▷ Baja la radio. Turn the radio down. ❽ to download (from internet); **bajarse de (1)** to get off (bus, train, plane) **(2)** to get out of (car)

bajo adj ❶ low ▷ una silla muy baja a very low chair; **la temporada baja** the low season ❷ short ▷ Mi hermano es muy bajo. My brother is very short.; **Hablaban en voz baja.** They spoke quietly.

▶ prep under ▷ Juan llevaba un libro bajo el brazo. Juan was carrying a book under his arm.; **bajo tierra** underground

▶ adv ❶ low ▷ El avión volaba muy bajo. The plane was flying very low. ❷ quietly ▷ ¡Habla bajo! Speak quietly!

▶ nm ❶ bass (instrument) ❷ ground floor

bala nf bullet

balcón (pl balcones) nm balcony

baldosa nf tile

baldosín (pl baldosines) nm tile

balear adj Balearic

Baleares nfpl the Balearic Islands

ballena nf whale

ballet (pl ballets) nm ballet

balneario nm spa

balón (pl balones) nm ball

baloncesto nm basketball

balonmano nm handball

balonvolea nm volleyball

balsa nf raft

banana nf (in Latin America) banana

bancario adj bank

banco nm ❶ bank (financial) ❷ bench ❸ pew

banda nf ❶ band ❷ gang ❸ sash; **la banda ancha** broadband; **la banda sonora** the soundtrack

bandeja nf tray

bandera nf flag

bandido nm bandit

bando nm side

banqueta nf ❶ stool ❷ (in Mexico) pavement

banquete nm banquet; **el banquete de bodas** the wedding reception

banquillo nm bench

bañador nm ❶ swimming trunks ❷ swimming costume

bañarse [26] vb ❶ to have a bath ❷ to go for a swim

bañera nf bath

baño nm bathroom; **darse un baño (1)** to have a bath **(2)** to go for a swim

bar nm bar

baraja nf pack of cards

barandilla nf ❶ banisters ❷ railing

barata nf (in Mexico) sale

barato adj cheap ▷ Esta marca es más barata que aquélla. This brand is cheaper than that one.
▶ adv cheaply

barba nf beard; **dejarse barba** to grow a beard

barbacoa nf barbecue

barbaridad nf atrocity; **Pablo come una barbaridad.** Pablo eats an awful lot.; **decir barbaridades** to talk nonsense; **¡Qué barbaridad!** Good grief!

barbilla nf chin

barca nf boat

barco nm ❶ ship; **un barco de guerra** a warship ❷ boat; **un barco de vela** a sailing boat

barda nf (in Mexico) fence

barniz (pl barnices) nm varnish

barnizar [14] vb to varnish

barra nf bar ▷ Me tomé un café en la barra. I had a coffee at the bar.; **las barras paralelas** the parallel bars; **una barra de pan** a French loaf; **una barra de labios** lipstick

barraca nf small farmhouse; **una barraca de feria** a fairground stall

barranco nm ravine

barrer [9] vb to sweep

barrera nf barrier; **una barrera de** seguridad a safety barrier

barriga nf belly; **Me duele la barriga.** I've got a sore stomach.

barril nm barrel

barrilete nm (in River Plate) kite

barrio nm area (of town, city); **la pescadería del barrio** the local fishmonger's; **el barrio chino** the red-light district

barro nm ❶ mud ❷ clay ▷ una vasija de barro a clay pot

barrote nm bar

barullo nm ❶ racket; **armar barullo** to make a racket ❷ mess

basarse [26] vb **Mi conclusión se basa en los datos.** My conclusion is based on the facts.; **¿En qué te basas para decir eso?** What grounds have you got for saying that?; **Para la novela me basé en la vida de mi abuela.** I based the novel on the life of my grandmother.

báscula nf scales

base nf ❶ base; **una base militar** a military base; **una base de datos** a database ❷ basis; **Lo consiguió a base de mucho trabajo.** She managed it through hard work.

básico adj basic

bastante adj ❶ enough ▷ Ya hay bastantes libros en casa. There are enough books in the house already. ❷ quite a lot of ▷ Vino bastante gente. Quite a lot of people came.; **Se tarda bastante tiempo en llegar.** It takes quite a while to get there.
▶ pron enough ▷ ¿Hay bastante? Is

there enough?

▶ *adv* ❶ quite ▷ *Son bastante ricos.*
They're quite rich. ❷ quite a lot
▷ *Ganan bastante.* They earn quite
a lot.; **Voy a tardar bastante.** I'm
going to be quite a while.

bastar [26] *vb* to be enough;
¡Basta! That's enough!; **bastarse**
to manage ▷ *Yo me basto solo.* I can
manage on my own.

basto *adj* coarse

bastón (*pl* bastones) *nm* stick; **un
bastón de esquí** a ski stick

bastos *nmpl* clubs

● Bastos are clubs, one of the
● suits in the Spanish card deck.

basura *nf* ❶ rubbish; **tirar algo a
la basura** to put something in the
bin ❷ litter; **la comida basura**
junk food; **el correo basura** spam

basurero, -a *nm/f* ❶ refuse
collector ❷ rubbish dump

bata *nf* ❶ dressing gown
❷ white coat ❸ lab coat

batalla *nf* battle

batería *nf* ❶ battery ❷ drums;
una batería de cocina a set of
kitchen equipment
▶ *nmf* drummer

batido *nm* milkshake ▷ *un batido de
fresa* a strawberry milkshake

batidora *nf* mixer

batir [59] *vb* ❶ to beat (*eggs*) ❷ to
whip (*cream*) ❸ to break (*a record*)

baúl *nm* ❶ chest ❷ trunk ❸ (*in
River Plate*) boot

bautizo *nm* christening

bayeta *nf* cloth

bebe, beba *nm/f* (*in River Plate*)
baby

bebé (*pl* bebés) *nm* baby

bebedero *nm* (*in Chile, Mexico*)
drinking fountain

beber [9] *vb* to drink

bebida *nf* drink; **bebidas
alcohólicas** alcoholic drinks

bebido *adj* drunk; **estar bebido**
to be drunk

beca *nf* ❶ grant ❷ scholarship

béisbol *nm* baseball

belén (*pl* belenes) *nm* crib

belga *nmf, adj* Belgian

Bélgica *nf* Belgium

belleza *nf* beauty

bello *adj* beautiful; **bellas artes**
fine art

bendecir [16] *vb* to bless

bendición (*pl* bendiciones) *nf*
blessing

beneficiar [26] *vb* to benefit;
beneficiarse de algo to benefit
from something

beneficio *nm* profit; **sacar
beneficio de algo** to benefit
from something; **a beneficio de**
in aid of

benéfico *adj* charity ▷ *un concierto
benéfico* a charity concert

berberecho *nm* cockle

berenjena *nf* aubergine

bermudas *nfpl* Bermuda shorts

berza *nf* cabbage

besar [26] *vb* to kiss; **Ana y Pepe
se besaron.** Ana and Pepe kissed
each other.

beso *nm* kiss; **dar un beso a
alguien** to give somebody a kiss

bestia *nf* beast

▶ adj **¡Qué bestia eres!** You're so rough!

besugo nm sea bream

betún nm shoe polish

biberón (pl **biberones**) nm baby's bottle; **Voy a dar el biberón al niño.** I'm going to give the baby his bottle.

Biblia nf Bible

biblioteca nf library

bicarbonato nm bicarbonate

bicho nm insect

bici nf bike

bicicleta nf bicycle; **una bicicleta de montaña** a mountain bike

bidé (pl **bidés**) nm bidet

bidón (pl **bidones**) nm drum

bien adv ❶ well ▷ Habla bien el español. He speaks Spanish well. ❷ good; **Lo pasamos muy bien.** We had a very good time. ❸ very ▷ un café bien caliente a very hot coffee; **¿Estás bien?** Are you OK?; **¡Está bien! Lo haré.** OK! I'll do it.; **¡Eso no está bien!** That's not very nice!; **Hiciste bien en decírselo.** You were right to tell him.; **¡Ya está bien!** That's enough!; **¡Qué bien!** Excellent!

▶ nm good ▷ Lo digo por tu bien. I'm telling you for your own good.; **los bienes** possessions

bienestar nm well-being

bienvenida nf **dar la bienvenida a alguien** to welcome somebody

bienvenido adj welcome ▷ Siempre serás bienvenido aquí. You will always be welcome here.

▶ excl welcome!

bife nm (in Chile, River Plate) steak

bifurcación (pl **bifurcaciones**) nf fork

bigote nm moustache

bikini nm bikini

bilingüe adj bilingual

billar nm billiards; **el billar americano** pool

billete nm ❶ ticket ▷ un billete de metro an underground ticket; **sacar un billete** to buy a ticket; **un billete de ida y vuelta** a return ticket; **un billete electrónico** an e-ticket ❷ note ▷ un billete de veinte euros a twenty-euro note

billón (pl **billones**) nm **un billón** a trillion

> The Spanish **billón** is equivalent to a million million while the English **billion** is only equivalent to a thousand million.

bingo nm ❶ bingo ▷ jugar al bingo to play bingo ❷ bingo hall

biodegradable adj biodegradable

biografía nf biography

biología nf biology

biológico adj ❶ organic ❷ biological

biquini nm bikini

birome nf (in River Plate) ballpoint pen

bisabuela nf great-grandmother

bisabuelo nm great-grandfather; **mis bisabuelos** my great-grandparents

bisagra nf hinge

bisiesto adj **un año bisiesto** a leap year

bisnieta nf great-granddaughter

bisnieto nm great-grandson; **tus bisnietos** your great-grandchildren

bistec (pl **bistecs**) nm steak

bisutería nf costume jewellery

bizco adj cross-eyed

bizcocho nm sponge cake

blanco adj white ▷ **un vestido blanco** a white dress
▶ nm white; **dar en el blanco** to hit the target; **dejar algo en blanco** to leave something blank; **Cuando iba a responder me quedé en blanco.** Just as I was about to reply my mind went blank.

blando adj soft ▷ **Este colchón es muy blando.** This mattress is very soft.

bloc (pl **blocs**) nm writing pad; **un bloc de dibujo** a drawing pad

bloque nm block; **un bloque de pisos** a block of flats

bloquear [26] vb to block

blusa nf blouse

bobada nf hacer bobadas to do silly things; **decir bobadas** to talk nonsense

bobina nf reel

bobo adj silly

boca nf mouth ▷ No debes hablar con la boca llena. You shouldn't talk with your mouth full.; **boca abajo** face down; **boca arriba** face up; **Me quedé con la boca abierta.** I was dumbfounded.; **la boca del metro** the entrance to the underground

bocacalle nf side street

bocadillo nm crusty filled roll; **Ya me he comido el bocadillo.** I've already had my roll.; **un bocadillo de queso** a cheese baguette

bocado nm ❶ bite; **No he probado bocado desde ayer.** I haven't had a bite to eat since yesterday. ❷ mouthful

bocata nm = **bocadillo**

bochorno nm Hace bochorno. It's muggy.

bocina nf ❶ horn ❷ (in Chile, River Plate) receiver

boda nf wedding; **las bodas de oro** golden wedding; **las bodas de plata** silver wedding

bodega nf ❶ cellar ❷ wine cellar ❸ wine shop ❹ hold (of plane)

bofetada nf slap; **dar una bofetada a alguien** to give somebody a slap

boicot (pl **boicots**) nm boycott

boina nf beret

bola nf ball; **una bola de nieve** a snowball

bolera nf bowling alley

boletería nf (in Latin America) ticket office

boletín (pl **boletines**) nm bulletin; **un boletín informativo** a news bulletin

boleto nm ticket ▷ **un boleto de lotería** a lottery ticket; **un boleto de quinielas** a pools coupon

boli nm pen

bolígrafo nm pen

bolillo nm (in Mexico) bun

Bolivia nf Bolivia

boliviano, -a nm/f, adj Bolivian

bollería nf pastries

bollo nm ❶ bun ❷ dent

bolos nmpl ❶ bowls ❷ tenpin bowling

bolsa nf ❶ bag ▷ *una bolsa de plástico* a plastic bag ▷ *una bolsa de viaje* a travel bag ❷ (in Mexico) handbag; **la Bolsa** the Stock Exchange

bolsillo nm pocket ▷ *Sacó las llaves del bolsillo.* He took his keys out of his pocket.; **un libro de bolsillo** a paperback

bolso nm bag

bomba nf ❶ bomb ❷ pump ▷ *una bomba de agua* a water pump; **pasarlo bomba** to have a brilliant time

bombacha nf (in River Plate) knickers

bombardear [26] vb to bombard

bombero, -a nm/f firefighter; **llamar a los bomberos** to call the fire brigade

bombilla nf lightbulb

bombita nf (in River Plate) lightbulb

bombo nm bass drum

bombón (pl bombones) nm chocolate

bombona nf gas cylinder

bondad nf kindness; **¿Tendría la bondad de …?** Would you be so kind as to …?

boniato nm sweet potato

bonito adj pretty
▶ nm tuna

bonobús (pl bonobuses) nm bus pass

boquerón (pl boquerones) nm fresh anchovy

boquete nm hole

borda nf echar algo por la borda to throw something overboard

bordar [26] vb to embroider

borde nm edge ▷ *al borde de la mesa* at the edge of the table; **estar al borde de algo** to be on the verge of something
▶ adj **¡No seas borde!** Don't be so horrible!

bordillo nm kerb

bordo nm **subir a bordo** to get on board

borrachera nf coger una borrachera to get drunk

borracho adj drunk ▷ *Estás borracho.* You're drunk.

borrador nm ❶ rough draft ❷ duster ▷ *Usó un trapo como borrador.* He used a rag as a duster.

borrar [26] vb ❶ to rub out ❷ to clean ▷ *Borra la pizarra.* Clean the board. ❸ to wipe ▷ *No borres esa cinta.* Don't wipe that tape.; **borrarse de** to take one's name off ▷ *Voy a borrarme de la lista.* I'm going to take my name off the list.

borrasca nf ❶ area of low pressure ❷ storm

borrón (pl borrones) nm stain

borroso adj blurred

Bosnia nf Bosnia

bosnio, -a nm/f, adj Bosnian

bosque nm ❶ wood ❷ forest

bostezar [14] vb to yawn

bota nf boot; **unas botas de agua**

a pair of wellingtons; **una bota de vino** a wineskin

botana nf (in Mexico) snack

botánica nf botany

botánico adj botanical

botar [26] vb ❶ to bounce ❷ to launch ❸ (in Latin America) to throw out

bote nm ❶ can ❷ tin ❸ jar ❹ boat; **un bote salvavidas** a lifeboat; **pegar un bote** to jump

botella nf bottle

botellín (pl botellines) nm bottle

botijo nm

• A **botijo** is an earthenware water container with spouts.

botín (pl botines) nm ❶ ankle boot ❷ haul

botiquín (pl botiquines) nm ❶ medicine cupboard ❷ first-aid kit ❸ sick bay

botón (pl botones) nm button; **pulsar un botón** to press a button

bóveda nf fly

boxeador, a nm/f boxer

boxear [26] vb to box

boxeo nm boxing

bragas nfpl knickers; **unas bragas** a pair of knickers

bragueta nf fly

brasa nf carne a la brasa grilled meat; **las brasas** the embers

brasier nm (in Mexico) bra

Brasil nm Brazil

brasileño, -a nm/f, adj Brazilian

brasilero, -a nm/f, adj (in Latin America) = **brasileño**

bravo excl well done!
▶ adj fierce

braza nf breaststroke; **nadar a braza** to do the breaststroke

brazalete nm bracelet

brazo nm arm ▷ Me duele el brazo. My arm hurts. ▷ Estaba sentada con los brazos cruzados. She was sitting with her arms folded.; **ir del brazo** to walk arm-in-arm; **un brazo de gitano** a swiss roll

brecha nf opening

breve adj ❶ brief ▷ por breves momentos for a few brief moments ❷ short ▷ un relato breve a short story; **en breve** shortly

bricolaje nm DIY

brillante adj ❶ shiny ❷ bright; **blanco brillante** brilliant white ❸ outstanding
▶ nm diamond

brillar [26] vb ❶ to shine ❷ to sparkle

brillo nm ❶ shine ❷ sparkle; **La pantalla tiene mucho brillo.** The screen is too bright.; **sacar brillo a algo** to polish something

brincar [49] vb to jump up and down; **brincar de alegría** to jump for joy

brinco nm pegar un brinco to jump; **Bajé tres escalones de un brinco.** I jumped down three steps.

brindar [26] vb brindar por to drink a toast to; **brindarse a hacer algo** to offer to do something

brindis (pl brindis) nm toast; **hacer un brindis** to make a toast

brisa nf breeze

británico, -a nm/f British person;

los británicos the British
▸ adj British
brocha nf ❶ paintbrush ❷ shaving brush
broche nm ❶ brooch ❷ clasp
broma nf joke; **gastar una broma a alguien** to play a joke on someone; **decir algo en broma** to say something as a joke; **una broma pesada** a practical joke
bromear [26] vb to joke
bromista nmf joker
bronca nf ❶ row; **echar una bronca a alguien** to tell somebody off ❷ fuss; **armar una bronca** to kick up a fuss
bronce nm bronze
bronceado adj tanned
▸ nm suntan
bronceador nm suntan lotion
bronquitis nf bronchitis
brotar [26] vb to sprout
bruces adv **Me caí de bruces.** I fell flat on my face.
bruja nf witch
brujo nm wizard
brújula nf compass
bruma nf mist
brusco adj ❶ sudden ❷ abrupt
bruto adj gross ▷ **el salario bruto** gross salary; **¡No seas bruto!** Don't be so rough!
bucear [26] vb to dive
buen adj = **bueno**
bueno adj good

> **bueno** is shortened to **buen** before masculine singular nouns.

▷ **Es un buen libro.** It's a good book.

▷ **Hace buen tiempo.** The weather's good. ▷ **Es buena persona.** He's a good person.; **ser bueno para** to be good for ▷ **Esta bebida es buena para la salud.** This drink is good for your health.; **Está muy bueno este bizcocho.** This sponge cake is lovely.; **Lo bueno fue que ni siquiera quiso venir.** The best thing was that he didn't even want to come.; **¡Bueno!** (1) OK! (2) (in Mexico) Hello!; **Bueno. ¿Y qué?** Well?; **¡Buenas!** Hello!; **Irás por las buenas o por las malas.** You'll go whether you like it or not.
buey nm ox
bufanda nf scarf
bufete nm **un bufete de abogados** a legal practice
buffet (pl buffets) nm buffet
buhardilla nf attic
búho nm owl
buitre nm vulture
bujía nf spark plug
Bulgaria nf Bulgaria
búlgaro, -a nm/f, adj Bulgarian
▸ nm Bulgarian (language)
bulto nm ❶ lump ▷ **Tengo un bulto en la frente.** I've got a lump on my forehead. ❷ figure ▷ **Sólo vi un bulto.** I only saw a figure.; **Llevábamos muchos bultos.** We were carrying a lot of bags.
buñuelo nm doughnut
buque nm ship; **un buque de guerra** a warship
burbuja nf bubble; **un refresco sin burbujas** a still drink; **un refresco con burbujas** a fizzy drink

burlarse [**26**] *vb* **burlarse de alguien** to make fun of someone

buró (*pl* **burós**) *nm* (*in Mexico*) bedside table

burocracia *nf* bureaucracy

burrada *nf* **hacer burradas** to do stupid things; **No hagas burradas con el coche.** Don't do anything stupid with the car.; **decir burradas** to talk nonsense

burro *adj* ❶ thick ❷ rough
▶ *nm* ❶ donkey ❷ idiot ▷ *Eres un burro.* You're an idiot.

busca *nf* **en busca de** in search of
▶ *nm* bleeper

buscador *nm* search engine

buscar [**49**] *vb* to look for ▷ *Ana busca trabajo.* Ana's looking for work.; **Te voy a buscar a la estación.** I'll come and pick you up at the station.; **buscar una palabra en el diccionario** to look up a word in the dictionary; **Él se lo ha buscado.** He was asking for it.

búsqueda *nf* search

butaca *nf* ❶ armchair ❷ seat

butano *nm* bottled gas

buzo *nm* diver

buzón (*pl* **buzones**) *nm*
❶ letterbox ❷ postbox; **echar una carta al buzón** to post a letter; **buzón de voz** voice mail

C

C/ *abbr* (= *calle*) St (= *Street*)

caballero *nm* gentleman; **¿Dónde está la sección de caballeros?** Where is the men's department?; **"Caballeros"** "Gents"

caballo *nm* ❶ horse; **¿Te gusta montar a caballo?** Do you like riding?; **un caballo de carreras** a racehorse ❸ knight (*in chess*)

cabaña *nf* hut

cabello *nm* hair

caber *vb* to fit ▷ *Tu guitarra no cabe en mi armario.* Your guitar won't fit in my cupboard.; **En mi coche caben dos maletas más.** There's room for two suitcases in my car.; **No cabe nadie más.** There's no room for anyone else.

cabeza *nf* head ▷ *Se rascó la cabeza.* He scratched his head.; **Se tiró**

al agua de cabeza. He dived headfirst into the water.; **estar a la cabeza de la clasificación** to be at the top of the league

cabina nf ❶ phone box ❷ booth ❸ cockpit ❹ cubicle

cable nm cable

cabo nm ❶ cape; **Cabo Cañaveral** Cape Canaveral ❷ corporal; **al cabo de dos días** after two days; **llevar algo a cabo** to carry something out

cabra nf goat

cabrá vb see **caber**

cabreado adj annoyed

caca nf **hacer caca** to do a poo

cacahuate nm (in Mexico) peanut

cacahuete nm peanut

cacao nm ❶ cocoa ❷ lipsalve

cacerola nf saucepan

cacharros nmpl pots and pans

cachondeo nm **Las clases eran un cachondeo.** The classes were a joke.; **No le hagas caso, está de cachondeo.** Don't pay any attention to him, he's having you on.

cachorro, -a nm/f ❶ puppy ❷ cub

cactus (pl cactus) nm cactus

cada adj ❶ each ▷ Cada libro es de un color distinto. Each book is a different colour.; **cada uno** each one ❸ every ▷ cada año every year ▷ cada vez que la veo every time I see her ▷ uno de cada diez one out of every ten; **Viene cada vez más gente.** More and more people are coming.; **Viene cada vez menos.**

He comes less and less often.; **Cada vez hace más frío.** It's getting colder and colder.; **¿Cada cuánto vas al dentista?** How often do you go to the dentist?

cadáver nm corpse

cadena nf ❶ chain; **tirar de la cadena del wáter** to flush the toilet; **la cadena de montaje** the assembly line; **una cadena montañosa** a mountain range ❷ channel ▷ Por la cadena 3 dan una película. There's a film on channel 3.; **cadena perpetua** life imprisonment

cadera nf hip

caducar [49] vb to expire; **Esta leche está caducada.** This milk is past its sell-by date.

caer [6] vb to fall; **El avión cayó al mar.** The plane came down in the sea.; **Su cumpleaños cae en viernes.** Her birthday falls on a Friday.; **Su hermano me cae muy bien.** I really like his brother.; **caerse** to fall ▷ El niño se cayó de la cama. The child fell out of bed. ▷ No te vayas a caer del caballo. Be careful not to fall off the horse.; **Se me cayeron las monedas.** I dropped the coins.

café (pl cafés) nm ❶ coffee; **un café con leche** a white coffee; **un café solo** a black coffee ❷ café

cafetera nf coffee pot

cafetería nf café

caída nf fall

caigo vb see **caer**

caimán (pl caimanes) nm

alligator

caja nf ❶ box ▷ *una caja de zapatos* a shoe box ❷ case ❸ crate ❹ checkout ❺ till ❻ cash desk; **la caja de ahorros** the savings bank; **la caja de cambios** the gearbox; **la caja fuerte** the safe

cajero, -a nm/f checkout operator; **Trabajo de cajera en un supermercado.** I work on the checkout in a supermarket.
▶ nm **un cajero automático** a cash dispenser

cajón (pl **cajones**) nm ❶ drawer ❷ crate (in Latin America) coffin

cajuela nf (in Mexico) boot

cala nf cove

calabacín (pl **calabacines**) nm courgette

calabacita nf (in Mexico) courgette

calabaza nf pumpkin

calado adj soaked; **Estaba calado hasta los huesos.** He was soaked to the skin.

calamar nm squid; **calamares a la romana** squid fried in batter

calambre nm ❶ cramp ▷ *Tengo un calambre en la pierna.* I've got cramp in my leg. ❷ electric shock ▷ *Si tocas el cable te dará calambre.* If you touch the cable you'll get an electric shock.

calar [26] vb to soak; **La lluvia me caló hasta los huesos.** I got soaked to the skin in the rain.

calavera nf skull

calcar [49] vb to trace

calcetín (pl **calcetines**) nm sock

calcio nm calcium

calculadora nf calculator

calcular [26] vb to calculate; **Calculo que nos llevará unos tres días.** I reckon that it will take us around three days.

cálculo nm calculation

caldo nm broth; **una pastilla de caldo** a stock cube

calefacción nf heating; **calefacción central** central heating

calendario nm calendar

calentador nm heater

calentamiento nm el **calentamiento global** global warming; **ejercicios de calentamiento** warm-up exercises

calentar [40] vb ❶ to heat up ❷ to warm up; **calentarse (1)** to heat up **(2)** to warm up

calentura nf temperature

calidad nf quality

caliente vb see **calentar**
▶ adj ❶ hot ▷ *Esta sopa está muy caliente.* This soup is very hot. ❷ warm ▷ *¡Esta cerveza está caliente!* This beer is warm!

calificación (pl **calificaciones**) nf mark; **boletín de calificaciones** school report

calificar [49] vb to mark; **Me calificó con sobresaliente.** He gave me an A.

callado adj quiet ▷ *Estuvo callado bastante rato.* He was quiet for quite a while.

callar [26] vb to be quiet; **callarse (1)** to keep quiet **(2)** to stop

talking; **¡Cállate!** Shut up!
calle nf ❶ street; **una calle
cortada** a cul-de-sac; **una calle de
sentido único** a one-way street;
una calle peatonal a pedestrian
precinct ❷ lane (on racetrack,
in pool)
callejero nm street map
callejón (pl **callejones**) nm alley
calma nf calm; **Todo estaba en
calma.** Everything was calm.;
Logró mantener la calma. He
managed to keep calm.; **Piénsalo
con calma.** Think about it calmly.;
Tómatelo con calma. Take it easy.
calmante nm ❶ painkiller
❷ tranquillizer
calmar [26] vb ❶ to calm down;
¡Cálmate! Calm down! ❷ to
relieve (pain)
calor nm heat ▷ No se puede trabajar
con este calor. It's impossible to
work in this heat.; **Hace calor.** It's
hot.; **Tengo calor.** I'm hot.
caloría nf calorie
caluroso adj hot
calvo adj bald; **Se está quedando
calvo.** He's going bald.
calzado nm footwear
calzoncillos nmpl underpants
calzones nmpl (in Chile) knickers
cama nf bed; **hacer la cama** to
make the bed; **Está en la cama.**
He's in bed.; **meterse en la cama**
to get into bed
cámara nf camera; **una cámara
digital** a digital camera; **a cámara
lenta** in slow motion
camarera nf ❶ waitress ❷ maid

camarero nm waiter
camarote nm cabin
cambiar [26] vb ❶ to change
▷ No has cambiado nada. You
haven't changed a bit. ▷ Quiero
cambiar este abrigo por uno más
grande. I want to change this coat
for a larger size.; **Tenemos que
cambiar de tren en París.** We
have to change trains in Paris.; **He
cambiado de idea.** I've changed
my mind. ❷ to swap ▷ Te cambio
mi bolígrafo por tu goma. I'll swap
my ballpoint for your rubber.;
cambiarse to get changed; **Se
han cambiado de coche.** They've
changed their car.; **cambiarse de
sitio** to move; **cambiarse de casa**
to move house
cambio nm ❶ change ▷ un
cambio brusco de temperatura a
sudden change in temperature
▷ ¿Tiene cambio de cincuenta?
Have you got change of a fifty?;
el cambio climático climate
change ❷ small change ▷ Necesito
cambio. I need some small change.
❸ exchange; **¿A cómo está el
cambio?** What's the exchange
rate?; **a cambio de** in return for;
en cambio on the other hand
camello nm ❶ camel ❷ drug
pusher
camilla nf ❶ stretcher ❷ couch
caminar [26] vb to walk
caminata nf long walk
camino nm ❶ path; **un camino
de montaña** a mountain track
❷ way ▷ ¿Sabes el camino a su

casa? Do you know the way to his house?; **A medio camino paramos a comer.** Half-way there, we stopped to eat.; **La farmacia me queda de camino.** The chemist's is on my way.

camión (*pl* **camiones**) *nm* **❶** lorry; **un camión cisterna** a tanker; **el camión de la basura** the dustcart **❷** (*in Mexico*) bus

camionero, -a *nm/f* lorry driver

camioneta *nf* van

camisa *nf* shirt

camiseta *nf* **❶** T-shirt **❷** vest

camisón (*pl* **camisones**) *nm* nightdress

camote *nm* (*in Mexico*) sweet potato

campamento *nm* camp

campana *nf* bell

campaña *nf* campaign; **la campaña electoral** the election campaign

campeón, -ona *nm/f* champion

campeonato *nm* championship

campesino, -a *nm/f* **❶** country person **❷** peasant

camping (*pl* **campings**) *nm* **❶** camping ▷ **ir de camping** to go camping **❷** campsite

campo *nm* **❶** country ▷ **Prefiero vivir en el campo.** I prefer living in the country. **Corrían campo a través.** They were running cross-country.; **el trabajo del campo** farm work **❷** countryside ▷ **El campo se pone verde en primavera.** The countryside turns green in springtime. **❸** field **❹** pitch;

un campo de deportes a sports ground; **un campo de golf** a golf course

cana *nf* grey hair; **Tiene canas.** He's got grey hair.; **Le están saliendo canas.** He's going grey.

Canadá *nm* Canada

canadiense *nmf, adj* Canadian

canal *nm* **❶** channel ▷ **Por el canal 2 dan una película.** They're showing a film on channel 2.; **el Canal de la Mancha** the English Channel **❷** canal; **el Canal de Panamá** the Panama Canal

canapé (*pl* **canapés**) *nm* canapé

Canarias *nfpl* the Canaries; **las Islas Canarias** the Canary Islands

canario *nm* canary

canasta *nf* basket

cancelar [**26**] *vb* to cancel

cáncer *nm* cancer ▷ **cáncer de mama** breast cancer

Cáncer *nm* Cancer (*sign*); **Soy cáncer.** I'm Cancer.

cancha *nf* **❶** court **❷** (*in Latin America*) pitch

canción (*pl* **canciones**) *nf* song; **una canción de cuna** a lullaby

candado *nm* padlock; **Estaba cerrado con candado.** It was padlocked.

candidato, -a *nm/f* candidate

canela *nf* cinnamon

canelones *nmpl* cannelloni

cangrejo *nm* **❶** crab **❷** crayfish

canguro *nm* kangaroo
▶ *nmf* baby-sitter; **hacer de canguro** to baby-sit

canica *nf* marble; **jugar a las**

canicas to play marbles

canilla nf (in River Plate) tap

canoa nf canoe

cansado adj ① tired ▷ Estoy muy cansado. I'm very tired. ② tiring ▷ Es un trabajo muy cansado. It's a very tiring job.

cansancio nm tiredness; ¡Qué cansancio! I'm so tired!

cansar [26] vb Es un viaje que cansa. It's a tiring journey.; **cansarse** to get tired; **Me cansé de esperarlo y me marché.** I got tired of waiting for him and I left.

cantante nmf singer

cantar [26] vb to sing

cantidad nf ① amount ▷ una cierta cantidad de dinero a certain amount of money ② quantity; ¡Qué cantidad de gente! What a lot of people!; **Había cantidad de turistas.** There were a lot of tourists.

cantimplora nf water bottle

canto nm ① edge ② singing

caña nf ① cane; **caña de azúcar** sugar cane ② glass of beer; **Me tomé dos cañas.** I had two beers.; **una caña de pescar** a fishing rod

cañería nf pipe

caos nm chaos

capa nf ① layer; **la capa de ozono** the ozone layer ② cloak

capacidad nf ① ability ② capacity

capaz (pl capaces) adj capable ▷ Es capaz de olvidarse el pasaporte. He's quite capable of forgetting his passport.; **Por ella sería capaz de cualquier cosa.** He would do anything for her.

capilla nf chapel

capital nf capital

capitán, -ana (mpl capitanes) nm/f captain

capítulo nm ① chapter ② episode

capricho nm whim; **Lo compré por capricho.** I bought it on a whim.; **Decidí viajar en primera para darme un capricho.** I decided to travel first class to give myself a treat.

Capricornio nm Capricorn (sign); **Soy capricornio.** I'm Capricorn.

capturar [26] vb to capture

capucha nf ① hood ② top

caqui (pl caqui) adj khaki

cara nf ① face ▷ Tiene la cara alargada. He has a long face.; **Tienes mala cara.** You don't look well.; **Tenía cara de pocos amigos.** He looked very unfriendly.; **No pongas esa cara.** Don't look like that. ② cheek ▷ ¡Qué cara! What a cheek! ③ side ▷ un folio escrito por las dos caras a sheet written on both sides; ¿**Cara o cruz?** Heads or tails?

caracol nm ① snail ② winkle

carácter (pl caracteres) nm nature; **tener buen carácter** to be good-natured; **tener mal carácter** to be bad-tempered; **La chica tiene mucho carácter.** The girl has a strong personality.

característica nf characteristic

caramba excl goodness!

a b c d e f g h i j k l m n o p q r s t u v w x y z

caramelo nm sweet

caravana nf caravan; **Había una caravana de dos kilómetros.** There was a two-kilometre tailback.

carbón nm coal; **carbón de leña** charcoal

carcajada nf **soltar una carcajada** to burst out laughing; **reírse a carcajadas** to roar with laughing

cárcel nf prison ▷ **Está en la cárcel.** He's in prison.

cardenal nm ❶ bruise ❷ cardinal

cardiaco adj heart ▷ **un ataque cardiaco** a heart attack

careta nf mask

carga nf ❶ load ▷ **carga máxima** maximum load ❷ burden ❸ refill

cargado adj ❶ loaded ❷ stuffy ❸ strong; **Venía cargada de paquetes.** She was laden with parcels.

cargamento nm ❶ cargo ❷ load

cargar [38] vb ❶ to load ▷ **Cargaron el coche de maletas.** They loaded the car with suitcases. ❷ to fill (pen, lighter) ❸ to charge (battery); **Tuve que cargar con todo.** I had to take responsibility for everything.

cargo nm post ▷ **un cargo de mucha responsabilidad** a very responsible post; **Está a cargo de la contabilidad.** He's in charge of keeping the books.

Caribe nm **el Caribe** the Caribbean

caribeño, -a nm/f, adj Caribbean

caricatura nf caricature

caricia nf caress; **Le hacía caricias al bebé.** She was caressing the baby.

caridad nf charity

caries (pl **caries**) nf ❶ tooth decay ❷ cavity

cariño nm affection; **Les tengo mucho cariño.** I'm very fond of them.; **Ven aquí, cariño.** Come here, darling.

cariñoso adj ❶ affectionate ❷ warm

carnaval nm carnival
- The **carnaval** is the traditional
- period of celebrating prior to
- the start of Lent.

carne nf meat ▷ **No como carne.** I don't eat meat.; **carne de cerdo** pork; **carne de puerco** (in Mexico) pork; **carne de cordero** lamb; **carne molida** (in Latin America) mince; **carne picada** mince; **carne de ternera** veal; **carne de vaca** beef; **carne de res** (in Mexico) beef

carnet (pl **carnets**) nm card; **el carnet de identidad** identity card; **un carnet de conducir** a driving licence

carnicería nf butcher's

carnicero, -a nm/f butcher

caro adj, adv expensive ▷ **Las entradas me costaron muy caras.** The tickets were very expensive.

carpeta nf folder

carpintería nf ❶ carpenter's shop ❷ carpentry

carpintero, -a nm/f carpenter

carrera nf ❶ race ▷ **una carrera de caballos** a horse race; **Me di**

una carrera para alcanzar el autobús. I had to run to catch the bus. ❸ degree ▷ *Está haciendo la carrera de derecho.* He's doing a law degree. ❸ career ▷ *Estaba en el mejor momento de su carrera.* He was at the height of his career. ❹ ladder (in tights)

carrete nm ❶ film ❷ reel

carretera nf road; **una carretera nacional** an A-road; **una carretera de circunvalación** a bypass

carretilla nf wheelbarrow

carril nm ❶ lane ❷ rail

carril-bici (pl carriles-bici) nm cycle lane

carrito nm trolley

carro nm ❶ cart ❷ trolley ❸ (in Latin America) car

carroza nf ❶ coach ❷ float

carta nf ❶ letter ▷ *Le he escrito una carta a Juan.* I've written Juan a letter.; **echar una carta** to post a letter ❷ card ▷ *jugar a las cartas* to play cards ❸ menu (in restaurant); **la carta de vinos** the wine list

cartel nm ❶ poster ❷ sign

cartelera nf ❶ billboard ❷ listings; **Estuvo tres años en la cartelera.** It ran for three years.

cartera nf ❶ wallet ❷ briefcase ❸ satchel ❹ (in Latin America) handbag ❺ postwoman

carterista nmf pickpocket

cartero nm postman

cartón (pl cartones) nm ❶ cardboard ▷ *una caja de cartón* a cardboard box ❷ carton

cartucho nm cartridge

cartulina nf card

casa nf ❶ house ▷ *una casa de dos plantas* a two-storey house ❷ home ▷ *Estábamos en casa.* We were at home. ▷ *Se fue a casa.* She went home.; **Estábamos en casa de Juan.** We were at Juan's.

casado adj married ▷ *una mujer casada* a married woman; **Está casado con una francesa.** He's married to a Frenchwoman.

casarse [26] vb to get married; **Se casó con una periodista.** He married a journalist.

cascabel nm small bell

cascada nf waterfall

cascar [49] vb to crack (nut, egg)

cáscara nf ❶ shell ❷ skin

casco nm helmet ▷ *El ciclista llevaba casco.* The cyclist was wearing a helmet.; **el casco antiguo de la ciudad** the old part of the town; **el casco urbano** the town centre; **los cascos** headphones

casero adj homemade

caseta nf ❶ kennel ❷ bathing hut ❸ stall

casete nm cassette player ▷ nm or nf cassette

casi adv almost ▷ *Son casi las cinco.* It's almost five o'clock.; **Casi me ahogo.** I nearly drowned.; **No queda casi nada en la nevera.** There's hardly anything left in the refrigerator.; **Casi nunca se equivoca.** He hardly ever makes a mistake.

casilla nf ❶ box ❷ square; **Casilla de Correos** (in River Plate) post-office box number

casino nm casino

caso nm case; **En ese caso** in that case; **En caso de que llueva, iremos en autobús.** If it rains, we'll go by bus.; **El caso es que no me queda dinero.** The thing is, I haven't got any money left.; **No le hagas caso.** Don't take any notice of him.; **Hazle caso que ella tiene más experiencia.** Listen to her, she has more experience.

caspa nf dandruff

cassette = **casete**

castaña nf chestnut

castaño adj chestnut ▷ Mi hermana tiene el pelo castaño. My sister has chestnut hair.

castañuelas nfpl castanets

castellano, -a nm/f, adj Castilian
　▶ nm Spanish (language)
　● Since the language we know
　● as Spanish originated in
　● Castile, it is commonly referred
　● to as **castellano**, especially
　● by Catalans, Basques and
　● Galicians, who have their own
　● regional official languages too.

castigar [38] vb to punish

castigo nm punishment

Castilla nf Castile

castillo nm castle

casualidad nf coincidence; **¡Qué casualidad!** What a coincidence!; **Nos encontramos por casualidad.** We met by chance.; **Da la casualidad que nacimos el mismo día.** It so happens that we were born on the same day.

catalán, -ana (mpl catalanes) nm/f, adj Catalan
　▶ nm Catalan (language)

catálogo nm catalogue

Cataluña nf Catalonia

catarro nm cold ▷ Vas a pillar un catarro. You're going to catch a cold.

catarata nf waterfall

catástrofe nf catastrophe

catedral nf cathedral

catedrático, -a nm/f ❶ professor ❷ principal teacher

categoría nf category; **un hotel de primera categoría** a first-class hotel; **un puesto de poca categoría** a low-ranking position

católico, -a nm/f, adj Catholic ▷ Soy católico. I am a Catholic.

catorce adj, pron fourteen; **el catorce de enero** the fourteenth of January

caucho nm rubber

causa nf cause; **a causa de** because of

causar [26] vb to cause; **Su visita me causó mucha alegría.** His visit made me very happy.; **Rosa me causó buena impresión.** Rosa made a good impression on me.

cava nm cava (sparkling wine)

cavar [26] vb to dig

caverna nf cave

cayendo vb see **caer**

caza nf ❶ hunting ❷ shooting

cazador nm hunter

cazadora nf ❶ jacket ❷ hunter

cazar [14] vb ❶ to hunt ❷ to shoot

cazo nm ❶ saucepan ❷ ladle

cazuela nf pot

CD (pl CDs) nm CD

CD-ROM (pl CD-ROMs) nm CD-ROM

cebo nm bait

cebolla nf onion

cebolleta nf ❶ spring onion ❷ pickled onion

cebra nf zebra; **un paso de cebra** a zebra crossing

ceder [9] vb ❶ to give in ▷ Al final tuve que ceder. In the end I had to give in. ❷ to give way ▷ La estantería cedió por el peso de los libros. The shelves gave way under the weight of the books.; **"Ceda el paso"** "Give way"

ceguera nf blindness

ceja nf eyebrow

celda nf cell

celebración (pl celebraciones) nf celebration

celebrar [26] vb ❶ to celebrate ❷ to hold

celo nm Sellotape®

celofán nm cellophane

celos nmpl jealousy ▷ Lo hizo por celos. He did it out of jealousy.; **Tiene celos de su mejor amiga.** She's jealous of her best friend.; **Lo hace para darle celos.** He does it to make her jealous.

celoso adj jealous

célula nf cell

cementerio nm cemetery; **un cementerio de coches** a scrapyard

cemento nm ❶ cement ❷ concrete; **el cemento armado** reinforced concrete ❸ (in Latin America) glue

cena nf dinner ▷ La cena es a las nueve. Dinner is at nine o'clock.

cenar [26] vb to have dinner; **¿Qué quieres cenar?** What do you want for dinner?

cenicero nm ashtray

ceniza nf ash

censura nf censorship

centavo nm cent (division of dollar)

centésima nf **una centésima de segundo** a hundredth of a second

centígrado adj centigrade

centímetro nm centimetre

céntimo nm cent (division of euro)

central adj central
   ▸ nf head office; **una central eléctrica** a power station; **una central nuclear** a nuclear power station

centralita nf switchboard

céntrico adj central ▷ Está en un barrio céntrico. It's in a central area.; **Es un piso céntrico.** The flat's in the centre of town.

centro nm centre ▷ en pleno centro de la ciudad right in the town centre; **Fui al centro a hacer unas compras.** I went into town to do some shopping.; **un centro comercial** a shopping centre; **un centro médico** a hospital

centroamericano, -a nm/f, adj Central American

ceñido adj tight

cepillar [26] vb to brush; **Se está cepillando los dientes.** He's brushing his teeth.

cepillo nm brush; **un cepillo de dientes** a toothbrush

cera nf wax

cerámica nf pottery ▷ *Me gusta la cerámica.* I like pottery.; **una cerámica** a piece of pottery

cerca adv near; **¿Hay algún banco por aquí cerca?** Is there a bank near here?; **cerca del cine** near the cinema; **cerca de dos horas** nearly two hours; **Quería verlo de cerca.** I wanted to see it close up.

cercanías nfpl outskirts

cercano adj nearby ▷ *Viven en un pueblo cercano.* They live in a nearby village.; **una de las calles cercanas a la catedral** one of the streets close to the cathedral

cerdo nm ❶ pig ❷ pork

cereal nm cereal; **Los niños desayunan cereales.** The children have cereal for breakfast.

cerebro nm brain

ceremonia nf ceremony

cereza nf cherry

cerilla nf match

cerillo nm (in Mexico) match

cero nm zero; **Estamos a cinco grados bajo cero.** It's five degrees below zero.; **cero coma tres** zero point three; **Van dos a cero.** The score is two-nil.; **Empataron a cero.** It was a no-score draw.; **quince a cero** fifteen-love

cerquillo nm (in Latin America) fringe

cerrado adj closed ▷ *Las tiendas están cerradas.* The shops are

closed.; **cerrado con llave** locked

cerradura nf lock

cerrar [40] vb ❶ to close ▷ *Cerró el libro.* He closed the book. ❷ to turn off ▷ *Cierra el grifo.* Turn off the tap.; **Cerré la puerta con llave.** I locked the door.; **La puerta se cerró de golpe.** The door slammed shut.

cerrojo nm bolt; **echar el cerrojo** to bolt the door

certificado nm certificate ▶ adj registered; **Mandé el paquete certificado.** I sent the parcel by registered post.

cervecería nf bar

cerveza nf beer; **la cerveza de barril** draught beer

cesar [26] vb to stop; **No cesa de hablar.** He never stops talking.; **No cesaba de repetirlo.** He kept repeating it.

césped nm grass ▷ *"no pisar el césped"* "keep off the grass"

cesta nf basket; **una cesta de Navidad** a Christmas hamper

cesto nm basket

chabacano nm (in Mexico) apricot

chabola nf shack; **un barrio de chabolas** a shantytown

chaleco nm waistcoat; **un chaleco salvavidas** a life-jacket

chalet (pl chalets) nm ❶ cottage ❷ villa ❸ house

champán (pl champanes) nm champagne

champiñón (pl champiñones) nm mushroom

champú (pl champús) nm

shampoo

chancho, -a nm/f (in River Plate) pig

chancleta nf flip-flop; **unas chancletas** a pair of flip-flops

chándal (pl **chándals**) nm tracksuit

chantaje nm blackmail; **hacer chantaje a alguien** to blackmail somebody

chapa nf ❶ badge ❷ top (of bottle) ❸ sheet (of metal) ❹ (in Latin America) number plate

chapado adj **chapado en oro** gold-plated

chaparrón (pl **chaparrones**) nm **Anoche cayó un buen chaparrón.** There was a real downpour last night.; **Es sólo un chaparrón.** It's just a shower.

chapuza nf botched job; **hacer chapuzas** to do odd jobs

chapuzón (pl **chapuzones**) nm **darse un chapuzón** to go for a dip

chaqueta nf ❶ cardigan ❷ jacket

charca nf pond

charco nm puddle

charcutería nf delicatessen (specializing in cold meats)

charla nf ❶ chat ▷ **Estuvimos de charla.** We had a chat. ❷ talk ▷ **Dio una charla sobre teatro clásico.** He gave a talk on classical theatre.

charlar [26] vb to chat

chasco nm disappointment; **llevarse un chasco** to be disappointed

chat nm chatroom

chatarra nf scrap metal

chatear [26] vb to chat (on internet)

chava nf (in Mexico) girl

chavo nm (in Mexico) boy

checar [49] vb (in Mexico) to check

checo, -a nm/f, adj Czech; **la República Checa** the Czech Republic
▶ nm Czech (language)

chef (pl **chefs**) nm chef

cheque nm cheque; **los cheques de viaje** traveller's cheques

chequeo nm check-up ▷ **hacerse un chequeo** to have a check-up

chévere adj, adv (in Latin America) great

chica nf girl; see also **chico**

chícharo nm (in Mexico) pea

chichón (pl **chichones**) nm bump ▷ **Me ha salido un chichón en la frente.** I've got a bump on my forehead.

chicle nm chewing gum

chico adj small
▶ nm ❶ boy ▷ **los chicos de la clase** the boys in the class ❷ guy ▷ **Me parece un chico muy majo.** He seems like a nice guy.; see also **chica**

Chile nm Chile

chileno, -a nm/f, adj Chilean

chillar [26] vb to scream

chimenea nf ❶ chimney ❷ fireplace

chimpancé (pl **chimpancés**) nm chimpanzee

China nf China

chinche nf (in Mexico, River Plate) drawing pin

chincheta nf drawing pin

chino, -a nm/f un chino a Chinese man; una china a Chinese woman; los chinos the Chinese
▶ nm Chinese (language)
▶ adj Chinese

Chipre nm Cyprus

chirimoya nf custard apple

chirriar [22] vb to squeak

chisme nm ❶ thing ❷ piece of gossip

chismorrear [26] vb to gossip

chismoso adj ¡No seas chismoso! Don't be such a gossip!

chiste nm ❶ joke ▷ contar un chiste to tell a joke; un chiste verde a dirty joke ❷ cartoon

chocar [49] vb to crash ▷ Los trenes chocaron de frente. The trains crashed head-on.; chocar con algo to crash into something; chocar contra (1) to hit (2) to bump into; Me choca que no sepas nada. I'm shocked that you don't know anything about it.

chocolate nm chocolate ▷ chocolate con leche milk chocolate; Nos tomamos un chocolate. We had a cup of hot chocolate.

chocolatina nf chocolate bar

chófer nmf ❶ driver ❷ chauffeur

chopo nm black poplar

choque nm ❶ crash ❷ clash (between people, cultures)

chorizo nm
● chorizo is a kind of spicy sausage.

chorrito nm dash ▷ Échame un chorrito de leche. Just a dash of milk,

please.

chorro nm jet; salir a chorros to gush out

choza nf hut

chubasco nm heavy shower

chubasquero nm cagoule

chuleta nf chop ▷ una chuleta de cerdo a pork chop

chulo, -a adj ❶ cocky ❷ neat ▷ ¡Qué mochila más chula! What a neat rucksack!

chupar [26] vb to suck

chupete nm dummy

churro nm
● A churro is a type of fritter
● typically served with a cup
● of hot chocolate at cafés or
● churrerías (churro stalls/
● shops).

cibercafé nm internet café

cibernauta nmf internet user

cicatriz (pl cicatrices) nf scar

ciclismo nm cycling; Mi hermano hace ciclismo. My brother is a cyclist.

ciclista nmf cyclist

ciclo nm cycle

ciego, -a nm/f un ciego a blind man; una ciega a blind woman; los ciegos the blind
▶ adj blind; quedarse ciego to go blind

cielo nm ❶ sky ❷ heaven

cien adj, pron a hundred ▷ Había unos cien invitados. There were about a hundred guests. ▷ cien mil a hundred thousand; cien por cien a hundred percent ▷ Es cien por cien algodón. It's a hundred percent cotton.

ciencia nf science ▷ *Me gustan mucho las ciencias.* I really enjoy science. ▷ *ciencias sociales* social sciences; **ciencias empresariales** business studies

ciencia-ficción nf science fiction

científico, -a nm/f scientist
▶ adj scientific

ciento adj, pron a hundred; **ciento cuarenta y dos libras** a hundred and forty two pounds; **Recibimos cientos de cartas.** We received hundreds of letters.; **el diez por ciento de la población** ten percent of the population

cierre nm ❶ clasp; **un cierre relámpago** (in River Plate) a zip ❷ closing-down

cierro vb see **cerrar**

cierto adj ❶ true ▷ *No, eso no es cierto.* No, that's not true. ❷ certain ▷ *Viene ciertos días a la semana.* He comes certain days of the week.; **por cierto** by the way

ciervo nm deer

cifra nf figure ▷ *un número de cuatro cifras* a four-figure number

cigarrillo nm cigarette

cigarro nm cigarette

cigüeña nf stork

cima nf top

cimientos nmpl foundations

cinco adj, pron five; **Son las cinco.** It's five o'clock.; **el cinco de enero** the fifth of January

cincuenta adj, pron fifty; **el cincuenta aniversario** the fiftieth anniversary

cine nm cinema; **ir al cine** to go to the cinema; **una actriz de cine** a film actress

cínico adj cynical

cinta nf ❶ ribbon ❷ tape; **una cinta de vídeo** a videotape; **cinta aislante** insulating tape; **cinta transportadora** a conveyor belt

cintura nf waist ▷ *¿Cuánto mides de cintura?* What's your waist size?

cinturón (pl cinturones) nm belt; **el cinturón de seguridad** the safety belt

ciprés (pl cipreses) nm cypress

circo nm circus

circuito nm ❶ track ❷ circuit; **circuito cerrado de televisión** closed-circuit television

circulación nf ❶ traffic ▷ *un accidente de circulación* a traffic accident ❷ circulation

circular [26] vb ❶ to drive; **¡Circulen!** Move along please! ❷ to circulate ❸ to go round

círculo nm circle

circunferencia nf circumference

circunstancia nf circumstance

ciruela nf plum; **una ciruela pasa** a prune

cirugía nf surgery; **hacerse la cirugía plástica** to have plastic surgery

cirujano, -a nm/f surgeon

cisne nm swan

cisterna nf tank

cita nf ❶ appointment ▷ *Tengo cita con el Sr. Pérez.* I've got an appointment with Mr Pérez.

❷ date ▷ No llegues tarde a la cita. Don't be late for your date. **❶** quotation ▷ una cita de Quevedo a quotation from Quevedo

citar [26] vb **❶** to quote **❷** to mention; **Nos han citado a las diez.** We've been given an appointment for ten o'clock.; **citarse con alguien** to arrange to meet somebody ▷ Me he citado con Elena. I've arranged to meet Elena.

ciudad nf **❶** city **❷** town; **la ciudad universitaria** the university campus

ciudadano, -a nm/f citizen

civil adj civil ▷ la guerra civil the Civil War

civilización (pl civilizaciones) nf civilization

civilizado adj civilized

clara nf **❶** white (of egg) **❷** shandy (drink)

clarinete nm clarinet

claro adj **❶** clear ▷ Lo quiero mañana. ¿Está claro? I want it tomorrow. Is that clear?; **Está claro que esconden algo.** It's obvious they're hiding something.; **No tengo muy claro lo que quiero hacer.** I'm not very sure about what I want to do. **❷** light ▷ una camisa azul claro a light blue shirt
▶ adv clearly ▷ Lo oí muy claro. I heard it very clearly.; **Quiero que me hables claro.** I want you to be frank with me.; **No he sacado nada en claro de la reunión.** I'm none the wiser after that

meeting.; **¡Claro!** (1) Sure! (2) Of course!

clase nf **❶** class ▷ A las diez tengo clase de física. I have a physics class at ten.; **Da clases de inglés.** He teaches English.; **Hoy no hay clase.** There's no school today.; **clases de conducir** driving lessons; **clases particulares** private classes **❷** classroom **❸** kind ▷ Había juguetes de todas clases. There were all kinds of toys.; **la clase media** the middle class

clásico adj **❶** classical ▷ Me gusta la música clásica. I like classical music. **❷** classic ▷ Es el clásico ejemplo de malnutrición. It's a classic case of malnutrition.

clasificación (pl clasificaciones) nf classification; **estar a la cabeza de la clasificación** to be at the top of the table

clasificar [49] vb to classify; **Esperan clasificarse para la final.** They hope to qualify for the final.; **Se clasificaron en tercer lugar.** They came third.

clavar [26] vb clavar una punta en algo to hammer a nail into something; **Las tablas están mal clavadas.** The boards aren't properly nailed down.; **Me he clavado una espina en el dedo.** I've got a thorn in my finger.

clave nf **❶** code; **un mensaje en clave** a coded message **❷** key ▷ la clave del éxito the key to success; **la clave de sol** the treble clef

clavel nm carnation

clavícula nf collar bone

clavo nm nail

clic nm click; **hacer clic en** to click on; **hacer doble clic en** to double-click on

clicar [49] vb to click; **clicar dos veces** to double-click

cliente, -a nm/f ❶ customer ❷ client ❸ guest

clima nm climate

climatizado adj ❶ air-conditioned ❷ heated

clínica nf hospital

clínico adj clinical

clip (pl **clips**) nm ❶ paper clip ❷ clip

cloaca nf sewer

clonar [26] vb to clone

cloro nm chlorine

club (pl **clubs**) nm club ▷ *el club de tenis* the tennis club

cobarde nmf coward
▶ adj cowardly

cobaya nf guinea-pig

cobija nf (in Latin America) blanket

cobrar [26] vb to charge ▷ *Me cobró treinta euros por la reparación.* He charged me thirty euros for the repair.; **cuando cobre el sueldo de este mes** when I get my wages this month; **¿Me cobra los cafés?** How much do I owe for the coffees?; **¡Cóbrese, por favor!** Can I pay, please?; **cobrar un cheque** to cash a cheque

cobre nm copper

cobro nm **llamar a cobro revertido** to reverse the charges

cocaína nf cocaine

cocer [7] vb ❶ to boil ❷ to cook; **Tarda diez minutos en cocerse.** It takes ten minutes to cook.

coche nm ❶ car ▷ *Fuimos a París en coche.* We went to Paris by car.; **un coche de carreras** a racing car ❷ **pram** ❸ **carriage;** **Fuimos en coche cama.** We took the sleeper.; **un coche de bomberos** a fire engine

cochino nm pig
▶ adj filthy

cocido nm stew
- The **cocido madrileño** is a stew of chickpeas, vegetables and meat.

cocina nf ❶ kitchen ❷ cooker ▷ *una cocina de gas* a gas cooker; **la cocina vasca** Basque cuisine; **un libro de cocina** a cookery book

cocinar [26] vb to cook ▷ *No sabe cocinar.* He can't cook.; **Cocinas muy bien.** You're a very good cook.

cocinero, -a nm/f cook

coco nm coconut

cocodrilo nm crocodile

código nm code; **el código de la circulación** the highway code; **el código postal** the postcode

codo nm elbow

codorniz (pl **codornices**) nf quail

coger [8] vb ❶ to take ▷ *Coja la primera calle a la derecha.* Take the first street on the right. ❷ to catch; **coger un resfriado** to catch a cold ❸ to pick up ❹ to get ▷ *¿Nos coges dos entradas?* Would you get us two tickets? ▷ *Voy a*

coger el autobús. I'm going to get the bus. ❷ to borrow ▷ *¿Te puedo coger el bolígrafo?* Can I borrow your pen?; **Iban cogidos de la mano.** They were walking hand in hand.

cohete nm rocket; **un cohete espacial** a rocket

cohibido adj inhibited; **sentirse cohibido** to feel inhibited

coincidencia nf coincidence; **¡Qué coincidencia!** What a coincidence!

coincidir [59] vb to match ▷ *Las huellas dactilares coinciden.* The fingerprints match.; **Coincidimos en el tren.** We happened to meet on the train.; **Es que esas fechas coinciden con mi viaje.** The problem is, those dates clash with my trip.

cojear [26] vb ❶ to limp ❷ to be lame ❸ to wobble (furniture)

cojín (pl cojines) nm cushion

cojo vb see coger
▶ adj ❶ lame ▷ *Está cojo.* He's lame. ❷ wobbly (furniture)

col nf cabbage; **las coles de Bruselas** Brussels sprouts

cola nf ❶ tail ❷ queue ▷ *Había mucha cola para los lavabos.* There was a long queue for the toilets.; **hacer cola** to queue ❸ glue

colaborar [26] vb ❶ to join in ❷ to contribute ❸ to cooperate

colador nm ❶ strainer ❷ sieve

colar [12] vb to strain; **colarse** to push in; **Nos colamos en el cine.** We sneaked into the cinema without paying.

colcha nf bedspread

colchón (pl colchones) nm mattress; **un colchón de aire** an air bed

colchoneta nf ❶ mat ❷ air bed

colección (pl colecciones) nf collection

coleccionar [26] vb to collect

colecta nf collection

colectivo nm (in River Plate) bus

colega nmf ❶ colleague ❷ mate

colegio nm school ▷ *Voy al colegio en bicicleta.* I cycle to school. ▷ *¿Todavía vas al colegio?* Are you still at school?; **un colegio de curas** a Catholic boys' school; **un colegio de monjas** a convent school; **un colegio público** a state school; **un colegio mayor** a hall of residence

coleta nf ponytail; **La niña llevaba coletas.** The girl wore her hair in bunches.

colgado adj hanging ▷ *Había varios cuadros colgados en la pared.* There were several pictures hanging on the wall.; **Debe de tener el teléfono mal colgado.** He must have left the telephone off the hook.

colgante nm pendant

colgar vb to hang; **¡No dejes la chaqueta en la silla, cuélgala!** Don't leave your jacket on the chair, hang it up!; **Me colgó el teléfono.** He hung up on me.; **¡Cuelga, por favor, que quiero hacer una llamada!** Hang up, please. I want to use the phone!;

No cuelgue, por favor. Please hold.

coliflor nf cauliflower

colilla nf cigarette end

colina nf hill

colisión (pl **colisiones**) nf collision

collar nm **①** necklace **②** collar

colmena nf beehive

colmillo nm **①** canine tooth **②** fang **③** tusk

colmo nm **¡Esto ya es el colmo!** This really is the last straw!; **Para colmo de males, empezó a llover.** To make matters worse, it started to rain.

colocar [49] vb **①** to put **②** to arrange; **colocarse** (1) to get a job (2) to get plastered (3) to get high; **¡Colocaos en fila!** Get into a line!; **El equipo se ha colocado en quinto lugar.** The team are now in fifth place.

Colombia nf Colombia

colombiano, -a nm/f, adj Colombian

colonia nf **①** perfume **②** colony **③** (in Mexico) district; **una colonia de verano** a summer camp

colonizar [14] vb to colonize

coloquial adj colloquial

color nm colour ▷ **¿De qué color son?** What colour are they?; **un vestido de color azul** a blue dress; **una televisión en color** a colour television

colorado adj red; **ponerse colorado** to blush

columna nf **①** column; **la columna vertebral** the spine

columpio nm swing

coma nf comma; **dos coma ocho** two point eight
▶ nm coma; **estar en coma** to be in a coma

comadrona nf midwife

comandante nmf major

comba nf skipping rope; **saltar a la comba** to skip

combate nm battle; **un piloto de combate** a fighter pilot; **un combate de boxeo** a boxing match

combinar [26] vb **①** to combine **②** to go ▷ **colores que combinan con el azul** colours that go with blue

combustible nm fuel

comedia nf comedy

comedor nm **①** dining room **②** refectory **③** canteen

comentar [26] vb **①** to say **②** to discuss; **Me han comentado que es una película muy buena.** I've heard it's a very good film.

comentario nm comment

comentarista nmf commentator

comenzar [20] vb to begin; **Comenzó a llover.** It began to rain.

comer [9] vb **①** to eat; **Me comí una manzana.** I had an apple. **②** to have lunch; **Hemos comido paella.** We had paella for lunch.; **¿Qué hay para comer?** What is there for lunch? **③** (in Latin America) to have dinner; **Le estaba dando de comer a su hijo.** She was feeding her son.; **No te comas el coco por eso.** Don't worry too much about it. .

comercial adj ❶ business ❷ trade ❸ commercial

comerciante nmf shopkeeper

comercio nm ❶ trade ❷ business ❸ shop

cometa nm comet ▸ nf kite

cometer [9] vb ❶ to commit ❸ to make

cómic (pl **cómics**) nm comic

cómico adj ❶ comical ▷ Fue muy cómico. It was very comical. ❷ comic ▷ un actor cómico a comic actor

comida nf ❶ food; **la comida basura** junk food ❷ lunch ▷ La comida es a la una y media. Lunch is at half past one. ❸ meal ▷ Es la comida más importante del día. It's the most important meal of the day. ❹ (in Latin America) supper

comienzo vb see **comenzar**

comillas nfpl quotation marks; **entre comillas** in quotation marks

comisaría nf police station

comité (pl **comités**) nm committee

como adv, conj ❶ like ▷ Tienen un perro como el nuestro. They've got a dog like ours.; **Sabe como a cebolla.** It tastes a bit like onion. ❷ as ▷ Lo usé como cuchara. I used it as a spoon. ▷ blanco como la nieve as white as snow ▷ Como ella no llegaba, me fui. As she hadn't arrived, I left.; **Hazlo como te dijo ella.** Do it the way she told you.;

Es tan alto como tú. He's as tall as you are.; **tal como lo había planeado** just as I had planned it; **como si** as if ❸ if ▷ Como lo vuelvas a hacer se lo digo a tu madre. If you do it again I'll tell your mother. ❹ about ▷ Vinieron como unas diez personas. About ten people came.

cómo adv how; **¿A cómo están las manzanas?** How much are the apples?; **¿Cómo es de grande?** How big is it?; **¿Cómo es su novio?** (1) What's her boyfriend like? (2) What does her boyfriend look like?; **Perdón, ¿cómo has dicho?** Sorry, what did you say?; **¡Cómo! ¿Mañana?** What? Tomorrow?; **¡Cómo corría!** Boy, was he running!

cómoda nf chest of drawers

comodidad nf ❶ comfort ❷ convenience

cómodo adj ❶ comfortable ❷ convenient

compact disc (pl **compact discs**) nm ❶ compact disc ❷ compact disc player

compadecer [13] vb to feel sorry for

compañero, -a nm/f ❶ classmate ❷ workmate ❸ partner; **un compañero de piso** a flatmate

compañía nf company ▷ una compañía de seguros an insurance company; **Ana vino a hacerme compañía.** Ana came to keep me company.; **una compañía aérea** an airline

comparación (pl **comparaciones**) nf comparison; **Mi coche no tiene comparación con el tuyo.** There's no comparison between my car and yours.; **en comparación con** compared to

comparar [26] vb to compare

compartir [59] vb to share

compás (pl **compases**) nm compass; **bailar al compás de la música** to dance in time to the music

compatible adj compatible

compensar [26] vb ❶ to make up for (lack, loss) ❷ to compensate; **No compensa viajar tan lejos por tan poco tiempo.** It's not worth travelling that far for such a short time.

competencia nf competition; **No quiere hacerle la competencia a su mejor amigo.** He doesn't want to compete with his best friend.

competente adj competent

competición (pl **competiciones**) nf competition

competir [39] vb to compete; **competir por un título** to compete for a title

complacer [12] vb to please

complejo nm complex

completar [26] vb to complete

completo adj ❶ complete ▷ **las obras completas de Lorca** the complete works of Lorca ❷ full ▷ **Los hoteles estaban completos.** The hotels were full.; **Me olvidé por completo.** I completely forgot.

complicado adj complicated

complicar [49] vb to complicate; **complicarse** to get complicated; **No quiero complicarme la vida.** I don't want to make life more difficult for myself.

cómplice nmf accomplice

componer [42] vb to compose

comportamiento nm behaviour

comportarse [26] vb to behave

compra nf shopping; **hacer la compra** to do the shopping; **ir de compras** to go shopping

comprar [26] vb to buy; **Le compré el coche a mi amigo.** I bought my friend's car.; **Quiero comprarme unos zapatos.** I want to buy a pair of shoes.

comprender [9] vb to understand

comprensivo adj understanding

compresa nf sanitary towel

comprimido nm pill

comprobante nm receipt

comprobar [12] vb to check

comprometerse [9] vb **Me he comprometido a ayudarlos.** I have promised to help them.; **No quiero comprometerme por si después no puedo ir.** I don't want to commit myself in case I can't go.

compromiso nm engagement; **Puede probarlo sin ningún compromiso.** You can try it with no obligation.; **Iba a ir pero sólo por compromiso.** I was going to go but only out of duty.; **poner a alguien en un compromiso** to put someone in a difficult situation

compruebo vb see **comprobar**

compuesto vb see **componer**
▶ adj **compuesto de** made up of

computador nm, **computadora** nf (in Latin America) computer; **un computador portátil** a laptop

común adj common ▶ un apellido muy común a very common surname; **No tenemos nada en común.** We have nothing in common.; **Hicimos el trabajo en común.** We did the work between us.; **las zonas de uso común** the communal areas

comunicación (pl **comunicaciones**) nf communication; **Se ha cortado la comunicación.** We've been cut off.

comunicar [49] vb to be engaged; **comunicarse** to communicate; **Los dos despachos se comunican.** The two offices are connected.

comunidad nf community; **una comunidad autónoma** an autonomous region

comunión (pl **comuniones**) nf communion; **Voy a hacer la primera comunión.** I'm going to make my first communion.

comunista adj, nmf communist

con prep with ▶ ¿Con quién vas a ir? Who are you going with?; **Lo he escrito con bolígrafo.** I wrote it in pen.; **Voy a hablar con Luis.** I'll talk to Luis.; **café con leche** white coffee; **Ábrelo con cuidado.** Open it carefully.; **Con estudiar un poco apruebas.** With a bit of studying

you should pass.; **Con que me digas tu teléfono basta.** If you just give me your phone number that'll be enough.; **con tal de que no llegues tarde** as long as you don't arrive late

concejal, a nm/f town councillor

concentrarse [26] vb ① to concentrate ▶ Me cuesta concentrarme. I find it hard to concentrate. ② to gather ▶ Los manifestantes se concentraron en la plaza. The demonstrators gathered in the square.

concertar [40] vb to arrange

concha nf shell

conciencia nf conscience; **Lo han estudiado a conciencia.** They've studied it thoroughly.

concierto nm ① concert ② concerto

conclusión (pl **conclusiones**) nf conclusion

concreto adj ① specific ▶ por poner un ejemplo concreto to take a specific example ② definite ▶ Todavía no hay fechas concretas. There are no definite dates yet.; **No me refiero a nadie en concreto.** I don't mean anyone in particular.; **Todavía no hemos decidido nada en concreto.** We still haven't decided anything definite.

concurrido adj busy (street, place)

concursante nmf competitor

concurso nm ① game show ② competition; **un concurso de belleza** a beauty contest; **un**

programa concurso a TV game show

conde nm count

condecoración (pl **condecoraciones**) nf decoration

condena nf sentence; **cumplir una condena** to serve a sentence

condenar [26] vb to sentence

condesa nf countess

condición (pl **condiciones**) nf condition; **a condición de que apruebes** on condition that you pass; **El piso está en muy malas condiciones.** The flat is in a very bad state.; **No está en condiciones de viajar.** He's not fit to travel.

condón (pl **condones**) nm condom

conducir [10] vb ❶ to drive; **No sé conducir.** I can't drive. ❷ to ride; **Enfadarse no conduce a nada.** Getting angry won't get you anywhere.; **La secretaria nos condujo hasta la salida.** The secretary showed us out.

conducta nf behaviour

conductor, a nm/f driver

conduzco vb see **conducir**

conectar [26] vb to connect

conejillo nm un **conejillo de Indias** a guinea pig

conejo nm rabbit

conexión (pl **conexiones**) nf connection

conferencia nf ❶ lecture ❷ conference ❸ long-distance call

confesar [40] vb ❶ to confess to ❸ to admit; **confesarse** to go to

confession

confeti nm confetti

confianza nf trust; **Tengo confianza en ti.** I trust you.; **No tiene confianza en sí mismo.** He has no self-confidence.; **un empleado de confianza** a reliable employee; **Se lo dije porque tenemos mucha confianza.** I told her about it because we're very close.; **Los alumnos se toman muchas confianzas con él.** The pupils take too many liberties with him.

confiar [22] vb **confiar en** to trust ▷ *No confío en ella.* I don't trust her.; **Confiaba en que su familia le ayudaría.** He was confident that his family would help him.; **No hay que confiarse demasiado.** You mustn't be over-confident.

confidencial adj confidential

confieso vb see **confesar**

confirmar [26] vb to confirm

confitería nf cake shop

conflicto nm conflict

conformarse [26] vb **conformarse con** to be satisfied with; **Se conforman con poco.** They're easily satisfied.; **Tendrás que conformarte con uno más barato.** You'll have to make do with a cheaper one.

conforme adj satisfied ▷ *No se quedó muy conforme con esa explicación.* He wasn't very satisfied with that explanation.; **estar conforme** to agree

confortable adj comfortable

confundir [59] vb ❶ to mistake ❷ to confuse; Confundí las fechas. I got the dates mixed up.; ¡Vaya! ¡Me he confundido! Oh! I've made a mistake!; Me confundí de piso. I got the wrong flat.

confusión (pl confusiones) nf confusion

confuso adj confused

congelado adj frozen

congelador nm freezer

congelar [26] vb to freeze; Me estoy congelando. I'm freezing.

congestionado adj ❶ blocked ❷ congested

congreso nm conference; un congreso médico a medical conference; el Congreso de los Diputados the lower chamber of the Spanish Parliament

conjunción (pl conjunciones) nf conjunction

conjunto nm ❶ collection ▷ El libro es un conjunto de poemas de amor. The book is a collection of love poems. ❷ group ▷ un conjunto de música pop a pop group; un conjunto de falda y blusa a matching skirt and blouse; Hay que estudiar esos países en conjunto. You have to study these countries as a whole.

conmemorar [26] vb to commemorate

conmigo pron with me ▷ ¿Por qué no vienes conmigo? Why don't you come with me? Rosa quiere hablar conmigo. Rosa wants to talk to me.

conmovedor, a adj moving

conmover [34] vb to move

cono nm cone; el Cono Sur the Southern Cone

conocer [13] vb ❶ to know; Nos conocemos desde el colegio. We know each other from school.; Me encantaría conocer China. I would love to visit China. ❷ to meet (for the first time)

conocido, -a nm/f acquaintance ▶ adj well-known

conocimiento nm consciousness; perder el conocimiento to lose consciousness; Tengo algunos conocimientos de francés. I have some knowledge of French.

conozco vb see **conocer**

conque conj so ▷ Hemos terminado, conque podéis iros. We've finished, so you can leave now.

conquistar [26] vb ❶ to conquer ❷ to win...over

consciente adj conscious ▷ El enfermo no estaba consciente. The patient wasn't conscious.; ser consciente de to be aware of

consecuencia nf consequence; a consecuencia de as a result of

consecutivo adj consecutive

conseguir [51] vb ❶ to get ▷ Él me consiguió el trabajo. He got me the job. ❷ to achieve ▷ Después de muchos intentos, al final lo consiguió. After many attempts, he finally succeeded.; Finalmente conseguí convencerla. I finally managed to convince her.; No conseguí que se lo comiera. I couldn't get him to eat it.

consejo nm advice ▷ Fui a pedirle consejo. I went to ask him for advice.; **¿Quieres que te dé un consejo?** Would you like me to give you some advice?

consentir [52] vb ❶ to allow ❷ to spoil

conserje nmf ❶ caretaker ❷ janitor ❸ porter

conserva nf atún en conserva tinned tuna; **conservas** tinned food

conservador, a adj conservative

conservar [26] vb ❶ to keep ▷ Debe conservarse en la nevera. It should be kept in the fridge. ❷ to preserve; **Enrique se conserva joven.** Enrique looks good for his age.

conservatorio nm music school

considerable adj considerable

considerado adj considerate; **Está muy bien considerada entre los profesores.** She's very highly regarded among the teachers.

considerar [26] vb to consider

consiento vb see **consentir**

consigna nf left-luggage office

consigo vb see **conseguir**
  ▶ pron ❶ with him ❷ with her ❸ with you

consiguiendo vb see **conseguir**

consintiendo vb see **consentir**

consistir [59] vb consistir en to consist of; **¿En qué consiste el trabajo?** What does the job involve?; **En eso consiste el secreto.** That's the secret.

consola nf console; **consola de videojuegos** games console

consolar [12] vb to console; **Para consolarme me compré un helado.** I bought an ice cream to cheer myself up.

consonante nf consonant

constante adj constant

constantemente adv constantly

constar [26] vb constar de to consist of; **¡Que conste que yo pagué mi parte!** Don't forget that I paid my share!

constipado adj estar constipado to have a cold

Be careful! **constipado** does not mean **constipated**.

  ▶ nm cold ▷ coger un constipado to catch a cold

constitución (pl constituciones) nf constitution

construcción (pl construcciones) nf construction

constructor, a nm/f builder

construir [11] vb to build

consuelo vb see **consolar**
  ▶ nm consolation

cónsul nmf consul

consulado nm consulate

consulta nf surgery; **horas de consulta** surgery hours; **un libro de consulta** a reference book

consultar [26] vb to consult

consumición (pl consumiciones) nf drink ▷ Con la entrada tienes una consumición. The admission price includes a drink.

consumir [59] vb ❶ to use ❷ to drink; **No podemos estar en el**

bar sin consumir. We can't stay in the pub without buying a drink.; **Sólo piensan en consumir.** Spending money is all they think about.

consumo nm consumption; **una charla sobre el consumo de drogas** a talk on drug use; **la sociedad de consumo** the consumer society

contabilidad nf accountancy

contable nmf accountant

contactar [26] vb contactar con **alguien** to contact someone

contacto nm ❶ contact ❷ touch ▷ *Nos mantenemos en contacto por teléfono.* We keep in touch by phone.; **Me puse en contacto con su familia.** I got in touch with her family.

contado: **al contado** adv **Lo pagué al contado.** I paid cash for it.

contador, a nm/f (in Latin America) accountant
  ▶ nm meter ▷ *el contador de la luz* the electricity meter

contagiar [26] vb to infect; **No quiero contagiarte.** I don't want to give it to you.; **Tiene la gripe y no quiere que los niños se contagien.** He's got flu and doesn't want the children to catch it.

contagioso adj infectious

contaminación nf pollution

contaminar [26] vb to pollute

contar [12] vb ❶ to count ▷ *Sabe contar hasta diez.* He can count to

ten. ❷ to tell ▷ *Cuéntame lo que pasó.* Tell me what happened.; **Cuento contigo.** I'm counting on you.; **¿Qué te cuentas?** How's things?

contendrá vb see **contener**

contener [54] vb to contain; **contenerse** to control oneself

contenido nm contents

contentarse [26] vb contentarse **con (1)** to be happy with **(2)** to be satisfied with

contento adj happy ▷ *Estaba contento porque era su cumpleaños.* He was happy because it was his birthday.; **estar contento con algo** to be pleased with something

contestación (pl **contestaciones**) nf reply; **No me des esas contestaciones.** Don't answer back.

contestador nm **el contestador automático** the answering machine

contestar [26] vb to answer; **Les he llamado varias veces y no contestan.** I've phoned them several times and there's no answer.; **Me escribieron y tengo que contestarles.** They wrote to me and I have to reply to them.

contigo pron with you ▷ *Quiero ir contigo.* I want to go with you.; **Necesito hablar contigo.** I need to talk to you.

continente nm continent

continuamente adv constantly

continuar [2] vb to continue;

Continuó estudiando toda la noche. He carried on studying right through the night.

continuo adj ❶ constant ❷ continuous

contra prep against ▷ *Eran dos contra uno.* It was two against one.; **Me choqué contra una farola.** I bumped into a lamppost.; **Estoy en contra de la pena de muerte.** I'm against the death penalty.

contrabajo nm double bass

contrabando nm smuggling ▷ *el contrabando de drogas* drug smuggling; **Lo trajeron al país de contrabando.** They smuggled it into the country.

contradecir [16] vb to contradict

contradicción (pl **contradicciones**) nf contradiction

contraria nf **llevar la contraria a alguien** (1) to contradict somebody (2) to do the opposite of what somebody wants

contrario adj ❶ opposing ❷ opposite ▷ *Los dos coches viajaban en dirección contraria.* The two cars were travelling in opposite directions.; **Ella opina lo contrario.** She thinks the opposite.; **Al contrario, me gusta mucho.** On the contrary, I like it a lot.; **De lo contrario, tendré que castigarte.** Otherwise, I will have to punish you.

contraseña nf password

contrastar [26] vb to contrast

contraste nm contrast

contratar [26] vb ❶ to hire ❷ to sign up

contrato nm contract

contribución (pl **contribuciones**) nf ❶ contribution ❷ tax ▷ *la contribución municipal* local tax

contribuir [11] vb to contribute

contribuyente nmf taxpayer

contrincante nmf opponent

control nm ❶ control ❷ road-block; **el control de pasaportes** passport control

controlar [26] vb to control **Tuve que controlarme para no pegarle.** I had to control myself, otherwise I would have hit him.; **No te preocupes, todo está controlado.** Don't worry, everything is under control.

convencer [13] vb ❶ to convince; **No me convence nada la idea.** I'm not convinced by the idea. ❷ to persuade ▷ *La convencimos para que nos acompañara.* We persuaded her to go with us.

convencional adj conventional

conveniente adj convenient; **Sería conveniente que se lo dijeras.** It would be advisable to tell him.

convenir [57] vb to suit ▷ *el método que más le convenga* the method that suits you best; **Te conviene descansar un poco.** You ought to get some rest.; **Quizá convenga recordar que ...** It might be appropriate to recall that ...

conversación (pl

conversaciones) nf conversation

convertir [52] vb **convertir algo en algo** to turn something into something ▷ *Convirtieron la casa en colegio.* They turned the house into a school.; **convertirse** to convert; **convertirse en** (1) to become (2) to turn into

convocar [49] vb to call

coñac (pl **coñacs**) nm brandy

cooperación nf cooperation

cooperar [26] vb to cooperate

copa nf ❶ glass ▷ *Sólo tomé una copa de vino.* I only had one glass of wine. ❷ drink; **Fuimos a tomar unas copas.** We went for a few drinks. ❸ top (of tree)
- **copas** are also goblets, one of the suits in the Spanish card deck.

copia nf copy ▷ *hacer una copia* to make a copy; **una copia impresa** a printout

copiar [26] vb to copy; **copiar y pegare** to copy and paste

copo nm **un copo de nieve** a snowflake

corazón (pl **corazones**) nm heart ▷ *Está mal del corazón.* He has heart trouble.; **Tiene muy buen corazón.** He is very kind-hearted.

corbata nf tie

corcho nm cork; **un tapón de corcho** a cork

cordel nm cord

cordero nm lamb ▷ *Comimos chuletas de cordero.* We had lamb chops.

cordón (pl **cordones**) nm

❶ shoelace ❷ cable

corneta nf bugle

coro nm ❶ choir ❷ chorus

corona nf crown; **una corona de flores** a garland

coronel nm colonel

corporal adj ❶ body ❷ corporal ❸ personal

corral nm ❶ farmyard ❷ playpen

correa nf ❶ belt ❷ lead ❸ strap

correcto adj correct

corredor, a nm/f runner

corregir [19] vb ❶ to correct ❷ to mark

correo nm post ▷ *Me lo mandó por correo.* He sent it to me by post.; **Correos** post office ▷ *Fui a Correos a comprar unos sellos.* I went to the post office to buy some stamps.; **correo electrónico** email

correr [9] vb ❶ to run; **El ladrón echó a correr.** The thief started to run. ❷ to hurry ▷ *Corre que llegamos tarde.* Hurry or we'll be late.; **No corras que te equivocarás.** Don't rush or you'll make a mistake. ❸ to go fast ▷ *No corras tanto, que hay hielo en la carretera.* Don't go so fast, the road's icy. ❹ to move; **¿Quieres que corra la cortina?** Do you want me to draw the curtains?

correspondencia nf correspondence

corresponder [9] vb **Me pagó lo que me correspondía.** He paid me my share.; **Estas fotos corresponden a otro álbum.** These photos belong to another album.; **No me corresponde a mí hacerlo.** It's not for me to do it.

correspondiente adj relevant; **los datos correspondientes al año pasado** the figures for last year

corresponsal nmf correspondent

corrida nf bullfight

corriente adj common ▷ *Pérez es un apellido muy corriente.* Pérez is a very common surname.; **Es un caso poco corriente.** It's an unusual case.; **Tengo que ponerle al corriente de lo que ha pasado.** I have to let him know what has happened.
  ▶ nf ❶ current; **Te va a dar corriente.** You'll get an electric shock. ❷ draught

corrijo vb see **corregir**

corro nm ring ▷ *Los niños hicieron un corro.* The children formed a ring.

corrupción nf corruption

cortado adj ❶ sour (milk)
  ❷ closed (street, road); **Juan estaba muy cortado con mis padres.** Juan was very shy with my parents.
  ▶ nm white coffee
  ● A **cortado** is a small white
  ○ coffee with only a little milk.

cortar [26] vb ❶ to cut ▷ *Corta la manzana por la mitad.* Cut the apple in half.; **Te vas a cortar.** You're going to cut yourself.; **Fui a cortarme el pelo.** I went to get my hair cut. ❷ to cut off ❸ to close; **De repente se cortó la comunicación.** Suddenly we

were cut off.

cortaúñas (pl cortaúñas) nm nail clippers

corte nm cut; **un corte de pelo** a hair-cut; **Me da corte pedírselo.** I'm embarrassed to ask him.

cortés (pl corteses) adj polite

cortesía nf courtesy; **por cortesía** as a courtesy

corteza nf ❶ crust ❷ rind ❸ bark

cortina nf curtain

corto adj short ▷ *Susana tiene el pelo corto.* Susana has short hair.; **ser corto de vista** to be short-sighted

cortocircuito nm short-circuit

cosa nf thing ▷ *Cogí mis cosas y me fui.* I picked up my things and left.; **cualquier cosa** anything; **¿Me puedes decir una cosa?** Can you tell me something?; **¡Qué cosa más rara!** How strange!

cosecha nf harvest

cosechar [26] vb to harvest

coser [9] vb to sew

cosmético nm cosmetic

cosquillas nfpl hacer cosquillas a alguien to tickle someone; **Tiene cosquillas.** He's ticklish.

costa nf coast; **Vive a costa de los demás.** He lives at the expense of others.

costado nm side; **Estaba tumbado de costado.** He was lying on his side.

costar [12] vb to cost ▷ *¿Cuánto cuesta?* How much does it cost? ▷ *Me costó diez euros.* It cost me ten euros.; **Las matemáticas**

a
b
c
d
e
f
g
h
i
j
k
l
m
n
o
p
q
r
s
t
u
v
w
x
y
z

le cuestan mucho. He finds maths very difficult.; **Me cuesta hablarle.** I find it hard to talk to him.

Costa Rica nf Costa Rica

costarricense nmf, adj Costa Rican

costarriqueño, -a nm/f, adj Costa Rican

coste nm cost ▷ el coste de la vida the cost of living

costilla nf rib

costo nm cost

costoso adj expensive

costra nf ❶ scab ❷ crust

costumbre nf ❶ habit ❷ custom; **Se le olvidó, como de costumbre.** He forgot, as usual.; **Nos sentamos en el sitio de costumbre.** We sat in our usual place.

costura nf ❶ seam ❷ sewing

cotidiano adj everyday ▷ la vida cotidiana everyday life

cotilla nmf gossip

cotillear [26] vb to gossip

cotilleo nm gossip

cráneo nm skull

creación (pl creaciones) nf creation

crear [26] vb to create; **No quiero crearme problemas.** I don't want to create problems for myself.

creativo adj creative

crecer [13] vb ❶ to grow ❷ to grow up

crecimiento nm growth

crédito nm ❶ loan ▷ Pedí un crédito al banco. I asked the bank for a

loan. ❷ credit ▷ comprar algo a crédito to buy something on credit

creencia nf belief

creer [31] vb ❶ to believe; **Eso no se lo cree nadie.** No one will believe that. ❷ to think ▷ No creo que pueda ir. I don't think I'll be able to go.; **Se cree muy lista.** She thinks she's pretty clever.; **Creo que sí.** I think so.; **Creo que no.** I don't think so.

creído adj **Es muy creído.** He's so full of himself.

crema nf cream; **crema de afeitar** shaving cream; **crema de champiñones** cream of mushroom soup; **una blusa de color crema** a cream-coloured blouse

cremallera nf zip ▷ Súbete la cremallera. Pull up your zip.

crematorio nm crematorium

creyendo vb see creer

creyente nmf believer

crezco vb see crecer

cría nf ❶ baby; **una cría de cebra** a baby zebra; **La leona tuvo dos crías.** The lioness had two cubs. ❷ girl

criada nf maid

criado nm servant

criar [22] vb ❶ to raise ❷ to breed ❸ to bring up ▷ Me criaron mis abuelos. My grandparents brought me up.; **Me crié en Sevilla.** I grew up in Seville.

crimen (pl crímenes) nm ❶ murder ❷ crime

criminal nmf criminal

crío nm ① baby; **¡no seas crío!** Don't be such a baby! ② boy; **los críos** the children

crisis (pl crisis) nf crisis; **una crisis nerviosa** a nervous breakdown

cristal nm ① glass ▷ *una botella de cristal* a glass bottle ② piece of glass ▷ *Me corté con un cristal.* I cut myself on a piece of glass.; **En el suelo había cristales rotos.** There was some broken glass on the floor. ③ window pane; **limpiar los cristales** to clean the windows ④ crystal

cristiano, -a nm/f, adj Christian

Cristo nm Christ

crítica nf ① criticism ② review ▷ *La película ha tenido muy buenas críticas.* The film got very good reviews.; *see also* **crítico**

criticar [49] vb to criticize

crítico, -a nm/f critic
  ▸ adj critical

croissant (pl croissants) nm croissant

cromo nm picture card

crónico adj chronic

cronometrar [26] vb to time

cronómetro nm stopwatch

croqueta nf croquette ▷ *croquetas de pollo* chicken croquettes

cruce nm crossroads; **un cruce de peatones** a pedestrian crossing

crucial adj crucial

crucifijo nm crucifix

crucigrama nm crossword

crudo adj ① raw ② underdone ▷ *El filete estaba crudo.* The fillet was underdone.

cruel adj cruel

crueldad nf cruelty

crujiente adj ① crunchy ② crusty

crujir [59] vb ① to rustle ② to creak ③ to crunch

cruz (pl cruces) nf cross; **la Cruz Roja** the Red Cross

cruzado adj **Había un tronco cruzado en la carretera.** There was a tree trunk lying across the road.

cruzar [14] vb ① to cross ② to fold; **Nos cruzamos en la calle.** We passed each other in the street.

cuaderno nm ① notebook ② exercise book

cuadra nf stable

cuadrado adj, nm square; **dos metros cuadrados** two square metres

cuadrar [26] vb to tally

cuadriculado adj **papel cuadriculado** squared paper

cuadro nm ① painting ▷ *un cuadro de Picasso* a painting by Picasso ② picture; **un mantel a cuadros** a checked tablecloth

cuajar [26] vb ① to set ② to lie; **cuajarse** to curdle

cual pron **el cual/la cual/los cuales/las cuales** (1) who ▷ *el primo del cual te estuve hablando* the cousin who I was speaking to you about (2) which ▷ *la ventana desde la cual nos observaban* the window from which they were watching us; **lo cual** which ▷ *Se ofendió, lo cual es comprensible.*

He took offence, which is understandable.; **con lo cual** with the result that; **sea cual sea la razón** whatever the reason may be

cuál pron ❶ what ▷ ¿Cuál es la solución? What's the answer? ▷ No sé cuál es la solución. I don't know what the answer is. ❷ which ▷ ¿Cuál te gusta más? Which do you like best?; ¿Cuáles quieres? Which ones do you want?

cualidad nf quality

cualquier adj = cualquiera

cualquiera adj any

> cualquiera is shortened to cualquier before singular nouns.

▷ en cualquier ciudad española in any Spanish town ▷ Puedes usar un bolígrafo cualquiera. You can use any pen.; **No es un empleo cualquiera.** It's not just any job.; **cualquier cosa** anything; **cualquier persona** anyone; **en cualquier sitio** anywhere ▶ pron ❶ anyone ▷ Cualquiera puede hacer eso. Anyone can do that. ❷ any one ▷ Me da igual, cualquiera. It doesn't matter, any one.; **en cualquiera de las habitaciones** in any one of the rooms; **cualquiera que elijas** whichever one you choose ❸ either ▷ ¿Cuál de los dos prefieres? - Cualquiera. Which of the two do you prefer? - Either.

cuando conj when ▷ cuando vienen a vernos when they come to see us

▷ Lo haré cuando tenga tiempo. I'll do it when I have time.; **Puedes venir cuando quieras.** You can come whenever you like.

cuándo adv when ▷ No sabe cuándo ocurrió. He doesn't know when it happened.; **¿Desde cuándo trabajas aquí?** Since when have you worked here?

cuanto, -a adj, pron **Termínalo cuanto antes.** Finish it as soon as possible.; **Cuanto más lo pienso menos lo entiendo.** The more I think about it, the less I understand it.; **Cuantas menos personas haya mejor.** The fewer people the better.; **En cuanto oí su voz me eché a llorar.** As soon as I heard his voice I began to cry.; **Había sólo unos cuantos invitados.** There were only a few guests.; **en cuanto a** as for

cuánto, -a adj, pron how much (pl how many) ▷ ¿Cuánto dinero? How much money? ▷ ¿Cuánto le debo? How much do I owe you? ▷ Me dijo cuánto costaba. He told me how much it was. ▷ ¿Cuántas sillas? How many chairs?; **¿A cuántos estamos?** What's the date?; **¡Cuánta gente!** What a lot of people!; **¿Cuánto hay de aquí a Bilbao?** How far is it from here to Bilbao?; **¿Cuánto tiempo llevas estudiando inglés?** How long have you been studying English?

cuarenta adj, pron forty; **el cuarenta aniversario** the fortieth anniversary

cuartel nm barracks; **el cuartel general** the headquarters

cuarto, -a adj, pron fourth ▷ Vivo en el cuarto piso. I live on the fourth floor.
▶ nm ❶ room; **el cuarto de estar** the living room; **el cuarto de baño** the bathroom ❷ quarter ▷ un cuarto de hora a quarter of an hour; **Son las once y cuarto.** It's a quarter past eleven.; **A las diez menos cuarto.** It's a quarter to ten.; **Es un cuarto para las diez.** (in Latin America) It's a quarter to ten.

cuatro adj, pron four; **Son las cuatro.** It's four o'clock.; **el cuatro de julio** the fourth of July

cuatrocientos, -as adj, pron four hundred

Cuba nf Cuba

cubano, -a nm/f, adj Cuban

cubertería nf cutlery

cúbico adj cubic

cubierta nf ❶ cover ❷ tyre ❸ deck

cubierto vb see cubrir
▶ adj covered ▷ Estaba todo cubierto de nieve. Everything was covered in snow.; **una piscina cubierta** an indoor swimming pool

cubiertos npl cutlery

cubito de hielo nm ice-cube

cubo nm bucket; **el cubo de la basura** the dustbin

cubrir vb to cover; **Las mujeres se cubren la cara con un velo.** The women cover their faces with a veil.

cucaracha nf cockroach

cuchara nf spoon

cucharada nf spoonful

cucharilla nf teaspoon

cucharón (pl cucharones) nm ladle

cuchichear [26] vb to whisper

cuchilla nf blade; **una cuchilla de afeitar** a razor blade

cuchillo nm knife

cuclillas: en cuclillas adv squatting; **ponerse en cuclillas** to squat down

cucurucho nm cone

cuelgo vb see colgar

cuello nm ❶ neck ❷ collar

cuenta nf ❶ bill ❷ account; **una cuenta corriente** a current account; **Ahora trabaja por su cuenta.** He's self-employed now.; **una cuenta de correo** an email account; **darse cuenta (1)** to realize ▷ Perdona, no me daba cuenta de que eras vegetariano. Sorry, I didn't realize you were a vegetarian. **(2)** to notice ▷ ¿Te has dado cuenta de que han cortado el árbol? Did you notice they've cut down that tree?; **tener algo en cuenta** to bear something in mind

cuento vb see contar
▶ nm story; **un cuento de hadas** a fairy tale

cuerda nf ❶ rope ❷ string ❸ skipping rope; **dar cuerda a un reloj** to wind up a watch

cuerno nm horn

cuero nm leather ▷ una chaqueta de

cuero a leather jacket

cuerpo nm body ▷ *el cuerpo humano* the human body; **el cuerpo de bomberos** the fire brigade

cuervo nm raven

cuesta vb see **costar**
▶ nf slope; **ir cuesta abajo** to go downhill; **ir cuesta arriba** to go uphill; **Llevaba la caja a cuestas.** He was carrying the box on his back.

cuestión (pl cuestiones) nf matter ▷ *Eso es otra cuestión.* That's another matter.

cueva nf cave

cuezo vb see **cocer**

cuidado nm care ▷ *He was driving carefully.*; **Pone mucho cuidado en su trabajo.** He takes great care over his work.; **Conducía con cuidado.** He was driving carefully.; **Debes tener mucho cuidado al cruzar la calle.** You must be very careful crossing the street.; **¡Cuidado!** Careful!; **Carlos está al cuidado de los niños.** Carlos looks after the children.; **cuidados intensivos** intensive care

cuidadoso adj careful

cuidar [26] vb to look after; **cuidarse** to look after oneself; **¡Cuídate!** Take care!

culebra nf snake

culebrón (pl culebrones) nm soap (on TV)

culo nm bum

culpa nf fault ▷ *La culpa es mía.* It's my fault.; **Tú tienes la culpa de todo.** It's all your fault.; **Siempre**

me echan la culpa a mí. They're always blaming me.; **por culpa del mal tiempo** because of the bad weather

culpable adj guilty ▷ *Se siente culpable de lo que ha pasado.* He feels guilty about what has happened.
▶ nmf culprit; **Ella es la culpable de todo.** She is to blame for everything.

cultivar [26] vb ❶ to grow ❷ to farm

culto adj ❶ cultured ❷ formal

cultura nf culture

culturismo nm body-building

cumbre nf summit

cumpleaños (pl cumpleaños) nm birthday; **¡Feliz cumpleaños!** Happy birthday!

cumplir [59] vb ❶ to carry out ❷ to keep ❸ to observe ❹ to serve; **Mañana cumplo dieciséis años.** I'll be sixteen tomorrow.; **El viernes se cumple el plazo para entregar las solicitudes.** Friday is the deadline for handing in applications.

cuna nf cradle

cuneta nf ditch

cuñada nf sister-in-law

cuñado nm brother-in-law

cuota nf fee

cupo vb see **caber**

cupón (pl cupones) nm ❶ voucher ❷ ticket

cura nf ❶ cure ❷ therapy
▶ nm priest

curar [26] vb ❶ to cure ❷ to treat;

Espero que te cures pronto. I hope you'll be better soon.

curiosidad *nf* curiosity; **Lo pregunté por curiosidad.** I asked out of curiosity.; **Tengo curiosidad por saber cuánto gana.** I'm curious to know how much he earns.

curioso *adj* ❶ curious; **¡Qué curioso!** How odd! ❷ nosy

curita *nf* (in Latin America) sticking plaster

cursillo *nm* course ▷ *un cursillo de cocina* a cookery course

curso *nm* ❶ year ▷ *un chico de mi curso* a boy in my year ▷ *Hago segundo curso.* I'm in the second year.; **el curso académico** the academic year ❷ course

curva *nf* ❶ bend ❷ curve

cuyo *adj* whose ▷ *El marido, cuyo nombre era Ricardo, estaba jubilado.* The husband, whose name was Ricardo, was retired. ▷ *La señora en cuya casa me hospedé* the lady whose house I stayed in

dado *nm* dice; **jugar a los dados** to play dice

dama *nf* lady ▷ *Damas y caballeros …* Ladies and gentlemen …; **las damas** draughts ▷ *jugar a las damas* to play draughts

damasco *nm* (in Latin America) apricot

danés, -esa (*mpl* **daneses**) *nm/f* Dane
▶ *nm* Danish (*language*)
▶ *adj* Danish

dañar [**26**] *vb* ❶ to damage ❷ to hurt; **Se dañó la pierna.** She hurt her leg.

daño *nm* damage; **ocasionar daños** to cause damage; **hacer daño a alguien** to hurt somebody; **hacerse daño** to hurt oneself

dar [**15**] *vb* ❶ to give ▷ *Le dio un*

bocadillo a su hijo. He gave his son a sandwich. ▷ Se lo di a Teresa. I gave it to Teresa.; **Me dio mucha alegría verla.** I was very pleased to see her.; **Déme 2 kilos.** 2 kilos please. ❷ to strike ▷ El reloj dio las 6. The clock struck 6.; **dar a** to look out onto; **dar con** to find; **Al final di con la solución.** I finally came up with the answer.; **El sol me da en la cara.** The sun's shining in my face.; **¿Qué más te da?** What does it matter to you?; **Se han dado muchos casos.** There have been a lot of cases.; **Se me dan bien las ciencias.** I'm good at science.; **darse un baño** to have a bath; **darse por vencido** to give up

dátil nm date

dato nm piece of information ▷ Ése es un dato importante. That's an important piece of information.; **Necesito más datos para poder juzgar.** I need more information to be able to judge.; **datos personales** personal details

de prep ❶ of ▷ un paquete de caramelos a packet of sweets; **una copa de vino (1)** a glass of wine **(2)** a wine glass; **la casa de Isabel** Isabel's house; **las clases de inglés** English classes; **un anillo de oro** a gold ring; **una máquina de coser** a sewing machine; **es de ellos** it's theirs; **a las 8 de la mañana** at 8 o'clock in the morning ❷ from ▷ Soy de Gijón. I'm from Gijón.; **salir del cine** to leave the cinema ❸ than ▷ Es más difícil de lo que

creía. It's more difficult than I thought it would be.; **más de 500 personas** over 500 people; **De haberlo sabido ...** If I'd known ...

dé vb see **dar**

debajo adv underneath ▷ Levanta la maceta, la llave está debajo. Lift up the flowerpot, the key's underneath.; **debajo de** under

debate nm debate

debatir [59] vb to debate

deber [9] vb ❶ must ▷ Debo intentar verla. I must try to see her. ▷ No debes preocuparte. You mustn't worry.; **Debería dejar de fumar.** I should stop smoking.; **No deberías haberla dejado sola.** You shouldn't have left her alone.; **como debe ser** as it should be; **deber de** must ▷ Debe de ser canadiense. He must be Canadian.; **No debe de tener mucho dinero.** He can't have much money. ❷ to owe ▷ ¿Cuánto le debo? How much do I owe you?; **deberse a** to be due to ▷ El retraso se debió a una huelga. The delay was due to a strike. ▶ nm duty ▷ Sólo cumplí con mi deber. I simply did my duty.; **los deberes** homework

debido adj **debido a** owing to ▷ Debido al mal tiempo, el vuelo se suspendió. Owing to the bad weather, the flight was cancelled.; **Habla como es debido.** Speak properly.

débil adj weak

debilidad nf weakness

debilitar [26] vb to weaken

década nf decade

decena nf ten ▷ decenas de miles de tens of thousands of; **Habrá una decena de libros.** There must be about ten books.

decente adj decent

decepción (pl decepciones) nf disappointment

 Be careful! **decepción** does not mean **deception**.

decepcionar [26] vb to disappoint; **La película me decepcionó.** The film was disappointing.

decidido adj determined ▷ Estoy decidido a hacerlo. I'm determined to do it.

decidir [59] vb to decide; **decidirse a hacer algo** to decide to do something; **decidirse por algo** to decide on something; **¡Decídete!** Make up your mind!

decimal adj, nm decimal

décimo, -a adj, pron tenth; **Vivo en el décimo.** I live on the tenth floor.

decir [16] vb ❶ to say ▷ ¿Qué dijo? What did he say? ▷ ¿Cómo se dice "casa" en inglés? How do you say "casa" in English?; **es decir** that is to say; **es un decir** it's a manner of speaking; **¡Diga!** Hello? ❷ to tell; **decirle a alguien que haga algo** to tell somebody to do something; **¡No me digas!** Really?; **querer decir** to mean

decisión (pl decisiones) nf decision ▷ tomar una decisión to take a decision

decisivo adj decisive

declaración (pl declaraciones) nf statement; **Prestó declaración ante el juez.** He gave evidence before the judge.; **una declaración de amor** a declaration of love; **la declaración de la renta** the income tax return

declarar [26] vb ❶ to declare ▷ ¿Algo que declarar? Anything to declare? ❷ to give evidence; **declarar culpable a alguien** to find somebody guilty; **declararse** (1) to declare oneself ▷ Se declaró partidario de hacerlo. He declared himself in favour of doing it. (2) to break out ▷ Se declaró un incendio en el bosque. A fire broke out in the forest.; **declararse a alguien** to propose to somebody

decorador, a nm/f interior decorator

decorar [26] vb to decorate

decreto nm decree

dedal nm thimble

dedicar [49] vb ❶ to devote ❷ to dedicate; **¿A qué se dedica?** What does he do for a living?; **Ayer me dediqué a arreglar los armarios.** I spent yesterday tidying the cupboards.

dedo nm ❶ finger ▷ Lleva un anillo en el dedo meñique. She wears a ring on her little finger.; **hacer dedo** to hitch a lift; **no mover un dedo** not to lift a finger ❷ toe; **el dedo gordo** (1) the thumb (2) the big toe

deducir [10] vb to deduce

defecto nm ❶ defect ❷ fault

defender [21] vb to defend;
defenderse to defend oneself; **Me
defiendo en inglés.** I can get by
in English.

defensa nf defence; **salir en
defensa de alguien** to come to
somebody's defence; **en defensa
propia** in self-defence

defensor, a nm/f defender

deficiente adj poor ▷ Su trabajo
es muy deficiente. His work is very
poor.

definición (pl **definiciones**) nf
definition

definir [59] vb to define

definitivo adj definitive; **en
definitiva** in short

defraudar [26] vb ❶ to
disappoint ❷ to defraud

dejar [26] vb ❶ to leave ▷ He
dejado las llaves en la mesa. I've left
the keys on the table. **¡Déjalo
ya!** Don't worry about it!; **Deja
mucho que desear.** It leaves a
lot to be desired. ❷ to let ▷ Mis
padres no me dejan salir de noche.
My parents won't let me go out at
night.; **dejar caer** to drop ▷ Dejó
caer la bandeja. She dropped the
tray. ❸ to lend ▷ Le dejé mi libro de
matemáticas. I lent him my maths
book. ❹ to give up ▷ Dejó el esquí
después del accidente. He gave up
skiing after the accident.; **dejar
de** to stop ▷ dejar de fumar to stop
smoking; **dejarse** to leave ▷ Se dejó
el bolso en un taxi. She left her bag
in a taxi.

del prep see **de**

delantal nm apron

delante adv in front; **de delante**
front; **la parte de delante** the
front; **delante de (1)** in front of
(2) opposite; **pasar por delante
de** to go past; **hacia delante**
forward

delantero adj front ▷ los asientos
delanteros the front seats; **la parte
delantera del coche** the front
of the car

delegación (pl **delegaciones**) nf
(in Mexico) police station

delegado, -a nm/f delegate;
el delegado de clase the class
representative

deletrear [26] vb to spell

delfín (pl **delfines**) nm dolphin

delgado adj ❶ slim ❷ thin

delicado adj ❶ delicate ▷ Estas
copas son muy delicadas. These
glasses are very delicate. ▷ Se trata
de un asunto muy delicado. It's a very
delicate subject. ❷ thoughtful
▷ Enviarte flores ha sido un gesto muy
delicado. Sending you flowers was
a very thoughtful gesture.

delicioso adj delicious

delincuente nmf criminal; **un
delincuente juvenil** a juvenile
delinquent

delito nm crime

demanda nf demand; **presentar
una demanda contra alguien** to
sue somebody

demás adj other ▷ los demás niños
the other children

▶ pron **los demás** the others; **lo
demás** the rest ▷ Yo limpio las

ventanas y lo demás lo limpias tú.
I'll clean the windows and you
clean the rest.; **todo lo demás**
everything else

demasiado adj too much (pl too
many) ▷ demasiado vino too much
wine ▷ demasiados libros too many
books

▶ adv ❶ too ▷ Es demasiado pesado
para levantarlo. It's too heavy to
lift. ▷ Caminas demasiado deprisa.
You walk too quickly. ❷ too much
▷ Hablas demasiado. You talk too
much.

democracia nf democracy

democrático adj democratic

demonio nm devil

demostración (pl
demostraciones) nf
❶ demonstration ❷ proof

demostrar [12] vb ❶ to
demonstrate ❷ to prove

densidad nf density

denso adj ❶ thick (fog, smoke)
❷ heavy (book)

dentadura nf teeth; la dentadura
postiza false teeth

dentífrico nm toothpaste

dentista nmf dentist

dentro adv inside ▷ ¿Qué hay
dentro? What's inside?; por dentro
inside; Está aquí dentro. It's in
here.; dentro de in; dentro de
poco soon; dentro de lo que cabe
as far as it goes

denuncia nf poner a alguien una
denuncia to report someone
▷ Voy a ponerle una denuncia por
hacer tanto ruido. I'm going to

report him for making so much
noise.

denunciar [26] vb to report

departamento nm
❶ department ❷ compartment
❸ (in Latin America) flat

depender [9] vb to depend;
depender de to depend on;
Depende. It depends.; No
depende de mí. It's not up to me.

dependiente, dependienta
nm/f sales assistant

deporte nm sport ▷ No hago mucho
deporte. I don't do much sport. ▷ los
deportes de invierno winter sports

deportista adj sporty ▷ Alicia es
poco deportista. Alicia is not very
sporty.

▶ nmf un deportista a sportsman;
una deportista a sportswoman

deportivo adj ❶ sports ▷ un club
deportivo a sports club ❷ sporting

depósito nm ❶ tank ❷ deposit

depresión (pl depresiones)
nf ❶ depression; tener una
depresión to be suffering from
depression ❷ hollow

deprimido adj depressed

deprimir [59] vb to depress;
deprimirse por algo to get
depressed about something

deprisa adv quickly; ¡Deprisa!
Hurry up!; Lo hacen todo deprisa
y corriendo. They do everything
in a rush.

derecha nf ❶ right hand ▷ Escribo
con la derecha. I write with my
right hand. ❷ right ▷ doblar a la
derecha to turn right; a la derecha

on the right ▷ *la segunda calle a la derecha* the second turning on the right; **conducir por la derecha** to drive on the right; **ser de derechas** to be right-wing ▷ *un partido de derechas* a right-wing party

derecho adj ❶ right ▷ *Me duele el ojo derecho.* I've got a pain in my right eye. ▷ *Escribo con la mano derecha.* I write with my right hand.; **a mano derecha** on the right-hand side ❷ straight ▷ *¡Ponte derecho!* Stand up straight!
▶ adv straight ▷ *Siga derecho.* Carry straight on.
▶ nm ❶ right ▷ *los derechos humanos* human rights; **tener derecho a hacer algo** to have the right to do something ▷ *No tienes derecho a decir eso.* You have no right to say that.; **¡No hay derecho!** It's not fair! ❷ law ▷ *Estudio derecho.* I'm studying law.

derramar [26] vb to spill

derrapar [26] vb to skid

derretir [39] vb to melt; **derretirse** to melt ▷ *El hielo se está derritiendo.* The ice is melting.; **derretirse de calor** to be melting

derribar [26] vb ❶ to demolish (building) ❷ to shoot down (plane) ❸ to overthrow (government)

derrota nf defeat

derrotar [26] vb to defeat

derrumbar [26] vb to pull down; **derrumbarse** to collapse

desabrochar [26] vb to undo; **desabrocharse** (1) to undo ▷ *Me desabroché la blusa.* I undid my blouse. (2) to come undone

desacuerdo nm disagreement

desafiar [22] vb to challenge

desafío nm challenge

desafortunado adj unfortunate

desagradable adj unpleasant

desagradecido adj ungrateful

desagüe nm ❶ wastepipe ❷ drain

desahogarse [38] vb *Se desahogó conmigo.* He poured out his heart to me.; **Lloraba para desahogarse.** He was crying to let off steam.

desalojar [26] vb to clear

desanimado adj downhearted

desanimar [26] vb to discourage; **desanimarse** to lose heart

desaparecer [13] vb to disappear; **¡Desaparece de mi vista!** Get out of my sight!

desaparición (pl desapariciones) nf disappearance

desapercibido adj pasar **desapercibido** to go unnoticed

desaprovechar [26] vb to waste

desarme nm disarmament ▷ *el desarme nuclear* nuclear disarmament

desarrollar [26] vb to develop; **desarrollarse** (1) to develop (2) to take place

desarrollo nm development; **un país en vías de desarrollo** a developing country

desastre nm disaster

desastroso adj disastrous

desatar [26] vb ❶ to undo ❷ to untie; **desatarse** to come undone

desayunar [26] vb ❶ to have breakfast ❷ to have...for breakfast ▷ *Desayuné café con leche y un bollo.* I had coffee and a roll for breakfast.

desayuno nm breakfast

descalzarse [14] vb to take one's shoes off

descalzo adj barefoot; **No entres en la cocina descalzo.** Don't come into the kitchen in bare feet.

descampado nm open space

descansar [26] vb ❶ to rest ❷ to sleep ▷ *¡Que descanses!* Sleep well!

descansillo nm landing

descanso nm ❶ rest ▷ *He caminado mucho, necesito un descanso.* I've done a lot of walking, I need a rest. ▷ **tomarse unos días de descanso** to take a few days off ❷ break ▷ *Cada dos horas me tomo un descanso.* I have a break every two hours. ❸ relief ▷ *¡Qué descanso!* What a relief! ❹ interval (in performance) ❺ half time (at a match)

descapotable nm convertible

descarado adj cheeky

descargar [38] vb ❶ to unload ❷ to take out; **descargarse** to go flat; **descargarse algo de Internet** to download something from the internet

descaro nm nerve ▷ *¡Qué descaro!* What a nerve!

descender [21] vb ❶ to go down ❷ to come down; **descender de** to be descended from

descendiente nmf descendant

descenso nm ❶ drop ▷ *el descenso de la temperatura* the drop in temperature ❷ descent ❸ relegation ▷ *el descenso a segunda división* relegation to the second division

descolgar vb ❶ to take down ❷ to pick up the phone; **descolgar el teléfono** to pick up the phone

descomponerse [42] vb (in Latin America) to break down

desconcertar [40] vb to disconcert; **desconcertarse** to be disconcerted

desconectar [26] vb ❶ to unplug ❷ to disconnect

desconfianza nf distrust

desconfiar [22] vb ❶ Desconfío de él. I don't trust him.; **Desconfía siempre de las apariencias.** Always beware of appearances.

descongelar [26] vb to defrost; **descongelarse** to defrost

desconocido, -a nm/f stranger ▶ adj unknown ▷ *un actor desconocido* an unknown actor

descontar [12] vb to deduct; **Descuentan el 5% si se paga en metálico.** They give a 5% discount if you pay cash.

descontento adj unhappy ▷ *Están descontentos de mis notas.* They're unhappy with my marks.

descoser [9] vb to unpick; **descoserse** to come apart at the seams

descremado adj skimmed

describir vb to describe

descripción (pl descripciones) nf description

descubierto nm overdraft

descubrimiento nm discovery

descubrir vb ❶ to discover ❷ to find out

descuento nm discount

descuidado adj ❶ careless ▷ Es muy descuidada con sus juguetes. She's very careless with her toys. ❷ neglected ▷ El jardín estaba descuidado. The garden was neglected.

descuidar [26] vb to neglect; **Descuida, que yo lo haré.** Don't worry, I'll do it.; **descuidarse** to let one's attention wander

descuido nm oversight

desde prep ❶ from ▷ Desde Burgos hasta mi casa hay 30 km. It's 30 km from Burgos to my house. ▷ Le llamaré desde la oficina. I'll ring him from the office. ❷ since ▷ La conozco desde niño. I've known her since I was a child. ▷ desde entonces since then; **Desde que llegó no ha salido.** He hasn't been out since he arrived.; **¿Desde cuándo vives aquí?** How long have you been living here?; **desde hace tres años** for three years; **desde ahora en adelante** from now on; **desde luego** of course

desdichado adj ❶ ill-fated ❷ unlucky

desdoblar [26] vb to unfold

desear [26] vb to wish ▷ Te deseo mucha suerte. I wish you lots of luck.; **Estoy deseando que esto**

termine. I'm longing for this to finish.; **¿Qué desea?** What can I do for you?; **dejar mucho que desear** to leave a lot to be desired

desechable adj disposable

desechos nmpl waste

desembarcar [49] vb ❶ to disembark ❷ to unload

desembarco nm landing

desembocar [49] vb desembocar en (1) to flow into (2) to lead into

desempacar [49] vb (in Latin America) to unpack

desempate nm play-off; **el partido de desempate** the deciding match

desempleado, -a nm/f unemployed person; **los desempleados** the unemployed

desempleo nm unemployment

desenchufar [26] vb to unplug

desengañar [26] vb Su traición la desengañó. His betrayal opened her eyes.; **¡Desengáñate! No está interesada en ti.** Stop kidding yourself! She isn't interested in you.

desengaño nm disappointment

desenredar [26] vb ❶ to untangle ❷ to resolve

desenrollar [26] vb ❶ to unwind ❷ to unroll

desenroscar [49] vb to unscrew

desenvolver [60] vb to unwrap; **desenvolverse** to cope

deseo nm wish ▷ Pide un deseo. Make a wish.

desequilibrado adj unbalanced

desértico adj desert ▷ una región desértica a desert region

desesperado, -a nm/f Corría como un desesperado. He was running like mad.
  ▶ adj desperate
desesperar [26] vb ❶ to drive... mad ▷ Los atascos me desesperan. Traffic jams drive me mad. ❷ to despair ▷ No desesperes y sigue intentándolo. Don't despair, just keep trying.; **desesperarse** to get exasperated
desfavorable adj unfavourable
desfiladero nm gorge
desfilar [26] vb to parade
desfile nm parade; **un desfile de modas** a fashion show
desgana nf ❶ loss of appetite ❷ reluctance; **hacer algo con desgana** to do something reluctantly
desgarrar [26] vb to tear up; **desgarrarse** to rip
desgarrón (pl **desgarrones**) nm rip
desgastar [26] vb ❶ to wear out ❷ to wear away; **desgastarse** to get worn out
desgaste nm ❶ wear and tear ❷ erosion
desgracia nf ❶ tragedy ❷ misfortune ▷ Ha tenido una vida llena de desgracias. He's had a lot of misfortune in his life.; **por desgracia** (1) sadly (2) unfortunately
desgraciado adj ❶ unhappy ▷ Desde que Ana le dejó ha sido muy desgraciado. He's been very unhappy since Ana left him.

❷ tragic ▷ Murió en un desgraciado accidente. He died in a tragic accident.
deshabitado adj ❶ uninhabited ❷ unoccupied
deshacer [27] vb ❶ to untie ❷ to unpack (case) ❸ to melt (ice, butter) ❹ to unpick (sewing, knitting); **deshacerse (1)** to come undone (knot, sewing) (2) to melt (ice, butter); **deshacerse de algo** to get rid of something
deshecho adj ❶ undone (knot) ❷ unmade (bed) ❸ melted; **Estoy deshecho.** (1) I'm exhausted. (2) I'm devastated.
deshielo nm thaw
deshinchar [26] vb to let down; **deshincharse (1)** to go down (balloon) (2) to go flat (tyre)
desierto adj deserted
  ▶ nm desert
desigual adj ❶ different (size) ❷ uneven (land, writing) ❸ unequal (fight)
desilusión (pl **desilusiones**) nf disappointment; **llevarse una desilusión** to be disappointed
desilusionar [26] vb ❶ to disappoint; **Su conferencia me desilusionó.** His lecture was disappointing.; **desilusionarse** to be disappointed
desinfectante nm disinfectant
desinfectar [26] vb to disinfect
desinflar [26] vb to let down
desinterés nm lack of interest
deslizarse [14] vb to slide
deslumbrar [26] vb to dazzle

desmayarse[26] vb to faint

desmayo nm faint; **sufrir un desmayo** to faint

desmontar[26] vb ❶ to take apart (furniture) ❷ to take down (tent)

desnatado adj ❶ skimmed ❷ low-fat

desnudar[26] vb to undress; **desnudarse** to get undressed

desnudo adj ❶ naked; **Duerme desnudo.** He sleeps in the nude. ❷ bare

desobedecer[13] vb to disobey

desobediente adj disobedient

desodorante nm deodorant

desorden (pl desórdenes) nm mess ▷ *Toda la casa estaba en desorden.* The whole house was in a mess.

desordenado adj untidy

desordenar[26] vb to mess up

desorganización nf disorganization

desorientar[26] vb to confuse; **desorientarse** to lose one's way

despabilar[26] vb to wake up; **despabilarse** (1) to wake up (2) to get a move on

despachar[26] vb ❶ to sell ❷ to serve ❸ to dismiss

despacho nm ❶ office; **una mesa de despacho** a desk ❷ study (room); **un despacho de billetes** a booking office

despacio adv slowly; **¡Despacio!** Take it easy!

despectivo adj ❶ contemptuous ❷ pejorative ▷ *una palabra*

despectiva a pejorative word

despedida nf farewell ▷ *una fiesta de despedida* a farewell party; **Le hicimos una buena despedida a Marta.** We gave Marta a good send-off.; **una despedida de soltero** a stag party; **una despedida de soltera** a hen party

despedir[39] vb ❶ to say goodbye to; **Fueron a despedirlo al aeropuerto.** They went to the airport to see him off. ❷ to dismiss; **despedirse** to say goodbye

despegar[38] vb to take off (plane); **despegarse** to come unstuck

despegue nm takeoff

despeinar[26] vb **despeinar a alguien** to mess somebody's hair up

despejado adj clear (sky, day, mind)

despejar[26] vb to clear; **¡Despejen!** Move along!; **Tomaré un café para despejarme.** I'll have a coffee to wake myself up.

despellejar[26] vb to skin

despensa nf larder

desperdiciar[26] vb ❶ to waste ❷ to throw away

desperdicio nm waste ▷ *Tirar toda esta comida es un desperdicio.* It's a waste to throw away all this food.; **los desperdicios** the scraps; **El libro no tiene desperdicio.** It's an excellent book from beginning to end.

desperezarse[14] vb to stretch

desperfecto nm flaw; **sufrir**

desperfectos to get damaged

despertador nm alarm clock

despertar [40] vb ❶ to wake up ▷ No me despiertes hasta las once. Don't wake me up until eleven o'clock.; **despertarse** to wake up

despido nm dismissal

despierto adj ❶ awake ❷ bright ▷ Es un niño muy despierto. He's a very bright boy.

despistado, -a nm/f scatterbrain ▶ adj absent-minded ▷ Es tan despistado que siempre se olvida las llaves. He's so absent-minded that he's always forgetting his keys.

despistar [26] vb ❶ to shake off ❷ to be misleading; **Me despisté y salí de la autopista demasiado tarde.** I wasn't concentrating and I turned off the motorway too late.

despiste nm absent-mindedness

desplazar [14] vb ❶ to move ❷ to take the place of

desplegar [35] vb ❶ to unfold ❷ to spread; **desplegarse** to be deployed

desplomarse [26] vb to collapse

despreciar [26] vb to despise

desprecio nm contempt

despreocuparse [26] vb to stop worrying; **despreocuparse de todo** to show no concern for anything

desprevenido adj pillar a alguien **desprevenido** to catch somebody unawares

después adv ❶ afterwards; **Primero cenaré y después saldré.** I'll have dinner first and go out after that. ❷ later ▷ un año después a year later ❸ next ▷ ¿Qué viene después? What comes next?; **después de** after; **después de todo** after all

destacar [49] vb ❶ to stress ❷ to stand out

destapador nm (in Latin America) bottle opener

destapar [26] vb ❶ to open ❷ to take the lid off; **destaparse** to get uncovered

desteñir [46] vb ❶ to run ❷ to fade; **desteñirse** to fade

desternillarse [26] vb **desternillarse de risa** to split one's sides laughing

destinar [26] vb ❶ to post (person) ❷ to earmark (funds); **El libro está destinado al público infantil.** The book is aimed at children.

destinatario, -a nm/f addressee

destino nm ❶ destination ▷ Por fin llegamos a nuestro destino. We finally arrived at our destination.; **el tren con destino a Valencia** the train to Valencia; **salir con destino a** to leave for ❷ posting ▷ Cada dos años me cambian de destino. They give me a new posting every two years. ❸ use ▷ Quiero saber qué destino tendrá este dinero. I want to know what use will be made of this money.

destornillador nm screwdriver

destornillar [26] vb to unscrew

destreza nf skill

destrozar [14] vb to wreck; **La**

noticia le destrozó el corazón.
The news broke his heart.

destrozos nmpl **damage**

destrucción nf **destruction**

destruir [11] vb ❶ to **destroy** ❷ to
ruin ▷ to **demolish**

desvalijar [26] vb ❶ to **burgle**
❷ to **rob**

desván (pl **desvanes**) nm **attic**

desventaja nf **disadvantage**;
estar en desventaja to be at a
disadvantage

desviación (pl **desviaciones**) nf
❶ **diversion** ❷ **detour**

desviar [22] vb to **divert**

desvío nm ❶ **turning** ▷ **Coge el
primer desvío a la derecha.** Take
the first turning on the right.
❷ **diversion**

detalle nm **detail** ▷ **No recuerdo
todos los detalles.** I don't remember
all the details.; **¡Qué detalle!** How
thoughtful!

detectar [26] vb to **detect**

detective nmf **detective** ▷ **un
detective privado** a private detective

detener [54] vb ❶ to **stop**
❷ to **arrest**; **detenerse** to stop
▷ **Nos detuvimos en el semáforo.**
We stopped at the lights.;
¡Deténgase! Stop!

detergente nm **detergent**

deteriorar [26] vb to **damage**;
deteriorarse to deteriorate

determinación nf
determination; **tomar una
determinación** to take a decision

determinado adj ❶ **certain**
▷ **En determinadas ocasiones es**
mejor callarse. There are certain
occasions when it's better to say
nothing.; **No hemos quedado
a una hora determinada.** We
haven't fixed a definite time.
❷ **particular** ▷ **¿Buscas algún libro
determinado?** Are you looking for a
particular book?

determinar [26] vb ❶ to
determine ▷ **Trataron de determinar
la causa del accidente.** They tried
to determine the cause of the
accident. ❷ to **fix** ▷ **determinar la
fecha de una reunión** to fix the date
of a meeting ❸ to **bring about** ▷ **Aquello determinó
la caída del gobierno.** That brought
about the fall of the government.
❹ to **state** ▷ **El reglamento determina
que...** The rules state that...

detestar [26] vb to **detest**

detrás adv **behind**; **detrás de**
behind ▷ **Se escondió detrás de un
árbol.** He hid behind a tree.; **uno
detrás de otro** one after another;
La critican por detrás. They
criticize her behind her back.

deuda nf **debt**; **contraer deudas**
to get into debt

devolución (pl **devoluciones**)
nf ❶ **return** (of letter, book)
❷ **repayment** (of money); **No se
admiten devoluciones.** Goods
cannot be returned.

devolver [60] vb ❶ to **give back**
▷ **Me devolvieron mal el cambio.**
They gave me the wrong change.;
**Te devolveré el favor cuando
pueda.** I'll return the favour when
I can. ❷ to **take back** (goods) ▷ to

throw up (vomit)

devorar [26] vb to devour;
devorar un bocadillo to wolf
down a sandwich

di vb see **decir**

día nm day ▷ Duerme de día y trabaja
de noche. He sleeps during the day
and works at night.; **Es de día.**
It's daylight.; **¿Qué día es hoy?**
(1) What's the date today? (2) What
day is it today?; **el día de mañana**
tomorrow; **al día siguiente** the
following day; **todos los días**
every day; **un día de estos** one
of these days; **un día sí y otro no**
every other day; **¡Buenos días!**
Good morning!; **un día de fiesta** a
public holiday; **un día feriado** (in
Latin America) a public holiday; **un
día laborable** a working day; **pan
del día** fresh bread

diabético, -a nm/f, adj diabetic

diablo nm devil

diagnóstico nm diagnosis

diagonal adj, nf diagonal; **en
diagonal** diagonally

dialecto nm dialect

dialogar [38] vb **dialogar con
alguien** to hold talks with
somebody

diálogo nm ❶ conversation
❷ dialogue

diamante nm diamond;
diamantes diamonds

diámetro nm diameter

diana nf ❶ bull's-eye ▷ dar
en la diana to get a bull's-eye
❷ dartboard

diapositiva nf slide

diario adj daily ▷ la rutina diaria the
daily routine; **la ropa de diario**
everyday clothes; **a diario** every
day ▷ Va al gimnasio a diario. He
goes to the gym every day.
▶ nm ❶ newspaper ❷ diary

diarrea nf diarrhoea

dibujante nmf ❶ artist
❷ cartoonist ❸ draughtsman

dibujar [26] vb to draw ▷ No sé
dibujar. I can't draw.

dibujo nm drawing ▷ el dibujo
técnico technical drawing; **los
dibujos animados** cartoons

diccionario nm dictionary

dicho vb see **decir**
▶ adj **en dichos países** in the
countries mentioned above;
mejor dicho or rather; **dicho y
hecho** no sooner said than done
▶ nm saying

dichoso adj ❶ happy ❷ lucky;
¡Dichoso ruido! Damned noise!

diciembre nm

Months start with a small
letter in Spanish.

December

diciendo vb see **decir**

dictado nm dictation ▷ La maestra
nos hizo un dictado. The teacher
gave us a dictation.

dictador, a nm/f dictator

dictadura nf dictatorship

dictar [26] vb to dictate

diecinueve adj, pron nineteen
▷ Tengo diecinueve años. I'm
nineteen.; **el diecinueve de julio**
the nineteenth of July

dieciocho adj, pron eighteen

▷ *Tengo dieciocho años*. I'm eighteen.; **el dieciocho de abril** the eighteenth of April

dieciséis adj, pron sixteen ▷ *Tengo dieciséis años*. I'm sixteen.; **el dieciséis de febrero** the sixteenth of February

diecisiete adj, pron seventeen ▷ *Tengo diecisiete años*. I'm seventeen.; **el diecisiete de enero** the seventeenth of January

diente nm tooth ▷ *lavarse los dientes* to clean one's teeth; **un diente de ajo** a clove of garlic

dieta nf diet; **estar a dieta** to be on a diet; **ponerse a dieta** to go on a diet; **dietas** expenses

diez adj, pron ten ▷ *Tengo diez años*. I'm ten.; **Son las diez**. It's ten o'clock.; **el diez de agosto** the tenth of August

diferencia nf difference; **a diferencia de** unlike ▷ *A diferencia de su hermana, a ella le encanta viajar*. Unlike her sister, she loves travelling.

diferenciar [26] vb ¿**En qué se diferencian?** What's the difference between them?; **Sólo se diferencian en el tamaño.** The only difference between them is their size.; **No diferencia el color rojo del verde.** He can't tell the difference between red and green.

diferente adj different

difícil adj difficult ▷ *Es un problema difícil de entender*. It's a difficult problem to understand. ▷ *Resulta difícil concentrarse*. It's difficult to

concentrate.

dificultad nf difficulty ▷ *con dificultad* with difficulty; **tener dificultades para hacer algo** to have difficulty doing something

dificultar [26] vb to make... difficult ▷ *La niebla dificultaba la visibilidad*. The fog made visibility difficult.

digerir [52] vb to digest

digestión nf digestion; **hacer la digestión** to digest

digestivo adj digestive

digital adj digital; **la radio digital** digital radio; **la televisión digital** digital television ▷ *un reloj digital* a digital watch; **una huella digital** a fingerprint

dignidad nf dignity

digno adj ❶ decent
❷ honourable; **digno de mención** worth mentioning

digo vb see **decir**

dije vb see **decir**

diluir [11] vb to dilute

diluviar [26] vb **Está diluviando.** It's pouring with rain.

diluvio nm downpour

dimensión (pl dimensiones) nf dimension

diminutivo nm diminutive

diminuto adj tiny

dimisión (pl dimisiones) nf resignation ▷ *presentar la dimisión* to hand in one's resignation

dimitir [59] vb to resign

Dinamarca nf Denmark

dinámico adj dynamic

dinero nm money ▷ *No tengo más*

dinero. I haven't got any more money.; **andar mal de dinero** to be short of money; **dinero suelto** loose change

dinosaurio nm dinosaur

dio vb see **dar**

Dios nm God ▷ **¡Gracias a Dios!** Thank God! ▷ **¡Dios mío!** My God!; **¡Por Dios!** For God's sake!; **¡Si Dios quiere!** God willing!; **No vino ni Dios.** Nobody turned up.

diploma nm diploma

diplomacia nf diplomacy

diplomático, -a nm/f diplomat
▶ adj diplomatic

diputado, -a nm/f Member of Parliament

dirá vb see **decir**

dirección (pl direcciones) nf
① direction ▷ **Íbamos en dirección equivocada.** We were going in the wrong direction.; **Tienes que ir en esta dirección.** You have to go this way.; **una calle de dirección única** a one-way street; **"dirección prohibida"** "no entry"; **"todas direcciones"** "all routes"
② address ② management
▷ **la dirección de la empresa** the management of the company

directo adj ① direct ▷ **Hay un tren directo a Valencia.** There's a direct train to Valencia. ② straight
▷ **Se fue directa a casa.** She went straight home.; **transmitir en directo** to broadcast live

director, a nm/f ① manager
② headteacher ③ director
④ conductor ⑤ editor

directorio nm ① directory ② (in Latin America) phone book

dirigente nmf ① leader
③ manager

dirigir [17] vb ① to manage (company) ② to lead (expedition)
③ to aim at ▷ **Este anuncio va dirigido a los niños.** This advertisement is aimed at children.; **no dirigir la palabra a alguien** not to speak to somebody
④ to direct (film) ⑤ to conduct (orchestra); **dirigirse a (1)** to address **(2)** to write to **(3)** to make one's way to

discapacitado adj disabled

discar [49] vb (in Latin America) to dial

disciplina nf discipline

disco nm ① record (for playing)
② light (traffic light) ③ discus; **un disco compacto** a compact disc; **el disco duro** the hard disk

discoteca nf disco

discreción nf discretion

discreto adj discreet

discriminación nf **la discriminación racial** racial discrimination

disculpa nf **pedir disculpas a alguien por algo** to apologize to somebody for something

disculpar [26] vb to excuse
▷ **Disculpa ¿me dejas pasar?** Excuse me, can I go past?; **disculparse** to apologize

discurso nm speech

discusión (pl discusiones) nf discussion; **tener una discusión**

con alguien to have an argument with somebody

discutir [59] vb ① to quarrel
▷ *Siempre discuten por dinero.* They're always quarrelling about money. ② to discuss ▷ *Tenemos que discutir el nuevo proyecto.* We've got to discuss the new project.

diseñar [26] vb to design

disfraz (pl disfraces) nm
① disguise ② costume; **una fiesta de disfraces** a fancy-dress party

disfrazarse [14] vb disfrazarse de (1) to disguise oneself as (2) to dress up as

disfrutar [26] vb to enjoy oneself ▷ *Disfruté mucho en la fiesta.* I really enjoyed myself at the party.; **Disfruto leyendo.** I enjoy reading.; **disfrutar de buena salud** to enjoy good health

disgustado adj upset

▌ Be careful **disgustado** does not mean **disgusted**.

disgustar [26] vb to upset; **disgustarse** to get upset; **disgustarse con alguien** to fall out with somebody

disgusto nm **dar un disgusto a alguien** to upset somebody; **llevarse un disgusto** to get upset

disimular [26] vb to hide; **No disimules, sé que has sido tú.** Don't bother pretending, I know it was you.

disminución (pl disminuciones) nf decrease

disminuido, -a nm/f un

disminuido mental a mentally handicapped person; **un disminuido físico** a physically handicapped person

disminuir [11] vb to fall

disolver [34] vb ① to dissolve ② to break up; **disolverse** to break up

disparar [26] vb to shoot; disparar a alguien to shoot at somebody; **Disparó dos tiros.** He fired two shots.

disparo nm shot

disponer [42] vb to arrange; **disponer de** to have; **disponerse a hacer algo** to get ready to do something

disponible adj available

dispuesto adj ① prepared ▷ *estar dispuesto a hacer algo* to be prepared to do something ② ready ▷ *Todo está dispuesto para la fiesta.* Everything's ready for the party.

disputa nf dispute

disquete nm diskette

distancia nf distance; **mantenerse a distancia** to keep at a distance; **¿Qué distancia hay entre Madrid y Barcelona?** How far is Madrid from Barcelona?; **¿A qué distancia está la estación?** How far's the station?; **a 20 kilómetros de distancia** 20 kilometres away

distinción (pl distinciones) nf distinction

distinguido adj distinguished

distinguir vb ① to distinguish;

Se parecen tanto que no los distingo. They're so alike that I can't tell them apart. ❸ to make out; distinguirse to stand out

distinto adj different ▷ Carlos es distinto a los demás. Carlos is different from other people.; distintos several ▷ distintas clases de coches several types of car

distracción (pl distracciones) nf pastime; En el pueblo hay pocas distracciones. There isn't much to do in the village.

distraer [55] vb ❶ to keep... entertained ▷ Les pondré un vídeo para distraerlos. I'll put a video on to keep them entertained. ❷ to distract ▷ No me distraigas, que tengo trabajo. Don't distract me, I've got work to do.; Me distrae mucho escuchar música. I really enjoy listening to music.; Me distraje un momento y me pasé de parada. I let my mind wander for a minute and missed my stop.

distraído adj absent-minded; Perdona, estaba distraído. Sorry, I wasn't concentrating.

distribución (pl distribuciones) nf ❶ layout ❷ distribution

distribuir [11] vb ❶ to distribute ❷ to hand out

distrito nm district

diversión (pl diversiones) nf entertainment

▌ Be careful! diversión does not mean diversion.

diverso adj different; diversos libros various books

divertido adj ❶ funny ❷ enjoyable; Fue muy divertido. It was great fun.

divertir [52] vb to entertain; divertirse to have a good time

dividir [59] vb to divide; dividirse (1) to divide (2) to share

divierto vb see divertir

divino adj divine

división (pl divisiones) nf division

divorciarse [26] vb to get divorced

divorcio nm divorce

divulgar [38] vb to spread

DNI abbr (= Documento Nacional de Identidad) ID card

doblar [26] vb ❶ to double ❷ to fold ❸ to turn ▷ Cuando llegues al cruce, dobla a la derecha. When you reach the junction, turn right. ❹ to dub ▷ Doblan todas las películas extranjeras. All foreign films are dubbed. ❺ to toll ▷ Las campanas de la iglesia doblan cuando hay un funeral. The church bells toll when there's a funeral.

doble adj double ▷ una habitación doble a double room
▶ nm twice as much ▷ Su sueldo es el doble del mío. His salary's twice as much as mine. ▷ Comes el doble que yo. You eat twice as much as I do.; Trabaja el doble que tú. He works twice as hard as you do.; jugar un partido de dobles to play doubles

doce adj, pron twelve ▷ Tengo doce años. I'm twelve.; Son las doce. It's twelve o'clock.

a
b
c
d
e
f
g
h
i
j
k
l
m
n
o
p
q
r
s
t
u
v
w
x
y
z

docena nf dozen

doctor, a nm/f doctor

doctrina nf doctrine

documental nm documentary

documento nm document;
el documento nacional de identidad the identity card
● All Spanish nationals over 14
● must have an identity card
● including their photo, personal
● details and fingerprint. In Spain
● this card is also known as the
● **DNI** or **carnet (de identidad)**,
● while in Latin American
● countries a similar card is called
● the **cédula de identidad**.
un documento adjunto an attachment

dólar nm dollar

doler [34] vb to hurt; **Me duele la cabeza.** I've got a headache.; **Me duele el pecho.** I've got a pain in my chest.; **Me duele la garganta.** I've got a sore throat.

dolor nm pain; **Tengo dolor de cabeza.** I've got a headache.; **Tengo dolor de estómago.** I've got stomachache.; **Tengo dolor de muelas.** I've got toothache.; **Tengo dolor de oídos.** I've got earache.; **Tengo dolor de garganta.** I've got a sore throat.

doméstico adj domestic;
las tareas domésticas the housework; **un animal doméstico** a pet

domicilio nm residence ▷ su domicilio particular their private residence; **servicio a domicilio**

home delivery

dominar [26] vb ❶ to dominate
❷ to control (temper) ❸ to be fluent in (language) ❹ to bring under control (fire); **dominarse** to control oneself

domingo nm
● Days of the week start with a
● small letter in Spanish.
Sunday ▷ el domingo pasado last Sunday ▷ el domingo que viene next Sunday

dominicano, -a adj, nm/f Dominican

dominio nm ❶ command (of subject) ❷ control ❸ domain

dominó nm ❶ domino
❷ dominoes ▷ jugar al dominó to play dominoes

don nm gift ▷ Tiene un don para la música. He has a gift for music.
● **Don** is used before a man's
● first name to show respect
● for someone older or more
● senior. Often abbreviated to
● **D.**, it is also seen on envelopes
● in combination with **Sr.**
● before a man's first name and
● surname(s).
▷ don Juan Gómez Mr Juan Gómez
▷ Sr. D. José Galera Real Mr José Galera Real

dona nf (in Mexico) doughnut

donante nmf donor

donativo nm donation

donde adv where ▷ La nota está donde la dejaste. The note's where you left it.

dónde adv where ▷ ¿Dónde vas?

Where are you going? ▷ ¿Sabes dónde está? Do you know where he is?; ¿De dónde eres? Where are you from?; ¿Por dónde se va al cine? How do you get to the cinema?

doña nf
- Doña is used before a woman's first name to show respect for someone older or more senior.
- Often abbreviated to Dña., it is also seen on envelopes in combination with Sra. before a woman's first name and surname(s).
▷ doña Marta García Mrs Marta García ▷ Sra. Dña. Ana Torre Martín Mrs Ana Torre Martín

dorado adj golden

dormir [18] vb to sleep; Se me ha dormido el brazo. My arm has gone to sleep.; dormir la siesta to have a nap; dormir como un tronco to sleep like a log; estar medio dormido to be half asleep; dormirse to fall asleep

dormitorio nm ❶ bedroom ❷ dormitory

dorso nm back ▷ Se apuntó el teléfono en el dorso de la mano. He wrote the telephone number on the back of his hand.; "véase al dorso" "see over"

dos adj, pron ❶ two ▷ ¿Tienes los dos libros que te dejé? Have you got the two books I lent you? ▷ Tiene dos años. He's two.; Son las dos. It's two o'clock.; de dos en dos in twos; el dos de enero the second

of January; cada dos por tres every five minutes ❷ both ▷ Al final vinieron los dos. In the end they both came. ▷ Los hemos invitado a los dos. We've invited both of them.

doscientos, -as adj, pron two hundred ▷ dos cientos cincuenta two hundred and fifty

dosis (pl dosis) nf dose

doy vb see **dar**

dragón (pl dragones) nm dragon

drama nm drama

dramático adj dramatic

droga nf drug ▷ las drogas blandas soft drugs ▷ las drogas duras hard drugs

drogadicto, -a nm/f drug addict

drogar [38] vb to drug; drogarse to take drugs

droguería nf
- A shop selling cleaning materials, paint and toiletries.

ducha nf shower ▷ darse una ducha to have a shower

ducharse [26] vb to have a shower

duda nf doubt ▷ Tengo mis dudas. I have my doubts.; sin duda no doubt; no cabe duda there's no doubt about it; Tengo una duda. I have a query.; ¿Alguna duda? Any questions?

dudar [26] vb to doubt; Dudo que sea cierto. I doubt if it's true.; Dudó si comprarlo o no. He wasn't sure whether to buy it or not.

dudoso adj ❶ doubtful ▷ Es dudoso que vengan. It's doubtful whether they'll come. ❷ dubious

duelo vb see **doler**

dueño, -a nm/f owner

duermo vb see **dormir**

Duero nm the Douro

dulce adj ❶ sweet ❷ gentle
▶ nm sweet

duración nf length; **una pila de larga duración** a long-life battery

duradero adj ❶ lasting ❷ hard-wearing

durante adv during; **durante toda la noche** all night long; **Habló durante una hora.** He spoke for an hour.

durar [26] vb to last ▷ *La película duraba dos horas.* The film lasted two hours.

durazno nm (in Latin America) peach

dureza nf ❶ hardness ❷ harshness

durmiendo vb see **dormir**

duro adj ❶ hard ▷ *Los diamantes son muy duros.* Diamonds are very hard. ❷ tough ▷ *Esta carne está dura.* This meat's tough. ❸ harsh ▷ *El clima es muy duro.* The climate is very harsh.; **a duras penas** with great difficulty; **ser duro de oído** to be hard of hearing
▶ adv hard ▷ *trabajar duro* to work hard
▶ nm five-peseta coin

DVD abbr (= *Disco de Vídeo Digital*) DVD

e conj

 e is used instead of y in front of words beginning with "i" and "hi", but not "hie".

and ▷ *Pablo e Inés.* Pablo and Inés.

echar [26] vb ❶ to throw ▷ *Échame las llaves.* Throw the keys over to me.; **Eché la carta en el buzón.** I posted the letter. ❷ to put; **Tengo que echar gasolina.** I need to put petrol in the car.; **¿Te echo más whisky?** Shall I pour you some more whisky? ❸ to throw out ▷ *Me echó de su casa.* He threw me out of his house. ❹ to expel ▷ *Lo han echado del colegio.* He's been expelled from school.; **La echaron del trabajo.** They sacked her.; **¿Qué echan hoy en la tele?** What's on TV today?;

echar de menos a alguien to miss somebody; **echar una ojeada (a)** to browse; **echarse (1)** to lie down **(2)** to jump

eco nm echo

ecología nf ecology

ecológico adj ecological; **un producto ecológico** an environmentally friendly product

ecologista adj environmental ▶ nmf environmentalist

economía nf ❶ economy ❷ economics

económico adj ❶ economic ▷ *una crisis económica* an economic crisis ❷ economical ▷ *un motor económico* an economical engine ❸ inexpensive ▷ *un restaurante económico* an inexpensive restaurant

economista nmf economist

economizar [14] vb to economize

Ecuador nm Ecuador

ecuatoriano, -a nm/f, adj Ecuadorean

edad nf age ▷ *Tenemos la misma edad.* We're the same age.; **¿Qué edad tienen?** How old are they?; **Está en la edad del pavo.** She's at that difficult age.

edición (pl ediciones) nf edition

edificar [49] vb to build

edificio nm building

Edimburgo nm Edinburgh

editar [26] vb to publish

editor, a nm/f publisher

editorial nf publisher

edredón (pl edredones) nm ❶ eiderdown ❷ duvet

educación nf ❶ education; **educación física** PE ❷ upbringing; **Señalar es de mala educación.** It's rude to point.; **Se lo pedí con educación.** I asked her politely.

educado adj polite; **Me contestó de forma educada.** He answered me politely.

educar [49] vb ❶ to educate ❷ to bring up

educativo adj educational

EE.UU. abbr (= *Estados Unidos*) USA

efectivamente adv **Efectivamente, estaba donde tú decías.** You were right, he was where you said.; **Entonces, ¿Es usted su padre? — Efectivamente.** So, are you his father? — That's right.

efectivo adj effective; **pagar en efectivo** to pay in cash

efecto nm effect; **hacer efecto** to take effect; **en efecto** indeed

efectuar [2] vb to carry out

eficaz adj ❶ effective ❷ efficient

eficiente adj efficient

egipcio, -a nm/f, adj Egyptian

Egipto nm Egypt

egoísmo nm selfishness

egoísta adj selfish ▶ nmf Maria es una egoísta. Maria's very selfish.

Eire nm Eire

eje nm ❶ axle ❷ axis

ejecución (pl ejecuciones) nf execution

ejecutar [26] vb ❶ to carry out ❷ to execute

a
b
c
d
e
f
g
h
i
j
k
l
m
n
o
p
q
r
s
t
u
v
w
x
y
z

ejecutivo, -a nm/f executive

ejemplar nm copy

ejemplo nm example; **por ejemplo** for example

ejercer vb **Ejerce de abogado.** He's a practising lawyer.; **Ejerce mucha influencia sobre sus hermanos.** He has a lot of influence on his brothers.

ejercicio nm exercise; **hacer ejercicio** to exercise

ejército nm army

ejote nm (in Mexico) green bean

el (fsg **la**, mpl **los**, fpl **las**) art the ▷ Perdí el autobús. I missed the bus.; **el del sombrero rojo** the one with the red hat; **Yo fui el que lo encontré.** I was the one who found it.

> You usually translate **el** as **my**, **his**, **her**, etc when it relates to a part of the body, clothes or belongings.

▷ Ayer me lavé la cabeza. I washed my hair yesterday. ▷ Me puse el abrigo. I put my coat on. ▷ Tiene un coche bonito, pero prefiero el de Juan. He's got a nice car, but I prefer Juan's.

> **el** isn't always translated into English.

▷ No me gusta el pescado. I don't like fish. ▷ Vendrá el lunes que viene. He's coming next Monday. ▷ Ha llamado el Sr. Sendra. Mr Sendra called.

él pron ❶ he ▷ Me lo dijo él. He told me. ❷ him ▷ Se lo di a él. I gave it to him. ▷ Su mujer es más alta que él. His wife's taller than he is.; **él mismo** himself; **de él** his ▷ El coche es de él. The car's his.

elaborar [26] vb to produce

elástico adj elastic ▷ una goma elástica an elastic band; **un tejido elástico** a stretchy material

elección (pl elecciones) nf ❶ election; **Han convocado elecciones generales.** They've called a general election. ❷ choice ▷ No tuve elección. I had no choice.

electoral adj **la campaña electoral** the election campaign

electricidad nf electricity

electricista nmf electrician

eléctrico adj ❶ electric ▷ una guitarra eléctrica an electric guitar ❷ electrical ▷ a causa de un fallo eléctrico due to an electrical fault

electrodoméstico nm domestic appliance

electrónica nf electronics

electrónico adj electronic; **el correo electrónico** email

elefante nm elephant

elegante adj smart

elegir [19] vb ❶ to choose ❷ to elect

elemento nm element

elevado adj high

elevar [26] vb to raise

eligiendo vb see **elegir**

elijo vb see **elegir**

eliminar [26] vb ❶ to remove ❷ to eliminate

elixir bucal nm mouthwash

ella pron ❶ she ▷ Ella no estaba en casa. She was not at home. ❷ her

▷ *El regalo es para ella.* The present's for her.; **ella misma** herself; **de ella** hers ▷ *Este abrigo es de ella.* This coat's hers.

ellos, -as *pron pl* ❶ they ▷ *Ellos todavía no lo saben.* They don't know yet. ❸ them ▷ *Yo me iré con ellas.* I'll leave with them. ▷ *Somos mejores que ellos.* We're better than they are.; **ellos mismos** themselves ▷ *Me lo dijeron ellos mismos.* They told me themselves.; **de ellos** theirs ▷ *El coche era de ellos.* The car was theirs.

elogiar [26] *vb* to praise

elote *nm* ❶ (in Mexico) corn on the cob ❷ sweetcorn

e-mail (pl e-mails) *nm* ❶ email (message, system); **mandar un e-mail a algn** to email someone ❷ email address

embajada *nf* embassy

embajador, a *nm/f* ambassador

embalar [26] *vb* to pack

embalse *nm* reservoir

embarazada *adj* pregnant ▷ *Estaba embarazada de cuatro meses.* She was four months pregnant.; **quedarse embarazada** to get pregnant

Be careful! **embarazada** does not mean **embarrassed**.

embarazoso *adj* embarrassing

embarcar [49] *vb* to board

embargo *nm* embargo; **sin embargo** nevertheless

emborracharse [26] *vb* to get drunk

embotellado *adj* bottled

embotellamiento *nm* traffic jam

embrague *nm* clutch

embrollarse [26] *vb* ❶ to get tangled up ❷ to get muddled up

embrollo *nm* tangle

embrujado *adj* haunted

embutido *nm* cold meats

emergencia (pl emergencias) *nf* emergency; **la salida de emergencia** the emergency exit

emigrar [26] *vb* to emigrate

emisión (pl emisiones) *nf* broadcast

emitir [59] *vb* ❶ to broadcast ❷ to give off

emoción (pl emociones) *nf* emotion; **Su carta me produjo gran emoción.** I was very moved by his letter.; **¡Qué emoción!** How exciting!

emocionado *adj* ❶ moved ❷ excited

emocionante *adj* ❶ moving ❷ exciting

emotivo *adj* ❶ moving ❷ emotional

empacharse [26] *vb* to get a tummy upset

empalagoso *adj* sickly

empalmar [26] *vb* ❶ to connect ❷ to join

empanada *nf* pasty

empañarse [26] *vb* to get steamed up

empapar [26] *vb* to soak; **estar empapado hasta los huesos** to be soaked to the skin

empapelar [26] *vb* to paper

empaquetar [26] *vb* to pack

emparedado nm (in Latin America) sandwich

emparejar [26] vb to pair up

empastar [26] vb **Me han empastado dos muelas.** I've had two fillings.

empaste nm filling

empatar [26] vb to draw

empate nm ❶ draw ❷ tie

empedernido adj **un fumador empedernido** a chronic smoker; **Es un lector empedernido.** He's a compulsive reader.

empeñado adj determined

empeñarse [26] vb **empeñarse en hacer algo** (1) to be determined to do something (2) to insist on doing something

empeorar [26] vb ❶ to get worse ❷ to make...worse ▷ Sólo empeorará las cosas. It will only make matters worse.

empezar [20] vb to start; **empezar a hacer algo** to start doing something; **volver a empezar** to start again

empinado adj steep

empleado, -a nm/f ❶ employee ❷ (in Latin America) shop assistant

emplear [26] vb ❶ to use ❷ to employ

empleo nm job; **estar sin empleo** to be unemployed; **"modo de empleo"** "how to use"

empollar [26] vb to swot

empollón, -ona (mpl **empollones**) nm/f swot

empresa nf firm

empresaria nf businesswoman

empresario nm businessman

empujar [26] vb to push

empujón (pl **empujones**) nm **Me dieron un empujón y caí a la piscina.** They pushed me and I fell into the pool.

en prep ❶ in ▷ Viven en Granada. They live in Granada. ▷ Nació en invierno. He was born in winter. ▷ Lo hice en dos días. I did it in two days. ▷ Está en el hospital. She's in hospital. ❷ into ▷ Entré en el banco. I went into the bank. ❸ on ▷ Las llaves están en la mesa. The keys are on the table. ▷ Está en la calle Pelayo. It's on Pelayo street. ▷ Está en el quinto piso. It's on the fifth floor. ❹ at ▷ Yo estaba en casa. I was at home. ▷ Vivía en el número 17. I was living at number 17. ▷ en ese momento at that moment ▷ en Navidades at Christmas ❺ by ▷ Vinimos en avión. We came by plane.; **ser el primero en llegar** to be the first to arrive

enamorado adj **estar enamorado de alguien** to be in love with somebody

enamorarse [26] vb to fall in love

enano, -a nm/f dwarf

encabezar [14] vb to head

encaminarse [26] vb **Nos encaminamos hacia el pueblo.** We headed towards the village.

encantado adj ❶ delighted ▷ Está encantada con su nuevo coche. She's delighted with her new car.; **¡Encantado de conocerle!** Pleased to meet you!

encantador, a adj charming

encantar [26] vb to love

encanto nm charm; **Eugenia es un encanto.** Eugenia is charming.

encarcelar [26] vb to imprison

encargado, -a nm/f manager ▶ adj **Estoy encargada de vender las entradas.** I'm in charge of selling the tickets.

encargar [38] vb to order

encariñarse [26] vb encariñarse con to grow fond of

encendedor nm lighter

encender [21] vb ❶ to light ❷ to switch on

encendido adj ❶ on ▷ La tele estaba encendida. The telly was on. ❷ lit (fire)

encerado nm board

encerrar [40] vb ❶ to shut up ❷ to lock up

enchilada nf (in Mexico) stuffed tortilla

enchufado, -a nm/f **Amelia es la enchufada del profesor.** Amelia's the teacher's pet.

enchufar [26] vb to plug in

enchufe nm ❶ plug ❷ socket

encía nf gum

enciclopedia nf encyclopaedia

enciendo vb see **encender**

encierro vb see **encerrar**

encima adv on ▷ Pon el cenicero aquí encima. Put the ashtray on here.; **No llevo dinero encima.** I haven't got any money on me.; **encima de** (1) on ▷ Ponlo encima de la mesa. Put it on the table. (2) on top of ▷ Mi maleta está encima del armario. My

case is on top of the wardrobe.; **Lo leí por encima.** I glanced at it.; **por encima de** (2) over; **¡Y encima no te da ni las gracias!** And on top of that he doesn't even thank you!

encina nf oak tree

encoger [8] vb to shrink; **Antonio se encogió de hombros.** Antonio shrugged his shoulders.

encontrar [12] vb to find; **No encuentro las llaves.** I can't find the keys.; **encontrarse** (1) to feel ▷ Ahora se encuentra mejor. She's feeling better now. (2) to meet; **Me encontré con Ana en la calle.** I bumped into Ana in the street.

encuentro nm meeting

encuesta nf survey

enderezar [14] vb to straighten

endulzar [14] vb to sweeten

endurecer [13] vb ❶ to harden ❷ to tone up (muscles)

enemigo, -a nm/f, adj enemy

enemistarse [26] vb to fall out

energía nf energy; **la energía solar** solar power; **la energía eléctrica** electricity

enérgico adj energetic

enero nm
⟩ Months start with a small letter in Spanish.
January

enfadado adj angry ▷ Estaba muy enfadado conmigo. He was very angry with me.; **Pilar y su novio están enfadados.** Pilar and her boyfriend have fallen out.

enfadarse [26] vb to be angry; **Se**

a
b
c
d
e
f
g
h
i
j
k
l
m
n
o
p
q
r
s
t
u
v
w
x
y
z

han enfadado. They've fallen out.

enfado nm **Ya se le ha pasado el enfado.** He isn't angry any more.

enfermarse [26] vb (in Latin America) to fall ill

enfermedad nf ❶ illness ❷ disease

enfermería nf sick bay

enfermero, -a nm/f nurse

enfermo, -a nm/f ❶ sick person ❷ patient
▸ adj ▸ ill ▸ **He estado enferma toda la semana.** I've been ill all week.; **¿Cuándo te pusiste enfermo?** When did you become ill?

enfocar [49] vb ❶ to focus on ❷ to approach

enfrentarse [26] vb **enfrentarse a algo** to face something

enfrente adv opposite; **La panadería está enfrente.** The baker's is across the street.; **de enfrente** opposite ▸ la casa de enfrente the house opposite; **enfrente de** opposite

enfriarse [22] vb ❶ to get cold ❷ to cool down ❸ to catch cold

enganchar [26] vb to hook; **engancharse** to get caught

engañar [26] vb ❶ to cheat ❷ to lie ❸ to cheat on; **Las apariencias engañan.** Appearances can be deceptive.

engaño nm ❶ con ❷ deception

engordar [26] vb ❶ to put on weight; **He engordado dos kilos.** I've put on two kilos. ❷ to be fattening

engreído adj conceited

enhorabuena nf **¡Enhorabuena!** Congratulations!; **Me dieron la enhorabuena por el premio.** They congratulated me on winning the prize.

enlace nm ❶ connection ❷ connecting flight ❸ link (in computing)

enlatado adj tinned

enlazar [14] vb to connect

enmarcar [49] vb to frame

enmoquetado adj carpeted

enojado adj angry ▸ Estaba muy enojado conmigo. He was very angry with me.; **Están enojados.** They've fallen out.

enojarse vb to be angry

enorme adj enormous

enredarse [26] vb ❶ to get tangled up ▸ Se me ha enredado el pelo. My hair's got all tangled up. ❷ to get into a muddle

enrevesado adj difficult

enriquecerse [13] vb to get rich

enrollar [26] vb to roll up

enroscar [49] vb ❶ to screw in ❷ to coil

ensalada nf salad

ensaladilla nf **una ensaladilla rusa** a Russian salad

ensanchar [26] vb to widen; **ensancharse** to stretch

ensayar [26] vb to rehearse

ensayo nm rehearsal

enseguida adv straight away; **Enseguida te atiendo.** I'll be with you in a minute.

enseñanza nf ❶ teaching ❷ education; la enseñanza

primaria primary education

enseñar [26] vb ❶ to teach ▷ Mi padre me enseñó a nadar. My father taught me to swim. ❷ to show; **Les enseñé el colegio.** I showed them round the school.

ensuciar [26] vb to get... dirty ▷ Vas a ensuciar el sofá. You'll get the sofa dirty.; **ensuciarse** to get dirty; **Te has ensuciado de barro los pantalones.** You've got mud on your trousers.

entender [21] vb to understand ▷ ¿Lo entiendes? Do you understand?; **Creo que lo he entendido mal.** I think I've misunderstood.; **Mi primo entiende mucho de coches.** My cousin knows a lot about cars.; **entenderse (1)** to get on ▷ Mi hermana y yo no nos entendemos. My sister and I don't get on. **(2)** to communicate; **Dio a entender que no le gustaba.** He implied that he didn't like it.

entendido, -a nm/f expert

enterarse [26] vb ❶ to find out; **Se enteraron del accidente por la tele.** They heard about the accident on the TV.; **Me sacaron una muela y ni me enteré.** They took out a tooth and I didn't notice a thing. ❷ to understand

entero adj whole ▷ Se pasó la noche entera estudiando. He spent the whole night studying.; **la leche entera** full-cream milk

enterrar [40] vb to bury

entiendo vb see **entender**

entierro vb see **enterrar**
▶ nm funeral

entonces adv ❶ then ▷ Me recogió y entonces fuimos al cine. He picked me up and then we went to the cinema.; **desde entonces** since then; **para entonces** by then ❷ so ▷ ¿Entonces, vienes o te quedas? So, are you coming or staying?

entorno nm surroundings

entrada nf ❶ entrance; **"entrada libre"** "free admission" ❷ ticket ▷ Tengo entradas para el teatro. I've got tickets for the theatre. ❸ entry; **"prohibida la entrada"** "no entry" ❹ deposit

entrante nm starter

entrar [26] vb ❶ to go in; **No me dejaron entrar.** They wouldn't let me in. ❷ to come in ❸ to fit ▷ La maleta no entra en el maletero. The case won't fit in the boot.; **El vino no entra en el precio.** The wine isn't included in the price.; **Le entraron ganas de reír.** She wanted to laugh.; **De repente le entró sueño.** He suddenly felt sleepy.

entre prep ❶ between ▷ Vendrá entre las diez y las once. He'll be coming between ten and eleven.; **Le compraremos un regalo entre todos.** We'll buy her a present between all of us. ❷ among ▷ Las mujeres hablaban entre sí. The women were talking among themselves. ❸ by ▷ 15 dividido entre 3 es 5. 15 divided by 3 is 5.

entreabierto adj ajar

entregar [38] vb ❶ to hand in ❷ to deliver ❸ to present...with ▷ *El director le entregó la medalla.* The director presented him with the medal.; **El ladrón se entregó a la policía.** The thief gave himself up.

entremeses nmpl appetizers

entrenador, a nm/f coach

entrenamiento nm training

entrenarse [26] vb to train

entretanto adv meanwhile

entretener [54] vb ❶ to entertain ❷ to keep ▷ *Una vecina me entretuvo hablando.* A neighbour kept me talking.; **entretenerse** to amuse oneself

entretenido adj entertaining

entrevista nf interview; **hacer una entrevista a alguien** to interview somebody

entrevistador, a nm/f interviewer

entrevistar [26] vb to interview

entrometerse [9] vb to meddle

entusiasmado adj excited

entusiasmarse [26] vb to get excited

entusiasmo nm enthusiasm; **con entusiasmo** enthusiastically

enumerar [26] vb to list

envase nm container; **"envase no retornable"** "non-returnable bottle"

envejecer [13] vb to age

enviar [22] vb to send; **Juan me envió el regalo por correo.** Juan posted me the present.

envidia nf envy; **¡Qué envidia!**

I'm so jealous!; **Le tiene envidia a Ana.** She's jealous of Ana.; **Le da envidia que mi coche sea mejor.** He's jealous that my car is better.

envidiar [26] vb to envy

envidioso adj envious

envolver [60] vb to wrap up

envuelto vb see **envolver**

epidemia nf epidemic

episodio nm episode

época nf time ▷ *en aquella época* at that time

equilibrado adj balanced

equilibrio nm balance ▷ *Perdí el equilibrio.* I lost my balance.

equipaje nm luggage; **equipaje de mano** hand luggage

equipo nm ❶ team ▷ *un equipo de baloncesto* a basketball team ❷ equipment ▷ *Me robaron todo el equipo de esquí.* They stole all my skiing equipment.; **el equipo de música** the stereo

equitación nf riding

equivaler [56] vb **equivaler a algo** to be equivalent to something

equivocación (pl **equivocaciones**) nf mistake

equivocado adj wrong ▷ *Estás equivocada.* You're wrong.

equivocarse [49] vb ❶ to make a mistake ❷ to be wrong; **Perdone, me he equivocado de número.** Sorry, wrong number.; **Se equivocaron de tren.** They caught the wrong train.

era vb see **ser**

eres vb see **ser**

erizo nm hedgehog; **un erizo de mar** a sea urchin

error nm mistake

eructar [26] vb to burp

eructo nm burp

es vb see **ser**

esa adj see **ese**

ésa pron see **ése**

esbelto adj slender

escala nf ❶ scale ▷ a escala nacional on a national scale
❷ stopover ▷ Tenemos una escala de tres horas en Bruselas. We've got a three-hour stopover in Brussels.

escalar [26] vb to climb

escalera nf stairs ▷ bajar las escaleras to go down the stairs; **una escalera de mano** a ladder; **la escalera de incendios** the fire escape; **una escalera mecánica** an escalator

escalofrío nm Tengo escalofríos. I'm shivering.

escalón (pl **escalones**) nm step

escama nf scale

escandalizar [14] vb to shock

escándalo nm ❶ scandal
❷ racket ▷ ¿Qué escándalo es éste? What's all this racket?

escandaloso adj noisy

escandinavo, -a adj, nm/f Scandinavian; **los escandinavos** the Scandinavians

escáner nm ❶ scanner ❷ scan; **hacerse un escáner** to have a scan

escapar [26] vb to escape; **escaparse** to escape; **Se me escapó un eructo.** I let out a burp.

escaparate nm shop window; **ir**

de escaparates to go window-shopping

escape nm leak ▷ Había un escape de gas. There was a gas leak.

escaquearse [26] vb escaquearse de clase to skip school

escarabajo nm beetle

escarbar [26] vb to dig

escarcha nf frost

escasez nf shortage

escaso adj scarce ▷ Los alimentos están muy escasos. Food is scarce.

escayola nf plaster

escayolar [26] vb to put...in plaster ▷ Le escayolaron la pierna. They put his leg in plaster.

escena nf scene

escenario nm stage

escéptico adj sceptical

esclavo, -a nm/f slave

escoba nf broom

escocer [7] vb to sting

escocés, -esa (mpl **escoceses**) nm/f ▷ un escocés a Scotsman; **una escocesa** a Scotswoman; **los escoceses** Scottish people
▶ adj Scottish; **una falda escocesa** a kilt

Escocia nf Scotland

escoger [8] vb to choose

escolar adj school ▷ el uniforme escolar school uniform

escombros nmpl rubble

esconder [9] vb to hide; **Me escondí debajo de la cama.** I hid under the bed.

escondidas nfpl hide-and-seek; **a escondidas** in secret

escondite nm jugar al escondite

to play hide-and-seek

escopeta nf shotgun

Escorpio nm Scorpio (sign); **Soy escorpio.** I'm Scorpio.

escorpión (pl escorpiones) nm scorpion

escribir [1] vb to write ▷ **Les escribí una carta.** I wrote them a letter.; **Nos escribimos de vez en cuando.** We write to each other from time to time.; **¿Cómo se escribe tu nombre?** How do you spell your name?; **escribir a máquina** to type

escrito vb see **escribir**
▷ adj written

escritor, a nm/f writer

escritorio nm ❶ desk ❷ (in Latin America) office

escritura nf writing

escrupuloso adj fussy

escuchar [26] vb ❶ to listen ❷ to listen to ▷ **Me gusta escuchar música.** I like listening to music.

escudo nm ❶ shield ❷ badge

escuela nf school; **la escuela primaria** primary school

esculcar vb (in Mexico) to search

escultura nf sculpture

escupir [59] vb to spit

escurridizo adj slippery

escurridor nm ❶ colander ❷ plate rack

escurrir [59] vb ❶ to wring ❷ to drain

ese, esa adj that ▷ **Dame ese libro.** Give me that book.

ése, ésa pron that one ▷ **Prefiero ésa.** I prefer that one.; **¿Quién es ése?** Who's that?

esencial adj essential

esforzarse vb to make an effort

esfuerzo nm effort

esfumarse [26] vb to vanish

esguince nm sprain; **Me hice un esguince en el tobillo.** I've sprained my ankle.

esmalte nm **el esmalte de uñas** nail varnish

ESO abbr = **Enseñanza Secundaria obligatoria**
  ● ESO is the compulsory
  ● secondary education course
  ● done by 12 to 16 year-olds.

eso pron that ▷ **Eso es mentira.** That's a lie. ▷ **¡Eso es!** That's it!; **a eso de las cinco** at about five; **En eso llamaron a la puerta.** Just then there was a ring at the door.; **Por eso te lo dije.** That's why I told you.

esos, -as adj pl those ▷ **Trae esas sillas aquí.** Bring those chairs over here.

ésos, -as pron pl those ones; **Ésos no son los que vimos ayer.** Those aren't the ones we saw yesterday.

espabilar [26] vb to wake up; **espabilarse (1)** to wake up **(2)** to get a move on

espacio nm ❶ room ▷ **El piano ocupa mucho espacio.** The piano takes up a lot of room. ❷ space; **un espacio en blanco** a gap; **viajar por el espacio** to travel in space

espada nf sword

- **espadas** are swords, one of the suits in the Spanish card deck.

espaguetis nmpl spaghetti

espalda nf back ▷ *Me duele la espalda.* My back's aching.; **Estaba tumbada de espaldas.** She was lying on her back.; **Ana estaba de espaldas a mí.** Ana had her back to me.; **Me encanta nadar a espalda.** I love swimming backstroke.

espantapájaros (pl **espantapájaros**) nm scarecrow

espantar [26] vb ❶ to frighten ❷ to frighten off ❸ to horrify ▷ *Me espantan los zapatos de tacón.* I hate high heels.; **espantarse** (*asustarse*) to get frightened

espantoso adj awful; *Hacía un frío espantoso.* It was awfully cold.

España nf Spain

español, a nm/f Spaniard; **los españoles** the Spaniards
  ▶nm Spanish (language) ▷ *¿Hablas español?* Do you speak Spanish?
  ▶adj Spanish

esparadrapo nm sticking plaster

espárrago nm asparagus

especia nf spice

especial adj special; **en especial** particularly ▷ *¿Desea ver a alguien en especial?* Is there anybody you particularly want to see?

especialidad nf speciality

especialista nmf specialist

especializarse [14] vb to specialize

especialmente adv ❶ especially ❷ specially

especie nf species

específico adj specific

espectacular adj spectacular

espectáculo nm performance; **Dio el espectáculo delante de todo el mundo.** He made a spectacle of himself in front of everyone.

espectador, a nm/f spectator; **los espectadores** the audience

espejo nm mirror; **un espejo retrovisor** a rearview mirror

espeluznante adj hair-raising

espera nf wait ▷ *tras una espera de tres horas* after a three-hour wait; **estar a la espera de algo** to be expecting something

esperanza nf hope; **No tengo esperanzas de aprobar.** I have no hope of passing.; **No pierdas las esperanzas.** Don't give up hope.

esperar [26] vb ❶ to wait; **Espera un momento, por favor.** Hang on a moment, please. ❷ to wait for ▷ *No me esperéis.* Don't wait for me.; **Me hizo esperar una hora.** He kept me waiting for an hour. ❸ to expect; **esperar un bebé** to be expecting a baby ❹ to hope; **¿Vendrás a la fiesta? - Espero que sí.** Are you coming to the party? - I hope so.; **¿Crees que Carmen se enfadará? - Espero que no.** Do you think Carmen will be angry? - I hope not.; **Fuimos a esperarla a la estación.** We went to the station to meet her.

espeso adj thick

espía *nmf* spy

espiar [22] *vb* to spy on

espina *nf* ❶ thorn ❷ bone

espinaca *nf* spinach

espinilla *nf* ❶ shin ❷ blackhead

espionaje *nm* spying; **una novela de espionaje** a spy story

espíritu *nm* spirit

espiritual *adj* spiritual

espléndido *adj* splendid

esponja *nf* sponge

esponjoso *adj* spongy

espontáneo *adj* spontaneous; **de manera espontánea** spontaneously

esposa *nf* wife; **las esposas** handcuffs

esposo *nm* husband

espuma *nf* ❶ foam ❷ head (on beer); **la espuma de afeitar** shaving cream

espumoso *adj* **vino espumoso** sparkling wine

esqueleto *nm* skeleton

esquema *nm* ❶ outline ❷ diagram

esquí (*pl* **esquís**) *nm* ❶ skiing; **el esquí acuático** water skiing; **una pista de esquí** a ski slope ❷ ski

esquiar [22] *vb* to ski

esquimal *adj, nmf* Eskimo

esquina *nf* corner; **doblar la esquina** to turn the corner

esquivar [26] *vb* to dodge

esta *adj see* **este**

ésta *pron see* **éste**

está *vb see* **estar**

estable *adj* stable

establecer [13] *vb* to establish;

Han logrado establecer contacto con el barco. They've managed to make contact with the boat.; **La familia se estableció en Madrid.** The family settled in Madrid.

establecimiento *nm* establishment

establo *nm* stable

estación (*pl* **estaciones**) *nf* ❶ station ▷ **la estación de autobuses** the bus station ▷ **la estación de ferrocarril** the railway station; **una estación de esquí** a ski resort; **una estación de servicio** a service station ❷ season ▷ **las cuatro estaciones** the four seasons

estacionar [26] *vb* to park

estacionarse [26] *vb* (in Chile, River Plate, Mexico) to park

estadía *nf* (in Latin America) stay

estadio *nm* stadium

estado *nm* state; **El Estado Español** The Spanish State; **estado civil** marital status; **María está en estado.** María is expecting.

Estados Unidos *npl* the United States ▷ **en Estados Unidos** in the United States

estadounidense *adj, nmf* American

estafar [26] *vb* to swindle

estallar [26] *vb* ❶ to explode (bomb) ❷ to burst (tyre, balloon) ❸ to break out (war)

estampilla *nf* (in Latin America) stamp

estancado *adj* stagnant

estancia *nf* ❶ stay ❷ ranch

estanco nm tobacconist's
- In Spain, an **estanco** is
- a government-licensed
- tobacconist's, recognizable by
- its brown and yellow "T" sign.
- The **estanco** also sells stamps,
- stationery, official forms and
- coupons for the **quiniela** or
- football pools.

estándar adj standard

estanque nm pond

estante nm shelf

estantería nf ❶ shelves
❷ bookshelves ❸ shelf unit

estaño nm tin

estar [23] vb ❶ to be

  estar is used to talk about
  location.

▷ ¿Dónde estabas? Where were you?
▷ Madrid está en el centro de España.
Madrid is in the centre of Spain.;
¿Está Mónica? Is Mónica there?

  estar is used to talk about
  temporary states and with
  past participles used as
  adjectives.

▷ ¿Cómo estás? How are you?
▷ Estoy muy cansada. I'm very tired.
▷ ¿Estás casado? Are you married?
▷ La radio está rota. The radio's
broken.; **Estamos de vacaciones.**
We're on holiday.

  estar is used in continuous
  tenses.

▷ Estamos esperando a Manolo.
We're waiting for Manolo.
▷ Estuvieron registrando la casa.
They were searching the house.

  estar is used with prices.

▷ ¿A cuánto está el kilo de naranjas?
How much are oranges a kilo?

  estar is used with dates and
  temperatures.

▷ Estamos a 30 de enero. It's 30th
January. ▷ Estábamos a 40°C. The
temperature was 40°C.; **¡Ya está!
Ya sé lo que podemos hacer.**
That's it! I know what we can do.
❷ to look

  estar is also used to say how
  someone or something looks.

▷ ¡Qué guapa estás esta noche!
You're looking really pretty
tonight!; **estarse** to be

estas adj see **estos**

éstas pron see **éstos**

estatal adj state

estatua nf statue

estatura nf height; **¿Cuál es tu
estatura?** How tall are you?; **Mide
casi dos metros de estatura.** He's
over six and a half feet tall.

este (1), esta adj this ▷ este libro
this book

este (2) nm, adj inv east ▷ en el este
de España in the East of Spain

éste, ésta pron this one ▷ Ésta me
gusta más. I prefer this one.; **Éste
no es el que vi ayer.** This is not the
one I saw yesterday.

esté vb see **estar**

estera nf mat

estéreo (pl **estéreos**) nm stereo

esterlina adj **diez libras
esterlinas** ten pounds sterling

estético adj **Se ha hecho la
cirugía estética.** He's had plastic
surgery.

estiércol nm manure

estilo nm style; **un estilo de vida similar al nuestro** a similar lifestyle to ours

estima nf **Lo tengo en gran estima.** I think very highly of him.

estimado adj **Estimado señor Pérez** Dear Mr Pérez

estimulante adj stimulating

estimular [26] vb ❶ to encourage ❷ to stimulate

estirar [26] vb to stretch

esto pron this ▷ *¿Para qué es esto?* What's this for?; **En esto llegó Juan.** Just then Juan arrived.

estofado nm stew

estómago nm stomach; **Me dolía el estómago.** I had stomach ache.

estorbar [26] vb to be in the way

estornudar [26] vb to sneeze

estos, -as adj pl these; **estas maletas** these cases

éstos, -as pron pl these ▷ *Éstos son los míos.* These ones are mine.; **Éstos no son los que vimos ayer.** These aren't the ones we saw yesterday.; **un día de éstos** one of these days

estoy vb see **estar**

estrangular [26] vb to strangle

estratégico adj strategic

estrechar [26] vb to take in ▷ *¿Me puedes estrechar esta falda?* Can you take in this skirt for me?; **La carretera se estrecha en el puente.** The road gets narrower over the bridge.; **Se estrecharon la mano.** They shook hands.

estrecho adj ❶ narrow ❷ tight ▷ *La falda me va muy estrecha.* The skirt's very tight on me. ▶ nm strait; **el estrecho de Gibraltar** the straits of Gibraltar

estrella nf star; **una estrella de cine** a film star

estrellarse [26] vb to smash

estrenar [26] vb to premiere; **Mañana estrenaré el vestido.** I'll wear the dress for the first time tomorrow.

estreno nm premiere

estreñido adj constipated

estrés nm stress

estricto adj strict

estridente adj loud

estropajo nm scourer

estropeado adj ❶ broken ❷ broken down

estropear [26] vb ❶ to break ❷ to ruin ▷ *La lluvia nos estropeó las vacaciones.* The rain ruined our holidays.; **estropearse** (1) to break ▷ *Se nos ha estropeado la tele.* The TV's broken. (2) **Se me estropeó el coche en la autopista.** My car broke down on the motorway.; **La fruta se está estropeando con este calor.** The fruit's going off in this heat.

estructura nf structure

estrujar [26] vb ❶ to squeeze ❷ to wring

estuche nm case

estudiante nmf student

estudiar [26] vb ❶ to study ❷ to learn

estudio nm ❶ studio ❷ studio flat ❸ study (room, activity); **Ha**

dejado los estudios. He's given up his studies.

estudioso adj studious

estufa nf ❶ heater ❷ (in Mexico) stove

estupendamente adv Me encuentro estupendamente. I feel great.; Nos lo pasamos estupendamente. We had a great time.

estupendo adj great ▷ Pasamos unas Navidades estupendas. We had a great Christmas.; ¡Estupendo! Great!

estupidez (pl estupideces) nf No dice más que estupideces. He just talks rubbish.; Lo que hizo fue una estupidez. What he did was stupid.

estúpido, -a nm/f idiot
▶ adj stupid

estuve vb see estar

etapa nf stage ▷ Lo hicimos por etapas. We did it in stages.

etc. abbr (= etcétera) etc.

eterno adj eternal

ética nf ethics

ético adj ethical

Etiopía nf Ethiopia

etiqueta nf label; traje de etiqueta formal dress

étnico adj ethnic

ETT abbr (= Empresa de Trabajo Temporal) temp agency

eufórico adj ecstatic

euro nm euro

Europa nf Europe

europeo, -a nm/f, adj European

Euskadi nm the Basque Country

euskera nm Basque
- Basque is one of Spain's four
- official languages, and there
- is Basque-language radio and
- television. It is not from the
- same family of languages as
- Spanish.

evacuar [26] vb to evacuate

evadir [59] vb ❶ to avoid ❷ to evade

evaluación (pl evaluaciones) nf assessment

evaluar [2] vb to assess

evangelio nm gospel

evaporarse [26] vb to evaporate

evasivo adj evasive

eventual adj un trabajo eventual a temporary job

evidencia nf evidence

evidente adj obvious

evidentemente adv obviously

evitar [26] vb ❶ to avoid ▷ Intento evitar a Luisa. I'm trying to avoid Luisa.; No pude evitarlo. I couldn't help it. ❷ to save ▷ Esto nos evitará muchos problemas. This will save us a lot of problems.

evolución (pl evoluciones) nf progress; la teoría de la evolución the theory of evolution

evolucionar [26] vb ❶ to develop ❷ to progress ❸ to evolve

ex prefix ex; su ex-marido her ex-husband

exactamente adv exactly

exactitud nf No lo sabemos con exactitud. We don't know exactly.

exacto adj ❶ exact ▷ el precio exacto the exact price; El tren salió a la hora exacta. The train left bang on time. ❷ accurate; **Tenemos que defender nuestros derechos. - ¡Exacto!** We have to stand up for our rights. - Exactly!

exageración (pl **exageraciones**) nf exaggeration

exagerar [26] vb to exaggerate

examen (pl **exámenes**) nm exam; **el examen de conducir** driving test

examinar [26] vb to examine; **Mañana me examino de inglés.** Tomorrow I've got an English exam.

excavadora nf digger

excavar [26] vb to dig

excelente adj excellent

excéntrico adj eccentric

excepción (pl **excepciones**) nf exception; **a excepción de** except for

excepcional adj exceptional

excepto prep except for

excesivo adj excessive

exceso nm excess; **exceso de equipaje** excess luggage

excitarse [26] vb **Se excitó mucho en la discusión.** He got very worked up in the argument.

exclamar [26] vb to exclaim

excluir [11] vb to exclude

exclusivo adj exclusive

excluyendo vb see **excluir**

excursión (pl **excursiones**) nf trip
▷ *Mañana vamos de excursión con el colegio.* Tomorrow we're going on a school trip.

excusa nf excuse

exhibición (pl **exhibiciones**) nf exhibition

exhibir [59] vb to exhibit; **Le gusta mucho exhibirse.** He likes drawing attention to himself.

exigente adj demanding

exigir [17] vb ❶ to demand; **La maestra nos exige demasiado.** Our teacher is too demanding. ❷ to require; **Exigen tres años de experiencia para el puesto.** They're asking for three years' experience for the job.

exiliado, -a nm/f exile

existir [59] vb to exist; **Existen dos maneras de hacerlo.** There are two ways of doing it.

éxito nm success; **Su película tuvo mucho éxito.** His film was very successful.

> Be careful! **éxito** does not mean **exit**.

exótico adj exotic

expansión (pl **expansiones**) nf expansion

expedición (pl **expediciones**) nf expedition

expediente nm file; **expediente académico** student record

expendio nm (in Latin America) shop

expensas nfpl **a expensas de su salud** at the cost of her health

experiencia nf experience; **con experiencia** experienced

experimentado adj experienced

experimental adj experimental

experimentar [26] vb ❶ to experiment ❷ to experience

experimento nm experiment

experto, -a nm/f expert

explicación (pl **explicaciones**) nf explanation

explicar [49] vb to explain; **¿Me explico?** Do I make myself clear?; **No me lo explico.** I can't understand it.

explorador, a nm/f explorer

explorar [26] vb to explore

explosión (pl **explosiones**) nf explosion; **El artefacto hizo explosión.** The device exploded.

explosivo nm explosive

explotación (pl **explotaciones**) nf exploitation

explotar [26] vb ❶ to exploit ❷ to explode

exponer [42] vb ❶ to display ❷ to present

exportación (pl **exportaciones**) nf export

exportar [26] vb to export

exposición (pl **exposiciones**) nf exhibition ▷ **montar una exposición** to put on an exhibition

expresamente adv ❶ specifically ❷ specially

expresar [26] vb to express

expresión (pl **expresiones**) nf expression

expresivo adj expressive

expreso nm ❶ express (train) ❷ espresso (coffee)

exprimir [59] vb to squeeze

expuesto vb see **exponer**

expulsar [26] vb ❶ to expel ❷ to send off

expulsión (pl **expulsiones**) nf expulsion

exquisito adj delicious

éxtasis nm ecstasy

extender [21] vb to spread; **El fuego se extendió rápidamente.** The fire spread quickly.; **extender los brazos** to stretch one's arms out

extendido adj outstretched

extensión (pl **extensiones**) nf ❶ area ▷ **una enorme extensión de tierra** an enormous area of land ❷ extension ▷ **¿Me pone con la extensión 212, por favor?** Can you put me through to extension 212, please?

extenso adj extensive

exterior (f **exterior**) adj ❶ outside (world) ❷ outer (layer) ❸ foreign (policy, trade) ▶ nm outside; **Salimos al exterior para ver qué pasaba.** We went outside to see what was going on.

externo adj ❶ outside ❷ outer

extiendo vb see **extender**

extinción nf putting out (of fire); **una especie en vías de extinción** an endangered species

extinguidor nm (in Latin America) fire extinguisher

extinguir vb to put out; **extinguirse** to become extinct; **El fuego se fue extinguiendo lentamente.** The fire was slowly going out.

extinto adj extinct

extintor nm fire extinguisher

extra adj extra ▷ **una manta extra** an extra blanket; **chocolate**

de calidad extra top quality chocolate

extractor *nm* extractor fan

extraer [55] *vb* **❶** to extract **❷** to draw

extraescolar *adj* **actividades extraescolares** extracurricular activities

extraigo *vb see* **extraer**

extranjero, -a *nm/f* foreigner; **vivir en el extranjero** to live abroad; **viajar al extranjero** to travel abroad
▸ *adj* foreign

extrañar [26] *vb* **❶** to miss ▷ *Extraña mucho a sus padres.* He misses his parents a lot. **❷** to surprise; **Me extraña que no haya llegado.** I'm surprised he hasn't arrived.; **¡Ya me extrañaba a mí!** I thought it was strange!; **extrañarse de algo** to be surprised at something

extrañeza *nf* **Nos miró con extrañeza.** He looked at us in surprise.

extraño *adj* strange; **¡Qué extraño!** How strange!

extraordinario *adj* extraordinary

extravagante *adj* extravagant

extraviado *adj* **❶** lost **❷** missing

extremista *adj, nmf* extremist

extremo, -a *adj* extreme
▸ *nm/f* winger *(in sports)*
▸ *nm* end *(of rope, street)*; **pasar de un extremo a otro** to go from one extreme to the other

extrovertido *adj* outgoing

exuberante *adj* lush

fábrica *nf* factory

⚠ Be careful! **fábrica** does not mean fabric.

fabricante *nmf* manufacturer

fabricar [49] *vb* to make; **"fabricado en China"** "made in China"

fachada *nf* **la fachada del edificio** the front of the building

fácil *adj* easy ▷ *El examen fue muy fácil.* The exam was very easy.; **Es fácil de entender.** It's easy to understand.; **Es fácil que venga.** He may well come.

facilidad *nf* **Se me rompen las uñas con facilidad.** My nails break easily.; **Pepe tiene facilidad para los idiomas.** Pepe has a gift for languages.; **Te dan facilidades de pago.** They offer credit facilities.

facilitar[26] *vb* to make...easier ▷ *Un ordenador facilita mucho el trabajo.* A computer makes work much easier.; **El banco me facilitó la información.** The bank provided me with the information.

factor *nm* factor

factura *nf* bill

facturar[26] *vb* to check in

facultad *nf* ❶ faculty; **la Facultad de Derecho** the Law Faculty ❷ university; **ir a la facultad** to go to university

faena *nf* work; **las faenas domésticas** housework

falda *nf* skirt

fallar[26] *vb* to fail (*brakes, engine, sight*); **Fallé el tiro.** I missed.

fallecer[13] *vb* to die

fallo *nm* ❶ fault ▷ *un pequeño fallo eléctrico* a small electrical fault ❷ failure ▷ *debido a un fallo de motor* due to engine failure ❸ mistake ▷ **¡Qué fallo!** What a stupid mistake!; **Fue un fallo humano.** It was human error.

falsificar[49] *vb* to forge

falso *adj* ❶ false ❷ forged; **Los diamantes eran falsos.** The diamonds were fakes.; **Eso es falso.** That's not true.

falta *nf* ❶ lack ▷ *la falta de dinero* lack of money ❷ foul ▷ *Ha sido falta.* It was a foul.; **Eso es una falta de educación.** That's bad manners.; **una falta de ortografía** a spelling mistake; **Me hace falta**

un ordenador. I need a computer.; **No hace falta que vengáis.** You don't need to come.

faltar[26] *vb* to be missing ▷ *Me falta un bolígrafo.* One of my pens is missing.; **Faltan varios libros del estante.** There are several books missing from the shelf.; **No podemos irnos. Falta Manolo.** We can't go. Manolo isn't here yet.; **A la sopa le falta sal.** There isn't enough salt in the soup.; **Falta media hora para comer.** There's half an hour to go before lunch.; **¿Te falta mucho?** Will you be long?; **faltar al colegio** to miss school

fama *nf* fame; **llegar a la fama** to become famous; **tener mala fama** to have a bad reputation; **Tiene fama de mujeriego.** He has a reputation for being a womanizer.

familia *nf* family; **una familia numerosa** a large family

familiar *adj* ❶ family ▷ *la vida familiar* family life ❷ familiar ▶ *nmf* relative ▷ *un familiar mío* a relative of mine

famoso *adj* famous

fan (*pl* **fans**) *nmf* fan

fantasía *nf* fantasy ▷ *un mundo de fantasía* a fantasy world ▷ *Son fantasías infantiles.* They're just children's fantasies.; **las joyas de fantasía** costume jewellery

fantasma *nm* ghost

fantástico *adj* fantastic

farmacéutico, -a *nm/f* chemist

farmacia nf chemist's; **una farmacia de guardia** a duty chemist's

faro nm ❶ lighthouse ❷ headlight ❸ lamp; **los faros antiniebla** foglamps

farol nm ❶ streetlamp ❷ lantern

farola nf ❶ streetlamp ❷ lamppost

fascículo nm part

fascinante adj fascinating

fascista adj, nmf fascist

fase nf phase

fastidiar [26] vb ❶ to annoy; **Esa actitud me fastidia mucho.** I find this attitude very annoying. ❷ to pester ▷ ¡Deja ya de fastidiarme! Will you stop pestering me! ❸ to spoil ▷ El accidente nos fastidió las vacaciones. The accident spoilt our holidays.

fastidio nm ¡Qué fastidio! What a nuisance!

fatal adj ❶ awful ▷ Me siento fatal. I feel awful. ▷ La obra estuvo fatal. The play was awful.; **Me parece fatal que le trates así.** I think it's rotten of you to treat him like that.
▶ adv **Lo pasé fatal.** I had an awful time.; **Lo hice fatal.** I made a mess of it.

favor nm favour ▷ ¿Puedes hacerme un favor? Can you do me a favour?; **por favor** please; **¡Haced el favor de callaros!** Will you please be quiet!; **estar a favor de algo** to be in favour of something

favorecer [13] vb to suit (dress, hairstyle)

favorito adj favourite

fax (pl **fax**) nm fax; **mandar algo por fax** to fax something

fe nf faith

febrero nm

> Months start with a small letter in Spanish.

February

fecha nf date ▷ ¿A qué fecha estamos? What's the date today?; **La carta tiene fecha del 21 de enero.** The letter is dated the 21st of January.; **la fecha de caducidad** the use-by date; **la fecha límite** the closing date; **la fecha tope** the deadline; **su fecha de nacimiento** his date of birth

felicidad nf happiness; **¡Felicidades!** (1) Happy birthday! (2) Congratulations!

felicitación (pl **felicitaciones**) nf congratulations

felicitar [26] vb to congratulate; **¡Te felicito!** Congratulations!; **felicitar a alguien por su cumpleaños** to wish somebody a happy birthday

feliz (pl **felices**) adj happy ▷ Se la ve muy feliz. She looks very happy.; **¡Feliz cumpleaños!** Happy birthday!; **¡Feliz Año Nuevo!** Happy New Year!; **¡Felices Navidades!** Happy Christmas!

felpudo nm doormat

femenino adj ❶ feminine (clothes, behaviour, pronoun) ❷ female (body, sex) ❸ women's (team, sport) ▷ el tenis femenino women's

tennis
▶ nm feminine ▷ El femenino de "lobo" es "loba". The feminine of "lobo" is "loba".

fenomenal adj, adv great ▷ Nos hizo un tiempo fenomenal. We had great weather.; **Lo pasé fenomenal.** I had a great time.

feo adj ugly

féretro nm coffin

feria nf ❶ fair; **una feria de muestras** a trade fair ❷ (in Mexico) small change ❸ (in Chile, River Plate) street market

ferretería nf ironmonger's

ferrocarril nm railway

fértil adj fertile

fertilizante nm fertilizer

festejar [26] vb (in Latin America) to celebrate

festival nm festival

festivo adj festive; **un día festivo** a holiday

feto nm foetus

fiable adj reliable

fiambres nmpl cold meats

fianza nf deposit

fiar [22] vb Es un hombre de fiar. He's completely trustworthy.; **fiarse de alguien** to trust somebody

fibra nf fibre

ficha nf ❶ index card ❷ counter; **una ficha de dominó** a domino

fichar [26] vb ❶ to clock in ❷ to clock out ❸ to sign up

fichero nm ❶ filing cabinet ❷ card index ❸ file

fideos nmpl ❶ noodles ❷ (in River Plate) pasta

fiebre nf ❶ temperature ▷ Le bajó la fiebre. His temperature came down.; **tener fiebre** to have a temperature ❷ fever ▷ la fiebre amarilla yellow fever

fiel adj faithful; **ser fiel a alguien** to be faithful to somebody

fiera nf wild animal

fiesta nf ❶ party; **una fiesta de cumpleaños** a birthday party ❷ holiday ▷ El lunes es fiesta. Monday is a holiday.

figura nf figure

figurar [26] vb to appear; **figurarse** to imagine; **¡Ya me lo figuraba!** I thought as much!

fijar [26] vb to fix; **fijarse (1)** to pay attention ▷ Tienes que fijarte más en lo que haces. You must pay more attention to what you're doing. **(2)** to notice ▷ No me fijé en la ropa que llevaba. I didn't notice what she was wearing.; **¡Fíjate en esos dos!** Just look at those two!

fijo adj ❶ fixed ▷ Gano un sueldo fijo. I earn a fixed salary. ❷ permanent; **Está fija en la empresa.** She's got a permanent job in the company.

fila nf ❶ row ▷ Estábamos sentados en segunda fila. We were sitting in the second row. ❷ line ▷ Los niños se pusieron en fila. The children got into line.

filete nm ❶ steak ▷ un filete con patatas fritas steak and chips ❷ fillet ▷ un filete de merluza a hake fillet

a b c d e f g h i j k l m n o p q r s t u v w x y z

Filipinas *nfpl* the Philippines

filmar [26] *vb* to film; **filmar una película** to shoot a film

filo *nm* **Tiene poco filo.** It isn't very sharp.

filoso *adj* (*in Latin America*) sharp

filosofía *nf* philosophy

filtrar [26] *vb* to filter; **filtrarse (1)** to seep **(2)** to filter

filtro *nm* filter

fin *nm* end ▷ *el fin de una era* the end of an era; **a fines de** at the end of ▷ *a fines de abril* at the end of April; **al fin** finally ▷ *Al fin llegaron a un acuerdo.* They finally reached an agreement.; **al fin y al cabo** after all; **En fin, ¡qué le vamos a hacer!** Oh well, what can we do about it!; **por fin** at last ▷ *¡Por fin hemos llegado!* We've got here at last!; **el fin de año** New Year's Eve; **el fin de semana** the weekend

final *adj* final ▷ *el resultado final* the final result
▶ *nm* end ▷ *Al final de la calle hay un semáforo.* At the end of the street there's a set of traffic lights.; **a finales de mayo** at the end of May; **al final** in the end ▷ *Al final tuve que darle la razón.* In the end I had to admit that he was right.; **un final feliz** a happy ending ▷ *la final de la copa* the cup final

finca *nf* country house

fingir [17] *vb* to pretend

finlandés, -esa (*mpl* **finlandeses**) *nm/f* Finn
▶ *nm* Finnish (*language*)

▶ *adj* Finnish

Finlandia *nf* Finland

fino *adj* **①** thin (*paper, layer*)
② fine (*hair, point, sand*)
③ slender (*fingers, neck*)

firma *nf* signature

firmar [26] *vb* to sign

firme *adj* **①** steady ▷ *Mantén la escalera firme.* Can you hold the ladder steady? **②** firm ▷ *Se mostró muy firme con ella.* He was very firm with her.

fiscal *nmf* public prosecutor

fisgar [38] *vb* to snoop

física *nf* physics; see also **físico**

físico, -a *nm/f* physicist
▶ *adj* physical

flaco *adj* thin

flama *nf* (*in Mexico*) flame

flamenco *nm* flamenco

flan *nm* crème caramel

flash (*pl* **flashes**) *nm* flash

flauta *nf* **①** recorder **②** flute

flecha *nf* arrow

flechazo *nm* **Fue un flechazo.** It was love at first sight.

flecos *nmpl* fringe ▷ *los flecos de la cortina* the curtain fringe

flequillo *nm* fringe

flexible *adj* flexible

flojo *adj* **①** loose (*knot, screw*) **②** slack (*cable, rope*) **③** weak (*tea, student, patient*); **Está flojo en matemáticas.** He's weak in maths.; **Todavía tengo las piernas muy flojas.** My legs are still very weak. **④** (*in Latin America*) lazy

flor *nf* flower ▷ *un ramo de flores* a

bunch of flowers
florero nm vase
floristería nf florist's
flotador nm ❶ rubber ring
❷ armband
flotar [26] vb to float
flote adv **a flote** afloat
fluir [11] vb to flow
fluorescente adj fluorescent
fluyendo vb see **fluir**
foca nf seal
foco nm ❶ spotlight ❷ floodlight
❸ (in Latin America) headlight
❹ (in Mexico) light bulb; **el foco de atención** the focus of attention
folio nm sheet of paper
folklore nm folklore
folleto nm ❶ brochure ❷ leaflet
fomentar [26] vb to promote
fonda nf ❶ boarding house
❷ restaurant
fondo nm ❶ bottom ▷ el fondo de la cazuela the bottom of the pan ▷ en el fondo del mar at the bottom of the sea ❸ end ▷ Mi habitación está al fondo del pasillo. My room's at the end of the corridor.; **estudiar una materia a fondo** to study a subject in depth; **un corredor de fondo** a long-distance runner; **en el fondo** deep down; **recaudar fondos** to raise funds
fontanero, -a nm/f plumber
footing nm jogging ▷ Hago footing todas las mañanas. I go jogging every morning.
forestal adj forest ▷ un incendio forestal a forest fire
forma nf ❶ shape; **en forma de**

pera pear-shaped ❷ way ▷ Me miraba de una forma extraña. She was looking at me in a strange way.; **de todas formas** anyway; **estar en forma** to be fit
formación (pl formaciones) nf training; **formación profesional** vocational training
formal adj responsible ▷ un chico muy formal a very responsible boy; **Sé formal y pórtate bien.** Be good and behave yourself.
formar [26] vb ❶ to form (circle, group, government); **Se formó una cola enorme en la puerta.** A huge queue formed at the door.; **estar formado por** to be made up of; **formar parte de algo** to be part of something ❷ to start (club)
formidable adj fantastic
fórmula nf formula
formulario nm form
forrar [26] vb ❶ to line ❷ to cover
forro nm lining ❷ cover
fortuna nf fortune ▷ Vale una fortuna. It's worth a fortune.; **por fortuna** luckily
forzar vb to force; **Estás forzando la vista.** You're straining your eyes.
fosa nf ❶ ditch ❷ grave
fósforo nm match
foto nf photo ▷ Les hice una foto a los niños. I took a photo of the children.
fotocopia nf photocopy
fotocopiadora nf photocopier
fotocopiar [26] vb to photocopy
fotografía nf ❶ photograph

a
b
c
d
e
f
g
h
i
j
k
l
m
n
o
p
q
r
s
t
u
v
w
x
y
z

▷ **una fotografía de mis padres**
a photograph of my parents
② photography
fotógrafo, -a nm/f photographer
fracasar [26] vb to fail
fracaso nm failure
fracción (pl **fracciones**) nf
fraction
fractura nf fracture
frágil adj fragile
fraile nm friar
frambuesa nf raspberry
francés, -esa (mpl **franceses**)
nm/f **un francés** a Frenchman;
una francesa a Frenchwoman; **los
franceses** the French
▶ nm French (language) ▷ **¿Hablas
francés?** Do you speak French?
▶ adj French
Francia nf France
franco adj frank; **para serte
franco ...** to be frank with you ...
franqueo nm postage
frasco nm bottle ▷ **un frasco de
perfume** a bottle of perfume
frase nf sentence; **una frase hecha**
a set phrase
fraude nm fraud
frazada nf (in Latin America)
blanket
frecuencia nf frequency; **Nos
vemos con frecuencia.** We
often see each other.; **¿Con
qué frecuencia tienen estos
síntomas?** How often do they get
these symptoms?
frecuente adj **①** common
② frequent
fregadero nm sink

fregar [35] vb to wash; **fregar los
platos** to wash the dishes; **Yo
estaba en la cocina fregando.** I
was in the kitchen washing the
dishes.; **fregar el suelo** to mop
the floor
fregona nf mop
freír [24] vb to fry
frenar [26] vb to brake
frenazo nm **Tuve que dar un
frenazo.** I had to brake suddenly.
freno nm brake; **Me quedé sin
frenos.** My brakes failed.; **el freno
de mano** the handbrake
frente nf forehead
▶ nm front ▷ **un frente común** a
united front; **frente a** opposite
▷ **Frente al hotel hay un banco.**
There's a bank opposite the hotel.;
Los coches chocaron de frente.
The cars collided head on.; **Viene
un coche de frente.** There's
a car coming straight for us.;
hacer frente a algo to face up to
something
fresa nf strawberry
fresco adj **①** cool (place, drink,
fabric) **②** fresh (fish, vegetables);
hace fresco (1) it's chilly **(2)** it's
cool
▶ nm **Hace fresco.** It's a bit chilly.
friego vb see **fregar**
frigorífico nm fridge
frijol nm (in Latin America) bean
frío vb see **freír**
▶ adj cold ▷ **Tengo las manos frías.**
My hands are cold.; **Estuvo muy
frío conmigo.** He was very cold
towards me.

▶ *nm* Hace frío. It's cold.; **Tengo mucho frío.** I'm very cold.

frito *vb see* **freír**

▶ *adj* fried ▷ **huevos fritos** fried eggs

frontera *nf* border ▷ *Nos pararon en la frontera.* We were stopped at the border.

frontón (*pl* **frontones**) *nm*
❶ pelota court **❷** pelota
pelota is a game in which two players use baskets or wooden rackets to hit a ball against a specially marked wall.

frotar [26] *vb* to rub; **El niño se frotaba las manos para calentarse.** The child was rubbing his hands to get warm.

fruncir *vb* **fruncir el ceño** to frown

frustrado *adj* frustrated

fruta *nf* fruit

frutería *nf* greengrocer's

frutilla *nf* (*in* River Plate) strawberry

fruto *nm* fruit; **los frutos secos** nuts

fue *vb see* **ir, ser**

fuego *nm* fire ▷ *encender el fuego* to light the fire; **prender fuego a algo** to set fire to something; **Puse la cazuela al fuego.** I put the pot on to heat.; **cocinar algo a fuego lento** to cook something on a low heat; **¿Tiene fuego, por favor?** Have you got a light, please?; **fuegos artificiales** fireworks

fuente *nf* **❶** fountain **❷** dish

fuera *vb see* **ir, ser**

▶ *adv* **❶** outside ▷ *Los niños estaban jugando fuera.* The children

were playing outside. ▷ *Por fuera es blanco.* It is white on the outside.; **fuera de mi casa** outside my house; **¡Estamos aquí fuera!** We are out here!; **Hoy vamos a cenar fuera.** We're going out for dinner tonight. **❷** away; **El enfermo está fuera de peligro.** The patient is out of danger.

fuerte *adj* **❶** strong (*material, smell, character*) **❷** loud (*noise*) **❸** hard (*knock*) **❹** bad (*pain, cold*); **"un beso muy fuerte"** "lots of love"

▶ *adv* loudly; **Agárrate fuerte.** Hold on tight.; **No le pegues tan fuerte.** Don't hit him so hard.

fuerza *nf* strength; **tener mucha fuerza** to be very strong; **Sólo lo conseguirás a fuerza de practicar.** You'll only manage it by practising.; **No te lo comas a la fuerza.** Don't force yourself to eat it.; **la fuerza de gravedad** the force of gravity; **la fuerza de voluntad** willpower

fuerzo *vb see* **forzar**

fugarse [26] *vb* to escape

fui *vb see* **ir, ser**

fumador, a *nm/f* smoker; **sección para no fumadores** non-smoking section

fumar [26] *vb* to smoke

función (*pl* **funciones**) *nf*
❶ function **❷** role **❸** show ▷ *Los niños representan una función en el colegio.* The children are putting on a show at school.

funcionar [26] *vb* to work ▷ *El*

ascensor no funciona. The lift isn't working.; **"No funciona."** "Out of order."; **Funciona con pilas.** It runs on batteries.

funcionario, -a nm/f civil servant

funda nf cover; **una funda de almohada** a pillowcase

fundamental adj basic; **Es fundamental que entendamos el problema.** It is essential that we understand the problem.

fundar [**26**] vb to found

fundirse [**59**] vb to melt; **Se han fundido los fusibles.** The fuses have blown.

funeral nm funeral

funeraria nf undertaker's

furgoneta nf van

furia nf fury

furioso adj furious ▷ Mi padre estaba furioso conmigo. My father was furious with me.

fusible nm fuse ▷ Han saltado los fusibles. The fuses have blown.

fusil nm rifle

fútbol nm football ▷ jugar al fútbol to play football

futbolín (pl futbolines) nm table football

futbolista nmf footballer

futuro adj, nm future ▷ su futuro marido your future husband; **la futura madre** the mother-to-be

gabardina nf raincoat

gabinete nm ❶ office; **el gabinete de prensa** press office ❷ cabinet (in government)

gafas nfpl glasses ▷ Tengo que llevar gafas. I have to wear glasses.; **las gafas de sol** sunglasses

gaita nf bagpipes

gajo nm segment

galaxia nf galaxy

galería nf gallery ▷ una galería de arte an art gallery; **una galería comercial** a shopping centre

Gales nm Wales; **el País de Gales** Wales

galés, -esa (mpl galeses) nm/f un galés a Welshman; **una galesa** a Welshwoman; **los galeses** the Welsh

▶ nm Welsh (language)

▸ *adj* Welsh

galgo *nm* greyhound

Galicia *nf* Galicia

gallego, -a *nm/f, adj* Galician
▸ *nm* Galician (*language*)

galleta *nf* biscuit

gallina *nf* hen; **Sólo pensarlo me
pone la carne de gallina.** It gives
me goosepimples just thinking
about it.; **jugar a la gallinita
ciega** to play blind man's buff

gallinero *nm* ❶ henhouse
❷ madhouse

gallo *nm* cock; **en menos que
canta un gallo** in an instant

galopar [26] *vb* to gallop

gama *nf* range ▷ *una amplia gama
de ordenadores* a wide range of
computers

gamba *nf* prawn

gamberro, -a *nm/f* hooligan

gana *nf* **Me visto como me da la
gana.** I dress the way I want to.;
¡No me da la gana! I don't want
to!; **tener ganas de hacer algo**
to feel like doing something;
hacer algo de mala gana to do
something reluctantly

ganadería *nf* cattle

ganado *nm* livestock; **el ganado
vacuno** cattle

ganador, -a *nm/f* winner
▸ *adj* winning ▷ *el equipo ganador*
the winning team

ganancia *nf* profit

ganar [26] *vb* ❶ to earn; **ganarse
la vida** to earn a living ❷ to win
❸ to beat; **Con eso no ganas
nada.** You won't achieve anything

by doing that.; **ganar tiempo**
to save time; **¡Te lo has ganado!**
You deserve it!; **salir ganando**
to do well

ganchillo *nm* crochet ▷ *una aguja
de ganchillo* a crochet hook; **hacer
ganchillo** to crochet

gancho *nm* ❶ hook ▷ *Colgué el
cuadro de un gancho.* I hung the
picture on a hook. ❷ (*in Latin
America*) hanger

gandul, a *nm/f* good-for-nothing
▸ *adj* lazy

ganga *nf* bargain

gángster (*pl* gángsters) *nm*
gangster

ganso, -a *nm/f* goose

garabato *nm* ❶ doodle
❷ scribble

garaje *nm* garage; **una plaza de
garaje** a parking space

garantía *nf* guarantee ▷ *bajo
garantía* under guarantee

garantizar [14] *vb* to guarantee

garbanzo *nm* chick pea

garganta *nf* throat ▷ *Me duele la
garganta.* I've got a sore throat.

gargantilla *nf* necklace

gárgaras *nfpl* **hacer gárgaras**
to gargle

garita *nf* sentry box

garra *nf* ❶ claw ❷ talon

garrafa *nf* carafe
  ● A **garrafa** is also a large bottle
    with handles.
vino de garrafa cheap wine

garúa *nf* (*in Latin America*) drizzle

gas (*pl* gases) *nm* gas; **agua
mineral sin gas** still mineral

water; **una bebida sin gas** a still drink; **agua mineral con gas** sparkling mineral water; **los gases del tubo de escape** exhaust fumes; **El niño tiene muchos gases.** The baby's got a lot of wind.; **Pasó una moto a todo gas.** A motorbike shot past at full speed.

gasa nf gauze

gaseosa nf
● A **gaseosa** is a drink of sweet fizzy water or lemonade.

gasoil nm diesel oil

gasóleo nm diesel oil

gasolina nf petrol ▷ **Tengo que poner gasolina.** I have to fill up with petrol.; **gasolina sin plomo** unleaded petrol

gasolinera nf petrol station

gastado adj worn ▷ **La moqueta está muy gastada.** The carpet is very worn.

gastar [26] vb ① to spend; **Javier gasta mucho en ropa.** Javier spends a lot of money on clothes. ② to use; **Gasté una caja de cerillas.** I used up a whole box of matches.; **¿Qué numero de zapato gastas?** What size shoes do you take?; **Le gastamos una broma a Juan.** We played a joke on Juan.; **Se han gastado las pilas.** The batteries have run out.; **Se me han gastado las suelas.** The soles of my shoes have worn out.

gasto nm expense ▷ **Este año hemos tenido muchos gastos.** We've had a lot of expenses this year.; **gastos**

de envío postage and packing

gatear [26] vb to crawl

gato, -a nm/f cat; **andar a gatas** to crawl ▷ **El niño todavía anda a gatas.** The baby is still crawling.
▶ nm jack

gaviota nf seagull

gay (pl **gays**) adj, nm gay

gazpacho nm
● **Gazpacho** is a refreshing soup made from tomatoes, cucumber, garlic, peppers, oil and vinegar and served cold.

gel nm gel ▷ **gel de baño** bath gel

gelatina nf jelly

gemelo, -a adj, nm/f identical twin ▷ **Son gemelos.** They're identical twins. ▷ **mi hermano gemelo** my identical twin

gemelos nmpl ① binoculars ② cufflinks

Géminis nm Gemini (sign); **Soy géminis.** I'm Gemini.

gen nm gene

generación (pl **generaciones**) nf generation

general adj general; **en general** in general; **por lo general** generally ▷ **Por lo general me acuesto temprano.** I generally go to bed early.
▶ nmf general

generalizar [14] vb to generalize

generalmente adv generally

generar [26] vb to generate

género nm ① gender ② kind ▷ **¿Qué género de música prefieres?** What kind of music do you prefer?; **el género humano** the human race ❸ material

generosidad nf generosity

generoso adj generous

genial adj brilliant ▷ *Antonio tuvo una idea genial.* Antonio had a brilliant idea. ▷ *El concierto estuvo genial.* It was a brilliant concert.

genio nm ❶ temper ▷ *¡Menudo genio tiene tu padre!* Your father has got such a temper!; **tener mal genio** to have a bad temper ❷ genius ▷ *¡Eres un genio!* You're a genius!

genitales nmpl genitals

genoma nm genome

gente nf people ▷ *Había poca gente en la sala.* There were few people in the room. ▷ *La gente está cansada de promesas.* People are tired of promises.; **Son buena gente.** They're good people.; **Óscar es buena gente.** Óscar's a good guy.; **la gente de la calle** the people in the street

geografía nf geography

geología nf geology

geometría nf geometry

geranio nm geranium

gerente nmf manager

germen (pl gérmenes) nm germ

germinar [26] vb to germinate

gesto nm **Hizo un gesto de alivio.** He looked relieved.; **Me hizo un gesto para que me sentara.** He made a sign for me to sit down.

gestoría nf

● A **gestoría** is a private agency
● which deals with government
● departments on behalf of its
● clients.

Gibraltar nm Gibraltar

gibraltareño, -a nm/f, adj Gibraltarian

gigante nmf giant

gigantesco adj gigantic

gimnasia nf gymnastics; **Mi madre hace gimnasia todas las mañanas.** My mother does exercises every morning.

gimnasio nm gym

gimnasta nmf gymnast

ginebra nf gin

ginecólogo, -a nm/f gynaecologist

gira nf tour ▷ *Hicimos una gira por toda Europa.* We did a tour all round Europe.; **estar de gira** to be on tour

girar [26] vb ❶ to turn ▷ *Gira a la derecha.* Turn right. ❷ to rotate; **La Luna gira alrededor de la Tierra.** The moon revolves around the Earth.

girasol nm sunflower

giro nm ❶ turn ▷ *El avión dio un giro de 90 grados.* The plane did a 90-degree turn. ❷ postal order

gitano, -a nm/f gypsy

glándula nf gland

global adj global

globo nm balloon; **un globo terráqueo** a globe

glorieta nf roundabout

glotón, -ona (mpl glotones) adj greedy

gobernar [40] vb to govern

gobierno nm government

gol nm goal; **meter un gol** to score a goal

golf nm golf; **jugar al golf** to play golf

golfo nm gulf

golondrina nf swallow

golosina nf sweet

goloso adj **ser goloso** to have a sweet tooth

golpe nm knock ▷ Oímos un golpe a la puerta. We heard a knock at the door.; **Me he dado un golpe en el codo.** I banged my elbow.; **Se dio un golpe contra la pared.** He hit the wall.; **El coche de atrás nos dio un golpe.** The car behind ran into us.; **de golpe** suddenly ▷ De golpe decidió dejar el trabajo. He suddenly decided to give up work.; **La puerta se cerró de golpe.** The door slammed shut.

golpear [26] vb ❶ to hit ❷ to bang; **Me golpeé la cabeza contra el armario.** I banged my head on the cupboard.

goma nf ❶ eraser; **una goma de borrar** an eraser; **unos guantes de goma** a pair of rubber gloves ❷ elastic band

gordo adj ❶ fat ▷ Estoy muy gordo. I'm very fat. ❷ thick ❸ big ▷ Debe de ser algo bastante gordo. It must be something pretty big.; **Su mujer me cae gorda.** I can't stand his wife.

gorila nm gorilla

gorra nf cap

gorrión (pl gorriones) nm sparrow

gorro nm hat; **un gorro de baño** a swimming cap

gorrón, -ona (mpl gorrones) nm/f scrounger

gota nf drop; **Están cayendo cuatro gotas.** It's spitting.

gotear [26] vb ❶ to drip ❷ to leak

gotera nf leak

gozar [14] vb **gozar de algo** to enjoy something

grabación (pl grabaciones) nf recording

grabadora nf recorder

grabar [26] vb ❶ to tape ❷ to record ❸ to engrave; **Lo tengo grabado en la memoria.** It's etched on my memory.

gracia nf **tener gracia** to be funny; **Yo no le veo la gracia.** I don't see what's so funny.; **Me hizo mucha gracia.** It was so funny.; **No me hace gracia tener que salir con este tiempo.** I'm not too pleased about having to go out in this weather.; **¡Muchas gracias!** Thanks very much!; **dar las gracias a alguien por algo** to thank somebody for something ▷ Vino a darme las gracias por las flores. He came to thank me for the flowers.; **Ni siquiera me dio las gracias.** He didn't even say thank you.; **gracias a** thanks to

gracioso adj funny ▷ ¡Qué gracioso! How funny!

gradas nfpl terraces

grado nm degree ▷ Estaban a diez grados bajo cero. It was ten degrees below zero.

graduado adj **gafas graduadas** prescription glasses

gradual adj gradual

graduar [2] vb to adjust;
  graduarse to graduate (student);
  Tengo que graduarme la vista.
  I've got to have my eyes tested.
gráfica nf graph
gráfico adj graphic
  ▶ nm table
gramática nf grammar
gramo nm gram
gran adj = **grande**
granada nf pomegranate; **una
granada de mano** a hand grenade
granate adj maroon

> When **granate** is used as an
> adjective, it never changes
> its ending.
>
> ▷ **una bufanda granate** a maroon
> scarf

Gran Bretaña nf Great Britain
grande adj

> **grande** is shortened to **gran**
> before singular nouns.

  ❶ big ▷ **Viven en una casa muy
grande.** They live in a very big
house.; **¿Cómo es de grande?**
How big is it?; **La camisa me
está grande.** The shirt is too big
for me. **❷** large ▷ **un gran número
de visitantes** a large number of
visitors ▷ **grandes sumas de dinero**
large sums of money **❸** great
▷ **un gran pintor** a great painter ▷ **Es
una ventaja muy grande.** It's a great
advantage.; **Me llevé una alegría
muy grande.** I felt very happy.;
Lo pasamos en grande. We had
a great time.; **unos grandes
almacenes** a department store
granel adv a granel in bulk

granero nm barn
granizado nm

  ● A **granizado** is a crushed ice
  drink.

granizar [14] vb to hail ▷ **Está
granizando.** It's hailing.
granizo nm hail
granja nf farm
granjero, -a nm/f farmer
grano nm **❶** grain (of sand, rice)
❷ bean (of coffee) **❸** spot ▷ **Me ha
salido un grano en la frente.** I've got
a spot on my forehead.; **ir al grano**
to get to the point
grapa nf staple
grapadora nf stapler
grasa nf **❶** fat ▷ **No te va bien tanta
grasa.** So much fat isn't good for
you. **❷** grease; **La cocina está
llena de grasa.** The cooker's really
greasy.
grasiento adj greasy
graso adj greasy
gratis (pl gratis) adj, adv free ▷ **La
entrada es gratis.** Entry is free.
gratuito adj free
grava nf gravel
grave adj **❶** serious ▷ **Tenemos un
problema grave.** We've got a serious
problem.; **Su padre está grave.**
His father is seriously ill. **❷** low
gravedad nf gravity ▷ **la ley de
la gravedad** the law of gravity;
estar herido de gravedad to be
seriously injured
gravemente adv seriously
Grecia nf Greece
griego, -a nm/f, adj Greek
  ▶ nm Greek (language)

grieta nf crack

grifo nm tap ▷ abrir el grifo to turn on the tap ▷ cerrar el grifo to turn off the tap

grillo nm cricket

gripe nf flu ▷ tener la gripe to have the flu

gris adj, nm grey ▷ una puerta gris a grey door

gritar [26] vb ❶ to shout ❷ to scream

grito nm ❶ shout; ¡No des esos gritos! Stop shouting like that! ❷ scream ▷ Oímos un grito en la calle. We heard a scream outside.; Es el último grito. It's all the rage.

grosella nf redcurrant

grosero adj rude

grosor nm thickness; La pared tiene 30cm de grosor. The wall is 30cm thick.

grúa nf crane

grueso, -a adj ❶ thick ❷ stout

grumo nm lump

gruñir vb to grumble

grupo nm ❶ group; el grupo sanguíneo blood group; Los alumnos trabajan en grupo. The students work in groups. ❷ band ▷ uno de los mejores grupos de rock one of the best rock bands

guacho, -a nm/f (in Andes, River Plate) homeless child

guante nm glove; unos guantes a pair of gloves

guapo adj ❶ handsome ❷ pretty ❸ beautiful; ¡Ven, guapo! Come here, love!

guarda nmf keeper; guarda jurado armed security guard

guardabarros (pl guardabarros) nm mudguard

guardaespaldas (mpl guardaespaldas) nmf bodyguard

guardar [26] vb ❶ to put away ▷ Los niños guardaron los juguetes. The children put away their toys. ❷ to keep ▷ Guarda el recibo. Keep the receipt.; No les guardo rencor. I don't bear them a grudge.; guardar las apariencias to keep up appearances; guardar un fichero to save a file

guardarropa nm cloakroom

guardería nf nursery

guardia nf de guardia on duty ▷ Estoy de guardia. I'm on duty.; la Guardia Civil the Civil Guard ▶ nmf police officer

guarro, -a nm/f ¡Eres un guarro! You're disgusting!

guay adj cool ▷ ¡Qué moto más guay! What a cool bike!

güero adj (in Mexico) blonde

guerra nf war; estar en guerra to be at war

guía nmf guide ▷ El guía vino a recogernos al aeropuerto. The guide came to pick us up at the airport. ▶ nf guidebook; una guía de hoteles a hotel guide; una guía telefónica a telephone directory

guiar [22] vb to guide; Nos guiamos por un mapa que teníamos. We found our way using a map that we had.

guijarro nm pebble

guinda nf cherry

guindilla nf chilli pepper

guiñar [26] vb to wink; **Me guiñó el ojo.** He winked at me.

guion (pl **guiones**) nm ❶ hyphen; **La palabra "self-defence" lleva guión.** The word "self-defence" is hyphenated. ❷ dash ❸ script

guisante nm pea

guisar [26] vb to cook

guitarra nf guitar

gusano nm ❶ worm ❷ maggot ❸ caterpillar

gustar [26] vb **Me gustan las uvas.** I like grapes.; **¿Te gusta viajar?** Do you like travelling?; **Me gustó como hablaba.** I liked the way he spoke.; **Me gustaría conocerla.** I would like to meet her.; **Me gusta su hermana.** I fancy his sister.; **Le gusta más llevar pantalones.** She prefers to wear trousers.

gusto nm taste ▷ *No tiene gusto para vestirse.* He has no taste in clothes. ▷ *Me he decorado la habitación a mi gusto.* I've decorated the room to my taste.; **un comentario de mal gusto** a tasteless remark; **Le noto un gusto a almendras.** It tastes of almonds.; **¡Con mucho gusto!** With pleasure!; **¡Mucho gusto en conocerle!** I'm very pleased to meet you!; **sentirse a gusto** to feel at ease

ha vb see **haber**

haba nm broad bean

Habana nf **La Habana** Havana

haber [25] vb to have ▷ *He comido.* I've eaten. ▷ *Hemos comido.* We've eaten. ▷ *Había comido.* I'd eaten. ▷ *Se ha sentado.* She has sat down.; **De haberlo sabido, habría ido.** If I'd known, I would have gone.; **¡Haberlo dicho antes!** You should have said so before!; **hay (1)** there is ▷ *Hay una iglesia en la esquina.* There's a church on the corner. ▷ *Hubo una guerra.* There was a war. **(2)** there are ▷ *Hay treinta alumnos en mi clase.* There are thirty pupils in my class. ▷ *¿Hay entradas?* Are there any tickets?; **¡No hay de qué!** Don't mention it!; **¿Qué hay?** How are things?; **¿Qué hubo?**

(in Mexico) How are things?; **Hay que ser respetuoso.** You must be respectful.; **¡Habrá que decírselo!** We'll have to tell him!

hábil adj skilful ▷ *Es un jugador muy hábil.* He's a very skilful player.; **Es muy hábil con las manos.** He's very good with his hands.; **Es muy hábil para los negocios.** He's a very able businessman.

habilidad nf skill; **Tiene mucha habilidad para los idiomas.** She's very good at languages.

habitación (pl **habitaciones**) nf ❶ bedroom ❷ room; **una habitación doble** a double room; **una habitación individual** a single room

habitante nmf inhabitant; **los habitantes de la zona** people living in the area

habitar [26] vb to live in; **La casa está todavía sin habitar.** The house is still unoccupied.

hábito nm habit

habitual adj usual; **un cliente habitual** a regular customer

habla nm speech; **Ha perdido el habla.** He's lost the power of speech.; **países de habla inglesa** English-speaking countries; **¿Señor López? - Al habla.** Señor López - Speaking.

hablador, a adj ❶ chatty ❷ gossipy

habladurías nfpl gossip

hablante nmf speaker

hablar [26] vb ❶ to speak ▷ *¿Hablas español?* Do you speak

Spanish?; **¿Quién habla?** Who's calling? ❷ to talk ▷ *Estuvimos hablando toda la tarde.* We were talking all afternoon.; **hablar con alguien (1)** to speak to someone ▷ *¿Has hablado ya con el profesor?* Have you spoken to the teacher yet? **(2)** to talk to someone ▷ *Necesito hablar contigo.* I need to talk to you.; **hablar de algo** to talk about something; **¡Ni hablar!** No way!

habré vb see **haber**

hacer [27] vb ❶ to make ▷ *Tengo que hacer la cama.* I've got to make the bed. ▷ *Voy a hacer una tortilla.* I'm going to make an omelette. ▷ *Están haciendo mucho ruido.* They're making a lot of noise. ❷ to do ▷ *¿Qué haces?* What are you doing? ▷ *Estoy haciendo los deberes.* I'm doing my homework. ▷ *Hago mucho deporte.* I do a lot of sport. ▷ *¿Qué hace tu padre?* What does your father do? ❸ to be ▷ *Hace calor.* It's hot. ▷ *Ojalá haga buen tiempo.* I hope the weather's nice. ▷ *Hizo dos grados bajo cero.* It was two degrees below zero.; **hace ... (1)** ▷ *Terminé hace una hora.* I finished an hour ago. **(2)** for ▷ *Hace un mes que voy.* I've been going for a month.; **¿Hace mucho que esperas?** Have you been waiting long?; **hacer hacer algo** to have something done ▷ *Hicieron pintar la fachada del colegio.* They had the front of the school painted.; **hacer a alguien**

hacer algo to make someone do something; **hacerse** to become; **Ya se está haciendo viejo.** He's getting old.

hacha nm axe

hacia prep **1** towards ▷ **Venía hacia mí.** He was coming towards me.; **hacia adelante** forwards; **hacia atrás** backwards; **hacia dentro** inside; **hacia fuera** outside; **hacia abajo** down; **hacia arriba** up **2** at about ▷ **Volveremos hacia las tres.** We'll be back at about three.

hada nm fairy; **un hada madrina** a fairy godmother; **un cuento de hadas** a fairy tale

hago vb see **hacer**

hala excl come on!

halagar[38] vb to flatter

hallar[26] vb to find; **hallarse** to be

hamaca nf **1** hammock **2** deckchair **3** (in River Plate) swing

hambre nm hunger; **tener hambre** to be hungry ▷ **Tengo mucha hambre.** I'm very hungry.

hamburguesa nf hamburger

hámster (pl hámsters) nm hamster

hardware nm hardware

haré vb see **hacer**

harina nf flour

hartar[26] vb **hartarse** to get fed up; **¡Me estás hartando!** You're getting on my nerves!; **Me harté de pasteles.** I stuffed myself with cakes.

harto adj **1** fed up; **estar harto de**

algo to be fed up with something ▷ **Estábamos hartos de repetirlo.** We were fed up with repeating it. ▷ **¡Me tienes harto!** I'm fed up with you! **2** (in Latin America) a lot of ▷ **Había harta comida.** There was a lot of food.

▶ adv **1** (in Latin America) very ▷ **Es un idioma harto difícil.** It's a very difficult language. **3** a lot ▷ **Tenemos harto que estudiar.** We've got a lot to study.

hasta adv even

▶ prep, conj **1** till ▷ **Está abierto hasta las cuatro.** It's open till four o'clock.; **¿Hasta cuándo?** How long? ▷ **¿Hasta cuándo te quedas?** - Hasta la semana que viene. How long are you staying? - Till next week.; **hasta ahora** up to now; **hasta que** until ▷ **Espera aquí hasta que te llamen.** Wait here until you're called. **2** up to ▷ **Caminamos hasta la puerta.** We walked up to the door. **3** as far as ▷ **Desde aquí se ve hasta el pueblo vecino.** From here you can see as far as the next town.; **¡Hasta luego!** See you!; **¡Hasta el sábado!** See you on Saturday!

hay vb see **haber**

haz vb see **hacer**

he vb see **haber**

▶ adv **He aquí un ejemplo.** Here's an example.; **He aquí unos ejemplos.** Here are some examples.; **he aquí por qué ...** that's why ...

hebilla nf buckle

hebreo nm Hebrew

hechizo nm spell

hecho vb see **hacer**
▶ adj made ▷ ¿De qué está hecho?
What's it made of?; **hecho a mano**
handmade; **hecho a máquina**
machine-made; **Me gusta la
carne bien hecha.** I like my meat
well done.; **un filete poco hecho**
a rare steak; **¡Bien hecho!** Well
done!
▶ nm ❶ fact ▷ el hecho de que ...
the fact that ...; **el hecho es que ...**
the fact is that ...; **de hecho** in fact
❷ event

helada nf frost

heladera nf (in River Plate)
refrigerator

heladería nf ice-cream parlour

helado adj ❶ frozen ▷ El lago
está helado. The lake's frozen
over. ❷ freezing ▷ Este cuarto
está helado. This room's freezing.
▷ ¡Estoy helado! I'm freezing!
▶ nm ice cream ▷ un helado de
chocolate a chocolate ice cream

helar [40] vb to freeze; **Anoche
heló.** There was a frost last night.;
helarse to freeze

helecho nm fern

helicóptero nm helicopter

hembra adj, nf female ▷ un elefante
hembra a female elephant

hemos vb see **haber**

heredar [26] vb to inherit

heredera nf heiress

heredero nm heir

herencia nf inheritance

herida nf ❶ wound ❷ injury

herido adj ❶ wounded ❷ injured

herir [52] vb ❶ to wound ❷ to
injure

hermana nf sister

hermanastra nf stepsister

hermanastro nm stepbrother;
mis hermanastros (1) my
stepbrothers (2) my stepbrothers
and sisters

hermano nm brother; **mis
hermanos** (1) my brothers (2) my
brothers and sisters

hermético adj airtight

hermoso adj beautiful

hermosura nf beauty; **¡Qué
hermosura de paisaje!** What a
beautiful landscape!

héroe nm hero

heroína nf heroine

heroinómano, -a nm/f heroin
addict

herradura nf horseshoe

herramienta nf tool

herrero nm blacksmith

hervir [52] vb to boil; **hervir agua**
to boil water

heterosexual adj, nmf
heterosexual

hice vb see **hacer**

hielo vb see **helar**
▶ nm ice

hierba nf ❶ grass ❷ herb; **una
mala hierba** a weed

hierbabuena nf mint

hierro nm iron ▷ una caja de hierro
an iron box

hígado nm liver

higiene nf hygiene

higiénico adj hygienic; **poco**

higiénico unhygienic

higo nm fig; **un higo chumbo** a prickly pear

higuera nf fig tree

hija nf daughter; **Soy hija única.** I'm an only child.; **Sí, hija mía, tienes razón.** Yes, my dear, you're right.

hijastra nf stepdaughter

hijastro nm stepson; **mis hijastros (1)** my stepsons **(2)** my stepsons and daughters

hijo nm son ▷ **su hijo mayor** his oldest son; **mis hijos (1)** my sons **(2)** my children; **Soy hijo único.** I'm an only child.

hilera nf ❶ row ❷ line ▷ **ponerse en hilera** to get into a line

hilo nm ❶ thread; **hilo de coser** sewing thread ❷ linen ❸ wire ▷ **los hilos del teléfono** the telephone wires

himno nm hymn; **el himno nacional** the national anthem

hincha nmf fan ▷ **los hinchas del fútbol** football fans

hinchado adj swollen

hipermercado nm hypermarket

hipo nm hiccups ▷ **Tengo hipo.** I've got hiccups.

hipócrita adj hypocritical; **¡No seas hipócrita!** Don't be such a hypocrite!
▶ nmf hypocrite

hipódromo nm racecourse

hipopótamo nm hippo

hipoteca nf mortgage

hiriendo vb see herir

hirviendo vb see hervir

hispanohablante nmf Spanish-speaker
▶ adj Spanish-speaking ▷ **los países hispanohablantes** Spanish-speaking countries

historia nf ❶ history ▷ **la historia de España** Spanish history ❷ story ▷ **El libro cuenta la historia de dos niños.** The book tells the story of two children.

historial nm record

histórico adj ❶ historic ▷ **una ciudad histórica** a historic city ❷ historical ▷ **un personaje histórico** a historical character

historieta nf comic strip

hizo vb see hacer

hobby nm hobby; **Lo hago por hobby.** I do it as a hobby.

> The "h" in **hobby** is pronounced like the Spanish "j".

hockey nm hockey; **el hockey sobre hielo** ice hockey

> The "h" in **hockey** is pronounced like the Spanish "j".

hogar nm home ▷ **en todos los hogares españoles** in every Spanish home; **productos para el hogar** household products

hoguera nf bonfire

hoja nf ❶ leaf ❷ sheet ▷ **una hoja de papel** a sheet of paper; **una hoja de cálculo** a spreadsheet; **una hoja de solicitud** an application form ❸ page; **una hoja de afeitar** a razor blade

hojaldre nm puff pastry

hojear [**26**] vb to leaf through

hola excl hello!

Holanda nf Holland

holandés, -esa (pl holandeses)
nm/f **un holandés** a Dutchman;
una holandesa a Dutchwoman;
los holandeses the Dutch
▶ nm Dutch (language)
▶ adj Dutch

holgazán, -ana (mpl holgazanes)
adj lazy

hollín nm soot

hombre nm man; **un hombre
de negocios** a businessman; **la
historia del hombre sobre la
tierra** the history of mankind
on earth

hombro nm shoulder; **encogerse
de hombros** to shrug one's
shoulders

homenaje nm tribute; **en
homenaje a** in honour of

homosexual adj, nmf homosexual

hondo adj deep ▷ **un pozo muy
hondo** a very deep well ▷ **Se ha
tirado por la parte honda de la
piscina.** He dived into the deep end
of the pool.

Honduras nf Honduras

hondureño, -a nm/f, adj
Honduran

honestidad nf ❶ honesty
❷ decency

honesto adj honest

hongo nm ❶ fungus ❷ (in Latin
America) mushroom

honor nm honour

honradez nf honesty

honrado adj honest

hora nf ❶ hour ▷ **El viaje dura una
hora.** The journey lasts an hour.
❷ time ▷ **¿Qué hora es?** What's
the time? ▷ **¿Tienes hora?** Have you
got the time? **¿A qué hora llega?**
What time is he arriving?; **llegar a
la hora** to arrive on time; **la hora
de cenar** dinner time; **a última
hora** at the last minute ❸ period;
**Después de inglés tenemos una
hora libre.** After English we have
a free period. ❹ appointment
▷ **Tengo hora para el dentista.**
I've got an appointment at the
dentist's; **horas extras** overtime;
en mis horas libres in my spare
time

horario nm timetable; **el horario
de trenes** the train timetable;
horario de visitas visiting hours

horchata nf
● Horchata is a milky looking
● drink made from tiger nuts and
● served cold.

horizontal adj horizontal

horizonte nm horizon

hormiga nf ant

hormigón nm concrete

hormigueo nm pins and needles

horno nm oven; **pescado al horno**
baked fish; **pollo al horno** roast
chicken; **un horno microondas** a
microwave oven

horóscopo nm horoscope

horquilla nf hairgrip

horrible adj awful ▷ **El tiempo ha
estado horrible.** The weather has
been awful.

horror nm horror; **tener horror a**

algo to be terrified of something
▷ *Les tengo horror a las arañas.* I'm terrified of spiders.; **¡Qué horror!** How awful!

horroroso *adj* ❶ **horrific** ▷ *un accidente horroroso* a horrific accident ❷ **hideous**

hortaliza *nf* **vegetable**

hortera *adj naff* ▷ *Tiene un gusto muy hortera.* He's got really naff taste.

hospedarse [26] *vb* **to stay**

hospital *nm* **hospital**

hospitalidad *nf* **hospitality**

hostal *nm* **small hotel**

hostia *nf* **host**

hotel *nm* **hotel**

hoy *adv* **today; desde hoy en adelante** from now on; **hoy en día** nowadays; **hoy por la mañana** this morning

hoyo *nm* **hole**

hube *vb see* **haber**

hucha *nf* **moneybox**

hueco *adj* **hollow**
▶ *nm* ❶ **space** ▷ *Deja un hueco para la respuesta.* Leave a space for the answer.; **Hazme un hueco para sentarme.** Make a bit of room so that I can sit down. ❷ **gap** ▷ *Entró por un hueco que había en la valla.* He got in through a gap in the fence. ❸ **free period** ▷ *Los lunes tengo un hueco entre clase y clase.* I have a free period between classes on Mondays.

huelga *nf* **strike; estar en huelga** to be on strike; **declararse en huelga** to go on strike

huelguista *nmf* **striker**

huella *nf* **footprint; huellas tracks; Desapareció sin dejar huella.** He disappeared without trace.; **huella digital** fingerprint

huelo *vb see* **oler**

huérfano, -a *nm/f* **orphan**
▶ *adj* **un niño huérfano** an orphan; **ser huérfano** to be an orphan; **Es huérfano de padre.** He's lost his father.; **quedarse huérfano** to be orphaned

huerta *nf* ❶ **vegetable garden** ❷ **orchard**

huerto *nm* ❶ **kitchen garden** ❷ **orchard**

hueso *nm* ❶ **bone** ❷ **stone** (in plum, peach); **aceitunas sin hueso** pitted olives

huésped *nmf* **guest**

huevo *nm* **egg; un huevo duro** a hard-boiled egg; **un huevo escalfado** a poached egg; **un huevo frito** a fried egg; **huevos revueltos** scrambled eggs; **un huevo pasado por agua** a soft-boiled egg

huida *nf* **escape**

huir [11] *vb* **to escape** ▷ *Huyó de la cárcel.* He escaped from prison.; **Huyeron del país.** They fled the country.; **salir huyendo** to run away

hule *nm* ❶ **oilcloth** ❷ (in Mexico) **rubber; una liga de hule** a rubber band

humanidad *nf* **humanity**

humano *adj* ❶ **human** ▷ *el cuerpo humano* the human body; **los**

seres humanos human beings ❷ humane
▶ *nm* human being

humareda *nf* cloud of smoke

humedad *nf* ❶ dampness ❷ humidity

húmedo *adj* ❶ damp ▷ *La ropa está todavía húmeda.* The clothes are still damp. ❷ humid ▷ *El día estaba muy húmedo.* It was a very humid day.

humilde *adj* humble ▷ *Era de familia humilde.* She was from a humble background.

humo *nm* smoke

humor *nm* mood; **estar de buen humor** to be in a good mood; **estar de mal humor** to be in a bad mood; **Tiene un gran sentido del humor.** He has got a good sense of humour.; **humor negro** black humour

hundirse [59] *vb* ❶ to sink ❷ to collapse

húngaro, -a *nm/f, adj* Hungarian
▶ *nm* Hungarian (language)

Hungría *nf* Hungary

huracán *nm* hurricane

hurgar [38] *vb* to rummage; **hurgarse la nariz** to pick one's nose

huyendo *vb see* **huir**

I.B. *abbr* = **Instituto de Bachillerato**
   In Spain the **Institutos de Bachillerato** are state secondary schools for 12- to 18-year-olds.

iba *vb see* **ir**

iberoamericano, -a *nm/f, adj* Latin American

iceberg (*pl* **icebergs**) *nm* iceberg

icono *nm* icon

ida *nf* single ▷ *¿Cuánto cuesta la ida?* How much does a single cost?; **El viaje de ida duró dos horas.** The journey there took two hours.; **un billete de ida y vuelta** a return ticket; **un boleto de ida y vuelta** (*in Latin America*) a return ticket; **a la ida** on the way there

idea *nf* idea; **¡Qué buena idea!**

What a good idea!; **No tengo ni idea.** I haven't the faintest idea.; **cambiar de idea** to change one's mind

ideal adj, nm ideal

idear [26] vb to devise

idéntico adj identical ▷ **Tiene una falda idéntica a la mía.** She has an identical skirt to mine.; **Es idéntica a su padre.** She's the spitting image of her father.

identificar [49] vb to identify; **identificarse con alguien** to identify with somebody

idioma nm language

idiota adj stupid ▷ **¡No seas tan idiota!** Don't be so stupid!
▸ nmf idiot

idiotez (pl idioteces) nf **Deja de decir idioteces.** Stop talking nonsense.

ídolo nm idol

iglesia nf church; **la Iglesia católica** the Catholic Church

ignorante adj ignorant

ignorar [26] vb ❶ not to know ▷ **Ignoramos su paradero.** We don't know his whereabouts. ❷ to ignore ▷ **Es mejor ignorarla.** It's best to ignore her.

igual adj ❶ equal; **X es igual a Y.** X is equal to Y. ❷ the same ▷ **Todas las casas son iguales.** All the houses are the same.; **Es igual a su madre.** (1) She looks just like her mother. (2) She's just like her mother.; **Tengo una falda igual que la tuya.** I've got a skirt just like yours.; **ir iguales** to be even;

Van quince iguales. It's fifteen all.; **Es igual hoy que mañana.** Today or tomorrow, it doesn't matter.; **Me da igual.** I don't mind.
▸ adv ❶ the same ▷ **Se visten igual.** They dress the same. ❷ maybe ▷ **Igual no lo saben todavía.** Maybe they don't know yet. ❸ anyway ▷ **No hizo nada pero la castigaron igual.** She didn't do anything but they punished her anyway.

igualdad nf equality ▷ **la igualdad racial** racial equality; **la igualdad de oportunidades** equal opportunities

igualmente adv the same to you ▷ **¡Feliz Navidad! --Gracias, igualmente.** Happy Christmas! --Thanks, the same to you.

ilegal adj illegal

ilegible adj illegible

ileso adj unhurt; **Todos resultaron ilesos.** No one was hurt.

iluminación nf lighting; **Se cortó la iluminación del estadio.** The stadium floodlighting went out.

iluminar [26] vb to light ▷ **Unas velas iluminaban la habitación.** The room was lit by candles.; **El flash le iluminó el rostro.** The flash lit up his face.; **Esta lámpara ilumina muy poco.** This lamp gives out very little light.; **Se le iluminó la cara.** His face lit up.

ilusión (pl ilusiones) nf ❶ hope ▷ **No te hagas muchas ilusiones.** Don't build your hopes up. ❸ illusion ▷ **una ilusión óptica** an optical illusion; **Le hace mucha**

ilusión que vengas. He's really looking forward to you coming.; **Tu regalo me hizo mucha ilusión.** I was delighted to get your present.; **¡Qué ilusión!** How wonderful!; **Mi mayor ilusión es llegar a ser médico.** My dream is to become a doctor.

ilusionado adj excited

ilusionar [26] vb **Me ilusiona mucho la idea.** I'm really excited about the idea.; **ilusionarse** to build up one's hopes; **ilusionarse con algo** to get really excited about something

ilustración (pl ilustraciones) nf illustration

imagen (pl imágenes) nf ❶ image; **ser la viva imagen de alguien** to be the spitting image of somebody ❷ picture

imaginación (pl imaginaciones) nf imagination; **Esas son imaginaciones tuyas.** You're imagining things.; **Ni se me pasó por la imaginación.** It never even occurred to me.

imaginarse [26] vb to imagine; **Me imagino que sí.** I imagine so.; **Me imagino que no.** I wouldn't think so.; **¿Se enfadó mucho? - ¡Imagínate!** Was he very angry? - What do you think!

imán (pl imanes) nm magnet

imbécil adj stupid
▶ nmf idiot

imitación (pl imitaciones) nf ❶ impression ▷ Es muy buena haciendo imitaciones. She's very good at doing impressions. ❷ imitation ▷ Es imitación cuero. It's imitation leather.

imitar [26] vb to copy; **imitar a alguien** to do an impression of somebody; **imitar un acento** to imitate an accent

impaciente adj impatient ▷ Se estaba empezando a poner impaciente. He was beginning to get impatient. ▷ Estarás impaciente por saberlo. You'll be impatient to know.

impar (f impar) adj odd ▷ un número impar an odd number
▶ nm odd number

imparcial adj impartial

impecable adj impeccable

impedir [39] vb ❶ to prevent ▷ impedir que alguien haga algo to prevent somebody from doing something ❷ to stop ❸ to block ▷ Un camión nos impedía el paso. A lorry was blocking our way.

imperdible nm safety pin

imperio nm empire

impermeable adj waterproof
▶ nm raincoat

impersonal adj impersonal

impertinente adj impertinent

impidiendo vb see **impedir**

impido vb see **impedir**

imponer [42] vb to impose; **imponerse** (1) to triumph (2) to assert oneself

importación (pl importaciones) nf import ▷ una empresa de importación/exportación an import-export business; **los artículos de**

importación imported goods

importancia nf importance; **dar importancia a algo** to attach importance to something; **La educación tiene mucha importancia.** Education is very important.; **¡Me he olvidado tu libro! - No tiene importancia.** I've forgotten your book! - It doesn't matter.

importante adj important; **lo importante** the important thing ▷ *Lo importante es que vengas.* The important thing is that you come.

importar[26] vb ❶ to import (goods) ❷ to matter; **no importa** (1) it doesn't matter (2) never mind; **No me importa levantarme temprano.** I don't mind getting up early. ▷ *¿Te importaría prestarme este libro?* Would you mind lending me this book? ▷ *¿Le importa que fume?* Do you mind if I smoke?; **¿Y a ti qué te importa?** What's it to you?; **Me importan mucho mis estudios.** My studies are very important to me.; **Me importa un bledo.** I couldn't care less.

imposible adj impossible ▷ *Es imposible predecir quién ganará.* It's impossible to predict who will win.; **Es imposible que lo sepan.** They can't possibly know.

impostor, a nm/f impostor

imprescindible adj essential

impresión (pl **impresiones**) nf impression ▷ *Le causó muy buena impresión a mis padres.* He made a very good impression on my parents.; **Tengo la impresión de que no va a venir.** I have a feeling he won't come.

impresionante adj ❶ impressive ❷ amazing

impresionar[26] vb ❶ to shock ▷ *Me impresionó mucho su palidez.* I was really shocked at how pale he was. ❷ to impress; **Impresiona lo rápido que es.** His speed is impressive.; **impresionarse** to be impressed

impreso nm form ▷ *un impreso de solicitud* an application form

impresora nf printer ▷ *una impresora láser* a laser printer

imprevisible adj ❶ unforeseeable ❷ unpredictable

imprevisto adj unexpected
▶ nm **si no surge algún imprevisto** if nothing unexpected comes up

imprimir[59] vb to print

improvisar[26] vb to improvise

imprudencia nf **Saltar la tapia fue una imprudencia.** It was unwise to jump over the wall.; **El accidente fue debido a una imprudencia del conductor.** The accident was caused by reckless driving.

imprudente adj unwise; **conductores imprudentes** reckless drivers

impuesto adj see **imponer**
▶ nm tax; **el impuesto sobre la renta** income tax; **libre de impuestos** duty-free

impulsar [26] vb ❶ to drive ❷ to boost

impulso nm impulse ▷ Actué por impulso. I acted on impulse.; **Mi primer impulso fue salir corriendo.** My first instinct was to run away.

inaceptable adj unacceptable

inadecuado adj unsuitable

inadvertido adj **pasar inadvertido** to go unnoticed

inapropiado adj unsuitable

inauguración (pl **inauguraciones**) nf opening; **la ceremonia de inauguración** the opening ceremony

inaugurar [26] vb to open

incapacidad nf inability; **la incapacidad física** physical disability; **la incapacidad mental** mental disability

incapaz (pl **incapaces**) adj incapable ▷ Es incapaz de estarse callado. He is incapable of keeping quiet.; **Hoy soy incapaz de concentrarme.** I can't concentrate today.

incendiarse [26] vb to catch fire

incendio nm fire

incentivo nm incentive

incidente nm incident

incierto adj uncertain

inclinar [26] vb to tilt ▷ Inclina un poco más la sombrilla. Can you tilt the umbrella a bit more?; **inclinar la cabeza** to nod; **inclinarse (1)** to bend down **(2)** to lean ▷ inclinarse sobre algo to lean over something ▷ inclinarse hacia

delante to lean forward **(3)** to bow; **Me inclino a pensar que ...** I'm inclined to think that ...

incluido adj included ▷ El servicio no está incluido en el precio. Service is not included.

incluir [11] vb to include

inclusive adv inclusive ▷ Está abierto de lunes a sábado inclusive. It's open from Monday to Saturday inclusive.

incluso adv even

incluyendo vb see **incluir**

incómodo adj uncomfortable

incompetente adj incompetent

incompleto adj incomplete

incomprensible adj incomprehensible

inconsciente adj ❶ unconscious ❷ thoughtless

inconveniente adj inconvenient ▶ nm ❶ problem ▷ Ha surgido un inconveniente. A problem has come up. ❷ drawback ▷ El plan tiene sus inconvenientes. The plan has its drawbacks.; **No tengo ningún inconveniente.** I have no objection.; **No tengo inconveniente en preguntárselo.** I don't mind asking him.; **¿Tienes algún inconveniente en que le dé tu teléfono?** Do you mind if I give him your telephone number?

incorrecto adj incorrect

increíble adj incredible

inculto adj ignorant

incurable adj incurable

indeciso adj indecisive; **Estoy indecisa, no sé cuál comprar.** I can't make up my mind, I don't know which to have.

indefenso adj defenceless

indemnización (pl **indemnizaciones**) nf compensation ▷ Recibieron mil dólares de indemnización. They received a thousand dollars in compensation.

indemnizar [14] vb to compensate; **Nos tienen que indemnizar.** They've got to pay us compensation.

independencia nf independence

independiente adj independent

independientemente adv independently

independizarse [14] vb to become independent

India nf La India India

indicación (pl **indicaciones**) nf sign; **Nos hizo una indicación para que siguiéramos.** He signalled to us to go on.; **indicaciones** (1) instructions (2) directions ▷ Me dio indicaciones de cómo llegar. He gave me directions for getting there.

indicar [49] vb ① to indicate ② to tell ▷ Un guardia me indicó el camino. A policeman told me the way. ③ to advise ▷ El médico me indicó que no fumara. The doctor advised me not to smoke.

índice nm ① index ② index finger

indiferencia nf indifference

indiferente adj indifferent; **Es indiferente que viva en Glasgow o Edimburgo.** It makes

no difference whether he lives in Glasgow or Edinburgh.; **Me es indiferente hacerlo hoy o mañana.** I don't mind whether I do it today or tomorrow.

indígena adj indigenous
▶ nmf native

indigestión nf indigestion

indignado adj angry

indignar [26] vb to infuriate; **indignarse por algo** to get angry about something; **indignarse con alguien** to be furious with somebody

indio, -a nm/f, adj Indian

indirecta nf hint ▷ lanzar una indirecta to drop a hint

indirecto adj indirect

indispensable adj essential

individual adj ① individual ② single (bed, room)
▶ nm singles ▷ la final del individual femenino the ladies' singles final

individuo nm individual

industria nf industry ▷ la industria petrolera the oil industry

industrial adj industrial

ineficiente adj inefficient

inesperado adj unexpected

inestable adj ① unsteady ② changeable

inevitable adj inevitable

inexacto adj inaccurate

inexperto adj inexperienced

inexplicable adj inexplicable

infantil adj ① children's (clothing, playground, programme) ② childish ▷ ¡No seas tan infantil! Don't be so childish!

infarto nm heart attack ▷ Le dio un infarto. He had a heart attack.

infección (pl infecciones) nf infection

infeliz (pl infelices) adj unhappy

inferior (f inferior) adj ❶ lower ❷ inferior; **un número inferior a nueve** a number below nine

infierno nm hell

infinitivo nm infinitive

inflable adj inflatable

inflación nf inflation

inflamable adj inflammable

inflar [26] vb ❶ to blow up ❷ to inflate

influencia nf influence

influenciar [26] vb to influence

influir [11] vb to influence; **influir en** to influence; **Mis padres influyeron mucho en mí.** My parents had a great influence on me.

información (pl informaciones) nf ❶ information; **una información muy importante** a very important piece of information; **Pregunta en información de dónde sale el tren.** Ask at the information desk which platform the train leaves from. ❷ news ▷ Este canal tiene mucha información deportiva. There's a lot of sports news on this channel. ❸ directory enquiries ▷ Llama a información y pide que te den el número. Call directory enquiries and ask them for the number.

informal adj ❶ informal; **Prefiero la ropa informal.** I prefer casual clothes. ❷ unreliable (person)

informar [26] vb to inform; **Les han informado mal.** You've been misinformed.; **¿Me podría informar sobre los cursos de inglés?** Could you give me some information about English courses?; **informarse de algo** to find out about something

informática nf ❶ computing ❷ computer science ❸ ICT; see also **informático**

informático, -a nm/f computer expert
▸ adj computer ▷ un programa informático a computer program; see also **informática**

informe nm report; **según mis informes** according to my information; **pedir informes** to ask for references

infusión (pl infusiones) nf herbal tea; **una infusión de manzanilla** a camomile tea

ingeniar [26] vb to devise; **ingeniárselas** to manage

ingeniería nf engineering

ingeniero, -a nm/f engineer

ingenio nm ❶ ingenuity ❷ wit; **un ingenio azucarero** (in Latin America) a sugar refinery

ingenioso adj ❶ ingenious ❷ witty

ingenuo adj naïve

Inglaterra nf England

inglés, -esa nm/f un inglés an Englishman; **una inglesa** an Englishwoman; **los ingleses** the

English
▶ *nm* English (language) ▷ *El inglés le resulta difícil.* He finds English difficult.
▶ *adj* English ▷ *la comida inglesa* English food

ingrediente *nm* ingredient

ingresar [26] *vb* to pay in ▷ *ingresar un cheque en una cuenta* to pay a cheque into an account; **ingresar en el hospital** to go into hospital; **Han vuelto a ingresar a mi abuela.** They've taken my grandmother into hospital again.; **ingresar en un club** to join a club

ingreso *nm* admission; **un examen de ingreso** an entrance exam; **los ingresos** income ▷ *Tiene unos ingresos muy bajos.* He has a very low income.

inicial *nf* initial

iniciativa *nf* initiative ▷ *Lo hizo por iniciativa propia.* He did it on his own initiative.

injusticia *nf* injustice

injusto *adj* unfair

inmaduro *adj* ❶ immature ❷ unripe

inmediatamente *adv* immediately

inmediato *adj* immediate; **inmediato a algo** next to something ▷ *en el edificio inmediato a la embajada* in the building next to the embassy; **de inmediato** immediately

inmenso *adj* immense; **la inmensa mayoría** the vast majority

inmigración *nf* immigration

inmigrante *nmf* immigrant

inmoral *adj* immoral

inmortal *adj* immortal

inmóvil *adj* motionless ▷ *Se quedó inmóvil.* He remained motionless.

innecesario *adj* unnecessary

inocente *adj* innocent ▷ *Es inocente.* He's innocent.; **El jurado la declaró inocente.** The jury found her not guilty.

inofensivo *adj* harmless

inolvidable *adj* unforgettable

inquietante *adj* worrying

inquietar [26] *vb* to worry; **inquietarse** to worry ▷ *¡No te inquietes!* Don't worry!

inquieto, -a *adj* ❶ worried ❷ restless

inquilino, -a *nm/f* ❶ tenant ❷ lodger

insatisfecho *adj* dissatisfied

inscribirse *vb* to enrol

inscripción (*pl* **inscripciones**) *nf* ❶ enrolment ❷ inscription

inscrito *adj* see **inscribirse**

insecto *nm* insect

inseguridad *nf* insecurity ▷ *la inseguridad en el trabajo* job insecurity; **la inseguridad ciudadana** the lack of safety on the streets

inseguro *adj* ❶ insecure ❷ unsafe

insensato *adj* foolish

insensible *adj* insensitive

insignia *nf* badge

insignificante *adj* insignificant

insinuar [2] *vb* to hint at;

¿Insinúas que miento? Are you insinuating that I'm lying?

insípido adj insipid

insistir [59] vb to insist

insolación nf sunstroke

insolente adj insolent

insoportable adj unbearable

inspector, a nm/f inspector

instalaciones nfpl facilities

instalar [26] vb ❶ to install ❷ to set up; **instalarse** to settle ▷ Decidieron instalarse en el centro. They decided to settle in the town centre.

instantáneo adj instantaneous; **el café instantáneo** instant coffee

instante nm moment ▷ por un instante for a moment; **A cada instante suena el teléfono.** The phone rings all the time.; **al instante** right away

instinto nm instinct

institución (pl instituciones) nf institution

instituto nm institute; **un instituto de enseñanza secundaria** a secondary school

instrucciones nfpl instructions

instructivo adj educational

instructor, a nm/f instructor ▷ un instructor de esquí a ski instructor ▷ un instructor de autoescuela a driving instructor

instrumento nm instrument

insuficiente adj insufficient
▸ nm fail; **Sacó un insuficiente en francés.** He failed French.

insulina nf insulin

insultar [26] vb to insult

insulto nm insult

intelectual adj, nmf intellectual

inteligencia nf intelligence

inteligente adj intelligent

intención (pl intenciones) nf intention ▷ No tengo la más mínima intención de hacerlo. I haven't got the slightest intention of doing it.; **tener intención de hacer algo** to intend to do something

intensivo adj intensive

intenso adj intense

intentar [26] vb to try

intento nm attempt ▷ Aprobó al primer intento. He passed at the first attempt.

intercambiar [26] vb ❶ to exchange ❷ to swap

intercambio nm exchange

interés (pl intereses) nm interest ▷ Tienes que poner más interés en tus estudios. You must take more of an interest in your studies.; **tener interés en hacer algo** to be interested in doing something

interesante adj interesting

interesar [26] vb to interest ▷ Eso es algo que siempre me ha interesado. That's something that has always interested me.; **Me interesa mucho la física.** I'm very interested in physics.; **interesarse por algo** to ask about something

interfono ❶ intercom ❷ entry phone

interior nm inside; **El tren se detuvo en el interior del túnel.** The train stopped inside the tunnel.

▶ adj ❶ inside (lane, pocket)
❷ inner (world) ❸ interior (space)
interiorista nmf interior designer
intermedio adj ❶ intermediate
❷ medium
▶ nm interval
interminable adj endless
intermitente adj ❶ intermittent
❷ flashing (light)
▶ nm indicator
internacional adj international
internado nm boarding school
internauta nmf internet user
Internet nm or nf the internet ▷ en Internet on the internet
interno, -a nm/f boarder
▶ adj **estar interno en un colegio** to be a boarder at a school
interpretación (pl interpretaciones) nf interpretation; **Todo fue producto de una mala interpretación.** It was all the result of a misunderstanding.
interpretar [26] vb ❶ to interpret; **No me interpretes mal.** Don't misunderstand me. ❷ to play ▷ Interpreta el papel de Victoria. She plays the part of Victoria. ❸ to perform (piece)
intérprete nmf interpreter
interrogar [38] vb to question
interrumpir [59] vb ❶ to interrupt (person) ❷ to cut short (holidays) ❸ to block ▷ Estás interrumpiendo el paso. You're blocking the way.
interrupción (pl interrupciones) nf interruption

interruptor nm switch
interurbano adj long-distance
intervalo nm interval
intervenir [57] vb ❶ to take part ▷ No intervino en el debate. He did not take part in the debate. ❷ to intervene
intimidad nf ❶ private life ❷ privacy; **La boda se celebró en la intimidad.** It was a private wedding.
intimidar [26] vb to intimidate
íntimo adj intimate; **Es un amigo íntimo.** He's a close friend.
introducción (pl introducciones) nf introduction
introducir [10] vb ❶ to insert ▷ Introdujo la moneda en la ranura. He inserted the coin in the slot. ❷ to bring in ▷ Esperan introducir un nuevo sistema de trabajo. They're hoping to bring in new working methods.; **Han introducido cambios en el horario.** They've made changes to the timetable.
introvertido adj introverted
intruso, -a nm/f intruder
intuición nf intuition
inundación (pl inundaciones) nf flood
inundar [26] vb to flood; **inundarse** to be flooded
inútil adj useless; **Es inútil tratar de hacerle entender.** It's no use trying to make him understand.; **Es inútil que esperes.** There's no point in your waiting.
▶ nmf **¡Es un inútil!** He's useless!
invadir [59] vb to invade

a
b
c
d
e
f
g
i
j
k
l
m
n
o
p
q
r
s
t
u
v
w
x
y
z

inválido, -a nm/f **un inválido** a disabled man; **una inválida** a disabled woman; **los inválidos** the disabled
▶ adj disabled

invasión (pl **invasiones**) nf invasion

inventar [26] vb ❶ to invent ❷ to make up (story)

invento nm invention

inventor, a nm/f inventor

invernadero nm greenhouse; **el efecto invernadero** the greenhouse effect

invernar [40] vb to hibernate

inverosímil adj unlikely

inversión (pl **inversiones**) nf investment

inverso adj reverse ▷ **en orden inverso** in reverse order; **a la inversa** the other way round

invertir [52] vb ❶ to invest (money) ❷ to spend (time) ❸ to reverse (order)

investigación (pl **investigaciones**) nf ❶ research ▷ **Está haciendo una investigación sobre el envejecimiento.** He's doing some research into ageing. ❷ investigation (by police) ❸ inquiry ▷ **Se hará una investigación pública.** There will be a public inquiry.

invierno nm winter ▷ **en invierno** in winter

invisible adj invisible

invitación (pl **invitaciones**) nf invitation

invitado, -a nm/f guest ▷ **Es el**

invitado de honor. He's the guest of honour.

invitar [26] vb to invite ▷ **Me invitó a una fiesta.** He invited me to a party.; **Te invito a un café.** I'll buy you a coffee.; **Esta vez invito yo.** This time it's on me.

inyección (pl **inyecciones**) nf injection ▷ **ponerle una inyección a alguien** to give someone an injection

inyectar [26] vb **Le tuvieron que inyectar insulina.** They had to give him an insulin injection.; **inyectarse algo** to inject oneself with something

ir [28] vb ❶ to go ▷ **Anoche fuimos al cine.** We went to the cinema last night. ▷ **¿A qué colegio vas?** What school do you go to?; **ir de vacaciones** to go on holiday; **ir a por** to go and get ▷ **Voy a por el paraguas.** I'll go and get the umbrella. ▷ **Ha ido a por el médico.** She has gone to get the doctor.; **Voy a hacerlo mañana.** I'm going to do it tomorrow.; **vamos** let's go ▷ **Vamos a casa.** Let's go home.; **¡Vamos!** Come on!; **¡Vamos a ver!** Let's see! ❷ to be ▷ **Iba con su madre.** He was with his mother. ▷ **como iba diciendo** as I was saying ❸ to come ▷ **¡Ahora voy!** I'm just coming!; **¿Puedo ir contigo?** Can I come with you?; **ir a pie** to walk; **ir en avión** to fly; **¿Cómo te va?** How are things?; **¿Cómo te va en los estudios?** How are you getting on with your studies?;

¡Que te vaya bien! Take care of yourself!; ¡Qué va! You must be joking!; ¡Vaya! ¡Qué haces tú por aquí? Well, what a surprise! What are you doing here?; ¡Vaya coche! What a car!; **irse (1)** to leave ▷ *Acaba de irse.* He has just left. **(2)** to go out ▷ *Se ha ido la luz.* The lights have gone out.; ¡Vámonos! Let's go!; ¡Vete! Go away!; **Vete a hacer los deberes.** Go and do your homework.

Irak nm Iraq

Irán nm Iran

iraní (pl **iraníes**) nmf, adj Iranian

iraquí (pl **iraquíes**) nmf, adj Iraqi

Irlanda nf Ireland ▷ *Irlanda del Norte* Northern Ireland

irlandés, -esa (mpl **irlandeses**) nm/f **un irlandés** an Irishman; **una irlandesa** an Irishwoman; **los irlandeses** the Irish
  ▶ nm Irish (language)
  ▶ adj Irish ▷ *un café irlandés* an Irish coffee

irónico adj ironic

irracional adj irrational

irrelevante adj irrelevant

irresistible adj irresistible

irresponsable adj irresponsible

irritante adj irritating

irritar [26] vb to irritate

irrompible adj unbreakable

isla nf island

Islam nm Islam

islámico adj Islamic

islandés, -esa (mpl **islandeses**) nm/f Icelander
  ▶ adj Icelandic

Islandia nf Iceland

isleño nm islander

Israel nm Israel

israelí (pl **israelíes**) nmf, adj Israeli

Italia nf Italy

italiano, -a nm/f, adj Italian
  ▶ nm Italian (language) ▷ *¿Hablas italiano?* Do you speak Italian?

itinerario nm ❶ route
  ❷ itinerary ▷ *Me gustaría incluir Roma en el itinerario.* I'd like to include Rome on our itinerary.

IVA abbr ❶ (= Impuesto sobre el Valor Añadido) VAT (= Value Added Tax)
  ❷ (in Latin America) (= Impuesto sobre el Valor Agregado) VAT (= Value Added Tax)

izar [14] vb to hoist

izquierda nf ❶ left hand; **Escribo con la izquierda.** I write with my left hand. ❷ left ▷ *doblar a la izquierda* to turn left; **a la izquierda** on the left ▷ *la segunda calle a la izquierda* the second turning on the left; **conducir por la izquierda** to drive on the left; **ser de izquierdas** to be left-wing ▷ *un partido de izquierdas* a left-wing party

izquierdo adj left ▷ *Levanta la mano izquierda.* Raise your left hand.; **a mano izquierda** on the left-hand side

j

jabón (pl **jabones**) nm soap

jaiba nf (in Latin America) crab

jalar [26] vb ❶ (in Latin America) to pull ▷ No le jales el pelo. Don't pull his hair. ❷ to take ▷ Jaló un folleto de la mesa. He took a leaflet from the table.

jamás adv never

jamón (pl **jamones**) nm ham ▷ un bocadillo de jamón a ham sandwich; **jamón serrano** cured ham; **jamón de York** cooked ham

Japón nm Japan

japonés, -esa (mpl **japoneses**) nm/f, adj Japanese
▶ nm Japanese (language)

jarabe nm syrup; **jarabe para la tos** cough syrup

jardín (pl **jardines**) nm garden; **jardín de infancia** nursery school

jardinera nf window box; see also **jardinero**

jardinería nf gardening

jardinero, -a nm/f gardener

jarra nf ❶ jug ❷ beer glass

jarro nm jug

jarrón (pl **jarrones**) nm vase

jaula nf cage

jefe, jefa nm/f ❶ boss ❷ head: **el jefe del departamento** the head of department; **el jefe de estado** the head of state; **el jefe del grupo guerrillero** the leader of the guerrilla group

jerez nm sherry

jeringuilla nf syringe

jersey (pl **jerseys**) nm jumper

Jesús excl ❶ Bless you! ❷ Good God!

jinete nm jockey

jirafa nf giraffe

jitomate nm (in Mexico) tomato

jornada nf **jornada de trabajo** working day; **trabajar a jornada completa** to work full-time; **trabajar a media jornada** to work part-time

joven (pl **jóvenes**) nmf **un joven** a young man; **una joven** a young woman; **los jóvenes** young people
▶ adj young ▷ un chico joven a young boy

joya nf jewel; **Me han robado mis joyas.** My jewellery has been stolen.

joyería nf jeweller's

joyero, -a nm/f jeweller
▶ nm jewellery box

jubilación (pl **jubilaciones**)

nf ❶ retirement ▷ La edad de jubilación es a los 65 años. The retirement age is 65. ❷ pension ▷ cobrar la jubilación to get one's pension

jubilado, -a nm/f pensioner
▶ adj retired; **estar jubilado** to be retired

jubilarse [26] vb to retire

judía nf bean; **judía blanca** haricot bean; **judía verde** green bean; see also **judío**

judío, -a nm/f Jew
▶ adj Jewish

judo nm judo

juego vb see **jugar**
▶ nm ❶ game ▷ un juego de ordenador a computer game; **juegos de cartas** card games; **juegos de mesa** board games ❷ gambling ▷ Lo perdió todo en el juego. He lost everything through gambling. ❸ set ▷ un juego de café a coffee set; **Las cortinas hacen juego con el sofá.** The curtains go with the sofa.

juerga nf **irse de juerga** to go out on the town

jueves (pl jueves) nm

Days of the week start with a small letter in Spanish.

Thursday

juez nm (mpl **jueces**) nm/f judge; **juez de línea** linesman

jugador, a nm/f player

jugar [29] vb ❶ to play; **jugar al fútbol** to play football ❷ to gamble; **jugar a la lotería** to do the lottery

jugo nm ❶ juice ❷ gravy

juguete nm toy; **un avión de juguete** a toy plane

juguetería nf toy shop

juicio nm trial; **llevar a alguien a juicio** to take someone to court

julio nm

Months start with a small letter in Spanish.

July

jungla nf jungle

junio nm

Months start with a small letter in Spanish.

June

junta nf committee; **La junta directiva tiene la última palabra.** The board of management has the final say.

juntar [26] vb ❶ to put together ▷ Vamos a juntar los pupitres. Let's put the desks together. ❷ to gather together ▷ Consiguieron juntar a mil personas. They managed to gather together one thousand people.; **juntarse** (1) to move closer together (2) to meet up ▷ Nos juntamos los domingos para comer. We meet up for dinner on Sundays.

junto adj ❶ close together ▷ Los muebles están demasiado juntos. The furniture is too close together. ❷ together ▷ Cuando estamos juntos apenas hablamos. We hardly talk when we're together.; **todo junto** all together ▷ Ponlo todo junto en una sola bolsa. Put it all together in one bag.

▶ *adv* **junto a** by; **junto con**
together with; **Mi apellido se
escribe todo junto.** My surname
is all in one word.

jurado *nm* ❶ jury ❷ panel (*in
competition*)

jurar [**26**] *vb* to swear

justicia *nf* justice

justificar [**49**] *vb* to justify

justo *adj* ❶ fair ▷ *Tuvo un juicio
justo.* He had a fair trial. ❷ right
▷ *Apareció en el momento justo.*
He appeared at the right time.
❸ tight ▷ *Me están muy justos
estos pantalones.* These trousers
are tight on me. ❹ just enough
▷ *Tengo el dinero justo para el billete.*
I have just enough money for
the ticket.
▶ *adv* just ▷ *La vi justo cuando
entrábamos.* I saw her just as
we were coming in.; **Me dio un
puñetazo justo en la nariz.** He
punched me right on the nose.

juvenil *adj* ❶ youth ❷ junior; **la
literatura juvenil** young people's
literature

juventud *nf* ❶ youth ▷ *en
su juventud* in his youth
❷ youngsters ▷ *La juventud viene
aquí a divertirse.* Youngsters come
here to have fun.

juzgado *nm* court

juzgar [**38**] *vb* to try (*in court*)

kárate *nm* karate

kilo *nm* kilo

kilogramo *nm* kilogramme

kilómetro *nm* kilometre
● A kilometre is about 0.6 miles.

kiosco *nm* news stand

la *art* the ▷ *la pared* the wall; **la del sombrero rojo** the girl in the red hat; **Yo fui la que te desperté.** It was I who woke you up.

> You usually translate **la** as **my, his, her,** etc when it relates to a part of the body, clothes or belongings.

Ayer me lavé la cabeza. I washed my hair yesterday.; **Abróchate la camisa.** Do your shirt up.; **Tiene una casa bonita, pero prefiero la de Juan.** He's got a lovely house, but I prefer Juan's.

> **la** isn't always translated into English.

▷ *No me gusta la fruta.* I don't like fruit. ▷ *Vendrá la semana que viene.* He'll come next week. ▷ *Me he encontrado a la Sra. Sendra.* I met Mrs Sendra.

▶ *pron* **①** her ▷ *La quiero.* I love her.; **La han despedido.** She has been sacked. **②** you ▷ *La acompaño hasta la puerta.* I'll see you out. **③** it ▷ *No la toques.* Don't touch it.

labio *nm* lip

labor *nf* work; **las labores domésticas** the housework

laborable *adj* **un día laborable** a working day

laboral *adj* **①** working (*conditions, day*) **②** at work (*accident*)

laboratorio *nm* laboratory

laca *nf* **①** hairspray **②** lacquer; **la laca de uñas** nail varnish

lácteo *adj* **los productos lácteos** dairy products

ladera *nf* hillside

lado *nm* side ▷ *a los dos lados de la carretera* on both sides of the road; **Hay gente por todos lados.** There are people everywhere.; **Tiene que estar en otro lado.** It must be somewhere else.; **Mi casa está aquí al lado.** My house is very near here.; **la mesa de al lado** the next table; **al lado de** beside ▷ *La silla que está al lado del armario.* The chair beside the wardrobe.; **Felipe se sentó a mi lado.** Felipe sat beside me.; **por un lado ..., por otro lado ...** on the one hand ..., on the other hand ...

ladrar [**26**] *vb* to bark

ladrillo *nm* brick

ladrón, -ona *nm/f* **①** thief **②** burglar **③** robber

lagarto *nm* lizard

lago nm lake

lágrima nf tear

laguna nf lake

lamentar [26] vb ❶ to be sorry about ▷ Lamento lo ocurrido. I'm sorry about what happened. ❷ to be sorry ▷ Lamentamos tener que decirle que … We're sorry to have to tell you that …; **lamentarse** to complain

lamer [9] vb to lick

lámpara nf lamp

lana nf wool; **una bufanda de lana** a woollen scarf

lancha nf motorboat; **una lancha de salvamento** a lifeboat

langosta nf lobster

langostino nm king prawn

lanzar [14] vb ❶ to throw (stone, ball, grenade) ❷ to launch (rocket, product); **lanzarse** to dive

lapicero nm pencil

lápida nf gravestone

lápiz (pl **lápices**) nm pencil ▷ Escribió mi dirección a lápiz. He wrote my address in pencil.; **los lápices de colores** crayons; **un lápiz de labios** lipstick; **un lápiz de ojos** an eyeliner

largo adj long ▷ Fue una conferencia muy larga. It was a very long conference. ▷ Esta cuerda es demasiado larga. This piece of string is too long.; **a lo largo del río** along the river; **a lo largo de la semana** throughout the week
▶ nm length; **¿Cuánto mide de largo?** How long is it?; **Tiene nueve metros de largo.** It's nine

metres long.; **Pasó de largo sin saludar.** He passed by without saying hello.

❚ Be careful! **largo** does not mean **large**.

las art pl the ▷ las paredes the walls; **las del estante de arriba** the ones on the top shelf

❚ You usually translate **las** as **my**, **his**, **her**, etc when it relates to a part of the body, clothes or belongings.

Me duelen las piernas. My legs hurt.; **Poneos las bufandas.** Put your scarves on.; **Estas fotos son bonitas, pero prefiero las de Pedro.** These photos are nice, but I prefer Pedro's.

❚ **las** isn't always translated into English.

No me gustan las arañas. I don't like spiders.; **Vino a las seis de la tarde.** He came at six in the evening.

▶ pron ❶ them ▷ Las vi por la calle. I saw them in the street.; **Las han despedido.** They've been sacked. ❷ you ▷ Las acompañaré hasta la puerta, señoras. I'll see you out, ladies.

láser nm laser

lástima nf Me da lástima de ella. I feel sorry for her.; **Es una lástima que no puedas venir.** It's a shame you can't come.; **¡Qué lástima!** What a shame!

lata nf ❶ tin ❷ can; **Deja de dar la lata.** Stop being a pain.

lateral adj side ▷ la puerta lateral

the side door
latido nm beat
látigo nm whip
latín nm Latin
Latinoamérica nf Latin America
latinoamericano, -a nm/f, adj Latin American
latir [59] vb to beat
laurel nm laurel; **una hoja de laurel** a bay leaf
lavabo nm ❶ sink ❷ toilet
lavado nm wash; **el lavado en seco** dry cleaning
lavadora nf washing machine
lavandería nf launderette
lavaplatos (pl lavaplatos) nm ❶ dishwasher ❷ (in Mexico) sink
lavar [26] vb to wash; **lavar la ropa** to do the washing; **lavarse** to wash; **Ayer me lavé la cabeza.** I washed my hair yesterday.; **Lávate los dientes.** Brush your teeth.
lavarropas (pl lavarropas) nm (in Mexico) washing machine
lavavajillas (pl lavavajillas) nm ❶ dishwasher ❷ washing-up liquid
lazo nm ❶ bow ❷ ribbon
le pron ❶ ▷ Le mandé una carta. I sent him a letter. ▷ Le miré con atención. I watched him carefully.; **Le abrí la puerta.** I opened the door for him. ❷ her ▷ Le mandé una carta. I sent her a letter.; **No le hablé de ti.** I didn't speak to her about you.; **Le busqué el libro.** I looked out the book for her. ❸ you ▷ Le presento a la Señora

Gutiérrez. Let me introduce you to Mrs Gutiérrez.; **Le he arreglado el ordenador.** I've fixed the computer for you.

Note how **le** and the definite article is translated by **his** or **her** with parts of the body, clothes and belongings.
▷ Le huelen los pies. His feet smell.
▷ Le arrastra la falda. Her skirt is trailing on the floor.

lealtad nf loyalty
lección (pl lecciones) nf lesson
leche nf milk; **la leche desnatada** skimmed milk; **la leche en polvo** powdered milk
lechuga nf lettuce
lector, a nm/f ❶ reader ❷ language assistant ▶ nm **un lector de CD** a CD player
lectura nf reading
leer [31] vb to read
legal adj legal
legumbre nf pulse
lejano adj distant ▷ un sitio muy lejano a very distant place
lejía nf bleach
lejos adv far; **De lejos parecía un avión.** From a distance it looked like a plane.
lencería nf lingerie
lengua nf ❶ tongue ▷ Me he mordido la lengua. I've bitten my tongue. ❷ language ▷ Habla varias lenguas. He speaks several languages.; **mi lengua materna** my mother tongue
lenguado nm sole
lenguaje nm language

a
b
c
d
e
f
g
h
i
j
k
l
m
n
o
p
q
r
s
t
u
v
w
x
y
z

lente nf lens; **las lentes de contacto** contact lenses

lenteja nf lentil

lentes nmpl (in Latin America) glasses; **los lentes de sol** sunglasses

lentilla nf contact lens

lento adj slow ▷ un proceso lento a slow process
  ▶ adv slowly

leña nf firewood

Leo nm Leo (sign); **Soy leo.** I'm Leo.

león (pl **leones**) nm lion

leona nf lioness

leopardo nm leopard

leotardos nmpl woolly tights

les pron ❶ them ▷ Les mandé una carta. I sent them a letter. ▷ Les miré con atención. I watched them carefully.; **Les abrí la puerta.** I opened the door for them.; **Les eché de comer a los gatos.** I gave the cats something to eat. ❷ you ▷ Les presento a la Señora Gutiérrez. Let me introduce you to Mrs Gutiérrez.; **Les he arreglado el ordenador.** I've fixed the computer for you.

> Note how **les** and the definite article is translated by **their** with parts of the body, clothes and belongings.

▷ Les huelen los pies. Their feet smell. ▷ Les arrastraban sus abrigos. Their coats were trailing on the floor.

lesbiana nf lesbian

lesión (pl **lesiones**) nf injury

lesionado adj injured

letra nf ❶ letter ▷ la letra "a" the letter "a" ❷ handwriting ▷ Tengo muy mala letra. My handwriting's very poor. ❸ lyrics

letrero nm sign

levantar [26] vb ❶ to lift; **Levantad la mano si tenéis alguna duda.** Raise your hand if you are unclear.; **levantarse** to get up

leve adj minor ▷ Sólo tiene heridas leves. He only has minor injuries.

ley (pl **leyes**) nf law

leyendo vb see **leer**

liar [22] vb ❶ to tie up (parcel) ❷ to confuse ▷ Me liaron con tantas explicaciones. They confused me with all their explanations.; **liarse** to get muddled up

Líbano nm Lebanon

liberal nmf, adj liberal

liberar [26] vb to free

libertad nf freedom; **No tengo libertad para hacer lo que quiera.** I'm not free to do what I want.; **poner a alguien en libertad** to release somebody

Libra nm Libra (sign); **Soy libra.** I'm Libra.

libra nf pound; **libra esterlina** pound sterling

librarse [26] vb librarse de (1) to get out of (2) to get rid of

libre adj free ▷ ¿Está libre este asiento? Is this seat free? ▷ El martes estoy libre, así que podemos quedar. I'm free on Tuesday so we can meet up.; **los 100 metros libres** the 100 metres freestyle

librería nf ❶ bookshop

❷ bookshelf

▌ Be careful! **librería** does not mean **library**.

librero nm (in Chile, Mexico) bookcase

libreta nf notebook

libro nm book; **un libro de bolsillo** a paperback; **un libro de texto** a text book

licencia nf licence; **estar de licencia** (in Latin America) to be on leave

licenciado, -a nm/f graduate

licenciatura nf degree

licor nm liqueur; **Bebimos cerveza y licores.** We drank beer and spirits.

líder nmf leader

liebre nf hare

liga nf ❶ league ❷ garter

ligar [38] vb **Ayer ligué con una chica.** I got off with a girl yesterday.

ligero adj ❶ light ▷ **Me gusta llevar ropa ligera.** I like to wear light clothing. ▷ **Comimos algo ligero.** We ate something light. ❷ slight ▷ **Tengo un ligero dolor de cabeza.** I have a slight headache.; **Andaba a paso ligero.** He walked quickly.

lila nf lilac

lima nf ❶ file ▷ **una lima de uñas** a nail file ❷ lime (fruit)

limitar [26] vb to limit; **España limita con Francia.** Spain has a border with France.; **Yo me limité a observar.** I just watched.

límite nm ❶ limit ▷ **el límite de velocidad** the speed limit; **fecha**

límite deadline ❷ boundary

limón (pl **limones**) nm lemon

limonada nf lemonade

limosna nf **pedir limosna** to beg

limpiaparabrisas (pl **limpiaparabrisas**) nm windscreen wiper

limpiar [26] vb ❶ to clean ❷ to wipe

limpieza nf cleaning ▷ **Yo hago la limpieza y tú paseas al perro.** I'll do the cleaning and you can walk the dog.; **limpieza en seco** dry cleaning

limpio adj clean ▷ **El baño está muy limpio.** The bathroom's very clean.

lindo adj ❶ pretty ❷ (in Latin America) nice ▷ **un día muy lindo** a very nice day

línea nf line; **Vaya en línea recta.** Go straight ahead.; **una línea aérea** an airline; **en línea** online

lino nm linen

linterna nf torch

lío nm mess; **En mi mesa hay un lío enorme de papeles.** My desk is in a real muddle with all these papers.; **hacerse un lío** to get muddled up ▷ **Se hizo un lío con tantos nombres.** He got muddled up with all the names.; **Te vas a meter en un lío.** You'll get yourself into a real mess.

liquidación nf sale

líquido adj, nm liquid

Lisboa nf Lisbon

liso adj ❶ smooth (surface) ❷ straight (hair) ❸ plain (colour)

lista nf list ▷ **la lista de espera** the

a
b
c
d
e
f
g
h
i
j
k
l
m
n
o
p
q
r
s
t
u
v
w
x
y
z

waiting list; **pasar lista** to call the register; **la lista de correo** mailing list

listo adj ❶ clever ▷ *Es una chica muy lista.* She's a very clever girl. ❷ ready ▷ *¿Estás listo?* Are you ready?

litera nf ❶ bunk bed ❷ berth

literatura nf literature

litro nm litre

liviano adj light

llaga nf sore

llama nf flame

llamada nf call; **una llamada telefónica** a phone call

llamar [26] vb ❶ to call ▷ *llamar a la policía* to call the police ❷ to phone; **llamar por teléfono a alguien** to phone somebody ❸ to knock; **llamarse** to be called; **¿Cómo te llamas?** What's your name?; **Me llamo Adela.** My name's Adela.

llano adj flat

llave nf ❶ key; **Echa la llave de la puerta cuando salgas.** Lock the door when you go out.; **una llave inglesa** a spanner ❷ (*in Latin America*) tap

llavero nm keyring

llegada nf ❶ arrival (*of train, plane, passengers*) ❷ finish (*of race*)

llegar [38] vb ❶ to get to; **¿A qué hora llegaste a casa?** What time did you get home? ❷ to arrive; **No llegues tarde.** Don't be late.; **Con tres euros no me llega.** Three euros isn't enough. ❸ to reach; **El agua me llegaba hasta las**

rodillas. The water came up to my knees.; **llegar a ser** to become

llenar [26] vb ❶ to fill (*container*) ❷ to fill in (*form*)

lleno adj full ▷ *El restaurante estaba lleno de gente.* The restaurant was full of people.

llevar [26] vb ❶ to take ▷ *¿Llevas los vasos a la cocina?* Can you take the glasses to the kitchen? ▷ *No llevará mucho tiempo.* It won't take long. ❷ to wear ▷ *María llevaba un abrigo muy bonito.* María was wearing a nice coat. ❸ to give a lift ▷ *Sofía nos llevó a casa.* Sofía gave us a lift home. ❹ to carry; **Sólo llevo diez euros.** I've only got ten euros on me.; **¿Cuánto tiempo llevas aquí?** How long have you been here?; **Llevo horas esperando aquí.** I've been waiting here for hours.; **Mi hermana mayor me lleva ocho años.** My elder sister is eight years older than me.; **llevarse algo** to take something; **Me llevo bien con mi hermano.** I get on well with my brother.

llorar [26] vb to cry

llover [32] vb to rain; **llover a cántaros** to pour down

lloviznar [26] vb to drizzle

llueve vb see **llover**

lluvia nf rain ▷ *bajo la lluvia* in the rain; **la lluvia ácida** acid rain

lluvioso adj rainy

lo art **Lo peor fue que no pudimos entrar.** The worst thing was we couldn't get in.; **No me gusta**

lo picante. I don't like spicy things.; **Pon en mi habitación lo de Pedro.** Put Pedro's things in my room.; **Lo mío son las matemáticas.** Maths is my thing.; **Lo de vender la casa no me parece bien.** I don't like this idea of selling the house.; **Olvida lo de ayer.** Forget what happened yesterday.

> lo followed by an adjective often corresponds to **how** in descriptions.

▷ **¡No sabes lo aburrido que es!** You don't know how boring he is!; **lo que (1)** what ▷ **Lo que más me gusta es nadar.** What I like best is swimming. **(2)** whatever ▷ **Ponte lo que quieras.** Wear whatever you like.; **más de lo que** more than ▷ **Cuesta más de lo que crees.** It costs more than you think.

▸ pron ❶ him ▷ **No lo conozco.** I don't know him.; **Lo han despedido.** He's been sacked. ❷ you ▷ **Yo a usted lo conozco.** I know you. ❸ it ▷ **No lo veo.** I can't see it. ▷ **Voy a pensarlo.** I'll think about it.; **No lo sabía.** I didn't know.; **No parece lista pero lo es.** She doesn't seem clever but she is.

lobo nm wolf

local adj local ▷ **un producto local** a local product
▸ nm premises

localidad nf ❶ town ❷ seat (in theatre)

localizar [14] vb ❶ to reach ▷ **Me puedes localizar en este teléfono.** You can reach me at this number. ❷ to locate ▷ **No han conseguido localizar a las víctimas.** They've been unable to locate the victims.

loción (pl lociones) nf lotion

loco, -a nm/f un loco a madman; una loca a madwoman
▸ adj ❶ mad ▷ volverse loco to go mad; **volver loco a alguien** to drive somebody mad ❷ crazy ▷ **¿Estás loco?** Are you crazy? ▷ **Está loco con su moto nueva.** He's crazy about his new motorbike.; **volver loco a alguien** to drive somebody mad; **Me vuelve loco el marisco.** I'm crazy about seafood.

locura nf madness ▷ **Es una locura ir solo.** It's madness to go on your own.

locutor, a nm/f newsreader

lógico adj ❶ logical ❷ natural; **Es lógico que no quiera venir.** It's only natural he doesn't want to come.

lograr [26] vb ❶ to get ▷ **Lograron lo que se proponían.** They got what they wanted. ❷ to manage ▷ **Logré que me concediera una entrevista.** I managed to get an interview with him.

lombriz (pl lombrices) nf worm

lomo nm ❶ back ❷ loin ❸ spine

lona nf canvas

loncha nf slice

Londres nm London

longitud nf length; **Tiene tres metros de longitud.** It's three metres long.

loro nm parrot

los *art* the ▷ *los barcos* the boats; **los de las bufandas rojas** the people in the red scarves

> You usually translate **los** as **my**, **his**, **her**, etc when it relates to a part of the body, clothes or belongings.

Se lavaron los pies en el río. They washed their feet in the river.; **Abrochaos los abrigos.** Button up your coats.; **Me gustan sus cuadros, pero prefiero los de Ana.** I like his paintings, but I prefer Ana's.

> **los** isn't always translated into English.

▷ *No me gustan los melocotones.* I don't like peaches. ▷ *Sólo vienen los lunes.* They only come on Mondays.

▶ *pron* **❶** them ▷ *Los vi por la calle.* I saw them in the street.; **Los han despedido.** They've been sacked. **❷** you ▷ *Los acompaño hasta la puerta, señores.* I'll see you to the door, gentlemen.

lotería *nf* lottery ▷ *Le tocó la lotería.* He won the lottery.

lucha *nf* fight; **lucha libre** wrestling

luchar[26] *vb* to fight

lucir *vb* to shine

luego *adv* **❶** then ▷ *Primero se puso de pie y luego habló.* First he stood up and then he spoke. **❷** later ▷ *Mi mujer viene luego.* My wife's coming later.; **desde luego** of course; **¡Hasta luego!** See you! **❸** (*in Chile, Mexico*) soon

▶ *conj* therefore

lugar *nm* place ▷ *Este lugar es muy bonito.* This is a lovely place.; **Llegó en último lugar.** He came last.; **en lugar de** instead of; **tener lugar** to take place

lujo *nm* luxury; **un coche de lujo** a luxury car

lujoso *adj* luxurious

luna *nf* **❶** moon **❷** window pane ▷ window; **la luna de miel** honeymoon

lunar *nm* mole; **una corbata de lunares** a spotted tie

lunes (*pl* lunes) *nm*

> Days of the week start with a small letter in Spanish.

Monday ▷ *el lunes pasado* last Monday ▷ *el lunes que viene* next Monday ▷ *Jugamos los lunes.* We play on Mondays.

lupa *nf* magnifying glass

luto *nm* **estar de luto por alguien** to be in mourning for somebody

Luxemburgo *nm* Luxembourg

luz (*pl* luces) *nf* **❶** light ▷ *Enciende la luz, por favor.* Put on the light please. **❷** electricity ▷ *No hay luz en todo el edificio.* There's no electricity in the whole building.; **dar a luz** to give birth

m

macarrones *nmpl* macaroni

macedonia *nf* fruit salad

maceta *nf* flowerpot

machacar [49] *vb* ❶ to crush ❷ to thrash

macho *adj, nm* male ▷ *un conejo macho* a male rabbit

madera *nf* wood; **un juguete de madera** a wooden toy; **Tiene madera de profesor.** He's got the makings of a teacher.

madrastra *nf* stepmother

madre *nf* mother; **¡Madre mía!** Goodness!

Madrid *nm* Madrid

madrileño *adj* from Madrid; **Soy madrileño.** I'm from Madrid.

madrina *nf* ❶ godmother ❷ matron of honour

madrugada *nf* early morning;

levantarse de madrugada (1) to get up early (2) to get up at daybreak; **a las 4 de la madrugada** at 4 o'clock in the morning

madrugar [38] *vb* to get up early

maduro *adj* ❶ mature ❷ ripe

maestro, -a *nm/f* teacher; **un maestro de escuela** a schoolteacher

magia *nf* magic

mágico *adj* magic ▷ *una varita mágica* a magic wand

magisterio *nm* **Estudia magisterio.** He's training to be a teacher.

magnífico *adj* splendid

mago, -a *nm/f* magician; **los Reyes Magos** the Three Wise Men

maíz (*pl* maíces) *nm* ❶ maize ❷ sweetcorn; **una mazorca de maíz** a corn cob

majestad *nf* **Su Majestad** (1) His Majesty (2) Her Majesty

majo *adj* ❶ nice ❷ pretty

mal *adj* = **malo**

▶ *adv* ❶ badly; **Esta habitación huele mal.** This room smells bad.; **Lo pasé muy mal.** I had a very bad time.; **Me entendió mal.** He misunderstood me.; **hablar mal de alguien** to speak ill of someone ❷ wrong ▷ *Han escrito mal mi apellido.* They've spelt my surname wrong.

▶ *nm* evil ▷ *el bien y el mal* good and evil

mala *nf* **la mala de la película** the villain in the film

malcriado adj badly brought up

maldito adj damned; **¡Maldita sea!** Damn it!

maleducado adj bad-mannered

malentendido nm misunderstanding

malestar nm discomfort

maleta nf suitcase; **hacer la maleta** to pack

maletero nm boot

maletín (pl **maletines**) nm briefcase

malgastar [26] vb to waste

malhumorado adj bad-tempered; **Hoy parece malhumorado.** He appears to be in a bad mood today.

malicia nf ❶ malice ❷ mischief

malicioso adj malicious

malla nf ❶ mesh ❷ leotard; **una malla de baño** (in River Plate) a swimsuit; **mallas (1)** tights **(2)** leggings

Mallorca nf Majorca

malo adj

> **malo** is shortened to **mal** before masculine singular nouns.

❶ bad ▷ un mal día a bad day ▷ Este programa es muy malo. This is a very bad programme. ▷ Soy muy mala para las matemáticas. I'm very bad at maths.; **Hace malo.** The weather's bad.; **Lo malo es que …** the trouble is that … ❷ naughty ▷ ¿Por qué eres tan malo? Why are you so naughty? ❸ off ▷ Esta carne está mala. This meat's off. ❹ ill ▷ Mi hija está mala. My daughter's

ill. ▷ Se puso malo después de comer. He started to feel ill after lunch.

maltratar [26] vb to ill-treat; **los niños maltratados** abused children

malvado adj evil

mama nf ❶ breast ❷ mum

mamá (pl **mamás**) nf mum ▷ tu mamá your mum ▷ ¡Hola mamá! Hi Mum!

mamífero nm mammal

manantial nm spring (of water)

mancha nf stain

manchar [26] vb to stain; **mancharse** to get dirty; **Me he manchado el vestido de tinta.** I've got ink stains on my dress.

mandar [26] vb ❶ to order; **Nos mandó callar.** He told us to be quiet.; **Aquí mando yo.** I'm the boss here. ❷ to send ▷ Me mandaron a hacer un recado. They sent me on an errand.; **mandar llamar a alguien** (in Latin America) to send for someone; **Se lo mandaremos por correo.** We'll post it to you.; **mandar a arreglar algo** (in Latin America) to have something repaired; **¿Mande?** (in Mexico) Pardon?

mandarina nf tangerine

mandíbula nf jaw

mando nm un alto mando a high-ranking officer; **Está al mando del proyecto.** He's in charge of the project.; **el mando a distancia** the remote control; **los mandos** the controls

manecilla nf hand ▷ las manecillas

del reloj the hands of the clock

manejable adj ❶ manoeuvrable ❷ easy to use

manejar [26] vb ❶ to use (tool) ❷ to operate (machine) ❸ to manage (business) ❹ (in Latin America) to drive; **un examen de manejar** (in Latin America) a driving test

manera nf way ▷ Lo hice a mi manera. I did it my way.; **de todas maneras** anyway; **No hay manera de convencerla.** There's nothing one can do to convince her.; **de manera que** (1) so ▷ No has hecho los deberes, de manera que no hay tele. You haven't done your homework so there's no TV. (2) so that ▷ Lo puse de manera que pudieran verlo. I positioned it so that they could see it.; **¡De ninguna manera!** No way!

manga nf sleeve; **de manga corta** short-sleeved; **de manga larga** long-sleeved

mango nm ❶ handle ❷ mango

manguera nf hose

manía nf **Tiene la manía de repetir todo lo que digo.** He has an irritating habit of repeating everything I say.; **El profesor me tiene manía.** The teacher has it in for me.

maniático adj fussy; **Es una maniática del orden.** She's obsessed with keeping things tidy.

manifestación (pl manifestaciones) nf demonstration

manifestante nmf demonstrator

manifestarse [40] vb to demonstrate

manillar nm handlebars

maniobra nf manoeuvre

manipular [26] vb ❶ to handle (food) ❷ to manipulate (opinion, person) ❸ to operate (equipment, machine)

maniquí (pl maniquíes) nmf model
▶ nm dummy

manivela nf crank

mano nf hand ▷ Dame la mano. Give me your hand.; **tener algo a mano** to have something to hand; **hecho a mano** handmade; **de segunda mano** secondhand; **echar una mano** to lend a hand; **estrechar la mano a alguien** to shake somebody's hand; **la mano de obra** labour; **una mano de pintura** a coat of paint

manojo nm bunch

manopla nf mitten; **una manopla de cocina** an oven glove

manso adj tame

manta nf blanket

manteca nf (in River Plate) butter; **manteca de cerdo** lard

mantel nm tablecloth

mantener [54] vb ❶ to keep
▷ mantener la calma to keep calm
❷ to support ▷ Mantiene a su familia. He supports his family.; **mantener una conversación** to have a conversation; **mantenerse** to support oneself; **mantenerse en forma** to keep fit

mantenimiento nm maintenance; **ejercicios de mantenimiento** keep-fit exercises

mantequilla nf butter

mantuve vb see **mantener**

manual adj, nm manual

manubrio nm (in Latin America) handlebars

manuscrito nm manuscript

manzana nf ❶ apple ❷ block (of buildings)

manzano nm apple tree

mañana nf morning ▷ Llegó a las nueve de la mañana. He arrived at nine o'clock in the morning.; **a media mañana** mid-morning; **Por la mañana voy al gimnasio.** In the mornings I go to the gym.
  ▶ adv tomorrow; **pasado mañana** the day after tomorrow; **mañana por la mañana** tomorrow morning; **mañana por la noche** tomorrow night

mapa nm map ▷ un mapa de carreteras a road map

maqueta nf model

maquillaje nm make-up

maquillarse [26] vb to put one's make-up on

máquina nf machine ▷ una máquina de coser a sewing machine ▷ una máquina expendedora a vending machine ▷ una máquina tragaperras a fruit machine; **una máquina de afeitar** a shaver; **una máquina fotográfica** a camera; **escrito a máquina** typed

maquinilla nf razor ▷ una maquinilla eléctrica an electric razor

mar nm sea; **por mar** by sea

Note that in certain idiomatic phrases, **mar** is feminine.

en alta mar on the high seas; **Lo hizo a la mar de bien.** He did it really well.

maratón (pl maratones) nm marathon

maravilla nf ¡Qué maravilla de casa! What a wonderful house!; **ser una maravilla** to be wonderful; **Se llevan de maravilla.** They get on wonderfully well together.

maravilloso adj marvellous

marca nf ❶ mark ▷ Había marcas de neumático en la arena. There were tyre marks in the sand. ❷ make ▷ ¿De qué marca es tu coche? What make's your car? ❸ brand; **la ropa de marca** designer clothes

marcador nm ❶ scoreboard ❷ bookmark (for webpage)

marcar [49] vb ❶ to mark; **marcar algo con una equis** to put a cross on something ❷ to dial (number) ❸ to score (goal) ❹ to set (hair); **Mi reloj marca las 2.** It's 2 o'clock according to my watch.

marcha nf ❶ departure ❷ gear ▷ cambiar de marcha to change gear; **salir de marcha** to go out on the town; **a toda marcha** at full speed; **estar en marcha (1)** to be running **(2)** to be underway; **No te subas nunca a un tren en marcha.** Never get onto a moving train.; **dar marcha atrás** to reverse

marcharse [26] vb to leave

marco nm frame

marea nf tide; **una marea negra**
an oil slick

mareado adj Estoy mareado. (1) I
feel dizzy. (2) I feel sick.

marear [26] vb to make...feel sick;
¡No me marees! Stop going on
at me!; **marearse** (1) to get dizzy
(2) to get seasick (3) to get carsick

mareo nm ❶ seasickness
❷ carsickness; Le dio un mareo
a causa del calor. The heat made
her feel ill.

marfil nm ivory

margarina nf margarine

margarita nf daisy

margen (pl márgenes) nm margin

marido nm husband

marinero nm sailor

mariposa nf butterfly

marisco nm shellfish ▷ No me gusta
el marisco. I don't like shellfish.

mármol nm marble

marrón (f marrón, pl marrones)
adj brown ▷ un traje marrón a
brown suit

Marruecos nm Morocco

martes (pl martes) nm

▌ Days of the week start with a
small letter in Spanish.

Tuesday ▷ el martes pasado last
Tuesday ▷ el martes que viene next
Tuesday

martillo nm hammer

marzo nm

▌ Months start with a small
letter in Spanish.

March ▷ en marzo in March

más adj, adv ❶ more;
Últimamente nos vemos más.
We've been seeing more of each
other lately.; ¿Quieres más?
Would you like some more?; No
tengo más dinero. I haven't
any more money.; hermoso
- más hermoso beautiful - more
beautiful ▷ deprisa - más deprisa
quickly - more quickly; joven
- más joven young - younger;
grande - más grande big - bigger;
más ... que more ... than ▷ Es más
guapo que yo. He's more handsome
than I am.; Es más grande que
el tuyo. It's bigger than yours.;
Trabaja más que yo. He works
harder than I do.; más de mil
libros more than a thousand
books; más de lo que yo creía
more than I thought; ¿Qué más?
What else?; ¡Qué perro más sucio!
What a filthy dog!; Tenemos uno
de más. We have one too many.;
Por más que estudio no apruebo.
However hard I study I still don't
pass.; más o menos more or less;
2 más 2 son 4 2 and 2 are 4; 14 más
20 menos 12 es igual a 22 14 plus
20 minus 12 equals 22 ❷ most ▷ su
película más innovadora his most
innovative film ▷ el más inteligente
de todos the most intelligent of all
of them; el bolígrafo más barato
the cheapest pen; el punto más
lejano the furthest point; Paco es
el que come más. Paco's the one
who eats the most.; Fue el que
más trabajó. He was the one who

worked the hardest.

masa nf ❶ dough ▷ *la masa de pan* bread dough ❷ mass ▷ *las masas* the masses; **en masa (1)** mass ▷ *la producción en masa* mass production **(2)** en masse ▷ *Fueron en masa a recibir al futbolista.* They went en masse to greet the footballer.

masaje nm massage

máscara nf mask

masculino adj ❶ masculine (voice, pronoun) ❷ male (body, sex) ❸ men's (team, sport) ▷ *la ropa masculina* men's clothing
▶ nm masculine

masticar [49] vb to chew

matar [26] vb to kill; **matarse** to be killed

matasellos (pl matasellos) nm postmark

mate adj matt
▶ nm checkmate

matemáticas nfpl mathematics

materia nf ❶ matter ▷ *materia orgánica* organic matter ❷ material ▷ *la materia prima* the raw material ❸ subject ▷ *Es un experto en la materia.* He's an expert on the subject.

material adj, nm material

materno adj maternal; **mi lengua materna** my mother tongue

matiz (pl matices) nm shade

matorral nm bushes

matrícula nf registration; **la matrícula del coche (1)** the registration number of the car **(2)** the number plate of the car

matricular [26] vb to register; **matricularse** to enrol

matrimonio nm ❶ marriage ❷ couple ▷ *un matrimonio feliz* a happy couple

maullar [26] vb to miaow

máximo adj maximum
▶ nm maximum; **como máximo (1)** at the most **(2)** at the latest

mayo nm

Months start with a small letter in Spanish.

May ▷ *en mayo* in May

mayonesa nf mayonnaise

mayor (f mayor) adj, pron ❶ older ▷ *Paco es mayor que Nacho.* Paco is older than Nacho. ▷ *Es tres años mayor que yo.* He is three years older than me.; **el hermano mayor (1)** the older brother **(2)** the oldest brother; **Soy el mayor. (1)** I'm the older. **(2)** I'm the oldest.; **Nuestros hijos ya son mayores.** Our children are grown-up now.; **la gente mayor** the elderly ❷ bigger ▷ *Necesitamos una casa mayor.* We need a bigger house.; **la mayor iglesia del mundo** the biggest church in the world
▶ nmf **un mayor de edad** an adult; **los mayores** grown-ups

mayoría nf majority; **La mayoría de los estudiantes son pobres.** Most students are poor.; **la mayoría de nosotros** most of us

mayúscula nf capital letter

mazapán (pl mazapanes) nm marzipan

me pron ❶ me ▷ *Me quiere.* He loves

me. ▷ *Me regaló una pulsera.* He gave me a bracelet.; **Me lo dio.** He gave it to me.; **¿Me echas esta carta?** Will you post this letter for me? ❸ myself ▷ *No me hice daño.* I didn't hurt myself.; **me dije a mí mismo** I said to myself

> Note how **me** and the definite article is translated by **my** with parts of the body, clothes and belongings.

▷ *Me duelen los pies.* My feet hurt. ▷ *Me puse el abrigo.* I put my coat on.

mear [26] *vb* to piss; **mearse** to wet oneself

mecánica *nf* mechanics; *see also* **mecánico**

mecánico, -a *nm/f* mechanic; *see also* **mecánica**
  ▶ *adj* mechanical

mecanismo *nm* mechanism

mecanografía *nf* typing

mecha *nf* ❶ wick ❷ fuse

mechero *nm* cigarette lighter

medalla *nf* medal

media *nf* average ▷ *Trabajo una media de seis horas diarias.* I work an average of six hours a day.; **medias** (1) stockings (2) tights (3) (*in Latin America*) socks; **medias bombachas** (*in River Plate*) tights; **a las cuatro y media** at half past four

mediados *npl* **a mediados de** around the middle of

mediano *adj* medium ▷ *de mediana estatura* of medium height; **de tamaño mediano** medium-sized;

el hijo mediano the middle son

medianoche *nf* midnight ▷ *a medianoche* at midnight

medicamento *nm* medicine

medicina *nf* medicine

médico, -a *nm/f* doctor ▷ *Quiere ser médica.* She wants to be a doctor. ▷ *el médico de cabecera* the family doctor; **ir al médico** to go to the doctor's

medida *nf* measure ▷ *tomar medidas contra la inflación* to take measures against inflation; **El sastre le tomó las medidas.** The tailor took his measurements.; **un traje a medida** a made-to-measure suit; **a medida que ...** as ... ▷ *Saludaba a los invitados a medida que iban llegando.* He greeted the guests as they arrived.

medio *adj* ❶ half ▷ *medio litro* half a litre ▷ *media hora* half an hour ▷ *una hora y media* an hour and a half; **Son las ocho y media.** It's half past eight. ❸ average ▷ *la temperatura media* the average temperature
  ▶ *adv* half
  ▶ *nm* ❶ middle ▷ *Está en el medio.* It's in the middle.; **en medio de** in the middle of ❸ means ▷ *un medio de transporte* a means of transport; **por medio de** by means of; **medios** means ▷ *por medios pacíficos* by peaceful means; **los medios de comunicación** the media; **el medio ambiente** the environment

mediodía *nm* **al mediodía** (1) at

midday **(2)** at lunchtime

medir [**39**] vb to measure; **¿Cuánto mides? - Mido 1.50 m.** How tall are you? - I'm 1.5 m tall.; **¿Cuánto mide esta habitación? - Mide 3 m por 4.** How big is this room? - It measures 3 m by 4.

Mediterráneo nm **el Mediterráneo** the Mediterranean

mediterráneo adj Mediterranean

medusa nf jellyfish

mejicano, -a nm/f, adj Mexican

Méjico nm Mexico

mejilla nf cheek

mejillón (pl **mejillones**) nm mussel

mejor (f **mejor**) adj, pron ❶ better ▷ **Éste es mejor que el otro.** This one is better than the other one.; **Es el mejor de los dos.** He's the better of the two. ❷ best ▷ **mi mejor amiga** my best friend ▷ **el mejor de la clase** the best in the class ▷ **Es el mejor de todos.** He's the best of the lot.

▶ adv ❶ better ❷ best; **a lo mejor** probably; **Mejor nos vamos.** We had better go.

mejora nf improvement

mejorar [**26**] vb to improve; **¡Que te mejores!** Get well soon!

mejoría nf improvement

melena nf ❶ long hair ▷ **Lleva una melena rubia.** She has long blond hair. ❷ mane (lion's)

mellizo, -a adj, nm/f twin ▷ **Son mellizos.** They're twins.

melocotón (pl **melocotones**) nm peach

melodía nf tune

melón (pl **melones**) nm melon

memoria nf memory; **aprender algo de memoria** to learn something by heart

memorizar [**14**] vb to memorize

mencionar [**26**] vb to mention

mendigo, -a nm/f beggar

menor (f **menor**) adj, pron ❶ younger ▷ **Es tres años menor que yo.** He's three years younger than me. ▷ **Juanito es menor que Pepe.** Juanito is younger than Pepe.; **el hermano menor (1)** the younger brother **(2)** the youngest brother; **Yo soy el menor. (1)** I'm the younger. **(2)** I'm the youngest. ❷ smaller ▷ **una talla menor** a smaller size; **No tiene la menor importancia.** It's not in the least important.

▶ nmf **un menor de edad** a minor; **los menores** the under-18s

Menorca nf Minorca

menos adj, adv ❶ less; **Últimamente nos vemos menos.** We've been seeing less of each other recently. ▷ **menos harina** less flour; **menos gatos** fewer cats ▷ **menos gente** fewer people; **menos...que** less...than ▷ **Me gusta menos que el otro.** I like it less than the other one. ▷ **Lo hizo menos cuidadosamente que ayer.** He did it less carefully than yesterday.; **Trabaja menos que yo.** He doesn't work as hard as I do.; **menos de 50 cajas** fewer than 50 boxes; **Tiene menos de dieciocho años.**

He's under eighteen. ❷ **least** ▷ *el chico menos desobediente de la clase* the least disobedient boy in the class; **Fue el que menos trabajó.** He was the one who worked the least hard.; **el examen con menos errores** the exam paper with the fewest mistakes; **No quiero verle y menos visitarle.** I don't want to see him, let alone visit him.; **¡Menos mal!** Thank goodness!; **al menos** at least; **por lo menos** at least; **a menos que** unless; **¡Ni mucho menos!** No way!
▶ *prep* **except;** *todos menos él* everyone except him; **5 menos 2 son 3** 5 minus 2 is 3

mensaje *nm* message; **un mensaje de texto** a text message; **el envío de mensajes con foto** picture messaging

mensajero, -a *nm/f* messenger

mensual *adj* monthly; **50 dólares mensuales** 50 dollars a month

menta *nf* mint ▷ *un caramelo de menta* a mint sweet

mentalidad *nf* mentality; **Tiene una mentalidad muy abierta.** He has a very open mind.

mente *nf* mind ▷ *No me lo puedo quitar de la mente.* I can't get it out of my mind.; **tener en mente hacer algo** to be thinking of doing something

mentir [52] *vb* to lie

mentira *nf* lie ▷ *No digas mentiras.* Don't tell lies.; **Parece mentira que aún no te haya pagado.** It's incredible that he still hasn't paid

you.; **una pistola de mentira** a toy pistol

mentiroso, -a *nm/f* liar

menú (*pl* menús) *nm* menu; **el menú del día** the set meal

menudo *adj* slight ▷ *Es una chica muy menuda.* She's a very slight girl.; **¡Menudo lío!** What a mess!; **a menudo** often

meñique *nm* little finger

mercado *nm* market

mercancía *nf* commodity

mercería *nf* haberdasher's

merecer [13] *vb* to deserve; **merece la pena** it's worthwhile

merendar [40] *vb* to have tea

merengue *nm* meringue

merienda *nf* tea

mérito *nm* merit

merluza *nf* hake

mermelada *nf* jam

mero *adv* (in Mexico) almost

mes (*pl* meses) *nm* month ▷ *el mes que viene* next month ▷ *a final de mes* at the end of the month

mesa *nf* table; **poner la mesa** to lay the table; **quitar la mesa** to clear the table

mesera *nf* (in Latin America) waitress

mesero *nm* (in Latin America) waiter

mesilla *nf* una mesilla de noche a bedside table

meta *nf* ❶ aim ❷ finishing line ❸ goal

metal *nm* metal

metálico *adj* metal ▷ *un objeto metálico* a metal object; **en**

metálico in cash

meter [9] vb to put; **meterse en** to go into; **meterse en política** to go into politics; **No te metas donde no te llaman.** Don't poke your nose in where it doesn't belong.; **meterse con alguien** to pick on somebody

método nm method

metro nm ❶ underground ▷ coger el metro to take the underground ❷ metre ▷ Mide tres metros de largo. It's three metres long.

mexicano, -a nm/f, adj Mexican

México nm Mexico

mezcla nf mixture

mezclar [26] vb to mix; **mezclarse en algo** to get mixed up in something

mezquino adj mean

mezquita nf mosque

mi (pl mis) adj my ▷ mis hermanas my sisters

mí pron me ▷ para mí for me; **Para mí que ...** I think that ...; **Por mí no hay problema.** There's no problem as far as I'm concerned.

microbio nm germ

micrófono nm microphone

microondas (pl microondas) nm microwave ▷ un horno microondas a microwave oven

microscopio nm microscope

midiendo vb see **medir**

miedo nm fear ▷ el miedo a la oscuridad fear of the dark; **tener miedo** to be afraid ▷ Le tenía miedo a su padre. He was afraid of his father. ▷ Tenemos miedo de que nos

ataquen. We're afraid that they may attack us.; **dar miedo a** to scare ▷ Me daba miedo hacerlo. I was scared of doing it.; **pasarlo de miedo** to have a fantastic time

miedoso adj **¡No seas tan miedoso!** Don't be such a coward!; **Mi hijo es muy miedoso.** My son gets frightened very easily.

miel nf honey

miembro nmf ❶ member ❷ limb

mientras adv, conj while; **Seguiré conduciendo mientras pueda.** I'll carry on driving for as long as I can.; **mientras que** while; **mientras tanto** meanwhile

miércoles (pl miércoles) nm

> Days of the week start with a small letter in Spanish.

Wednesday ▷ el miércoles pasado last Wednesday ▷ el miércoles que viene next Wednesday

mierda nf shit; **Esta película es una mierda.** This film's a load of crap.; **¡Vete a la mierda!** Go to hell!

miga nf crumb

mil adj, pron thousand ▷ miles de personas thousands of people ▷ dos mil euros two thousand euros; **miles de veces** hundreds of times

milagro nm miracle

mili nf military service

milímetro nm millimetre

militar nmf soldier; **los militares** the military
  ▶ adj military

milla nf mile

millón (pl millones) nm million
  ▷ millones de personas millions of

people; **mil millones** a billion

millonario, -a nm/f millionaire

mimado adj spoiled

mina nf mine

mineral adj, nm mineral

minero, -a nm/f miner

miniatura nf miniature; **una casa en miniatura** a miniature house

minidisco nm Minidisc®

minifalda nf miniskirt

mínimo adj minimum ▷ **el salario mínimo** the minimum wage; **No tienes ni la más mínima idea.** You haven't the faintest idea.
▶ nm minimum ▷ **un mínimo de 10 euros** a minimum of 10 euros; **lo mínimo que puede hacer** the least he can do; **Como mínimo podrías haber llamado.** You could at least have called.

ministerio nm ministry

ministro, -a nm/f minister

minoría nf minority

minucioso adj thorough

minúscula nf small letter

minusválida nf disabled woman

minusválido nm disabled man; **los minusválidos** the disabled

minuto nm minute ▷ **Espera un minuto.** Wait a minute.

mío, -a adj, pron mine ▷ **Estos caballos son míos.** Those horses are mine. ▷ **Es mía.** Whose scarf is this? - It's mine. ▷ **El mío está en el armario.** Mine's in the cupboard. ▷ **Éste es el mío.** This one's mine.; **un amigo mío** a friend of mine

miope adj short-sighted

mirada nf look ▷ **con una mirada de odio** with a look of hatred; **echar una mirada a algo** to have a look at something

mirar [26] vb to look; **mirar algo** to look at something; **mirar por la ventana** to look out of the window; **mirar algo fijamente** to stare at something; **¡Mira que es tonto!** What an idiot!; **mirarse al espejo** to look at oneself in the mirror; **Se miraron asombrados.** They looked at each other in amazement.

misa nf mass ▷ **la misa del gallo** midnight mass ▷ **ir a misa** to go to mass

miseria nf ❶ poverty ❷ pittance

misión (pl **misiones**) nf mission

misionero, -a nm/f missionary

mismo adj same ▷ **Nos gustan los mismos libros.** We like the same books.; **yo mismo** myself ▷ **Lo hice yo mismo.** I did it myself.
▶ adv **Hoy mismo le escribiré.** I'll write to him today.; **Nos podemos encontrar aquí mismo.** We can meet right here.; **enfrente mismo del colegio** right opposite the school
▶ pron **lo mismo** the same ▷ **Yo tomaré lo mismo.** I'll have the same.; **Da lo mismo.** It doesn't matter.; **No ha llamado pero lo mismo viene.** He hasn't phoned but he may well come.

misterio nm mystery

misterioso adj mysterious

mitad nf half ▷ **Se comió la mitad del**

pastel. He ate half the cake. ▷ *más de la mitad de los trabajadores* more than half the workers; **La mitad son chicas.** Half of them are girls.; **a mitad de precio** half-price; **a mitad de camino** halfway there; **Corta el pan por la mitad.** Cut the loaf in half.

mito nm myth

mixto adj mixed

mobiliario nm furniture

mochila nf rucksack

moco nm **Límpiate los mocos.** Wipe your nose.; **tener mocos** to have a runny nose

moda nf fashion; **estar de moda** to be in fashion; **pasado de moda** old-fashioned

modales nmpl manners ▷ *buenos modales* good manners

modelo adj, nm/f model ▷ *una niña modelo* a model child ▷ *Quiero ser modelo.* I want to be a model.

moderado adj moderate

modernizar [14] vb to modernize; **modernizarse** to get up to date

moderno adj modern

modestia nf modesty

modesto adj modest

modificar [49] vb to modify

modisto, -a nm/f dressmaker

modo nm way ▷ *Le gusta hacerlo todo a su modo.* She likes to do everything her own way.; **de todos modos** anyway; **de modo que** (1) so ▷ *No has hecho los deberes, de modo que no puedes salir.* You haven't done your homework so you can't go out. (2) so that

▷ *Mueve la tele de modo que todos la podamos ver.* Move the TV so that we can all see it.; **los buenos modos** good manners; **los malos modos** bad manners; **"modo de empleo"** "instructions for use"

moho nm ❶ mould ❷ rust

mojado adj wet

mojar [26] vb to get...wet ▷ *¡No mojes la alfombra!* Don't get the carpet wet!; **Moja el pan en la salsa.** Dip the bread into the sauce.; **mojarse** to get wet

molde nm mould

moler [34] vb to grind; **Estoy molido.** I'm knackered.

molestar [26] vb ❶ to bother ❷ to disturb; **molestarse** to get upset; **molestarse en hacer algo** to bother to do something

molestia nf **tomarse la molestia de hacer algo** to take the trouble to do something; **"perdonen las molestias"** "we apologize for any inconvenience"

molesto adj annoying (noise, cough); **estar molesto** to be annoyed

molinillo nm **un molinillo de café** a coffee grinder

molino nm mill ▷ *un molino de viento* a windmill

momento nm moment ▷ *Espera un momento.* Wait a moment. ▷ *en un momento* in a moment; **en este momento** at the moment; **de un momento a otro** any moment now; **por el momento** for the moment; **Llegó el momento de**

irnos. The time came for us to go.

momia nf mummy

monarca nmf monarch

monarquía nf monarchy

monasterio nm monastery

moneda nf coin ▷ una moneda de 2 euros a 2-euro coin; **la moneda extranjera** foreign currency

monedero nm purse

monitor, -a nm/f instructor
▶ nm monitor (on computer)

monja nf nun

monje nm monk

mono adj pretty ▷ ¡Qué piso tan mono! What a pretty flat!; ¡Qué niña tan mona! What a sweet little girl!
▶ nm ❶ monkey ❷ overalls ❸ dungarees

monopatín (pl monopatines) nm skateboard

monótono adj monotonous

monstruo nm monster

montaña nf ❶ mountain; **la montaña rusa** the roller coaster

montañoso adj mountainous

montar [26] vb ❶ to assemble (machinery, furniture) ❷ to set up (business); **montar una tienda** to put up a tent; **montar a caballo** to ride a horse; **montar en bici** to ride a bike; **montarse** to get on

monte nm mountain

montón (pl montones) nm pile; **un montón de ...** loads of ... ▷ un montón de gente loads of people

monumento nm monument

moño nm bun ▷ Mi abuela siempre lleva moño. My grandmother always wears her hair in a bun.

moqueta nf carpet

mora nf ❶ blackberry ❷ mulberry

morado adj purple ▷ un vestido morado a purple dress

moral adj moral
▶ nf ❶ morale; **levantar la moral a alguien** to cheer somebody up; **estar bajo de moral** to be down ❷ morals ▷ No tienen moral. They have no morals.

moraleja nf moral

morcilla nf black pudding

morder [34] vb to bite; **morderse las uñas** to bite one's nails

mordisco nm bite ▷ Dame un mordisco de tu bocadillo. Let me have a bite of your sandwich.; **dar un mordisco** to bite ▷ Me dio un mordisco. He bit me.

moreno adj ❶ dark; **Es moreno.** (1) He has dark hair. (2) He is dark-skinned.; **ponerse moreno** to get brown ❷ brown (bread, sugar)

morir [33] vb to die; **morirse de hambre** to starve; **morirse de vergüenza** to die of shame; **Me muero de ganas de ir a nadar.** I'm dying to go for a swim.

mortal adj ❶ fatal (accident, injury) ❷ deadly (disease, poison) ❸ mortal (enemy, danger)

mosca nf fly; **por si las moscas** just in case

mosquito nm mosquito

mostaza nf mustard

mostrador nm counter

mostrar [12] vb to show;

mostrarse amable to be kind

mote nm nickname

motivo nm ❶ reason ▷ por motivos personales for personal reasons; **sin motivo** for no reason ❷ motive
▷ ¿Cuál fue el motivo del crimen? What was the motive for the crime?

moto nf motorbike

motocicleta nf motorbike

motor nm motor

motorista nmf motorcyclist

mover [34] vb to move; **moverse** to move

móvil adj mobile
▶ nm ❶ mobile (phone) ❷ motive (for murder)

movimiento nm movement

moza nf girl

mozo nm ❶ youth ❷ waiter; **un mozo de estación** a porter

MP3 nm MP3 ▷ un reproductor de MP3 an MP3 player

muchacha nf ❶ girl ❷ maid

muchacho nm boy

muchedumbre nf crowd

mucho adj ❶ a lot of ▷ Había mucha gente. There were a lot of people. ❷ much (pl many) ▷ No tenemos mucho tiempo. We haven't got much time. ▷ Muchas personas creen que … Many people think that …; **no hace mucho tiempo** not long ago; **Hace mucho calor.** It's very hot.; **Tengo mucho frío.** I'm very cold.
▶ pron ❶ a lot ▷ Tengo mucho que hacer. I've got a lot to do. ▷ ¿Cuántos había? - Muchos. How many were

there? - A lot. ❷ much (pl many)
▷ No tengo mucho que hacer. I haven't got much to do. ▷ ¿Hay manzanas? - Sí pero no muchas. Are there any apples? - Yes, but not many.; **¿Vinieron muchos?** Did many people come?
▶ adv ❶ very much ▷ No me gusta mucho la carne. I don't like meat very much.; **Me gusta mucho el jazz.** I really like jazz. ❷ a lot; **mucho más** a lot more; **mucho antes** long before; **No tardes mucho.** Don't be long.; **Como mucho leo un libro al mes.** At most I read one book a month.; **Fue, con mucho, el mejor.** He was by far the best.; **Por mucho que lo quieras no debes mimarlo.** No matter how much you love him, you shouldn't spoil him.

mudanza nf move

mudarse [26] vb to move; **mudarse de casa** to move house

mudo adj dumb; **quedarse mudo de asombro** to be dumbfounded

mueble nm un mueble a piece of furniture; **los muebles** furniture; **seis muebles** six pieces of furniture

muela nf tooth; **una muela del juicio** a wisdom tooth

muelle nm ❶ spring (in mattress)
❷ quay

muelo vb see **moler**

muerdo vb see **morder**

muero vb see **morir**

muerte nf death ▷ Lo condenaron a muerte. He was sentenced to death.; **Nos dio un susto de muerte.** He nearly frightened us to death.; **un hotel de mala muerte** a grotty hotel

muerto, -a nm/f **un muerto** a dead man; **una muerta** a dead woman; **los muertos** the dead; **Hubo tres muertos.** Three people were killed.; **hacer el muerto** to float

▶ **dead**; **Está muerto de cansancio.** He's dead tired.

▶ vb see **morir**

muestra nf ❶ sample ❷ sign **dar muestras de** to show signs of ❸ token ▷ *Me lo regaló como muestra de afecto.* She gave it to me as a token of affection.

muestro vb see **mostrar**

muevo vb see **mover**

mujer nf ❶ woman ❷ wife

muleta nf crutch

● In bullfighting, the **muleta** is
● a special stick with a red cloth
● attached to it that the matador
● uses.

multa nf fine ▷ *una multa de 50 euros* a 50-euro fine; **poner una multa a alguien** to fine somebody

múltiple adj **múltiples** many ▷ *un sistema con múltiples inconvenientes* a system with many drawbacks

multiplicar [49] vb to multiply; **la tabla de multiplicar** the multiplication tables

multitud nf crowd; **multitud de** lots of

mundial adj ❶ world (*war, history*) ❷ worldwide (*problem,*

recognition)

▶ nm world championship

mundo nm world; **todo el mundo** everybody; **No la cambiaría por nada del mundo.** I wouldn't change it for anything in the world.

municipal adj ❶ council (*office, employee*) ❷ local (*tax*) ❸ public (*baths*)

municipio nm ❶ municipality ❷ town council

muñeca nf ❶ wrist ❷ doll

muñeco nm doll; **un muñeco de peluche** a soft toy

muralla nf city wall

murciélago nm bat

murmullo nm murmur

muro nm wall

músculo nm muscle

museo nm museum; **un mueso de arte** an art gallery

música nf music; **la música pop** pop music; see also **músico**

músico, -a nm/f musician

muslo nm thigh

musulmán, -ana (mpl **musulmanes**) nm/f, adj Muslim

mutuo adj mutual ▷ *de mutuo acuerdo* by mutual agreement

muy adv very; **Eso es muy español.** That's typically Spanish.; **No me gusta por muy guapa que sea.** No matter how pretty she is, I don't like her.; **Muy señor mío ...** Dear Sir ...

n

nabo nm turnip

nacer vb to be born ▷ Nació en 1994. He was born in 1994.

nacimiento nm ❶ birth ❷ crib

nación (pl naciones) nf nation; **las Naciones Unidas** the United Nations

nacional adj ❶ national ❷ home; **vuelos nacionales** domestic flights

nacionalidad nf nationality

nacionalismo nm nationalism

nacionalista adj, nmf nationalist

nada pron ❶ nothing ▷ ¿Qué has comprado? - Nada. What have you bought? - Nothing. ▷ No dijo nada. He said nothing. ❷ anything ▷ No quiero nada. I don't want anything.; **No dijo nada más.** He didn't say anything else.; **Quiero uno nada más.** I only want one, that's all.; **Encendió la tele nada más llegar.** He turned on the TV as soon as he came in.; **¡Gracias! - De nada.** Thanks! - Don't mention it.; **Se lo advertí, pero como si nada.** I warned him but he paid no attention.; **No sabe nada de español.** He knows no Spanish at all.; **No me dio nada de nada.** He gave me absolutely nothing.
   ▶ adv at all ▷ Esto no me gusta nada. I don't like this at all.

nadar [26] vb to swim

nadie pron ❶ nobody ▷ Nadie habló. Nobody spoke. ▷ No había nadie. There was nobody there. ❷ anybody ▷ No quiere ver a nadie. He doesn't want to see anybody.

nafta nf (in River Plate) petrol

naipe nm playing card

nalgas nfpl buttocks

nana nf lullaby

naranja nf orange (fruit)
   ▶ nm orange (colour)
   ▶ adj orange

   When **naranja** is used as an adjective, it never changes its ending.

   ▷ un anorak naranja an orange anorak

naranjo nm orange tree

narcotráfico nm drug trafficking

nariz (pl narices) nf nose; **No metas las narices en mis asuntos.** Don't poke your nose into my business.; **estar hasta las narices de algo** to be totally fed up with something

narración (*pl* **narraciones**) *nf* story

narrar [26] *vb* to tell

narrativa *nf* fiction

nata *nf* cream; **la nata líquida** single cream; **la nata montada** whipped cream

natación *nf* swimming

natal *adj* home ▷ **su pueblo natal** his home town

natillas *nfpl* custard

nato *adj* **un actor nato** a born actor

natural *adj* natural ▷ **Comes mucho y es natural que estés gordo.** You eat a lot, so it's only natural you're fat.; **Es natural de Alicante.** He's from Alicante.

naturaleza *nf* nature; **Es despistado por naturaleza.** He's naturally absent-minded.

naufragio *nm* shipwreck

náuseas *nfpl* **tener náuseas** to feel sick

náutico *adj* **club náutico** yacht club

navaja *nf* clasp knife; **una navaja de afeitar** a razor

Navarra *nf* Navarre

nave *nf* ship; **una nave espacial** a spaceship

navegador *nm* browser; **un navegador de Web** a web browser

navegar [38] *vb* to sail; **navegar por Internet** to surf the Net

Navidad *nf* Christmas; **¡Feliz Navidad!** Happy Christmas!

neblina *nf* mist

necesario *adj* necessary ▷ **No**

estudié más de lo necesario. I didn't study any more than necessary.; **No es necesario que vengas.** You don't have to come.

necesidad *nf* ❶ need ▷ **No hay necesidad de hacerlo.** There is no need to do it. ❷ necessity; **Hizo sus necesidades.** He did his business.

necesitar [26] *vb* to need ▷ **Necesito cien euros.** I need a hundred euros.; **"Se necesita camarero"** "Waiter wanted"

negar [35] *vb* ❶ to deny; **negar con la cabeza** to shake one's head ❷ to refuse; **Se negó a pagar la multa.** He refused to pay the fine.

negativo *adj* negative
▶ *nm* negative

negociación (*pl* **negociaciones**) *nf* negotiation

negociar [26] *vb* to negotiate; **negociar en or con** to deal in; **Su empresa negocia con armas.** His company deals in arms.

negocio *nm* business ▷ **Hemos montado un negocio de videojuegos.** We set up a video games business.; **el mundo de los negocios** the business world

negro, -a *adj* black
▶ *nm* black (colour)
▶ *nm/f* **un negro** a black man; **una negra** a black woman

nervio *nm* nerve; **Me pone de los nervios.** He gets on my nerves.

nerviosismo *nm* **Me entra nerviosismo cuando la veo.** I get nervous when I see her.

nervioso adj nervous ▷ Me pongo muy nervioso en los exámenes. I get very nervous during exams.; **¡Me pone nervioso!** He gets on my nerves!

neumático nm tyre

neutral adj neutral

nevada nf snowfall

nevar [40] vb to snow

nevera nf refrigerator

ni conj ❶ or ▷ No bebe ni fuma. He doesn't drink or smoke. ❷ neither ▷ Ella no fue, ni yo tampoco. She didn't go and neither did I.; **ni ... ni** neither ... nor ▷ No vinieron ni Carlos ni Sofía. Neither Carlos nor Sofía came.; **No me gustan ni el bacalao ni el hígado.** I don't like either cod or liver.; **No compré ni uno ni otro.** I didn't buy either of them.; **Ni siquiera me saludó.** He didn't even say hello.

Nicaragua nf Nicaragua

nicaragüense nmf, adj Nicaraguan

nido nm nest

niebla nf fog; **Hay niebla.** It's foggy.

niego vb see **negar**

nieta nf granddaughter

nieto nm grandson; **los nietos** grandchildren

nieva vb see **nevar**

nieve nf snow

NIF abbr = **número de identificación fiscal**
  • This is an ID number used for tax purposes in Spain.

ningún pron = **ninguno**

ninguno, -a
  │ **ninguno** is shortened to **ningún** before masculine singular nouns.

adj, pron ❶ no ▷ No tengo ningún interés en ir. I have no interest in going. ❷ any ▷ No vimos ninguna serpiente en el río. We didn't see any snakes in the river. ❸ none ▷ ¿Cuál eliges? - Ninguno. Which do you want? - None of them. ▷ No me queda ninguno. I have none left. ▷ Ninguno de nosotros va a ir a la fiesta. None of us are going to the party.; **No lo encuentro por ningún sitio.** I can't find it anywhere.; **ninguno de los dos** (1) neither of them ▷ A ninguna de los dos les gusta el café. Neither of them likes coffee. (2) either of them ▷ No me gusta ninguno de los dos. I don't like either of them.

niña nf girl

niñera nf nanny

niñez nf childhood He's still very young.

niño nm boy; **de niño** as a child; **los niños** the children

nitrógeno nm nitrogen

nivel nm ❶ level ▷ el nivel del agua the water level ❷ standard; **el nivel de vida** the standard of living

no adv ❶ no ▷ ¿Quieres venir? - No. Do you want to come? - No.; **¿Puedo salir esta noche? - ¡Que no!** Can I go out tonight? - I said no! ❷ not ▷ no mucho not much;

No me gusta. I don't like it.; **Esto es tuyo, ¿no?** This is yours, isn't it?; **Fueron al cine, ¿no?** They went to the cinema, didn't they?; **los fumadores** non-smokers

noble *adj* noble

noche *nf* night; **¡Buenas noches!** (1) Good evening! (2) Good night!; **esta noche** tonight; **hoy por la noche** tonight; **por la noche** at night ▷ *Estudia por la noche.* He studies at night. ▷ *el sábado por la noche* on Saturday night; **Era de noche cuando llegamos a casa.** It was night time when we got back home.; **No me gusta conducir de noche.** I don't like driving at night.

Nochebuena *nf* Christmas Eve
- In Spanish-speaking
- countries, the main Christmas
- celebrations are on Christmas
- Eve. This is the night when
- people have their Christmas
- dinner and go to the Misa de
- Gallo (Midnight Mass).

Nochevieja *nf* New Year's Eve
- At midnight on New Year's Eve
- in Spain it is traditional to eat
- **las uvas de la suerte** (twelve
- good-luck grapes) to the chimes
- of Madrid's **Puerta del Sol** clock,
- which are broadcast live.

nociones *nfpl* **Tengo nociones de informática.** I know a little about computers.

nocturno *adj* ❶ night ❷ evening

nomás *adv* (in Latin America) just; **así nomás** just like that

nombrar [26] *vb* ❶ to appoint ❷ to mention

nombre *nm* ❶ name; **nombre de pila** first name; **nombre y apellidos** full name ❷ noun

nómina *nf* pay slip; **estar en nómina** to be on the payroll

nordeste *nm* northeast

noreste *nm* northeast

noria *nf* big wheel

norma *nf* rule

normal *adj* ❶ normal ▷ *una persona normal* a normal person ▷ *Es normal que quiera divertirse.* It's only normal that he wants to enjoy himself. ❷ ordinary ▷ *¿Es guapo? - No, normal.* Is he handsome? - No, just ordinary.

normalmente *adv* normally

noroeste *nm* northwest

norte *nm* north

norteamericano, -a *nm/f, adj* American

Noruega *nf* Norway

noruego, -a *nm/f, adj* Norwegian
▶ *nm* Norwegian (language)

nos *pron* ❶ us ▷ *Nos vinieron a ver.* They came to see us. ▷ *Nos dio un consejo.* He gave us some advice.; **Nos lo dio.** He gave it to us.; **Nos tienen que arreglar el ordenador.** They have to fix the computer for us. ❷ ourselves ▷ *Tenemos que defendernos.* We must defend ourselves.; **Nos levantamos a las ocho.** We got up at eight o'clock. ❸ each other ▷ *No nos hablamos desde hace tiempo.* We haven't spoken to each other for a long time.

> Note how **nos** and the definite article is translated by **our** with parts of the body, clothes and belongings.

▷ *Nos dolían los pies.* Our feet were hurting. ▷ *Nos pusimos los abrigos.* We put our coats on.

nosotros, -as pron ❶ we
▷ *Nosotros no somos italianos.* We're not Italian. ❷ us ▷ *¿Quién es? - Somos nosotros.* Who is it? - It's us. ▷ *Tu hermano vino con nosotros.* Your brother came with us. ▷ *Llegaron antes que nosotros.* They arrived before us.; **nosotros mismos** ourselves

nota nf ❶ mark ▷ *Saca muy malas notas.* He gets very bad marks. ❷ note ▷ *Tomó muchas notas en la conferencia.* He took a lot of notes during the lecture.

notar [26] vb ❶ to notice ❷ to feel; **Se nota que has estudiado mucho este trimestre.** You can tell that you've studied a lot this term.

notario, -a nm/f notary

noticia nf news ▷ *Tengo una buena noticia que darte.* I've got some good news for you. ▷ *Vi las noticias de las nueve.* I watched the nine o'clock news.; **Fue una noticia excelente para la economía.** It was an excellent piece of news for the economy.; **No tengo noticias de Juan.** I haven't heard from Juan.

▌ Be careful **noticia** does not mean **notice**.

notificar [49] vb to notify

novato, -a nm/f beginner

novecientos, -as adj, pron nine hundred

novedad nf **Las últimas novedades en moda infantil.** The latest in children's fashions.; **¿Cómo sigue tu hijo? - Sin novedad.** How's your son? - There's no change.

novela nf novel; **una novela policíaca** a detective story

noveno, -a adj, pron ninth; **Vivo en el noveno.** I live on the ninth floor.

noventa adj, pron ninety; **el noventa aniversario** the ninetieth anniversary

novia nf ❶ girlfriend ❷ fiancée ❸ bride

noviazgo nm ❶ relationship ❷ engagement

noviembre nm

> Months start with a small letter in Spanish in November ▷ *en noviembre* in November

novillos nmpl **hacer novillos** to play truant

novio nm ❶ boyfriend ❷ fiancé ❸ bridegroom; **los novios** the bride and groom

nube nf cloud

nublado adj cloudy

nublarse [26] vb to cloud over

nuboso adj cloudy

nuca nf nape

nuclear adj nuclear; **una central nuclear** a nuclear power station

núcleo nm **el núcleo urbano** the

city centre

nudo *nm* knot; **atar con un nudo** to tie in a knot

nuera *nf* daughter-in-law

nuestro, -a *adj, pron* ❶ our ▷ *nuestro perro* our dog ▷ *nuestras bicicletas* our bicycles ❷ ours ▷ *¿De quién es esto? - Es nuestro.* Whose is this? - It's ours. ▷ *Esta casa es la nuestra.* This house is ours.; **un amigo nuestro** a friend of ours

nueve *adj, pron* nine; **Son las nueve.** It's nine o'clock.; **el nueve de marzo** the ninth of March

nuevo *adj* new ▷ *Necesito un ordenador nuevo.* I need a new computer.; **Tuve que leer el libro de nuevo.** I had to read the book again.

nuez *(pl* nueces*) nf* ❶ walnut; **la nuez moscada** nutmeg ❷ Adam's apple

número *nm* ❶ number; **Calle Aribau, sin número.** Aribau street, no number.; **número de teléfono** telephone number ❷ size ❸ issue; **montar un número** to make a scene

nunca *adv* ❶ never; **No le veré nunca más.** I'll never see him again. ❷ ever ▷ *Casi nunca me escribe.* He hardly ever writes to me.

nutria *nf* otter

nylon *nm* nylon

ñoño *adj* soppy

ñu *nm* gnu

O

o conj or ▷ ¿Quieres té o café? Would you like tea or coffee?; **o ... o ...** either ... or ... ▷ O ha salido o no coge el teléfono. Either he's out or he's not answering the phone.; **O te callas o no sigo hablando.** If you're not quiet I won't go on.

obedecer [13] vb to obey; **obedecer a alguien** to obey someone

obediente adj obedient

obeso adj obese

obispo nm bishop

objeción (pl objeciones) nf objection

objetivo nm objective; **Nuestro principal objetivo es ganar las elecciones.** Our main aim is to win the elections.

objeto nm object; ¿Cuál es el objeto de su visita? What's the reason for your visit?; **los objetos de valor** valuables

obligación (pl obligaciones) nf obligation

obligado adj **verse obligado a hacer algo** to be forced to do something ▷ Se vieron obligados a vender su casa. They were forced to sell their house.; **No estás obligado a venir si no quieres.** You don't have to come if you don't want to.

obligar [38] vb ① to force ▷ Nadie te obliga a aceptar este empleo. Nobody's forcing you to accept this job. ② to make ▷ No puedes obligarme a ir. You can't make me go.

obligatorio adj compulsory

obra nf ① work; **una obra de arte** a work of art; **la obra completa de Neruda** the complete works of Neruda; **una obra de teatro** a play; **una obra maestra** a masterpiece ② building site; **"obras"** "roadworks"

obrero, -a nm/f worker

obsequio nm gift ▷ como obsequio as a gift

observación (pl observaciones) nf ① observation ② comment

observador, a adj observant

observar [26] vb ① to observe ② to remark

obsesión (pl obsesiones) nf obsession

obsesionar [26] vb **Es un tema que le obsesiona.** He's obsessed by the subject.

obstáculo nm obstacle ▷ *Nos puso muchos obstáculos.* He put many obstacles in our way.

obstante adv no obstante nevertheless

obstinado adj obstinate

obstinarse [26] vb to insist ▷ *¿Por qué te obstinas en hacerlo?* Why do you insist on doing it?

obtener [54] vb to obtain

obvio adj obvious

oca nf goose

ocasión (pl ocasiones) nf
① opportunity ② occasion
▷ *en varias ocasiones* on several occasions; **un libro de ocasión** a secondhand book

ocasionar [26] vb to cause

occidental adj western; **los países occidentales** the West

occidente nm **el Occidente** the West

océano nm ocean ▷ *el océano Atlántico* the Atlantic Ocean

ochenta adj, pron eighty ▷ *Tiene ochenta años.* He's eighty.; **el ochenta aniversario** the eightieth anniversary

ocho adj, pron eight; **Son las ocho.** It's eight o'clock.; **el ocho de agosto** the eighth of August

ochocientos, -as adj, pron eight hundred

ocio nm **en mis ratos de ocio** in my spare time

octavo, -a adj, pron eighth; **Vivo en el octavo.** I live on the eighth floor.

octubre nm

▌ Months start with a small letter in Spanish.

October ▷ *en octubre* in October

oculista nmf eye specialist ▷ *Es oculista.* He's an eye specialist.

ocultar [26] vb to conceal; **No nos ocultes la verdad.** Don't try to hide the truth from us.; **ocultarse** to hide

ocupación (pl ocupaciones) nf
① activity ② occupation

ocupado adj ① busy ▷ *Estoy muy ocupado.* I'm very busy. ② engaged ▷ *Si la línea está ocupada vuelva a llamar.* If the line's engaged please call back later.; **"ocupado"** "engaged"; **¿Está ocupado este asiento?** Is this seat taken?

ocupar [26] vb ① to occupy
② to take up ▷ *Ocupa casi todo mi tiempo.* It takes up almost all my time.; **ocuparse de algo** to look after something; **Yo me ocuparé de decírselo.** I'll tell him.

ocurrencia nf **Juan tuvo la ocurrencia de decírselo a la cara.** Juan had the bright idea to tell her to her face.; **¡Qué ocurrencia!** Him and his crazy ideas!

ocurrir [59] vb to happen; **¿Qué te ocurre?** What's the matter?; **Se nos ocurrió una idea brillante.** We had a brilliant idea.

odiar [26] vb to hate

odio nm hate

oeste nm, adj west ▷ *en la costa oeste* on the west coast; **Viajábamos hacia el oeste.**

a b c d e f g h i j k l m n o p q r s t u v w x y z

We were travelling west.; **una película del oeste** a western (film)

ofender [9] vb to offend; **ofenderse** to take offence

ofensa nf insult

oferta nf offer; **una oferta especial** a special offer; **estar de oferta** to be on special offer; **"ofertas de trabajo"** "situations vacant"

oficial adj official

▶ nmf officer ▷ **Es oficial de marina.** He's an officer in the navy.

oficina nf office; **la oficina de turismo** the tourist office; **la oficina de empleo** the job centre; **la oficina de correos** the post office; **la oficina de objetos perdidos** the lost property office

oficio nm trade ▷ **Es carpintero de oficio.** He's a carpenter by trade.

ofrecer [13] vb to offer; **ofrecerse para hacer algo** to offer to do something; **¿Qué se le ofrece?** What can I get you?

ofrecimiento nm offer

oído nm ❶ hearing ❷ ear; **tener buen oído** to have a good ear

oír [36] vb ❶ to hear ❷ to listen to; **oír la radio** to listen to the radio; **¡Oye!** Hey!; **¡Oiga, por favor!** Excuse me!

ojalá excl ❶ I hope ▷ **¡Ojalá Toni venga hoy!** I hope Toni comes today! ❷ if only ▷ **¡Ojalá pudiera!** If only I could!

ojeras nfpl **tener ojeras** to have bags under one's eyes

ojo nm eye; **ir con ojo** to keep one's eyes open for trouble; **costar un**

ojo de la cara to cost an arm and a leg; **¡Ojo! Es muy mentiroso.** Be careful! He's an awful liar.

ola nf wave

oler [37] vb to smell; **Huele a tabaco.** It smells of cigarette smoke.; **oler bien** to smell nice; **oler mal** to smell awful

olfato nm sense of smell

Olimpiadas nfpl Olympics

olímpico adj Olympic; **los Juegos Olímpicos** the Olympic Games

oliva nf olive; **el aceite de oliva** olive oil

olivo nm olive tree

olla nf pot; **una olla a presión** a pressure cooker

olor nm smell ▷ **un olor a tabaco** a smell of cigarette smoke; **¡Qué mal olor!** What a horrible smell!

olvidar [26] vb ❶ to forget; **olvidarse de hacer algo** to forget to do something; **Se me olvidó por completo.** I completely forgot. ❷ to leave ▷ **Olvidé las llaves encima de la mesa.** I left the keys on top of the table.

olvido nm **Ha sido un olvido imperdonable.** It was an unforgivable oversight.

ombligo nm navel

omitir [59] vb to leave out

once adj, pron eleven ▷ **Tengo once años.** I'm eleven.; **Son las once.** It's eleven o'clock.; **el once de agosto** the eleventh of August

onda nf wave; **onda corta** short wave

ondear [26] vb to fly

ondulado adj wavy

ONU nf (= Organización de las Naciones Unidas) UN (= United Nations)

opaco adj ❶ opaque ❷ dull (not shiny)

opción (pl opciones) nf option ▷ No tienes otra opción. You have no option.

ópera nf opera

operación (pl operaciones) nf operation

operar [26] vb to operate on; Me van a operar del corazón. I'm going to have a heart operation.; **operarse** to have an operation

opinar [26] vb to think

opinión (pl opiniones) nf opinion; en mi opinión in my opinion

oponerse [42] vb to oppose; No me opongo. I don't object.

oportunidad nf chance ▷ No tuvo la oportunidad de hacerlo. He didn't have a chance to do it.; **dar otra oportunidad a alguien** to give someone another chance

oportuno adj en el momento oportuno at the right time

oposición (pl oposiciones) nf opposition; **las oposiciones** public examinations

- oposiciones are exams held
- periodically for posts in the
- public sector, state education
- and the judiciary. Such posts
- are permanent, so the number
- of candidates is high and the
- exams very hard.

optar [26] vb optar por hacer algo

to choose to do something

optativo adj optional ▷ las asignaturas optativas optional subjects

óptica nf optician's

optimismo nm optimism

optimista nmf optimist
  ▸ adj optimistic

óptimo adj optimum

opuesto adj ❶ conflicting ❷ opposite

opuse vb see oponer

oración (pl oraciones) nf ❶ prayer ❷ sentence (phrase)

orador, a nm/f speaker

oral adj oral; por vía oral orally; un examen oral an oral exam

orden (pl órdenes) nm order; por orden alfabético in alphabetical order; **La casa está en orden.** The house is tidy.
  ▸ nf order; ¡Deja de darme órdenes! Stop bossing me about!

ordenado adj tidy

ordenador nm computer; un ordenador portátil a laptop

ordenar [26] vb ❶ to tidy up ❷ to order ▷ El policía nos ordenó que saliéramos del edificio. The policeman ordered us to get out of the building.

ordeñar [26] vb to milk

ordinario adj ❶ common ❷ ordinary; de ordinario usually

oreja nf ear

orgánico adj organic

organismo nm organization

organización (pl organizaciones) nf organization

organizar [14] vb to organize;
organizarse to organize oneself

órgano nm organ

orgullo nm pride

orgulloso adj proud

orientación (pl orientaciones) nf
tener sentido de la orientación
to have a good sense of direction;
la orientación profesional
careers advice

oriente nm **el Oriente** the East

origen (pl orígenes) nm origin

original adj original

originalidad nf originality

orilla nf ① shore ② bank; **a orillas
de** (1) on the shores of (2) on the
banks of; **un paseo a la orilla del
mar** a walk along the seashore

orina nf urine

orinar [26] vb to urinate

oro nm gold ▷ un collar de oro a gold
necklace

● **oros** or "golden coins" are also
one of the suits in the Spanish
card deck.

orquesta nf orchestra; **una
orquesta de jazz** a jazz band

ortodoxo adj orthodox

ortografía nf spelling

oruga nf caterpillar

os pron ① you ▷ No os oigo. I can't
hear you. ▷ Os he comprado un
libro a cada uno. I've bought each
of you a book.; **Os lo doy.** I'll give
it to you.; **¿Os han arreglado
ya el ordenador?** Have they
fixed the computer for you yet?
② yourselves ▷ ¿Os habéis hecho
daño? Did you hurt yourselves?; **Os**

**tenéis que levantar antes de las
ocho.** You have to get up before
eight. ③ each other ▷ Quiero que
os pidáis perdón. I want you to say
sorry to each other.

> Note how **os** and the definite
> article is translated by **your**
> with parts of the body, clothes
> and belongings.
>
> ▷ Lavaos las manos. Wash your
> hands. ▷ No hace falta que os quitéis
> el abrigo. You don't need to take
> your coats off.

oscilar [26] vb to fluctuate

oscurecer [13] vb to get dark

oscuridad nf darkness; **Estaban
hablando en la oscuridad.** They
were talking in the dark.

oscuro adj dark ▷ una habitación
muy oscura a very dark room ▷ azul
oscuro dark blue; **a oscuras** in
darkness

oso, -a nm/f bear; **un oso de
peluche** a teddy bear

ostión (pl ostiones) nm (in Mexico)
oyster

ostra nf oyster; **¡Ostras!** Good
grief!

OTAN nf (= Organización del Tratado
del Atlántico Norte) NATO (= North
Atlantic Treaty Organization)

otoño nm autumn ▷ en otoño in
autumn

otro adj, pron ① another ▷ otro
coche another car; **¿Has perdido
el lápiz? - No importa, tengo
otro.** Have you lost your pencil? - It
doesn't matter, I've got another
one.; **¿Hay alguna otra manera**

de hacerlo? Is there any other way of doing it?; **No quiero éste, quiero el otro.** I don't want this one, I want the other one.; **Quiero otra cosa.** I want something else.; **otra vez** again; **Que lo haga otro.** Let someone else do it.; **Están enamorados el uno del otro.** They're in love with each other.

❷ other ▷ **Tengo otros planes.** I have other plans.; **otros tres libros** another three books

ovalado *adj* oval

oveja *nf* sheep

ovillo *nm* ball ▷ **un ovillo de lana** a ball of wool

OVNI *nm* (= objeto volador no identificado) UFO (= unidentified flying object)

oxidado *adj* rusty

oxidarse [26] *vb* to rust

oxígeno *nm* oxygen

oyendo *vb see* oír

oyente *nmf* ❶ listener ❷ unregistered student

paciencia *nf* patience; **¡Ten paciencia!** Be patient!

paciente *adj, nmf* patient

Pacífico *nm* the Pacific

pacífico *adj* peaceful

pacifista *adj, nmf* pacifist; **el movimiento pacifista** the peace movement

pacto *nm* agreement ▷ **hacer un pacto** to make an agreement

padecer [13] *vb* ❶ to suffer from; **Padece del corazón.** He has heart trouble. ❷ to suffer

padrastro *nm* stepfather

padre *nm* father; **Es padre de familia.** He's a family man.; **mis padres** my parents; **rezar el Padre Nuestro** to say the Lord's Prayer

padrino *nm* godfather; **mis**

padrinos my godparents
- At a wedding, the **padrino** is the person who escorts the bride down the aisle and gives her away, usually her father.

paella nf paella

paga nf ❶ pocket money ❷ pay
- In Spain, most people receive two extra payments (**pagas extras**) a year, each equivalent to a month's salary.

pagar [38] vb ❶ to pay ▷ Se puede pagar con tarjeta de crédito. You can pay by credit card. ❸ to pay for

página nf page; **una página web** a Web page

pago nm payment

país (pl **países**) nm country; **el País Vasco** the Basque Country; **los Países Bajos** the Netherlands

paisaje nm ❶ landscape ❷ scenery

paja nf ❶ straw ▷ un sombrero de paja a straw hat ❷ padding ▷ El resto del texto es sólo paja. The rest of the text is just padding.

pajarita nf bow tie

pájaro nm bird

pajita nf drinking straw

pala nf ❶ spade ❷ shovel ❸ bat (for table tennis)

palabra nf word ▷ Cumplió su palabra. He was true to his word. ▷ sin decir palabra without a word; **No me dirige la palabra.** He doesn't speak to me.

palabrota nf swearword; **soltar palabrotas** to swear

palacio nm palace

paladar nm palate

palanca nf lever; **la palanca de cambio** gear lever

palangana nf washbasin

palco nm box

Palestina nf Palestine

palestino, -a nm/f, adj Palestinian

paleta nf ❶ trowel ❷ palette (painter's)

pálido adj pale ▷ Se puso pálida. She turned pale.

palillo nm ❶ toothpick ❷ chopstick

paliza nf beating ▷ Si mi padre se entera me va a dar una paliza. If my father finds out he'll give me a beating.; **Sus clases son una paliza.** His classes are a real pain.

palma nf palm; **dar palmas** to clap

palmera nf palm tree

palo nm ❶ stick ❷ club (in golf) ❸ suit (in cards); **una cuchara de palo** a wooden spoon

paloma nf ❶ pigeon ▷ una paloma mensajera a carrier pigeon ❷ dove ▷ la paloma de la paz the dove of peace

palomitas nfpl **las palomitas de maíz** popcorn

palpar [26] vb to feel

palpitación (pl **palpitaciones**) nf palpitation

palpitar [26] vb ❶ to pound ▷ El corazón me palpitaba de miedo. My heart was pounding with fear. ❷ to beat ▷ El corazón del enfermo dejó de palpitar. The patient's heart stopped beating.

palta nf (in Chile, River Plate) avocado

pan nm ❶ bread ▷ pan con mantequilla bread and butter ▷ pan integral wholemeal bread ▷ pan de molde sliced bread ▷ una barra de pan a loaf of bread; **pan rallado** breadcrumbs; **pan tostado** toast ❷ loaf ▷ Compré dos panes. I bought two loaves.

pana nf corduroy

panadería nf bakery

panadero, -a nm/f baker ▷ Es panadero. He's a baker.

Panamá nm Panama

panameño, -a nm/f, adj Panamanian

pancarta nf banner

pancito nm (in Latin America) bread roll

panda nm panda

pandereta nf tambourine

pandilla nf gang

panfleto nm pamphlet

pánico nm panic; **Me entró pánico.** I panicked.

pantaletas nfpl (in Mexico) knickers

pantalla nf ❶ screen ❷ lampshade

pantalones nmpl trousers; **unos pantalones** a pair of trousers; **pantalones cortos** shorts; **pantalones vaqueros** jeans

pantano nm reservoir

pantera nf panther

pantimedias nfpl (in Mexico) tights

pantis nmpl tights

pantorrilla nf calf

pants nmpl (in Mexico) tracksuit

pañal nm nappy

paño nm cloth; **un paño de cocina** a dishcloth

pañuelo nm ❶ handkerchief ❷ scarf ❸ headscarf

papa nm pope; **el Papa** the Pope ▶ nf (in Latin America) potato; **pescado frito con papas fritas** fish and chips; **un paquete de papas fritas** a packet of crisps

papá (pl papás) nm dad; **mis papás** my mum and dad; **Papá Noel** Father Christmas

papalote nm (in Mexico) kite

papel nm ❶ paper ▷ una bolsa de papel a paper bag ❷ piece of paper; **papel de aluminio** tinfoil; **papel higiénico** toilet paper; **papel pintado** wallpaper ❸ role ▷ la actriz que tiene el papel principal the actress who has the leading role; **Jugó un papel muy importante en las negociaciones.** He played a very important part in the negotiations.; **¿Qué papeles te piden para sacar el pasaporte?** What documents do you need to get a passport?

papeleo nm paperwork

papelera nf ❶ wastepaper bin ❷ litter bin

papelería nf stationer's

papeleta nf ❶ results slip (with exam results) ❷ ballot paper ❸ raffle ticket

paperas nfpl mumps

papilla nf baby food

paquete nm ❶ packet (of biscuits, cigarettes) ❸ parcel ▷ Me mandaron un paquete por correo. I got a parcel in the post.

Paquistán nm Pakistan

paquistaní (pl paquistaníes) nmf, adj Pakistani

par (f par) adj **número par** even number
　▶ nm ❶ couple ▷ un par de horas al día a couple of hours a day ❷ pair ▷ un par de calcetines a pair of socks; **Abrió la ventana de par en par.** He opened the window wide.

para prep ❶ for ▷ Es para ti. It's for you. ▷ Tengo muchos deberes para mañana. I have a lot of homework to do for tomorrow. ▷ el autobús para Marbella the bus for Marbella; **¿Para qué lo quieres?** What do you want it for?; **¿Para qué sirve?** What's it for?; **para siempre** forever; **Para entonces ya era tarde.** It was already too late by then. ❷ to ▷ Estoy ahorrando para comprarme una moto. I'm saving up to buy a motorbike. ▷ Son cinco para las ocho. (in Latin America) It's five to eight.; **Entré despacio para no despertarla.** I went in slowly so as not to wake her.; **para que te acuerdes de mí** so that you remember me

parabólica nf satellite dish

parabrisas (pl parabrisas) nm windscreen

paracaídas (pl paracaídas) nm parachute

paracaidista nmf ❶ paratrooper ❷ parachutist

parachoques (pl parachoques) nm bumper

parada nf stop; **una parada de autobús** a bus stop; **una parada de taxis** a taxi rank

paradero nm (in Latin America) bus stop

parado adj unemployed ▷ Está parada. She's unemployed.

parador nm
　◦ The **paradores** are a group
　◦ of luxury Spanish hotels
　◦ occupying castles, monasteries
　◦ and other historical buildings
　◦ and sited in scenic areas.

paraguas (pl paraguas) nm umbrella

Paraguay nm Paraguay

paraguayo, -a nm/f, adj Paraguayan

paraíso nm paradise

paralelo adj, nm parallel

parálisis (pl parálisis) nf paralysis

paralítico adj **Está paralítico.** He's paralysed.

parapente nm ❶ paragliding ❷ paraglider

parar [26] vb to stop; **Nos equivocamos de tren y fuimos a parar a Manchester.** We got on the wrong train and ended up in Manchester; **pararse** (1) to stop (2) (in Latin America) to stand up; **hablar sin parar** to talk non-stop

pararrayos (pl pararrayos) nm lightning conductor

parcela nf plot of land

parche nm patch

parchís nm

- **parchís** is a Spanish version of **ludo**.

parcial adj ❶ partial; **a tiempo parcial** part time ❷ biased
▶ nm mid-term exam

parecer [13] vb ❶ to seem ▷ *Parece muy simpática*. She seems very nice.; **Parece mentira que ya haya pasado tanto tiempo.** I can't believe it has been so long. ❷ to look ▷ *Parece más joven.* He looks younger.; **Parece una modelo.** She looks like a model.; **Parece que va a llover.** It looks as if it's going to rain.; **¿Qué te pareció la película?** What did you think of the film?; **Me parece que sí.** I think so.; **Me parece que no.** I don't think so.; **si te parece bien** if that's all right with you; **parecerse** to look alike; **parecerse a** to look like

parecido adj similar ▷ *Tu blusa es parecida a la mía.* Your blouse is similar to mine.; **o algo parecido** or something like that

pared nf wall

pareja nf ❶ couple ▷ *Había varias parejas bailando.* There were several couples dancing. ❷ pair ▷ *En este juego hay que formar parejas.* For this game you have to get into pairs. ❸ partner ▷ *Vino con su pareja.* He came with his partner.

parejo adj (in Latin America) even

paréntesis (pl paréntesis) nm bracket ▷ *entre paréntesis* in brackets

pariente nmf relative ▷ *Es pariente mío.* He's a relative of mine.

> Be careful! **pariente** does not mean **parent**.

París nm Paris

parisiense nmf, adj Parisian

parisino, -a nm/f, adj Parisian

parking (pl parkings) nm car park

parlamento nm parliament

parlanchín, -ina (mpl parlanchines) adj chatty

parlante nm (in Latin America) loudspeaker

paro nm ❶ unemployment; **Estoy en paro.** I'm on the dole.; **cobrar el paro** to get the dole ❷ strike ▷ *un paro de tres días* a three-day strike

parpadear [26] vb to blink

párpado nm eyelid

parque nm park; **un parque de atracciones** an amusement park; **un parque infantil** a children's playground; **un parque temático** a theme park; **un parque zoológico** a zoo

parquímetro nm parking meter

parra nf vine

párrafo nm paragraph

parrilla nf grill; **carne a la parrilla** grilled meat

parrillada nf grill

párroco nm parish priest

parroquia nf parish

parte nf ❶ part ▷ *¿De qué parte de Inglaterra eres?* What part of England are you from? ❷ share ▷ *mi parte de la herencia* my share of the inheritance; **Tengo que**

a b c d e f g h i j k l m n o p q r s t u v w x y z

haberlo dejado en alguna parte.
I must have left it somewhere.;
por todas partes everywhere;
en parte partly ▷ *Se debe en parte
a su falta de experiencia.* It's partly
due to his lack of experience.; **la
mayor parte de los españoles**
most Spanish people; **la parte
delantera** the front; **la parte de
atrás** the back; **la parte de arriba**
the top; **la parte de abajo** the
bottom; **por una parte ..., por
otra ...** on the one hand ..., on the
other hand ...; **Llamo de parte
de Juan.** I'm calling on behalf of
Juan.; **¿De parte de quién?** Who's
calling please?; **Estoy de tu parte.**
I'm on your side.

participar [**26**] *vb* to take part

participio *nm* participle

particular *adj* private ▷ **clases
particulares** private classes;
**El vestido no tiene nada de
particular.** The dress is nothing
special.; **en particular** in
particular

partida *nf* ❶ game ▷ *echar una
partida de cartas* to have a game of
cards ❷ certificate ▷ *partida de
nacimiento* birth certificate

partidario, -a *nm/f* supporter
  ▶ *adj* **ser partidario de algo** to be
in favour of something

partido *nm* ❶ party (political)
❷ match ❸ (in Latin America)
game ▷ *un partido de ajedrez* a game
of chess

partir [**59**] *vb* ❶ to cut (cake,
melon) ❷ to crack (nut) ❸ to

break off (branch, piece of chocolate)
❹ to leave ▷ *La expedición partirá
mañana de París.* The expedition
is to leave from Paris tomorrow.;
a partir de enero from January;
partirse to break; **partirse de risa**
to split one's sides laughing

partitura *nf* score

parto *nm* birth; **estar de parto** to
be in labour

pasa *nf* raisin

pasado *adj* ❶ last ▷ *el verano
pasado* last summer ❷ after
▷ *Pasado el semáforo verás un cine.*
After the traffic lights you'll see
a cinema. ▷ *Volvió pasadas las tres
de la mañana.* He returned after
three in the morning.; **pasado
mañana** the day after tomorrow;
un sombrero pasado de moda an
old-fashioned hat
  ▶ *nm* past ▷ *en el pasado* in the past

pasador *nm* ❶ hair slide ❷ tiepin

pasaje *nm* ❶ ticket ❷ passage

pasajero, -a *nm/f* passenger
  ▶ *adj* ❶ temporary (pain, upset)
❷ passing (fashion, phase)

pasamanos (*pl* pasamanos) *nm*
banister

pasaporte *nm* passport

pasar [**26**] *vb* ❶ to pass; **Cuando
termines pásasela a Isabel.**
When you've finished pass it on
to Isabel.; **La foto fue pasando de
mano en mano.** The photo was
passed around.; **Un momento, te
paso con Pedro.** Just a moment,
I'll put you on to Pedro. ❷ to go
past ▷ *Pasaron varios coches.* A

number of cars went past.; **¡Pase, por favor!** Please come in.; **El tiempo pasa deprisa.** Time goes so quickly.; **Pasaron cinco años.** Five years went by.; **Ya ha pasado una hora.** It's been an hour already. ❹ to spend (time) ▷ **Me pasé el fin de semana estudiando.** I spent the weekend studying. ❺ to happen ▷ **pase lo que pase** whatever happens; **¿Qué pasa? (1)** What's the matter? **(2)** What's happening?; **¿Qué le pasa a Juan?** What's the matter with Juan?; **pasarlo bien** to have a good time; **pasarlo mal** to have a bad time; **Hemos pasado mucho frío.** We were very cold.; **Están pasando hambre.** They are starving.; **¡Paso de todo!** I couldn't care less!; **pasar por (1)** to go through ▷ **No pasamos por la ciudad.** We don't go through the city. **(2)** to go past; **Podrían perfectamente pasar por gemelos.** They could easily pass for twins.; **No puedo pasar sin teléfono.** I can't get by without a telephone.; **pasarse de moda** to go out of fashion

pasatiempo nm hobby

Pascua nf Easter; **¡Felices Pascuas!** Happy Christmas!

pase nm pass ▷ **un pase gratis** a free pass; **un pase de modelos** a fashion show

pasear[26] vb to walk; **ir a pasear** to go for a walk

paseo nm walk ▷ **Salimos a dar un paseo.** We went out for a walk.;

ir de paseo to go for a walk; **el paseo marítimo** the promenade; **un paseo en barco** a boat trip; **un paseo en bicicleta** a bike ride

pasillo nm ❶ corridor ❷ aisle (in cinema, plane)

pasión (pl **pasiones**) nf passion

pasivo adj passive

pasmado adj amazed

paso nm ❶ step ▷ **Dio un paso hacia atrás.** He took a step backwards. ▷ **paso a paso** step by step; **He oído pasos.** I heard footsteps.; **Vive a un paso de aquí.** He lives very near here. ❷ way ▷ **Han cerrado el paso.** They've blocked the way.; **"Ceda el paso"** "Give way"; **"Prohibido el paso"** "No entry"; **El banco me pilla de paso.** The bank is on my way.; **Están de paso por Barcelona.** They're just passing through Barcelona.; **un paso de peatones** a pedestrian crossing; **un paso de cebra** a zebra crossing; **un paso a nivel** a level crossing

pasta nf ❶ pasta ❷ dosh; **pastas de té** biscuits; **pasta de dientes** toothpaste

pastar[26] vb to graze

pastel nm cake

pastelería nf patisserie

pastilla nf ❶ pill; **pastillas para la tos** cough sweets ❷ bar (of soap) ❸ piece (of chocolate); **pastillas de caldo** stock cubes

pasto nm (in Latin America) grass

pastor nm shepherd; **un pastor alemán** an Alsatian; **un perro**

a
b
c
d
e
f
g
h
i
j
k
l
m
n
o
p
q
r
s
t
u
v
w
x
y
z

pastor a sheepdog

pastora nf shepherdess

pata nf leg; ¡He vuelto a meter la pata! I've gone and put my foot in it again!; **Me parece que he metido la pata en el examen de física.** I think I messed up my physics exam.

patada nf **Me dio una patada.** He kicked me.

Patagonia nf Patagonia

patata nf potato; **un filete con patatas fritas** steak and chips; **una bolsa de patatas fritas** a bag of crisps

paté (pl **patés**) nm pâté

patera nf small boat

paterno adj paternal

patilla nf sideburn

patín (pl **patines**) nm ❶ roller skate ❷ ice-skate ❸ pedal boat

patinaje nm ❶ roller skating ❷ ice skating; **patinaje artístico** figure skating

patinar [26] vb ❶ to roller-skate ❷ to ice-skate ❸ to skid

patinete nm scooter

patio nm ❶ playground ❸ courtyard; **el patio de butacas** the stalls

pato nm duck

patoso adj clumsy

patria nf homeland

patriota adj patriotic

patrocinador, a nm/f sponsor

patrocinar [26] vb to sponsor

patrón (pl **patrones**) nm ❶ patron saint ❷ boss ❸ landlord

patrona nf ❶ patron saint

❷ boss ❸ landlady

patrulla nf patrol ▷ **estar de patrulla** to be on patrol

pausa nf ❶ pause (during speech, reading) ❷ break (in meeting, programme)

pavimento nm ❶ paving ❷ surface

pavo nm turkey; **un pavo real** a peacock

payaso, -a nm/f clown; **Deja de hacer el payaso.** Stop clowning around.

paz (pl **paces**) nf peace; ¡Déjame en paz! Leave me alone!; **Ha hecho las paces con su novio.** She's made it up with her boyfriend.

PC abbr PC

P.D. abbr (= posdata) P.S.

peaje nm toll

peatón (pl **peatones**) nm pedestrian

peca nf freckle

pecado nm sin

pecar [49] vb to sin

pecho nm ❶ chest ❷ breast; **dar el pecho a un niño** to breastfeed a baby

pechuga nf breast

pedal nm pedal ▷ **el pedal del freno** the brake pedal

pedalear [26] vb to pedal

pedante adj pedantic

pedazo nm piece ▷ **un pedazo de pan** a piece of bread; **hacer pedazos** (1) to smash (2) to tear up

pediatra nmf paediatrician

pedido nm order ▷ **hacer un pedido**

to place an order

pedir [39] vb ❶ to ask for ▷ Le pedí dinero a mi padre. I asked my father for some money. ❷ to ask ▷ ¿Te puedo pedir un favor? Can I ask you a favour?; Pedí que me enviaran la información por correo. I asked them to mail me the information. ❸ to order ▷ Yo pedí paella. I ordered paella.; Le pedí disculpas. I apologized to him.; Tuve que pedir dinero prestado. I had to borrow some money.

pega nf snag; Me pusieron muchas pegas. They made things very difficult for me.

pegadizo adj catchy

pegajoso adj ❶ sticky ❷ (in Latin America) catchy

pegamento nm glue

pegar [38] vb ❶ to hit ▷ Andrés me ha pegado. Andrés hit me. ❷ to stick ▷ Lo puedes pegar con celo. You can stick it on with sticky tape. ❸ to give; Pegó un grito. He shouted.; Le pegaron un tiro. They shot him. ❹ to look right ▷ Esta camisa no pega con el traje. This shirt doesn't look right with the suit.; El niño se pegó a su madre. The boy clung to his mother.

pegatina nf sticker

peinado nm hairstyle

peinar [26] vb ❶ to comb; Péinate antes de salir. Comb your hair before you go out. ❷ to brush; Mañana voy a peinarme. I'm going to have my hair done tomorrow.

peine nm comb

p.ej. abbr (= por ejemplo) e.g.

pelar [26] vb ❶ to peel; Se me está pelando la espalda. My back is peeling.; Hace un frío que pela. It's bitterly cold. ❷ to shell

peldaño nm ❶ step ❷ rung

pelea nf ❶ fight ❷ argument ▷ Tuvo una pelea con su novio. She had an argument with her boyfriend.

peleado adj Están peleados. They've fallen out.

pelear [26] vb ❶ to fight ❷ to argue

pelícano nm pelican

película nf film ▷ A las ocho ponen una película. There's a film on at eight.; una película de dibujos animados a cartoon; una película del oeste a western; una película de suspense a thriller

peligro nm danger ▷ Está fuera de peligro. He's out of danger.

peligroso adj dangerous

pelirrojo adj Es pelirrojo. He has red hair.

pellejo nm skin; arriesgar el pellejo to risk one's neck

pellizcar [49] vb to pinch

pellizco nm pinch ▷ un pellizco de sal a pinch of salt

pelmazo, -a nm/f bore

pelo nm hair ▷ Tiene el pelo rizado. He has curly hair.; No perdí el avión por un pelo. I only just caught the plane.; Se me pusieron los pelos de punta. It made my hair stand on end.; **Me estás tomando el pelo.** You're pulling my leg.

pelota nf ❶ ball ▷ **jugar a la pelota** to play ball ❷ pelota (Basque game)

● pelota is a game in which two
● players use baskets or wooden
● rackets to hit a ball against a
● specially marked wall.

peluca nf wig

peludo adj hairy

peluquería nf hairdresser's

peluquero, -a nm/f hairdresser

pena nf ❶ shame ▷ **Es una pena que no puedas venir.** It's a shame you can't come. ▷ ¡**Qué pena!** What a shame!; **Me dio tanta pena el pobre animal.** I felt so sorry for the poor animal.; **Me da pena tener que marcharme.** I'm so sad to have to go away.; **No tengas pena.** (in Latin America) Don't be embarrassed.; **Vale la pena.** It's worth it.; **No vale la pena gastarse tanto dinero.** It's not worth spending so much money.; **la pena de muerte** the death penalty

penalty (pl penaltys) nm penalty

pendiente adj **Tenemos un par de asuntos pendientes.** We have a couple of matters to sort out.; **Tiene una asignatura pendiente.** He has to resit one subject.; **Estaban pendientes de ella.** They were watching her intently.

▶ nm earring

▶ nf slope

pene nm penis

penetrar [26] vb **penetrar en** to find one's way into

penicilina nf penicillin

península nf peninsula; **la Península Ibérica** the Iberian Peninsula

penique nm penny

pensamiento nm ❶ thought ❷ pansy

pensar [40] vb ❶ to think ▷ ¿**Qué piensas de Manolo?** What do you think of Manolo? ▷ ¿**Qué piensas del aborto?** What do you think of abortion? ❷ to think about ▷ **Tengo que pensarlo.** I'll have to think about it.; **Estaba pensando en ir al cine esta tarde.** I was thinking of going to the cinema this evening.; ¡**Ni pensarlo!** No way!; **pensándolo bien ...** on second thoughts ...; **Piénsatelo.** Think it over.

pensativo adj thoughtful

pensión (pl pensiones) nf ❶ pension ❷ guest house; **pensión completa** full board; **media pensión** half board

pensionista nmf pensioner

penúltimo, -a nm/f **Soy el penúltimo.** I'm second to last.

▶ adj **la penúltima estación** the last station but one

peñón (pl peñones) nm **el Peñón de Gibraltar** the Rock of Gibraltar

peón (pl peones) nm ❶ labourer ❷ pawn

peonza nf spinning top

peor (f peor) adj, adv ❶ worse ▷ **Su**

caso es peor que el nuestro. His case is worse than ours. ▷ *Hoy me siento peor.* I feel worse today. ❷ worst ▷ *El peor día de mi vida* the worst day of my life; **el restaurante donde peor se come** the restaurant with the worst food; **y lo peor es que ...** and the worst thing is that ...; **Si no viene, peor para ella.** If she doesn't come, too bad for her.

pepinillo nm gherkin

pepino nm cucumber; **Me importa un pepino lo que piense.** I couldn't care less what he thinks.

pepita nf ❶ pip (in fruit) ❷ nugget (of gold)

pequeño adj small ▷ *Prefiero los coches pequeños.* I prefer small cars. ▷ *Estos zapatos me quedan pequeños.* These shoes are too small for me.; **¿Cuál prefieres? - El pequeño.** Which one do you prefer? - The small one.; **mi hermana pequeña** my younger sister; **La pequeña estudia medicina.** The youngest is studying medicine.; **Tuvimos un pequeño problema.** We had a slight problem.

pequinés nm Pekinese

pera nf pear

percha nf ❶ coat hanger ❷ coat hook

perchero nm ❶ coat rack ❷ coat stand

percibir [59] vb ❶ to notice ❷ to see ❸ to sense

percusión nf percussion

perdedor, a nm/f loser ▷ *Eres mal perdedor.* You're a bad loser.
▶ adj losing ▷ *la pareja perdedora* the losing pair

perder [21] vb ❶ to lose ▷ *He perdido el monedero.* I've lost my purse.; **Se le perdieron las llaves.** He lost his keys. ❷ to miss; **¡No te lo pierdas!** Don't miss it!; **¡Me estás haciendo perder el tiempo!** You're wasting my time!; **Ana es la que saldrá perdiendo.** Ana is the one who will lose out.; **Tenía miedo de perderme.** I was afraid of getting lost.

pérdida nf ❶ loss ❷ leak (of liquid, gas); **Fue una pérdida de tiempo.** It was a waste of time.

perdido adj ❶ lost ▷ *la oficina de objetos perdidos* the lost property office ❷ remote ▷ *un pueblecito perdido en la montaña* a remote little village in the mountains

perdigón (pl perdigones) nm pellet

perdiz (pl perdices) nf partridge

perdón nm **Le pedí perdón.** I apologized to him.; **¡Perdón!** (1) Sorry! (2) Excuse me!

perdonar [26] vb to forgive; **¡Perdona! ¿Tienes hora?** Excuse me, do you have the time?; **¡Perdona! ¿Te he hecho daño?** I'm so sorry. Did I hurt you?

peregrino, -a nm/f pilgrim

perejil nm parsley

pereza nf laziness; **¡Qué pereza tengo!** I feel so lazy!; **Me da pereza levantarme.** I can't be bothered to get up.

perezoso adj lazy

perfeccionar [26] vb to improve

perfectamente adv perfectly

perfecto adj perfect

perfil nm profile

perfume nm perfume

perfumería nf perfume shop

periódico adj periodic
▸ nm newspaper

periodismo nm journalism

periodista nmf journalist

periodo nm period

periquito nm budgerigar

perjudicar [49] vb ❶ to damage
❷ to be harmful to; El cambio ha perjudicado sus estudios. The change has had an adverse effect on his studies.

perjudicial adj damaging; El tabaco es perjudicial para la salud. Smoking damages your health.

perla nf pearl

permanecer [13] vb to remain

permanente adj permanent
▸ nf perm; hacerse la permanente to have a perm

permiso nm ❶ permission; ¡Con permiso! Excuse me. ❷ leave
▷ Mi hermano está de permiso. My brother is on leave. ❸ permit
▷ Necesitas un permiso de trabajo. You need a work permit.; un permiso de conducir a driving licence

permitir [59] vb to allow; No me lo puedo permitir. I can't afford it.; ¿Me permite? May I?

pero conj but

perpendicular adj at right angles

perplejo adj puzzled

perrera nf dog's home

perrito nm un perrito caliente a hot dog

perro nm dog; un perro callejero a stray dog; un perro guardián a guard dog

perseguir [51] vb ❶ to chase ❷ to persecute

persiana nf blind

persiguiendo vb see perseguir

persona nf person ▷ Es una persona encantadora. He's a charming person.; en persona in person; personas people ▷ Había unas diez personas en la sala. There were about ten people in the hall.

personaje nm ❶ character ❷ figure ▷ un personaje público a public figure

personal adj personal
▸ nm staff

personalidad nf personality

personalmente adv personally

perspectiva nf perspective
▷ en perspectiva in perspective; perspectivas prospects ▷ buenas perspectivas económicas good economic prospects

persuadir [59] vb to persuade

pertenecer [13] vb pertenecer a to belong to

pertenencias nfpl belongings

pértiga nf pole; el salto con pértiga the pole vault

Perú nm Peru

peruano, -a nm/f, adj Peruvian

perverso adj wicked

pervertido, -a nm/f pervert

pesa nf weight; **hacer pesas** to do weight training

pesadez nf Es una pesadez tener que madrugar. It's such a pain having to get up early.; **¡Qué pesadez de película!** What a boring film!

pesadilla nf nightmare

pesado, -a adj ❶ heavy ❷ tiring ❸ boring; **¡No seas pesado!** Don't be a pain in the neck!
▸ nm/f **Mi primo es un pesado.** My cousin is a pain in the neck.

pésame nm condolences ▷ Fuimos a darle el pésame. We went to offer our condolences.

pesar [26] vb ❶ to weigh ▷ ¿Cuánto pesas? How much do you weigh? ▷ Tengo que pesarme. I must weigh myself. ❷ to be heavy; **pesar poco** to be very light; **Me pesa haberlo hecho.** I regret having done it.; **a pesar del mal tiempo** in spite of the bad weather; **a pesar de que la quiero** even though I love her

pesca nf fishing ▷ ir de pesca to go fishing

pescadería nf fishmonger's

pescadilla nf whiting

pescado nm fish

pescador nm fisherman

pescar [49] vb ❶ to fish ❷ to catch

pesero nm (in Mexico) minibus

peseta nf peseta

pesimista adj pessimistic; **No seas pesimista.** Don't be a pessimist.
▸ nmf pessimist

pésimo adj terrible ▷ La comida era pésima. The food was terrible.

peso nm ❶ weight ▷ ganar peso to gain weight ▷ Ha perdido mucho peso. He's lost a lot of weight.; **La fruta se vende a peso.** Fruit is sold by weight. ❷ scales ▷ peso

pesquero adj fishing ▷ un pueblecito pesquero a fishing village

pestaña nf eyelash

pestañear [26] vb to blink

peste nf ❶ plague ❷ stink

pesticida nm pesticide

pestillo nm ❶ bolt ❷ latch

pétalo nm petal

petardo nm firecracker

petición (pl peticiones) nf ❶ request ▷ a petición de la pareja at the request of the couple ❷ petition ▷ firmar una petición to sign a petition

petirrojo nm robin

petróleo nm oil

petrolero nm oil tanker

pez (pl peces) nm fish; **un pez de colores** a goldfish

pezuña nf hoof

pianista nmf pianist

piano nm piano; **un piano de cola** a grand piano

piar [22] vb to chirp

pibe, piba nm/f (in River Plate) kid

picada nf (in Latin America); **El avión cayó en picada.** The plane nose-dived.

picado adj ❶ bad (tooth) ❷ choppy (sea); **El avión cayó en**

picado. The plane nose-dived.

picadura nf ❶ bite ❷ sting

picante adj hot (food, sauce)

picaporte nm door handle

picar [49] vb ❶ to bite (insect, snake) ❷ to sting ❸ to chop up ❹ to mince; **La salsa pica bastante**. The sauce is quite hot.; **Saqué algunas cosas para picar.** I put out some nibbles.; **Me pica la espalda.** I've got an itchy back.; **Me pica la garganta.** My throat tickles.

pichi nm pinafore

picnic (pl **picnics**) nm picnic

pico nm ❶ beak ❷ peak (of mountain) ❸ pick (tool); **Eran las tres y pico**. It was just after three.; **doscientos euros y pico** just over two hundred euros; **cuello de pico** V-neck; **la hora pico** (in Latin America) the rush hour

picoso adj (in Mexico) hot

pidiendo vb see **pedir**

pie nm foot ▷ Fuimos a pie. We went on foot. ▷ Al pie de la página hay una explicación. There's an explanation at the foot of the page.; **Estaba de pie junto a mi cama.** He was standing next to my bed.; **ponerse de pie** to stand up; **de pies a cabeza** from head to foot

piedad nf mercy

piedra nf stone; **una piedra preciosa** a precious stone

piel nf ❶ skin ▷ Tengo la piel grasa. I have greasy skin. ❷ fur ▷ un abrigo de pieles a fur coat ❸ leather ▷ un bolso de piel a leather bag ❹ peel

pienso vb see **pensar**

pierdo vb see **perder**

pierna nf leg; **una pierna de cordero** a leg of lamb

pieza nf piece; **una pieza de recambio** a spare part

pijama nm pyjamas

pijo adj posh

pila nf ❶ battery ❷ pile ▷ una pila de revistas a pile of magazines ❸ sink

pilar nm pillar

píldora nf pill

pileta nf (in River Plate) sink

pillar [26] vb ❶ to catch; **Se pilló los dedos en la puerta.** He caught his fingers in the door. ❷ to hit ▷ La pilló una moto. She was hit by a motorbike.; **La estación nos pilla cerca de casa.** The station is pretty close to our house.

pillo adj ❶ crafty ❷ naughty

piloto nmf ❶ pilot ❷ driver; **piloto de carreras** racing driver

pimentón nm paprika

pimienta nf pepper ▷ pimienta negra black pepper

pimiento nm pepper ▷ un pimiento morrón a red pepper

pin (pl **pins**) nm badge

pincel nm paintbrush

pinchadiscos (pl **pinchadiscos**) nmf disk jockey

pinchar [26] vb ❶ to prick ▷ Me pinché con un alfiler. I pricked myself on a pin. ❷ to burst; **Me pincharon en el brazo.** They gave me an injection in the arm.; **Se me pinchó una rueda.** I had a

puncture.; **Los cactus pinchan.**
Cactuses are prickly.

pinchazo nm ❶ puncture ▷ *Tuve un pinchazo en la autopista.* I got a puncture on the motorway. ❷ sharp pain

pincho nm ❶ thorn ❷ snack; **un pincho moruno** a kebab

ping-pong nm table tennis ▷ *jugar al ping-pong* to play table tennis

pingüino nm penguin

pino nm pine tree; **hacer el pino** to do a headstand

pinta nf **tener buena pinta** to look good; **Con esas gafas tienes pinta de maestra.** You look like a teacher with those glasses on.

pintadas nfpl graffiti

pintalabios (pl pintalabios) nm lipstick

pintar [26] vb ❶ to paint ❷ to colour in; **Nunca me pinto.** I never wear makeup.; **pintarse los labios** to put on lipstick; **pintarse las uñas** to paint one's nails

pintor, a nm/f painter

pintoresco adj picturesque

pintura nf ❶ paint ❷ painting ▷ *pintura al óleo* oil painting

pinza nf ❶ clothes peg ❷ hairgrip ❸ pincer; **unas pinzas** a pair of tweezers

piña nf ❶ pine cone ❷ pineapple

piñón (pl piñones) nm pine nut

piojo nm louse

pipa nf ❶ pipe ▷ *Fuma en pipa.* He smokes a pipe. ❷ seed; **comer pipas** to eat sunflower seeds

pipí nm wee ▷ *hacer pipí* to have

a wee

piragua nf canoe

piragüismo nm canoeing

pirámide nf pyramid

pirata adj pirate
▶ nmf pirate; **un pirata informático** a hacker

Pirineos nmpl **los Pirineos** the Pyrenees

piropo nm compliment

pirulí (pl pirulís) nm lollipop

pisada nf ❶ footprint ❷ footstep

pisapapeles (pl pisapapeles) nm paperweight

pisar [26] vb ❶ to walk on ▷ *¿Se puede pisar el suelo de la cocina?* Can I walk on the kitchen floor? ❷ to tread on ▷ *Perdona, te he pisado.* Sorry, I trod on your toe.; **Pisé el acelerador a fondo.** I put my foot down.

piscina nf swimming pool

Piscis nm Pisces (sign); **Soy piscis.** I'm Pisces.

piso nm ❶ flat ❷ floor ▷ *Está en el segundo piso.* It's on the second floor.

pista nf ❶ clue ▷ *¿Te doy una pista?* Shall I give you a clue? ❷ track (of animal) ❸ court; **la pista de aterrizaje** the runway; **la pista de baile** the dance floor; **la pista de carreras** the racetrack; **la pista de esquí** the ski slope; **la pista de patinaje** the ice rink

pistola nf pistol

pitar [26] vb ❶ to blow one's whistle ❷ to hoot; **Salió pitando.** He was off like a shot.

a
b
c
d
e
f
g
h
i
j
k
l
m
n
o
p
q
r
s
t
u
v
w
x
y
z

pitear [26] vb (in Latin America) to whistle

pito nm whistle; **Me importa un pito.** I don't give a hoot.

piyama nm (in Latin America) pyjamas

pizarra nf ❶ blackboard; **una pizarra blanca** a whiteboard; **una pizarra interactiva** an interactive whiteboard ❷ slate

pizca nf pinch

pizza nf pizza

placa nf ❶ plaque ❷ badge ❸ hotplate; **una placa de matrícula** a number plate

placer nm pleasure

plaga nf ❶ pest ❷ plague

plan nm plan ▷ ¿Qué planes tienes para este verano? What are your plans for the summer?; **viajar en plan económico** to travel cheap; **Lo dije en plan de broma.** I said it as a joke.; **el plan de estudios** the syllabus

plancha nf iron; **pescado a la plancha** grilled fish

planchar [26] vb ❶ to iron ❷ to do the ironing

planeador nm glider

planear [26] vb ❶ to plan ❷ to glide

planeta nm planet

planificar [49] vb to plan

plano adj flat
  ▶ nm ❶ street plan ❷ plan; **en primer plano** in close-up

planta nf ❶ plant ❷ floor ▷ la planta baja the ground floor; **la planta del pie** the sole of the foot

plantado adj **dejar a alguien plantado** to stand someone up

plantar [26] vb to plant

plantilla nf ❶ insole ❷ staff

plástico nm plastic

plastilina® nf Plasticine®

plata nf ❶ silver ❷ (in Latin America) money

plataforma nf platform; **una plataforma petrolífera** an oil rig

plátano nm banana

platicar [49] vb ❶ (in Mexico) to talk ❷ to tell

platillo nm **un platillo volante** a flying saucer; **los platillos** the cymbals

platino nm platinum

plato nm ❶ plate ❷ dish; **un plato combinado** a complete main course; **el plato del día** the dish of the day ❸ course ▷ ¿Qué hay de segundo plato? What's for the main course? ❹ saucer

playa nf ❶ beach ❷ seaside

playera nf ❶ canvas shoe ❷ (in Mexico) T-shirt

plaza nf ❶ square ▷ la plaza mayor the main square ❷ market ▷ No había pescado en la plaza. There was no fish at the market. ❸ place ▷ Todavía quedan plazas. There are still some places left.; **una plaza de toros** a bullring

plazo nm ❶ period ▷ en un plazo de diez días within a period of ten days; **El viernes se cumple el plazo.** Friday is the deadline.; **una solución a corto plazo** a short-term solution ❷ instalment

▷ **pagar a plazos** to pay in instalments

plegable adj folding

plegar [35] vb to fold

pleno adj **en pleno verano** in the middle of summer; **a plena luz del día** in broad daylight

pletina nf tape deck

pliegue vb see **plegar**
▶ nm ❶ fold ❷ pleat

plomero, -a nm/f (in Latin America) plumber

plomo nm lead; **gasolina sin plomo** unleaded petrol; **Se han fundido los plomos.** The fuses have blown.

pluma nf ❶ feather ❷ pen; **una pluma atómica** (in Latin America) a ballpoint pen; **una pluma estilográfica** a fountain pen

plural adj, nm plural

población (pl poblaciones) nf
❶ population ❷ town

pobre adj poor ▷ **Somos pobres.** We're poor. ▷ **¡Pobre Pedro!** Poor Pedro!; **los pobres** the poor

pobreza nf poverty

poco adj, adv, pron not much (pl not many) ▷ **Hay poca leche.** There isn't much milk. ▷ **Tiene pocos amigos.** He hasn't got many friends.; **Tenemos muy poco tiempo.** We have very little time.; **Sus libros son poco conocidos aquí.** His books are not very well known here.; **un poco** a bit ▷ **¿Me das un poco?** Can I have a bit?; **Tomé un poco de vino.** I had a little wine.; **unos pocos** a few ▷ **Me llevé unos**

pocos. I took a few with me.; **poco a poco** little by little; **poco después** shortly after; **dentro de poco** in a short time; **hace poco** not long ago; **por poco** nearly ▷ **Por poco me caigo.** I nearly fell.

podar [26] vb to prune

poder [41] vb ❶ can ▷ **¿Puedo usar tu teléfono?** Can I use your phone? ▷ **¡No puede ser!** That can't be true! ▷ **Pudiste haberte hecho daño.** You could have hurt yourself. ▷ **Me lo podías haber dicho!** You could have told me! ▷ **Aquí no se puede fumar.** You can't smoke here. ❷ to be able to ▷ **Creo que mañana no voy a poder ir.** I don't think I'll be able to come tomorrow.; **¿Se puede?** May I?; **Puede que llegue mañana.** He might arrive tomorrow.; **Puede ser.** It's possible.; **No puedo con tanto trabajo.** I can't cope with so much work.
▶ nm power ▷ **estar en el poder** to be in power

poderoso adj powerful

podólogo, -a nm/f chiropodist

podrido adj rotten

podrirse vb = **pudrirse**

poema nm poem

poesía nf ❶ poetry ❷ poem

poeta nmf poet

póker nm poker

polaco, -a nm/f Pole; **los polacos** the Poles
▶ nm Polish (language)
▶ adj Polish

polémica nf controversy

polémico adj controversial

polen nm pollen; **alergia al polen** hay fever

policía nf ❶ police ▷ Llamamos a la policía. We called the police.
❷ policewoman
▸ nm policeman

policíaco adj **una novela policíaca** a detective novel

polideportivo nm sports centre

polilla nf moth

polio nf polio

política nf ❶ politics ❷ policy; see also **político**

político, -a nm/f politician
▸ adj political

pollo nm chicken; **pollo asado** roast chicken

polluelo nm chick

polo nm ❶ ice lolly ❷ polo shirt; **el Polo Norte** the North Pole; **el Polo Sur** the South Pole

Polonia nf Poland

polvo nm dust; **quitar el polvo** to do the dusting; **quitar el polvo a algo** to dust something; **en polvo** powdered ▷ leche en polvo powdered milk; **polvos de talco** talcum powder; **Estoy hecho polvo.** I'm shattered.

pólvora nf gunpowder

pomada nf ointment

pomelo nm grapefruit

pomo nm handle

pompa nf bubble ▷ pompas de jabón soap bubbles

pómulo nm cheekbone

ponchar [26] vb (in Mexico) **Se nos ponchó una llanta.** We had a puncture.

ponche nm punch

poncho nm poncho

pondrá vb see **poner**

poner [42] vb ❶ to put ▷ ¿Dónde pongo mis cosas? Where shall I put my things? ❷ to put on ▷ ¿Pongo música? Shall I put some music on?; **Me puse el abrigo.** I put on my coat.; **No sé que ponerme.** I don't know what to wear.; **Ponlo más alto.** Turn it up.; **¿Ponen alguna película esta noche?** Is there a film on tonight? ❸ to set ▷ Puse el despertador para las siete. I set the alarm for seven o'clock. ▷ poner la mesa to set the table ❹ to put in ▷ Queremos poner calefacción. We want to put in central heating.; **¿Me pone con el Sr. García, por favor?** Could you put me through to Mr. Garcia, please?; **Le pusieron Mónica.** They called her Monica.; **¿Qué te pongo?** What can I get you?; **Cuando se lo dije se puso muy triste.** He was very sad when I told him.; **¡Qué guapa te has puesto!** You look beautiful!; **Se puso a mi lado en clase.** He sat down beside me in class.; **ponerse a hacer algo** to start doing something

poney (pl poneys) nm pony

pongo vb see **poner**

pop (f pop, pl pop) adj pop ▷ música pop pop music

popote nm (in Mexico) straw

popular adj popular

por prep ❶ for ▷ Lo hice por mis padres. I did it for my parents.

▷ *Lo vendió por 100 euros.* He sold it for 100 euros. ▷ *Me castigaron por mentir.* I was punished for lying. ❸ **through** ▷ *La conozco por mi hermano.* I know her through my brother. ▷ *por la ventana* through the window ▷ *Pasamos por Valencia.* We went through Valencia. ❹ **by** ▷ *Fueron apresados por la policía.* They were captured by the police. ▷ *por correo* by post ▷ *Me agarró por el brazo.* He grabbed me by the arm. ❺ **along** ▷ *Paseábamos por la playa.* We were walking along the beach. ❻ **around** ▷ *viajar por el mundo* to travel around the world ▷ *Viven por esta zona.* They live around this area. ❼ **because of** ▷ *Tuvo que suspenderse por el mal tiempo.* It had to be cancelled because of bad weather. ❽ **per** ▷ *100 kilómetros por hora* 100 kilometres per hour ▷ *diez euros por persona* ten euros per person; **por aquí cerca** near here; **por escrito** in writing; **por la mañana** in the morning; **por la noche** at night; **por mí** ... as far as I'm concerned ...; **¿Por qué?** Why?

porcelana *nf* porcelain

porcentaje *nm* percentage

porche *nm* porch

porción (*pl* porciones) *nf* portion

pornografía *nf* pornography

poro *nm* ❶ pore ❷ (*in Mexico*) leek

poroto *nm* (*in Chile, River Plate*) bean

porque *conj* because

porquería *nf* Este CD es una

porquería. This CD's rubbish.

porra *nf* truncheon

porrazo *nm* **Me di un porrazo en la rodilla.** I banged my knee.; **Daba porrazos en la puerta.** He was banging on the door.

portada *nf* ❶ front page ❷ cover

portal *nm* ❶ hallway ❷ portal (*on internet*); **el portal de Belén** the nativity scene

portarse [26] *vb* **portarse bien** to behave well; **portarse mal** to behave badly; **Se portó muy bien conmigo.** He treated me very well.

portátil *adj* portable

portavoz (*pl* portavoces) *nm* spokesman
▶ *nf* spokeswoman

portazo *nm* **Dio un portazo.** He slammed the door.

portera *nf* ❶ caretaker ❷ goalkeeper

portería *nf* goal

portero *nm* ❶ caretaker ❷ goalkeeper; **un portero automático** an entryphone

portorriqueño, -a *nm/f, adj* Puerto Rican

Portugal *nm* Portugal

portugués, -esa (*mpl* portugueses) *nm/f, adj* Portuguese
▶ *nm* Portuguese (*language*)
▷ **¿Hablas portugués?** Do you speak Portuguese?

porvenir *nm* future

posar [26] *vb* to pose; **posarse** to land

posdata *nf* postscript

poseer [31] vb to possess

posguerra nf **durante la posguerra** during the postwar period

posibilidad nf ❶ possibility ▷ Es una posibilidad. It's a possibility. ❷ chance ▷ Tendrás la posibilidad de viajar. You'll have the chance to travel.; **Tiene muchas posibilidades de ganar.** He has a good chance of winning.

posible adj possible ▷ Es posible. It's possible.; **hacer todo lo posible** to do everything possible; **Es posible que ganen.** They might win.

posición (pl posiciones) nf position; **Está en primera posición.** He's in first place.

positivo adj positive

posponer [42] vb to postpone

posta: a posta adv on purpose

postal nf postcard

poste nm ❶ post ❷ pole

póster (pl pósters) nm poster

posterior (f posterior) adj rear ▷ los asientos posteriores the rear seats; **la parte posterior** the rear

postizo adj false
▶ nm hairpiece

postre nm dessert ▷ De postre tomé un helado. I had ice cream for dessert. ▷ ¿Qué hay de postre? What's for dessert?

postura nf position

potable adj **agua potable** drinking water

potaje nm stew

potencia nf power

potencial adj potential

potente adj powerful

potro nm ❶ colt ❷ horse

pozo nm well

práctica nf practice ▷ No tengo mucha práctica. I haven't had much practice.; **en la práctica** in practice

prácticamente adv practically

practicante adj practising
▶ nmf nurse

practicar [49] vb to practise; **No practico ningún deporte.** I don't do any sports.

práctico adj practical

prado nm meadow

precaución (pl precauciones) nf precaution ▷ tomar precauciones to take precautions; **con precaución** with caution

precavido adj **Es muy precavida.** She's always very well-prepared.

precinto nm seal

precio nm price ▷ Han subido los precios. Prices have gone up.; **¿Qué precio tiene?** How much is it?

preciosidad nf **La casa es una preciosidad.** The house is beautiful.

precioso adj beautiful ▷ ¡Es precioso! It's beautiful!

precipicio nm precipice

precipitarse [26] vb to rush ▷ No hay que precipitarse. There's no need to rush into anything.

precisamente adv precisely

precisar [26] vb ¿Puedes precisar un poco más? Can you be a little more specific?; **Precisó que no**

se trataba de un virus. He said specifically that it was not a virus.

preciso adj ❶ precise ▷ en ese preciso momento at that precise moment ❷ accurate ▷ un reloj muy preciso a very accurate watch; **si es preciso** if necessary; **No es preciso que vengas.** There's no need for you to come.

precoz (pl precoces) adj precocious

predecir [16] vb to predict

predicar [49] vb to preach

predicción (pl predicciones) nf prediction

predicho vb see **predecir**

preescolar adj pre-school

prefabricado adj prefabricated

preferencia nf ❶ preference ▷ No tengo ninguna preferencia. I have no preference. ❷ priority ▷ Tienen preferencia los coches que vienen por la derecha. Cars coming from the right have priority.

preferido adj favourite

preferir [52] vb to prefer; **Prefiero ir mañana.** I'd rather go tomorrow.

prefiero vb see **preferir**

prefijo nm code ▷ ¿Cuál es el prefijo de Andorra? What is the code for Andorra?

pregunta nf question ▷ hacer una pregunta to ask a question

preguntar [26] vb to ask; **Me preguntó por ti.** He asked after you.; **preguntarse** to wonder ▷ Me pregunto si estará enterado. I wonder if he's heard yet.

prehistórico adj prehistoric

prejuicio nm prejudice; **Yo no tengo prejuicios.** I'm not prejudiced.

prematuro adj premature

premiar [26] vb ❶ to award a prize to; **el director premiado** the award-winning director ❷ to reward

premio nm ❶ prize ▷ llevarse un premio to get a prize ❷ reward; **el premio gordo** the jackpot

prenda nf garment

prender [9] vb ❶ to catch (person) ❷ to light (match, cigarette) ❸ (in Latin America) to switch on; **prender fuego a algo** to set fire to something

prensa nf press ▷ una conferencia de prensa a press conference

preocupación (pl preocupaciones) nf worry

preocupado adj worried; **estar preocupado por algo** to be worried about something

preocupar [26] vb to worry; **preocuparse por algo** to worry about something; **Si llego un poco tarde se preocupa.** If I arrive a bit late he gets worried.

preparar [26] vb ❶ to prepare ❷ to prepare for ▷ ¿Te has preparado el examen? Have you prepared for the exam? ❸ to cook; **Me estaba preparando para salir.** I was getting ready to go out.

preparativos nmpl preparations

presa nf ❶ dam ❷ prey; see also

preso

prescindir [59] vb **prescindir de** to do without

presencia nf presence ▷ *en presencia de un sacerdote* in the presence of a priest

presenciar [26] vb to witness

presentador, a nm/f ❶ presenter ❷ newsreader

presentar [26] vb ❶ to introduce ❷ to hand in ❸ to present; **presentarse** (1) to turn up (2) to introduce oneself; **presentarse a un examen** to sit an exam

presente adj, nm present ▷ *Juan no estaba presente.* Juan was not present.; **el presente** the present; **los presentes** those present; **¡Presente!** Present!

presentimiento nm premonition

preservativo nm condom

presidente, presidenta nm/f ❶ president ❷ chairperson

presión (pl **presiones**) nf pressure; **la presión sanguínea** blood pressure

presionar [26] vb ❶ to put pressure on ❷ to press

preso, -a nm/f prisoner
▶ adj **Estuvo tres años preso.** He was in prison for three years.; **llevarse a alguien preso** to take someone prisoner

prestado adj **La cinta no es mía, es prestada.** It's not my tape, someone lent it to me.; **Le pedí prestada la bicicleta.** I asked if I could borrow his bicycle.; **Me dejó el coche prestado.** He lent

me his car.

préstamo nm loan; **un préstamo hipotecario** a mortgage

prestar [26] vb to lend ▷ *Un amigo me prestó el traje.* A friend lent me the suit.; **¿Me prestas el boli?** Can I borrow your pen?; **Tienes que prestar atención.** You must pay attention.

prestigio nm prestige

presumido adj vain

presumir [59] vb to show off; **Luis presume de guapo.** Luis thinks he's really handsome.

presupuesto nm ❶ budget ❷ estimate

pretender [9] vb ❶ to intend; **¿Qué pretendes decir con eso?** What do you mean by that? ❷ to expect ▷ *¡No pretenderás que te pague la comida!* You're not expecting me to pay for your meal, are you?

▌ Be careful! **pretender** does not mean **pretend**.

pretexto nm excuse ▷ *Era sólo un pretexto.* It was only an excuse.; **Vino con el pretexto de ver al abuelo.** He came in order to see Granddad, or so he said.

prevención nf prevention

prevenir [57] vb ❶ to prevent ❷ to warn

prever [58] vb ❶ to foresee; **Han previsto nevadas en el norte.** Snow is forecast for the north. ❷ to plan; **Tienen previsto acabar el metro para el 2008.** They plan to finish the metro by the year 2008.

previo adj previous

previsible adj foreseeable

previsto vb see **prever**

▸ adj Tengo previsto volver
mañana. I plan to return
tomorrow.; **El avión tiene
prevista su llegada a las dos.**
The plane is due in at two o'clock.;
Como estaba previsto, ganó él.
As expected, he was the winner.

primario adj la educación
primaria primary education

primavera nf spring ▸ en primavera
in spring

primer adj see **primero**

primero, -a

> primero is shortened to
> **primer** before masculine
> singular nouns.

adj, pron first ▸ el primer día the
first day ▸ Primer plato: sopa. First
course: soup. ▸ Primero vamos a
comer. Let's eat first.; **en primera
fila** in the front row; **En primer
lugar, veamos los datos.** Firstly,
let's look at the facts.; **primer
ministro** prime minister; **Vivo en
el primero.** I live on the first floor.;
Fui la primera en llegar. I was the
first to arrive.; **Lo primero es la
salud.** The most important thing
is your health.; **El examen será a
primeros de mayo.** The exam will
be at the beginning of May.

primitivo adj primitive

primo, -a nm/f cousin; **primo
segundo** second cousin

princesa nf princess

principal adj main; **Lo principal es
estar sano.** The main thing is to
stay healthy.

principalmente adv mainly

príncipe nm prince

principiante nmf beginner

principio nm ❶ beginning; **Al
principio parecía fácil.** It seemed
easy at first.; **a principios de
año** at the beginning of the year
❷ principle; **En principio me
parece una buena idea.** On the
face of it, it's a good idea.

prioridad nf priority

prisa nf rush; **Con las prisas me
olvidé el paraguas.** In the rush I
forgot my umbrella.; **¡Date prisa!**
Hurry up!; **Tengo prisa.** I'm in
a hurry.

prisión (pl prisiones) nf prison

prisionero, -a nm/f prisoner

prismáticos nmpl binoculars

privado adj private ▸ un colegio
privado a private school

privarse [26] vb En vacaciones no
me privo de nada. When I'm on
holiday I really spoil myself.

privilegio nm privilege

pro nm los pros y contras the pros
and cons

probabilidades nfpl Tiene
muchas probabilidades de
ganar. He has a very good chance
of winning.; **No tengo muchas
probabilidades de aprobar.** I don't
have much chance of passing.

probable adj likely ▸ Es muy
probable. It's very likely.; **Es
probable que llegue tarde.** He'll

probably arrive late.

probablemente adv probably

probador nm changing room

probar [12] vb ❶ to prove ▷ La policía no pudo probarlo. The police could not prove it. ❷ to taste ▷ Probé la sopa para ver si le faltaba sal. I tasted the soup to see if it needed more salt. ❸ to try ▷ Pruébalo antes para ver si funciona bien. Try it first and see if it works properly.; **Me probé un vestido.** I tried on a dress.

probeta nf test tube; **un niño probeta** a test-tube baby

problema nm problem; **Este coche nunca me ha dado problemas.** This car has never given me any trouble.; **tener problemas de estómago** to have stomach trouble

procedente adj procedente de from ▷ el tren procedente de Barcelona the train from Barcelona

procesador nm processor; **un procesador de textos** a word processor

procesión (pl procesiones) nf procession

proceso nm process; **el proceso de datos** data processing

proclamar [26] vb to proclaim

procurar [26] vb to try; **Procura terminarlo mañana.** Try to finish it tomorrow.

producción (pl producciones) nf production; **la producción en serie** mass production

producir [10] vb ❶ to produce

❷ to cause; **¿Cómo se produjo el accidente?** How did the accident happen?

producto nm product; **los productos del campo** farm produce

productor, a nm/f producer

profesión (pl profesiones) nf profession

profesional adj, nmf professional

profesor, a nm/f teacher; **mi profesor particular** my private tutor; **un profesor universitario** a university lecturer

> Be careful! **profesor** does not mean **professor**.

profundamente adv deeply

profundidad nf depth; **Tiene dos metros de profundidad.** It's two metres deep.

profundo adj deep; **una piscina poco profunda** a shallow pool

programa nm ❶ programme ▷ un programa de televisión a television programme; **un programa-concurso** a quiz show; **el programa de estudios** the syllabus ❷ program (on computer)

programación nf ❶ programmes ❷ programming

programador, a nm/f programmer

programar [26] vb to program (computer)

progresar [26] vb to progress

progreso nm progress; **Carmen ha hecho muchos progresos este trimestre.** Carmen has made great progress this term.

prohibir [43] vb to ban; **Queda terminantemente prohibido.** It is strictly forbidden.; **"prohibido fumar"** "no smoking"

prolijo adj (in River Plate) neat

prólogo nm prologue

prolongar [38] vb to extend

promedio nm average

promesa nf promise

prometer [9] vb to promise; **¡Te lo prometo!** I promise!

promoción nf promotion; **Está en promoción.** It's on offer.

pronombre nm pronoun

pronosticar [49] vb to forecast

pronóstico nm **el pronóstico del tiempo** the weather forecast

pronto adv ➊ soon; **lo más pronto posible** as soon as possible; **¡Hasta pronto!** See you soon! ➋ early; **De pronto, empezó a nevar.** All of a sudden it began to snow.

pronunciar [26] vb to pronounce

propaganda nf ➊ advertising; **Han hecho mucha propaganda del concierto.** The concert has been well-advertised. ➋ junk mail

propagarse [38] vb to spread

propiedad nf property

propietario, -a nm/f owner

propina nf tip

propio adj ➊ own ▷ **Tengo mi propia habitación.** I have my own room. ➋ himself ▷ **Lo anunció el propio ministro.** It was announced by the minister himself. ➌ typical; **un nombre propio** a proper noun

proponer [42] vb ➊ to suggest; **Me propuso un trato.** He made me a proposition. ➋ to nominate; **Se ha propuesto adelgazar.** He's decided to lose some weight.

proporción (pl proporciones) nf proportion

proporcional adj proportional

proporcionar [26] vb to provide

propósito nm purpose ▷ **¿Cuál es el propósito de su visita?** What's the purpose of your visit?; **Lo hizo a propósito.** He did it on purpose.; **A propósito, ya tengo los billetes.** By the way, I've got the tickets.

propuesta nf proposal

propuesto vb see **proponer**

prórroga nf ➊ extension ➋ extra time

prospecto nm leaflet

prosperar [26] vb to do well

próspero adj **¡Próspero Año Nuevo!** A prosperous New Year!

prostituta nf prostitute

protagonista nmf ➊ main character; **El protagonista es Tom Cruise.** Tom Cruise plays the lead.

protección nf protection

protector, a adj protective ▷ **una funda protectora** a protective cover

proteger [8] vb to protect; **Nos protegimos de la lluvia en la cabaña.** We sheltered from the rain in the hut.

protesta nf protest ▷ **como protesta por los despidos** as a protest against redundancies

protestante *nmf, adj* Protestant

protestar [26] *vb* ① to protest
② to complain

provecho *nm* ¡**Buen provecho!**
Enjoy your meal!; **Sacó mucho
provecho del curso.** He got a lot
out of the course.

proverbio *nm* proverb

provincia *nf* province

provisional *adj* provisional

provisiones *nfpl* provisions

provocar [49] *vb* ① to provoke
② to cause; **El incendio fue
provocado.** The fire was started
deliberately.

provocativo *adj* provocative

próximo *adj* wise ▷ **Lo haremos la
próxima semana.** We'll do it next
week. ▷ **la próxima vez** next time
▷ **la próxima calle a la izquierda** the
next street on the left

proyecto *nm* ① plan ▷ **¿Tienes
algún proyecto para este verano?**
Have you got any plans for the
summer? ② project ▷ **el proyecto
en el que estamos trabajando** the
project we are working on

proyector *nm* projector

prudente *adj* wise ▷ **Lo más
prudente sería esperar.** It would be
wisest to wait.; **Debería ser más
prudente.** He should be more
careful.

prueba *vb see* **probar**
▶ *nf* ① test ▷ **El médico me hizo más
pruebas.** The doctor did some more
tests.; **pruebas nucleares** nuclear
tests ② proof ▷ **Eso es la prueba**

de que lo hizo él. This is the proof
that he did it.; **El fiscal presentó
nuevas pruebas.** The prosecutor
presented new evidence. ③ heat
▷ **la prueba de los cien metros valla**
the hundred metres hurdles heat;
a prueba de balas bullet-proof

pruebo *vb see* **probar**

psicología *nf* psychology

psicológico *adj* psychological

psicólogo, -a *nm/f* psychologist

psiquiatra *nmf* psychiatrist

psiquiátrico *adj* psychiatric

ptas. *abbr* (= pesetas) pesetas

púa *nf* ① plectrum ② tooth (of
comb)

pub (*pl* pubs) *nm* bar

publicar [49] *vb* to publish

publicidad *nf* ① advertising
② publicity

público *adj* public
▶ *nm* ① public ② audience (at
concert, play) ③ spectators (at
match)

pude *vb see* **poder**

pudrirse *vb* to rot

pueblo *nm* ① village ② town
③ people

puedo *vb see* **poder**

puente *nm* bridge; **el puente
aéreo** the shuttle service; **hacer
puente** to make a long weekend
of it

　● When a public holiday falls on
　　a Tuesday or Thursday people
　　often take off Monday or Friday
　　as well to give themselves a
　　long weekend.

puerco *nm* ① pig ② (in Mexico)

pork

puerro nm leek

puerta nf ① door ▷ Llaman a la puerta. There's somebody at the door.; **Susana me acompañó a la puerta.** Susana saw me out. ② gate; **la puerta de embarque** boarding gate

puerto nm port ▷ un puerto pesquero a fishing port; **un puerto deportivo** a marina; **un puerto de montaña** a mountain pass

Puerto Rico nm Puerto Rico

puertorriqueño, -a nm/f, adj Puerto Rican

pues conj ① then ▷ Tengo sueño. - ¡Pues vete a la cama! I'm tired. - Then go to bed! ② well ▷ Pues, como te iba contando … Well, as I was saying … ▷ ¡Pues no lo sabía! Well I didn't know!; **¡Pues claro!** Yes, of course!

puesta nf **la puesta de sol** sunset; **la puesta en libertad de dos presos** the release of two prisoners

puesto vb see **poner**
▶ nm ① place ▷ Acabé la carrera en primer puesto. I finished in first place. ② stall ▷ un puesto de verduras a vegetable stall; **un puesto de trabajo** a job; **un puesto de socorro** a first aid station; **puesto que** since ▷ Puesto que no lo querías, se lo di a Pedro. Since you didn't want it, I gave it to Pedro.

pulga nf flea

pulgada nf inch

pulgar nm thumb

pulir[59] vb to polish

pulmón(pl pulmones) nm lung

pulpería nf (in Latin America) shop

púlpito nm pulpit

pulpo nm octopus

pulsar[26] vb to press

pulsera nf bracelet; **un reloj de pulsera** a wrist watch

pulso nm pulse

pulverizador nm spray

punta nf ① tack ② tip (of finger, tongue) ③ point (of pen, knife); **Sácale punta al lápiz.** Sharpen your pencil.; **Vivo en la otra punta del pueblo.** I live at the other end of the town.; **la hora punta** the rush hour

puntapié(pl puntapiés) nm **Le dio un puntapié a la piedra.** He kicked the stone.

puntería nf **tener buena puntería** to be a good shot

puntiagudo adj pointed

puntilla nf lace edging; **andar de puntillas** to tiptoe; **ponerse de puntillas** to stand on tiptoe

punto nm ① point ▷ desde ese punto de vista from that point of view ② stitch; **Me gusta hacer punto.** I like knitting. ③ dot ④ full stop; **punto y seguido** full stop, new sentence; **punto y aparte** full stop, new paragraph; **punto y coma** semi-colon; **dos puntos** colon; **Estábamos a punto de salir cuando llamaste.** We were about to go out when you phoned.; **Estuve a punto**

a b c d e f g h i j k l m n o p q r s t u v w x y z

de perder el tren. I very nearly missed the train.; **a la una en punto** at one o'clock sharp

puntuación (*pl* **puntuaciones**) *nf* ❶ punctuation ❷ score

puntual *adj* punctual ▷ **Sé puntual.** Be punctual.; **Jamás llega puntual.** He never arrives on time.

puntualidad *nf* punctuality

puntuar *vb* **Este trabajo no puntúa para la nota final.** This essay doesn't count towards the final mark.; **un profesor que puntúa muy bajo** a teacher who gives very low marks

puñado *nm* handful

puñal *nm* dagger

puñalada *nf* **Le dieron una puñalada.** He was stabbed.

puñetazo *nm* punch; **Le pegó un puñetazo.** He punched him.

puño *nm* ❶ fist ❷ cuff

pupitre *nm* desk

puré (*pl* **purés**) *nm* **puré de verduras** puréed vegetables; **puré de patatas** mashed potato

puro *adj* pure ▷ **por pura casualidad** by pure chance; **Es la pura verdad.** That's the absolute truth.
　▶ *nm* cigar

puse *vb see* **poner**

que *conj* ❶ than ▷ **Es más alto que tú.** He's taller than you.; **Yo que tú, iría.** I'd go if I were you. ❷ that ▷ **José sabe que estás aquí.** José knows that you're here.

　■ **que** isn't always translated into English.

　▷ **Dijo que vendría.** He said he'd come.; **¡Que te mejores!** Get well soon!; **¿De verdad que te gusta? — ¡Que sí!** Do you really like it? – Of course I do!; **Dile a Rosa que me llame.** Ask Rosa to call me.

　▶ *pron* ❶ which ▷ **la película que ganó el premio** the film which won the award

　■ **que** isn't always translated into English.

　▷ **el sombrero que te compraste** the hat you bought ▷ **el libro del que** *te hablé* the book I spoke to you about ❷ who ▷ *el hombre que vino ayer* the man who came yesterday

▌*que* isn't always translated into English.

▷ *la chica que conocí* the girl I met

qué *adj, adv, pron* ❶ what ▷ *¿Qué fecha es hoy?* What's today's date? ▷ *No sabe qué es.* He doesn't know what it is. ▷ *No sé qué hacer.* I don't know what to do.; **¿qué?** what? ❷ which ▷ *¿Qué película quieres ver?* Which film do you want to see? **¡Qué asco!** How revolting!; **¡Qué día más bonito!** What a glorious day!; **¿Qué tal?** How are things?; **¿Qué tal está tu madre?** How's your mother?; **No lo he hecho. ¿Y qué?** I haven't done it. So what?

quebrado *nm* fraction

quebrar [40] *vb* to go bankrupt; **quebrarse** (*in Latin America*) to break

quedar [26] *vb* ❶ to be left; **Me quedan quince euros.** I've got fifteen euros left. ❷ to be ▷ *Eso queda muy lejos de aquí.* That's a long way from here. ❸ to arrange to meet ▷ *He quedado con ella en el cine.* I've arranged to meet her at the cinema.; **¿Quedamos en la parada?** Shall we meet at the bus stop? ❹ to suit ▷ *No te queda bien ese vestido.* That dress doesn't suit you.; **quedarse** to stay; **quedarse atrás** to fall behind; **quedarse sordo** to go deaf; **quedarse con algo** to keep something ▷ *Quédate con el cambio.* Keep the change.

quehaceres *nmpl* **los quehaceres de la casa** the household chores

queja *nf* complaint

quejarse [26] *vb* to complain; **quejarse de algo** to complain about something; **quejarse de que ...** to complain that ...

quejido *nm* ❶ moan ❷ whine

quemado *adj* burnt

quemadura *nf* burn; **quemaduras de sol** sunburn

quemar [26] *vb* ❶ to burn ❷ to be burning hot; **quemarse** to burn oneself

quepa *vb see* caber

querer [44] *vb* ❶ to want; **Quiero que vayas.** I want you to go.; **¿Quieres un café?** Would you like some coffee? ❷ to love ▷ *Te quiero.* I love you. ❸ to mean ▷ *Lo hice sin querer.* I didn't mean to do it.; **querer decir** to mean

querido *adj* dear

querré *vb see* querer

queso *nm* cheese

quicio *nm* **sacar a alguien de quicio** to drive somebody up the wall

quiebra *nf* **ir a la quiebra** to go bankrupt

quien *pron* who ▷ *Fue Juan quien nos lo dijo.* It was Juan who told us.

▌**quien** isn't always translated into English.

▷ *Vi al chico con quien sales.* I saw the boy you're going out with.

quién *pron* who ▷ *¿Quién es ésa?* Who's that? ▷ *¿A quién viste?* Who did you see? ▷ *No sé quién es.* I don't

know who he is.; ¿De quién es ...?
Whose is ...? ▷ ¿De quién es este
libro? Whose is this book?; ¿Quién
es? (1) Who's there? (2) Who's
calling?

quiero vb see **querer**

quieto adj still ▷ ¡Estáte quieto!
Keep still!

química nf chemistry; see also
químico

químico, -a nm/f chemist
▶ adj chemical

quince adj, pron fifteen; **el quince
de enero** the fifteenth of January;
quince días a fortnight

quinceañero, -a nm/f teenager

quincena nf fortnight

quincenal adj fortnightly

quiniela nf football pools

quinientos, -as adj, pron five
hundred

quinto, -a adj, pron fifth; **Vivo en
el quinto.** I live on the fifth floor.

quiosco nm ❶ news stand
❷ drinks stand ❸ flower stall
❹ bandstand

quirófano nm operating theatre

quirúrgico adj surgical; **una
intervención quirúrgica** an
operation

quise vb see **querer**

quitaesmalte nm nail polish
remover

quitamanchas (pl
quitamanchas) nm stain
remover

quitanieves (pl **quitanieves**) nf
snowplough

quitar [26] vb ❶ to remove ❷ to

take away; **Me han quitado
la cartera.** I've had my wallet
stolen.; **Esto te quitará el
dolor.** This will relieve the pain.;
quitarse to take off; **¡Quítate de
en medio!** Get out of the way!

quizá adv = **quizás**

quizás adv perhaps

r

rábano nm radish; **¡Me importa un rábano!** I don't give a monkey's!

rabia nf ❶ rage ▷ *Lo hizo por rabia.* He did it out of rage.; **Me da mucha rabia.** It's really annoying. ❷ rabies

rabieta nf tantrum

rabo nm tail

racha nf **una racha de buen tiempo** a spell of good weather; **una racha de viento** a gust of wind; **pasar una mala racha** to go through a bad patch

racial adj racial

racimo nm bunch

ración (pl **raciones**) nf portion

racionar [26] vb to ration

racismo nm racism

racista adj, nmf racist

radar nm radar

radiación nf radiation

radiactividad nf radioactivity

radiactivo adj radioactive

radiador nm radiator

radio nf radio ▷ *Por la mañana escucho la radio.* In the morning I listen to the radio.; **Lo oí por la radio.** I heard it on the radio.
▶ nm ❶ radius ❷ (in Latin America) radio ❸ spoke

radiocasete nm radio cassette player

radiografía nf X-ray; **Tengo que hacerme una radiografía.** I've got to have an X-ray.

raíl nm rail

raíz (pl **raíces**) nf root; **La planta está echando raíces.** The plant's taking root.; **a raíz de** as a result of

raja nf ❶ crack ❷ tear ❸ slice

rajarse [26] vb ❶ to crack ❷ to split

rallar [26] vb to grate

rally (pl **rallys**) nm rally

rama nf branch

ramo nm bunch ▷ *un ramo de claveles* a bunch of carnations

rampa nf ramp

rana nf frog

rancho nm ranch

rancio adj rancid

rango nm rank; **políticos de alto rango** high-ranking politicians

ranura nf slot ▷ *Introduzca la moneda en la ranura.* Put the coin in the slot.

rapar [26] vb ❶ to crop ❷ to shave

rape nm monkfish

rápidamente adv quickly

rapidez nf ❶ speed; **con rapidez** quickly

rápido adj ❶ fast ▷ *un coche muy rápido* a very fast car ❷ quick ▷ *Fue una visita muy rápida.* It was a very quick visit.

▶ adv fast; **Lo hice tan rápido como pude.** I did it as quickly as I could.; **¡Rápido!** Hurry up!

raptar [26] vb to kidnap

rapto nm kidnapping

raqueta nf ❶ racket ❷ bat

raramente adv rarely

raro adj ❶ strange ▷ **¡Qué raro!** How strange! **Sabe un poco raro.** It tastes a bit funny. ❷ rare; **Es raro que haga tan buen tiempo.** It's unusual to have such good weather.; **rara vez** seldom

rascacielos (pl **rascacielos**) nm skyscraper

rascar [49] vb ❶ to scratch ❷ to scrape; **rascarse** to scratch

rasgar [38] vb to rip

rasgo nm feature

rasguño nm scratch

rastrillo nm ❶ rake ❷ (in Mexico) razor

rastro nm ❶ trail ❷ trace ▷ *Desaparecieron sin dejar rastro.* They vanished without trace. ❸ fleamarket

rasurarse [26] vb (in Latin America) to shave

rata nf rat

rato nm while ▷ *después de un rato* after a while; **Estaba aquí hace un rato.** He was here a few minutes

ago.; **al poco rato** shortly after; **pasar el rato** to while away the time; **pasar un buen rato** to have a good time; **Pasamos un mal rato.** We had a dreadful time.; **en mis ratos libres** in my free time

ratón (pl **ratones**) nm mouse

raya nf ❶ line ▷ *trazar una raya* to draw a line; **pasarse de la raya** to overstep the mark ❷ stripe; **un jersey a rayas** a striped jumper ❸ parting ▷ *Me hago la raya en medio.* I have my parting in the middle. ❹ crease (in trousers) ❺ dash (punctuation mark)

rayar [26] vb to scratch

rayo nm ❶ lightning ▷ *Cayó un rayo en la torre de la iglesia.* The church tower was struck by lightning. ❷ ray ▷ *un rayo de luz* a ray of light; **los rayos X** X-rays

raza nf ❶ race ▷ *la raza humana* the human race ❷ breed ▷ *¿De qué raza es tu gato?* What breed's your cat?; **un perro de raza** a pedigree dog

razón (pl **razones**) nf reason ▷ *¿Cuál era la razón de su visita?* What was the reason for his visit?; **tener razón** to be right; **dar la razón a alguien** to agree that somebody is right; **no tener razón** to be wrong

razonable adj reasonable

reacción (pl **reacciones**) nf reaction

reaccionar [26] vb to react

reactor nm ❶ jet plane ❷ jet engine; **un reactor nuclear** a to be wrong nuclear reactor

real *adj* ❶ real; **La película está basada en hechos reales.** The film is based on actual events. ❷ royal

realidad *nf* reality; **en realidad** actually; **Mi sueño se hizo realidad.** My dream came true.; **realidad virtual** virtual reality

realista *adj* realistic

realizar [14] *vb* ❶ to carry out; **Has realizado un buen trabajo.** You've done a good job. ❷ to realize; **realizarse** to come true

realmente *adv* ❶ really ❷ actually

rebaja *nf* ❶ discount ▷ *Me hizo una rebaja por pagar al contado.* He gave me a discount for paying cash. ❷ reduction; **las rebajas** the sales; **Todos los grandes almacenes están de rebajas.** There are sales on in all the department stores.

rebajar [26] *vb* to reduce

rebanada *nf* slice

rebaño *nm* flock ▷ *un rebaño de ovejas* a flock of sheep

rebeca *nf* cardigan

rebelarse [26] *vb* to rebel

rebelde *adj* rebellious ▶ *nmf* rebel

rebelión (*pl* rebeliones) *nf* rebellion

rebobinar [26] *vb* to rewind

rebotar [26] *vb* to bounce; **La pelota rebotó en el poste.** The ball bounced off the post.

rebozado *adj* ❶ breaded ❷ battered

recado *nm* ❶ message ▷ *Dejé recado de que me llamara.* I left a message for him to call me. ❷ errand ▷ *Fui a hacer unos recados.* I went to do some errands.

recaída *nf* relapse

recalcar [49] *vb* to stress

recámara *nf* (in Mexico) bedroom

recambio *nm* ❶ spare ▷ *la rueda de recambio* the spare wheel; **una pieza de recambio** a spare part ❷ refill

recargar [38] *vb* ❶ to recharge ❷ to fill up

recargo *nm* **El taxista me cobró un recargo por el equipaje.** The taxi driver charged me extra for my luggage.

recaudar [26] *vb* to collect

recepción (*pl* recepciones) *nf* reception

recepcionista *nmf* receptionist

receptor *nm* receiver

recesión (*pl* recesiones) *nf* recession

receta *nf* ❶ recipe ❷ prescription ▷ *Los antibióticos sólo se venden con receta.* Antibiotics are only available on prescription.

> Be careful! **receta** does not mean **receipt**.

recetar [26] *vb* to prescribe

rechazar [14] *vb* ❶ to reject ❷ to turn down

rechoncho *adj* stocky

recibidor *nm* entrance hall

recibir [59] *vb* ❶ to receive; **Recibí muchos regalos.** I got a lot of presents. **②** to meet ▷ *Vinieron a recibirnos al aeropuerto.* They came and met us at the airport.; **El director me recibió en su despacho.** The manager saw me in his office.

recibo nm **①** receipt **②** bill

reciclaje nm recycling

reciclar [26] vb to recycle

recién adv just ▷ *El comedor está recién pintado.* The dining room has just been painted.; **Recién se fueron.** (in Latin America) They've just left.; **los recién casados** the newly-weds; **un recién nacido** a newborn baby; **"recién pintado"** "wet paint"

reciente adj recent; **pan reciente** fresh bread

recientemente adv recently

recipiente nm container

recital nm recital

recitar [26] vb to recite

reclamación (pl reclamaciones) nf complaint ▷ *presentar una reclamación* to make a complaint; **el libro de reclamaciones** the complaints book

reclamar [26] vb **①** to complain **②** to demand

reclamo nm (in Latin America) complaint

recluta nmf recruit

recogedor nm dustpan

recoger [8] vb **①** to pick up; **recoger fruta** to pick fruit **②** to collect **③** to clear up; **Recogí los platos y los puse en el fregadero.** I cleared away the plates and put

them in the sink.; **recoger la mesa** to clear the table

recogida nf collection

recomendación (pl recomendaciones) nf **①** recommendation ▷ *por recomendación de* on the recommendation of **②** advice ▷ *Hago régimen por recomendación del médico.* I'm on a diet on my doctor's advice.

recomendar [40] vb to recommend

recompensa nf reward

reconciliarse [26] vb **reconciliarse con alguien** to make it up with somebody

reconocer [13] vb **①** to recognize **②** to admit

reconocimiento nm checkup ▷ *hacerse un reconocimiento médico* to have a checkup

reconquista nf reconquest

reconstruir [11] vb to rebuild

récord (pl récords) nm record

recordar [26] vb **①** to remember ▷ *No recuerdo dónde lo puse.* I can't remember where I put it. **②** to remind ▷ *Recuérdame que hable con Daniel.* Remind me to speak to Daniel. ▷ *Me recuerda a su padre.* He reminds me of his father.

▌ Be careful! **recordar** does not mean **record**.

recorrer [9] vb **①** to travel around **②** to do

recorrido nm ¿Qué recorrido hace este autobús? Which route does this bus take?; **un recorrido**

turístico a tour; **un tren de largo recorrido** an inter-city train

recortar[26] vb to cut out; **recortar gastos** to cut costs

recorte nm **recortes de prensa** press cuttings; **recortes de personal** staff cutbacks

recostarse[12] vb to lie down

recreo nm break ▷ **Tenemos 20 minutos de recreo.** We have a 20-minute break.

recta nf straight line; **la recta final** the home straight

rectangular adj rectangular

rectángulo nm rectangle

recto adj, adv straight ▷ **una línea recta** a straight line; **todo recto** straight on ▷ **Siga todo recto.** Go straight on.

recuadro nm box

recuerdo vb see **recordar**
  ▶ nm ❶ memory ❷ souvenir; **un recuerdo de familia** a family heirloom; **¡Recuerdos a tu madre!** Give my regards to your mother!; **Dale recuerdos de mi parte.** Give him my regards.

recuperación(pl **recuperaciones**) nf ❶ recovery ❷ resit

recuperar[26] vb to get back; **recuperar fuerzas** to get one's strength back; **recuperarse de** (1) to get over (2) to recover from; **recuperar el tiempo perdido** to make up for lost time

recurrir[59] vb recurrir a algo to resort to something; **recurrir a alguien** to turn to somebody

recurso nm **como último recurso** as a last resort; **recursos** resources ▷ **recursos naturales** natural resources

red nf ❶ net ❷ network; **la Red** the Net; **una red de tiendas** a chain of shops

redacción(pl **redacciones**) nf essay; **hacer una redacción sobre algo** to do an essay on something; **el equipo de redacción** the editorial staff

redactar[26] vb to write

redactor, a nm/f editor

redada nf raid

redondo adj round ▷ **una mesa redonda** a round table; **Todo salió redondo.** Everything worked out perfectly.

reducción(pl **reducciones**) nf reduction

reducir[10] vb ❶ to reduce ❷ to cut

reembolsar[26] vb to refund

reembolso nm refund; **enviar algo contra reembolso** to send something cash on delivery

reemplazar[14] vb to replace

referencia nf reference; **con referencia a** with reference to; **hacer referencia a** to refer to; **referencias** references

referéndum(pl **referéndums**) nm referendum

referente adj referente a concerning

referirse[52] vb referirse a to refer to; **¿A qué te refieres?** (1) What exactly do you mean? (2) What are you referring to?

refinería nf refinery

refiriendo vb see **referir**

reflejar [26] vb to reflect

reflejo nm reflection; **reflejos**
(1) reflexes ▷ Estás bien de
reflejos. You have good reflexes.
(2) highlights (in hair)

reflexión (pl **reflexiones**) nf
reflection

reflexionar [26] vb to think;
**Reflexiona bien antes de tomar
una decisión.** Think it over
carefully before taking a decision.

reflexivo adj reflexive

reforma nf ❶ reform
❷ alteration ▷ Estamos haciendo
reformas en el piso. We're having
alterations made to the flat.;
"Cerrado por reformas" "Closed
for refurbishment"

reformar [26] vb ❶ to reform
❷ to do up

refrán (pl **refranes**) nm saying

refrescante adj refreshing

refrescar [49] vb to get cooler;
refrescarse to freshen up

refresco nm soft drink

refrigerador nm fridge

refugiado, -a nm/f refugee

refugiarse [26] vb ❶ to shelter
❷ to take refuge

refugio nm refuge ▷ un refugio de
montaña a mountain refuge; **un
refugio antiaéreo** an air-raid
shelter

regadera nf ❶ watering can
❷ (in Mexico) shower; **estar como
una regadera** to be as mad as

a hatter

regalar [26] vb ❶ to give; **Ayer
fue mi cumpleaños. - ¿Qué te
regalaron?** It was my birthday
yesterday. - What did you get?
❷ to give away

regaliz nm liquorice

regalo nm present ▷ hacer un
regalo a alguien to give somebody
a present; **una tienda de regalos**
a gift shop; **papel de regalo**
wrapping paper; **de regalo** free
▷ un CD de regalo con la compra del
radiocasete a free CD when you buy
the radio cassette

regañadientes: a regañadientes
adv reluctantly

regañar [26] vb to tell off

regar [35] vb to water

regata nf yacht race

regatear [26] vb ❶ to haggle
❷ to dodge past

régimen (pl **regímenes**) nm
❶ diet; **estar a régimen** to be on a
diet; **ponerse a régimen** to go on
a diet ❷ regime

regimiento nm regiment

región (pl **regiones**) nf region

regional adj regional

registrar [26] vb ❶ to search ▷ Me
registraron. They searched me.
❷ to register ❸ to check in; **Me
registré en el hotel.** I checked
into the hotel.

registro nm ❶ search; **realizar un
registro en un lugar** to carry out
a search of a place ❷ register; **el
registro civil** the registry office

regla nf ❶ rule ▷ saltarse las reglas

to break the rules ❷ period
▷ *Estoy con la regla.* I've got my
period. ❸ *ruler* ▷ *Trazó la línea
con una regla.* He drew the line
with a ruler.; **por regla general**
generally; **tener todo en regla** to
have everything in order
reglamento *nm* regulations
regresar [26] *vb* ❶ to go back
❷ to come back; **Regresamos
tarde.** We got back late. ❸ (*in
Latin America*) to give back;
regresarse (1) (*in Latin America*)
to go back (2) (*in Latin America*) to
come back
regreso *nm* return; **a nuestro
regreso** on our return; **de regreso**
on the way back
regulable *adj* adjustable
regular *adj* regular; **La obra
estuvo regular.** The play was
pretty ordinary.
　▶ *adv* **El examen me fue regular.**
My exam didn't go brilliantly.;
¿Cómo te encuentras? - Regular.
How are you? - Not too bad.
rehacer [27] *vb* to redo
rehén (*pl* rehenes) *nmf* hostage
reina *nf* queen
reinado *nm* reign
reino *nm* kingdom
Reino Unido *nm* the United
Kingdom
reír [45] *vb* to laugh; **echarse a
reír** to burst out laughing; **reírse**
to laugh; **reírse de** to laugh at;
Siempre nos reímos con él. We
always have a good laugh with
him.

reivindicación (*pl
reivindicaciones*) *nf* claim
reja *nf* grille; **estar entre rejas** to
be behind bars
relación (*pl* relaciones) *nf* ❶ link
❷ relationship; **con relación a** in
relation to; **relaciones públicas**
public relations
relacionar [26] *vb* to link; **Le
gusta relacionarse con niños
mayores que él.** He likes mixing
with older children.; **No se
relaciona mucho con la gente.**
He doesn't mix much.
relajado *adj* ❶ relaxed ▷ *¿Estás
relajado?* Are you feeling relaxed?
❷ laid-back ▷ *Es un tipo muy
relajado.* He's a very laid-back guy.
relajante *adj* relaxing
relajar [26] *vb* to relax; **¡Relájate!**
Relax!
relámpago *nm* flash of lightning;
No me gustan los relámpagos. I
don't like lightning.
relativamente *adv* relatively
relativo *adj* relative; **en lo relativo
a** concerning
relato *nm* story
relevo *nm* **una carrera de relevos**
a relay race; **tomar el relevo
a alguien** to take over from
somebody
religión (*pl* religiones) *nf* religion
religioso *adj* religious
rellano *nm* landing
rellenar [26] *vb* ❶ to stuff ❷ to
fill in
relleno *adj* stuffed ▷ *aceitunas
rellenas* stuffed olives; **relleno de**

a
b
c
d
e
f
g
h
i
j
k
l
m
n
o
p
q
r
s
t
u
v
w
x
y
z

algo filled with something

reloj nm ❶ clock; **un reloj despertador** an alarm clock; **un reloj de cuco** a cuckoo clock; **contra reloj** against the clock ❷ watch ▷ *Se me ha parado el reloj.* My watch has stopped.; **un reloj digital** a digital watch; **un reloj de sol** a sundial

relojera nf watchmaker

relojería nf watchmaker's

relojero nm watchmaker

relucir vb to shine

remar [26] vb ❶ to paddle ❷ to row

remediar [26] vb to solve; **Me eché a reír, no lo pude remediar.** I began to laugh, I couldn't help it.

remedio nm remedy ▷ *un remedio contra la tos* a cough remedy; **No tuve más remedio que hacerlo.** I had no choice but to do it.

remite nm name and address of sender

remitente nmf sender

remo nm ❶ oar ❷ rowing

remojar [26] vb to soak

remojo nm **poner algo en remojo** to leave something to soak

remolacha nf beetroot

remolcar [49] [26] vb to tow

remolque nm trailer

remordimiento nm remorse

remoto adj remote

remover [34] vb ❶ to stir (coffee, cooking) ❷ to toss (salad) ❸ to turn over (earth)

renacuajo nm tadpole

rencor nm ill-feeling; **guardar**

rencor a alguien to bear a grudge against somebody

rencoroso adj **No soy rencoroso.** I don't bear grudges.

rendido adj worn out ▷ *Estaba rendido de tanto andar.* I was worn out after so much walking.

rendija nf ❶ crack ❷ gap

rendimiento nm performance

rendir [39] vb **Este negocio no rinde.** This business doesn't pay.; **rendirse (1)** to give up **(2)** to surrender

renglón (pl **renglones**) nm line

reno nm reindeer

renovable adj renewable

renovar [12] vb ❶ to renew ❷ to renovate ❸ to change

renta nf ❶ income ❷ rent

rentable adj profitable; **una fábrica poco rentable** an uneconomic factory

rentar [26] vb (in Mexico) to rent

reñido adj hard-fought

reñir [46] vb ❶ to tell somebody off ❷ to quarrel ❸ to fall out

reparación (pl **reparaciones**) nf repair; **"reparaciones en el acto"** "repairs while you wait"

reparar [26] vb to repair

repartir [59] vb ❶ to hand out ❷ to share out ❸ to deliver ❹ to deal

reparto nm ❶ delivery; **reparto a domicilio** home delivery service ❷ cast ▷ *un reparto estelar* a star cast

repasar [26] vb ❶ to check ❷ to revise; **repasar para un examen**

to revise for an exam

repaso nm revision; **Tengo que darles un repaso a los apuntes.** I must revise my notes.

repente adv **de repente** suddenly

repentino adj sudden

repertorio nm repertoire

repetición (pl **repeticiones**) nf repetition

repetidamente adv repeatedly

repetir [39] vb ❶ to repeat ❷ to have a second helping

repetitivo adj repetitive

repisa nf shelf; **la repisa de la chimenea** the mantelpiece

repitiendo vb see **repetir**

repollo nm cabbage

reportaje nm ❶ documentary ❷ article

reposacabezas (pl **reposacabezas**) nm headrest

reposición (pl **reposiciones**) nf ❶ repeat ❷ revival

repostar [26] vb to refuel

repostería nf confectionery

representación (pl **representaciones**) nf performance

representante nmf ❶ representative ❷ agent

representar [26] vb ❶ to represent ❷ to put on ▷ Los niños van a representar una obra de teatro. The children are going to put on a play. ❸ to play ▷ Representa el papel de Don Juan. He's playing the part of Don Juan.

representativo adj representative

reprobar [12] vb (in Latin America) to fail

reprochar [26] vb **Me reprochó que no la hubiera invitado.** He reproached me for not having invited her.

reproducción (pl **reproducciones**) nf reproduction

reproducirse [10] vb to reproduce

reproductor nm **un reproductor de CD** a CD player

reptil nm reptile

república nf republic

República Dominicana nf the Dominican Republic

republicano, -a adj, nm/f republican

repuesto nm spare part; **de repuesto** spare ▷ la rueda de repuesto the spare wheel

repugnante adj revolting

reputación (pl **reputaciones**) nf reputation; **tener buena reputación** to have a good reputation

requesón nm cottage cheese

requisito nm requirement

resaca nf hangover; **tener resaca** to have a hangover

resaltar [26] vb ❶ to stand out ❷ to highlight

resbaladizo adj slippery

resbalar [26] vb ❶ to be slippery ❷ to skid; **resbalarse** to slip

rescatar [26] vb to rescue

rescate nm ❶ rescue ▷ un equipo de rescate a rescue team ❷ ransom; **pedir un rescate por alguien** to hold somebody to ransom

reserva nmf reserve

▶ nf ❶ reservation; **Tengo mis reservas al respecto.** I've got reservations about it. ❷ reserve ▷ una reserva natural a nature reserve

reservado adj reserved

reservar [26] vb to reserve

resfriado adj estar resfriado to have a cold

▶ nm cold; **agarrarse un resfriado** to catch a cold

resfriarse [22] vb to catch a cold

resguardo nm ❶ ticket ❷ receipt

residencia nf residence ▷ un permiso de residencia a residence permit; **una residencia de ancianos** an old people's home; **una residencia de estudiantes** a hall of residence; **una residencia sanitaria** a hospital

residencial adj residential

residuos nmpl waste ▷ residuos radiactivos radioactive waste

resistencia nf resistance; **resistencia física** stamina

resistente adj tough; **resistente al calor** heat-resistant

resistir [59] vb ❶ to resist ❷ to take ❸ to stand; **Se resisten a cooperar.** They are refusing to cooperate.

resolver [34] vb to solve

respaldar [26] vb to back up

respaldo nm back

respectivamente adv respectively

respecto nm con respecto a with regard to

respetable adj respectable

respetar [26] vb ❶ to respect ❷ to obey

respeto nm respect; tener respeto a alguien to respect somebody; **No le faltes al respeto.** Don't be disrespectful to him.

respiración nf breathing; **quedarse sin respiración** to be out of breath; **la respiración boca a boca** the kiss of life; **la respiración artificial** artificial respiration

respirar [26] vb to breathe

responder [9] vb ❶ to answer; **Eso no responde a mi pregunta.** That doesn't answer my question. ❷ to reply ❸ to respond

responsabilidad nf responsibility

responsable adj responsible ▷ Cada cual es responsable de sus acciones. Everybody is responsible for their own actions.

▶ nmf **Tú eres la responsable de lo ocurrido.** You're responsible for what happened.; **Los responsables serán castigados.** Those responsible will be punished.; **Juan es el responsable de la cocina.** Juan is in charge of the kitchen.

respuesta nf answer

resquebrajarse [26] vb to crack

resta nf subtraction

restante adj remaining

restar [26] vb to subtract

restauración (pl **restauraciones**) nf restoration

restaurante nm restaurant

restaurar [26] vb to restore

resto nm rest ▷ Yo haré el resto. I'll do the rest.; **los restos (1)** the leftovers **(2)** the wreckage

restregar [38] vb to rub

restricción (pl **restricciones**) nf restriction

resuelto vb see **resolver**

resuelvo vb see **resolver**

resultado nm ❶ result ❷ score; **dar resultado** to work

resultar [26] vb to turn out; **Me resultó violento decírselo.** I found it embarrassing to tell him.

resumen (pl **resúmenes**) nm summary; **hacer un resumen de algo** to summarize something; **en resumen** in short

resumir [59] vb to summarize; **Dijo, resumiendo, que el viaje había sido un desastre.** He said, in short, that the trip had been a disaster.

retar [26] vb ❶ to challenge ❷ (in Chile, River Plate) to tell off

retirar [26] vb ❶ to take away ❷ to withdraw; **retirarse** to retire

reto nm challenge

retorcer vb to twist; **retorcerse de risa** to double up with laughter

retransmisión (pl **retransmisiones**) nf broadcast

retransmitir [59] vb to broadcast

retrasado adj ❶ behind ▷ Voy retrasado con este trabajo. I'm behind with this work. ❷ slow ▷ Este reloj va retrasado veinte minutos. This clock is twenty minutes slow.; **Tienen un hijo un poco retrasado.** They've got a son with learning difficulties.

retrasar [26] vb ❶ to postpone ❷ to delay ❸ to put back; **retrasarse** to be late; **Tu reloj se retrasa.** Your watch is slow.

retraso nm delay; **Perdonad por el retraso.** Sorry I'm late.; **ir con retraso** to be running late; **llegar con retraso** to be late

retrato nm portrait; **hacer un retrato a alguien** to paint somebody's portrait

retrete nm toilet

retroceder [9] vb to go back

retrovisor nm rear-view mirror

retuerzo vb see **retorcer**

reúma nm rheumatism

reunión (pl **reuniones**) nf ❶ meeting ❷ gathering

reunir [47] vb ❶ to gather together ❷ to satisfy ❸ to raise; **reunirse (1)** to gather **(2)** to get together **(3)** to meet

revelar [26] vb ❶ to develop; **Llevé los carretes a revelar.** I took the films to be developed. ❷ to reveal

reventar [40] vb to burst

revés (pl **reveses**) nm backhand; **al revés (1)** the other way round **(2)** inside out ▷ Te has puesto los calcetines al revés. You've put your socks on inside out. **(3)** back to front (**4**) upside down ▷ *El dibujo está al revés.* The picture's upside down.

reviento vb see **reventar**

revisar [**26**] vb ❶ to check; **Tengo que ir a que me revisen el coche.** I must take my car for a service. ❷ (*in Latin America*) to search

revisión (*pl* revisiones) nf service ▷ *He llevado el coche a revisión.* I've taken the car for a service.; **una revisión médica** a checkup

revisor, a nm/f ticket inspector

revista nf magazine

revoltoso adj naughty

revolución (*pl* revoluciones) nf revolution

revolucionario, -a nm/f revolutionary

revolver [**60**] vb ❶ to mess up; **No revuelvas mis papeles.** Don't muddle my papers up. ❸ to turn upside down ❸ to rummage in

revólver (*pl* revólveres) nm revolver

revuelto vb see **revolver**

▶ adj in a mess; **Las fotos están revueltas.** The photos are muddled up.; **El tiempo está muy revuelto.** The weather's very unsettled.; **Tengo el estómago revuelto.** I've got an upset stomach.

rey (*pl* reyes) nm king; **Los reyes visitaron China.** The King and Queen visited China.; **los Reyes** **Magos** the Three Wise Men ● As part of the Christmas ● festivities, the Spanish ● celebrate **el día de Reyes** ● (Epiphany) on 6th of January, ● when the Three Wise Men bring ● presents to children.

rezar [**14**] vb to pray; **rezar el Padrenuestro** to say the Lord's Prayer

ría nf estuary

riachuelo nm stream

ribera nf bank

rico, -a nm/f **un rico** a rich man; **una rica** a rich woman; **los ricos** the rich

▶ adj ❶ rich ▷ *Son muy ricos.* They're very rich. ❷ delicious ▷ *¡Qué rico!* How delicious!

ridiculizar [**14**] vb to ridicule

ridículo adj ridiculous; **hacer el ridículo** to make a fool of oneself; **poner a alguien en ridículo** to make a fool of somebody

riel nm rail

riendas nfpl reins

riendo vb see **reír**

riesgo nm risk; **correr riesgos** to take risks; **Corres el riesgo de que te despidan.** You run the risk of being dismissed.; **un seguro a todo riesgo** a fully comprehensive insurance policy

rifa nf raffle

rifle nm rifle

rígido adj ❶ stiff ❷ strict

riguroso adj ❶ strict ❷ severe

rima nf rhyme

rímel nm mascara

rincón (pl **rincones**) nm corner

rinoceronte nm rhinoceros

riña nf ❶ row ❷ brawl

riñendo vb see **reñir**

riñón (pl **riñones**) nm kidney; **Me duelen los riñones.** I've got a pain in my lower back.

riñonera nf bum bag

río vb see **reír**
▶ nm river ▷ el río Ebro the River Ebro

riqueza nf ❶ wealth ❷ richness

risa nf laugh ▷ una risa contagiosa an infectious laugh; **Me da risa.** It makes me laugh.; **¡Qué risa!** What a laugh!; **partirse de risa** to split one's sides laughing

ritmo nm ❶ rhythm; **Daban palmas al ritmo de la música.** They were clapping in time to the music. ❷ pace

ritual nm ritual

rival adj, nmf rival

rivalidad nf rivalry

rizado adj curly

rizar [14] vb ❶ to curl ❷ to perm

rizo nm curl

robar [26] vb ❶ to steal ▷ Me han robado la cartera. My wallet has been stolen. ❷ to rob ❸ to break into

roble nm oak

robo nm ❶ theft ❷ robbery ❸ burglary; **¡Estos precios son un robo!** This is daylight robbery!

robot (pl **robots**) nm robot; **el robot de cocina** the food processor

robusto adj strong

roca nf rock

rociar [22] vb to spray

rocío nm dew

rodaja nf slice ▷ cortar algo en rodajas to cut something into slices

rodaje nm shooting

rodar [12] vb ❶ to roll ❷ to shoot

rodear [26] vb to surround; **rodeado de** surrounded by

rodilla nf knee; **ponerse de rodillas** to kneel down

rodillo nm ❶ rolling pin ❷ roller

rogar vb ❶ to beg ❷ to pray; **"Se ruega no fumar"** "Please do not smoke"

rojo adj, nm red ▷ Va vestida de rojo. She's wearing red.; **ponerse rojo** to go red

rollo nm roll ▷ un rollo de papel higiénico a roll of toilet paper; **La conferencia fue un rollo.** The lecture was really boring.; **¡Qué rollo de película!** What a boring film.; **Nos soltó el rollo de siempre.** He gave us the same old lecture.

Roma nf Rome

romano, -a nm/f, adj Roman

romántico, -a adj, nm/f romantic

rombo nm rhombus

rompecabezas (pl **rompecabezas**) nm ❶ jigsaw ❷ puzzle

romper [1] vb ❶ to break ❷ to tear up; **Se ha roto una sábana.** A sheet has got torn.; **Se me han roto los pantalones.** I've torn my trousers.; **romper con alguien** to

a
b
c
d
e
f
g
h
i
j
k
l
m
n
o
p
q
r
s
t
u
v
w
x
y
z

finish with somebody

ron nm rum

roncar [49] vb to snore

ronco adj hoarse; **quedarse ronco** to go hoarse

ronda nf round ▷ Esta ronda la pago yo. I'll get this round.; **hacer la ronda** to be on patrol

ronquido nm snore

ronronear [26] vb to purr

ropa nf clothes ▷ Voy a cambiarme de ropa. I'm going to change my clothes.; **la ropa interior** underwear; **ropa de deporte** sportswear; **la ropa de cama** bed linen; **la ropa sucia** the dirty washing

rosa adj pink

> When **rosa** is used as an adjective, it never changes its ending.

▷ Llevaba unos calcetines rosa. He was wearing pink socks.
▶ nm pink (colour) ▷ Va vestida de rosa. She's wearing pink.
▶ nf rose

rosado adj rosé (wine)

rosal nm rosebush

rostro nm face

roto vb see **romper**
▶ adj ❶ broken ❷ torn ❸ worn out
▶ nm hole

rotonda nf roundabout

rotulador nm ❶ felt-tip pen ❷ highlighter pen

rótulo nm sign

rozar [14] vb to rub against

rubio adj ❶ fair ▷ Luis tiene el pelo

rubio. Luis has got fair hair.; **Es rubia con los ojos azules.** She has got fair hair and blue eyes. ❷ blond

ruborizarse [14] vb to blush

rudimentario adj basic

rueda nf ❶ wheel ▷ la rueda delantera the front wheel ▷ la rueda trasera the back wheel; **Se te ha pinchado la rueda.** You've got a puncture.; **una rueda de prensa** a press conference

ruedo vb see **rodar**

ruego vb see **rogar**

rugby nm rugby ▷ jugar al rugby to play rugby

rugir [17] vb to roar

ruido nm noise ▷ No hagáis tanto ruido. Don't make so much noise.

ruidoso adj noisy

ruina nf Su socio lo llevó a la ruina. His business partner ruined him financially.; **las ruinas** the ruins ▷ El castillo está en ruinas. The castle is in ruins.

rulo nm roller

rulot (pl **rulots**) nf caravan

Rumanía nf Romania

rumano, -a nm/f, adj Romanian

rumba nf rumba

rumor nm ❶ rumour ❷ murmur

rural adj rural

Rusia nf Russia

ruso, -a nm/f, adj Russian

ruta nf route

rutina nf routine; **la rutina diaria** the daily routine; **un chequeo de rutina** a routine check-up

S

sábado *nm*

> Days of the week start with a small letter in Spanish.

Saturday ▷ *La vi el sábado.* I saw her on Saturday.

sábana *nf* sheet

saber [48] *vb* ❶ to know ▷ *No lo sé.* I don't know.; **Lo dudo, pero nunca se sabe.** I doubt it, but you never know. ❷ to find out ▷ *En cuanto lo supimos fuimos a ayudarle.* As soon as we found out, we went to help him.; **No sé nada de ella.** I haven't heard from her.; **que yo sepa** as far as I know ❸ can ▷ *No sabe nadar.* She can't swim. ❹ to taste ▷ *Sabe a pescado.* It tastes of fish.; **saberse** to know

sabio *adj* wise

sabor *nm* ❶ taste ❷ flavour

sabotaje *nm* sabotage

sabré *vb see* **saber**

sabroso *adj* tasty

sacacorchos (*pl* **sacacorchos**) *nm* corkscrew

sacapuntas (*pl* **sacapuntas**) *nm* pencil sharpener

sacar [49] *vb* ❶ to take out ▷ *Voy a sacar dinero del cajero.* I'm going to take some money out of the machine. ▷ *sacar la basura* to take the rubbish out; **Me han sacado una muela.** I've had a tooth taken out.; **sacar a pasear al perro** to take the dog out for a walk ❷ to get ▷ *Yo sacaré las entradas.* I'll get the tickets. ▷ *sacar buenas notas* to get good marks ❸ to release ▷ *Han sacado un nuevo CD.* They've released a new CD.; **sacar algo adelante** to conclude; **sacar una foto a alguien** to take a photo of somebody; **sacar la lengua a alguien** to stick your tongue out at somebody; **sacarse el carnet de conducir** to pass one's driving test; **sacarse el título de abogado** to qualify as a lawyer; **sacarse las botas** to take off one's boots

sacarina *nf* saccharin

sacerdote *nm* priest

saco *nm* ❶ sack ▷ *un saco de harina* a sack of flour; **un saco de dormir** a sleeping bag ❷ (*in Latin America*) jacket

sacrificio *nm* sacrifice

sacudir [59] *vb* to shake

Sagitario *nm* Sagittarius; **Soy sagitario.** I'm a Sagittarius.

sagrado adj ❶ sacred ❷ holy

sal nf salt

sala nf ❶ room ❷ ward ❸ hall; **sala de embarque** departure lounge; **sala de espera** waiting room; **sala de estar** living room; **sala de fiestas** nightclub

salado adj ❶ salty ▷ *La carne está muy salada.* The meat's very salty. ❷ savoury ▷ *¿Es dulce o salado?* Is it sweet or savoury?

salario nm pay

salchicha nf sausage

salchichón (pl **salchichones**) nm spiced salami sausage

saldo nm balance; **saldos** sales

saldré vb see **salir**

salero nm salt cellar

salgo vb see **salir**

salida nf ❶ exit; **salida de emergencia** emergency exit; **a la salida del teatro** on the way out of the theatre ❷ departure ❸ start (of race); **la salida del sol** sunrise

salir [50] vb ❶ to come out ❷ to go out; **Ha salido.** She's out. ❸ **salir con alguien** to go out with somebody ❹ to get out ❺ to leave ❻ to appear ▷ *Su foto salió en todos los periódicos.* Her picture appeared in all the newspapers.; **Sale a 15 euros por persona.** It works out at 15 euros each.; **Me está saliendo una muela del juicio.** One of my wisdom teeth is coming through.; **No sé cómo vamos a salir adelante.** I don't know how we're going to go

on.; **salir bien** to work out well; **Espero que todo salga bien.** I hope everything works out all right.; **Les salió mal el proyecto.** Their plan didn't work out.; **¡Qué mal me ha salido el dibujo!** My drawing hasn't come out very well, has it!; **salirse** (1) to boil over ▷ *Se ha salido la leche.* The milk's boiled over. (2) to leak ▷ *Se salía el aceite del motor.* Oil was leaking out of the engine. (3) to come off ▷ *Nos salimos de la carretera.* We came off the road. (4) to come out ▷ *Se ha salido el enchufe.* The plug has come out.

saliva nf saliva

salmón (pl **salmones**) nm salmon; **rosa salmón** salmon pink

salón (pl **salones**) nm ❶ living room; **salón de actos** meeting hall; **salón de belleza** beauty salon; **salón de juegos recreativos** amusement arcade ❸ (in Mexico) classroom

salpicadera nf (in Mexico) mudguard

salpicadero nm dashboard

salpicar [49] vb to splash

salsa nf ❶ sauce ▷ *salsa de tomate* tomato sauce ❷ salsa

saltamontes (pl **saltamontes**) nm grasshopper

saltar [26] vb to jump; **hacer saltar algo por los aires** to blow something up; **saltarse** to skip; **saltarse un semáforo en rojo** to go through a red light

salto nm ❶ jump; **dar un salto** to

jump; **salto de altura** high jump; **salto de longitud** long jump; **salto mortal** somersault ❷ **dive**

salud nf health
▶ excl ❶ cheers! ❷ bless you!

saludable adj healthy

saludar [26] vb ❶ to say hello ❷ to greet; **Lo saludé desde la otra acera.** I waved to him from the other side of the street. ❸ to salute

saludo nm ❶ greeting ❷ regards ▷ *Carolina te manda un saludo.* Carolina sends her regards. ▷ *Saludos cordiales.* Kind regards.; **¡Saludos a Teresa de mi parte!** Say hello to Teresa for me!

salvaje adj wild

salvapantallas nm screensaver

salvar [26] vb to save

salvavidas (pl **salvavidas**) nm lifebelt

salvo prep except ▷ *todos salvo yo* everyone except me; **salvo que** unless; **estar a salvo** to be safe; **Consiguieron ponerse a salvo.** They managed to reach safety.

San adj Saint ▷ *San Pedro* Saint Peter

sandalia nf sandal

sandía nf watermelon

sandwich (pl **sandwiches**) nm ❶ sandwich ❷ toasted sandwich

sangrar [26] vb to bleed

sangre nf blood; **echar sangre** to bleed

sangría nf sangria

sanidad nf public health

sano adj healthy; **sano y salvo** safe

and sound

■ Be careful! **sano** does not mean **sane**.

santa nf saint ▷ *Santa Clara* Saint Clara

santo adj holy
▶ nm ❶ saint ▷ *Santo Domingo* Saint Dominic ❷ name day
● Besides birthdays, some
● Spaniards also celebrate the
● feast day of the saint they are
● named after.

sapo nm toad

saque nm service; **saque de esquina** corner; **saque inicial** kick-off

sarampión (pl **sarampiones**) nm measles

sarcástico adj sarcastic

sardina nf sardine

sargento nmf sergeant

sarpullido nm rash ▷ *Le ha salido un sarpullido en la cara.* His face has come out in a rash.

sarro nm tartar

sarta nf **Nos contó una sarta de mentiras.** He told us a pack of lies.

sartén (pl **sartenes**) nf frying pan
▶ nm (in Latin America) frying pan

sastre nmf tailor

satélite nm satellite

satisfacción (pl **satisfacciones**) nf satisfaction

satisfacer [27] vb to satisfy

satisfactorio adj satisfactory

satisfecho adj satisfied ▷ *No estoy satisfecho con el resultado.* I'm not satisfied with the result.

sauna nf sauna

saxofón (pl **saxofones**) nm
saxophone

sazonar [26] vb to season

se pron

When **se** is used as an indirect object in combination with a direct-object pronoun, it is usually translated by **to him**, **to her**, **to you** or **to them**. Sometimes **to** is substituted by **for** or else there is no preposition in English.

▷ *Pedro necesitaba la calculadora y se la dejé.* Pedro needed the calculator and I lent it to him. ▷ *He hablado con mis padres y se lo he explicado.* I've talked to my parents and explained it to them. ▷ *Aquí tiene las flores. ¿Se las envuelvo, señor?* Here are your flowers. Shall I wrap them for you, sir? ; **No quiero que Rosa lo sepa. No se lo digas.** I don't want Rosa to know. Don't tell her.

se isn't translated when it is used in combination with a and a name or other noun.

▷ *Dáselo a Enrique.* Give it to Enrique. ▷ *No se lo digas a Susana.* Don't tell Susana. ▷ *¿Se lo has preguntado a tus padres?* Have you asked your parents about it?

When **se** is used reflexively, it can be translated as **himself**, **herself**, **yourself**, **itself**, **yourselves** or **themselves**, though very often a non-reflexive construction is used in English.

▷ *Marcos se ha cortado con un cristal.* Marcos cut himself on a piece of broken glass. ▷ *Margarita se estaba preparando para salir.* Margarita was getting herself ready to go out. ▷ *La calefacción se apaga sola.* The heating turns itself off automatically. ▷ *¿Se ha hecho usted daño?* Have you hurt yourself? ; **Se está afeitando.** He's shaving. ; **Mi hermana nunca se queja.** My sister never complains.

Note how **se** and the definite article is translated with **his**, **her**, **your** or **their** with parts of the body and clothes.

▷ *Pablo se lavó los dientes.* Pablo brushed his teeth. ▷ *Carmen no podía abrocharse el vestido.* Carmen couldn't do up her dress.

Sometimes **se** is translated by **each other**.

▷ *Se dieron un beso.* They gave each other a kiss.

When **se** is used impersonally, it is usually translated by **it** or **you**.

▷ *Se cree que el tabaco produce cáncer.* It is believed that smoking causes cancer. ▷ *Es lo que pasa cuando se come tan deprisa.* That's what happens when you eat so fast. ; **"se vende"** "for sale"

sé vb see **saber**

sea vb see **ser**

secador nm hair dryer

secadora nf ❶ tumble dryer
❷ (in Mexico) hair dryer

secar [49] vb to dry; **secarse** to

dry; **¿Se ha secado ya la ropa?**
Is the washing dry yet?; **Se han
secado las plantas.** The plants
have dried up.

sección (pl **secciones**) nf
1 section **2** department

seco adj **1** dry ▷ El suelo ya está
seco. The floor's dry now. **2** dried
▷ flores secas dried flowers

secretario, -a nm/f secretary

secreto nm secret; **en secreto**
in secret
▶ adj secret

secta nf sect

sector nm sector

secuencia nf sequence

secuestrador, a nm/f
1 kidnapper **2** hijacker

secuestrar [26] vb **1** to kidnap
2 to hijack

secuestro nm **1** kidnapping
2 hijack

secundario adj secondary

sed nf thirst; **tener sed** to be
thirsty

seda nf silk ▷ una camisa de seda a
silk shirt

sedal nm fishing line

sedante nm sedative

sede nf **1** headquarters **2** venue

sediento adj thirsty

segar vb **1** to reap **2** to mow

seguido adj in a row ▷ La he visto
tres días seguidos. I've seen her
three days in a row.; **en seguida**
straight away; **En seguida
termino.** I'm just about to finish.;
todo seguido straight on ▷ Vaya
todo seguido hasta la plaza y luego …

Go straight on until the square
and then …

seguir [51] vb **1** to carry on
▷ Siguió mirándola. He carried on
looking at her.

> Note how the verb **seguir** is
> often translated into English
> using **still** and a verb.

Sigue lloviendo. It's still raining.;
El ascensor sigue estropeado.
The lift's still not working.; **Sigo
sin comprender.** I still don't
understand. **2** to follow; **seguir
adelante** to go ahead

según prep **1** according to ▷ Según
tú, no habrá problemas de entradas.
According to you there won't be
any problems with the tickets.
2 depending on ▷ Iremos o no,
según esté el tiempo. We might go,
depending on the weather.

segundo (f **segunda**) adj, pron
second; **el segundo plato** the
main course; **Vive en el segundo.**
He lives on the second floor.
▶ nm second ▷ Es un segundo nada
más. It'll only take a second.

seguramente adv probably

seguridad nf **1** safety **2** security
▷ Las medidas de seguridad son muy
estrictas. The security measures
are very strict. **3** certainty ▷ con
toda seguridad with complete
certainty; **seguridad en uno
mismo** self-confidence; **la
seguridad social** social security

seguro adj **1** safe ▷ Este avión es
muy seguro. This plane is very safe.
▷ Aquí estaremos seguros. We'll be

a
b
c
d
e
f
g
h
i
j
k
l
m
n
o
p
q
r
s
t
u
v
w
x
y
z

safe here. ❷ sure ▷ *Estoy segura de que ganaremos.* I'm sure we'll win. ▷ *Está muy seguro de sí mismo.* He's very sure of himself. ❸ certain ▷ *No es seguro que vayan a venir.* It's not certain that they're going to come.

▶ *nm* insurance ▷ *el seguro del coche* car insurance; **seguro de vida** life assurance

seis *adj, pron* six; **Son las seis.** It's six o'clock.; **el seis de enero** the sixth of January

seiscientos, -as *adj, pron* six hundred

selección (*pl* **selecciones**) *nf* ❶ selection ❷ team

seleccionar [**26**] *vb* to pick

selectividad *nf* university entrance exam

sellar [**26**] *vb* ❶ to seal (*letter, parcel*) ❷ to stamp (*passport*) ❸ to sign on (*for unemployment benefit*)

sello *nm* stamp ▷ *Colecciona sellos.* He collects stamps.

selva *nf* jungle; **la selva tropical** the rainforest

semáforo *nm* traffic lights; **un semáforo en rojo** a red light

semana *nf* week ▷ *dentro de una semana* in a week's time ▷ *una vez a la semana* once a week; **entre semana** during the week; **Semana Santa** Holy Week

semanal *adj* weekly

sembrar [**40**] *vb* ❶ to plant ❷ to sow

semejante *adj* ❶ similar ❷ such ▷ *Nunca he dicho semejante cosa.* I've

never said such a thing.

semicírculo *nm* semicircle

semifinal *nf* semi-final

semilla *nf* seed

senado *nm* senate

senador, a *nm/f* senator

sencillamente *adv* simply

sencillo *adj* ❶ simple ▷ *Es muy sencillo.* It's really simple. ❷ modest

▶ *nm* ❶ single ❷ (*in Latin America*) small change

senderismo *nm* trekking

sendero *nm* path

sensación (*pl* **sensaciones**) *nf* ❶ feeling ▷ *Tengo la sensación de que mienten.* I get the feeling they're lying. ▷ *una sensación de picor* an itchy feeling

sensacional *adj* sensational

sensato *adj* sensible

sensible *adj* ❶ sensitive ❷ appreciable

> Be careful! **sensible** does not mean **sensible**.

sensual *adj* sensuous

sentado *adj* **estar sentado** to be sitting down

sentar [**40**] *vb* ❶ to suit ▷ *Ese vestido te sienta muy bien.* That dress really suits you. ❷ to agree with ▷ *No me sienta bien cenar tanto.* Having so much dinner doesn't agree with me.; **Le ha sentado mal que no lo invitaras a la boda.** He was put out that you didn't invite him to the wedding.; **sentarse** to sit down

sentencia *nf* sentence

sentido nm ❶ sense; **sentido común** common sense; **sentido del humor** sense of humour; **una calle de sentido único** a one-way street; **en algún sentido** in some respects ❷ meaning

sentimental adj sentimental

sentimiento nm feeling

sentir [52] vb ❶ to feel ▷ *Sentí un dolor en la pierna.* I felt a pain in my leg. ❷ to hear ❸ to be sorry ▷ *Lo siento mucho.* I'm very sorry.; **sentirse** to feel

seña nf sign ▷ *Les hice una seña.* I made a sign to them.; **señas** address

señal nf ❶ sign; **señal de tráfico** road sign; **señal indicadora** signpost; **señal de llamada** dialling tone ❷ signal ❸ deposit

señalar [26] vb ❶ to point; **señalar con el dedo** to point ❷ to mark

señalizar [14] vb to indicate

señor nm ❶ man ▷ *Este señor ha llegado antes que yo.* This man was before me.; **¿Le ocurre algo, señor?** Is there something the matter? ❷ sir ▷ *¿Qué le pongo, señor?* What would you like, sir? ❸ Mr ▷ *el señor Delgado* Mr Delgado; **Muy señor mío ...** Dear Sir ...; **el señor alcalde** the mayor

señora nf ❶ lady ▷ *Deja pasar a esta señora.* Let the lady past.; **¿Le ocurre algo, señora?** Is there something the matter? ❷ madam ▷ *¿Qué le pongo, señora?* What would you like, madam?

❸ Mrs ▷ *la señora Delgado* Mrs Delgado ❹ Ms ▷ *la señora Delgado* Ms Delgado ❺ wife ▷ *Vino con su señora.* He came with his wife.

señorita nf ❶ young lady ▷ *Deja pasar a esta señorita.* Let the young lady past. ❷ Miss ▷ *la señorita Delgado* Miss Delgado ❸ Ms ▷ *la señorita Delgado* Ms Delgado

sepa vb see **saber**

separación (pl separaciones) nf ❶ separation ❷ gap

separado adj ❶ separate; **por separado** separately ❷ separated ▷ *Está separado de su mujer.* He's separated from his wife.

separar [26] vb to separate; **separarse** (1) to separate (2) to split up

septiembre nm

> Months start with a small letter in Spanish.

September

séptimo, -a adj, pron seventh; **Vivo en el séptimo.** I live on the seventh floor.

sequía nf drought

ser [53] vb to be

> **ser** is used with adjectives describing permanent or inherent states.

▷ *Es muy alto.* He's very tall. ▷ *Es azul.* It's blue.

> **ser** is used with nouns to say what someone or something is.

▷ *Es médico.* He's a doctor. ▷ *París es la capital de Francia.* Paris is the capital of France.; **Soy Lucía.** It's Lucía.; **Éramos cinco en el coche.** There were five of us in the car.

> ser is used in passive constructions.

▷ *Fue construido en 1960.* It was built in 1960.

> ser is used to talk about the time and date.

▷ *Son las seis y media.* It's half past six. ▷ *¿Qué fecha es hoy?* What's the date today?; **Era de noche.** It was night.

> ser is also used in other expressions.

¡Es cierto! That's right!; **Me es imposible asistir.** It's impossible for me to attend.; **ser de (1) Es de Joaquín.** It's Joaquín's. **(2)** to be from ▷ *¿De dónde eres?* Where are you from? **(3)** to be made of; **a no ser que …** unless …; **O sea, que no vienes.** So you're not coming.; **mis hijos, o sea, Juan y Pedro** my children, that is, Juan and Pedro ▶ *nm* being; **un ser humano** a human being

serie *nf* series

serio *adj* serious; **en serio** seriously ▷ *No hablaba en serio.* I wasn't speaking seriously.; **¿Lo dices en serio?** Do you really mean it?

sermón (*pl* **sermones**) *nm* sermon

serpiente *nf* snake; **una serpiente de cascabel** a rattlesnake

serrar [**40**] *vb* to saw

serrucho *nm* saw

servicial *adj* helpful

servicio *nm* ① service ▷ *El servicio no va incluido.* Service is not included.; **estar de servicio** to be on duty ② toilet ▷ *Está en el servicio.* He's in the toilet.; **el servicio de caballeros** the gents'; **el servicio de señoras** the ladies'

servidor *nm* server

servilleta *nf* napkin

servir [**39**] *vb* ① to be useful for; **¿Para qué sirve esto?** What's this for?; **Esta radio aún sirve.** This radio still works. ② to serve; **Sírveme un poco más de vino.** Give me a little bit more wine.; **no servir para nada** to be useless; **¿En qué puedo servirlo?** How can I help you?

sesenta *adj, pron* sixty ▷ *Tiene sesenta años.* He's sixty.; **el sesenta aniversario** the sixtieth anniversary

sesión (*pl* **sesiones**) *nf* ① session ② showing

seta *nf* mushroom; **seta venenosa** toadstool

setecientos, -as *adj, pron* seven hundred

setenta *adj, pron* seventy ▷ *Tiene setenta años.* He's seventy.; **el setenta aniversario** the seventieth anniversary

seto *nm* hedge

seudónimo *nm* pseudonym

severo *adj* ① strict ② harsh

Sevilla *nf* Seville

sexista *adj, nmf* sexist

sexo *nm* sex

sexto, -a *adj, pron* sixth; **Vivo en el**

sexto. I live on the sixth floor.

sexual adj sexual

sexualidad nf sexuality

si conj ❶ if ▷ Si quieres, te dejo el coche. I'll lend you the car if you like. ▷ ¿Sabes si hemos cobrado ya? Do you know if we've been paid yet?; ¿Y si llueve? And what if it rains?; Si me hubiera tocado la lotería ... If I had won the lottery ... ❷ whether ▷ No sé si ir o no. I don't know whether to go or not.; si no (1) otherwise ▷ Ponte crema. Si no, te quemarás. Put some cream on, otherwise you'll get sunburned. (2) if...not ▷ Avísame si no podéis venir. Let me know if you can't come.

sí adv yes; ¿Te gusta? - Sí. Do you like it? - Yes, I do.; Creo que sí. I think so.; Él no quiere pero sí yo. He doesn't want to but I do.

▶ pron

When **sí** is used in reflexive constructions, it can be translated as **himself, herself, yourself, itself, yourselves** or **themselves**, though very often a non-reflexive construction is used in English.

▷ Sólo habla de sí mismo. He only talks about himself. ▷ Se perjudica a sí misma. She's harming herself. ▷ Pregúntese a sí mismo el motivo. Ask yourself the reason. ▷ La pregunta en sí no era difícil. The question itself wasn't difficult. ▷ Hablaban entre sí. They were

talking among themselves.

When it is used in impersonal constructions, it is translated by **yourself**.

▷ Es mejor aprender las cosas por sí mismo. It's better to learn things by yourself.

Sicilia nf Sicily

sida nm AIDS

sidra nf cider

siego vb see segar

siembro vb see sembrar

siempre adv always; como siempre as usual; para siempre forever; siempre y cuando provided

siendo vb see ser

siento vb see sentir

sierra nf ❶ saw ❷ mountain range

siesta nf nap; echarse la siesta to have a nap

siete adj, pron seven; Son las siete. It's seven o'clock.; el siete de marzo the seventh of March

siglas nfpl abbreviation

siglo nm century ▷ el siglo 21 the 21st century

significado nm meaning

significar [49] vb ❶ to mean ❷ to stand for

significativo adj significant

signo nm sign; ¿De qué signo del zodíaco eres? What star sign are you?; signo de admiración exclamation mark; signo de interrogación question mark

siguiendo vb see seguir

siguiente adj next ▷ el siguiente

vuelo the next flight ▷ *Al día siguiente visitamos Toledo.* The next day we visited Toledo.; **¡Que pase el siguiente, por favor!** Next please!

sílaba nf syllable

silbar [26] vb to whistle

silbato nm whistle

silbido nm whistle

silencio nm silence; **guardar silencio** to keep quiet; **¡Silencio!** Quiet!

silencioso adj silent

silla nf chair; **silla de montar** saddle; **silla de paseo** pushchair; **silla de ruedas** wheelchair

sillín (pl sillines) nm saddle

sillón (pl sillones) nm armchair

silueta nf outline; **Tiene una silueta perfecta.** She has a perfect figure.

símbolo nm symbol

simpatía nf ❶ kindness ❷ friendly nature; **Les tengo simpatía.** I like them.

simpático adj nice ▷ *Estuvo muy simpática con todos.* She was very nice to everybody. ▷ *Los cubanos son muy simpáticos.* Cubans are very nice people.; **Me cae simpático.** I think he's really nice.

▌ Be careful! **simpático** does not mean **sympathetic**.

simple adj simple

simplemente adv simply

simultáneo adj simultaneous

sin prep without ▷ *Es peligroso ir en moto sin casco.* It's dangerous to ride a motorbike without a

helmet. ▷ *Salió sin hacer ruido.* She went out without making a noise. ▷ *Se fue él se diera cuenta* without him realizing; **la gente sin hogar** the homeless

sincero adj honest

sindicalista nmf trade unionist

sindicato nm trade union

sinfonía nf symphony

singular adj, nm singular

siniestro adj sinister

sino conj but ▷ *No son ingleses sino galeses.* They're not English, but Welsh.; **No hace sino pedirnos dinero.** All he does is ask us for money.; **no sólo ... sino...** not only ... but...

sintético adj synthetic

sintiendo vb see **sentir**

síntoma nm symptom

sinvergüenza nmf crook; **Es una sinvergüenza.** She's shameless.

siquiera adv **ni siquiera** not even

sirena nf ❶ siren ❷ mermaid

sirviendo vb see **servir**

sirvienta nf maid

sirviente nm servant

sistema nm system

sitio nm ❶ place; **cambiar algo de sitio** to move something around; **en cualquier sitio** anywhere; **en algún sitio** somewhere; **en ningún sitio** nowhere ❷ room ▷ *Hay sitio de sobra.* There's room to spare.; **un sitio web** website

situación (pl situaciones) nf situation

situado adj **está situado en ...** it's situated in ...

sobaco nm armpit

soborno nm ❶ bribery ❷ bribe

sobra nf Tenemos comida de sobra. We've got more than enough food.; Sabes de sobra que yo no lo he sido. You know full well that it wasn't me.; las sobras the leftovers

sobrar [26] vb ❶ to be left over ❷ to be spare; Este ejemplo sobra. This example is unnecessary.; Con este dinero sobrará. This money will be more than enough.

sobre prep ❶ on ▷ Dejó el dinero sobre la mesa. He left the money on the table. ❷ about ▷ información sobre vuelos information about flights; sobre las seis at about six o'clock; sobre todo above all
▶ nm envelope

sobredosis (pl sobredosis) nf overdose

sobrenatural adj supernatural

sobresaliente nm distinction

sobrevivir [59] vb to survive

sobrina nf niece

sobrino nm nephew; mis sobrinos (1) my nephews (2) my nieces and nephews

sobrio adj sober

social adj social

socialismo nm socialism

socialista adj, nmf socialist

sociedad nf society; una sociedad anónima a limited company

socio, -a nm/f ❶ partner (in business) ❷ member (of club, organization)

sociología nf sociology

socorrista nmf lifeguard

socorro nm help; pedir socorro to ask for help
▶ excl help!

soda nf soda

sofá (pl sofás) nm sofa; un sofá-cama a sofa bed

sofisticado adj sophisticated

software nm software

sois vb see ser

soja nf soya

sol nm sun; Hace sol. It's sunny.; tomar el sol to sunbathe

solamente adv only

soldado nm soldier

soleado adj sunny

soledad nf loneliness

soler [34] vb

When in the present tense, soler followed by the infinitive is normally translated by usually and a verb.

▷ Suele salir a las ocho. He usually leaves at eight.

When in the past tense, soler followed by the infinitive is normally translated by used to and a verb.

▷ Solíamos ir todos los años a la playa. We used to go to the beach every year.

solicitar [26] vb ❶ to ask for ❷ to apply for

solicitud nf ❶ request ❷ application

sólido adj solid

solitario adj solitary

a b c d e f g h i j k l m n o p q r s t u v w x y z

sollozar [14] vb to sob

solo adj ❶ alone ▷ ¡Déjame solo! Leave me alone! ▷ Me quedé solo. I was left alone.; ¿Estás solo? Are you on your own?; **Lo hice solo.** I did it on my own. ❷ lonely ❸ single ▷ No hubo una sola queja. There wasn't a single complaint.; **Habla solo.** He talks to himself.; **un café solo** a black coffee ▸ nm solo

sólo adv only; **no sólo ... sino ...** not only ... but...

solomillo nm sirloin

soltar [12] vb ❶ to let go of; ¡Suéltame! Let me go! ❷ to put down ▷ Soltó la bolsa de la compra en un banco. She put her shopping bag down on a bench. ❸ to release ▷ Han soltado a los rehenes. They've released the hostages. ❹ to let out (sigh)

soltero, -a nm/f **un soltero** a bachelor; **una soltera** a single woman ▸ adj single ▷ Es soltero. He's single.

solución (pl soluciones) nf ❶ solution ❷ answer

solucionar [26] vb to solve; **un problema sin solucionar** an unsolved problem

sombra nf ❶ shade ▷ Prefiero quedarme a la sombra. I prefer to stay in the shade. ❷ shadow; **sombra de ojos** eye shadow

sombrero nm hat

sombrilla nf ❶ parasol ❷ sunshade

somier nm mattress base

somnífero nm sleeping pill

sonajero nm rattle

sonar [12] vb ❶ to sound ▷ Escríbelo tal y como suena. Write it down just the way it sounds. ❷ to play (music) ❸ to ring (bell, telephone) ❹ to go off (alarm clock); **Me suena esa cara.** That face rings a bell.; **sonarse la nariz** to blow one's nose

sondeo nm **un sondeo de opinión** an opinion poll

sonido nm sound

sonreír [45] vb to smile

sonrisa nf smile

sonrojarse [26] vb to blush

soñar [12] vb to dream

sopa nf soup ▷ sopa de pescado fish soup

soplar [26] vb to blow

soportar [26] vb to stand

> Be careful! **soportar** does not mean **support**.

soprano nf soprano

sorber [9] vb to sip

sordo adj deaf; **quedarse sordo** to go deaf

sordomudo adj deaf and dumb

sorprendente adj surprising

sorprender [9] vb to surprise; **Me sorprendí al verlo allí.** I was surprised to see him there.

sorpresa nf surprise; **coger a alguien de sorpresa** to take somebody by surprise

sorteo nm draw

sortija nf ring

soso adj ❶ dull ❷ bland

sospecha nf suspicion

sospechar [26] vb to suspect; **Sospechan de él.** They suspect him.

sospechoso, -a nm/f suspect
▷ adj suspicious

sostén (pl sostenes) nm bra

sostener [54] vb ❶ to support ❷ to hold; **¿Puedes sostener la puerta un momento?** Can you hold the door open for a moment?

sota nf jack

sótano nm ❶ basement ❷ cellar

soy vb see **ser**

spot nm **un spot publicitario** a commercial

Sr. abbr (= señor) Mr

Sra. abbr ❶ (= señora) Mrs ❷ Ms

Sres. abbr (= señores) Messrs

Srta. abbr ❶ (= señorita) Miss ❷ Ms

su adj ❶ his ▷ su máquina de afeitar his razor ▷ sus padres his parents ❷ her ▷ su falda her skirt ▷ sus amigas her friends ❸ its ▷ un oso y su cachorro a bear and its cub ▷ el coche y sus accesorios the car and its fittings ❹ their ▷ su equipo favorito their favourite team ▷ sus amigos their friends ▷ your ▷ Su abrigo, señora. Your coat, madam. ▷ No olviden sus paraguas. Don't forget your umbrellas.

suave adj ❶ smooth (skin, surface) ❷ soft (hair) ❸ gentle (breeze, voice, squeeze) ❹ mild (climate, temperature)

suavizante nm ❶ conditioner ❷ fabric conditioner

subasta nf auction

subcampeón, -ona (mpl subcampeones) nm/f runner-up

subdesarrollado adj underdeveloped

subdirector, a nm/f ❶ deputy head ❷ deputy director ❸ deputy manager

subida nf ❶ rise ▷ una subida de los precios a rise in prices ❷ ascent

subir [59] vb ❶ to go up ▷ Subimos la cuesta. We went up the hill. ▷ La gasolina ha vuelto a subir. Petrol's gone up again. ❷ to come up ▷ Sube, que te voy a enseñar unos discos. Come up, I've got some records to show you. ❸ to climb ▷ subir una montaña to climb a mountain ❹ to take up ▷ ¿Me puedes ayudar a subir las maletas? Can you help me take the cases up? ❺ to put up (prices, fares) ❻ to raise ▷ Sube los brazos. Raise your arms. ❼ to turn up (volume, radio); **subirse a (1)** to get into (car) **(2)** to get onto (bike) **(3)** to get on (bus, train, plane); **subirse a un árbol** to climb a tree

subjuntivo nm subjunctive

submarino nm submarine

subrayar [26] vb to underline

subsidio nm subsidy; **subsidio de paro** unemployment benefit

subte nm (in River Plate) underground

subterráneo adj underground

subtitulado adj subtitled

subtítulos nmpl subtitles

suburbio nm slum area

subvención (pl subvenciones)
nf subsidy

subvencionar [26] vb to
subsidize

suceder [9] vb to happen

suceso nm ❶ event ❷ incident;
**Acudieron rápidamente al lugar
del suceso.** They rushed to the
scene.

> Be careful! **suceso** does not
> mean **success**.

suciedad nf dirt

sucio adj dirty ▷ **Tienes las manos
sucias.** You've got dirty hands.

sucursal nf branch

sudadera nf sweatshirt

Sudáfrica nf South Africa

Sudamérica nf South America

sudamericano, -a nm/f, adj
South American

sudar [26] vb to sweat

sudeste nm southeast

sudoeste nm southwest

sudor nm sweat

sudoroso adj sweaty

Suecia nf Sweden

sueco, -a nm/f Swede
> ▶ nm Swedish (language)
> ▶ adj Swedish

suegra nf mother-in-law

suegro nm father-in-law; **mis
suegros** my in-laws

suela nf sole

sueldo nm ❶ salary ❷ wages

suelo nm ❶ floor ❷ ground; **Me
caí al suelo.** I fell over.
> ▶ vb see **soler**

suelto vb see **soltar**
> ▶ adj loose ▷ **Lleva el pelo suelto.**

She wears her hair loose. ▷ **No
dejes al perro suelto.** Don't let the
dog loose.
> ▶ nm change

sueno vb see **sonar**

sueño vb see **soñar**
> ▶ nm ❶ dream ❷ sleep; **Tengo
sueño.** I'm sleepy.

suerte nf luck; **¡Qué mala suerte!**
What bad luck!; **¡Qué suerte!**
How lucky!; **Tuvo suerte.** She was
lucky.; **por suerte** luckily

suéter nm sweater

suficiente adj enough ▷ **No tenía
dinero suficiente.** I didn't have
enough money.

suficientemente adv sufficiently

sufrir [59] vb ❶ to have ▷ **Sufrió un
ataque al corazón.** He had a heart
attack. ❷ to suffer; **sufrir un
colapso** to collapse

sugerencia nf suggestion;
hacer una sugerencia to make a
suggestion

sugerir [52] vb to suggest

sugiero vb see **sugerir**

suicidio nm suicide

Suiza nf Switzerland

suizo, -a adj, nm/f Swiss; **los
suizos** the Swiss

sujetador nm bra

sujetar [26] vb ❶ to hold ❷ to
fasten

sujeto nm subject

suma nf sum ▷ **una suma de dinero**
a sum of money; **hacer una suma**
to do a sum

sumar [26] vb to add up

suministrar [26] vb to supply

suministro nm supply

supe vb see **saber**

súper adj **gasolina súper** four-star petrol

superar [26] vb ❶ to get over (illness, problem) ❷ to beat (record) ❸ to pass (test) ❹ exceed (expectations)

superficie nf ❶ surface ❷ area

superior (f superior) adj ❶ upper ▷ **el labio superior** the upper lip ❷ top ▷ **el piso superior** the top floor; **superior a** superior to; **Su inteligencia es superior a la media.** He has above-average intelligence.; **un curso de inglés de nivel superior** an advanced level English course

supermercado nm supermarket

superviviente nmf survivor

suplemento nm supplement

suplente nmf ❶ reserve ❷ supply teacher ❸ locum

suplicar [49] vb to beg

suponer [42] vb ❶ to suppose; **Supongo que sí.** I suppose so. ❷ to think ▷ **Supusimos que no vendrías.** We didn't think you would be coming. ❸ to involve ▷ **Tener un coche supone más gastos.** Having a car involves having more expenses.

supositorio nm suppository

suprimir [59] vb to delete

supuesto vb see **suponer** ▶ nm **¿Y en el supuesto de que no venga?** And supposing he doesn't come?; **por supuesto** of course; **¡Por supuesto que no!** Of

course not!

supuse vb see **suponer**

sur nm, adj south

sureño adj southern

sureste nm southeast

surf nm surfing; **surf a vela** windsurfing; **practicar el surf** to surf

surgir [17] vb to come up

suroeste nm southwest

surtido adj assorted ▷ **pasteles surtidos** assorted cakes; **estar bien surtido** to have a good selection ▶ nm selection

surtidor nm petrol pump

susceptible adj touchy

suscripción (pl suscripciones) nf subscription

suspender [9] vb ❶ to call off ❷ to postpone; **El partido se suspendió a causa de la lluvia.** The game was rained off. ❸ to fail

suspense nm suspense; **una película de suspense** a thriller

suspenso nm (in Latin America) suspense; **una película de suspenso** a thriller; **Tengo un suspenso en inglés.** I failed English.

suspicaz (pl suspicaces) adj suspicious

suspirar [26] vb to sigh

suspiro nm sigh

sustancia nf substance

sustantivo nm noun

sustituir [11] vb ❶ to replace ❷ to stand in for

sustituto, -a nm/f ❶ replacement ❷ substitute

sustituyendo vb see **sustituir**

susto nm fright ▷ ¡Qué susto! What a fright!; **dar un susto a alguien** to give somebody a fright

susurrar [26] vb to whisper

sutil adj subtle

suyo, -a pron, adj ❶ his ▷ Todas estas tierras son suyas. All this land is his. ▷ ¿Es éste su cuarto? - No, el suyo está abajo. Is this his room? - No, his is downstairs.; **un amigo suyo** a friend of his ▷ Es suyo. It's hers. ▷ ¿Es éste su abrigo? - No, el suyo es marrón. Is this her coat? - No, hers is brown.; **un amigo suyo** a friend of hers ❸ theirs ▷ Es suyo. It's theirs. ▷ ¿Es ésta su casa? - No, la suya está más adelante. Is this their house? - No, theirs is further on.; **un amigo suyo** a friend of theirs ❹ yours ▷ Todos estos libros son suyos. All these books are yours. ▷ ¿Es ésta nuestra habitación? - No, la suya está arriba. Is this our room? - No, yours is upstairs.; **un amigo suyo** a friend of yours

tabaco nm ❶ tobacco ❷ cigarettes

taberna nf bar

tabique nm partition

tabla nf plank; **la tabla de multiplicar** the multiplication table; **una tabla de cocina** a chopping board; **la tabla de planchar** the ironing board; **la tabla de surf** the surfboard; **quedar en tablas** to draw

tablao nm ❶ flamenco show ❷ flamenco venue

tablero nm board; **el tablero de ajedrez** the chessboard; **el tablero de mandos** the dashboard

tableta nf ❶ bar (of chocolate) ❷ tablet (pill)

tablón (pl **tablones**) nm plank; **el tablón de anuncios** the notice board

tabú (pl **tabúes**) nm taboo

taburete nm stool

tacaño, -a nm/f skinflint
▶ adj mean

tachar [26] vb to cross out

taco nm ① rawlplug ② stud
③ cube ④ cue ⑤ swearword;
soltar tacos to swear ④ (in Chile,
River Plate) heel

tacón (pl **tacones**) nm heel;
zapatos de tacón high-heeled
shoes

táctica nf tactics

tacto nm ① touch ② tact; **Lo dijo
con mucho tacto.** He said it very
tactfully.

tajada nf slice

tajante adj ① emphatic ② sharp
(tone)

tal adj, pron such ▷ En tales casos
es mejor consultar con un médico.
In such cases it's better to see a
doctor. ▷ ¡En el aeropuerto había
tal confusión! There was such
confusion at the airport!; **Lo dejé
tal como estaba.** I left it just as
it was.; **con tal de que** as long as
▷ con tal de que regreséis antes de las
once as long as you get back before
eleven; **¿Qué tal?** How are things?;
¿Qué tal has dormido? How did
you sleep?; **tal vez** perhaps

taladradora nf ① pneumatic drill
② punch

taladrar [26] vb to drill

taladro nm drill

talento nm talent

talla nf size

tallar [26] vb ① to carve ② to
sculpt ③ (in Chile, River Plate)
to scrub

tallarines nmpl noodles

taller nm ① garage ▷ Tengo el coche
en el taller. My car is in the garage.
② workshop

tallo nm stem

talón (pl **talones**) nm ① heel
② cheque ▷ cobrar un talón to cash
a cheque

talonario nm ① chequebook
② book of tickets ③ receipt book

tamaño nm size; **¿Qué tamaño
tiene?** What size is it?

tambalearse [26] vb ① to wobble
② to stagger

también adv also; **Tengo hambre.
-Yo también.** I'm hungry. -So
am I.; **Yo estoy de acuerdo. -
Nosotros también.** I agree. -So
do we.

tambor nm drum

Támesis nm Thames

tamiz (pl **tamices**) nm sieve

tampoco adv ① either ▷ Yo
tampoco lo compré. I didn't buy it
either. ② neither ▷ Yo no la vi. -Yo
tampoco. I didn't see her. -Neither
did I.

tampón (pl **tampones**) nm
tampon

tan adv ① so ▷ No creía que vendrías
tan pronto. I didn't think you'd
come so soon.; **¡Qué hombre tan
amable!** What a kind man!; **tan ...
que ... so ... that ...** ▷ Habla tan
deprisa que no la entiendo. She talks
so fast that I can't understand her.

❸ such ▷ No era una idea tan buena. It wasn't such a good idea.; **tan... como** as...as ▷ Vine tan pronto como pude. I came as soon as I could.

tanque nm tank

tantear [26] vb to weigh up

tanto, -a adj, adv, pron **❶** so much (pl so many) ▷ Ahora no bebo tanta leche. I don't drink so much milk now. ▷ Se preocupa tanto que no puede dormir. He worries so much that he can't sleep. ▷ ¡Tengo tantas cosas que hacer hoy! I have so many things to do today! ▷ Vinieron tantos que no cabían en la sala. So many people came that they couldn't fit into the room.; **No recibe tantas llamadas como yo.** He doesn't get as many calls as I do.; **Gano tanto como tú.** I earn as much as you. **❷** so often ▷ Ahora no la veo tanto. I don't see her so often now.; **¡No corras tanto!** Don't run so fast!; **tanto tú como yo** both you and I; **tanto si viene como si no** whether he comes or not; **¡Tanto gusto!** How do you do?; **entre tanto** meanwhile; **por lo tanto** therefore
▶ nm **❶** goal ▷ Juárez marcó el segundo tanto. Juárez scored the second goal. **❷** amount ▷ Me paga un tanto fijo cada semana. He pays me a fixed amount each week.; **un tanto por ciento** a percentage; **Había cuarenta y tantos invitados.** There were forty-odd guests.; **Manténme al tanto.** Keep me informed.

tapa nf **❶** lid **❷** top **❸** cover **❹** tapa ▷ Pedimos unas tapas en el bar. We ordered some tapas in the bar.

tapadera nf lid

tapado nm (in River Plate) coat

tapar [26] vb to cover; **Tapa la olla.** Put the lid on the pan.; **Me estás tapando el sol.** You're keeping the sun off me.; **Tápate bien que hace frío.** Wrap up well as it's cold.

tapete nm **❶** embroidered tablecloth **❷** (in Mexico) rug

tapia nf wall

tapicería nf **❶** upholstery **❷** upholsterer's

tapiz (pl tapices) nm tapestry

tapizar [14] vb to upholster

tapón (pl tapones) nm **❶** plug **❷** top **❸** cork; **tapón de rosca** screw top

taquigrafía nf shorthand

taquilla nf **❶** box office **❷** ticket office **❸** locker

tararear [26] vb to hum

tardar [26] vb to be late; **Tardaron una semana en contestar.** They took a week to reply.; **En avión se tarda dos horas.** The plane takes two hours.

tarde nf **❶** afternoon ▷ a las tres de la tarde at three in the afternoon; **¡Buenas tardes!** Good afternoon!; **por la tarde** in the afternoon; **hoy por la tarde** this afternoon **❷** evening ▷ a las ocho de la tarde at eight in the evening; **¡Buenas tardes!** Good evening!; **por la tarde** in the evening; **hoy por la**

tarde this evening
▶ *adv* late ▷ *Se está haciendo tarde.*
It's getting late.; **más tarde** later;
tarde o temprano sooner or
later; **Llegaré a las nueve como
muy tarde.** I'll arrive at nine at
the latest.

tarea *nf* task; **las tareas
domésticas** the chores; **las tareas**
(*in Latin America*) homework

tarifa *nf* ❶ rate ❷ fare; **tarifa
de precios** price list

tarima *nf* platform

tarjeta *nf* card; **una tarjeta de
Navidad** a Christmas card; **una
tarjeta de cajero automático**
a cash card; **una tarjeta de
crédito** a credit card; **una tarjeta
telefónica** a phonecard; **una
tarjeta de embarque** a boarding
pass

tarro *nm* ❶ jar ❷ (*in Mexico*) mug

tarta *nf* ❶ cake; **una tarta de
cumpleaños** a birthday cake
❷ tart

tartamudear [26] *vb* to stammer

tartamudo *adj* **ser tartamudo**
to stutter

tasa *nf* rate ▷ *la tasa de natalidad*
the birth rate

tasar [26] *vb* to value

tasca *nf* tavern

tata *nm* ❶ (*in Latin America*) daddy
❷ grandpa

tatuaje *nm* tattoo

tatuar [2] *vb* to tattoo

Tauro *nm* Taurus (*sign*); **Soy tauro.**
I'm Taurus.

taxi *nm* taxi ▷ *tomar un taxi* to

take a taxi

taxímetro *nm* taximeter

taxista *nmf* taxi driver

taza *nf* ❶ cup ▷ *Tomamos una taza
de café.* We had a cup of coffee.
❷ cupful ▷ *una taza de arroz* a
cupful of rice ❸ bowl (*of toilet*)

tazón (*pl* **tazones**) *nm* bowl

te *pron* ❶ you ▷ *Te quiero.* I love
you. ▷ *Te voy a dar un consejo.* I'm
going to give you some advice.;
Me gustaría comprártelo. I'd like
to buy it for you. ❷ yourself ▷ *¿Te
has hecho daño?* Have you hurt
yourself?

> Note how **te** and the definite
> article is translated by **your**
> with parts of the body and
> clothes.

▷ *¿Te duelen los pies?* Do your feet
hurt? ▷ *Te tienes que poner el abrigo.*
You should put your coat on.

té (*pl* **tés**) *nm* tea; **Me hice un té.** I
made myself a cup of tea.

teatro *nm* theatre; **una obra de
teatro** a play

tebeo *nm* comic

techo *nm* ❶ ceiling ❷ (*in Latin
America*) roof

tecla *nf* key; **pulsar una tecla** to
press a key

teclado *nm* keyboard

teclear [26] *vb* to type

técnica *nf* ❶ technique
❷ technology; *see also* **técnico**

técnico, -a *nm/f* technician ▷ *un
técnico de laboratorio* a laboratory
technician
▶ *adj* technical

tecno nm techno

tecnología nf technology

tecnológico adj technological

teja nf tile

tejado nm roof

tejanos nmpl jeans

tejer [9] vb ❶ to weave ❷ to knit

tejido nm ❶ fabric ❷ tissue

tel. abbr (= teléfono) tel.

tela nf fabric; **tela metálica** wire netting

telaraña nf cobweb

tele nf TV ▷ Estábamos viendo la tele. We were watching TV.

telecomunicaciones nfpl telecommunications

telediario nm news

teledirigido adj remote-controlled

teleférico nm cable car

telefonear [26] vb to phone

telefónico adj telephone; **la guía telefónica** the telephone directory

telefonista nmf telephonist

teléfono nm telephone; **Hablamos por teléfono.** We spoke on the phone.; **Está hablando por teléfono.** He's on the phone.; **colgar el teléfono a alguien** to hang up on somebody; **un teléfono de tarjeta** a card phone; **un teléfono móvil** a mobile phone; **un teléfono celular** a cellphone; **un teléfono con cámara** a camera phone

telegrama nm telegram

telenovela nf soap opera

telepatía nf telepathy

telerrealidad nf reality TV

telescopio nm telescope

telesilla nm chairlift

telespectador, a nm/f viewer

telesquí (pl **telesquís**) nm ski-lift

teletexto nm Teletext®

televentas nfpl telesales

televisar [26] vb to televise

televisión (pl **televisiones**) nf television ▷ ¿Qué ponen en la televisión esta noche? What's on the television tonight?; **la televisión por cable** cable television; **la televisión digital** digital TV

televisor nm television set

telón (pl **telones**) nm curtain ▷ Subió el telón. The curtain rose.

tema nm ❶ topic ❷ subject ▷ Luego hablaremos de ese tema. We'll talk about that subject later.; **cambiar de tema** to change the subject; **temas de actualidad** current affairs

temblar [40] vb to tremble; **temblar de miedo** to tremble with fear; **temblar de frío** to shiver

temblor de tierra nm earthquake

tembloroso adj trembling

temer [9] vb ❶ to be afraid ❷ to be afraid of ▷ Le teme al profesor. He's afraid of the teacher.

temible adj fearsome

temor nm fear ▷ el temor a la oscuridad fear of the dark

temperamental adj temperamental

temperamento nm

temperament

temperatura nf temperature

tempestad nf storm

templado adj ❶ lukewarm (water, meal) ❷ mild (climate)

templo nm temple

temporada nf season ▷ la temporada alta the high season ▷ la temporada baja the low season

temporal adj temporary
▶ nm storm

temporario adj (in Latin America) temporary

temprano adv early; **por la mañana temprano** early in the morning

ten vb see **tener**

tenaz (pl **tenaces**) adj tenacious

tenazas nfpl pliers

tendedero nm ❶ clothes line ❷ clothes horse

tendencia nf tendency

tender [21] vb ❶ to hang out ❷ to lay out; **Me tendió la mano.** He stretched out his hand to me.; **tender a hacer algo** to tend to do something; **tenderse en el sofá** to lie down on the sofa; **tender la cama** (in Latin America) to make the bed; **tender la mesa** (in Latin America) to lay the table

tendero, -a nm/f shopkeeper

tendido adj **La ropa estaba tendida.** The washing was hanging out.; **Lo encontré tendido en el suelo.** I found him lying on the floor.

tendón (pl **tendones**) nm tendon

tendrá vb see **tener**

tenedor nm fork

tener [54] vb ❶ to have ▷ Tengo dos hermanas. I have two sisters.; **¿Cuántos años tienes?** How old are you?; **Tiene cinco metros de largo.** It's five metres long.; **Ten cuidado.** Be careful.; **No tengas miedo.** Don't be afraid.; **Tenía el pelo mojado.** His hair was wet. ❷ to hold ▷ Tenía el pasaporte en la mano. He was holding his passport in his hand.; **tener que hacer algo** to have to do something; **Tendrías que comer más.** You should eat more.; **No tienes por qué ir.** There's no reason why you should go.; **Eso no tiene nada que ver.** That's got nothing to do with it.; **¡Tenga!** Here you are!; **tenerse en pie** to stand

tenga vb see **tener**

teniente nmf lieutenant

tenis nm tennis; **¿Juegas al tenis?** Do you play tennis?; **tenis de mesa** table tennis

tenista nmf tennis player

tenor nm tenor

tensar [26] vb to tighten

tensión (pl **tensiones**) nf ❶ tension ❷ blood pressure ▷ El médico me tomó la tensión. The doctor took my blood pressure.

tenso adj ❶ tense ❷ taut

tentación (pl **tentaciones**) nf temptation; **caer en la tentación** to give in to temptation

tentador, a adj tempting

tentar [40] vb to tempt; **No me tienta la idea.** The idea isn't very tempting.

tentativa nf attempt

tentempié (pl **tentempiés**) nm snack

tenue adj faint

teñir [46] vb to dye

teología nf theology

teoría nf theory ▷ En teoría es fácil. In theory it's easy.

teórico adj theoretical

terapéutico adj therapeutic

terapia nf therapy

tercer adj = **tercero**

tercero, -a adj, pron third

> **tercero** is shortened to **tercer** before masculine singular nouns.

▷ la tercera vez the third time
▷ Llegué el tercero. I arrived third.; **una tercera parte de la población** a third of the population; **Vivo en el tercero.** I live on the third floor.; **el Tercer Mundo** the Third World

tercio nm third

terciopelo nm velvet

terco adj obstinate

tergiversar [26] vb to distort

terminal nm terminal
▶ nf terminal

terminante adj ❶ categorical ❷ strict

terminantemente adv strictly

terminar [26] vb ❶ to finish; **cuando terminó de hablar** when he finished talking ❷ to end; **Terminaron peleándose.** They ended up fighting.; **Se nos ha terminado el café.** We've run

out of coffee.; **He terminado con Andrés.** I've broken up with Andrés.

término nm term ▷ un término médico a medical term; **por término medio** on average

termita nf termite

termo® nm Thermos flask®

termómetro nm thermometer; **Le puse el termómetro.** I took his temperature.

termostato nm thermostat

ternera nf veal

ternero, -a nm/f calf

ternura nf tenderness; **con ternura** tenderly

terrateniente nmf landowner

terraza nf ❶ balcony ❷ roof terrace

terremoto nm earthquake

terreno nm ❶ land; **un terreno** a piece of land ❷ field; **el terreno de juego** the pitch; **Lo decidiremos sobre el terreno.** We'll decide as we go along.

terrestre adj land

terrible adj terrible; **Tenía un cansancio terrible.** I was awfully tired.

terrier (pl **terriers**) nmf terrier

territorio nm territory

terrón (pl **terrones**) nm lump

terror nm terror; **Les tiene terror a los perros.** He's terrified of dogs.; **una película de terror** a horror film

terrorismo nm terrorism

terrorista adj, nmf terrorist; **un terrorista suicida** a suicide bomber

tesis (*pl* **tesis**) *nf* thesis

tesón *nm* determination

tesorero, -a *nm/f* treasurer

tesoro *nm* treasure; **Ven aquí, tesoro.** Come here, darling.

test (*pl* **tests**) *nm* test ▷ **Hoy nos han hecho un test.** We had a test today.

testamento *nm* will; **hacer testamento** to make one's will; **el Antiguo Testamento** the Old Testament; **el Nuevo Testamento** the New Testament

testarudo *adj* stubborn

testigo *nmf* witness; **Fui testigo del accidente.** I witnessed the accident.

testimonio *nm* evidence

tétanos *nm* tetanus

tetera *nf* **①** teapot **②** (*in Chile, Mexico*) kettle **③** (*in Mexico*) baby's bottle

tetina *nf* teat

textil *adj, nm* textile

texto *nm* text; **un libro de texto** a textbook

textura *nf* texture

tez *nf* complexion

ti *pron* you ▷ **una llamada para ti** a call for you; **Sólo piensas en ti mismo.** You only think of yourself.

tía *nf* **①** aunt ▷ **mi tía** my aunt **②** girl ▷ **Es una tía majísima.** She's a really nice girl.

tibio *adj* lukewarm

tiburón (*pl* **tiburones**) *nm* shark

tic *nm* tic ▷ **un tic nervioso** a nervous tic

tictac *nm* tick-tock

tiemblo *vb see* **temblar**

tiempo *nm* **①** time ▷ **No tengo tiempo.** I don't have time. ▷ **¿Qué haces en tu tiempo libre?** What do you do in your spare time? ▷ **Me llevó bastante tiempo.** It took me quite a long time.; **¿Cuánto tiempo hace que vives aquí?** How long have you been living here?; **Hace mucho tiempo que no la veo.** I haven't seen her for a long time.; **al mismo tiempo** at the same time; **perder el tiempo** to waste time; **al poco tiempo** soon after; **a tiempo** in time ▷ **Llegamos a tiempo de ver la película.** We got there in time to see the film. **②** weather; **¿Qué tiempo hace ahí?** What's the weather like there?; **Hizo buen tiempo.** The weather was fine. **③** half ▷ **Metieron el gol durante el segundo tiempo.** They scored the goal during the second half. **④** tense (*of verb*)

tienda *nf* shop; **una tienda de comestibles** a grocer's shop; **ir de tiendas** to go shopping; **una tienda de campaña** a tent

tiendo *vb see* **tender**

tiene *vb see* **tener**

tiento *vb see* **tentar**

tierno *adj* **①** tender **②** fresh

tierra *nf* **①** land; **la Tierra Santa** the Holy Land; **tierra adentro** inland **②** soil; **la Tierra** the Earth

tieso *adj* **①** stiff **②** straight ▷ **Ponte tiesa.** Stand up straight.

tiesto *nm* flowerpot

tigre nm tiger

tijeras nfpl scissors

timar [26] vb ① to con ② to rip off

timbrazo nm ring

timbre nm ① bell ▷ Ya ha sonado el timbre. The bell has already gone.; **llamar al timbre** to ring the bell ② (in Mexico) stamp

timidez nf shyness

tímido adj shy

timo nm ① con ② rip off; ¡Vaya timo! What a rip-off!

tinta nf ink; **tinta China** Indian ink; **sudar tinta** to sweat blood

tinte nm dye

tintero nm inkwell

tinto nm red wine
▷ adj red (wine)

tintorería nf dry cleaner's

tiñendo vb see **teñir**

tío nm ① uncle; **mis tíos** my uncle and aunt ② guy ▷ Es un tío muy simpático. He's a really nice guy.

tiovivo nm merry-go-round

típicamente adv typically

típico adj typical

tipo nm ① kind ▷ No me gusta este tipo de fiestas. I don't like this kind of party.; **todo tipo de ...** all sorts of ... ② figure ▷ Marisa tiene un tipo muy bonito. Marisa has a lovely figure. ③ bloke ▷ un tipo de aspecto sospechoso a suspicious-looking bloke

tíquet (pl **tíquets**) nm ① ticket ② receipt

tira nf strip ▷ una tira de papel a strip of paper ▷ una tira cómica a comic strip

tirada nf ① print run ② circulation; **de una tirada** in one go

tirado adj ① dirt-cheap ② dead easy

tirador nm handle

tirana nf tyrant

tiránico adj tyrannical

tirano nm tyrant

tirante adj ① tight ② tense
▷ nm strap; **tirantes** braces

tirar [26] vb ① to throw ② to throw away; **tirar algo a la basura** to throw something out ③ to knock down; **tirar al suelo** to knock over ④ to drop; **tirar a la derecha** to turn right; **tirar de algo** to pull something; **tirar la cadena** (in Latin America) to pull the chain; **Vamos tirando.** We're getting by.; **tirarse al agua** to plunge into the water; **tirarse de cabeza** to dive in head first; **tirarse en el sofá** (in Latin America) to lie down on the sofa; **Se tiró toda la mañana estudiando.** He spent the whole morning studying.

tirita nf plaster

tiritar [26] vb to shiver; **tiritar de frío** to shiver with cold

tiro nm shot; **Lo mataron de un tiro.** They shot him dead.; **tiro al blanco** target practice; **un tiro libre** a free kick

tiroteo nm shoot-out

títere nm puppet

titubear [26] vb to hesitate

titulado adj qualified

titular [26] nm headline

▶ nmf ❶ holder ❷ owner

▶ vb to call; **¿Cómo vas a titular el trabajo?** What title are you going to give the essay?

título nm ❶ title ❷ qualification ▷ *Tiene el título de enfermera.* She has a nursing qualification. ❸ certificate

tiza nf chalk; **una tiza** a piece of chalk

toalla nf towel

tobillo nm ankle ▷ *Me he torcido el tobillo.* I've twisted my ankle.

tobogán (pl **toboganes**) nm ❶ slide ❷ toboggan

tocadiscos (pl **tocadiscos**) nm record player

tocador nm dressing table

tocar [49] vb ❶ to touch ❷ to play (*instrument, waltz*) ❸ to ring (*bell*) ❹ to blow (*horn*); **tocar a la puerta** (*in Latin America*) to knock on the door; **Te toca fregar los platos.** It's your turn to do the dishes.; **Le tocó la lotería.** He won the lottery.

tocino nm pork fat

todavía adv ❶ still ▷ *¿Todavía estás en la cama?* Are you still in bed? ❷ yet ▷ *Todavía no han llegado.* They haven't arrived yet.

todo, -a adj, pron ❶ all ▷ *todos los niños* all the children ▷ *Todos son caros.* They're all expensive. ▷ *el más bonito de todos* the prettiest of all; **toda la noche** all night; **todos vosotros** all of you; **todos los que quieran venir** all those

who want to come ❷ every ▷ *todos los días* every day ❸ the whole ▷ *He limpiado toda la casa.* I've cleaned the whole house.; **Ha viajado por todo el mundo.** He has travelled throughout the world.; **Todo el mundo lo sabe.** Everybody knows. ❹ everything ▷ *Lo sabemos todo.* We know everything. ▷ *todo lo que me dijeron* everything they told me ❺ everybody ▷ *Todos estaban de acuerdo.* Everybody agreed.; **Vaya todo seguido.** Keep straight on.; **todo lo contrario** quite the opposite

toldo nm ❶ sun blind ❷ awning ❸ sunshade

tolerar [26] vb to tolerate; **Sus padres le toleran demasiado.** His parents let him get away with too much.

tomar [26] vb ❶ to take; **tomarse algo a mal** to take something badly ❷ to have ▷ *¿Qué quieres tomar?* What are you going to have? ▷ *De postre tomé un helado.* I had an ice cream for dessert.; **Toma, esto es tuyo.** Here, this is yours.; **tomar el pelo a alguien** to pull somebody's leg; **tomar el aire** to get some fresh air; **tomar el sol** to sunbathe; **tomar nota de algo** to note something down

tomate nm tomato; **ponerse como un tomate** to turn as red as a beetroot

tomillo nm thyme

tomo nm volume

tonel nm barrel

tonelada nf ton

tónica nf tonic

tono nm ❶ tone ▷ *Lo dijo en tono cariñoso.* He said it in an affectionate tone.; **un tono de llamada** a ringtone ❷ shade (of colour)

tontería nf piece of nonsense; **tonterías** nonsense ▷ *¡Eso son tonterías!* That's nonsense! ▷ *¡No digas tonterías!* Don't talk nonsense!

tonto, -a nm/f fool; **hacer el tonto** to act the fool; **hacerse el tonto** to act dumb
▶ adj silly ▷ *¡Qué error más tonto!* What a silly mistake!

toparse[26] vb **toparse con alguien** to bump into somebody

topes nmpl **El autobús iba hasta los topes.** The bus was packed.

tópico nm cliché

topo nm mole

toque nm **dar los últimos toques a algo** to put the finishing touches to something

torcedura nf **una torcedura de tobillo** a sprained ankle

torcer vb ❶ to twist; **torcerse el tobillo** to sprain one's ankle ❷ to turn ▷ *torcer a la derecha* to turn right

torcido adj ❶ crooked ❷ bent

torear[26] vb to fight

toreo nm bullfighting

torero, -a nm/f bullfighter

tormenta nf storm; **Hubo tormenta.** There was a storm.; **un**

día de tormenta a stormy day

torneo nm tournament

tornillo nm ❶ screw; **A tu hermana le falta un tornillo.** Your sister's got a screw loose. ❷ bolt

toro nm bull; **los toros** bullfighting; **ir a los toros** to go to a bullfight

toronja nf (in Latin America) grapefruit

torpe adj clumsy

torre nf ❶ tower ▷ *la torre de control* the control tower ❷ pylon ❸ rook (in chess)

torta nf ❶ small flat cake ❷ (in Latin America) pie ❸ (in Mexico) filled roll; **pegar una torta a alguien** to give somebody a slap; **No entiendo ni torta.** I don't understand a thing.

tortilla nf ❶ omelette; **una tortilla de patatas** a Spanish omelette ❷ tortilla

tortuga nf ❶ tortoise ❷ turtle

torturar[26] vb to torture

tos (pl toses) nf cough; **Tengo mucha tos.** I have a bad cough.

toser[9] vb to cough

tostada nf ❶ piece of toast; **tostadas** toast ▷ *Tomé café con tostadas.* I had coffee and toast. ❷ (in Mexico) fried corn tortilla

tostado adj ❶ toasted ❷ roasted ❸ tanned

tostador nm toaster

tostar[12] vb ❶ to toast ❷ to roast

total adj, nm total; **un cambio total** a complete change; **En total**

éramos catorce. There were fourteen of us altogether.
▶ adv Total, que perdí mi trabajo. So, in the end, I lost my job.

totalitario adj totalitarian

totalmente adv ❶ totally ❷ completely; ¿Estás seguro? -Totalmente. Are you sure? -Absolutely.

tóxico adj toxic

toxicómano, -a nm/f drug addict

tozudo adj obstinate

trabajador, a nm/f worker
▶ adj hard-working

trabajar[26] vb to work; ¿En qué trabajas? What's your job?; Trabajo de camarero. I work as a waiter.; trabajar jornada completa to work full-time; trabajar media jornada to work part-time

trabajo nm ❶ work; estar sin trabajo to be unemployed; trabajo en equipo teamwork; el trabajo de la casa the housework; trabajos manuales handicrafts ❷ job ▷ No encuentro trabajo. I can't find a job.; quedarse sin trabajo to find oneself out of work ❸ essay ▷ Tengo que entregar dos trabajos mañana. I have to hand in two essays tomorrow.

tractor nm tractor

tradición (pl tradiciones) nf tradition

tradicional adj traditional

traducción (pl traducciones) nf translation

traducir[10] vb to translate

traductor, a nm/f translator

traer[55] vb ❶ to bring ▷ He traído el paraguas por si acaso. I've brought the umbrella just in case. ❷ to carry ▷ ¿Qué traes es esa bolsa? What are you carrying in that bag? ❸ to wear ▷ Traía un vestido nuevo. She was wearing a new dress.

traficante nmf dealer ▷ traficantes de armas arms dealers

tráfico nm traffic; un accidente de tráfico a road accident; tráfico de drogas drug-trafficking

tragar[38] vb to swallow; No la trago. I can't stand her.

tragedia nf tragedy

trágico adj tragic

trago nm drink ▷ ¿Te apetece un trago? Do you fancy a drink?; de un trago in one gulp

traición (pl traiciones) nf ❶ betrayal ❷ treason

traicionar[26] vb to betray

traicionero adj treacherous

traidor, a nm/f traitor

traigo vb see traer

tráiler (pl tráilers) nm ❶ trailer ❷ articulated lorry

traje nm ❶ suit; un traje de chaqueta a suit ❷ dress; el traje de novia the bridal gown; un traje de baño (1) a pair of swimming trunks (2) a swimsuit

trama nf plot

tramitar[26] vb Estoy tramitando un préstamo con el banco. I'm negotiating a loan with the bank.; Estamos tramitando el divorcio. We are going through divorce proceedings.

tramo nm ❶ section ❷ flight

trampa nf trap ▷ caer en la trampa to fall into the trap; **Les tendió una trampa.** He set a trap for them.; **hacer trampa** to cheat

trampolín (pl **trampolines**) nm ❶ diving board ❷ trampoline

tramposo, -a nm/f cheat

tranquilamente adv ❶ calmly ❷ peacefully

tranquilidad nf peace and quiet; **Respondió con tranquilidad.** He answered calmly.; **Llévatelo a casa y léelo con tranquilidad.** Take it home with you and read it at your leisure.

tranquilizar [14] vb ❶ to calm down ❷ to reassure

tranquilo adj ❶ calm ❷ relaxed ❸ peaceful

transatlántico nm ocean liner

transbordador nm ferry; **el transbordador espacial** the space shuttle

transbordo nm Hay que hacer transbordo en París. You have to change trains in Paris.

transcurrir vb to pass

transeúnte nmf passer-by

transferencia nf transfer ▷ transferencia bancaria bank transfer

transformación (pl **transformaciones**) nf transformation

transformar [26] vb ❶ to transform ❷ to convert ▷ Hemos

transformado el garaje en sala de estar. We've converted the garage into a living room.; **transformarse** to turn into

transfusión (pl **transfusiones**) nf Me hicieron una transfusión de sangre. They gave me a blood transfusion.

transgénico adj genetically modified

tránsito nm traffic; **en tránsito** in transit

transmisión (pl **transmisiones**) nf broadcast ▷ una transmisión en directo a live broadcast

transmitir [59] vb ❶ to transmit ❷ to broadcast

transparente adj transparent

transpiración nf perspiration

transportar [26] vb to carry

transporte nm transport; **el transporte público** public transport

transportista nmf carrier

tranvía nm tram

trapo nm cloth; **un trapo de cocina** a dishcloth; **Pásale un trapo al espejo.** Give the mirror a wipe over.; **el trapo del polvo** the duster

tráquea nf windpipe

tras prep after ▷ Salimos corriendo tras ella. We ran out after her. ▷ semana tras semana week after week

trasero adj back ▷ la rueda trasera de la bici the back wheel of the bike ▶ nm bottom

trasladar [26] vb ❶ to move ❷ to

transfer

traslado nm move; **He pedido
traslado a Barcelona.** I've asked
for a transfer to Barcelona.; **los
gastos de traslado de la oficina**
the office's relocation expenses

trasluz nm **al trasluz** against
the light

trasnochar [26] vb to stay up late

trasplante nm transplant

trastero nm storage room

trastes nmpl (in Mexico) pots and
pans; **lavar los trastes** to do the
dishes

trasto nm piece of junk; **El desván
está lleno de trastos.** The loft is
full of junk.

trastornado adj disturbed

trastorno nm disruption
▷ La huelga ha causado muchos
trastornos. The strike has caused
a lot of disruption.; **trastornos
mentales** mental disorders

tratado nm treaty

tratamiento nm treatment;
Está en tratamiento médico.
He's having medical treatment.;
tratamiento de datos data
processing

tratar [26] vb ① to treat ② to
deal with ▷ Trataremos este tema
en la reunión. We'll deal with that
subject at the meeting.; **Trato con
todo tipo de gente.** I deal with all
sorts of people.; **tratar de hacer
algo** to try to do something; **¿De
qué se trata?** What's it about?; **La
película trata de un adolescente
en Nueva York.** The film is about a

teenager in New York.

trato nm deal ▷ hacer un trato to
make a deal; **¡Trato hecho!** It's
a deal; **No tengo mucho trato
con él.** I don't have much to do
with him.; **recibir malos tratos
de alguien** to be treated badly by
somebody

trauma nm trauma

través prep **a través de** (1) across
▷ Nadó a través del río. He swam
across the river. (2) through ▷ Se
enteraron a través de un amigo. They
found out through a friend.

travesía nf ① crossing ② side-
street

travesura nf prank; **hacer
travesuras** to get up to mischief

travieso adj naughty

trayecto nm ① journey ② way;
¿Qué trayecto hace el 34? What
way does the 34 go?

trazar [14] vb ① to draw ② to
draw up

trébol nm clover; **tréboles** clubs

trece adj, pron thirteen ▷ Tengo
trece años. I'm thirteen.; **el trece de
enero** the thirteenth of January

treinta adj, pron thirty ▷ Tiene
treinta años. He's thirty.; **el
treinta aniversario** the thirtieth
anniversary

tremendo adj ① terrible; **Hacía
un frío tremendo.** It was terribly
cold. ② tremendous

tren nm train; **viajar en tren** to
travel by train; **Tomé un tren
directo.** I took a through train.;
con este tren de vida with such

a hectic life

trenza nf plait; **Le hice una trenza.** I plaited her hair.

trepadora nf climber

trepar [26] vb to climb; **trepar a un árbol** to climb a tree

tres adj, pron three; **Son las tres.** It's three o'clock.; **Tiene tres años.** He's three.; **el tres de febrero** the third of February

trescientos, -as adj, pron three hundred

triángulo nm triangle

tribu nf tribe

tribuna nf ① platform ② stand

tribunal nm ① court ② board of examiners

tridimensional adj three-dimensional

trigo nm wheat

trillizos, -as nmpl/nfpl triplets

trimestral adj quarterly; **los exámenes trimestrales** the end-of-term exams

trimestre nm term

trinchar [26] vb to carve

trineo nm ① sledge ② sleigh

trío nm trio

tripa nf gut

triple adj three; **Esta habitación es el triple de grande.** This room is three times as big.; **Gastan el triple que nosotros.** They spend three times as much as we do.

triplicar [49] vb to treble

tripulación (pl **tripulaciones**) nf crew

triste adj ① sad ▷ **Me puse muy triste cuando me enteré de la noticia.**

I was very sad when I heard the news. ② gloomy

tristeza nf sadness

triturar [26] vb ① to crush ② to grind

triunfar [26] vb to triumph

triunfo nm triumph

trivial adj trivial

trocear [26] vb to cut up

trofeo nm trophy

trombón (pl **trombones**) nm trombone

trompa nf ① trunk ② horn

trompeta nf trumpet

tronar [12] vb to thunder

troncharse [26] vb **Yo me tronchaba de risa.** I was killing myself laughing.

tronco nm ① trunk ② log; **dormir como un tronco** to sleep like a log

trono nm throne

tropas nfpl troops

tropezar [20] vb to trip; **tropezar con una piedra** to trip on a stone; **tropezar contra un árbol** to bump into a tree; **Me tropecé con Juan en el banco.** I bumped into Juan in the bank.

tropezón (pl **tropezones**) nm trip; **dar un tropezón** to trip

tropical adj tropical

tropiece vb see **tropezar**

trotar [26] vb to trot

trozo nm piece ▷ **un trozo de madera** a piece of wood

trucha nf trout

truco nm trick; **Ya le he cogido el truco.** I've got the hang of it already.

truena *vb see* **tronar**

trueno *nm* Oímos un trueno. We heard a clap of thunder.; Me despertaron los truenos. The thunder woke me up.

tu *adj your* ▷ *tu coche* your car ▷ *tus familiares* your relations

tú *pron you* ▷ *Cuando tú quieras.* Whenever you like. ▷ *Llegamos antes que tú.* We arrived before you.

tubería *nf* pipe ▷ *Ha reventado una tubería.* A pipe has burst.

tubo *nm* ❶ pipe ▷ *el tubo de escape* the exhaust pipe; **el tubo de desagüe** the drainpipe ❷ tube

tuerca *nf* nut

tuerzo *vb see* **torcer**

tuétano *nm* marrow

tulipán *(pl* **tulipanes***) nm* tulip

tumba *nf* ❶ grave ❷ tomb

tumbar [26] *vb* to knock down; **tumbarse** to lie down

tumbona *nf* deck chair

tumor *nm* tumour

túnel *nm* tunnel; **un túnel de lavado** a car wash

Túnez *nm* Tunisia

turbante *nm* turban

turbina *nf* turbine

turbio *adj* cloudy

turbulento *adj* turbulent

turco, -a *nm/f* Turk
  ▷ *nm* Turkish *(language)*
  ▷ *adj* Turkish

turismo *nm* ❶ tourism; **casas de turismo rural** holiday cottages; **la oficina de turismo** the tourist office ❷ tourists ▷ *En verano hay mucho turismo.* In summer there

are a lot of tourists. ❸ car

turista *nmf* tourist

turístico *adj* tourist

turnarse [26] *vb* to take it in turns
  ▷ *Nos turnamos para fregar los platos.* We take it in turns to do the washing-up.

turno *nm* ❶ turn ▷ *cuando me tocó el turno* when it was my turn ❷ shift ▷ *Hago el turno de tarde.* I do the afternoon shift.

turquesa *adj, nf* turquoise ▷ *un anorak turquesa* a turquoise anorak

Turquía *nf* Turkey

turrón *(pl* **turrones***) nm*
  ● Turrón is a kind of nougat
  ● traditionally eaten at Christmas.

tutear [26] *vb* tutear a algn (1) to address someone as "tú" (2) to be on familiar terms with someone; **Se tutean.** They address each other as "tú".

tutor, a *nm/f* ❶ tutor ❷ guardian

tuve *vb see* **tener**

tuyo, -a *adj, pron yours* ▷ *¿Es tuyo este abrigo?* Is this coat yours? ▷ *La tuya está en el armario.* Yours is in the cupboard. ▷ *mis amigos y los tuyos* my friends and yours; **un amigo tuyo** a friend of yours

u _conj_ or
  u is used instead of o before words starting with o- or ho-.
  ▷ ¿Minutos u horas? Minutes or hours?

ubicado _adj_ situated

Ud. _abbr_ = usted

Uds. _abbr_ = ustedes

UE _abbr_ (= Unión Europea) EU

uf _excl_ **①** phew! **②** ugh!

úlcera _nf_ ulcer

últimamente _adv_ recently

ultimátum (_pl_ ultimátums) _nm_ ultimatum

último, -a _adj_ **①** last ▷ _la última vez que hablé con ella_ the last time I spoke to her **②** top ▷ _No llego al último estante._ I can't reach the top shelf. **③** back ▷ _Nos sentamos en la última fila._ We sat in the back row.; **la última moda** the latest fashion; **a última hora** at the last minute; **llegar en último lugar** to come last
  ▶ _nm/f_ the last one; **a últimos de mes** towards the end of the month; **por último** lastly

ultra _nmf_ right-wing extremist

ultrasónico _adj_ ultrasonic

ultravioleta _adj_ ultraviolet

un, a _art_ **①** a ▷ _una silla_ a chair **②** an ▷ _un paraguas_ an umbrella **③** some (in plural) ▷ _Fui con unos amigos._ I went with some friends.; **Tiene unas uñas muy largas.** He has very long nails.; **Había unas 20 personas.** There were about 20 people.; **Me he comprado unos zapatos de tacón.** I've bought a pair of high heels.

unánime _adj_ unanimous

undécimo, -a _adj, pron_ eleventh

únicamente _adv_ only

único, -a _adj_ **①** only ▷ _el único día que tengo libre_ the only day I have free; **Soy hija única.** I'm an only child.; **Lo único que no me gusta ...** The only thing I don't like ... **②** unique
  ▶ _nm/f_ **el único que me queda** the only one I've got left

unidad _nf_ **①** unit; **unidad de cuidados intensivos** intensive care unit **②** unity

unido _adj_ close ▷ _una familia muy unida_ a very close family

uniforme _adj_ even ▷ _una superficie uniforme_ an even surface
  ▶ _nm_ uniform ▷ _Llevaba el uniforme_

del colegio. He was wearing his school uniform.

unión (*pl* **uniones**) *nf* union; **la Unión Europea** the European Union

unir [**59**] *vb* ❶ to link ▷ *Este pasaje une los dos edificios.* This passage links the two buildings. ❷ to join ▷ *Unió los dos extremos con una cuerda.* He joined the two ends with some string. ❸ to unite ▷ *Es la persona perfecta para unir al partido.* He's the ideal person to unite the party. ❹ to bring together ▷ *La enfermedad de la madre ha unido a los hijos.* The mother's illness has brought the children together.; **unirse a algo** to join something; **Más adelante los dos caminos se unen.** The two paths join further on.; **Los dos bancos se han unido.** The two banks have merged.

universal *adj* universal

universidad *nf* university; **Universidad a Distancia** Open University

universitario, -a *nm/f* ❶ university student ❷ graduate ▶ *adj* university ▷ *estudiantes universitarios* university students

universo *nm* universe

uno, -a *adj, pron* one ▷ *Vivo en el número uno.* I live at number one. ▷ *Uno de ellos era mío.* One of them was mine.; **unos pocos** a few; **uno mismo** oneself; **Entraron uno a uno.** They came in one by one.;

unas diez personas about ten people; **el uno de abril** the first of April; **Es la una.** It's one o'clock.; **Unos querían ir, otros no.** Some of them wanted to go, others didn't.; **Se miraron uno al otro.** They looked at each other.

untar [**26**] *vb* **untar algo con algo** to spread something on something; **Te has untado las manos de chocolate.** You've got chocolate all over your hands.; **Unta el molde con aceite.** Grease the baking dish with oil.

uña *nf* ❶ nail ❷ claw

uranio *nm* uranium

urbanización (*pl* **urbanizaciones**) *nf* housing estate

urgencia *nf* emergency ▷ *en caso de urgencia* in an emergency ▷ *los servicios de urgencia* the emergency services; **urgencias** casualty ▷ *Tuvimos que ir a urgencias.* We had to go to casualty.; **con urgencia** urgently

urgente *adj* urgent; **Lo mandé por correo urgente.** I sent it express.

urna *nf* ballot box

Uruguay *nm* Uruguay

uruguayo, -a *nm/f, adj* Uruguayan

usado *adj* ❶ secondhand ▷ *una tienda de ropa usada* a secondhand clothes shop ❷ worn ▷ *Estas zapatillas están ya muy usadas.* These slippers are very worn now.

usar [**26**] *vb* ❶ to use ▷ *Uso una afeitadora eléctrica.* I use an electric razor. ❷ to wear ▷ *¿Qué número*

a
b
c
d
e
f
g
h
i
j
k
l
m
n
o
p
q
r
s
t
u
v
w
x
y
z

de zapato usas? What size shoe do you take?

uso nm use ▷ instrucciones de uso instructions for use

usted pron sg you ▷ Quisiera hablar con usted en privado. I'd like to speak to you in private.

ustedes pron pl you ▷ Quisiera hablar con ustedes en privado. I'd like to speak to you in private.

usual adj usual

usuario, -a nm/f user

utensilio nm utensil

útil adj useful

utilizar[14] vb to use

uva nf grape

va vb see **ir**

vaca nf ❶ cow ❷ beef ▷ No como carne de vaca. I don't eat beef.

vacaciones nfpl holidays; **las vacaciones de Navidad** the Christmas holidays; **La secretaria está de vacaciones.** The secretary is on holiday.; **En Agosto me voy de vacaciones.** I'm going on holiday in August.

vacante adj ❶ vacant ❷ unoccupied
▶ nf vacancy

vaciar[22] vb to empty

vacilar[26] vb to hesitate; **sin vacilar** without hesitating

vacío adj empty
▶ nm ❶ vacuum ❷ void

vacuna nf vaccine

vacunar[26] vb to vaccinate

vado nm "vado permanente" "no parking - in constant use"

vagabundo, -a nm/f tramp
▶ adj stray

vagar [38] vb to wander

vago, -a nm/f layabout; **hacer el vago** to laze around
▶ adj ❶ lazy ❷ vague

vagón (pl vagones) nm carriage; **vagón cama** sleeper; **vagón restaurante** restaurant car

vaho nm steam

vainilla nf vanilla

vajilla nf dishes ▷ La vajilla está en el lavaplatos. The dishes are in the dishwasher.; **Me regaló una vajilla de porcelana.** She gave me a china dinner service.

vale nm ❶ voucher; **un vale-regalo** a gift voucher; **un vale de descuento** a money-off coupon ❷ credit note

valenciano, -a nm/f, adj Valencian

valentía nf bravery; **con valentía** bravely

valer [56] vb ❶ to cost ▷ ¿Cuánto vale? How much does it cost? ❷ to be worth; **vale la pena** it's worth it; **vale la pena hacer el esfuerzo.** It's worth the effort.; **no vale la pena** it's not worth it; **No vale la pena gastar tanto dinero.** It's not worth spending that much money.; **No vale mirar.** You're not allowed to look.; **¡Eso no vale!** That's not fair!; **Este cuchillo no vale para nada.** This knife is useless.; **Yo no valdría para**

enfermera. I'd make a hopeless nurse.; **¿Vale? OK?; ¿Vamos a tomar algo? -¡Vale!** Shall we go for a drink? - OK!; **Más vale que te lleves el abrigo.** You'd better take your coat.; **No puede valerse por sí mismo.** He can't look after himself.

válido adj valid

valiente adj brave

valija nf (in River Plate) suitcase

valioso adj valuable

valla nf fence; **valla publicitaria** hoarding; **los cien metros vallas** the hundred metre hurdles

valle nm valley

valor nm ❶ value; **una pulsera de gran valor** an extremely valuable bracelet ❷ courage ▷ armarse de valor to pluck up courage; **objetos de valor** valuables

valorar [26] vb to value

vals nm waltz; **bailar un vals** to waltz

válvula nf valve

vampiro, -a nm/f vampire

vandalismo nm vandalism

vanguardia nf avant-garde; **de vanguardia** avant-garde

vanidad nf vanity

vanidoso adj vain

vano adj vain ▷ un intento vano a vain attempt; **en vano** in vain

vapor nm steam; **plancha de vapor** steam iron; **al vapor** steamed

vaquero adj denim ▷ una falda vaquera a denim skirt
▶ nm cowboy; **una película de**

a
b
c
d
e
f
g
h
i
j
k
l
m
n
o
p
q
r
s
t
u
v
w
x
y
z

vaqueros a western; **vaqueros** jeans

variable adj variable

variado adj varied

variar [22] vb to vary; **Decidí ir en tren, para variar.** I decided to go by train for a change.

varicela nf chicken pox

variedad nf variety

varilla nf rod; **la varilla del aceite** the dipstick

varios, -as adj, pron several ▷ Estuve enfermo varios días. I was ill for several days.; **Le hicimos un regalo entre varios.** Several of us clubbed together to get him a present.

variz (pl varices) nf varicose vein

varón (pl varones) adj male ▷ los herederos varones the male heirs
▶ nm ❶ Tiene dos hembras y un varón. She has two girls and a boy.; **Sexo: varón.** Sex: male.

Varsovia nf Warsaw

vasco, -a nm/f, adj Basque; **el País Vasco** the Basque Country
▶ nm Basque (language)

vasija nf vessel

vaso nm ❶ glass ▷ un vaso de leche a glass of milk; **un vaso de plástico** a plastic cup; **un vaso sanguíneo** a blood vessel

váter nm loo

Vaticano nm Vatican

vatio nm watt

vaya vb see ir

Vd. abbr = **usted**

Vds. abbr = **ustedes**

ve vb see ir, ver

vecindario nm neighbourhood

vecino, -a nm/f ❶ neighbour
▷ los vecinos de al lado the next door neighbours ❷ inhabitant ▷ todos los vecinos de Torrevieja all the inhabitants of Torrevieja
▶ adj neighbouring ▷ las ciudades vecinas the neighbouring towns

vegetación (pl vegetaciones) nf vegetation

vegetal adj, nm vegetable ▷ aceite vegetal vegetable oil

vegetariano, -a nm/f, adj vegetarian

vehículo nm vehicle

veinte adj, pron twenty ▷ Tiene veinte años. He's twenty.; **el veinte de enero** the twentieth of January; **el siglo veinte** the twentieth century

vejez nf old age

vejiga nf bladder

vela nf ❶ candle ❷ sail
❸ sailing; **un barco de vela** a yacht; **Pasé la noche en vela.** I had a sleepless night.

velarse [26] vb **Se han velado las fotos.** The photos got exposed by accident.

velero nm yacht

vello nm ❶ hair ▷ Tiene mucho vello. He's very hairy. ❷ down (on face)

velo nm veil

velocidad nf ❶ speed ▷ Pasó una moto a toda velocidad. A motorbike went past at full speed.; **¿A qué velocidad ibas?** How fast were you going? ❷ gear ▷ cambiar de velocidad to change gear

velocímetro nm speedometer

velocista nmf sprinter

velódromo nm cycle track

veloz (pl veloces) adj swift

ven vb see **ir, ver**

vena nf vein

vencedor, a nm/f winner
▶ adj winning ▷ el equipo vencedor
the winning team

vencer vb ❶ to defeat ❷ to
overcome (fear, obstacle) ❸ to
expire ▷ El pasaporte me vence
mañana. My passport expires
tomorrow.

vencido adj darse por vencido
to give up

venda nf ❶ bandage; Me
pusieron una venda en el
brazo. They bandaged my arm.
❷ blindfold

vendar [26] vb to bandage;
vendar los ojos a alguien to
blindfold someone

vendedor, a nm/f un vendedor
a salesman; una vendedora
a saleswoman; un vendedor
ambulante a pedlar; un vendedor
de periódicos a newspaper seller

vender [9] vb to sell; Venden
la oficina de arriba. The office
upstairs is for sale.; "se vende" "for
sale"; venderse por to sell for

vendimia nf grape harvest

vendré vb see **venir**

veneno nm ❶ poison ❷ venom

venenoso adj poisonous

venezolano, -a nm/f, adj
Venezuelan

Venezuela nf Venezuela

venganza nf revenge

vengarse vb to take revenge;
vengarse de alguien to take
revenge on someone; vengarse
de algo to avenge something

vengo vb see **venir**

venida nf arrival; La venida la
hicimos en autobús. We came
here by bus.

venir [57] vb ❶ to come ▷ Vino en
taxi. He came by taxi.; ¡Venga,
vámonos! Come on, let's go!;
¡Venga ya! Come off it!; el año
que viene next year ❷ to be ▷ La
noticia venía en el periódico. The
news was in the paper.; La casa se
está viniendo abajo. The house is
falling apart.; Mañana me viene
mal. Tomorrow isn't good for
me.; ¿Te viene bien el sábado? Is
Saturday alright for you?

venta nf sale; estar en venta to
be for sale

ventaja nf advantage

ventana nf window

ventanilla nf ❶ window (of
vehicle, at bank) ❷ box office

ventilación nf ventilation

ventilar [26] vb to air

ventisca nf ❶ gale force winds
❷ blizzard

ver [58] vb ❶ to see; Voy a ver
si está en su despacho. I'll see
if he's in his office.; Quedamos
en vernos en la estación. We
arranged to meet at the station.;
¡Luego nos vemos! See you later!;
Eso no tiene nada que ver. That
has nothing to do with it.; ¡No la

puede ver! He can't stand her!; **A ver …** Let's see …; **Se ve que no tiene idea de informática.** It's clear he's got no idea about computers. ❷ **to watch** ▷ *ver la televisión* to watch television

veranear [**26**] *vb* **to spend the summer holidays** ▷ *Veraneamos en Calpe.* We spend our summer holidays in Calpe.

veraneo *nm* **lugar de veraneo** summer resort; **No pudimos ir de veraneo el año pasado.** We couldn't go on holiday last summer.

verano *nm* **summer**

veras *nfpl* **de veras** really

veraz (*pl* **veraces**) *adj* **truthful**

verbena *nf* **open-air dance**; **la verbena de San Roque** the festival of San Roque

verbo *nm* **verb**

verdad *nf* **truth** ▷ *Les dije la verdad.* I told them the truth.; **¡Es verdad!** It's true!; **La verdad es que no tengo ganas.** I don't really feel like it.; **¿De verdad?** Really?; **De verdad que yo no dije eso.** I didn't say that, honestly.; **No era un policía de verdad.** He wasn't a real policeman.; **Es bonito, ¿verdad?** It's pretty, isn't it?; **No te gusta, ¿verdad?** You don't like it, do you?

verdadero *adj* **real**

verde *adj* ❶ **green** ▷ *Tiene los ojos verdes.* She has green eyes. ❷ **dirty** ▷ *un chiste verde* a dirty joke; **los verdes** the Green Party

▶ *nm* **green**

verdugo *nm* ❶ **executioner** ❷ **hangman**

verdulería *nf* **greengrocer's**

verdura *nf* **vegetables** ▷ *Comemos mucha verdura.* We eat a lot of vegetables.

vereda *nf* ❶ **path** ❷ (*in Chile, River Plate*) **pavement**

vergonzoso *adj* ❶ **shy** ❷ **disgraceful**

vergüenza *nf* ❶ **embarrassment** ▷ *Casi me muero de vergüenza.* I almost died of embarrassment.; **¡Qué vergüenza!** How embarrassing!; **Le da vergüenza pedírselo.** He's embarrassed to ask her. ❷ **shame** ▷ *No tienen vergüenza.* They have no shame.; **¡Es una vergüenza!** It's disgraceful!

verídico *adj* **true**

verificar [**49**] *vb* **to check**

verja *nf* ❶ **railings** ❷ **gate**

vermut *nm* **vermouth**

verruga *nf* ❶ **wart** ❷ **verruca**

versión (*pl* **versiones**) *nf* **version**; **una película francesa en versión original** a film in the original French version

verso *nm* ❶ **line** ❷ **verse**

vértebra *nf* **vertebra**

vertedero *nm* **rubbish tip**

verter [**21**] *vb* ❶ **to pour** ❷ **to dump**

vertical *adj* **vertical**; **Ponlo vertical.** Put it upright.

vértigo *nm* **vertigo**; **Me da vértigo.** It makes me dizzy.

Vespa® nf scooter

vespertino adj evening ▷ un diario vespertino an evening paper

vestíbulo nm ❶ hall ❷ foyer

vestido adj Iba vestida de negro. She was dressed in black.; **Yo iba vestido de payaso.** I was dressed as a clown.; **un hombre bien vestido** a well-dressed man ▶ nm dress; **el vestido de novia** the wedding dress

vestir[39] vb to wear; **vestir a alguien** to dress someone; **vestir bien** to dress well; **vestirse** to get dressed; **Se vistió de princesa.** She dressed up as a princess.; **ropa de vestir** smart clothes

vestón (pl **vestones**) nm (in Chile, River Plate) jacket

vestuario nm ❶ changing room (at baths, gym) ❷ wardrobe (for film, play)

veterinario, -a nm/f vet

vez (pl **veces**) nf time ▷ la próxima vez next time ▷ ¿Cuántas veces al año? How many times a year?; **a la vez** at the same time; **a veces** sometimes; **algunas veces** sometimes; **muchas veces** often; **cada vez más** more and more; **cada vez menos** less and less; **de una vez** once and for all; **de vez en cuando** from time to time; **en vez de** instead of; **¿La has visto alguna vez?** Have you ever seen her?; **otra vez** again; **tal vez** maybe; **una vez** once ▷ La veo una vez a la semana. I see her once a week.; **dos veces** twice; **una y**

otra vez again and again

vi vb see **ver**

vía nf ❶ track ❷ platform ▷ Nuestro tren sale por la vía dos. Our train leaves from platform two.; **por vía aérea** by airmail; **Madrid-Berlín vía París** Madrid-Berlin via Paris

viajar[26] vb to travel

viaje nm ❶ trip; **¡Buen viaje!** Have a good trip!; **un viaje de negocios** a business trip ❷ journey ▷ Es un viaje muy largo. It's a very long journey.; **estar de viaje** to be away; **salir de viaje** to go away; **una agencia de viajes** a travel agency; **el viaje de novios** honeymoon

viajero, -a nm/f passenger

víbora nf viper

vibración (pl **vibraciones**) nf vibration

vibrar[26] vb to vibrate

vicepresidenta nf ❶ vice president ❷ chairwoman

vicepresidente nm ❶ vice president ❷ chairman

viceversa adv vice versa

viciarse[26] vb to deteriorate; **viciarse con las drogas** to become addicted to drugs

vicio nm vice; **Tengo el vicio de morderme las uñas.** I have the bad habit of biting my nails.

víctima nf victim

victoria nf victory; **su primera victoria fuera de casa** their first away win

vid nf vine

vida nf life ▷ Llevan una vida muy tranquila. They lead a very quiet life. ▷ ¡Esto sí que es vida! This is the life!; **la media de vida de un televisor** the average life span of a television set; **vida nocturna** nightlife; **estar con vida** to survive; **salir con vida** to come out alive; **Se gana la vida haciendo traducciones.** He earns his living by translating.; **¡Vida mía!** My darling!

vídeo nm (in Latin America) video

vídeo nm video ▷ Tengo la película en vídeo. I've got the film on video.; **cinta de vídeo** videotape

videocámara nf video camera

videojuego nm video game

videollamada nf video call

videoteléfono nm videophone

vidriera nf ❶ stained glass window ❷ (in Latin America) shop window

vidrio nm ❶ glass ❷ piece of glass ❸ windowpane

viejo, -a nm/f **un viejo** an old man; **una vieja** an old woman; **los viejos** old people; **llegar a viejo** to reach old age

▸ adj old ▷ un viejo amigo mío an old friend of mine ▷ Estos zapatos ya están muy viejos. These shoes are very old now.; **hacerse viejo** to get old

viene vb see **venir**

viento nm wind; **Hace mucho viento.** It's very windy.

vientre nm stomach; **hacer de vientre** to go to the toilet

viernes (pl **viernes**) nm

▮ Days of the week start with a small letter in Spanish.

Friday ▷ el viernes pasado last Friday ▷ el viernes que viene next Friday; **Viernes Santo** Good Friday

vierta vb see **verter**

vietnamita nmf, adj Vietnamese; **los vietnamitas** the Vietnamese

viga nf ❶ beam ❷ girder

vigilancia nf ❶ surveillance ▷ bajo vigilancia policial under police surveillance ❷ vigilance; **patrulla de vigilancia** security patrol

vigilante nmf ❶ security guard; **un vigilante jurado** a security guard; **un vigilante nocturno** a night watchman ❷ store detective

vigilar [26] vb ❶ to guard ❷ to watch ▷ Nos vigilan. They're watching us. ❸ to keep an eye on ▷ ¿Me vigilas el bolso un momento? Can you keep an eye on my bag for a minute?

VIH abbr (= virus de inmunodeficiencia humana) HIV

villa nf ❶ town ❷ villa

villancico nm carol

vinagre nm vinegar

vínculo nm bond

vine vb see **venir**

viniendo vb see **venir**

vino nm wine; **vino blanco** white wine; **vino tinto** red wine; **vino de la casa** house wine

viña nf vineyard

viñedo nm vineyard

violación (pl **violaciones**) nf ❶ rape ❷ violation

violador nm rapist

violar [26] vb ❶ to rape ❷ to violate

violencia nf violence

violento adj ❶ violent ❷ embarrassing ▷ *Era una situación violenta.* It was an embarrassing situation.; **Me resulta violento decírselo.** I'm embarrassed to tell him.

violeta adj purple

> When **violeta** is used as an adjective, it never changes its ending.
>
> ▷ *unas cortinas violeta* some purple curtains
> ▶ nm purple (colour)
> ▶ nf violet (flower)

violín (pl **violines**) nm violin

violinista nmf violinist

violón (pl **violones**) nm double bass

violonchelista nmf cellist

violonchelo nm cello

virgen (pl **vírgenes**) adj ❶ virgin ❷ blank
> ▶ nf virgin; **la Virgen** the Virgin

Virgo nm Virgo (sign); **Soy virgo.** I'm Virgo.

viril adj virile

virilidad nf virility

virtud nf virtue

viruela nf smallpox

virus (pl **virus**) nm virus

visa nf (in Latin America) visa

visado nm visa

visera nf ❶ peak (of cap) ❷ visor

visibilidad nf visibility

visible adj visible

visillo nm net curtain

visión (pl **visiones**) nf ❶ vision ❷ view; **Tú estás viendo visiones.** You're seeing things.

visita nf ❶ visit; **hacer una visita a alguien** to visit someone; **horario de visita** visiting hours ❷ visitor ▷ *Tienes visita.* You've got visitors. ❸ hit (on website)

visitante nmf visitor

visitar [26] vb to visit

visón (pl **visones**) nm mink; **un abrigo de visón** a mink coat

víspera nf the day before ▷ *la víspera de la boda* the day before the wedding; **la víspera de Navidad** Christmas Eve

vista nf ❶ sight (sense); **a primera vista** at first glance; **alzar la vista** to look up; **bajar la vista** to look down; **perder la vista** to lose one's sight; **volver la vista** to look back; **conocer a alguien de vista** to know someone by sight; **hacer la vista gorda** to turn a blind eye; **¡Hasta la vista!** See you! ❷ view ▷ *una habitación con vistas al mar* a room with a sea view

vistazo nm **echar un vistazo a algo** to have a look at something

vistiendo vb see **vestir**

visto vb see **ver**
> ▶ adj **Está visto que ...** It's clear that ...; **Hurgarse la nariz está mal visto.** Picking your nose is frowned upon.; **por lo visto** apparently; **dar el visto bueno**

a algo to give something one's approval

vistoso adj showy

vital adj vital

vitalidad nf vitality

vitamina nf vitamin

vitorear [26] vb to cheer

vitrina nf ❶ glass cabinet ❷ (in Latin America) shop window

viudo, -a nm/f **un viudo** a widower; **una viuda** a widow
▶ adj **Es viuda.** She's a widow.; **quedarse viudo** to be widowed; **Se quedó viuda a los 50 años.** She was widowed at 50.

vivaracho adj lively

víveres nmpl provisions

vivero nm nursery

vivienda nf ❶ house ❷ flat ❸ housing ▷ la escasez de la vivienda the housing shortage

vivir [59] vb ❶ to live ▷ ¿Dónde vives? Where do you live?; **vivir de algo** to live on something ▷ Viven de su pensión. They live on his pension.; **¡Viva!** Hurray! ❷ to be alive ▷ ¿Todavía vive? Is he still alive?

vivo, -a adj ❶ alive ▷ Estaba vivo. He was alive. ❷ bright (colour, eyes); **en vivo** live ▷ una retransmisión en vivo a live broadcast

vocabulario nm vocabulary

vocación (pl vocaciones) nf vocation

vocal nf vowel

vodka nm vodka

volante nm steering wheel;

volantes flounce

volar [12] vb ❶ to fly ▷ El helicóptero volaba muy bajo. The helicopter was flying very low.; **Tuvimos que ir volando al hospital.** We had to rush to the hospital. ❷ to blow up ▷ Volaron el puente. They blew up the bridge.

volcán (pl volcanes) nm volcano

volcar vb ❶ to knock over (glass, container) ❷ to capsize (boat) ❸ to overturn (car, lorry); **volcarse** to get tipped over (drink, container)

voleibol nm volleyball

voltaje nm voltage

voltereta nf ❶ forward roll; **dar una voltereta** to do a forward roll ❷ somersault

voltio nm volt

volumen (pl volúmenes) nm volume; **bajar el volumen** to turn the volume down; **subir el volumen** to turn the volume up

voluntad nf ❶ will ▷ Lo hizo contra mi voluntad. He did it against my will. ❷ willpower

voluntario, -a nm/f volunteer; **ofrecerse voluntario para algo** to volunteer for something
▶ adj voluntary

volver [60] vb ❶ to come back ❷ to go back ❸ to turn ▷ Me volvió la espalda. He turned away from me.; **volver a hacer algo** to do something again; **volver en sí** to come round; **volverse** (1) to turn round ▷ Me volví para ver quién era. I turned round to see who it was. (2) to become; **Se ha vuelto**

muy cariñoso. He's become very affectionate.

vomitar [26] vb to be sick; **Vomitó todo lo que había comido.** He threw up everything he'd eaten.

vos pron (in River Plate) you

vosotros, -as pron pl you
▷ **Vosotros vendréis conmigo.** You'll come with me.; **Hacedlo vosotros mismos.** Do it yourselves.

votación (pl **votaciones**) nf Hicimos una votación. We took a vote.; **Salió elegida por votación.** She was voted in.

votar [26] vb to vote; **Votaron a los socialistas.** They voted for the Socialists.

voy vb see **ir**

voz (pl **voces**) nf voice; **hablar en voz alta** to speak loudly; **dar voces** to shout

vuelco vb see **volcar**
▶ nm **dar un vuelco** (1) to overturn (car) (2) to capsize (boat); **Me dio un vuelco el corazón.** My heart missed a beat.

vuelo vb see **volar**
▶ nm flight; **vuelo chárter** charter flight; **vuelo regular** scheduled flight

vuelta nf ❶ return ▷ un billete de ida y vuelta a return ticket ❷ lap ▷ Di tres vueltas a la pista. I did three laps of the track. ❸ change ▷ Quédese con la vuelta. Keep the change.; **a vuelta de correo** by return of post; **Vive a la vuelta de la esquina.** He lives round the corner.; **El coche dio la vuelta.**

The car turned round.; **dar la vuelta a la página** to turn the page; **dar la vuelta al mundo** to go round the world; **No le des más vueltas a lo que dijo.** Stop worrying about what he said.; **dar una vuelta** (1) to go for a walk (2) to go for a drive; **dar media vuelta** to turn round; **estar de vuelta** to be back; **vuelta ciclista** cycle race

vuelto vb see **volver**
▶ nm (in Latin America) change

vuelvo vb see **volver**

vuestro, -a adj, pron ❶ your ▷ vuestra casa your house ▷ vuestros amigos your friends; **un amigo vuestro** a friend of yours ❷ yours ▷ ¿Son vuestros? Are they yours?; **¿Es ésta la vuestra?** Is this one yours?; **¿Y los bocadillos? - Los vuestros están aquí.** Where are the sandwiches? - Yours are over here.

vulgar adj vulgar

W X

walkie-talkie (*pl* **walkie-talkies**) *nm* walkie-talkie

walkman® (*pl* **walkmans**) *nm* Walkman®

wáter *nm* loo

web *nf* ❶ web page ❷ (World Wide) Web

western (*pl* **westerns**) *nm* western

whisky (*pl* **whiskys**) *nm* whisky

windsurf *nm* ❶ windsurfing ❷ windsurf

xenófobo *adj* xenophobic

xilófono *nm* xylophone

y

y *conj* already ▷ *Andrés y su novia.* Andrés and his girlfriend.; **Yo quiero una ensalada. ¿Y tú?** I'd like a salad. What about you?; **¡Y yo!** Me too!; **¿Y qué?** So what?; **Son las tres y cinco.** It's five past three.

ya *adv* already; **ya no** any more ▷ *Ya no salimos juntos.* We're not going out any more.; **Estos zapatos ya me están pequeños.** These shoes are too small for me now.; **ya que** since; **Ya lo sé.** I know.; **Ya veremos.** We'll see.; **Rellena el impreso y ya está.** Fill in the form and that's it.; **¡Ya voy!** I'm coming!

yacimiento *nm* site; **un yacimiento petrolífero** an oilfield

yanqui *(mpl yanquis) adj, nmf* Yank

yate *nm* ❶ pleasure cruiser ❷ yacht

yedra *nf* ivy

yegua *nf* mare

yema *nf* ❶ yolk ❷ fingertip

yendo *vb see* **ir**

yerno *nm* son-in-law

yeso *nm* plaster

yo *pron* ❶ I ▷ *Carlos y yo no fuimos.* Carlos and I didn't go. ❷ me ▷ *¿Quién ha visto la película?* –Ana y yo. Who's seen the film? –Ana and me. ▷ *Es más alta que yo.* She's taller than me. ▷ *Soy yo, María.* It's me, María.; **¡Yo también!** Me too!; **yo mismo** myself ▷ *Lo hice yo misma.* I did it myself.; **yo que tú** if I were you

yoga *nm* yoga

yogur *nm* yoghurt

yudo *nm* judo

Yugoslavia *nf* Yugoslavia ▷ *en la antigua Yugoslavia* in the former Yugoslavia

Z

zafiro *nm* sapphire

zambullirse[26] *vb* to dive underwater

zamparse *vb* to wolf down

zanahoria *nf* carrot

zancadilla *nf* poner la zancadilla a alguien to trip someone up

zancudo *nm* (*in Latin America*) mosquito

zanja *nf* ditch

zanjar[26] *vb* to settle

zapatería *nf* ❶ shoe shop ❷ shoe repairer's

zapatero, -a *nm/f* shoemaker

zapatilla *nf* slipper; zapatillas de ballet ballet shoes; zapatillas de deporte training shoes

zapato *nm* shoe; zapatos de tacón high-heeled shoes; zapatos planos flat shoes

zarpa *nf* paw

zarpar[26] *vb* to set sail

zarza *nf* bramble

zarzamora *nf* blackberry bush

zigzag *nm* zigzag; una carretera en zigzag a winding road

Zimbabue *nm* Zimbabwe

zíper(*pl* zípers) *nm* (*in Latin America*) zip

zócalo *nm* ❶ skirting board ❷ (*in Latin America*) main square

zodíaco *nm* zodiac ▷ los signos del zodíaco the signs of the zodiac

zona *nf* area ▷ Viven en una zona muy tranquila. They live in a very quiet area.; Fue declarada zona neutral. It was declared a neutral zone.; una zona azul a pay-and-display area; una zona verde a green space; una zona industrial an industrial park; una zona peatonal a pedestrian precinct

zoo *nm* zoo

zoología *nf* zoology

zoológico *nm* zoo

zoólogo, -a *nm/f* zoologist

zoom(*pl* zooms) *nm* zoom lens

zorro *nm* fox

zueco *nm* clog

zumbar[26] *vb* to buzz ▷ Me zumban los oídos. My ears are buzzing.

zumo *nm* juice ▷ zumo de naranja orange juice

zurcir *vb* to darn

zurdo *adj* ❶ left-handed ❷ left-footed

zurrar[26] *vb* to thrash

a *indef art*

Use **un** for masculine nouns, **una** for feminine nouns.

① un *m* ▷ *a book* un libro ◆ **②** una *f* ▷ *an apple* una manzana

Sometimes **a** is not translated, particularly if referring to professions. ▷ *He's a butcher.* Es carnicero. ▷ *I haven't got a car.* No tengo coche.; **70 kilometres an hour** 70 kilómetros por hora; **30 pence a kilo** 30 peniques el kilo

abandon *vb* abandonar

abbey *n* abadía *f*

abbreviation *n* abreviatura *f*

ability *n* capacidad *f*; **to have the ability to do something** tener la capacidad de hacer algo

able *adj* **to be able to do**

something poder hacer algo ▷ *Will you be able to come on Saturday?* ¿Puedes venir el sábado?

abolish *vb* abolir

abortion *n* aborto *m*; **to have an abortion** abortar

about *prep, adv* **①** sobre ▷ *a book about London* un libro sobre Londres ▷ *I don't know anything about it.* No sé nada sobre eso.; **I'm phoning you about tomorrow's meeting.** Te llamo por lo de la reunión de mañana.; **What's it about?** ¿De qué trata? **②** (*approximately*) unos (*f* unas) ▷ *It takes about 10 hours.* Se tarda unas 10 horas.; **at about 11 o'clock** sobre las 11 **③** por ▷ *to walk about the town* caminar por la ciudad; **What about me?** ¿Y yo?; **to be about to do something** estar a punto de hacer algo ▷ *I was about to go out.* Estaba a punto de salir.; **How about going to the cinema?** ¿Qué tal si vamos al cine?

above *prep, adv*

When something is located above something, use **encima de**. When there is movement involved, use **por encima de**.

① encima de ▷ *There was a picture above the fireplace.* Había un cuadro encima de la chimenea. **②** por encima de ▷ *He put his hands above his head.* Puso las manos por encima de la cabeza.; **above all** sobre todo **③** (*more than*) más de ▷ *above 40 degrees* más de 40 grados

abroad adv **to go abroad** ir al extranjero; **to live abroad** vivir en el extranjero

absence n ❶ (of people) ausencia f ❷ (of things) falta f ▷ absence from school la falta de asistencia a clase

absent adj ausente

absent-minded adj distraído

absolutely adv totalmente ▷ I absolutely refuse to do it. Me niego totalmente a hacerlo.; **Jill's absolutely right.** Jill tiene toda la razón.; **It's absolutely delicious!** ¡Está riquísimo!; **They did absolutely nothing to help him.** No hicieron absolutamente nada para ayudarle.

abuse n (of power) abuso m; **to shout abuse at somebody** insultar a alguien
  ▶ vb maltratar; **abused children** niños maltratados

academic adj académico ▷ the academic year el año académico

academy n academia f

accelerate vb acelerar

accelerator n acelerador m

accent n acento m ▷ He's got a Spanish accent. Tiene acento español.

accept vb aceptar ▷ She accepted the offer. Aceptó la oferta.; **to accept responsibility for something** asumir la responsabilidad de algo

acceptable adj aceptable

access n acceso m ▷ He has access to confidential information. Tiene acceso a información reservada.;

Her ex-husband has access to the children. Su ex marido puede ver a los niños.

accessory n accesorio m ▷ fashion accessories los accesorios de moda

accident n accidente m ▷ to have an accident sufrir un accidente; **by accident (1)** (by chance) por casualidad ▷ They made the discovery by accident. Lo descubrieron por casualidad. **(2)** (by mistake) sin querer ▷ The burglar killed him by accident. El ladrón lo mató sin querer.

accidental adj I didn't do it deliberately, it was accidental. No lo hice adrede, fue sin querer.

accommodation n alojamiento m

accompany vb acompañar

according to prep según ▷ According to him, everyone had gone. Según él, todos se habían ido.

account n ❶ (with bank, at shop) cuenta f; **to do the accounts** llevar la contabilidad ❷ (report) informe m; **to take something into account** tener algo en cuenta; **by all accounts** a decir de todos; **on account of** (because of) a causa de

accountancy n contabilidad f

accountant n contable mf (LatAm contador m, contadora f) ▷ She's an accountant. Es contable.

accuracy n exactitud f

accurate adj exacto

accurately adv con exactitud

accuse vb **to accuse somebody**

of something acusar a alguien de algo ▷ *The police are accusing her of murder.* La policía la acusa de asesinato.

ace n **as** m ▷ *the ace of hearts* el as de corazones

ache n **dolor** m ▷ *stomach ache* dolor de estómago
▶ vb **My leg's aching.** Me duele la pierna.

achieve vb **conseguir**

achievement n **logro** m

acid n **ácido** m

acid rain n **lluvia f ácida**

acne n **acné** m

acrobat n **acróbata** mf

across prep, adv ❶ **al otro lado de** ▷ *He lives across the river.* Vive al otro lado del río. ❷ **a través de** ▷ *an expedition across the Sahara* una expedición a través del Sahara; **to run across the road** cruzar la calle corriendo

act vb **actuar** ▷ *The police acted quickly.* La policía actuó con rapidez. ▷ *He acts really well.* Actúa muy bien.
▶ n **acto** m ▷ *in the first act* en el primer acto; **It was all an act.** Era todo un cuento.

action n **acción** f (pl **acciones**)

active adj **activo** ▷ *He's a very active person.* Es una persona muy activa.

activity n **actividad** f

actor n **actor** m

actress n **actriz** f (pl **actrices**)

actual adj **real** ▷ *The film is based on actual events.* La película está basada en hechos reales.

> ▍ Be careful not to translate **actual** by the Spanish word **actual**.

actually adv ❶ **realmente** ▷ *Did it actually happen?* ¿Ocurrió realmente? ❷ **de hecho** ▷ *I was so bored I actually fell asleep!* ¡Me aburría tanto que de hecho me quedé dormido!; **Fiona's awful, isn't she? - Actually, I quite like her.** Fiona es una antipática, ¿verdad? - Pues a mí me cae bien.; **Actually, I don't know him at all.** La verdad es que no lo conozco de nada.

AD abbr (= *Anno Domini*) **d.C.** (= *después de Cristo*) ▷ *in 800 AD* en el año 800 d.C.

ad n **anuncio** m

adapt vb **adaptar** ▷ *His novel was adapted for television.* Su novela fue adaptada para la televisión.; **to adapt to something** adaptarse a algo ▷ *He adapted to his new school very quickly.* Se adaptó a su nuevo colegio muy rápidamente.

adaptor n ❶ (*for several plugs*) **ladrón** m (pl **ladrones**) ❷ (*for different types of plugs*) **adaptador** m

add vb **añadir** ▷ *Add more flour to the dough.* Añada más harina a la masa.

add up vb **sumar** ▷ *Add up the figures.* Suma las cifras.

addict n **adicto** m, **adicta** f; **a drug addict** un drogadicto ▷ *She's a drug addict.* Es drogadicta.; **Martin's a football addict.** Martin es un fanático del fútbol.

addicted adj **to be addicted to** drogas ser drogadicto; **She's addicted to heroin.** Es heroinómana.; **She's addicted to soaps.** Es una apasionada de las telenovelas.

addition n **in addition** además; **in addition to** además de

address n dirección f (pl direcciones)

adjective n adjetivo m

adjust vb ❶ (temperature, height) regular ❷ (mechanism) ajustar; **to adjust to something** adaptarse a algo ▷ He adjusted to his new school very quickly. Se adaptó a su nuevo colegio muy rápidamente.

adjustable adj regulable

administration n administración f

admiral n almirante m

admire vb admirar

admission n entrada f ▷ "admission free" "entrada gratuita"

admit vb reconocer ▷ He admitted that he'd done it. Reconoció que lo había hecho.

adolescent n adolescente mf

adopt vb adoptar

adopted adj adoptivo

adoption n adopción f (pl adopciones)

adore vb adorar

adult n adulto m, adulta f; **adult education** la educación de adultos

advance vb avanzar ▷ Technology has advanced a lot. La tecnología ha

avanzado mucho.
▶ n **in advance** con antelación ▷ They bought the tickets a month in advance. Compraron los billetes con un mes de antelación.

advanced adj avanzado

advantage n ventaja f ▷ Going to university has many advantages. Ir a la universidad tiene muchas ventajas.; **to take advantage of something** aprovechar algo ▷ He took advantage of his day off to have a rest. Aprovechó su día libre para descansar.; **to take advantage of somebody** aprovecharse de alguien ▷ The company was taking advantage of its employees. La compañía se aprovechaba de sus empleados.

adventure n aventura f

adverb n adverbio m

advert n anuncio m

advertise vb anunciar ▷ Jobs are advertised in the papers. Las ofertas de empleo se anuncian en los periódicos.

advertisement n anuncio m

advertising n publicidad f

advice n consejo m ▷ to ask for advice pedir consejo ▷ I'd like to ask your advice. Quería pedirte consejo.; **to give somebody advice** aconsejar a alguien; **a piece of advice** un consejo

advise vb aconsejar ▷ He advised me to wait. Me aconsejó que esperara. ▷ He advised me not to go there. Me aconsejó que no fuera.

   aconsejar que has to be
   followed by a verb in the
   subjunctive.

aerial n antena f

aerobics n ① aerobic m ▷ I do
aerobics. Hago aerobic.

aeroplane n avión m (pl aviones)

aerosol n aerosol m

affair n ① aventura f ▷ to have
an affair with somebody tener una
aventura con alguien ② asunto m
▷ The government has mishandled the
affair. El gobierno ha llevado mal
el asunto.

affect vb afectar

affectionate adj cariñoso

afford vb permitirse ▷ I can't
afford a new pair of jeans. No
puedo permitirme comprar
otros vaqueros.; **We can't afford
to go on holiday.** No podemos
permitirnos el lujo de ir de
vacaciones.

afraid adj **to be afraid of
something** tener miedo de algo
▷ I'm afraid of spiders. Tengo miedo
de las arañas.; **I'm afraid I can't
come.** Me temo que no puedo ir.;
I'm afraid so. Me temo que sí.; **I'm
afraid not.** Me temo que no.

Africa n África f

African adj africano
   ▶ n africano m, africana f

after prep, conj, adv ① después
de ▷ after the match después
del partido ▷ After watching the
television I went to bed. Después de
ver la televisión me fui a la cama.

② **después de que**
   When there's a change of
   subject in an **after** clause, use
   después de que with a verb in
   an appropriate tense instead
   of **después de +** infinitive.
▷ I met her after she had left the
company. La conocí después de que
dejó la empresa.

   después de que has to be
   followed by a verb in the
   subjunctive when referring to
   an event in the future.
▷ I'll help you after we've finished
this. Te ayudaré después de que
terminemos esto.; **after dinner**
después de cenar; **He ran after
me.** Corrió detrás de mí.; **after all**
después de todo; **soon after** poco
después

afternoon n tarde f ▷ in the
afternoon por la tarde ▷ 3 o'clock in
the afternoon las 3 de la tarde ▷ on
Saturday afternoon el sábado por
la tarde

afters n postre m ▷ What's for
afters? ¿Qué hay de postre?

aftershave n aftershave m

afterwards adv después ▷ She
left not long afterwards. Se marchó
poco después.

again adv otra vez ▷ I'd like to hear
it again. Me gustaría escucharlo
otra vez.

   In Spanish you often use
   the verb **volver a** and an
   infinitive to talk about doing
   something **again**.
▷ I'd like to hear it again. Me

gustaría volver a escucharlo.; **Can you tell me again?** ¿Me lo puedes repetir?; **Do it again!** ¡Vuelve a hacerlo!; **again and again** una y otra vez

against prep **①** contra ▷ He leant against the wall. Se apoyó contra la pared. **②** en contra de ▷ I'm against nuclear testing. Estoy en contra de las pruebas nucleares.

age n edad f ▷ an age limit un límite de edad; **at the age of sixteen** a los dieciséis años; **I haven't been to the cinema for ages.** Hace siglos que no voy al cine.

agenda n orden m del día

Be careful not to translate **agenda** by the Spanish word **agenda**.

agent n agente mf

aggressive adj agresivo

ago adv **two days ago** hace dos días; **How long ago did it happen?** ¿Cuánto hace que ocurrió?

agony n **to be in agony** sufrir mucho dolor

agree vb estar de acuerdo ▷ I don't agree! ¡No estoy de acuerdo! ▷ I agree with Carol. Estoy de acuerdo con Carol.; **to agree to do something** (1) (when someone requests) aceptar hacer algo ▷ He agreed to go with her. Aceptó acompañarla. (2) (arrange) acordar hacer algo ▷ They agreed to meet again next week. Acordaron volver a reunirse la semana próxima.; **to agree that...** reconocer que... ▷ I

agree it's difficult. Reconozco que es difícil.; **Garlic doesn't agree with me.** El ajo no me sienta bien.

agreement n acuerdo m; **to be in agreement** estar de acuerdo

agricultural adj agrícola

agriculture n agricultura f

ahead adv delante ▷ She looked straight ahead. Miró hacia delante.; **to plan ahead** hacer planes con antelación; **The Spanish are five points ahead.** Los españoles llevan cinco puntos de ventaja.; **Go ahead! Help yourself!** ¡Venga! ¡Sírvete!

aid n ayuda f; **in aid of children** a beneficio de la infancia

AIDS n sida m

aim vb **to aim at** apuntar a ▷ He aimed a gun at me. Me apuntó con una pistola.; **The film is aimed at children.** La película está dirigida a los niños.; **to aim to do something** pretender hacer algo ▶ n propósito m

air n aire m ▷ To get some fresh air tomar un poco el aire; **by air** en avión

air-conditioned adj con aire acondicionado

air conditioning n aire m acondicionado

Air Force n ejército m del aire

air hostess n azafata f ▷ She's an air hostess. Es azafata.

airline n línea f aérea

airmail n **by airmail** por correo aéreo

airplane n (in US) avión m (pl

aviones)

airport n aeropuerto m

aisle n (in plane, cinema) pasillo m

alarm n alarma f ▷ a fire alarm una alarma contra incendios

alarm clock n despertador m

album n álbum m

alcohol n alcohol m

alcoholic n alcohólico m, alcohólica f
  ▶ adj alcohólico ▷ alcoholic drinks bebidas alcohólicas

alert adj ❶ (lively) despierto
  ❷ (vigilant) atento ▷ We must stay alert. Hay que estar atentos.

A levels npl bachillerato
  Under the reformed Spanish
  Educational System, if students
  stay on at school after the age
  of 16, they can do a two-year
  course - **bachillerato**. In
  order to get in to university,
  they sit an entrance exam - **la
  selectividad** - in the subjects
  they have been studying for the
  bachillerato.

Algeria n Argelia f

alien n ❶ (foreigner) extranjero m, extranjera f ❷ (extraterrestrial) extraterrestre m f

alike adv **to look alike** parecerse ▷ The two sisters look alike. Las dos hermanas se parecen.

alive adj vivo

all adj, pron, adv todo ▷ all day todo el día ▷ all the apples todas las manzanas; **All of us went.** Fuimos todos.; **all alone** completamente solo; **not at all** en absoluto

▷ I'm not at all tired. No estoy en absoluto cansado.; **Thank you.
- Not at all.** Gracias. - De nada.; **The score is five all.** El marcador es de empate a cinco.

allergic adj alérgico ▷ to be allergic to something ser alérgico a algo

allergy n alergia f

allow vb **to allow somebody to do something** dejar a alguien hacer algo ▷ His mum allowed him to go out. Su madre le dejó salir. ▷ He's not allowed to go out at night. No le dejan salir por la noche.; **Smoking is not allowed.** Está prohibido fumar.

all right adv, adj bien ▷ Everything turned out all right. Todo salió bien. ▷ Are you all right? ¿Estás bien?; **Is that all right with you?** ¿Te parece bien?; **The film was all right.** La película no estuvo mal.; **We'll talk about it later.
- All right.** Lo hablamos después.
- Vale.

almond n almendra f

almost adv casi ▷ It's almost finished. Está casi terminado.

alone adj, adv solo ▷ She lives alone. Vive sola.; **to leave somebody alone** dejar en paz a alguien ▷ Leave her alone! ¡Déjala en paz!; **to leave something alone** no tocar algo ▷ Leave my things alone! ¡No toques mis cosas!

along prep, adv por ▷ Chris was walking along the beach. Chris paseaba por la playa.; **all along** desde el principio ▷ He was lying to me all along. Me había mentido desde el principio.

aloud adv en voz alta

alphabet n alfabeto m

Alps npl Alpes mpl

already adv ya ▷ Liz had already gone. Liz ya se había ido.

also adv también

alter vb cambiar

alternate adj **on alternate days** en días alternos

alternative n alternativa f ▷ You have no alternative. No tienes otra alternativa.; **Fruit is a healthy alternative to chocolate.** La fruta es una opción más sana que el chocolate.; **There are several alternatives.** Hay varias posibilidades.
▷ adj otro ▷ They made alternative plans. Hicieron otros planes.; **alternative medicine** la medicina alternativa

alternatively adv **Alternatively, we could just stay at home.** Si no, podemos simplemente quedarnos en casa.

although conj aunque ▷ Although she was tired, she stayed up late. Aunque estaba cansada, se quedó levantada hasta tarde.

altogether adv ❶ (in total) en total ▷ You owe me £20 altogether. En total me debes 20 libras. ❷ (completely) del todo ▷ I'm not altogether happy with your work. No estoy del todo satisfecho con tu trabajo.

aluminium (US **aluminum**) n

aluminio m

always adv siempre ▷ He's always moaning. Siempre está quejándose.

am vb see **be**

a.m. abbr de la mañana ▷ at 4 a.m. a las 4 de la mañana

amateur n amateur mf (pl amateurs)

amazed adj asombrado ▷ I was amazed that I managed to do it. Estaba asombrado de haberlo conseguido.

amazing adj ❶ asombroso ▷ That's amazing news! ¡Es una noticia asombrosa! ❷ extraordinario ▷ Vivian's an amazing cook. Vivian es una cocinera extraordinaria.

ambassador n embajador m, embajadora f

ambition n ambición f (pl ambiciones)

ambitious adj ambicioso

ambulance n ambulancia f

amenities npl **The town has many amenities.** La ciudad ofrece gran variedad de servicios.

America n ❶ (United States) Estados mpl Unidos ❷ (continent) América f

American adj norteamericano
▷ n norteamericano m, norteamericana f ▷ the Americans los norteamericanos

among prep entre

amount n cantidad f ▷ a huge amount of rice una cantidad enorme de arroz; **a large amount of money** una alta suma de dinero

amp n ❶ (amplifier) amplificador m
❸ (ampere) amperio m

amplifier n amplificador m

amuse vb ❶ (make laugh) divertir
▷ The thought seemed to amuse
him. La idea parecía divertirle.
❷ (entertain) entretener ▷ He was
most amused by the story. El cuento
le entretuvo mucho.

amusement arcade n salón m
de juegos

an indef art see **a**

analyse vb analizar

analysis n análisis m (pl análisis)

analyze vb (in US) analizar

ancestor n antepasado m

anchor n ancla f

> Although it's a feminine noun,
> remember that you use **el** and
> **un** with **ancla**.

ancient adj antiguo ▷ ancient
Greece la antigua Grecia;
an ancient monument un
monumento histórico

and conj y ▷ Mary and Jane. Mary
y Jane.

> Use **e** to translate **and** before
> words beginning with "i" or
> "hi" but not "hie".
> ▷ Miguel and Ignacio. Miguel e
> Ignacio.

> **and** is not translated when
> linking numbers.
> ▷ two hundred and fifty doscientos
> cincuenta; **Please try and come!**
> ¡Procura venir!; **He talked and
> talked.** No paraba de hablar.;
> **better and better** cada vez mejor

angel n ángel m

anger n enfado m (LatAm enojo m)

angle n ángulo m

angry adj enfadado (LatAm
enojado) ▷ to be angry with
somebody estar enfadado con
alguien ▷ Your father looks very
angry. Tu padre parece estar muy
enfadado.; **to get angry** enfadarse
(LatAm enojarse)

animal n animal m

ankle n tobillo m ▷ I've twisted my
ankle. Me he torcido el tobillo.

anniversary n aniversario m
▷ wedding anniversary aniversario
de bodas

announce vb anunciar

announcement n anuncio m

annoy vb molestar ▷ Make a note of
the things that annoy you. Haz una
lista de las cosas que te molestan.;
He's really annoying me. Me
está fastidiando de verdad.; **to
be annoyed with somebody**
estar molesto con alguien; **to
get annoyed** enfadarse (LatAm
enojarse) ▷ Don't get annoyed! ¡No
te enfades!

annoying adj molesto ▷ the most
annoying problem el problema más
molesto; **I find it very annoying.**
Me molesta mucho.

annual adj anual

anorak n anorak m (pl anoraks)

anorexia n anorexia f

another adj, pron otro ▷ Have
you got another skirt? ¿Tienes otra
falda?; **Another two kilometres.**
Dos kilómetros más.

answer vb responder ▷ Can you

answer my question? ¿Puedes contestar a mi pregunta?; **to answer the phone** contestar al teléfono; **to answer the door** abrir la puerta ▷ *Can you answer the door please?* ¿Puedes ir a abrir la puerta?

▶ *n* ❶ *(to question)* respuesta *f* ❷ *(to problem)* solución *f* (*pl* soluciones)

answering machine *n* contestador *m* automático

ant *n* hormiga *f*

Antarctic *n* **the Antarctic** el Antártico

anthem *n* **the national anthem** himno nacional

antibiotic *n* antibiótico *m*

antique *n* antigüedad *f*

antique shop *n* tienda *f* de antigüedades

antiseptic *n* antiséptico *m*

anxious *adj* preocupado

any *adj, adv*

> In questions and negative sentences **any** is usually not translated.

▷ *Have you got any change?* ¿Tienes cambio? ▷ *Are there any beans left?* ¿Quedan alubias? ▷ *He hasn't got any friends.* No tiene amigos.

> Use **algún/alguna** + singular noun in questions and **ningún/ninguna** + singular noun in negatives where **any** is used with plural nouns and the number of items is important.

▷ *Do you speak any foreign languages?* ¿Hablas algún idioma

extranjero? ▷ *I haven't got any books by Cervantes.* No tengo ningún libro de Cervantes.

> Use **cualquier** in affirmative sentences.

▷ *Any teacher will tell you.* Cualquier profesor te lo dirá.; **Come any time you like.** Ven cuando quieras.; **Would you like any more coffee?** ¿Quieres más café?; **I don't love him any more.** Ya no le quiero.

▶ *pron* ❶ *(in questions)* alguno *(f* alguna) ▷ *I need a stamp. Have you got any?* Necesito un sello. ¿Te queda alguno?

> Only use **alguno/alguna** if **any** refers to a countable noun. Otherwise don't translate it.

▷ *I fancy some soup. Have we got any?* Me apetece sopa. ¿Tenemos? ❷ *(in negatives)* ninguno *(f* ninguna) ▷ *I don't like any of them.* No me gusta ninguno.

> Only use **ninguno/ninguna** if **any** refers to a countable noun. Otherwise don't translate it.

▷ *Did you buy the oranges? - No, there weren't any.* ¿Compraste las naranjas? - No, no había.

anybody *pron* ❶ alguien

> Use **alguien** in questions.

▷ *Has anybody got a pen?* ¿Tiene alguien un bolígrafo? ❷ nadie

> Use **nadie** in negative sentences.

▷ *I can't see anybody.* No veo a

nadie. ❷ <u>cualquiera</u>
▮ Use **cualquiera** in affirmative sentences.
▷ Anybody can learn to swim. Cualquiera puede aprender a nadar.

anyhow adv = **anyway**

anyone pron = **anybody**

anything pron ❶ <u>algo</u>
▮ Use **algo** in questions.
▷ Do you need anything? ¿Necesitas algo? ▷ Would you like anything to eat? ¿Quieres algo de comer?
❷ <u>nada</u>
▮ Use **nada** in negative sentences.
▷ I can't hear anything. No oigo nada. ❸ <u>cualquier cosa</u>
▮ Use **cualquier cosa** in affirmative sentences.
▷ Anything could happen. Puede pasar cualquier cosa.

anyway adv <u>de todas maneras</u>

anywhere adv ❶ <u>en algún sitio</u>
▮ Use **en** or **a algún sitio** in questions.
▷ Have you seen my coat anywhere? ¿Has visto mi abrigo en algún sitio? ▷ Are we going anywhere? ¿Vamos a algún sitio? ❷ <u>en ningún sitio</u>
▮ Use **en** or **a ningún sitio** in negative sentences.
▷ I can't find it anywhere. No lo encuentro en ningún sitio. ▷ I can't go anywhere. No puedo ir a ningún sitio. ❸ <u>en cualquier sitio</u>
▮ Use **en cualquier sitio** in affirmative sentences.

▷ You can buy stamps almost anywhere. Se pueden comprar sellos casi en cualquier sitio.; **You can sit anywhere you like.** Siéntate donde quieras.

apart adv **The two towns are 10 kilometres apart.** Los dos pueblos están a 10 kilómetros el uno del otro.; **It was the first time we had been apart.** Era la primera vez que estábamos separados.; **apart from** aparte de ▷ Apart from that, everything's fine. Aparte de eso, todo va bien.

apartment n <u>piso</u> m (LatAm <u>apartamento</u> m)

apologize vb <u>disculparse</u> ▷ He apologized for being late. Se disculpó por llegar tarde.; **I apologize!** ¡Lo siento!

apology n <u>disculpa</u> f

apostrophe n <u>apóstrofo</u> m

apparent adj ❶ <u>aparente</u> ▷ for no apparent reason sin razón aparente ❷ <u>claro</u> ▷ It was apparent that he disliked me. Estaba claro que no le caigo bien.

apparently adv <u>por lo visto</u> (LatAm <u>dizque</u>) ▷ Apparently he was abroad when it happened. Por lo visto estaba en el extranjero cuando ocurrió.

appeal vb ❶ <u>hacer un llamamiento</u> ▷ They appealed for help. Hicieron un llamamiento de ayuda. ❷ <u>atraer</u> ▷ Greece doesn't appeal to me. Grecia no me atrae.
▶ n <u>llamamiento</u> m ▷ They have launched an appeal for unity. Han

hecho un llamamiento a la unidad.

appear vb ❶ aparecer ▷ The bus appeared around the corner. El autobús apareció por la esquina.; **to appear on TV** salir en la tele ❷ parecer ▷ She appeared to be asleep. Parecía estar dormida.

appendicitis n apendicitis f ▷ She's got appendicitis. Tiene apendicitis.

appetite n apetito m

applaud vb aplaudir

applause n aplausos mpl

apple n manzana f; **an apple tree** un manzano

applicant n candidato m, candidata f

application n **a job application** una solicitud de empleo

application form n impreso m de solicitud

apply vb **to apply for a job** solicitar un empleo; **to apply to** afectar a ▷ This rule doesn't apply to us. Esta norma no nos afecta.

appointment n cita f ▷ to make an appointment with someone concertar una cita con alguien; **I've got a dental appointment.** Tengo hora con el dentista.

appreciate vb agradecer ▷ I really appreciate your help. Agradezco de veras tu ayuda.

apprentice n aprendiz m, aprendiza f (mpl aprendices)

approach vb ❶ acercarse a ▷ He approached the house. Se acercó a la casa. ❷ abordar ▷ to approach a problem abordar un problema

appropriate adj apropiado ▷ That dress isn't very appropriate for an interview. Ese vestido no es muy apropiado para una entrevista.; **Tick the appropriate box.** Marque la casilla que corresponda.

approval n aprobación f

approve vb **I don't approve of his choice.** No me parece bien su elección.; **They didn't approve of his girlfriend.** No veían con buenos ojos a su novia.

approximate adj aproximado

apricot n albaricoque m

April n abril m ▷ in April en abril ▷ on 4 April el 4 de abril; **April Fool's Day** el día de los Santos Inocentes
- In Spanish-speaking countries
- **el día de los Santos Inocentes** falls on the 28th of December.
- People play practical jokes in the same way as they do on April Fool's Day.

apron n delantal m

Aquarius n (sign) Acuario m; **I'm Aquarius.** Soy acuario.

Arab adj árabe
▶ n árabe mf ▷ the Arabs los árabes

Arabic adj árabe

arch n arco m

archaeologist n arqueólogo m, arqueóloga f ▷ He's an archaeologist. Es arqueólogo.

archaeology n arqueología f

archbishop n arzobispo m

archeologist n (in US) arqueólogo m, arqueóloga f

archeology n (in US) arqueología f

architect n arquitecto m, arquitecta f ▷ She's an architect. Es arquitecta.

architecture n arquitectura f

Arctic n the Arctic el Ártico

are vb see be

area n ❶ zona f ▷ a mountainous area of Spain una zona montañosa de España ❷ superficie f

Argentina n Argentina f

Argentinian adj argentino
▶ n argentino m, argentina f

argue vb discutir ▷ They never stop arguing. Siempre están discutiendo.

argument n discusión f (pl discusiones); **to have an argument** discutir

Aries n (sign) Aries m; **I'm Aries.** Soy aries.

arithmetic n aritmética f

arm n brazo m ▷ I burnt my arm. Me quemé el brazo.

armchair n sillón m (pl sillones)

army n ejército m

around prep, adv ❶ alrededor de ▷ She wore a scarf around her neck. Llevaba una bufanda alrededor del cuello. ▷ It costs around £100. Cuesta alrededor de 100 libras.; **She ignored the people around her.** Ignoró a la gente que estaba a su alrededor.; **Shall we meet at around 8 o'clock?** ¿Quedamos sobre las 8? ❷ por ▷ I've been walking around the town. He estado paseando por la ciudad. ▷ We walked around for a while.

Paseamos por ahí durante un rato.; **around here** por aquí ▷ Is there a chemist's around here? ¿Hay alguna farmacia por aquí?

arrange vb organizar ▷ to arrange a party organizar una fiesta; **to arrange to do something** quedar en hacer algo ▷ They arranged to go out together on Friday. Quedaron en salir juntos el viernes.

arrangement n **to make an arrangement to do something** quedar en hacer algo; **a flower arrangement** un arreglo floral; **arrangements** los preparativos ▷ Pamela is in charge of the travel arrangements. Pamela se encarga de los preparativos para el viaje.

arrest vb detener
▶ n detención f (pl detenciones); **You're under arrest!** ¡Queda detenido!

arrival n llegada f ▷ the airport arrivals hall la sala de llegadas del aeropuerto

arrive vb llegar ▷ I arrived at 5 o'clock. Llegué a las 5.

arrow n flecha f

art n arte m; **works of art** las obras de arte; **art school** la escuela de Bellas Artes

artery n arteria f

art gallery n ❶ (state-owned) museo m ❷ (private) galería f de arte

article n artículo m

artificial adj artificial

artist n artista mf ▷ She's an artist. Es artista.

artistic adj artístico

as conj, adv ① cuando ▷ He came in as I was leaving. Entró cuando yo me iba. ② mientras ▷ All the jury's eyes were on him as he continued. Todo el jurado la observaba mientras él proseguía. ③ como ▷ As it's Sunday, you can have a lie-in. Como es domingo, puedes quedarte en la cama hasta tarde. ④ de ▷ He works as a waiter in the holidays. En vacaciones trabaja de camarero.; **as...as** tan...como ▷ Peter's as tall as Michael. Peter es tan alto como Michael.; **as much...as** tanto...como ▷ I haven't got as much energy as you. No tengo tanta energía como tú. ▷ Her coat cost twice as much as mine. Su abrigo costó el doble que el mío.; **as soon as possible** cuanto antes; **as from tomorrow** a partir de mañana; **as if** or **as though** como si

▎**como si** has to be followed by a verb in the subjunctive.
▷ She acted as if or as though she hadn't seen me. Hizo como si no me hubiese visto.

ash n ① (from fire, cigarette) ceniza f ② (tree, wood) fresno m

ashamed adj **to be ashamed** estar avergonzado ▷ I'm ashamed of myself for shouting at you. Estoy avergonzado de gritarte.; **You should be ashamed of yourself!** ¡Debería darte vergüenza!

ashtray n cenicero m

Asia n Ásia f

Asian adj asiático
▶ n asiático m, asiática f

ask vb ① preguntar ▷ "Have you finished?" she asked. "¿Has terminado?" preguntó.; **to ask somebody something** preguntar algo a alguien; **to ask about something** preguntar por algo ▷ I asked about train times to Leeds. Pregunté por el horario de trenes a Leeds.; **to ask somebody a question** hacer una pregunta a alguien ② pedir ▷ She asked him to do the shopping. Le pidió que hiciera la compra.

▎**pedir que** has to be followed by a verb in the subjunctive.

to ask for something pedir algo
▷ He asked for a cup of tea. Pidió una taza de té.; **Peter asked her out.** Peter le pidió que saliera con él. ③ invitar ▷ Have you asked Matthew to the party? ¿Has invitado a Matthew a la fiesta?

asleep adj **to be asleep** estar dormido; **to fall asleep** quedarse dormido

AS level n certificado académico que se hace entre los 'GCSEs' y los 'A levels'

asparagus n espárragos mpl

aspirin n aspirina f

assembly n (at school) reunión f general de todos los alumnos

assignment n (at school) tarea f

assistance n ayuda f

assistant n ① (in shop) dependiente m, dependienta f ② (helper) ayudante mf

association n asociación f (pl

asociaciones)

assortment n surtido m

assume vb suponer ▷ I assume she won't be coming. Supongo que no vendrá.

assure vb asegurar ▷ He assured me he was coming. Me aseguró que venía.

asthma n asma f

> Although it's a feminine noun, remember that you use **el** with **asma**.
>
> ▷ He's got asthma. Tiene asma.

astonish vb pasmar

astrology n astrología f

astronaut n astronauta mf

astronomy n astronomía f

at prep ❶ en ▷ at home en casa ▷ at school en la escuela ▷ at work en el trabajo ❷ a ▷ at 50 km/h a 50 km/h ▷ at 4 o'clock a las cuatro; **at night** por la noche; **at Christmas** en Navidad; **What are you doing at the weekend?** ¿Qué haces este fin de semana?; **at sign** (in email address) la arroba

ate vb see **eat**

Athens n Atenas f

athlete n atleta mf

athletic adj atlético

athletics n atletismo m ▷ I enjoy watching the athletics on television. Me gusta ver el atletismo en la televisión.

Atlantic n Atlántico m

atlas n atlas m (pl atlas)

atmosphere n atmósfera f

atom n átomo m

atomic adj atómico

attach vb atar ▷ They attached a rope to the car. Ataron una cuerda al coche.

attached adj to be attached to somebody tener cariño a alguien; Please find attached a cheque for £10. Se adjunta cheque de 10 libras.

attachment n (to email) archivo m adjunto

attack vb atacar
▶ n ataque m; to be under attack ser atacado

attempt n intento m
▶ vb to attempt to do something intentar hacer algo ▷ I attempted to write a song. Intenté escribir una canción.

attend vb asistir a ▷ to attend a meeting asistir a una reunión

attention n atención f; to pay attention to prestar atención a ▷ He didn't pay attention to what I was saying. No prestó atención a lo que estaba diciendo.; **Don't pay any attention to him!** ¡No le hagas caso!

attic n desván m (pl desvanes) (LatAm altillo m)

attitude n actitud f

attorney n (in US) abogado m, abogada f

attract vb atraer ▷ Oxford attracts lots of tourists. Oxford atrae a muchos turistas.

attraction n atracción f (pl atracciones) ▷ a tourist attraction una atracción turística

attractive adj atractivo

aubergine n berenjena f

auction n subasta f

audience n público m

August n agosto m ▷ in August en agosto ▷ on 13 August el 13 agosto

aunt n tía f; **my aunt and uncle** mis tíos

aunty n tía f

au pair n au pair f (pl au pairs)

Australia n Australia f

Australian adj australiano
▶ n australiano m, australiana f
▷ the Australians los australianos

Austria n Austria f

Austrian adj austríaco
▶ n austríaco m, austríaca f ▷ the Austrians los austríacos

author n autor m, autora f ▷ the author of the book el autor del libro; **a famous author** un escritor famoso

autobiography n autobiografía f

autograph n autógrafo m

automatic adj automático

automatically adv automáticamente

autumn n otoño m ▷ in autumn en el otoño

availability n disponibilidad f

available adj disponible
▷ According to the available information, it can't be done. De acuerdo con la información disponible, no se puede hacer.; **Free brochures are available on request.** Disponemos de folletos gratuitos para quien los solicite.; **Is Mr Cooke available today?** ¿Está libre el señor Cooke hoy?

avalanche n alud m

avenue n avenida f

average n media f ▷ on average de media
▶ adj medio ▷ the average price el precio medio

avocado n aguacate m

avoid vb evitar ▷ Avoid going out on your own at night. Evite salir solo por la noche.

awake adj to be awake estar despierto

award n premio m ▷ the award for the best actor el premio al mejor actor

aware adj to be aware that saber que; to be aware of something ser consciente de algo; not that I am aware of que yo sepa, no

away adj, adv It's two kilometres away. Está a dos kilómetros de distancia.; The holiday was two weeks away. Faltaban dos semanas para las vacaciones.; to be away estar fuera ▷ Jason was away on a business trip. Jason estaba fuera en viaje de negocios.; He's away for a week. Se ha ido una semana.; Go away! ¡Vete!; away from lejos de ▷ away from family and friends lejos de la familia y los amigos; It's 30 miles away from town. Está a 30 millas de la ciudad.

away match n It is their last away match. Es el último partido que juegan fuera.

awful adj horrible ▷ The weather's awful. Hace un tiempo horrible.;

I feel awful. Me siento fatal.; **We met and I thought he was awful.** Nos conocimos y me cayó fatal.; **an awful lot of work** un montón de trabajo

awkward *adj* ❶ (*uncomfortable: situation, shape*) incómodo; **Mike's being awkward about letting me have the car.** Mike no hace más que ponerme pegas para dejarme el coche. ❷ (*clumsy: gesture, movement*) torpe

axe *n* hacha *f*

> Although it's a feminine noun, remember that you use **el** and **un** with **hacha**.

baby *n* bebé *mf* (*pl* bebés)
baby carriage *n* (*in US*) cochecito *m* de niño
babysit *vb* hacer de canguro
babysitter *n* canguro *mf*
babysitting *n* **I don't like babysitting.** No me gusta hacer de canguro.
bachelor *n* soltero *m*
back *n* ❶ (*of person*) espalda *f* ❷ (*of animal*) lomo *m* ❸ (*of chair*) respaldo *m* ❹ (*of cheque, hand*) dorso *m*; **at the back of the house** en la parte de atrás de la casa; **in the back of the car** en la parte trasera del coche; **at the back of the class** al fondo de la clase
▶ *adj, adv* trasero ▷ *the back seat* el asiento trasero; **the back door** la puerta de atrás; **He's not back**

yet. Todavía no ha vuelto.; **to get back** volver ▷ *What time did you get back?* ¿A qué hora volviste?; **I'll call back later.** Volveré a llamar más tarde.

▷ *vb* respaldar ▷ *The union is backing his claim for compensation.* El sindicato respalda su demanda de compensación.; **to back a horse** apostar por un caballo; **She backed into the parking space.** Aparcó dando marcha atrás.

back up *vb* respaldar ▷ *She complained, and her colleagues backed her up.* Presentó una queja y sus colegas la respaldaron.

backache *n* dolor *m* de espalda ▷ *to have backache* tener dolor de espalda

backbone *n* columna *f* vertebral

backfire *vb* (*go wrong*) tener el efecto contrario

background *n* (*of picture*) fondo *m* ▷ *a house in the background* una casa en el fondo; **background noise** ruido de fondo; **his family background** su historial familiar

backhand *n* revés *m* (*pl* reveses)

backing *n* apoyo *m*

backpack *n* mochila *f*

backpacker *n* mochilero *m*, mochilera *f*

backside *n* trasero *m*

backstroke *n* espalda *f*

backup *n* apoyo *m* ▷ *We have extensive computer backup.* Tenemos amplio apoyo informático.; **a backup file** una copia de seguridad

backwards *adv* hacia atrás ▷ *to take a step backwards* dar un paso hacia atrás; **to fall backwards** caerse de espaldas

bacon *n* bacon *m* (LatAm tocino *m*) ▷ *bacon and eggs* los huevos fritos con bacon

bad *adj* ❶ malo

Use **mal** before a masculine singular noun.

▷ *bad weather* mal tiempo; **to be in a bad mood** estar de mal humor; **to be bad at something** ser malo para algo ▷ *I'm really bad at maths.* Soy muy malo para las matemáticas. ❷ (*serious*) grave ▷ *a bad accident* un accidente grave; **to go bad** (*food*) echarse a perder; **I feel bad about it.** (*guilty*) Me siento un poco culpable.; **How are you? - Not bad.** ¿Cómo estás? - Bien; **That's not bad at all.** No está nada mal.; **bad language** las palabrotas

badge *n* ❶ (*metal, plastic*) chapa *f* ❷ (*cloth*) escudo *m*

badly *adv* mal ▷ *badly paid* mal pagado; **badly wounded** gravemente herido; **He badly needs a rest.** Le hace muchísima falta un descanso.

badminton *n* bádminton *m* ▷ *to play badminton* jugar al bádminton

bad-tempered *adj* **to be bad-tempered (1)** (*by nature*) tener mal genio ▷ *He's very bad-tempered.* Tiene muy mal genio. **(2)** (*temporarily*) estar de mal humor ▷ *He was very bad-tempered* yesterday. Ayer estaba de muy mal humor.

bag n bolsa f

baggage n equipaje m

baggage reclaim n recogida f de equipajes

baggy adj (trousers) ancho

bagpipes npl gaita f sg

bake vb **to bake bread** hacer pan; **She loves to bake.** Le gusta cocinar al horno.

baked beans npl alubias fpl blancas en salsa de tomate

baked potato n patatas fpl asadas con piel (LatAm papas fpl asadas con cáscara)

baker n panadero m, panadera f ▷ He's a baker. Es panadero. ▷ at the baker's en la panadería

bakery n panadería f

balance n equilibrio m ▷ to lose one's balance perder el equilibrio ▶ vb mantener el equilibrio ▷ I balanced on the window ledge. Mantenía el equilibrio en el poyo de la ventana.; **She balanced on one leg.** Se mantenía a la pata coja.; **The boxes were carefully balanced.** Las cajas estaban cuidadosamente contrapesadas.

balanced adj equilibrado

balcony n balcón m (pl balcones)

bald adj calvo

ball n ❶ (for tennis, basketball, rugby) pelota f ▷ a golf ball una pelota de golf ❷ (for football) balón m (pl balones)

ballet n ballet m (pl ballets) ▷ ballet lessons las clases de ballet

ballet dancer n bailarín m, bailarina f (mpl bailarines)

ballet shoes npl zapatillas fpl de ballet

balloon n globo m; **a hot-air balloon** un globo aerostático

ballpoint pen n bolígrafo m

ballroom dancing n baile m de salón

ban n prohibición f (pl prohibiciones)
▶ vb prohibir

banana n plátano m ▷ a banana skin una piel de plátano

band n ❶ (pop, rock) grupo m ❷ (military) banda f ❸ (at a dance) orquesta f

bandage n venda f
▶ vb vendar ▷ The nurse bandaged his arm. La enfermera le vendó el brazo.

Band-Aid® n (in US) tirita f

bang n ❶ (noise) estallido m ▷ I heard a loud bang. Oí un fuerte estallido. ❷ (blow) golpe m ▷ a bang on the head un golpe en la cabeza
▶ vb golpear ▷ I banged my head. Me golpeé la cabeza.; **to bang on the door** aporrear la puerta; **to bang the door** dar un portazo

bank n ❶ (financial) banco m ❷ (of river, lake) orilla f

bank account n cuenta f bancaria

banker n banquero m, banquera f ▷ He's a banker. Es banquero.

bank holiday n día m festivo

banknote n billete m de banco

bar n ❶ (pub) bar m ❷ (counter)

a b c d e f g h i j k l m n o p q r s t u v w x y z

a
b
c
d
e
f
g
h
i
j
k
l
m
n
o
p
q
r
s
t
u
v
w
x
y
z

barra f; **a bar of chocolate**
(1) (*large*) una tableta de chocolate
(2) (*small*) una chocolatina; **a bar**
of soap una pastilla de jabón
barbecue n barbacoa f ▷ **to have a**
barbecue hacer una barbacoa
bare adj desnudo
barefoot adj, adv descalzo ▷ **The**
children go around barefoot. Los
niños van descalzos.
barely adv apenas ▷ **I could barely**
hear what she was saying. Apenas
oía lo que estaba diciendo.
bargain n ganga f ▷ **It was a**
bargain! ¡Era una ganga!
barge n barcaza f
bark vb ladrar
barmaid n camarera f ▷ **She's a**
barmaid. Es camarera.
barman n barman m (*pl* barmans)
▷ **He's a barman.** Es barman.
barn n granero m
barrel n **❶** (*container*) barril m
❷ (*of gun*) cañón m (*pl* cañones)
barrier n barrera f
bartender n (*in US*) barman m (*pl*
barmans) ▷ **He's a bartender.** Es
barman.
base n base f
baseball n béisbol m ▷ **to play**
baseball jugar al béisbol; **a**
baseball cap una gorra de béisbol
based adj **based on** basado en
basement n sótano m ▷ **a**
basement flat un apartamento en
el sótano
bash vb golpear con fuerza
  ▶ n **I'll have a bash at it.** Lo
intentaré.

basic adj básico ▷ **It's a basic**
model. Es un modelo básico.; **The**
accommodation was pretty
basic. El alojamiento tenía sólo lo
imprescindible.
basically adv básicamente ▷ **They**
are basically the same thing. Son
básicamente lo mismo.; **Basically,**
I don't like him. Simplemente, no
me gusta.
basics npl principios mpl básicos
basin n **❶** (*washbasin*) lavabo
m **❷** (*for cooking, mixing food*)
cuenco m
basis n base f ▷ **On the basis of**
what you've said. En base a lo
que has dicho.; **on a daily basis**
diariamente; **on a regular basis**
regularmente
basket n cesto m
basketball n **❶** baloncesto m ▷ **to**
play basketball jugar al baloncesto
bass n (*voice*) bajo m; **a bass**
guitar un bajo; **a double bass** un
contrabajo
bass drum n bombo m
bassoon n fagot m (*pl* fagots)
bat n **❶** (*for baseball, cricket*) bate
m **❷** (*for table tennis*) raqueta f
❸ (*animal*) murciélago m
bath n **❶** baño m ▷ **a hot bath** un
baño caliente; **to have a bath**
bañarse **❷** (*bathtub*) bañera f
bathe vb bañarse
bathing suit n (*in US*) traje m
de baño
bathroom n cuarto m de baño
bath towel n toalla f de baño
batter n masa f para rebozar

battery n ❶ (for torch, toy) pila f ❷ (for car) batería f

battle n batalla f ▷ the Battle of Hastings la batalla de Hastings; **It was a battle, but we managed in the end.** Fue muy difícil, pero al final lo conseguimos.

bay n bahía f

BC abbr (= before Christ) a.C. (= antes de Cristo)

be vb

> There are two basic verbs to translate **be** into Spanish: **estar** and **ser**. **estar** is used to form continuous tenses; to talk about where something is; and with adjectives describing a temporary state. It is also used with past participles used adjectivally even if these describe a permanent state.

❶ estar ▷ What are you doing? ¿Qué estás haciendo? ▷ Edinburgh is in Scotland. Edimburgo está en Escocia. ▷ I've never been to Madrid. No he estado nunca en Madrid. ▷ I'm very happy. Estoy muy contento. ▷ He's dead. Está muerto.

> **ser** is used to talk about the time and date; with adjectives describing permanent and inherent states such as nationality and colour; with nouns to say what somebody or something is; and to form the passive.

❷ ser ▷ It's four o'clock. Son las cuatro. ▷ It's the 28th of October today. Hoy es 28 de octubre. ▷ She's English. Es inglesa. ▷ He's a doctor. Es médico. ▷ Paris is the capital of France. París es la capital de Francia. ▷ He's very tall. Es muy alto. ▷ The house was destroyed by an earthquake. La casa fue destruida por un terremoto.

> Passive constructions are not as common in Spanish as in English. Either the active or a reflexive construction are preferred.

▷ He was killed by a terrorist. Lo mató un terrorista. ▷ These cars are produced in Spain. Estos coches se fabrican en España.

> When referring to the weather, use **hacer**.

It's a nice day, isn't it? Hace buen día, ¿verdad?; **It's cold.** Hace frío.; **It's too hot.** Hace demasiado calor.

> When using certain adjectives such as **cold**, **hot**, **hungry**, and **thirsty** to describe how you feel, use **tener** with a noun.

I'm cold. Tengo frío.; **I'm hungry.** Tengo hambre.

> When saying how old somebody is, use **tener**.

I'm fourteen. Tengo catorce años.; **How old are you?** ¿Cuántos años tienes?

beach n playa f

bead n cuenta f

beak n pico m

beam n (of light) rayo m

beans npl alubias fpl; **beans on toast** las alubias blancas en salsa de tomate sobre una tostada; **green beans** las judías verdes

bear n oso m
▶ vb aguantar ▷ I can't bear it! ¡No lo aguanto!

beard n barba f ▷ He's got a beard. Lleva barba. ▷ a man with a beard un hombre con barba

bearded adj con barba

beat n ritmo m
▶ vb ganar ▷ We beat them three-nil. Les ganamos tres a cero.; **Beat it!** ¡Lárgate! (informal)

beat up vb dar una paliza a

beautiful adj precioso

beauty n belleza f

beauty spot n (place) lugar m pintoresco

became vb see **become**

because conj porque; **because of** a causa de

become vb llegar a ser

bed n cama f; **to go to bed** acostarse; **to go to bed with somebody** irse a la cama con alguien

bed and breakfast n pensión f (pl pensiones) ▷ We stayed in a bed and breakfast. Nos quedamos en una pensión.; **How much is it for bed and breakfast?** ¿Cuánto es la habitación con desayuno?

bedclothes npl ropa f de cama

bedding n ropa f de cama

bedroom n dormitorio m

bedsit n estudio m

bedspread n colcha f

bedtime n Ten o'clock is my usual **bedtime.** Normalmente me voy a la cama a las diez.; **Bedtime!** ¡A la cama!

bee n abeja f

beef n carne f de vaca; **roast beef** el rosbif

beefburger n hamburguesa f

been vb see **be**

beer n cerveza f

beetle n escarabajo m

beetroot n remolacha f

before prep, conj, adv ❶ antes de ▷ before Tuesday antes del martes ▷ I'll phone before leaving. Llamaré antes de salir. ❷ antes de que

> ▌ **antes de que** has to be followed by a verb in the subjunctive.

▷ I'll call her before she leaves. La llamaré antes de que se vaya.; **I've seen this film before.** Esta película ya la he visto.; **the week before** la semana anterior

beforehand adv con antelación

beg vb ❶ (for money, food) mendigar ❷ suplicar

> ▌ **suplicar que** has to be followed by a verb in the subjunctive.

▷ He begged me to stop. Me suplicó que parara.

began vb see **begin**

beggar n mendigo m, mendiga f

begin vb empezar; **to begin doing something** empezar a hacer algo

beginner n principiante mf

beginning n comienzo m; **in the beginning** al principio

begun vb see **begin**

behalf n **on behalf of somebody** de parte de alguien

behave vb comportarse ▷ He behaved like an idiot. Se comportó como un idiota.; **to behave oneself** portarse bien ▷ Did the children behave themselves? ¿Se portaron bien los niños?; **Behave!** ¡Compórtate!

behaviour (US behavior) n comportamiento m

behind prep, adv detrás de ▷ behind the television detrás de la televisión; **to be behind** (late) ir atrasado ▷ I'm behind with my work. Voy atrasado con mi trabajo.
▶ n trasero m

beige adj beige (f + pl beige)
Pronounce this word like the English word **base**.

Belgian adj belga ▷ He's Belgian. Es belga.
▶ n belga mf ▷ the Belgians los belgas

Belgium n Bélgica f

believe vb creer ▷ I don't believe you. No te creo.; **I don't believe it!** ¡No me lo creo!; **to believe in something** creer en algo ▷ Do you believe in ghosts? ¿Crees en los fantasmas?

bell n **❶** (of door, in school) timbre m ▷ The bell goes at nine o'clock. El timbre suena a las nueve. **❷** (of church) campana f **❸** (of toy, on animal) cascabel m

belong vb **to belong to somebody** pertenecer a alguien ▷ This ring

belonged to my grandmother. Este anillo pertenecía a mi abuela.; **Who does it belong to?** ¿De quién es?; **That belongs to me.** Eso es mío.; **Do you belong to any clubs?** ¿Eres miembro de algún club?

belongings npl (things) cosas fpl ▷ my belongings mis cosas; **personal belongings** los efectos personales

below prep, adv **❶** debajo de ▷ the apartment directly below ours el apartamento que está justo debajo del nuestro **❷** abajo ▷ seen from below visto desde abajo ▷ on the floor below en el piso de abajo; **ten degrees below freezing** diez grados bajo cero

belt n cinturón m (pl cinturones)

bench n banco m

bend n curva f
▶ vb **❶** doblar ▷ I can't bend my arm. No puedo doblar el brazo. **❷** torcerse ▷ It bends easily. Se tuerce fácilmente.

bend down vb agacharse

bend over vb inclinarse

beneath prep bajo

benefit n beneficio m; **unemployment benefit** el subsidio de desempleo
▶ vb beneficiar ▷ This will benefit us all. Esto nos beneficiará a todos.; **He'll benefit from the change.** Se beneficiará con el cambio.

bent vb see **bend**
▶ adj torcido ▷ a bent fork un tenedor torcido; **to be bent**

on doing something estar empeñado en hacer algo

beret n boina f

berth n (bunk) litera f

beside prep al lado de ▷ *beside the television* al lado de la televisión.; **He was beside himself.** Estaba fuera de sí.; **That's beside the point.** Eso no viene al caso.

besides adv además ▷ *Besides, it's too expensive.* Además, es demasiado caro.; **... and much more besides.** ... y mucho más todavía.

best adj, adv mejor ▷ *He's the best player in the team.* Es el mejor jugador del equipo. ▷ *Janet's the best at maths.* Janet es la mejor en matemáticas. ▷ *Emma sings best.* Emma es la que canta mejor.; **That's the best I can do.** No puedo hacer más.; **to do one's best** hacer todo lo posible ▷ *It's not perfect, but I did my best.* No es perfecto, pero he hecho todo lo posible.; **You'll just have to make the best of it.** Tendrás que arreglártelas con lo que hay.

best man n padrino m de boda

bet n apuesta f

▶ vb apostar ▷ *I bet you he won't come.* Te apuesto a que no viene.

better adj, adv mejor ▷ *This one's better than that one.* Éste es mejor que aquél. ▷ *Are you feeling better now?* ¿Te sientes mejor ahora?; **That's better!** ¡Así está mejor!; **to get better (1)** (improve) mejorar ▷ *I hope the weather gets better soon.*

Espero que el tiempo mejore pronto. **(2)** (from illness) mejorarse ▷ *I hope you get better soon.* Espero que te mejores pronto.; **You'd better do it straight away.** Más vale hacerlo enseguida.; **I'd better go home.** Tengo que irme a casa.

between prep entre ▷ *between 15 and 20 minutes* entre 15 y 20 minutos

beware vb **Beware of the dog!** ¡Cuidado con el perro!

beyond prep, adv al otro lado de ▷ *There is a lake beyond the mountains.* Hay un lago al otro lado de las montañas.; **We have no plans beyond next year.** No tenemos planes para después del año que viene.; **the wheat fields and the mountains beyond** los campos de trigo y las montañas al fondo; **it's beyond me** no lo entiendo; **beyond belief** increíble; **beyond repair** irreparable

Bible n Biblia f

bicycle n bicicleta f

big adj grande ▷ *a big house* una casa grande ▷ *a big car* un coche grande

▊ Use **gran** before a singular noun.

▷ *it's a big business* es un gran negocio; **my big brother** mi hermano mayor; **He's a big guy.** Es un tipo grandote.; **Big deal!** ¡Vaya cosa!

bigheaded adj **to be bigheaded** ser engreído

bike n ❶ (bicycle) bici f ▷ *by bike* en

bici ❷ (*motorbike*) moto f

Although **moto** ends in -**o**, it is actually a feminine noun.

bikini n bikini m

bilingual adj bilingüe

bill n ❶ (*in restaurant*) cuenta f ▷ *Can we have the bill, please?* ¿Nos trae la cuenta, por favor? ❷ (*for gas, electricity, telephone*) factura f ▷ *the gas bill* la factura del gas ❸ (*in US*) billete m ▷ *a five-dollar bill* un billete de cinco dólares

billiards n billar m ▷ *to play billiards* jugar al billar

billion n mil millones mpl ▷ *two billion dollars* dos mil millones de dólares

bin n ❶ (*in kitchen*) cubo m de la basura ❷ (*for paper*) papelera f

binoculars npl prismáticos mpl; **a pair of binoculars** unos prismáticos

biochemistry n bioquímica f

biography n biografía f

biology n biología f

bird n pájaro m

birdwatching n He likes to go **birdwatching on Sundays.** Los domingos le gusta ir a ver pájaros.

Biro® n bolígrafo m

birth n nacimiento m ▷ *date of birth* la fecha de nacimiento

birth certificate n partida f de nacimiento

birth control n control m de natalidad

birthday n cumpleaños m (pl cumpleaños) ▷ *a birthday cake* un pastel de cumpleaños ▷ *a birthday*

card una tarjeta de cumpleaños ▷ *a birthday party* una fiesta de cumpleaños ▷ *When's your birthday?* ¿Cuándo es tu cumpleaños?

biscuit n galleta f

bishop n obispo m

bit vb see **bite**
▶ n ❶ (*piece*) trozo m; **a bit** un poco ▷ *He's a bit mad.* Está un poco loco.; **a bit of (1)** (*piece of*) un trozo de ▷ *a bit of cake* un trozo de pastel (2) (*a little*) un poco de ▷ *a bit of music* un poco de música; **It's a bit of a nuisance.** Es un poco fastidioso.; **to fall to bits** caerse a pedazos; **to take something to bits** desmontar algo; **bit by bit** poco a poco

bite vb ❶ (*person, dog*) morder ▷ *My dog's never bitten anyone.* Mi perro nunca ha mordido a nadie. ❷ (*insect*) picar ▷ *I got bitten by mosquitoes.* Me picaron los mosquitos.; **to bite one's nails** morderse las uñas
▶ n ❶ (*insect bite*) picadura f ❷ (*animal bite*) mordisco m; **to have a bite to eat** comer alguna cosa

bitter adj ❶ amargo ▷ *It tastes bitter.* Sabe amargo. ❷ glacial ▷ *It's bitter today.* Hoy hace un frío glacial.
▶ n cerveza británica a base de lúpulos

black adj negro ▷ *a black jacket* una chaqueta negra ▷ *She's black.* Es negra.; **black and white** blanco y negro

blackberry n mora f
blackbird n mirlo m
blackboard n pizarra f
black coffee n café m solo
blackcurrant n grosella f negra
blackmail n chantaje m
▶ vb chantajear
black pudding n morcilla f
blade n hoja f
blame vb echar la culpa a ▷ Don't blame me! ¡No me eches la culpa a mí!; **He blamed it on my sister.** Le echó la culpa a mi hermana.
blank adj ❶ (sheet of paper) en blanco ❷ (cassette) virgen (pl vírgenes); **My mind went blank.** Me quedé en blanco.
▶ n espacio m en blanco ▷ Fill in the blanks. Rellene los espacios en blanco.
blanket n manta f
blast n **a bomb blast** una explosión
blaze n incendio m
blazer n blazer m (pl blazers)
bleach n lejía f
bleed vb sangrar; **to bleed to death** morir desangrado; **My nose is bleeding.** Me sangra la nariz.
blender n licuadora f
bless vb bendecir; **Bless you!** (after sneezing) ¡Jesús! (LatAm ¡Salud!)
blew vb see **blow**
blind adj ciego
▶ n (for window) persiana f
blindfold n venda f
blink vb parpadear
blister n ampolla f

blizzard n ventisca f de nieve
block n bloque m ▷ a block of flats un bloque de apartamentos
▶ vb bloquear
blog n blog m
blonde adj rubio ▷ She's got blonde hair. Tiene el pelo rubio.
blood n sangre f
blood pressure n presión f sanguínea; **to have high blood pressure** tener la tensión alta
blood test n análisis m de sangre (pl análisis de sangre)
blouse n blusa f
blow n golpe m
▶ vb ❶ soplar ▷ A cold wind was blowing. Soplaba un viento frío. ❷ (whistle, trumpet) sonar; **to blow one's nose** sonarse la nariz
blow out vb apagar ▷ Blow out the candles! ¡Apaga las velas!
blow up vb ❶ volar ▷ They blew up a plane. Volaron un avión. ❷ inflar ▷ We've blown up the balloons. Hemos inflado los globos. ❸ saltar por los aires ▷ The house blew up. La casa saltó por los aires.
blow-dry n secado m con secador de mano; **Cut and blow-dry.** Corte y secado a mano.
blue adj azul ▷ a blue dress un vestido azul; **out of the blue** en el momento menos pensado
blues npl (music) blues m (pl blues)
blunder n metedura f de pata
blunt adj ❶ (person) directo ❷ (knife) desafilado
blush vb ruborizarse
board n ❶ (plank) tabla

f ❷ (blackboard) pizarra

f ❸ (noticeboard) tablón m
de anuncios (pl tablones de
anuncios) **❹** (for diving) trampolín
m (pl trampolines) **❺** (for games)
tablero m; **a chopping board** una
tabla de picar; **on board** a bordo;
"full board" "pensión completa"

boarder n interno m, interna f

board game n juego m de mesa

boarding card n tarjeta f de
embarque

boarding school n internado m

boast vb alardear; **to boast about
something** alardear de algo; **Stop
boasting!** ¡Deja ya de presumir!

boat n barco m

body n ❶ cuerpo m ▷ the human
body el cuerpo humano ❷ (corpse)
cadáver m

bodybuilding n culturismo m

bodyguard n guardaespaldas
m (pl guardaespaldas) ▷ He's a
bodyguard. Es guardaespaldas.

boil n furúnculo m
▶ vb ❶ (water) hervir ▷ The water's
boiling. El agua está hirviendo.
❷ (egg) cocer

boil over vb salirse

boiled adj hervido; **a boiled egg** un
huevo pasado por agua

boiling adj **It's boiling in here!**
¡Aquí dentro se asa uno!

bolt n ❶ (on door, window) cerrojo
m ❷ (type of screw) tornillo m

bomb n bomba f
▶ vb bombardear

bomber n (plane) bombardero m

bombing n bombardeo m

bone n ❶ (of human, animal) hueso
m ❷ (of fish) espina f

bonfire n hoguera f

bonnet n (of car) capó m

bonus n ❶ (extra payment) plus m
❷ (added advantage) ventaja f

book n libro m
▶ vb reservar; **We haven't
booked.** No hemos hecho reserva.

bookcase n librería f

booklet n folleto m

bookshelf n estantería f

bookshop n librería f

boot n ❶ (of car) maletero m
❷ (fashion boots) bota f ❸ (for
hiking) borceguí m (pl borceguíes);
football boots las botas de fútbol

border n frontera f

bore vb see **bear**

bored adj aburrido ▷ to be bored
estar aburrido; **to get bored**
aburrirse

boring adj aburrido ▷ It's boring.
Es aburrido.

born adj **to be born** nacer ▷ I was
born in 1992. Nací en 1992.

borne vb see **bear**

borrow vb pedir prestado;
**to borrow something from
somebody** pedir algo prestado a
alguien ▷ I borrowed some money
from a friend. Le pedí dinero
prestado a un amigo.; **Can I
borrow your pen?** ¿Me prestas el
bolígrafo?

Bosnia n Bosnia f

Bosnian adj bosnio

boss n jefe m, jefa f

boss around vb **to boss**

a
b
c
d
e
f
g
h
i
j
k
l
m
n
o
p
q
r
s
t
u
v
w
x
y
z

a
b
c
d
e
f
g
h
i
j
k
l
m
n
o
p
q
r
s
t
u
v
w
x
y
z

somebody around mandonear a alguien

bossy adj **mandón** (f **mandona**) (mpl **mandones**)

both adj, pron, adv los dos ▷ We both went. Fuimos los dos. ▷ Both of your answers are wrong. Tus respuestas están las dos mal. ▷ Both of them play the piano. Los dos tocan el piano.; **He has houses in both France and in Spain.** Tiene casas tanto en Francia como en España.

bother vb ❶ (worry) preocupar ▷ What's bothering you? ¿Qué es lo que te preocupa? ❷ (disturb) molestar ▷ I'm sorry to bother you. Siento molestarle.; **Don't bother!** ¡No te preocupes! ; **to bother to do something** tomarse la molestia de hacer algo ▷ He didn't bother to tell me about it. Ni se tomó la molestia de decírmelo.

▶ n **molestia** f ▷ no bother no es ninguna molestia

bottle n **botella** f

bottle bank n **contenedor** m del vidrio

bottle-opener n **abrebotellas** m (pl **abrebotellas**)

bottom n ❶ (of container, bag, sea) **fondo** m; **at the bottom of the page** al final de la página; **He was always bottom of the class.** Siempre era el último de la clase. ❷ (buttocks) **trasero** m

▶ adj **de abajo** ▷ the bottom shelf el estante de abajo

bought vb see **buy**

bounce vb **rebotar**

bouncer n **gorila** m

> Although **gorila** ends in -a, it is actually a masculine noun in this case.

bound adj **He's bound to fail.** Seguro que suspende.; **She's bound to come.** Es seguro que vendrá.

boundary n **límite** m

bow n ❶ (knot) **lazo** m ▷ to tie a bow hacer un lazo ❷ **arco** m ▷ a bow and arrow un arco y flecha

▶ vb hacer una reverencia

bowl n ❶ (for soup, cereals) **tazón** m (pl **tazones**) ❷ (for cooking, mixing food) **cuenco** m

▶ vb lanzar la pelota

bowling n **bolos** mpl; **to go bowling** jugar a los bolos; **a bowling alley** una bolera

bowls npl juego de los bolos

bow tie n **pajarita** f

box n ❶ **caja** f ▷ a box of matches una caja de cerillas ▷ a cardboard box una caja de cartón ❷ (on form) **casilla** f

boxer n **boxeador** m

boxer shorts npl **bóxers** mpl; **a pair of boxer shorts** unos bóxers

boxing n **boxeo** m

Boxing Day n el 26 de diciembre

boy n ❶ (young man) **muchacho** m ▷ a boy of fifteen un muchacho de quince años ❷ (child) **niño** m ▷ a boy of seven un niño de siete años; **She has two boys and a girl.** Tiene dos niños y una niña.; **a baby boy** un niño

boyfriend n **novio** m ▷ Have you got

a boyfriend? ¿Tienes novio?

bra n sostén m (pl sostenes)

brace n (on teeth) aparato m
▷ *Richard wears a brace.* Richard lleva un aparato.

bracelet n pulsera f

brackets npl **in brackets** entre paréntesis

brain n cerebro m

brainy adj inteligente

brake n freno m
▶ vb frenar

branch n ❶ (of tree) rama f ❷ (of bank) sucursal f

brand n marca f ▷ *a well-known brand of coffee* una marca de café muy conocida

brand-new adj flamante

brandy n coñac m (pl coñacs)

brass n (metal) latón m; **the brass section** los bronces

brass band n banda f de música

brave adj valiente

Brazil n Brasil m

bread n pan m; **bread and butter** el pan con mantequilla

break n ❶ (rest) pausa f ▷ *to take a break* hacer una pausa ❷ (at school) recreo m; **the Christmas break** las vacaciones de Navidad; **Give me a break!** ¡Déjame en paz!
▶ vb ❶ romper ▷ *Careful, you'll break something!* ¡Cuidado, que vas a romper algo!; **I broke my leg.** Me rompí la pierna. ❷ romperse ▷ *Careful, it'll break!* ¡Ten cuidado, que se va a romper!; **to break a promise** faltar a una promesa; **to break a record** batir un récord

break down vb averiarse; **The car broke down.** El coche se averió.

break in vb (burglar) entrar
▷ *The thief had broken in through a window.* El ladrón había entrado por una ventana.

break into vb (house) entrar en

break out vb ❶ (war) estallar
❷ (fire, fighting) desencadenarse
❸ (prisoner) escaparse; **He broke out in a rash.** Le salió un sarpullido.

break up vb ❶ disolver ▷ *Police broke up the demonstration.* La policía disolvió la demostración.
❷ (crowd) dispersarse
❸ (marriage) fracasar ▷ *More and more marriages are breaking up.* Cada día fracasan más matrimonios. ❹ (two lovers) romper ▷ *Richard and Marie have broken up.* Richard y Marie han roto.; **to break up a fight** poner fin a una pelea; **We break up next Wednesday.** El miércoles que viene empezamos las vacaciones.; **You're breaking up.** (on phone) Se corta.

breakdown n ❶ crisis f nerviosa (pl crisis nerviosas) ▷ *He had a breakdown because of the stress.* Sufrió una crisis nerviosa debida al estrés. ❷ (in vehicle) avería f ▷ *to have a breakdown* tener una avería

breakdown van n grúa f

breakfast n desayuno m; **to have breakfast** desayunar

break-in n **There have been a lot of break-ins in my area.** Han

a
b
c
d
e
f
g
h
i
j
k
l
m
n
o
p
q
r
s
t
u
v
w
x
y
z

entrado a robar en muchas casas de mi barrio.

breast n pecho m; **chicken breast** la pechuga de pollo

breaststroke n braza f

breath n aliento m ▷ *He's got bad breath.* Tiene mal aliento.; **I'm out of breath.** Estoy sin aliento.; **to get one's breath back** recobrar el aliento

breathe vb respirar

breathe in vb aspirar

breathe out vb espirar

breed vb (reproduce) reproducirse; **to breed dogs** criar perros
▶ n raza f

breeze n brisa f

brewery n fábrica f de cerveza

bribe n soborno m
▶ vb sobornar

brick n ladrillo m

bride n novia f

bridegroom n novio m

bridesmaid n dama f de honor

bridge n ❶ puente m ▷ *a suspension bridge* un puente colgante ❷ (card game) bridge m ▷ *to play bridge* jugar al bridge

brief adj breve

briefcase n maletín m (pl maletines)

briefly adv brevemente

briefs npl calzoncillos mpl; **a pair of briefs** unos calzoncillos

bright adj ❶ vivo ▷ *a bright colour* un color vivo; **bright red** rojo vivo ❷ (light) brillante ❸ listo ▷ *He's not very bright.* No es muy listo.

brilliant adj ❶ estupendo; **We**

had a brilliant time! ¡Lo pasamos estupendo! ❷ genial ▷ *a brilliant scientist* un científico genial

bring vb traer ▷ *Can I bring a friend?* ¿Puedo traer a un amigo?

bring back vb (book) devolver; **That song brings back memories.** Esa canción me trae recuerdos.

bring up vb criar ▷ *She brought up five children on her own.* Crió a cinco hijos ella sola.

Britain n Gran Bretaña f

British adj británico; **the British** los británicos; **the British Isles** las Islas Británicas; **She's British.** Es británica.

broad adj ancho

broadband n banda f ancha

broad bean n haba f

> Although it's a feminine noun, remember that you use **el** and **un** with **haba**.

broadcast n emisión f (pl emisiones)
▶ vb emitir ▷ *The interview was broadcast all over the world.* La entrevista se emitió a todo el mundo.; **to broadcast live** emitir en directo

broccoli n brécol m

brochure n folleto m

broil vb ❶ (in US: in cooker) hacer al grill ❷ (barbecue) asar a la parrilla

broke vb see **break**
▶ adj **to be broke** estar sin blanca (informal)

broken vb see **break**
▶ adj roto ▷ *It's broken.* Está roto.

▷ He's got a broken arm. Tiene un brazo roto.

bronchitis n bronquitis f

bronze n bronce m ▷ the bronze medal la medalla de bronce

brooch n broche m

broom n escoba f

brother n hermano m

brother-in-law n cuñado m

brought vb see **bring**

brown adj ❶ (clothes) marrón (mpl marrones) ❷ (hair, eyes) castaño ❸ (tanned) moreno; **brown bread** el pan integral

Brownie n niña f exploradora

bruise n moretón m (pl moretones)

brush n ❶ (for hair, teeth) cepillo m ❷ (paintbrush) pincel m
▶ vb cepillar; **to brush one's hair** cepillarse el pelo; **to brush one's teeth** cepillarse los dientes ▷ I brush my teeth every night. Me cepillo los dientes todas las noches.

Brussels n Bruselas f

Brussels sprouts npl coles fpl de Bruselas

bubble n ❶ (of soap) pompa f ❷ (of air, gas) burbuja f

bubble bath n baño m de espuma

bubble gum n chicle m

bucket n cubo m

buckle n (on belt, watch, shoe) hebilla f

Buddhism n budismo m

Buddhist adj budista

buddy n (in US) amiguete m, amigueta f

budget n presupuesto m

budgie n periquito m

buffet n buffet m

buffet car n coche m restaurante

bug n ❶ (insect) insecto m ❷ (illness, in computer) virus m (pl virus) ▷ There's a bug going round. Hay un virus en el ambiente.; **a stomach bug** una gastroenteritis

build vb construir ▷ They're going to build houses here. Van a construir viviendas aquí.

builder n ❶ (contractor) contratista mf ❷ (worker) albañil m

building n edificio m

built vb see **build**

bulb n ❶ (electric) bombilla f ❷ (of flower) bulbo m

bull n toro m

bullet n bala f

bullfighting n Do you like bullfighting? ¿Te gustan los toros?

bullring n plaza f de toros

bully n matón m (pl matones) ▷ He's a big bully. Es un matón.
▶ vb intimidar

bum n culo m (informal)

bum bag n riñonera f

bump n ❶ (on head) chichón m (pl chichones) ❷ (on surface) bulto m ❸ (on road) bache m ❹ (minor accident) golpe m; **We had a bump.** Nos dimos un golpe.
▶ vb I bumped my head on the wall. Me di con la cabeza en la pared.

bump into vb ❶ tropezarse con ▷ I bumped into Paul yesterday. Me

a b c d e f g h i j k l m n o p q r s t u v w x y z

tropecé con Paul ayer. ❷ **darse contra** ▷ We bumped into a tree. Nos dimos contra un árbol.

bumper n parachoques m (pl parachoques)

bumpy adj (road) lleno de baches

bun n (bread) bollo m

bunch n ❶ (of flowers) ramo m ▷ a bunch of flowers un ramo de flores ❷ (of grapes) racimo m ❸ (of keys) manojo m

bunches npl coletas fpl ▷ She has her hair in bunches. Lleva coletas.

bungalow n bungalow m

bunk n litera f

burger n hamburguesa f

burglar n ladrón m, ladrona f (mpl ladrones)

burglarize vb (in US) entrar a robar en

burglary n robo m

burgle vb entrar a robar en ▷ Her house was burgled. Le entraron a robar en casa.

burn n quemadura f
▶ vb (rubbish, documents) quemar ▷ I burned the rubbish. Quemé la basura.; **I burned the cake.** Se me quemó el pastel.; **to burn oneself** quemarse; **I've burned my hand.** Me quemé la mano.

burn down vb quedar reducido a cenizas ▷ The factory burned down. La fábrica quedó reducida a cenizas.

burst vb reventarse ▷ The balloon burst. El globo se reventó.; **to burst a balloon** reventar un globo; **to burst out laughing** echarse a

reír; **to burst into tears** romper a llorar; **to burst into flames** incendiarse

bury vb enterrar

bus n autobús m (pl autobuses) ▷ by bus en autobús; **the school bus** el autocar escolar; **a bus ticket** un billete de autobús

bush n arbusto m

business n ❶ (firm) negocio m ▷ He's got his own business. Tiene su propio negocio. ❷ negocios mpl ▷ He's away on business. Está en un viaje de negocios.; **a business trip** un viaje de negocios; **It's none of my business.** No es asunto mío.

businessman n hombre m de negocios

businesswoman n mujer f de negocios

busker n músico m callejero, música f callejera

bus pass n bonobús m (pl bonobuses)

bus station n estación f de autobuses (pl estaciones de autobuses)

bus stop n parada f de autobús

bust n busto m

busy adj ❶ (person, telephone line) ocupado ▷ She's a very busy woman. Es una mujer muy ocupada. ❷ (day, week) ajetreado ▷ It's been a very busy day. Ha sido un día muy ajetreado. ❸ (street, shop) concurrido

but prep, conj ❶ pero ▷ I'd like to come, but I'm busy. Me gustaría

venir, pero tengo trabajo. **②** sino
Use **sino** when you want to
correct a previous negative
statement.
▷ He's not English but French. No
es inglés sino francés. **③** menos;
**They won all but two of their
matches.** Ganaron todos los
partidos menos dos.; **the last but
one** el penúltimo

butcher n carnicero m, carnicera f;
He's a butcher. Es carnicero. ▷ at
the butcher's en la carnicería

butter n mantequilla f

butterfly n (insect, swimming)
mariposa f▷ Her favourite stroke is
the butterfly. Su estilo favorito es
mariposa.

button n **①** botón m (pl botones)
② (in US: metal, plastic) chapa f

buy vb comprar ▷ He bought me
an ice cream. Me compró un
helado.; **to buy something from
somebody** comprar algo a alguien
▷ I bought a watch from him. Le
compré un reloj.
▶ n **It was a good buy.** Fue una
buena compra.

by prep **①** por ▷ The thieves were
caught by the police. Los ladrones
fueron capturados por la policía.
② de ▷ a painting by Picasso un
cuadro de Picasso **③** en ▷ by car
en coche ▷ by train en tren ▷ by
bus en autobús **④** (next to) junto
a **⑤** para ▷ We have to be there by
4 o'clock. Tenemos que estar allí
para las cuatro.; **by the time...**
cuando... ▷ By the time I got there it

was too late. Cuando llegué allí ya
era demasiado tarde.; **That's fine
by me.** Por mí no hay problema.;
all by himself él solo; **by the way**
a propósito

bye excl ¡adiós!

bypass n (road) carretera f de
circunvalación

a
b
c
d
e
f
g
h
i
j
k
l
m
n
o
p
q
r
s
t
u
v
w
x
y
z

C

cab n taxi m ▷ *I'll go by cab.* Iré en taxi.

cabbage n berza f

cabin n ❶ (on ship) camarote m ❷ (on aeroplane) cabina f

cable n cable m

cable car n teleférico m

cable television n televisión f por cable

cactus n cacto m

café n cafetería f

cage n jaula f

cagoule n canguro m

cake n pastel m

calculate vb calcular

calculation n cálculo m

calculator n calculadora f

calendar n calendario m

calf n ❶ (of cow) ternero m ❷ (of leg) pantorrilla f

call n llamada f ▷ *Thanks for your call.* Gracias por su llamada. ▷ *a phone call* una llamada telefónica; **to be on call** (doctor) estar de guardia
▶ vb llamar ▷ *We called the police.* Llamamos a la policía. ▷ *I'll tell him you called.* Le diré que has llamado.; **to be called** llamarse ▷ *He's called Fluffy.* Se llama Fluffy. ▷ *What's she called?* ¿Cómo se llama?

call back vb volver a llamar ▷ *I'll call back later.* Volveré a llamar más tarde.; **Can I call you back?** ¿Puedo llamarte más tarde?

call for vb pasar a recoger ▷ *Shall I call for you at seven thirty?* ¿Paso a recogerte a las siete y media?

call off vb suspender ▷ *The match was called off.* El partido se suspendió.

call box n cabina f telefónica

call centre n centro m de atención al cliente

calm adj tranquilo

calm down vb calmarse ▷ *Calm down!* ¡Cálmate!

calorie n caloría f

calves npl see **calf**

camcorder n videocámara f

came vb see **come**

camel n camello m

camera n cámara f

cameraman n cámara m

camera phone n teléfono m con cámara

camp vb acampar
▶ n campamento m ▷ *a summer camp* un campamento de verano;

a **refugee camp** un campo de refugiados

campaign n campaña f
▸ vb hacer campaña ▷ *They are campaigning for a change in the law.* Están haciendo campaña a favor de un cambio legislativo.

camper n campista mf; **a camper van** una caravana

camping n **to go camping** ir de camping

campsite n camping m (pl campings)

can n lata f ▷ **a can of beer** una lata de cerveza; **a can of petrol** un bidón de gasolina
▸ vb ❶ (be able to, be allowed to) poder ▷ *Can I use your phone?* ¿Puedo usar el teléfono? ▷ *I can't do that.* No puedo hacer eso. ▷ *I'll do it as soon as I can.* Lo haré tan pronto como pueda. ▷ *That can't be true!* ¡No puede ser cierto! ▷ *You could hire a bike.* Podrías alquilar una bici. ▷ *He couldn't concentrate because of the noise.* No se podía concentrar a causa del ruido.
❷ (know how to) saber ▷ *I can swim.* Sé nadar. ▷ *He can't drive.* No sabe conducir.

⏸ **can** is sometimes not translated.

▷ *I can't hear you.* No te oigo. ▷ *I can't remember.* No me acuerdo. ▷ *Can you speak French?* ¿Hablas francés?; **You could be right.** Es posible que tengas razón.

Canada n Canadá m

Canadian adj canadiense

▸ n canadiense mf

canal n canal m

Canaries n **the Canaries** las Canarias

canary n canario m; **the Canary Islands** las islas Canarias

cancel vb cancelar ▷ *Our flight was cancelled.* Cancelaron nuestro vuelo.

cancer n cáncer m ▷ *He's got cancer.* Tiene cáncer.; **I'm Cancer.** Soy cáncer.

candidate n candidato m, candidata f

candle n ❶ vela f ❷ (in church) cirio m

candy n (in US) dulces mpl ▷ *I love candy.* Me encantan los dulces.; **a candy** un caramelo

candyfloss n algodón m de azúcar

canned adj (food) en lata inv

cannot vb = **can not**

canoe n canoa f

canoeing n **We went canoeing.** Fuimos a hacer piragüismo.

can-opener n abrelatas m (pl abrelatas)

can't vb = **can not**

canteen n cantina f

canvas n lona f

cap n ❶ (of bottle, tube) tapón m (pl tapones) ❷ (hat) gorra f

capable adj capaz; **to be capable of doing something** ser capaz de hacer algo ▷ *She's capable of doing much more.* Es capaz de hacer mucho más.

capacity n capacidad f

capital n ❶ capital f ▷ *Cardiff is*

a
b
c
d
e
f
g
h
i
j
k
l
m
n
o
p
q
r
s
t
u
v
w
x
y
z

the capital of Wales. Cardiff es la capital del país de Gales. **②** (letter) mayúscula f ▷ in capitals en mayúsculas

capitalism n capitalismo m

Capricorn n (sign) Capricornio m; **I'm Capricorn.** Soy capricornio.

captain n capitán m, capitana f (mpl capitanes)

capture vb capturar

car n coche m; **to go by car** ir en coche ▷ **We went by car.** Fuimos en coche.; **a car crash** un accidente de coche

caramel n caramelo m

caravan n caravana f ▷ **a caravan site** un cámping de caravanas

card n **①** tarjeta f ▷ **I got lots of cards and presents on my birthday.** Recibí muchas tarjetas y regalos para mi cumpleaños. **②** (playing card) carta f; **a card game** un juego de cartas

cardboard n cartón m ▷ **a cardboard box** una caja de cartón

cardigan n chaqueta f de punto

cardphone n teléfono m de tarjeta

care n cuidado m ▷ **with care** con cuidado; **to take care of** cuidar a ▷ **I take care of the children on Saturdays.** Yo cuido a los niños los sábados.; **Take care! (1)** (be careful) ¡Ten cuidado! **(2)** (look after yourself) ¡Cuídate!

▶ vb **to care about** preocuparse por ▷ **They don't care about their image.** No se preocupan por su imagen.; **I don't care!** ¡No me importa!; **Who cares?** ¿Y a quién

le importa?

care for vb cuidar ▷ **They employed a nurse to care for her.** Emplearon a una enfermera para cuidarla.

career n carrera f

careful adj **Be careful!** ¡Ten cuidado!

carefully adv (cautiously) con cuidado ▷ **Drive carefully!** ¡Conduce con cuidado!; **Think carefully!** ¡Piénsalo bien!; **She carefully avoided talking about it.** Tuvo mucho cuidado de no hablar del tema.

careless adj **①** (work) poco cuidado; **a careless mistake** un error de descuido **②** (person) poco cuidadoso ▷ **She's very careless.** Es muy poco cuidadosa.; **a careless driver** un conductor imprudente

caretaker n conserje mf; **school caretaker** el bedel

car ferry n ferry m (pl ferrys)

cargo n cargamento m

car hire n alquiler m de coches

Caribbean adj caribeño
　▶ n **We're going to the Caribbean.** Vamos al Caribe.; **the Caribbean** (sea) el mar Caribe

caring adj bondadoso

carnation n clavel m

carnival n carnaval m

carol n **A Christmas carol** un villancico

car park n aparcamiento m

carpenter n carpintero m, carpintera f ▷ **He's a carpenter. Es** carpintero.

carpet n **①** (fitted) moqueta f

❷ alfombra f ▷ *a Persian carpet* una alfombra persa

car rental n (in US) alquiler m de coches

carriage n (of train) vagón m (pl vagones)

carrier bag n bolsa f de plástico

carrot n zanahoria f

carry vb **❶** llevar ▷ *I'll carry your bag.* Te llevo la bolsa. **❷** transportar ▷ *a plane carrying 100 passengers* un avión que transporta 100 pasajeros

carry on vb seguir ▷ *She carried on talking.* Siguió hablando.; **Carry on!** ¡Sigue! ▷ *Am I boring you? - No, carry on!* ¿Te estoy aburriendo? - ¡No, sigue!

carrycot n moisés m (pl moisés)

cart n carro m

carton n (of milk, fruit juice) cartón m (pl cartones)

cartoon n **❶** (film) dibujos mpl animados **❷** (in newspaper) chiste m

cartridge n cartucho m

carve vb trinchar ▷ *Dad carved the roast.* Papá trinchó el asado.; **a carved oak chair** una silla de roble tallado

case n **❶** maleta f ▷ *I've packed my case.* He hecho mi maleta. **❷** caso m ▷ *in some cases* en algunos casos; **in case it rains** por si llueve; **just in case** por si acaso ▷ *Take some money with you, just in case.* Llévate algo de dinero por si acaso.

cash n dinero m ▷ *I'm a bit short of cash.* Ando un poco justo de

dinero.; **in cash** en efectivo ▷ *£200 in cash* 200 libras esterlinas en efectivo; **to pay cash** pagar al contado

▶ vb **to cash a cheque** cobrar un cheque

cash card n tarjeta f de cajero automático

cash desk n caja f

cash dispenser n cajero m automático

cashew nut n anacardo m

cashier n cajero m, cajera f

cashmere n cachemir m ▷ *a cashmere sweater* un suéter de cachemir

casino n casino m

cassette n casete m; **a cassette player** un casete; **a cassette recorder** un casete

cast n reparto m ▷ *The cast of the film includes many famous actors.* El reparto de la película incluye a muchos actores famosos.; **After the play, we met the cast.** Cuando terminó la obra charlamos con los actores.

castle n castillo m

casual adj **❶** informal ▷ *I prefer casual clothes.* Prefiero la ropa informal. **❷** despreocupado ▷ *a casual attitude* una actitud despreocupada ▷ *It's just a casual job.* Es sólo un trabajo eventual.

casualty n **❶** (hospital department) urgencias ▷ *He was taken to casualty after the accident.* Lo llevaron a urgencias después del accidente. ❷ víctima f ▷ The casualties include a young boy. Entre las víctimas se encuentra un niño.

cat n gato m, gata f

catalogue n catálogo m

catastrophe n catástrofe f

catch vb ❶ coger (Sp) (LatAm agarrar)

> Be very careful with the verb **coger**: in most of Latin America this is an extremely rude word that should be avoided. Use **tomar** in Latin America instead if catching a train, bus etc. However, in Spain this verb is common and not rude at all.

▷ They caught the thief. Cogieron al ladrón. ▷ We caught the last train. Cogimos el último tren.; **My cat catches birds.** Mi gato caza pájaros. ❷ agarrar ▷ He caught her arm. La agarró del brazo.; **to catch a cold** resfriarse; **I didn't catch his name.** No me enteré de su nombre.; **He caught her stealing.** La pilló robando.; **If they catch you smoking you'll be in trouble.** Si te pillan fumando te la vas a cargar.

catch up vb ❶ ponerse al día ▷ I've got to catch up on my work. Tengo que ponerme al día con el trabajo. ❷ alcanzar ▷ She caught me up. Me alcanzó.

catering n **The hotel did all the catering for the wedding.** El hotel se encargó de organizar el banquete de bodas.

cathedral n catedral f

Catholic adj católico
▶ n católico m, católica f ▷ I'm a Catholic. Soy católico.

cattle npl ganado m

caught vb see **catch**

cauliflower n coliflor f

cause n causa f
▶ vb causar

cautious adj prudente

cave n cueva f

CD n CD m (pl CDs)

CD player n reproductor m de CD

CD-ROM n CD-ROM m

ceiling n techo m

celebrate vb celebrar

celebration n celebración f

celebrity n celebridad f

celery n apio m

cell n ❶ (of prisoner) celda f ❷ (in biology) célula f

cellar n ❶ sótano m; **a wine cellar** una bodega

cello n violonchelo m

cement n cemento m

cemetery n cementerio m

cent n ❶ (division of dollar) centavo m ❷ (division of euro) céntimo m

centenary n centenario m

center n (in US) centro m

centigrade adj centígrado ▷ 20 degrees centigrade 20 grados centígrados

centimetre (US **centimeter**) n centímetro m

central adj central

central heating n calefacción f central

centre n centro m

century n siglo m ▷ the twentieth century el siglo veinte

cereal n cereales mpl ▷ I have cereal for breakfast. Desayuno cereales.

ceremony n ceremonia f

certain adj ❶ (particular) cierto ▷ a certain person cierta persona ❷ (definite) seguro ▷ I am certain he's not coming. Estoy seguro de que no viene.; **for certain** con certeza; **to make certain** cerciorarse ▷ I made certain the door was locked. Me cercioré de que la puerta estaba cerrada con llave.

certainly adv por supuesto ▷ I shall certainly be there. Por supuesto que estaré allí. ▷ Certainly not! ¡Por supuesto que no!; **So it was a surprise? - It certainly was!** ¿Así que fue una sorpresa? - ¡Ya lo creo!

certificate n certificado m

chain n cadena f ▷ a gold chain una cadena de oro

chair n ❶ silla f ▷ a table and four chairs una mesa y cuatro sillas ❷ (armchair) sillón m (pl sillones)

chairlift n telesilla m

> Although **telesilla** ends in **-a**, it is actually a masculine noun.

chairman n presidente m, presidenta f

chalet n chalet m (pl chalets)

chalk n tiza f; **a piece of chalk** una tiza

challenge n reto m
▶ vb retar ▷ She challenged me to a race. Me retó a echar una carrera.

chambermaid n camarera f

champagne n champán m

champion n campeón m, campeona f (mpl campeones)

championship n campeonato m

chance n ❶ posibilidad f ▷ The team's chances of winning are very good. El equipo tiene muchas posibilidades de ganar. ❷ oportunidad f ▷ I had the chance of working in Brazil. Tuve la oportunidad de trabajar en Brasil.; **I'll write when I get the chance.** Te escribiré cuando tenga un momento.; **by chance** por casualidad; **No chance!** ¡Ni en broma!; **to take a chance** arriesgarse ▷ I'm taking no chances! ¡No me quiero arriesgar!

change vb ❶ cambiar ▷ The town has changed a lot. La ciudad ha cambiado mucho. ▷ I'd like to change £50. Quisiera cambiar 50 libras esterlinas. ❷ cambiar de ▷ He wants to change his job. Quiere cambiar de trabajo.; **I'm going to change my shoes.** Voy a cambiarme de zapatos.; **to get changed** cambiarse; **to change one's mind** cambiar de idea ▶ n ❶ cambio m ▷ There's been a change of plan. Ha habido un cambio de planes.; **a change of clothes** una muda; **for a change** para variar ❷ dinero m suelto ▷ I haven't got any change. No tengo dinero suelto.; **Can you give me change for a pound?** ¿Me puede cambiar una libra?; **There's your**

a b **c** d e f g h i j k l m n o p q r s t u v w x y z

change. Aquí tiene el cambio.
changing room n ❶ (in shop)
probador m ❷ (for sport)
vestuario m
channel n (TV) canal m; **the
English Channel** el Canal de la
Mancha; **the Channel Islands** las
islas del Canal de la Mancha; **the
Channel Tunnel** el túnel del Canal
de la Mancha
chaos n caos m
chapel n capilla f
chapter n capítulo m
character n ❶ carácter m (pl
los caracteres) ▷ Can you give me
some idea of his character? ¿Puede
describirme un poco su carácter?
❷ (in film, book) personaje m;
She's quite a character. Es todo
un personaje.
characteristic n característica f
charcoal n ❶ (for barbecue)
carbón m vegetal ❷ (for drawing)
carboncillo m
charge n **Is there a charge for
delivery?** ¿Cobran por el envío?;
an extra charge un suplemento;
free of charge gratuito; **I'd like
to reverse the charges.** Quisiera
llamar a cobro revertido.; **to be
in charge** ser el responsable ▷ She
was in charge of the group. Ella era la
responsable del grupo.
▶ vb ❶ cobrar ▷ How much did
he charge you? ¿Cuánto te cobró?
❷ (with crime) acusar ▷ The police
have charged him with murder.
La policía lo ha acusado de
asesinato.

charity n (organization)
organización f benéfica (pl
organizaciones benéficas) ▷ He
gave the money to charity. Donó
el dinero a una organización
benéfica.; **to collect for charity**
recaudar dinero para obras
benéficas; **charity shop** tienda de
artículos de segunda mano que
dedica su recaudación a causas
benéficas
charm n encanto m
charming adj encantador (f
encantadora)
chart n gráfico m ▷ The chart
shows the rise of unemployment. El
gráfico muestra el aumento del
desempleo.; **the charts** la lista
de éxitos ▷ His record has been in
the charts for 10 weeks. Su disco
ha estado en la lista de éxitos
durante 10 semanas.
charter flight n vuelo m chárter
chase vb ❶ perseguir ▷ The
policeman chased the thief along the
road. El policía persiguió al ladrón
a lo largo de la calle. ❷ ir detrás
de ▷ He's always chasing the girls.
Siempre va detrás de las chicas.
▶ n persecución f (pl
persecuciones) ▷ a car chase una
persecución en coche
chat n charla f; **to have a chat**
charlar
▶ vb ❶ (talk) charlar ❷ (on
internet) chatear
chat up vb intentar ligarse a ▷ Jake
was chatting up one of the girls. Jake
estaba intentando ligarse a una

de las chicas.

chatroom n chat m

chat show n programa m de entrevistas

> Although **programa** ends in -a, it is actually a masculine noun.

cheap adj barato ▷ a cheap T-shirt una camiseta barata ▷ It's cheaper by bus. Es más barato en autobús.; **a cheap flight** un vuelo económico

cheat vb ① (at cards) hacer trampa ▷ You're cheating! ¡Estás haciendo trampa! ② (in exam) copiar
▶ n tramposo m, tramposa f

check n ① control m ▷ a security check un control de seguridad ② (in US) cheque m ▷ to write a check extender un cheque ③ (in US) cuenta f ▷ The waiter brought us the check. El camarero nos trajo la cuenta.
▶ vb comprobar ▷ Could you check the oil, please? ¿Podría comprobar el aceite, por favor?; **to check with somebody** preguntarle a alguien ▷ I'll check with the driver what time the bus leaves. Le preguntaré al conductor a qué hora sale el autobús.

check in vb ① (at airport) facturar ② (in hotel) registrarse

check out vb dejar el hotel

checked adj a cuadros inv

checkers n (in US) damas fpl ▷ to play checkers jugar a las damas

check-in n facturación f de equipajes

checkout n caja f

check-up n reconocimiento m

cheek n ① mejilla f ▷ He kissed her on the cheek. La besó en la mejilla.; **What a cheek!** ¡Qué cara!

cheeky adj descarado ▷ Don't be cheeky! ¡No seas descarado!; **a cheeky smile** una sonrisilla maliciosa

cheer n Three cheers for the winner! ¡Viva el ganador!; **Cheers!**
(1) (when drinking) ¡Salud! **(2)** (thank you) ¡Gracias!
▶ vb vitorear; **to cheer somebody up** levantar el ánimo a alguien ▷ I was trying to cheer him up. Estaba intentando levantarle el ánimo.; **Cheer up!** ¡Anímate!

cheerful adj alegre

cheese n queso m

chef n chef mf (pl chefs)

chemical n sustancia f química

chemist n ① (dispenser) farmacéutico m, farmacéutica f ② (shop) farmacia f ▷ You get it from the chemist. Se compra en la farmacia.
● Chemist's shops in Spain are
● identified by a special green
● cross outside the shop.
③ (scientist) químico m, química f

chemistry n química f ▷ the chemistry lab el laboratorio de química

cheque n cheque m ▷ to write a cheque extender un cheque ▷ to pay by cheque pagar con cheque

chequebook n talonario m de cheques

cherry n cereza f

chess n ajedrez m ▷ He likes playing chess. Le gusta jugar al ajedrez.

chessboard n tablero m de ajedrez

chest n pecho m ▷ I've got a pain in my chest. Tengo un dolor en el pecho.

chestnut n castaña f

chest of drawers n cómoda f

chew vb masticar

chewing gum n chicle m; a piece of chewing gum un chicle

chick n polluelo m

chicken n ❶ (animal) gallina f ❷ (food) pollo m

chickenpox n varicela f ▷ I've got chickenpox. Tengo la varicela.

chickpeas npl garbanzos mpl

chief n jefe m, jefa f ▷ The chief of security el jefe de seguridad

child n ❶ niño m, niña f ▷ a child of six un niño de seis años ❷ hijo m, hija f ▷ Susan is our eldest child. Susan es nuestra hija mayor. ▷ They've got three children. Tienen tres hijos.

childish adj infantil

child minder n niñera f

children npl see child

Chile n Chile m

chill vb (drink, food) poner a enfriar; Serve chilled. Sírvase bien frío. ▶ n to catch a chill resfriarse

chilli n chile m; chilli con carne el chile con carne

chilly adj frío

chimney n chimenea f

chin n barbilla f; Keep your chin up! ¡No pierdas el ánimo!

china n porcelana f ▷ a china plate un plato de porcelana

China n China f

Chinese adj chino; a Chinese man un chino; a Chinese woman una china
▶ n (language) chino m; the Chinese los chinos

chip n ❶ (food) patata f frita (LatAm papa f frita) ❷ (in computer) chip m (pl chips)

chiropodist n podólogo m, podóloga f ▷ He's a chiropodist. Es podólogo.

chives npl cebollinos mpl

chocolate n ❶ chocolate m ▷ a chocolate cake un pastel de chocolate ▷ a cup of hot chocolate una taza de chocolate ❷ bombón m (pl bombones) ▷ a box of chocolates una caja de bombones

choice n elección f (pl elecciones); I had no choice. No tenía otro remedio.

choir n coro m

choke vb (on food) atragantarse

choose vb elegir

chop vb ❶ (onion, herbs) picar ❷ (meat) cortar en trozos pequeños
▶ n chuleta f ▷ a pork chop una chuleta de cerdo

chopsticks npl palillos mpl

chose, chosen vb see choose

Christ n Cristo m

christening n bautismo m

Christian n cristiano m, cristiana f
▶ adj cristiano

Christian name n nombre m de pila

Christmas n Navidad f ▷ *Happy Christmas!* ¡Feliz Navidad!; **Christmas Day** el día de Navidad; **on Christmas Day** el día de Navidad; **Christmas Eve** Nochebuena; **a Christmas tree** un árbol de Navidad; **Christmas dinner** la comida de Navidad

- As well as lunch on Christmas Day, Spaniards also have a special supper on Christmas Eve.

a Christmas present un regalo de Navidad

- In Spain Christmas presents are traditionally given on 6th January although more and more people are exchanging gifts on Christmas Eve.

Christmas pudding el pudín de Navidad; **Christmas card** la tarjeta de Navidad; **at Christmas** en Navidad

chunk n pedazo m ▷ *Cut the meat into chunks.* Córtese la carne en pedazos.

church n iglesia f; **the Church of England** la Iglesia Anglicana

cider n sidra f

cigar n puro m

cigarette n cigarrillo m

cigarette lighter n mechero m

cinema n cine m

cinnamon n canela f

circle n círculo m

circular adj circular

circumstances npl

circunstancias fpl ▷ *in the circumstances* dadas las circunstancias; **under no circumstances** bajo ningún concepto

circus n circo m

citizen n ciudadano m, ciudadana f

citizenship n (*school subject*) civismo m

city n ciudad f ▷ *the city centre* el centro de la ciudad

civilization n civilización f (pl civilizaciones)

civil servant n funcionario m, funcionaria f ▷ *He's a civil servant.* Es funcionario.

civil war n guerra f civil

claim vb ❶ asegurar ▷ *He claims he found the money.* Asegura haber encontrado el dinero. ❷ reclamar ▷ *He's claiming compensation from the company.* Reclama una indemnización por parte de la empresa. ❸ cobrar ▷ *She's claiming unemployment benefit.* Cobra subsidio de desempleo.; **We claimed on our insurance.** Reclamamos al seguro.

▶ n ❶ (*on insurance policy*) reclamación f (pl reclamaciones); **to make a claim** reclamar al seguro ❷ afirmación f (pl afirmaciones) ▷ *The manufacturer's claims are obviously untrue.* Las afirmaciones del fabricante son obviamente falsas.

clap vb aplaudir; **to clap one's hands** dar palmadas

clarinet n clarinete m

clash vb **①** (colours) desentonar
▷ Red clashes with orange. El rojo desentona con el naranja. **②** (events) coincidir ▷ The party clashes with the meeting. La fiesta coincide con la reunión.

clasp n (of necklace) cierre m

class n clase f ▷ We're in the same class. Estamos en la misma clase. ▷ I go to dancing classes. Voy a clases de baile.

classic adj clásico ▷ a classic example un ejemplo clásico
▶ n clásico m

classical adj clásico ▷ classical music la música clásica

classmate n compañero m de clase, compañera f de clase

classroom n clase f

claw n **①** (of lion, eagle) garra f **②** (of cat, parrot) uña f **③** (of crab, lobster) pinza f

clean adj limpio
▶ vb limpiar; **I clean my teeth after every meal.** Me lavo los dientes después de cada comida.

cleaner n **①** (person) hombre m de la limpieza, mujer f de la limpieza **②** (substance) producto m de limpieza

cleaner's n tintorería f ▷ He took his coat to the cleaner's. Llevó el abrigo a la tintorería.

cleanser n crema f limpiadora

clear adj **①** claro ▷ a clear explanation una explicación clara ▷ It's clear you don't believe me. Está claro que no me crees.; **Have I**

made myself clear? ¿Me explico? **②** despejado ▷ Wait till the road is clear. Espera hasta que la carretera esté despejada. ▷ a clear day un día despejado **③** transparente ▷ It comes in a clear plastic bottle. Viene en una botella de plástico transparente.
▶ vb **①** despejar ▷ They are clearing the road. Están despejando la carretera. **②** (fog, mist) despejarse; **She was cleared of murder.** La absolvieron del cargo de asesinato.; **to clear the table** quitar la mesa

clear up vb **①** ordenar ▷ Who's going to clear all this up? ¿Quién va a ordenar todo esto? **②** resolver ▷ I'm sure we can clear up this problem right away. Estoy seguro de que podemos resolver este problema enseguida.; **I think it's going to clear up.** (weather) Creo que va a despejar.

clearly adv claramente ▷ to speak clearly hablar claramente; **Clearly this project will cost money.** Evidentemente este proyecto costará dinero.

clementine n clementina f

clever adj **①** listo ▷ She's very clever. Es muy lista. **②** ingenioso ▷ a clever system un sistema ingenioso; **What a clever idea!** ¡Qué idea más genial!

click on vb (computing) hacer clic en; **to click on the mouse** hacer clic con el ratón; **to click on an icon** hacer clic en un icono

client n cliente m, clienta f

cliff n acantilado m

climate n clima m

> Although **clima** ends in **-a**, it is actually a masculine noun.

climate change el cambio climático

climb vb ❶ escalar ▷ Her ambition is to climb Mount Everest. Su ambición es escalar el Monte Everest. ❷ trepar a ▷ They climbed a tree. Treparon a un árbol.; **to climb the stairs** subir las escaleras

climber n escalador m, escaladora f

climbing n montañismo m; **to go climbing** hacer montañismo ▷ We're going climbing in Scotland. Vamos a hacer montañismo en Escocia.

cling film n plástico m para envolver alimentos

clinic n ❶ (in NHS hospital) consultorio m ❷ (private hospital) clínica f

clip n ❶ (for hair) horquilla f ❷ secuencia f ▷ some clips from Johnny Depp's latest film unas secuencias de la última película de Johnny Depp

cloakroom n ❶ (for coats) guardarropa m

> Although **guardarropa** ends in **-a**, it is actually a masculine noun.

❷ (toilet) servicios mpl

clock n reloj m; **an alarm clock** un despertador; **a clock radio** un radio-despertador

clone n clon m
▶ vb clonar ▷ to clone a sheep clonar una oveja; **a cloned sheep** una oveja clónica

close adj, adv ❶ cerca ▷ The shops are very close. Las tiendas están muy cerca. ▷ The hotel is close to the station. El hotel está cerca de la estación.; **Come closer.** Acércate más.; **She was close to tears.** Estaba a punto de llorar. ❷ cercano ▷ We have only invited close relations. Sólo hemos invitado a parientes cercanos. ❸ íntimo ▷ She's a close friend of mine. Es amiga íntima mía.; **I'm very close to my sister.** Estoy muy unida a mi hermana. ❹ reñido ▷ It was a very close contest. Fue un concurso muy reñido.; **It's close this afternoon.** Hace bochorno esta tarde.
▶ vb ❶ cerrar ▷ The shops close at five thirty. Las tiendas cierran a las cinco y media. ▷ Please close the door. Cierra la puerta, por favor. ❷ cerrarse ▷ The doors close automatically. Las puertas se cierran automáticamente.

closed adj cerrado

closely adv (look, examine) de cerca; **This will be a closely fought race.** Será una carrera muy reñida.

cloth n (material) tela f; **a cloth** un trapo ▷ Wipe it with a damp cloth. Límpialo con un trapo húmedo.

clothes npl ropa f; **clothes line** la cuerda de tender; **clothes peg** la pinza para tender la ropa

cloud n nube f

cloudy adj nublado

clove n **a clove of garlic** un diente de ajo

clown n payaso m

club n ① club m ▷ *the youth club* el club juvenil; **a golf club (1)** (*society*) un club de golf; **(2)** (*stick*) un palo de golf ② discoteca f ▷ *We had dinner and went on to a club.* Cenamos y fuimos a una discoteca.; **clubs** (*at cards*) los tréboles ▷ *the ace of clubs* el as de tréboles

clubbing n **to go clubbing** ir de discotecas

clue n pista f ▷ *an important clue* una pista clave; **I haven't a clue.** No tengo ni idea.

clumsy adj torpe

clutch n (*of car*) embrague m ▶ vb agarrar ▷ *She clutched my arm and begged me not to go.* Me agarró el brazo y me suplicó que no me marchara.

coach n ① autobús m ▷ *by coach* en autobús ▷ *the coach station* la estación de autobuses ▷ *a coach trip* una excursión en autobús ② (*trainer*) entrenador m, entrenadora f; **the Spanish coach** el entrenador del equipo español

coal n carbón m; **a coal mine** una mina de carbón; **a coal miner** un minero de carbón

coarse adj ① basto ▷ *The bag was made of coarse black cloth.* La bolsa estaba hecha de una tela basta de

color negro. ② grueso ▷ *The sand is very coarse on that beach.* La arena es muy gruesa en esa playa.

coast n costa f ▷ *It's on the west coast of Scotland.* Está en la costa oeste de Escocia.

coastguard n guardacostas m (pl guardacostas)

coat n abrigo m ▷ *a woollen coat* un abrigo de lana; **a coat of paint** una mano de pintura

coat hanger n percha f

cobweb n telaraña f

cocaine n cocaína f

cockerel n gallo m

cocoa n cacao m; **a cup of cocoa** una taza de chocolate

coconut n coco m

cod n bacalao m

code n ① clave f ▷ *It's written in code.* Está escrito en clave. ② (for *telephone*) prefijo m ▷ *What is the code for London?* ¿Cuál es el prefijo de Londres?

coffee n café m (pl cafés) ▷ *a cup of coffee* una taza de café; **A cup of coffee, please.** Un café, por favor.

coffee table n mesa f de centro

coffin n ataúd m

coin n moneda f ▷ *a 20p coin* una moneda de 20 peniques

coincidence n coincidencia f

Coke® n Coca-Cola® f

colander n colador m

cold adj frío ▷ *The water's cold.* El agua está fría.; **Are you cold?** ¿Tienes frío? ▶ n ① frío m ▷ *I can't stand the cold.* No soporto el frío. ② (*illness*)

resfriado m; **to catch a cold**
resfriarse; **to have a cold** estar
resfriado

cold sore n calentura f

coleslaw n ensalada de col,
zanahoria, cebolla y mayonesa

collapse vb ❶ venirse abajo ▷ The
bridge collapsed during the storm. El
puente se vino abajo en medio de
la tormenta. ❷ sufrir un colapso
▷ He collapsed while playing tennis.
Sufrió un colapso mientras
jugaba al tenis.

collar n ❶ (of coat, shirt) cuello m
❷ (for animal) collar m

collarbone n clavícula f

colleague n colega mf

collect vb ❶ recoger ▷ The teacher
collected the exercise books. El
maestro recogió los cuadernos.
▷ Their mother collects them from
school. Su madre los recoge del
colegio. ❷ coleccionar ▷ He
collects stamps. Colecciona
sellos. ❸ hacer una colecta
▷ I'm collecting for UNICEF. Estoy
haciendo una colecta para la
UNICEF.

collection n ❶ colección f (pl
colecciones) ▷ my CD collection mi
colección de CDs ❷ colecta f ▷ a
collection for charity una colecta
para obras benéficas

collector n coleccionista mf

college n (university) universidad f

collide vb chocar

collision n colisión f (pl colisiones)

colon n (punctuation mark) dos
puntos

colonel n coronel mf

colour (US color) n color m ▷ What
colour is it? ¿De qué color es?; **a
colour TV** una televisión en color

colourful (US colorful) adj de
colores muy vistosos

colouring (US coloring) n (for
food) colorante m

comb n peine m
▶ vb **You haven't combed your
hair.** No te has peinado.

combination n combinación f (pl
combinaciones)

combine vb ❶ combinar ▷ The
film combines humour with suspense.
La película combina el humor con
el suspense. ❷ compaginar ▷ It's
difficult to combine a career with a
family. Es difícil compaginar la
profesión con la vida familiar.

come vb ❶ venir ▷ Helen came with
me. Helen vino conmigo. ▷ Come
home. Ven a casa. ▷ Come and see us
soon. Ven a vernos pronto.; **Where
do you come from?** ¿De dónde
eres? ❷ llegar ▷ They came late.
Llegaron tarde. ▷ The letter came
this morning. La carta llegó esta
mañana.; **I'm coming!** ¡Ya voy!

come back vb volver ▷ My brother
is coming back tomorrow. Mi
hermano vuelve mañana.

come down vb bajar

come in vb entrar ▷ Come in!
¡Entra!

come on vb **Come on!**
(1) (expressing encouragement,
urging haste) ¡Venga! **(2)** (expressing
disbelief) ¡Venga ya!

a
b
c
d
e
f
g
h
i
j
k
l
m
n
o
p
q
r
s
t
u
v
w
x
y
z

come out vb ▷ salir ▷ *We came out of the cinema at 10.* Salimos del cine a las 10. ❷ *irse* ▷ *I don't think this stain will come out.* No creo que esta mancha se vaya a quitar.

come up vb ❶ subir ▷ *Come up here!* ¡Sube aquí! ❷ surgir ▷ *Something's come up so I'll be late home.* Ha surgido algo, así es que llegaré tarde a casa.; **to come up to somebody** acercarse a alguien ▷ *She came up to me and kissed me.* Se me acercó y me besó.

comedian n cómico m, cómica f

comedy n comedia f

comfortable adj ❶ cómodo ▷ *comfortable shoes* zapatos cómodos ▷ *Make yourself comfortable!* ¡Ponte cómodo! ❸ (house, room) confortable ▷ *Their house is small but comfortable.* Su casa es pequeña pero confortable.

comic n comic m (pl comics)

comic strip n tira f cómica

comma n coma f

command n orden f (pl órdenes)

comment n comentario m ▷ *He made no comment.* No hizo ningún comentario.; **No comment!** ¡Sin comentarios!
　▷ vb hacer comentarios ▷ *The police have not commented on these rumours.* La policía no ha hecho comentarios sobre estos rumores.

commentary n crónica f

commentator n comentarista mf

commercial n spot m publicitario (pl spots publicitarios)

　▷ adj comercial

commit vb **to commit a crime** cometer un crimen; **to commit suicide** suicidarse; **I don't want to commit myself.** No quiero comprometerme.

committee n comité m

common adj común (pl comunes) ▷ *"Smith" is a very common surname.* "Smith" es un apellido muy común.; **in common** en común ▷ *We've got a lot in common.* Tenemos mucho en común.

Commons npl **the House of Commons** la Cámara de los Comunes

common sense n sentido m común

communicate vb comunicar

communication n comunicación f (pl comunicaciones)

communion n comunión f (pl comuniones)

communism n comunismo m

communist n comunista mf

community n comunidad f ▷ *the local community* el vecindario; **community service** el trabajo comunitario

commute vb **She commutes between Oxford and London.** Para ir al trabajo se desplaza diariamente de Oxford a Londres.

compact disc n disco m compacto; **compact disc player** el lector de discos compactos

company n empresa f ▷ *He works for a big company.* Trabaja para una empresa grande.

❸ compañía f ▷ *an insurance company* una compañía de seguros ▷ *a theatre company* una compañía de teatro; **to keep somebody company** hacerle compañía a alguien

comparatively *adv* relativamente

compare *vb* comparar ▷ *People always compare him with his brother.* La gente siempre lo compara con su hermano.; **compared with** con comparación a ▷ *Oxford is small compared with London.* Oxford es pequeño en comparación a Londres.

comparison *n* comparación f (*pl* comparaciones)

compartment *n* compartimento m

compass *n* brújula f

compensation *n* indemnización f ▷ *They got £2000 compensation.* Recibieron 2.000 libras esterlinas de indemnización.

compete *vb* **to compete in** competir en ▷ *I'm competing in the marathon.* Compito en el maratón.; **to compete for something** competir por algo ▷ *There are 50 students competing for 6 places.* Hay 50 estudiantes compitiendo por 6 puestos.

competent *adj* competente

competition *n* ❶ concurso m ▷ *a singing competition* un concurso de canto ❷ competencia f ▷ *Competition in the computer sector is fierce.* La competencia en el

sector de la informática es muy intensa.

competitive *adj* competitivo

competitor *n* ❶ (*contestant*) concursante mf ❷ rival mf

complain *vb* ❶ reclamar ▷ *We're going to complain to the manager.* Vamos a reclamar al director. ❷ quejarse ▷ *She's always complaining about her husband.* Siempre se está quejando de su marido.

complaint *n* queja f

complete *adj* completo

completely *adv* completamente

complexion *n* cutis m (*pl* cutis)

complicated *adj* complicado

compliment *n* cumplido m; **to pay somebody a compliment** hacerle un cumplido a alguien ▶ *vb* felicitar ▷ *They complimented me on my Spanish.* Me felicitaron por mi español.

compose *vb* (*music*) componer; **to be composed of** componerse de

composer *n* compositor m, compositora f

comprehension *n* (*school exercise*) ejercicio m de comprensión

comprehensive school *n* instituto m

compulsory *adj* obligatorio

computer *n* ordenador m (*LatAm* computador m, computadora f)

computer game *n* juego m de ordenador

computer programmer *n* programador m, programadora f

computer science *n*

informática f

computing n informática f

concentrate vb concentrarse ▷ I couldn't concentrate. No me podía concentrar. ▷ I was concentrating on my homework. Me estaba concentrando en los deberes.

concentration n concentración f

concerned adj preocupado ▷ His mother is concerned about him. Su madre está preocupada por él.; **as far as the new project is concerned ...** en lo que respecta al nuevo proyecto ...; **As far as I'm concerned,** you can come any time you like. Por mí, puedes venir cuando quieras.; **It's a stressful situation for everyone concerned.** Es una situación estresante para todos los involucrados.

concert n concierto m

conclusion n conclusión f

concrete n hormigón m

condemn vb condenar

condition n condición f (pl condiciones) ▷ I'll do it, on one condition. Lo haré, con una condición.; **in good condition** en buen estado

conditional n condicional m

conditioner n (for hair) suavizante m (LatAm enjuague m)

condom n preservativo m

conduct vb (orchestra) dirigir

conductor n ❶ (of orchestra) director m de orquesta, directora f de orquesta ❷ (on bus) cobrador m, cobradora f

cone n ❶ cucurucho m ▷ an ice cream cone un cucurucho ❷ (geometric shape) cono m; **a traffic cone** un cono para señalizar el tráfico

conference n conferencia f

confess vb confesar ▷ He confessed to the murder. Confesó haber cometido el asesinato.

confession n confesión f (pl confesiones)

confidence n ❶ confianza f ▷ I've got a lot of confidence in him. Tengo mucha confianza en él. ❷ confianza f en sí mismo ▷ She lacks confidence. Le falta confianza en sí misma.; **I told you that story in confidence.** Te conté esa historia de manera confidencial.

confident adj ❶ (sure of something) seguro ▷ I'm confident everything will be okay. Estoy seguro de que todo saldrá bien. ❷ (self-assured) seguro de sí mismo ▷ She seems quite confident. Parece muy segura de sí misma.

confidential adj confidencial

confirm vb confirmar

confuse vb confundir

confused adj (person) confuso

confusing adj poco claro ▷ The traffic signs are confusing. Las señales de tráfico están poco claras.

confusion n confusión f

congratulate vb felicitar ▷ My friends congratulated me on passing my test. Mis amigos me felicitaron por aprobar el examen.

congratulations npl
enhorabuena f ▷ *Congratulations on
your new job!* ¡Enhorabuena por tu
nuevo empleo!

conjunction n conjunción f

conjurer n prestidigitador m,
prestidigitadora f

connection n ❶ conexión f (pl
conexiones) ▷ *There's no connection
between the two events.* No hay
ninguna conexión entre los dos
sucesos. ❷ *(on journey)* enlace
m ▷ *We missed our connection.*
Perdimos el enlace.

conscience n conciencia f; **to
have a guilty conscience** tener
remordimientos de conciencia

conscious adj consciente ▷ *He
was still conscious when the doctor
arrived.* Estaba todavía consciente
cuando llegó el médico. ▷ *She was
conscious of Max looking at her.* Era
consciente de que Max la miraba.;
**He made a conscious decision
to tell nobody.** Tomó la firme
decisión de no decírselo a nadie.

consciousness n conocimiento
m ▷ *I lost consciousness.* Perdí el
conocimiento.

consequence n consecuencia f

consequently adv por
consiguiente

conservation n conservación
f; **energy conservation** la
conservación de la energía

conservative adj conservador (f
conservadora); **the Conservative
Party** el partido Conservador

Conservative n conservador

m, conservadora f; **to vote
Conservative** votar a favor del
partido Conservador

conservatory n invernadero m

consider vb ❶ considerar ▷ *He
considers it a waste of time.* Lo
considera una pérdida de tiempo.
❷ pensar en ▷ *We considered
cancelling our holiday.* Pensamos en
cancelar nuestras vacaciones.

considerate adj considerado

considering prep ❶ teniendo en
cuenta ▷ *Considering we were there
for a month we did not spend too
much money.* Teniendo en cuenta
que estuvimos allí durante un mes
no nos gastamos mucho dinero.
❷ después de todo ▷ *I got a good
mark, considering.* Saqué buena
nota, después de todo.

consist vb **to consist of** consistir
en

consonant n consonante f

constant adj constante

constantly adv constantemente

constipated adj estreñido ▷ *I'm
constipated.* Estoy estreñido.

  Be careful not to translate
constipated by **constipado**.

construct vb construir

construction n construcción f (pl
construcciones)

consult vb consultar

consumer n consumidor m,
consumidora f

contact n contacto m ▷ *I'm in
contact with her.* Estoy en contacto
con ella.
▶ vb ponerse en contacto con

▷ *Where can we contact you?* ¿Dónde podemos ponernos en contacto contigo?

contact lenses npl lentillas fpl (LatAm lentes mpl de contacto)

contain vb contener

container n recipiente m

contents npl contenido m

contest n competición f (pl competiciones) ▷ *a fishing contest* una competición de pesca; **a beauty contest** un concurso de belleza

contestant n concursante mf

context n contexto m

continent n continente m; **the Continent** el continente europeo

continental breakfast n desayuno m continental

continue vb continuar ▷ *She continued talking to her friend.* Continuó hablando con su amiga.

continuous adj continuo; **continuous assessment** la evaluación continua

contraceptive n anticonceptivo m

contract n contrato m

contradict vb contradecir

contrary n **on the contrary** al contrario

contrast n contraste m

contribute vb **to contribute to** contribuir a ▷ *Everyone contributed to the success of the play.* Todos contribuyeron al éxito de la obra. ▷ *She contributed £10 to the collection.* Contribuyó 10 libras esterlinas a la colecta.

contribution n contribución f (pl contribuciones)

control n control m; **to lose control** (of vehicle) perder el control; **He always seems to be in control.** Parece que siempre está en control de la situación.; **She can't keep control of the class.** No sabe controlar a la clase.; **out of control** fuera de control ▷ *That boy is out of control.* Ese muchacho está fuera de control.

▶ vb controlar ▷ *He can't control the class.* No sabe controlar a la clase. ▷ *Please control yourself, everyone's looking at us.* Por favor contrólate, todos nos están mirando.

controversial adj polémico ▷ *It's a controversial subject.* Es un tema polémico.

convenient adj (place) bien situado ▷ *The hotel's convenient for the airport.* El hotel está bien situado con respecto al aeropuerto.; **It's not a convenient time for me.** A esa hora no me va bien.; **Would Monday be convenient for you?** ¿Te iría bien el lunes?

conventional adj convencional

conversation n conversación f (pl conversaciones) ▷ *We had a long conversation.* Tuvimos una larga conversación.

convert vb convertir ▷ *We've converted the loft into a bedroom.* Hemos convertido el desván en un dormitorio.

convict vb declarar culpable ▷ *He*

was convicted of the murder. Fue declarado culpable del asesinato.

convince vb convencer; **I'm not convinced.** No me convence.

cook vb ① cocinar ▷ *I can't cook.* No sé cocinar.; **The chicken isn't cooked.** El pollo no está hecho. ② preparar ▷ *She's cooking lunch.* Está preparando el almuerzo.
▶ n cocinero m, cocinera f ▷ *She is a cook in a hotel.* Es cocinera en un hotel. ▷ *Maria's an excellent cook.* María es una cocinera excelente.

cookbook n libro m de cocina

cooker n cocina f ▷ *a gas cooker* una cocina de gas

cookery n cocina f

cookie n (*in US*) galleta f

cooking n cocina f ▷ *French cooking* la cocina francesa; **I like cooking.** Me gusta cocinar.

cool adj ① fresco ▷ *a cool place* un lugar fresco; **to stay cool** (*keep calm*) mantenerse en calma ▷ *He stayed cool throughout the crisis.* Se mantuvo en calma durante toda la crisis. ② (*great*) guay; **Cool!** (*ok*) ¡Vale!

cooperation n cooperación f

cop n poli mf (*informal*)

cope vb arreglárselas ▷ *It was hard, but we coped.* Fue difícil, pero nos las arreglamos.; **She's got a lot of problems to cope with.** Tiene muchos problemas a los que hacer frente.

copper n ① cobre m ▷ *a copper bracelet* un brazalete de cobre ② (*informal: policeman*) poli mf

copy n ① (*of letter, document*) copia f ② (*of book*) ejemplar m
▶ vb copiar; **to copy and paste** (*computing*) copiar y pegar

core n (*of fruit*) corazón m (pl corazones)

cork n corcho m

corkscrew n sacacorchos m (pl sacacorchos)

corn n ① (*wheat*) trigo m ② (*sweetcorn*) maíz m; **corn on the cob** la mazorca de maíz

corner n esquina f ▷ *the shop on the corner* la tienda de la esquina ▷ *He lives just round the corner.* Vive a la vuelta de la esquina. ② rincón m (pl rincones) ▷ *in a corner of the room* en un rincón de la habitación ③ (*in football*) saque m de esquina

cornflakes npl copos mpl de maíz

Cornwall n Cornualles m

corpse n cadáver m

correct adj correcto ▷ *That's correct!* ¡Correcto! ▷ *the correct answer* la respuesta correcta; **You're absolutely correct.** Tienes toda la razón.
▶ vb corregir

correction n corrección f (pl correcciones)

correctly adv correctamente

corridor n pasillo m

corruption n corrupción f

cosmetics npl productos mpl de belleza

cost vb costar ▷ *The meal cost £20.* La comida costó 20 libras esterlinas. ▷ *How much does it cost?* ¿Cuánto cuesta?

▶ n coste m (LatAm costo m) ▷ the cost of living el coste de vida; **at all costs** a toda costa

costume n traje m

cosy adj acogedor (f acogedora) ▷ a cosy room una habitación acogedora

cot n cuna f

cottage n chalet m (pl chalets)

cotton n algodón m ▷ a cotton shirt una camisa de algodón

cotton wool n algodón m

couch n sofá m (pl sofás)

cough vb toser
▶ n tos f ▷ I've got a cough. Tengo tos.; **cough mixture** el jarabe para la tos

could vb see **can**

council n (in town) ayuntamiento m ▷ He's on the council. Es concejal del ayuntamiento.; **a council estate** un barrio de viviendas de protección oficial; **a council house** una casa de protección oficial

councillor n concejal m, concejala f

count vb contar

count on vb contar con ▷ You can count on me. Puedes contar conmigo.

counter n ❶ (in shop) mostrador m ❷ (in bank, post office) ventanilla f ❸ (in game) ficha f

country n ❶ país m ▷ the border between the two countries la frontera entre los dos países ❷ campo m ▷ I live in the country. Vivo en el campo.; **country dancing** la danza folklórica

countryside n campo m

county n condado m

couple n ❶ pareja f ▷ the couple who live next door la pareja que vive al lado ❷ par m ▷ a couple of hours un par de horas

courage n valor m

courgette n calabacín m (pl calabacines)

courier n ❶ (for tourists) guía mf ❷ (delivery service) servicio m de mensajero ▷ They sent it by courier. Lo enviaron por servicio de mensajero.

course n ❶ curso m ▷ a Spanish course un curso de español ▷ to go on a course hacer un curso ❷ plato m ▷ the main course el segundo plato ▷ the first course el primer plato ❸ campo m ▷ a golf course un campo de golf; **of course** por supuesto ▷ Do you love me? - Of course I do! ¿Me quieres? - ¡Por supuesto que te quiero!

court n (of law) tribunal m; **a tennis court** una pista de tenis (LatAm una cancha de tenis)

courtyard n patio m

cousin n primo m, prima f

cover n ❶ (of book) tapa f ❷ (of duvet) funda f
▶ vb cubrir ▷ My face was covered with mosquito bites. Tenía la cara cubierta de picaduras de mosquito. ▷ Our insurance didn't cover it. Nuestro seguro no lo cubría.

cow n vaca f

coward n cobarde mf

cowboy n vaquero m

crab n cangrejo m

crack n ❶ (in wall) grieta f ❷ (in cup, window) raja f ❸ (drug) crack m; **He opened the door a crack.** Abrió la puerta un poquito.; **I'll have a crack at it.** Lo intentaré.
▶ vb (nut, egg) cascar; **He cracked his head on the pavement.** Se dio con la cabeza en la acera.; **I think we've cracked it!** ¡Creo que lo hemos resuelto!; **to crack a joke** contar un chiste

cracked adj ❶ (cup, window) rajado ❷ (wall) resquebrajado

cracker n (biscuit) galleta f salada; **Christmas cracker** la sorpresa navideña

craft n artesanía f; **a craft shop** una tienda de objetos de artesanía

crane n (machine) grúa f

crash vb chocar ▷ **The two cars crashed.** Los dos coches chocaron.; **to crash into something** chocar con algo; **He's crashed his car.** Ha tenido un accidente con el coche.; **The plane crashed.** El avión se estrelló.
▶ n accidente m; **a crash helmet** un casco protector; **a crash course** un curso intensivo

crawl vb (baby) gatear
▶ n crol m; **to do the crawl** nadar estilo crol

crazy adj loco

cream adj de color crema inv ▷ a cream silk blouse una blusa de seda de color crema
▶ n nata f (LatAm crema f de leche) ▷ strawberries and cream fresas con nata ▷ a cream cake un pastel de nata; **cream cheese** el queso cremoso ❷ (for skin) crema f ▷ sun cream la crema solar

crease n ❶ (in clothes, paper) arruga f ❷ (in trousers) raya f

creased adj arrugado

create vb crear

creative adj creativo

creature n criatura f

crèche n guardería f infantil

credit n crédito m ▷ on credit a crédito; **He's a credit to his family.** Hace honor a su familia.

credit card n tarjeta f de crédito

crew n ❶ (of plane, boat) tripulación f (pl tripulaciones); **a film crew** un equipo de rodaje

crew cut n pelo m cortado al rape

cricket n ❶ críquet m ▷ I play cricket. Juego al críquet. ❷ (insect) grillo m

crime n ❶ (offence) delito m ▷ He committed a crime. Cometió un delito. ▷ the scene of the crime el lugar del delito ❷ (very serious) crimen m (pl crímenes) ▷ a crime against humanity un crimen contra la humanidad ❸ (activity) delincuencia f ▷ Crime is rising. La delincuencia va en aumento.

criminal n delincuente mf
▶ adj **It's a criminal offence.** Constituye un delito.; **to have a criminal record** tener antecedentes penales

a
b
c
d
e
f
g
h
i
j
k
l
m
n
o
p
q
r
s
t
u
v
w
x
y
z

crisis n crisis f (pl crisis)

crisp adj (food) crujiente

crisps npl patatas fpl fritas (LatAm papas fpl fritas) ▷ a bag of crisps una bolsa de patatas fritas

critical adj crítico

criticism n crítica f

criticize vb criticar

Croatia n Croacia f

crochet vb hacer ganchillo ▷ She enjoys crocheting. Le gusta hacer ganchillo.

crocodile n cocodrilo m

crook n sinvergüenza mf

crop n cosecha f ▷ a good crop of apples una buena cosecha de manzanas

cross n cruz f (pl cruces)
 ▶ adj enfadado (LatAm enojado)
 ▷ He was cross about something. Estaba enojado por algo.
 ▶ vb (road, river) cruzar

cross out vb tachar

cross-country n a **cross-country race** una carrera (pl unos cross); **cross-country skiing** el esquí de fondo

crossing n ❶ travesía f ▷ a 10-hour crossing una travesía de 10 horas ❷ (for pedestrians) paso m de peatones

crossroads n cruce m

crossword n crucigrama m

 Although **crucigrama** ends in -a, it is actually a masculine noun.

crouch down vb agacharse

crow n cuervo m

crowd n ❶ muchedumbre f ❷ (at sports match) público m

crowded adj abarrotado de gente

crown n corona f

crude adj vulgar ▷ crude language lenguaje vulgar; **crude oil** el petróleo en crudo

cruel adj cruel

cruise n crucero m

crumb n miga f

crunchy adj crujiente

crush vb ❶ (box, fingers) aplastar ❷ machacar ▷ Crush two cloves of garlic. Machacar dos dientes de ajo.

crutch n muleta f

cry n grito m ▷ He gave a cry of pain. Dio un grito de dolor.; **She had a good cry.** Se dio una buena de llorar.
 ▶ vb ❶ llorar ▷ The baby's crying. El bebé está llorando. ❷ gritar ▷ "You're wrong", he cried. "No es cierto", gritó.

crystal n cristal m

cub n ❶ (animal) cachorro m ❷ (scout) lobato m

cube n ❶ (geometric shape) cubo m ❷ dado m ▷ Cut the meat into cubes. Cortar la carne en dados. ❸ (of sugar) terrón m (pl terrones)

cubic adj a **cubic metre** un metro cúbico

cucumber n pepino m

cuddle vb abrazar

cue n (for snooker, pool) taco m

culture n cultura f

cunning adj ❶ (person) astuto ❷ ingenioso ▷ a cunning plan un plan ingenioso

cup n ❶ taza f ▷ *a china cup* una taza de porcelana; **a cup of coffee** un café ❷ (*trophy*) copa f

cupboard n armario m

cure vb curar
  ▶ n cura f ▷ *There is no simple cure for the common cold.* No hay una cura sencilla para el catarro común.

curious adj curioso; **to be curious about something** sentir curiosidad por algo

curl n rizo m

curly adj rizado

currant n pasa f

currency n moneda f ▷ *foreign currency* la moneda extranjera

current n corriente f ▷ *The current is very strong.* La corriente es muy fuerte.
  ▶ adj ❶ actual ▷ *the current situation* la situación actual ❷ presente ▷ *the current financial year* el presente año financiero

current affairs npl temas mpl de actualidad

curriculum n plan m de estudios

curriculum vitae n currículum m vitae

curry n curry m (pl curries)

curtain n cortina f

cushion n cojín m (pl cojines)

custard n natillas fpl

custody n custodia f ▷ *The mother has custody of the children.* La madre tiene la custodia de los hijos.; **to be remanded in custody** estar detenido

custom n costumbre f ▷ *It's an old custom.* Es una vieja costumbre.

customer n cliente m, clienta f

customs npl aduana f; **to go through customs** pasar por la aduana

customs officer n oficial mf de aduanas

cut n ❶ corte m ▷ *He's got a cut on his forehead.* Tiene un corte en la frente. ❷ (*in price, spending*) reducción f (pl reducciones)
  ▶ vb ❶ cortar ▷ *I'll cut some bread.* Voy a cortar pan. ▷ *I cut my foot on a piece of glass.* Me corté el pie con un cristal.; **to cut oneself** cortarse ❷ (*price, spending*) reducir

cut down vb ❶ (*tree*) cortar ❷ (*reduce*) **I'm cutting down on coffee and cigarettes.** Estoy intentando tomar menos café y fumar menos.

cut off vb cortar ▷ *The electricity has been cut off.* Han cortado la electricidad. ▷ *We've been cut off.* Se ha cortado la comunicación.

cut up vb (*vegetables, meat*) picar

cute adj (*baby, pet*) mono ▷ *Isn't he cute!* ¡Qué mono es!

cutlery n cubertería f

CV n currículum m vitae

cycle vb ir en bicicleta ▷ *I cycle to school.* Voy al colegio en bicicleta.
  ▶ n bicicleta f ▷ *a cycle ride* un paseo en bicicleta

cycle lane n carril-bici m

cycling n ciclismo m; **The roads round here are ideal for cycling.** Las carreteras de por aquí son ideales para ir en bicicleta.

cyclist n ciclista mf
cylinder n cilindro m
Cyprus n Chipre f
Czech n ❶ (person) checo m,
   checa f ▷ the Czechs los checos
   ❷ (language) checo m
   ▶ adj checo; **the Czech Republic**
   la República Checa

dad n ❶ padre m ▷ my dad mi
   padre ❷ papá ▷ I'll ask Dad. Se lo
   preguntaré a papá.
daffodil n narciso m
daft adj estúpido
daily adj, adv ❶ diario ▷ daily life
   la vida diaria; **It's part of my**
   daily routine. Forma parte de mi
   rutina diaria.; **a daily paper** un
   periódico ❷ todos los días ▷ The
   pool is open daily. La piscina abre
   todos los días.
dairy products npl productos
   mpl lácteos
daisy n margarita f
dam n presa f
damage n daños mpl ▷ The storm
   did a lot of damage. La tormenta
   provocó muchos daños.
   ▶ vb dañar

damn n **I don't give a damn!** ¡Me importa un rábano! (informal); **Damn!** ¡Maldita sea! (informal)

damp adj húmedo

dance n baile m
▶ vb bailar

dancer n ❶ bailador m, bailadora f; **He is not a very good dancer.** No baila muy bien. ❷ (professional) bailarín m, bailarina f (mpl bailarines)

dancing n **to go dancing** ir a bailar

dandruff n caspa f

D & T n (= design and technology) dibujo y tecnología

Dane n danés m, danesa f (mpl daneses); **the Danes** los daneses

danger n peligro m; **in danger** en peligro; **We were in danger of missing the plane.** Corríamos el riesgo de perder el avión.

dangerous adj peligroso

Danish adj danés (f danesa)
▶ n (language) danés m

dare vb atreverse ▷ I didn't dare to tell my parents. No me atrevía a decírselo a mis padres.; **Don't you dare!** ¡Ni se te ocurra!; **I dare you!** ¡A que no te atreves!

daring adj atrevido

dark adj oscuro ▷ a dark green sweater un jersey verde oscuro ▷ It's dark in here. Está oscuro aquí dentro. ▷ She's got dark hair. Tiene el pelo oscuro.; **He's got dark skin.** Tiene la piel morena.; **It's getting dark.** Está oscureciendo.
▶ n (darkness) oscuridad f ▷ I'm

afraid of the dark. Me da miedo la oscuridad.

darkness n oscuridad f ▷ in the darkness en la oscuridad; **The room was in darkness.** La habitación estaba a oscuras.

darling n cariño ▷ Thank you, darling. Gracias, cariño.

dart n dardo m ▷ to play darts jugar a los dardos

data npl datos mpl

database n base f de datos

date n ❶ fecha f ▷ my date of birth mi fecha de nacimiento; **What's the date today?** ¿A qué estamos hoy?; **He's got a date with his girlfriend.** Ha quedado con su novia.; **out of date** (1) (document) caducado ▷ My passport's out of date. Tengo el pasaporte caducado. **(2)** (technology, idea) anticuado ❷ (fruit) dátil m

daughter n hija f

daughter-in-law n nuera f

dawn n amanecer m ▷ at dawn al amanecer

day n día m

▌ Although **día** ends in **-a**, it is actually a masculine noun.
▷ during the day por el día ▷ It's a lovely day. Hace un día precioso. ▷ every day todos los días ▷ a day off un día libre; **the day after tomorrow** pasado mañana; **the day before yesterday** anteayer; **a day return** un billete de ida y vuelta para el día

dead adj muerto ▷ He was dead. Estaba muerto.; **He was shot**

dead. Lo mataron de un tiro.
▶ *adv* **You're dead right!** ¡Tienes toda la razón!; **It was dead easy.** Fue facilísimo.; **dead on time** a la hora exacta

dead end *n* callejón *m* sin salida

deadline *n* fecha *f* tope

deaf *adj* sordo

deafening *adj* ensordecedor (*f* ensordecedora)

deal *n* trato *m* ▶ *He made a deal with the kidnappers.* Hizo un trato con los secuestradores. ▶ *It's a deal!* ¡Trato hecho!; **Big deal!** ¡Vaya cosa!; **It's no big deal.** No pasa nada.; **a great deal** mucho ▶ *a great deal of money* mucho dinero
▶ *vb* dar cartas ▶ *It's your turn to deal.* Te toca dar cartas.

deal with *vb* ocuparse de ▶ *He promised to deal with it immediately.* Prometió ocuparse de ello enseguida.

dealer *n* **a drug dealer** un traficante de drogas (*f* una traficante de drogas); **an antique dealer** un anticuario (*f* una anticuaria)

dealt *vb see* **deal**

dear *adj* ❶ querido ▶ *Dear Paul* Querido Paul; **Dear Mrs Smith** Estimada señora Smith; **Dear Sir** Muy señor mío; **Dear Madam** Estimada señora; **Dear Sir/ Madam** (*in a circular*) Estimados Sres.; **Oh dear! I've spilled my coffee.** ¡Oh, no! He derramado el café. ❸ (*expensive*) caro ▶ *These shoes are too dear.* Estos zapatos

son demasiado caros.

death *n* muerte *f* ▶ *after his death* después de su muerte; **I was bored to death.** Estaba aburrido como una ostra.

debate *n* debate *m*
▶ *vb* discutir

debt *n* deuda *f* ▶ *heavy debts* grandes deudas; **to be in debt** estar endeudado

decade *n* década *f*

decaffeinated *adj* descafeinado

December *n* diciembre *m*; **in December** en diciembre; **on 22 December** el 22 de diciembre

decent *adj* decente

decide *vb* ❶ decidir ▶ *I decided to write to her.* Decidí escribirle. ❷ decidirse ▶ *Haven't you decided yet?* ¿Aún no te has decidido?

decimal *adj* decimal ▶ *decimal point* la coma decimal

decision *n* decisión *f* (*pl* decisiones); **to make a decision** tomar una decisión

deck *n* ❶ (*of ship*) cubierta *f*; **on deck** en cubierta ❷ (*of bus*) piso *m*; **a deck of cards** una baraja

deckchair *n* tumbona *f*

declare *vb* declarar

decorate *vb* ❶ decorar ▶ *I decorated the cake with glacé cherries.* Decoré el pastel con guindas confitadas. ❷ (*paint*) pintar ❸ (*wallpaper*) empapelar

decorations *npl* adornos *mpl* ▶ *Christmas decorations* adornos de Navidad

decrease n disminución f (pl disminuciones) ▷ There has been a decrease in the number of unemployed people. Ha habido una disminución del número de desempleados.
▸vb disminuir

deduct vb descontar

deep adj ❶ profundo ▷ deep water agua profunda; **a hole four metres deep** un agujero de cuatro metros de profundidad; **How deep is the lake?** ¿Qué profundidad tiene el lago? ❷ espeso ▷ a deep layer of snow una espesa capa de nieve ❸ grave ▷ He's got a deep voice. Tiene la voz grave.; **to take a deep breath** respirar hondo

deeply adv profundamente ▷ deeply grateful profundamente agradecido

deer n ciervo m

defeat n derrota f
▸vb derrotar

defect n defecto m

defence n defensa f

defend vb defender

defender n ❶ (of person, ideas) defensor m, defensora f ❷ (in sports) defensa mf

defense n (in US) defensa f

define vb definir

definite adj ❶ concreto ▷ I haven't got any definite plans. No tengo planes concretos. ❷ definitivo ▷ It's too soon to give a definite answer. Es pronto aún para dar una respuesta definitiva. ❸ seguro ▷ Maybe we'll go to Spain, but it's not definite. Quizá vayamos a España, pero no es seguro.; **He was definite about it.** Fue rotundo acerca de esto. ❹ claro ▷ It's a definite improvement. Es una clara mejoría.

definitely adv sin duda ▷ He's definitely the best player. Es sin duda el mejor jugador.; **He's the best player. - Definitely!** Es el mejor jugador. - ¡Desde luego!; **Are you going to go out with him? - Definitely not!** ¿Vas a salir con él? - ¡En absoluto!

definition n definición f (pl definiciones)

degree n ❶ (measure of temperature) grado m ▷ 30 degrees 30 grados ❷ (from university) licenciatura f ▷ a degree in English una licenciatura en filología inglesa; **She's got a degree in English.** Es licenciada en filología inglesa.

delay vb retrasar ▷ We decided to delay our departure. Decidimos retrasar la salida.; **to be delayed** retrasarse ▷ Our flight was delayed. Nuestro vuelo se retrasó.
▸n retraso m ▷ The tests have caused some delay. Las pruebas han ocasionado algún retraso.

delete vb suprimir

deliberate adj intencionado

deliberately adv a propósito

delicate adj delicado

delicatessen n tienda especializada en comida exótica

delicious adj delicioso

delight n placer m

delighted adj encantado ▷ He'll be delighted to see you. Estará encantado de verte.

deliver vb ❶ repartir ▷ I deliver newspapers. Reparto periódicos. ❷ entregar ▷ The package was delivered in the morning. Entregaron el paquete por la mañana.; **Doctor Hamilton delivered the twins.** El Doctor Hamilton asistió en el parto de los gemelos.

delivery n ❶ entrega f ▷ Allow 28 days for delivery. La entrega se realizará en un plazo de 28 días. ❷ (of baby) parto m

demand vb exigir ▷ I demand an explanation. Exijo una explicación. ▶ n ❶ (firm request) petición f (pl peticiones) ▷ His demand for compensation was rejected. Rechazaron su petición de indemnización. ❷ (commercial) demanda f ▷ Demand for coal is down. Ha bajado la demanda de carbón.

democracy n democracia f

democratic adj democrático

demolish vb derribar

demonstrate vb ❶ demostrar ▷ You have to demonstrate that you are reliable. Tienes que demostrar que se puede confiar en ti.; **She demonstrated the technique.** Hizo una demostración de la técnica. ❷ manifestarse ▷ They demonstrated outside the court. Se manifestaron a las puertas del tribunal.

demonstration n ❶ (of method, product) demostración f (pl demostraciones) ❷ (protest) manifestación f (pl manifestaciones)

demonstrator n manifestante mf

denim n **a denim jacket** una cazadora vaquera

Denmark n Dinamarca f

dense adj (smoke, fog) denso

dent n abolladura f
▶ vb abollar

dental adj dental ▷ dental treatment el tratamiento dental; **a dental appointment** una cita con el dentista; **dental floss** la seda dental

dentist n dentista mf ▷ Catherine is a dentist. Catherine es dentista. ▷ at the dentist's en el dentista

deny vb negar ▷ She denied everything. Lo negó todo.

deodorant n desodorante m

depart vb ❶ (person) partir ▷ He departed at three o'clock precisely. Partió a las tres en punto. ❷ salir ▷ Trains depart for the airport every half hour. Los trenes salen para el aeropuerto cada media hora.

department n ❶ (in shop) sección f (pl secciones) ▷ the toy department la sección de juguetes ❷ (in school) departamento m ▷ the English department el departamento de inglés

department store n grandes almacenes mpl

departure n salida f ▷ The

departure of this flight has been delayed. Se ha retrasado la salida de este vuelo.

departure lounge n sala f de embarque

depend vb **to depend on**
(1) depender de ▷ *The price depends on the quality*. El precio depende de la calidad. (2) (rely on) confiar en ▷ *You can depend on him*. Puedes confiar en él.; **depending on** según

▌**según** has to be followed by a verb in the subjunctive.
▷ *depending on the weather* según el tiempo que haga; **It depends.** Depende.

deposit n ❶ (on hired goods) depósito m ▷ *You get the deposit back when you return the bike*. Al devolver la bici te devuelven el depósito. ❷ (advance payment) señal f ▷ *You have to pay a deposit when you book*. Se paga una señal al hacer la reserva. ❸ (in house buying) entrada f ▷ *He paid a £2000 deposit on the house*. Dio una entrada de 2.000 libras para la casa.

depressed adj deprimido ▷ *I'm feeling depressed*. Estoy deprimido.

depressing adj deprimente

depth n profundidad f ▷ *14 feet in depth* 14 pies de profundidad

deputy head n subdirector m, subdirectora f

descend vb descender

describe vb describir

description n descripción f (pl descripciones)

desert n desierto m

desert island n isla f desierta

deserve vb merecer

design n ❶ (of aircraft, equipment) diseño m; **fashion design** diseño de modas; **design and technology** dibujo y tecnología ❷ (pattern) motivo m
▶ vb diseñar ▷ *She designed the dress herself*. Ella misma diseñó el vestido.

designer n (of clothes) modista mf; **designer clothes** la ropa de diseño

desire n deseo m
▶ vb desear

desk n ❶ (in office) escritorio m ❷ (for pupil) pupitre m ❸ (in hotel, at airport) mostrador m

despair n desesperación f ▷ *a feeling of despair* un sentimiento de desesperación; **to be in despair** estar desesperado

desperate adj desesperado ▷ *a desperate situation* una situación desesperada; **I was starting to get desperate.** Estaba empezando a desesperarme.

desperately adv
❶ tremendamente ▷ *We're desperately worried*. Estamos tremendamente preocupados.
❷ desesperadamente ▷ *He was desperately trying to persuade her*. Intentaba desesperadamente convencerla.

despise vb despreciar

despite prep a pesar de

dessert n postre m ▷ for dessert de postre

destination n destino m

destroy vb destruir

destruction n destrucción f

detached house n casa f no adosada

detail n detalle m ▷ I can't remember the details. No recuerdo los detalles.; **in detail** detalladamente

detailed adj detallado

detective n detective mf ▷ He's a detective. Es detective. ▷ a private detective un detective privado; **a detective story** una novela policíaca

detention n to get a detention quedarse castigado después de clase

detergent n detergente m

determined adj decidido ▷ She's determined to succeed. Está decidida a triunfar.

detour n desvío m

devastated adj deshecho ▷ I was devastated when they told me. Cuando me lo dijeron me quedé deshecho.

develop vb ❶ (idea, quality) desarrollar ▷ I developed his original idea. Yo desarrollé su idea original. ❷ desarrollarse ▷ Girls develop faster than boys. Las chicas se desarrollan más rápido que los chicos. ❸ (photo) revelar ▷ to get a film developed revelar un carrete; **to develop into** convertirse en ▷ The argument developed into a

fight. La discusión se convirtió en una pelea.

developing adj **a developing country** un país en vías de desarrollo

development n desarrollo m ▷ economic development in Pakistan el desarrollo económico de Pakistán; **the latest developments** los últimos acontecimientos

devil n diablo m

devoted adj (friend) leal; **a devoted wife** una abnegada esposa; **He's completely devoted to her.** Está totalmente entregado a ella.

diabetes n diabetes f

diabetic adj diabético ▷ I'm diabetic. Soy diabético.

diagonal adj diagonal

diagram n diagrama m

> Although **diagrama** ends in **-a**, it is actually a masculine noun.

dial vb marcar (LatAm discar)

dialling tone n señal f de marcar

dialogue n diálogo m

diamond n diamante m ▷ a diamond ring un anillo de diamantes; **diamonds** (at cards) los diamantes ▷ the ace of diamonds el as de diamantes

diaper n (in US) pañal m

diarrhoea n diarrea f ▷ to have diarrhoea tener diarrea

diary n ❶ agenda f ▷ I've got her phone number in my diary. Tengo su número de teléfono en la agenda. ❷ diario m ▷ I keep a diary. Estoy escribiendo un diario.

dice n dado m

dictation n dictado m

dictionary n diccionario m

did vb see **do**

didn't = **did not**

die vb morir ▷ He died last year. Murió el año pasado. ▷ She's dying. Se está muriendo.; **to be dying to do something** morirse de ganas de hacer algo

diesel n (fuel) gasoil m

diet n ① dieta f ▷ a healthy diet una dieta sana ② régimen m (pl regímenes) ▷ I'm on a diet. Estoy a régimen.; **a diet Coke®** una Coca-Cola® light

difference n diferencia f ▷ There's not much difference in age between us. No hay mucha diferencia de edad entre nosotros.; **Good weather makes all the difference.** Con buen tiempo la cosa cambia mucho.; **It makes no difference.** Da lo mismo.

different adj distinto

difficult adj difícil ▷ It was difficult to choose. Era difícil escoger.

difficulty n dificultad f ▷ What's the difficulty? ¿Cuál es la dificultad?; **to have difficulty doing something** tener dificultades para hacer algo

dig vb cavar ▷ They're digging a hole in the road. Están cavando un hoyo en la calle.

digestion n digestión f

digital camera n cámara f digital

digital television n televisión f digital

digital watch n reloj m digital (pl relojes digitales)

dim adj ① (light) tenue ② (person) lerdo

dimension n dimensión f (pl dimensiones)

din n ① (of traffic, machinery) estruendo m ② (of crowd, voices) jaleo m

diner n (in US) restaurante m barato

dinghy n **a rubber dinghy** una lancha neumática

dining room n comedor m

dinner n ① (at midday) comida f ② (in the evening) cena f (LatAm comida f); **The children have dinner at school.** Los niños comen en la escuela.

dinner jacket n esmoquin m (pl esmóquines)

dinner party n cena f

dinner time n ① (at midday) hora f de la comida ② (in the evening) hora f de la cena

dinosaur n dinosaurio m

diploma n diploma m

> Although **diploma** ends in -a, it is actually a masculine noun.

direct adj, adv directo ▷ the most direct route el camino más directo; **You can't fly to Manchester direct from Seville.** No hay vuelos directos a Manchester desde Sevilla.
> vb dirigir

direction n dirección f (pl direcciones) ▷ We're going in the wrong direction. Vamos en la dirección equivocada.; **to ask somebody for directions** preguntar el camino a alguien

director n director m, directora f

directory n ❶ (telephone) guía f telefónica; **directory enquiries** información telefónica ❸ (in computing) directorio m

dirt n suciedad f

dirty adj sucio ▷ It's dirty. Está sucio.; **to get dirty** ensuciarse; **to get something dirty** ensuciarse algo ▷ He got his hands dirty. Se ensució las manos.

disabled adj minusválido; **disabled people** los minusválidos

disadvantage n desventaja f; **to be at a disadvantage** estar en desventaja

disagree vb no estar de acuerdo ▷ He disagrees with me. No está de acuerdo conmigo.

disagreement n desacuerdo m

disappear vb desaparecer

disappearance n desaparición f (pl desapariciones)

disappointed adj decepcionado ▷ I'm disappointed. Estoy decepcionado.

disappointment n decepción f (pl decepciones)

disaster n desastre m

disastrous adj desastroso

disc n disco m

discipline n disciplina f

disc jockey n discjockey mf (pl discjockeys) ▷ He's a disc jockey. Es discjockey.

disco n ❶ (place) discoteca f ❷ (occasion) baile m ▷ There's a disco at school tonight. Esta noche hay baile en la escuela.

disconnect vb (appliance) desconectar; **to disconnect the water supply** cortar el agua

discount n descuento m ▷ a 20% discount un descuento del 20 por ciento

discourage vb (dishearten) desanimar; **to get discouraged** desanimarse; **to discourage somebody from doing something** disuadir a alguien de hacer algo

discover vb descubrir

discovery n descubrimiento m

discrimination n discriminación f ▷ racial discrimination la discriminación racial

discuss vb ❶ discutir ▷ I'll discuss it with my parents. Lo discutiré con mis padres. ❷ (topic) discutir sobre ▷ We discussed the topic at length. Discutimos sobre el tema largo y tendido.

discussion n discusión f (pl discusiones)

disease n enfermedad f

disgraceful adj vergonzoso

disguise n disfraz m (pl disfraces); **in disguise** disfrazado

disgusted adj indignado ▷ I was completely disgusted. Estaba totalmente indignado.

▌ Be careful not to translate **disgusted** by **disgustado**.

disgusting adj ❶ (food, smell)

asqueroso ▷ It looks disgusting.
Tiene un aspecto asqueroso.
❷ (disgraceful) indignante ▷ That's
disgusting! ¡Es indignante!
dish n plato m ▷ a china dish un
plato de porcelana ▷ a vegetarian
dish un plato vegetariano; **to
do the dishes** fregar los platos;
a satellite dish una antena
parabólica
dishonest adj poco honrado
dish soap n (in US) lavavajillas m
(pl lavavajillas)
dishwasher n lavaplatos m (pl
lavaplatos)
disinfectant n desinfectante m
disk n disco m ▷ The hard disk el
disco duro
dislike vb I dislike it. No me gusta.
dismiss vb (employee) despedir
disobedient adj desobediente
display n The assistant took
the watch out of the display.
El dependiente sacó el reloj de
la vitrina.; **There was a lovely
display of fruit in the window.**
Había un estupendo surtido de
fruta en el escaparate.; **to be on
display** estar expuesto; **a
firework display** fuegos
artificiales
▶ vb ❶ mostrar ▷ She proudly
displayed her medal. Mostró con
orgullo su medalla. ❷ (in shop
window) exponer
disposable adj desechable ▷ a
disposable razor una maquinilla
desechable
disqualify vb descalificar; **to be**

disqualified ser descalificado
▷ They were disqualified from the
competition. Fueron descalificados
del campeonato.
disrupt vb interrumpir
dissolve vb disolver
distance n distancia f ▷ a distance
of forty kilometres una distancia de
cuarenta kilómetros.; **It's within
walking distance.** Se puede
ir andando.; **in the distance** a
lo lejos
distant adj lejano ▷ in the distant
future en un futuro lejano
distract vb distraer
distribute vb distribuir
district n ❶ (of town) barrio m
❷ (of country) región f (pl regiones)
disturb vb molestar ▷ I'm sorry to
disturb you. Siento molestarte.
ditch n zanja f
▶ vb dejar ▷ She's just ditched her
boyfriend. Acaba de dejar al novio.
dive n ❶ (into water) salto m de
cabeza ❷ (under water) buceo m
▶ vb ❶ (into water) tirarse de
cabeza ❷ (under water) bucear
diver n buzo mf
diversion n (for traffic) desvío m
Be careful not to translate
diversion by diversión.
divide vb ❶ dividir ▷ Divide the
pastry in half. Divide la masa
en dos.; **12 divided by 3 is 4.** 12
dividido entre 3 es 4. ❷ dividirse
▷ We divided into two groups. Nos
dividimos en dos grupos.
diving n ❶ (under water) buceo
m ▷ diving equipment equipo de

buceo ❷ (*into water*) salto m de trampolín ▷ *a diving competition* una competición de saltos de trampolín

diving board n trampolín m (pl trampolines)

division n división f (pl divisiones)

divorce n divorcio m

divorced adj divorciado ▷ *My parents are divorced.* Mis padres están divorciados.; **to get divorced** divorciarse

DIY n bricolaje m ▷ *a DIY shop* una tienda de bricolaje

dizzy adj **I feel dizzy.** Estoy mareado.

DJ n discjockey mf (pl discjockeys) ▷ *He's a DJ.* Es discjockey.

do vb ❶ hacer ▷ *What are you doing this evening?* ¿Qué vas a hacer esta noche? ▷ *I want to do physics at university.* Quiero hacer física en la universidad.; **What does your father do?** ¿A qué se dedica tu padre? ❷ ir ▷ *She's doing well at school.* Va bien en el colegio.; **How are you doing?** ¿Qué tal?; **How do you do?** Mucho gusto. ❸ valer ▷ *It's not very good, but it'll do.* No es muy bueno, pero valdrá. ▷ *Will £10 do?* ¿Valdrá con diez libras?; **That'll do, thanks.** Así está bien, gracias.

Do is not translated when used to form questions.

▷ *Do you speak English?* ¿Hablas inglés? ▷ *Where does he live?* ¿Dónde vive? ▷ *Where did you go for your holidays?* ¿Dónde te fuiste de vacaciones?

Use **no** in negative sentences for **don't**.

▷ *I don't understand.* No entiendo. ▷ *He didn't come.* No vino.

Do is not translated when it is used in place of another verb.

▷ *I hate maths. - So do I.* Odio las matemáticas. - Yo también. ▷ *I didn't like the film. - Neither did I.* No me gustó la película. - A mí tampoco. ▷ *Do you speak English? - Yes, I do.* ¿Hablas inglés? - Sí. ▷ *Do you like horses? - No, I don't.* ¿Te gustan los caballos? - No.

Use **¿no?** or **¿verdad?** to check information.

▷ *You go swimming on Fridays, don't you?* Los viernes vas a nadar, ¿no? ▷ *It doesn't matter, does it?* No importa, ¿verdad?

do up vb ❶ (*shoes*) atarse ▷ *Do up your shoes!* ¡Átate los zapatos! ❷ (*shirt, cardigan, coat*) abrocharse ▷ *Do your coat up.* Abróchate el abrigo.; **Do up your zip!** ¡Súbete la cremallera! ❸ (*house, room*) reformar

do with vb (*be connected with*) tener que ver con ▷ *What has it got to do with you?* ¿Qué tiene que ver contigo?; **I could do with a holiday.** Me vendrían bien unas vacaciones.

do without vb pasar sin ▷ *I can't do without my computer.* Yo no puedo pasar sin el ordenador.

doctor n médico m, médica f ▷ *He's a doctor.* Es médico. ▷ *at the doctor's* en el médico

document n documento m

documentary n documental m

dodge vb (attacker, blow) esquivar

dodgems npl coches mpl de choque

does vb see do

doesn't = does not

dog n perro m ▷ Have you got a dog? ¿Tienes perro?

do-it-yourself n bricolaje m

dole n subsidio m de paro; He's on the dole. Está parado.; to go on the dole quedarse parado

doll n muñeca f

dollar n dólar m

dolphin n delfín m (pl delfines)

dominoes npl to have a game of dominoes echar una partida al dominó

donate vb donar

done vb see do

▶ adj listo ▷ Is the pasta done? ¿Está lista la pasta?; How do you like your steak? - Well done. ¿Cómo quieres el filete? - Muy hecho.

donkey n burro m

don't = do not

door n puerta f

doorbell n timbre m

doorstep n peldaño m de la puerta; on my doorstep en mi puerta

dormitory n dormitorio m

dot n punto m; on the dot en punto ▷ He arrived at nine on the dot. Llegó a las nueve en punto.

double vb ❶ doblar ▷ They doubled their prices. Doblaron los precios.

❷ doblarse ▷ The number of attacks has doubled. El número de agresiones se ha doblado.

▶ adj, adv doble ▷ a double helping una ración doble ▷ to cost double costar el doble; a double bed una cama de matrimonio; a double room una habitación doble

double bass n contrabajo m

double-click vb hacer doble clic ▷ to double-click on an icon hacer doble clic en un icono

double-decker bus n autobús m de dos pisos

double glazing n doble acristalamiento m

doubles npl (in tennis) dobles mpl ▷ to play mixed doubles jugar un partido de dobles mixtos

doubt n duda f ▷ I have my doubts. Tengo mis dudas.; no doubt sin duda ▷ as you no doubt know como sin duda sabrá

▶ vb dudar ▷ I doubt it. Lo dudo. Use the subjunctive after dudar que.

▷ I doubt that he'll agree. Dudo que vaya a estar de acuerdo.

doubtful adj dudoso ▷ It's doubtful. Es dudoso.; to be doubtful about doing something no estar seguro de hacer algo ▷ I'm doubtful about going by myself. No estoy seguro de ir solo.; You sound doubtful. No pareces muy convencido.

dough n masa f

doughnut n buñuelo m ▷ a jam doughnut un buñuelo de

mermelada

down adv ❶ abajo ▷ It's down there. Está allí abajo. ❷ al suelo ▷ He threw down his racket. Tiró la raqueta al suelo.
▶ prep **to go down the road** ir calle abajo; **They live just down the road.** Viven más adelante en esta calle.
▶ adj desanimado; **to feel down** estar desanimado; **The computer's down.** El ordenador no funciona.

download vb descargar ▷ to download a file descargar un fichero

downstairs adv, adj ❶ abajo ▷ The bathroom's downstairs. El baño está abajo.; **to go downstairs** bajar ❷ de abajo ▷ the downstairs bathroom el baño de abajo ▷ the neighbours downstairs los vecinos de abajo

downtown adv ❶ (in US: go, come) al centro de la ciudad ❷ (live, be) en el centro de la ciudad

doze vb dormitar

doze off vb quedarse dormido

dozen n docena f ▷ a dozen eggs una docena de huevos; **dozens of times** cientos de veces

draft n (in US) corriente f de aire

drag vb (thing, person) arrastrar
▶ n **It's a real drag!** ¡Es una verdadera lata! (informal)

dragon n dragón m (pl dragones)

drain n ❶ (of house) desagüe m ❸ (in street) alcantarilla f
▶ vb (vegetables, pasta) escurrir

drama n ❶ (play) drama m
Although **drama** ends in **-a**, it is actually a masculine noun.
▷ a TV drama un drama para televisión ❷ (theatre) teatro m ▷ Drama is my favourite subject. Mi asignatura favorita es teatro.; **drama school** la escuela de arte dramático

dramatic adj espectacular ▷ a dramatic improvement una espectacular mejoría

drank vb see **drink**

drapes npl (in US) cortinas fpl

draught n corriente f de aire ▷ There's a draught from the window. Entra corriente por la ventana.

draughts n damas fpl ▷ to play draughts jugar a las damas

draw n ❶ (in game, match) empate m ▷ The game ended in a draw. El partido terminó en empate. ❷ (of lottery) sorteo m
▶ vb ❶ (a scene, a person) dibujar; **to draw a picture** hacer un dibujo; **to draw a picture of somebody** hacer un retrato de alguien; **to draw a line** trazar una línea ❷ empatar ▷ We drew two all. Empatamos a dos.; **to draw the curtains (1)** (open) descorrer las cortinas **(2)** (close) correr las cortinas

drawback n inconveniente m

drawer n cajón m (pl cajones)

drawing n dibujo m; **He's good at drawing.** Se le da bien dibujar.

drawing pin n chincheta f

drawn vb see **draw**

dreadful adj ❶ terrible ▷ *a dreadful mistake* un terrible error ❷ horrible ▷ *The weather was dreadful.* Hizo un tiempo horrible.; **You look dreadful.** Tienes muy mal aspecto.; **I feel dreadful about not having phoned.** Me siento muy mal por no haber llamado.

dream vb soñar ▷ *Do you dream every night?* ¿Sueñas todas las noches? ▷ *She dreamt about her baby.* Soñó con su bebé.
▶ n sueño m

drench vb **I got drenched.** Me puse empapado.

dress n vestido m
▶ vb vestirse ▷ *I got up, dressed and went downstairs.* Me levanté, me vestí y bajé.; **to get dressed** vestirse

dress up vb disfrazarse ▷ *I dressed up as a ghost.* Me disfracé de fantasma.

dressed adj vestido ▷ *I'm not dressed yet.* Aún no estoy vestido. ▷ *She was dressed in white.* Iba vestida de blanco.

dresser n (furniture) aparador m

dressing gown n bata f

dressing table n tocador m

drew vb see **draw**

dried adj seco ▷ *dried flowers* flores secas; **dried milk** la leche en polvo; **dried fruits** las frutas pasas

drier = **dryer**

drift n *a snow drift* un ventisquero
▶ vb ❶ (boat) ir a la deriva
❷ (snow) amontonarse

drill n taladradora f
▶ vb taladrar; **He drilled a hole in the wall.** Hizo un agujero en la pared.

drink vb beber (LatAm tomar) ▷ *What would you like to drink?* ¿Qué te apetece beber? ▷ *She drank three cups of tea.* Se bebió tres tazas de té.
▶ n ❶ (soft) bebida f ▷ *a cold drink* una bebida fría ❷ (alcoholic) copa f ▷ *They've gone out for a drink.* Han salido a tomar una copa.; **to have a drink** tomar algo ▷ *Would you like a drink?* ¿Quieres tomar algo?

drive n ❶ paseo m en coche ▷ *to go for a drive* ir a dar un paseo en coche; **We've got a long drive tomorrow.** Mañana nos espera un largo viaje en coche. ❷ camino m de entrada a la casa ▷ *He parked his car in the drive.* Aparcó el coche en el camino de entrada a la casa.; **disk drive** la unidad de disco
▶ vb ❶ (a car) conducir (LatAm manejar) ▷ *Can you drive?* ¿Sabes conducir? ❷ (go by car) ir en coche ▷ *We never drive into the town centre.* Nunca vamos en coche al centro. ❸ (transport) llevar en coche ▷ *My mother drives me to school.* Mi madre me lleva al colegio en coche.; **to drive somebody home** acercar a alguien a su casa en coche; **to drive somebody mad** volver loco a alguien ▷ *He drives her mad.* La vuelve loca.

driver n conductor m, conductora f ▷ *He's a bus driver.* Es conductor de autobús.; **She's an excellent driver.** Conduce muy bien.

driver's license n (in US) permiso m de conducir

driving instructor n profesor m de autoescuela, profesora f de autoescuela ▷ He's a driving instructor. Es profesor de autoescuela.

driving lesson n clase f de conducir

driving licence n permiso m de conducir

driving test n to take one's **driving test** hacer el examen de conducir; **She's just passed her driving test.** Acaba de sacarse el carnet de conducir.

drop n ❶ (of liquid) gota f ▷ Would you like some milk? - Just a drop. ¿Quieres leche? - Una gota nada más. ❷ (fall) bajada f ▷ a drop in temperature una bajada de las temperaturas
▶ vb ❶ bajar ▷ The temperature will drop tonight. La temperatura bajará esta noche. ❷ soltar ▷ The cat dropped the mouse at my feet. El gato soltó al ratón junto a mis pies.; **I dropped the glass.** Se me cayó el vaso. ❸ dejar ▷ Could you drop me at the station? ¿Me puedes dejar en la estación?; **I'm going to drop chemistry.** No voy a dar más química.

drought n sequía f

drove vb see **drive**

drown vb ahogarse ▷ A boy drowned here yesterday. Un chico se

ahogó ayer aquí.

drug n ❶ (medicine) medicamento m ▷ They need food and drugs. Necesitan comida y medicamentos. ❷ (illegal) droga f ▷ hard drugs drogas duras; **to take drugs** drogarse; **a drug addict** un drogadicto

drugstore n (in US) tienda de comestibles, periódicos y medicamentos

drum n tambor m ▷ an African drum un tambor africano; **a drum kit** una batería; **to play the drums** tocar la batería

drummer n (in rock group) batería mf

drunk vb see **drink**
▶ adj borracho ▷ He was drunk. Estaba borracho.; **to get drunk** emborracharse
▶ n borracho m, borracha f

dry adj seco ▷ The paint isn't dry yet. Aún no está seca la pintura.
▶ vb ❶ secar ▷ to dry the dishes secar los platos ❷ secarse ▷ The washing will dry quickly in the sun. La colada se secará rápido al sol.; **to dry one's hair** secarse el pelo

dry-cleaner's n tintorería f

dryer n a tumble dryer una secadora; **a hair dryer** un secador de pelo

dubbed adj doblado ▷ The film was dubbed into Spanish. La película estaba doblada al español.

duck n pato m

due adj, adv He's due to arrive tomorrow. Debe llegar mañana.;

The plane's due in half an hour.
El avión llegará en media hora.;
When's the baby due? ¿Para
cuándo nacerá el niño?; **due to**
debido a ▷ *The trip was cancelled
due to bad weather.* El viaje se
suspendió debido al mal tiempo.

dug *vb see* **dig**

dull *adj* ❶ (*uninteresting*) soso
▷ *He's nice, but a bit dull.* Es
simpático, pero un poco soso.
❷ (*grey*) gris ▷ *It's always dull and
wet.* El tiempo está siempre gris
y lluvioso.

dumb *adj* ❶ (*unable to speak*) mudo
❷ (*stupid*) bobo

dummy *n* (*for baby*) chupete *m*

dump *n* **It's a real dump!** ¡Es una
auténtica pocilga!; **a rubbish
dump** un vertedero
▶ *vb* (*waste*) verter

dungarees *npl* mono *m* (*LatAm*
overol *m*)

dungeon *n* mazmorra *f*

during *prep* durante

dusk *n* anochecer *m*; **at dusk** al
anochecer

dust *n* polvo *m*
▶ *vb* limpiar el polvo de ▷ *I dusted
the shelves.* Limpié el polvo de las
estanterías.

dustbin *n* cubo *m* de la basura
(*LatAm* balde *m*)

dustman *n* basurero *m*

dusty *adj* polvoriento

Dutch *adj* holandés (*f* holandesa)
▷ *She's Dutch.* Es holandesa.
▶ *n* (*language*) holandés *m*; **the
Dutch** los holandeses

Dutchman *n* holandés *m*

Dutchwoman *n* holandesa *f*

duty *n* deber *m* ▷ *It was his duty
to tell the police.* Su deber era
decírselo a la policía.; **to be on
duty** ❶ (*policeman*) estar de
servicio ❷ (*doctor, nurse*) estar
de guardia

duty-free *adj* libre de impuestos

duvet *n* edredón *m* (*pl* edredones)

DVD *n* DVD *m* ▷ *a DVD player* un
lector de DVD

dwarf *n* enano *m*, enana *f*

dye *n* tinte *m* ▷ *hair dye* el tinte
para el pelo
▶ *vb* teñir ▷ *to dye sth red* teñir
algo de rojo ▷ *She has dyed her
hair blonde.* Se ha teñido el pelo
de rubio.

dying *vb see* **die**

dynamic *adj* dinámico

dyslexia *n* dislexia *f*

a b c d e f g h i j k l m n o p q r s t u v w x y z

e

each _adj, pron_ ❶ cada ▷ _each day_ cada día; **Each house has its own garden.** Todas las casas tienen jardín. ❷ cada uno (_f_ cada una) ▷ _The plates cost £5 each._ Los platos cuestan 5 libras cada uno. ▷ _He gave each of us £10._ Nos dio 10 libras a cada uno.

> Use a reflexive verb to translate **each other**.

▷ _They hate each other._ Se odian.
▷ _They don't know each other._ No se conocen.

eagle _n_ águila _f_

> Although it's a feminine noun, remember that you use **el** and **un** with **águila**.

ear _n_ oreja _f_

earache _n_ **to have earache** tener dolor de oídos

earlier _adv_ ❶ antes ▷ _I saw him earlier._ Lo vi antes. ❷ (_in the morning_) más temprano ▷ _I ought to get up earlier._ Debería levantarme más temprano.

early _adv, adj_ ❶ temprano ▷ _I have to get up early._ Tengo que levantarme temprano.; **to have an early night** irse a la cama temprano ❷ (_ahead of time_) pronto ▷ _I came early to avoid the heavy traffic._ Vine pronto para evitar el tráfico denso.

earn _vb_ ganar ▷ _She earns £5 an hour._ Gana 5 libras esterlinas a la hora.

earnings _npl_ (_income_) ingresos _mpl_

earring _n_ pendiente _m_ (_LatAm_ arete _m_)

earth _n_ tierra _f_; **What on earth are you doing here?** ¿Qué diablos haces aquí?

earthquake _n_ terremoto _m_

easily _adv_ fácilmente

east _n_ (_direction, region_) este _m_ ▷ _in the east of the country_ al este del país
▶ _adj_ **an east wind** un viento del este; **the east coast** la costa oriental
▶ _adv_ hacia el este ▷ _We were travelling east._ Viajábamos hacia el este.; **east of** al este de ▷ _It's east of London._ Está al este de Londres.

Easter _n_ Pascua _f_; **Easter egg** el huevo de Pascua; **the Easter holidays** las vacaciones de Semana Santa

eastern _adj_ oriental ▷ _the eastern part of the island_ la parte oriental

de la isla; **Eastern Europe** la
Europa del Este

easy adj fácil

eat vb comer ▷ Would you like
something to eat? ¿Quieres comer
algo?

echo n eco m

eco-friendly adj ecológico

ecology n ecología f

economic adj ❶ (growth,
development, policy) económico
❷ (profitable) rentable

economical adj económico ▷ My
car is very economical to run. Mi
coche me sale muy económico.

economics n economía f ▷ the
economics of the third world
countries la economía de los países
tercermundistas; **He's doing
economics at university.** Estudia
económicas en la universidad.

economy n economía f

ecstasy n (drug) éxtasis m; **to be in
ecstasy** estar en éxtasis

eczema n eczema m

Although **eczema** ends in
-a, it is actually a masculine
noun.

▷ She's got eczema. Tiene eczema.

edge n borde m ▷ on the edge of
the desk en el borde del escritorio;
**They live on the edge of the
town.** Viven en los límites de la
ciudad. ❷ (of lake) orilla f

Edinburgh n Edimburgo m

editor n ❶ (of newspaper,
magazine) director m, directora
f ❷ redactor m, redactora f ▷ the
sports editor el redactor de la

sección de deportes

education n ❶ educación f
▷ There should be more investment in
education. Debería invertirse más
dinero en educación. ❷ (teaching)
enseñanza f ▷ She works in
education. Trabaja en la enseñanza.

educational adj ❶ (toy)
educativo ❷ (experience, film)
instructivo

effect n efecto m ▷ special effects los
efectos especiales

effective adj eficaz (pl eficaces)

efficient adj ❶ eficiente ▷ His
secretary is very efficient. Su
secretaria es muy eficiente.
❷ eficaz (pl eficaces) ▷ It's a very
efficient system. Es un sistema
muy eficaz.

effort n esfuerzo m; **to make
an effort to do something**
esforzarse en hacer algo

e.g. abbr p.ej.

egg n huevo m ▷ a boiled egg (soft)
un huevo pasado por agua ▷ a
hard-boiled egg un huevo duro

egg cup n huevera f

eggplant n (in US) berenjena f

Egypt n Egipto m

eight num ocho ▷ She's eight. Tiene
ocho años.

eighteen num dieciocho ▷ She's
eighteen. Tiene dieciocho años.

eighteenth adj decimoctavo;
the eighteenth floor la planta
dieciocho; **the eighteenth of
August** el dieciocho de agosto

eighth adj octavo ▷ the eighth
floor el octavo piso; **the eighth of**

August el ocho de agosto
eighty num ochenta ▷ He's eighty. Tiene ochenta años.
Eire n Eire m
either adj, conj, pron, adv tampoco ▷ I don't like milk, and I don't like eggs either. No me gusta la leche, y tampoco me gustan los huevos.; **either...or...** o...o...▷ You can have either ice cream or yoghurt. Puedes tomar o helado o yogur.; **I don't like either of them.** No me gusta cualquiera de los dos.; **Choose either of them.** Elige cualquiera de los dos.; **on either side of the road** a ambos lados de la carretera
elastic n elástico m
elastic band n goma f elástica
elbow n codo m
elder adj mayor ▷ my elder sister mi hermana mayor
elderly adj anciano; **an elderly man** un anciano; **the elderly** los ancianos
eldest adj, n mayor ▷ my eldest sister mi hermana mayor; **He's the eldest.** Él es el mayor.
elect vb elegir
election n elección f (pl elecciones)
electric adj eléctrico ▷ an electric fire una estufa eléctrica
electrical adj eléctrico ▷ electrical engineering la ingeniería eléctrica
electrician n electricista mf ▷ He's an electrician. Es electricista.
electricity n electricidad f
electronic adj electrónico

electronics n electrónica f
elegant adj elegante
elementary school n (in US) escuela f primaria
elephant n elefante m
elevator n (in US) ascensor m
eleven num once ▷ She's eleven. Tiene once años.
eleventh adj undécimo; **the eleventh floor** el piso once; **the eleventh of August** el once de agosto
else adv somebody else otra persona; **something else** otra cosa; **somewhere else** en algún otro sitio; **nobody else** nadie más; **nothing else** nada más; **Did you look anywhere else?** ¿Miraste en otro sitio?; **I didn't look anywhere else.** No miré en ningún otro sitio.; **Would you like anything else?** ¿Desea alguna otra cosa?; **I don't want anything else.** No quiero nada más.
email n e-mail m
▷ vb **to email somebody** enviar un e-mail a alguien; **I'll email you the details.** Te mandaré la información por e-mail.
email address n dirección f de e-mail ▷ My email address is Jones at collins dot com. Mi dirección de e-mail es jones arroba collins punto com.
embankment n (of railway) terraplén m (pl terraplenes)
embarrassed adj **I was really embarrassed.** Me dio mucha

vergüenza.

> Be careful not to translate **embarrassed** by **embarazada**.

embarrassing adj (mistake, situation) embarazoso; **It was so embarrassing.** Fue una situación muy violenta.; **How embarrassing!** ¡Qué vergüenza!

embassy n embajada f

embroider vb bordar

embroidery n bordado m; **I do embroidery in the afternoon.** Bordo por las tardes.

emergency n emergencia f ▷ *This is an emergency!* ¡Es una emergencia!; **in an emergency** en caso de emergencia; **an emergency exit** una salida de emergencia; **an emergency landing** un aterrizaje forzoso; **the emergency services** los servicios de urgencia

emigrate vb emigrar

emotion n emoción f (pl emociones)

emotional adj emotivo ▷ *She's very emotional.* Es una persona muy emotiva.; **He got very emotional at the farewell party.** Se emocionó mucho en la fiesta de despedida.

emperor n emperador m

emphasize vb recalcar ▷ *He emphasized the importance of the issue.* Recalcó la importancia de la cuestión.; **to emphasize that** subrayar que

empire n imperio m

employ vb emplear ▷ *The factory employs 600 people.* La fábrica emplea a 600 trabajadores.; **Thousands of people are employed in tourism.** Miles de personas trabajan en el sector de turismo.

employee n empleado m, empleada f

employer n empresario m, empresaria f

employment n empleo m

empty adj vacío
▶ vb vaciar; **to empty something out** vaciar algo

encourage vb animar ▷ *to encourage somebody to do something* animar a alguien a hacer algo

encouragement n estímulo m

encyclopedia n enciclopedia f

end n ❶ (of corridor, holidays) final m ▷ *the end of the film* el final de la película ▷ *at the end of the street* al final de la calle; **in the end** al final ▷ *In the end I decided to stay at home.* Al final decidí quedarme en casa. ❷ (of table) extremo m ▷ *at the other end of the table* al otro extremo de la mesa; **for hours on end** durante horas enteras
▶ vb terminar ▷ *What time does the film end?* ¿A qué hora termina la película?; **to end up doing something** terminar haciendo algo ▷ *I ended up walking home.* Terminé yendo a casa andando.

ending n final m ▷ *a happy ending* un final feliz

endless adj interminable ▷ *The*

journey seemed endless. El viaje parecía interminable.

enemy n enemigo m, enemiga f

energetic adj activo ▷ *She's very energetic.* Es muy activa.

energy n energía f

engaged adj ❶ (telephone, toilet) ocupado ❷ prometido ▷ *Brian and Mary are engaged.* Brian y Mary están prometidos.; **to get engaged** prometerse

engagement n compromiso ▷ *They announced their engagement yesterday.* Anunciaron su compromiso ayer.; **The engagement lasted 10 months.** El noviazgo duró 10 meses.; **engagement ring** anillo de compromiso

engine n ❶ (of vehicle) motor m ❷ (of train) locomotora f

engineer n ingeniero m, ingeniera f ▷ *He's an engineer.* Es ingeniero.

engineering n ingeniería f

England n Inglaterra f

English adj inglés (f inglesa) (mpl ingleses)
▶ n (language) inglés m ▷ *the English teacher* el profesor de inglés; **the English** (people) los ingleses

Englishman n inglés m (pl ingleses)

Englishwoman n inglesa f

enjoy vb **Did you enjoy the film?** ¿Te gustó la película?; **to enjoy oneself** divertirse ▷ *Did you enjoy yourselves at the party?* ¿Os divertisteis en la fiesta?

enjoyable adj agradable

enlargement n (of photo) ampliación f (pl ampliaciones)

enormous adj enorme

enough adj, pron, adv bastante ▷ *I didn't have enough money.* No tenía bastante dinero.; **big enough** suficientemente grande; **I've had enough!** ¡Ya estoy harto!; **That's enough!** ¡Ya basta!

enquire vb **to enquire about something** informarse acerca de algo

enquiry n (official investigation) investigación f (pl investigaciones)

enter vb entrar en ▷ *He entered the room and sat down.* Entró en la habitación y se sentó.; **to enter a competition** presentarse a un concurso

entertain vb (guests) recibir

entertaining adj (book, movie) entretenido

enthusiasm n entusiasmo m

enthusiast n entusiasta mf ▷ *She's a DIY enthusiast.* Es una entusiasta del bricolaje.

enthusiastic adj (response, welcome) entusiasta; **She didn't seem very enthusiastic about your idea.** No pareció muy entusiasmada con tu idea.

entire adj entero ▷ *the entire world* el mundo entero

entirely adv completamente ▷ *an entirely new approach* un enfoque completamente nuevo; **I agree entirely.** Estoy totalmente de acuerdo.

entrance n entrada f; **an entrance exam** un examen de ingreso; **entrance fee** la cuota de entrada

entry n entrada f; **"no entry" (1)** (on door) "prohibido el paso" **(2)** (on road sign) "dirección prohibida"; **an entry form** un impreso de inscripción

entry phone n portero m automático

envelope n sobre m

envious adj envidioso

environment n (surroundings) entorno m; **the environment** el medio ambiente

environmental adj medioambiental ▷ environmental pollution contaminación ambiental; **environmental groups** grupos ecologistas

environment-friendly adj ecológico

envy n envidia f
▶ vb envidiar

epileptic n epiléptico m, epiléptica f

episode n episodio m

equal adj igual ▷ The cake was divided into 12 equal parts. El pastel se dividió en 12 partes iguales.; **Women demand equal rights at work.** Las mujeres exigen igualdad de derechos en el trabajo.

equality n igualdad f

equalize vb (in sport) empatar

equator n ecuador m

equipment n equipo m ▷ skiing equipment el equipo de esquí

equipped adj equipado ▷ This caravan is equipped for four people. Esta caravana está equipada para cuatro personas.; **equipped with** provisto de ▷ All rooms are equipped with phones, computers and faxes. Todas las habitaciones están provistas de teléfonos, ordenadores y fax.; **He was well equipped for the job.** Estaba bien preparado para el puesto.

equivalent adj equivalente; **to be equivalent to something** equivaler a algo

error n error m

escalator n escalera f mecánica

escape n (from prison) fuga f; **We had a narrow escape.** Nos salvamos por muy poco.
▶ vb escaparse ▷ A lion has escaped. Se ha escapado un león.; **We escaped unhurt.** Salimos ilesos.; **to escape from prison** fugarse de la cárcel

escort n escolta f ▷ a police escort una escolta policial

especially adv especialmente ▷ It's very hot there, especially in the summer. Allí hace mucho calor, especialmente en verano.

essay n trabajo m ▷ a history essay un trabajo de historia

essential adj esencial ▷ It's essential to bring warm clothes. Es esencial traer ropa de abrigo.

estate n ❶ (housing estate) urbanización f (pl urbanizaciones) ❷ (country estate) finca f

estate agent n agente

m inmobiliario, agente *f* inmobiliaria ▷ She's an estate agent. Es agente inmobiliaria.

estate agent's *n* agencia *f* inmobiliaria

estate car *n* ranchera *f*

estimate *vb* calcular ▷ They estimated it would take three weeks. Calcularon que llevaría tres semanas.

etc *abbr* (= et cetera) etc.

Ethiopia *n* Etiopía *f*

ethnic *adj* **①** étnico ▷ an ethnic minority una minoría étnica; **ethnic cleansing** la limpieza étnica **②** (restaurant, food) exótico

EU *n* (= European Union) UE *f*

euro *n* euro *m*

Europe *n* Europa *f*

European *adj* europeo
▶ *n* europeo *m*, europea *f*

European Union *n* Unión *f* Europea

eve *n* **Christmas Eve** la Nochebuena; **New Year's Eve** la Nochevieja

even *adv* incluso ▷ I like all animals, even snakes. Me gustan todos los animales, incluso las serpientes.; **not even** ni siquiera ▷ He didn't even say hello. Ni siquiera saludó.; **even if** aunque

> Use the subjunctive after **aunque** when translating **even if**.

▷ I'd never do that, even if you asked me. Nunca haría eso, aunque me lo pidieras.; **even though** aunque ▷ He's never got any money, even

though his parents are quite rich. Nunca tiene dinero aunque sus padres son bastante ricos.; **even more** aún más ▷ I liked Granada even more than Seville. Me gustó Granada aún más que Sevilla.
▶ *adj* uniforme ▷ an even layer of snow una capa de nieve uniforme; **an even surface** una superficie lisa; **an even number** un número par; **to get even with somebody** vengarse en alguien

evening *n* **①** (before dark) tarde *f* **②** (after dark) noche *f* ▷ in the evening por la tarde/noche; **Good evening!** ¡Buenas tardes/noches!; **evening class** la clase nocturna

event *n* **①** (happening) acontecimiento *m* ▷ It was one of the most important events in his life. Fue uno de los acontecimientos más importantes de su vida. **②** (in sport) prueba *f*; **in the event of** en caso de ▷ in the event of an accident en caso de accidente

eventful *adj* (race, journey) lleno de incidentes

eventually *adv* finalmente

ever *adv* Have you ever been to Portugal? ¿Has estado alguna vez en Portugal?; **Have you ever seen her?** ¿La has visto alguna vez?; **the best I've ever seen** el mejor que he visto; **for the first time ever** por primera vez; **ever since** desde que ▷ ever since I met him desde que lo conozco; **ever since then** desde entonces; **ever so** (very) muy ▷ It's ever so kind of you. Es muy amable de su parte.

every adj cada ▷ every time cada vez; **every day** todos los días; **every now and then** de vez en cuando

everybody pron todo el mundo ▷ Everybody makes mistakes. Todo el mundo se equivoca.; **Everybody had a good time.** Todos se lo pasaron bien.

everyone pron = everybody

everything pron todo ▷ You've thought of everything! ¡Has pensado en todo!

everywhere adv en todas partes ▷ I looked everywhere, but I couldn't find it. Miré en todas partes, pero no lo encontré.; I **see him everywhere I go.** Lo veo dondequiera que vaya.

> **dondequiera** has to be followed by a verb in the subjunctive.

evil adj ❶ (person) malvado ❷ (plan, spirit) maligno

ex- prefix ex- ▷ his ex-wife su ex-esposa

exact adj exacto

exactly adv exactamente ▷ exactly the same exactamente igual; **It's exactly 10 o'clock.** Son las 10 en punto.

exaggerate vb exagerar

exaggeration n exageración f (pl exageraciones)

exam n examen m (pl exámenes) ▷ a French exam un examen de francés

examination n examen m (pl exámenes)

examine vb examinar ▷ The doctor examined him. El médico lo examinó.

examiner n examinador m, examinadora f

example n ejemplo m ▷ for example por ejemplo

excellent adj excelente

except prep excepto ▷ everyone except me todos excepto yo; **except for** excepto; **except that** salvo que ▷ The weather was great, except that it was a bit cold. El tiempo fue estupendo, salvo que hizo un poco de frío.

> **salvo que** may be followed by a verb in subjunctive.

exception n excepción f (pl excepciones) ▷ to make an exception hacer una excepción

exchange vb cambiar ▷ I exchanged the book for a CD. Cambié el libro por un CD.
▶ n intercambio m ▷ I'd like to do an exchange with an English student. Me gustaría hacer un intercambio con un estudiante inglés.; **in exchange for** a cambio de

exchange rate n tipo m de cambio

excited adj entusiasmado

excitement n emoción f

exciting adj emocionante

exclamation mark n signo m de admiración

excuse n excusa f
▶ vb **Excuse me! (1)** (to attract attention, apologize) ¡Perdón!

(2) (when you want to get past) ¡Con permiso!

exercise n ejercicio m ▷ page ten, exercise three página diez, ejercicio tres ▷ to take some exercise hacer un poco de ejercicio; **exercise book** el cuaderno

exhaust n tubo m de escape

exhausted adj agotado

exhaust fumes npl gases mpl de escape

exhaust pipe n tubo m de escape

exhibition n exposición f (pl exposiciones)

exist vb existir

exit n salida f

> Be careful not to translate **exit** by **éxito**.

expect vb ❶ esperar ▷ I'm expecting him for dinner. Lo espero para cenar. ▷ She's expecting a baby. Está esperando un bebé. ❷ imaginarse ▷ I expect he'll be late. Me imagino que llegará tarde.; **I expect so.** Me imagino que sí.

expedition n expedición f (pl expediciones).

expel vb to get expelled (from school) ser expulsado

expenses npl gastos mpl

expensive adj caro

experience n experiencia f

experienced adj an experienced teacher un maestro con experiencia; She's very experienced in looking after children. Tiene mucha experiencia en cuidar niños.

experiment n experimento m

expert n experto m, experta f ▷ He's a computer expert. Es un experto en informática. ▶ adj experto ▷ He's an expert cook. Es un experto cocinero.

expire vb caducar ▷ My passport has expired. Mi pasaporte ha caducado.

explain vb explicar

explanation n explicación f (pl explicaciones)

explode vb estallar

explore vb (place) explorar

explosion n explosión f (pl explosiones)

export vb exportar

> n exportación f

express vb expresar; **to express oneself** expresarse ▷ It's not easy to express oneself in a foreign language. No es fácil expresarse en un idioma extranjero.

expression n expresión f (pl expresiones) ▷ It's an English expression. Es una expresión inglesa.

expressway n (in US) autopista f

extension n ❶ (of building) ampliación f (pl ampliaciones) ❷ (telephone) extensión f (pl extensiones) ▷ Extension three one three seven, please. Con la extensión tres uno tres siete, por favor.

extent n to some extent hasta cierto punto

extinct adj extinto ▷ Dinosaurs are extinct. Los dinosaurios están extintos.; **to become extinct**

extinguirse

extinguisher n extintor m (*LatAm* extinguidor m)

extra adj, adv **He gave me an extra blanket.** Me dio una manta más.; **to pay extra** pagar un suplemento; **Breakfast is extra.** El desayuno no está incluido.; **Be extra careful!** ¡Ten muchísimo cuidado!

extraordinary adj extraordinario

extravagant adj (*person*) derrochador (f derrochadora)

extreme adj extremo; **with extreme caution** con sumo cuidado

extremely adv sumamente

extremist n extremista mf

eye n ojo m ▷ **I've got green eyes.** Tengo los ojos verdes.; **to keep an eye on something** vigilar algo

eyebrow n ceja f

eyelash n pestaña f

eyelid n párpado m

eyeliner n lápiz m de ojos (pl lápices de ojos)

eye shadow n sombra f de ojos

eyesight n vista f ▷ **to have good eyesight** tener buena vista

fabric n tela f

█ Be careful not to translate **fabric** by **fábrica**.

fabulous adj fabuloso

face n ❶ (*of person, mountain*) cara f ❷ (*of clock*) esfera f; **in the face of these difficulties** en vista de estas dificultades; **face to face** cara a cara

▷ vb ❶ estar frente a ▷ **They stood facing each other.** Estaban de pie el uno frente al otro.; **The garden faces south.** El jardín da al sur. ❷ enfrentarse a ▷ **They face serious problems.** Se enfrentan a graves problemas.; **Let's face it, we're lost.** Tenemos que admitirlo, estamos perdidos.

face cloth n toallita f para lavarse

facilities npl instalaciones

fpl ▷ This school has excellent facilities. Esta escuela tiene unas instalaciones magníficas.; **The youth hostel has cooking facilities.** El albergue juvenil dispone de cocina.

fact *n* **the fact that ...** el hecho de que ...

Use the subjunctive after **el hecho de que.**

▷ The fact that you are very busy is of no interest to me. El hecho de que estés muy ocupado no me interesa.; **facts and figures** datos y cifras; **in fact** de hecho

factory *n* fábrica *f*

fail *vb* ① suspender ▷ He failed his driving test. Suspendió el examen de conducir. ② fallar ▷ The lorry's brakes failed. Al camión le fallaron los frenos. ③ fracasar ▷ The plan failed. El plan fracasó.; **to fail to do something** no lograr hacer algo ▷ They failed to reach the quarter finals. No lograron llegar a los cuartos de final.; **The bomb failed to explode.** La bomba no llegó a estallar.

failure *n* ① fracaso *m* ▷ The attempt was a complete failure. El intento fue un completo fracaso. ② fallo *m* ▷ a mechanical failure un fallo mecánico

faint *adj* débil ▷ His voice was very faint. Tenía la voz muy débil.; **to feel faint** sentirse mareado
▶ *vb* desmayarse

fair *adj* ① justo ▷ That's not fair. Eso no es justo.; **I paid more than**

my fair share. Pagué más de lo que me correspondía. ② rubio ▷ He's got fair hair. Tiene el pelo rubio. ③ blanco ▷ people with fair skin la gente con la piel blanca; **I have a fair chance of winning.** Tengo bastantes posibilidades de ganar. ④ considerable ▷ That's a fair distance. Esa es una distancia considerable.
▶ *n* ① (travelling funfair) feria *f* ② (on permanent site) parque *m* de atracciones; **a trade fair** una feria de muestras

fair-haired *adj* rubio

fairly *adv* ① equitativamente ▷ The cake was divided fairly. La tarta se repartió equitativamente. ② bastante ▷ My car is fairly new. Mi coche es bastante nuevo. ▷ The weather was fairly good. El tiempo fue bastante bueno.

fairy *n* hada *f*

Although it's a feminine noun, remember that you use **el** and **un** with **hada.**

fairy tale *n* cuento *m* de hadas

faith *n* ① (trust) confianza *f* ▷ People have lost faith in the government. La gente ha perdido la confianza en el gobierno. ② (religion) fe *f*

faithful *adj* fiel

faithfully *adv* **Yours faithfully...** (in letter) le saluda atentamente...

fake *n* falsificación *f* (pl falsificaciones) ▷ The painting was a fake. El cuadro era una falsificación.

▶ adj **falso** ▷ a fake banknote un billete falso; **a fake fur coat** un abrigo de piel sintética

fall n ❶ (of sport) caída f ▷ She had a nasty fall. Tuvo una mala caída.; **a fall of snow** una nevada ❷ (in US: autumn) otoño m

▶ vb ❶ (bomb, rain, leaves) caer

⬛ When the action of falling is not deliberate, use **caerse**.

▷ He tripped and fell. Tropezó y se cayó. ▷ The book fell off the shelf. El libro se cayó de la estantería.; **to fall in love with someone** enamorarse de alguien ❷ (price, temperature) bajar

fall apart vb romperse ▷ The book fell apart when he opened it. El libro se rompió cuando lo abrió.

fall down vb caerse ▷ She's fallen down. Se ha caído.

fall out vb reñir ▷ Sarah's fallen out with her boyfriend. Sarah ha reñido con su novio.

false adj falso; **a false alarm** una falsa alarma; **false teeth** la dentadura postiza

fame n fama f

familiar adj familiar ▷ The name sounded familiar to me. El nombre me sonaba familiar.; **a familiar face** un rostro conocido; **to be familiar with something** conocer bien algo ▷ I'm familiar with his work. Conozco bien su obra.

family n familia f ▷ the Cooke family la familia Cooke

famine n hambruna f

famous adj famoso ▷ Oxford is famous for its university. Oxford es famoso por su universidad.

fan n ❶ (of sport) hincha mf ❷ (of pop star) fan mf (pl fans) ▷ the Oasis fan club el club de fans de Oasis; **I'm one of his greatest fans.** Soy uno de sus mayores admiradores. ❸ (enthusiast) aficionado m, aficionada f ▷ a rap music fan un aficionado al rap ❹ (to keep cool) abanico m; **an electric fan** un ventilador

fanatic n fanático m, fanática f

fancy vb apetecer ▷ I fancy an ice cream. Me apetece un helado. ▷ What do you fancy doing? ¿Qué te apetece hacer?

⬛ **apetecer que** has to be followed by a verb in the subjunctive.

▷ Do you fancy going to the cinema sometime? ¿Te apetece que vayamos al cine algún día?; **He fancies her.** Le gusta ella.

fancy dress n disfraz m (pl disfraces); **a fancy dress ball** un baile de disfraces

fantastic adj fantástico

far adj, adv lejos ▷ Is it far? ¿Está lejos? ▷ It's not far from London. No está lejos de Londres.; **How far is it to Madrid?** ¿A qué distancia está Madrid?; **at the far end of the swimming pool** al otro extremo de la piscina; **as far as I know** por lo que yo sé; **so far** hasta ahora

fare n tarifa f ▷ Rail fares are very high in Britain. Las tarifas de tren son muy altas en Gran Bretaña.; **He didn't have the bus fare.** No tenía dinero para el autobús.; **full fare** el precio del billete completo; **Children pay half fare on the bus.** Los niños pagan la mitad en el autobús.

Far East n the Far East el Extremo Oriente

farm n granja f (LatAm estancia f)

farmer n granjero m, granjera f (LatAm estanciero m, estanciera f) ▷ He's a farmer. Es granjero.

farmhouse n caserío m

farming n agricultura f ▷ organic farming agricultura biológica

fascinating adj fascinante

fashion n moda f; **to be in fashion** estar de moda; **to go out of fashion** pasar de moda

fashionable adj de moda inv ▷ That colour is very fashionable. Ese color está muy de moda.; **Jane wears fashionable clothes.** Jane viste a la moda.

fast adj, adv rápido ▷ a fast car un coche rápido ▷ They work very fast. Trabajan muy rápido.; **That clock's fast.** Ese reloj va adelantado.; **He's fast asleep.** Está profundamente dormido.

fat adj gordo ▷ She thinks she's too fat. Piensa que está demasiado gorda.
▸ n ❶ (on meat, in food) grasa f ▷ It's very high in fat. Es muy rico en grasas. ❷ (used for cooking) manteca f

fatal adj ❶ mortal ▷ a fatal accident

un accidente mortal ❷ fatal ▷ a fatal mistake un error fatal

father n padre m; **Father Christmas** Papá Noel

father-in-law n suegro m

faucet n (in US) grifo m

fault n ❶ culpa f ▷ It wasn't my fault. No fue culpa mía. ❷ defecto m ▷ He has his faults, but I still like him. Tiene sus defectos, pero aun así me gusta.; **a mechanical fault** un fallo mecánico

favour (US favor) n favor m (pl favores) ▷ Could you do me a favour? ¿Me harías un favor?; **to be in favour of something** estar a favor de algo

favourite (US favorite) adj favorito ▷ Blue's my favourite colour. El azul es mi color favorito.

fax n fax m (pl faxes)
▸ vb mandar por fax ▷ I'll fax you the details. Te mandaré la información por fax.

fear n miedo m
▸ vb temer ▷ You have nothing to fear. No tienes nada que temer.

feather n pluma f

feature n característica f ▷ an important feature una característica importante

February n febrero m ▷ in February en febrero ▷ on 18 February el 18 de febrero

fed vb see **feed**

fed up adj **to be fed up with something** estar harto de algo

feed vb dar de comer a ▷ Have you fed the cat? ¿Le has dado de comer al gato? ▷ He worked hard to feed his family. Trabajaba mucho para dar de comer a su familia.

feel vb ❶ (pain, heat) sentir ❷ sentirse ▷ I don't feel well. No me siento bien. ❸ How do you feel? ¿Cómo te sientes?

Use **tener** to say that you feel hungry, thirsty, hot or cold.
▷ I was feeling hungry. Tenía hambre. ❸ (touch) tocar ▷ The doctor felt his forehead. El médico le tocó la frente.; **to feel like doing something** tener ganas de hacer algo ▷ I don't feel like going out tonight. No tengo ganas de salir esta noche.; **Do you feel like an ice cream?** ¿Te apetece un helado?

feeling n ❶ sensación f (pl sensaciones) ▷ a burning feeling una sensación de escozor ❷ sentimiento m ▷ He was afraid of hurting my feelings. Tenía miedo de herir mis sentimientos.; **What are your feelings about it?** ¿Tú qué opinas de ello?

feet npl see **foot**

fell vb see **fall**

felt vb see **feel**

felt-tip pen n rotulador m

female adj ❶ hembra inv ▷ a female bat un murciélago hembra ❷ femenino ▷ the female sex el sexo femenino
▶ n (animal) hembra f

feminine adj femenino

feminist n feminista mf

fence n valla f

fern n helecho m

ferry n ferry m

festival n festival m ▷ a jazz festival un festival de jazz

fetch vb ❶ ir a por ▷ Fetch the bucket. Ve a por el cubo.; **to fetch something for someone** traer algo a alguien ▷ Fetch me a glass of water. Tráeme un vaso de agua. ❷ venderse por ▷ His painting fetched £5000. Su cuadro se vendió por 5.000 libras esterlinas.

fever n fiebre f

few adj, pron ❶ pocos ▷ He has few friends. Tiene pocos amigos.; **a few** unos ▷ She was silent for a few seconds. Se quedó callada unos segundos. ❷ algunos ▷ a few of them algunos de ellos; **quite a few people** bastante gente

fewer adj menos ▷ There were fewer people than yesterday. Había menos gente que ayer.

fiancé n novio m

fiancée n novia f

fiction n ficción f

field n (on farm) campo m ▷ He's an expert in his field. Es un experto en su campo.

fierce adj ❶ feroz (pl feroces) ▷ a fierce Alsatian un pastor alemán feroz ❷ encarnizado ▷ There's fierce competition between the companies. Existe una encarnizada competencia entre las empresas. ❸ violento ▷ a fierce attack un violento ataque

fifteen num quince ▷ I'm fifteen. Tengo quince años.

fifteenth adj decimoquinto; **the fifteenth of August** el quince de agosto

fifth adj quinto ▷ the fifth floor el quinto piso; **the fifth of August** el cinco de agosto

fifty num cincuenta ▷ He's fifty. Tiene cincuenta años.

fight n ① pelea f ▷ There was a fight in the pub. Hubo una pelea en el pub.; **She had a fight with her best friend.** Se peleó con su mejor amiga. ② lucha f ▷ the fight against cancer la lucha contra el cáncer

▶ vb ① pelearse ▷ The fans started fighting. Los hinchas empezaron a pelearse. ② luchar ▷ She has fought against racism all her life. Ha luchado toda su vida contra el racismo.; **The doctors tried to fight the disease.** Los médicos intentaron combatir la enfermedad.

fight back vb defenderse

figure n ① cifra f ▷ Can you give me the exact figures? ¿Me puedes dar las cifras exactas? ② silueta f ▷ Helen saw the figure of a man on the bridge. Helen vio la silueta de un hombre en el puente.; **She's got a good figure.** Tiene buen tipo.; **I have to watch my figure.** Tengo que mantener la línea. ③ figura f ▷ She's an important political figure. Es una importante figura política.

figure out vb ① calcular ▷ I'll try to figure out how much it'll cost.

Intentaré calcular lo que va a costar. ② llegar a comprender ▷ I couldn't figure out what it meant. No llegué a comprender lo que significaba.

file n ① expediente m ▷ There was stuff in that file that was private. Había cosas privadas en ese expediente.; **The police have a file on him.** Está fichado por la policía. ② carpeta f ▷ She put the photocopy into her file. Metió la fotocopia en su carpeta. ③ lima f ▷ a nail file una lima de uñas ④ (on computer) fichero m

▶ vb ① archivar ▷ You have to file all these documents. Tienes que archivar todos estos documentos. ② limarse ▷ She was filing her nails. Se estaba limando las uñas.

fill vb llenar ▷ She filled the glass with water. Llenó el vaso de agua.

fill in vb ① rellenar ▷ Can you fill in this form, please? Rellene este impreso, por favor. ② llenar ▷ He filled the hole in with soil. Llenó el agujero de tierra.

film n ① (movie) película f ② carrete m ▷ I need a 36-exposure film. Quería un carrete de 36.

film star n estrella f de cine

filthy adj mugriento

final adj ① último ▷ a final attempt un último intento ② definitivo ▷ a final decision una decisión definitiva; **I'm not going and that's final.** He dicho que no voy y se acabó.

▶ n final f ▷ *Roger Federer is in the final.* Roger Federer ha llegado a la final.

finally adv ❶ por último ▷ *Finally, I would like to say thank you to all of you.* Por último me gustaría darles las gracias a todos. ❷ al final ▷ *They finally decided to leave on Saturday.* Al final decidieron salir el sábado.

financial adj ❶ (services, adviser, institution) financiero ❷ (problems) económico

find vb encontrar ▷ *I can't find the exit.* No encuentro la salida.

find out vb averiguar ▷ *I found out what happened.* Averigüé lo que ocurrió.; **to find out about** enterarse de ▷ *Find out as much as possible about the town.* Entérate de todo lo que puedas sobre la ciudad.

fine adj, adv ❶ estupendo ▷ *He's a fine musician.* Es un músico estupendo.; **How are you? - I'm fine.** ¿Qué tal estás? - Bien.; **I feel fine.** Me siento bien.; **It'll be ready tomorrow. - That's fine, thanks.** Mañana estará listo. - Muy bien, gracias.; **The weather is fine today.** Hoy hace muy buen tiempo. ❷ fino ▷ *She's got very fine hair.* Tiene el pelo muy fino.
▶ n multa f ▷ *I got a fine for driving through a red light.* Me pusieron una multa por saltarme un semáforo en rojo.

finger n dedo m; **my little finger** el meñique

fingernail n uña f

finish n ❶ fin m ▷ *from start to finish* de principio a fin ❷ (of race) llegada f
▶ vb terminar ▷ *I've finished!* ¡Ya he terminado! ▷ *to finish doing something* terminar de hacer algo ▷ *Have you finished eating?* ¿Has terminado de comer?

Finland n Finlandia

Finn n finlandés m, finlandesa f (mpl finlandeses) ▷ *the Finns* los finlandeses

Finnish adj finlandés (f finlandesa) (mpl finlandeses)
▶ n (language) finlandés m

fire n ❶ (flames) fuego m ▷ *The fire spread quickly.* El fuego se extendió rápidamente. ❷ (accidental) incendio m ▷ *The house was destroyed by a fire.* La casa fue destruida por un incendio. ❸ (bonfire) hoguera f ▷ *He made a fire to warm himself up.* Encendió una hoguera para calentarse. ❹ (heater) estufa f ▷ *an electric fire* una estufa eléctrica; **to be on fire** estar ardiendo
▶ vb (shoot) disparar ▷ *She fired at him.* Le disparó.; **to fire a gun** disparar; **to fire somebody** despedir a alguien ▷ *He was fired from his job.* Le despidieron del trabajo.

fire alarm n alarma f contra incendios

fire brigade n cuerpo m de bomberos

fire engine n coche m de

bomberos

fire escape n escalera f de incendios

fire extinguisher n extintor m

fireman n bombero m ▷ He's a fireman. Es bombero.

fireplace n chimenea f

fire station n parque m de bomberos

fireworks npl fuegos mpl artificiales

firm adj ❶ firme ▷ to be firm with somebody mostrarse firme con alguien ❷ duro ▷ a firm mattress un colchón duro
▷ n empresa f

first adj, n, adv ❶ primero ▷ for the first time por primera vez

> Use **primer** before a masculine singular noun.

▷ my first job mi primer trabajo ▷ Rachel came first in the race. Rachel quedó primera en la carrera. ❷ She was the first to arrive. Fue la primera en llegar.; **the first of September** el uno de septiembre; **at first** al principio ❷ antes ▷ I want to get a job, but first I have to pass my exams. Quiero conseguir un trabajo, pero antes tengo que aprobar los exámenes.; **first of all** ante todo

first aid n primeros auxilios mpl; **a first aid kit** un botiquín

first-class adj ❶ de primera clase inv ▷ a first-class ticket un billete de primera clase ❷ de primera inv ▷ a first-class meal una comida de primera; **a first-class stamp** un

sello para correo urgente

● In Spain there is no first-class
● or second-class postage. If you
● want your mail to arrive fast,
● you must have it sent express
● - **urgente** - from a post office.

firstly adv en primer lugar

first name n nombre m de pila

fish n ❶ (animal) pez m (pl peces) ▷ I caught three fish. Pesqué tres peces. ❷ (food) pescado m ▷ fish and chips pescado rebozado con patatas fritas
▷ vb pescar; **to go fishing** ir a pescar

fisherman n pescador m ▷ He's a fisherman. Es pescador.

fishing n pesca f ▷ I enjoy fishing. Me gusta la pesca.; **a fishing boat** un barco pesquero; **fishing rod** la caña de pescar

fishing tackle n aparejos mpl de pesca

fishmonger's n pescadería f

fist n puño m

fit adj en forma ▷ He felt relaxed and fit after his holiday. Se sentía relajado y en forma tras las vacaciones.; **Will he be fit to play next Saturday?** ¿Estará en condiciones de jugar el próximo sábado?
▷ n **to have a fit** (1) (epileptic) sufrir un ataque de epilepsia (2) (be angry) ponerse hecho una furia ▷ My Mum will have a fit when she sees the carpet! ¡Mi madre se va a poner hecha una furia cuando vea la moqueta!

▶vb ❶ (go into a space) caber ▷ It's
small enough to fit into your pocket.
Es lo bastante pequeño como para
que caber en el bolsillo. ❷ encajar
▷ Make sure the cork fits well into
the bottle. Asegúrese de que el
corcho encaja bien en la botella.
❸ (install) instalar ▷ He fitted an
alarm in his car. Instaló una alarma
en el coche. ❹ (attach) poner
▷ She fitted a plug to the hair dryer.
Le puso un enchufe al secador.; to
fit somebody estar bien a alguien
▷ These trousers don't fit me. Estos
pantalones no me están bien.;
Does it fit? ¿Te está bien?

fit in vb ❶ encajar ▷ That story
doesn't fit in with what he told us.
Esa historia no encaja con lo que
él nos contó. ❷ adaptarse ▷ She
fitted in well at her new school. Se
adaptó bien al nuevo colegio.

fitted carpet n moqueta f

five num cinco ▷ He's five. Tiene
cinco años.

fix vb ❶ arreglar ▷ Can you fix my
bike? ¿Me puedes arreglar la bici?
❷ fijar ▷ Let's fix a date for the party.
Vamos a fijar una fecha para la
fiesta.

fizzy adj gaseoso

flag n bandera f

flame n llama f

flan n ❶ (sweet) tarta f ▷ a raspberry
flan una tarta de frambuesa
❷ (savoury) pastel m ▷ a cheese
and onion flan un pastel de queso
y cebolla

flap vb (wings) batir ▷ The bird

flapped its wings. El pájaro batió
las alas.

flash n (of camera) flash m; a flash
of lightning un relámpago; in a
flash en un abrir y cerrar de ojos
▶vb They flashed a torch in
his face. Le enfocaron con una
linterna en la cara.

flask n (vacuum flask) termo m

flat adj llano ▷ a flat surface una
superficie llana; flat shoes
zapatos bajos; I've got a flat tyre.
Tengo una rueda desinflada.
▶n piso m (LatAm apartamento m)

flavour n sabor m (pl sabores)
▷ Which flavour of ice cream would
you like? ¿De qué sabor quieres el
helado?

flea n pulga f

flew vb see fly

flexible adj flexible ▷ flexible
working hours un horario de
trabajo flexible

flick vb to flick through a book
hojear un libro

flight n vuelo m ▷ What time is the
flight to Paris? ¿A qué hora es el
vuelo para París?; a flight of stairs
un tramo de escaleras

flight attendant n auxiliar mf
de vuelo

fling vb arrojar ▷ He flung the
dictionary onto the floor. Arrojó el
diccionario al suelo.

float vb flotar

flood n inundación f (pl
inundaciones) ▷ The rain
has caused many floods. La
lluvia ha provocado muchas

inundaciones.; **He received a flood of letters.** Recibió un aluvión de cartas.
▶ vb inundar ▷ *The river has flooded the village.* El río ha inundado el pueblo.

floor n ❶ (of room) suelo m (LatAm piso m); **the dance floor** la pista de baile ❷ (storey) piso m ▷ *on the first floor* en el primer piso

floppy disk n disquete m

florist n florista mf

flour n harina f

flower n flor f (pl flores)
▶ vb florecer

flown vb see **fly**

flu n gripe f ▷ *I've got flu.* Tengo gripe.

fluent adj **He speaks fluent Spanish.** Habla español con fluidez.

flung vb see **fling**

flush vb **to flush the toilet** tirar de la cadena

flute n flauta f

fly n mosca f
▶ vb volar ▷ *He flew from London to Glasgow.* Voló de Londres a Glasgow. ▷ *The bird flew away.* El pájaro salió volando.

focus n centro m ▷ *He was the focus of attention.* Era el centro de atención.; **to be out of focus** estar desenfocado
▶ vb enfocar ▷ *Try to focus the binoculars.* Intenta enfocar los prismáticos.; **to focus on something (1)** (with camera, telescope) enfocar algo ▷ *The* cameraman focused on the bird. El cámara enfocó al pájaro. **(2)** (concentrate on) centrarse en algo

fog n niebla f

foggy adj **It's foggy.** Hay niebla.; **a foggy day** un día de niebla

foil n (kitchen foil) papel m de aluminio

fold n pliegue m
▶ vb doblar ▷ *He folded the newspaper in half.* Dobló el periódico por la mitad.; **to fold one's arms** cruzarse de brazos

folder n carpeta f

follow vb seguir ▷ *You go first and I'll follow.* Ve tú primero y yo te sigo.

following adj siguiente ▷ *the following day* al día siguiente

fond adj **to be fond of somebody** tener cariño a alguien ▷ *I'm very fond of her.* Le tengo mucho cariño.

food n comida f ▷ *cat food* comida para gatos ▷ *We need to buy some food.* Hay que comprar comida.

fool n idiota mf

foot n ❶ (of person) pie m ▷ *My feet are aching.* Me duelen los pies.; **on foot** a pie

- In Spain measurements are in metres and centimetres rather than feet and inches. A foot is about 30 centimetres.

▷ *Dave is six foot tall.* Dave mide un metro ochenta. ❷ (of animal) pata f

football n ❶ fútbol m ▷ *I like playing football.* Me gusta jugar al fútbol. ❸ balón m (pl balones)

▷ *Paul threw the football over the fence.* Paul lanzó el balón por encima de la valla.

footballer n futbolista mf

footpath n sendero m

for prep

> There are three basic ways of translating **for** into Spanish: **para**, **por** and **durante**. Check the boxes at the beginning of each translation to find the meaning or example you need. If you can't find it look at the phrases at the end of the entry.

❶ para

> **para** is used to indicate destination, employment, intention and purpose.

▷ *a present for me* un regalo para mí ▷ *He works for the government.* Trabaja para el gobierno. ▷ *What for?* ¿Para qué? ▷ *What's it for?* ¿Para qué es? **❷ por**

> **por** is used to indicate reason or cause. Use it also when talking about amounts of money.

▷ *I'll do it for you.* Lo haré por ti. ▷ *What did he do that for?* ¿Por qué ha hecho eso? ▷ *I sold it for £5.* Lo vendí por 5 libras. **❸ durante**

> When referring to periods of time, use **durante** to refer to the future and completed actions in the past. Note that it can often be omitted, as in the next two examples.

▷ *She will be away for a month.*

Estará fuera (durante) un mes. ▷ *He worked in Spain for two years.* Trabajó (durante) dos años en España.

> Use **hace...que** and the present to describe actions and states that started in the past and are still going on. Alternatively use the present and **desde hace**. Another option is **llevar** and an **-ando/-iendo** form.

▷ *He has been learning French for two years.* Hace dos años que estudia francés. ▷ *I haven't seen her for two years.* No la veo desde hace dos años. ▷ *She's been learning German for four years.* Lleva cuatro años estudiando alemán.

> See how the tenses change when talking about something that **had** happened or **had been** happening **for** a time.

▷ *He had been learning French for two years.* Hacía dos años que estudiaba francés. ▷ *I hadn't seen her for two years.* No la veía desde hacía dos años. ▷ *She had been learning German for four years.* Llevaba cuatro años estudiando alemán. **❹** (*in favour of*) a favor de ▷ *Are you for or against the idea?* ¿Estás a favor o en contra de la idea?; **There are roadworks for three kilometres.** Hay obras en tres kilómetros.; **What's the English for "león"?** ¿Cómo se dice "león" en inglés?; **It's time for**

lunch. Es la hora de comer.; **Can you do it for tomorrow?** ¿Puedes hacerlo para mañana?

forbid vb prohibir; **to forbid somebody to do something** prohibir a alguien que haga algo

force n fuerza f ▷ the force of the explosion la fuerza de la explosión; **UN forces** las fuerzas de la ONU; **in force** (law, rules) en vigor
▷ vb obligar ▷ They forced him to open the safe. Le obligaron a abrir la caja fuerte.

forecast n **the weather forecast** el pronóstico del tiempo

forehead n frente f

foreign adj extranjero ▷ a foreign language una lengua extranjera

foreigner n extranjero m, extranjera f

forest n bosque m

forever adv **①** para siempre ▷ He's gone forever. Se ha ido para siempre. **②** siempre ▷ She's forever complaining. Siempre se está quejando.

forgave vb see **forgive**

forge vb falsificar ▷ She forged his signature. Falsificó su firma.

forget vb olvidar ▷ I've forgotten his name. He olvidado su nombre.;
to forget to do something olvidarse de hacer algo ▷ I forgot to close the window. Me olvidé de cerrar la ventana.; **I'm sorry, I had completely forgotten!** ¡Lo siento, se me había olvidado por completo!; **Forget it!** ¡No importa!

forgive vb perdonar ▷ I forgive you.

Te perdono.; **to forgive somebody for doing something** perdonar a alguien que haya hecho algo

forgot, forgotten vb see **forget**

fork n (for eating) tenedor m

form n **①** (document) impreso m (LatAm planilla f) ▷ to fill in a form rellenar un impreso **②** (shape) forma f ▷ I'm against hunting in any form. Estoy en contra de cualquier forma de caza. **③** (at school) clase f

formal adj formal ▷ In English, "residence" is a formal term. En inglés, "residence" es un término formal.

⬛ Put **antiguo** before the noun when translating **former**.

▷ a former pupil un antiguo alumno

fort n fuerte m

fortnight n a fortnight quince días ▷ I'm going on holiday for a fortnight. Me voy quince días de vacaciones.

fortunate adj **He was extremely fortunate to survive.** Tuvo la gran suerte de salir vivo.; **It's fortunate that I remembered the map.** Menos mal que me acordé de traer el mapa.

fortunately adv afortunadamente

fortune n fortuna f ▷ He made his fortune in car sales. Consiguió su fortuna con la venta de coches.; **Kate earns a fortune!** ¡Kate gana un dineral!; **to tell somebody's fortune** decir la buenaventura a alguien

forty num cuarenta ▷ He's forty. Tiene cuarenta años.

forward adv hacia delante ▷ to look forward mirar hacia delante; **to move forward** avanzar

foster child n niño m acogido en una familia

fought vb see **fight**

foul adj ❶ horrible ▷ The weather was foul. El tiempo era horrible. ❷ asqueroso ▷ It smells foul. Huele asqueroso.; **Brenda is in a foul mood.** Brenda está de muy mal humor.
▶ n (in sports) falta f

found vb see **find**

fountain n fuente f

fountain pen n pluma f estilográfica (LatAm plumafuente f)

four num cuatro ▷ She's four. Tiene cuatro años.

fourteen num catorce ▷ I'm fourteen. Tengo catorce años.

fourteenth adj decimocuarto; **the fourteenth of July** el catorce de julio

fourth adj cuarto ▷ the fourth floor el cuarto piso; **the fourth of July** el cuarto de julio

fox n zorro m

fragile adj frágil

frame n marco m ▷ a silver frame un marco de plata; **glasses with plastic frames** gafas con montura de plástico

France n Francia

frantic adj frenético ▷ I was going frantic. Me estaba poniendo

frenético.; **to be frantic with worry** estar muerto de preocupación

fraud n ❶ fraude m ▷ He was jailed for fraud. Lo encarcelaron por fraude. ❷ impostor m, impostora f ▷ You're a fraud! ¡Eres un impostor!

freckles npl pecas fpl

free adj ❶ gratuito ▷ a free brochure un folleto gratuito; **You can get it for free.** Se puede conseguir gratis. ❷ libre ▷ Is this seat free? ¿Está libre este asiento? ▷ Are you free after school? ¿Estás libre después de clase?
▶ vb liberar

freedom n libertad f

freeway n (in US) autopista f

freeze vb ❶ congelar ▷ She froze the rest of the raspberries. Congeló el resto de las frambuesas. ❷ helarse ▷ The water had frozen. El agua se había helado.

freezer n congelador m

freezing adj **It's freezing!** ¡Hace un frío que pela! (informal); **I'm freezing!** ¡Me estoy congelando!

French adj francés (ffrancesa) (mpl franceses)
▶ n (language) francés m ▷ the French teacher el profesor de francés; **the French** los franceses

French beans npl judías fpl verdes

French fries npl patatas fpl fritas (LatAm papas fpl fritas)

French horn n trompa f de llaves

French loaf n barra f de pan

Frenchman n francés m (pl franceses)

French windows npl
puertaventana f

Frenchwoman n francesa f

frequent adj frecuente

fresh adj fresco ▷ I always buy fresh
fish. Siempre compro pescado
fresco.; **I need some fresh air.**
Necesito tomar el aire.

Friday n viernes m (pl viernes) ▷ I
saw her on Friday. La vi el viernes.
▷ **every Friday** todos los viernes
▷ **last Friday** el viernes pasado
▷ **next Friday** el viernes que viene
▷ **on Fridays** los viernes

fridge n nevera f (LatAm
refrigeradora f)

fried adj frito ▷ a fried egg un
huevo frito

friend n amigo m, amiga f

friendly adj simpático ▷ She's
really friendly. Es muy simpática.;
Liverpool is a friendly city.
Liverpool es una ciudad
acogedora.; **a friendly match** un
partido amistoso

friendship n amistad f

fright n susto m ▷ She gave us a
fright. Nos dio un susto. ▷ **to get a
fright** llevarse un susto

frighten vb asustar ▷ She was
trying to frighten him. Intentaba
asustarlo.; **Horror films frighten
him.** Le dan miedo las películas
de terror.

frightened adj **to be frightened**
tener miedo ▷ I'm frightened!
¡Tengo miedo!; **Anna's frightened
of spiders.** A Anna le dan miedo
las arañas.

frightening adj aterrador (f
aterradora)

fringe n flequillo m ▷ She's got a
fringe. Lleva flequillo.

frog n rana f

from prep **①** de ▷ Where do you
come from? ¿De dónde eres? ▷ a
letter from my sister una carta de mi
hermana ▷ The hotel is one kilometre
from the beach. El hotel está a
un kilómetro de la playa. ▷ The
price was reduced from £10 to £5.
Rebajaron el precio de 10 a 5 libras
esterlinas. **②** desde ▷ Breakfast
is available from 6 a.m. Se puede
desayunar desde las 6 de la
mañana. ▷ I can't see anything from
here. Desde aquí no veo nada.

> In the following phrases
> de and desde are
> interchangeable. Use a to
> translate to if you have chosen
> de and hasta if you have opted
> for desde.

He flew from London to Bilbao.
Voló de Londres a Bilbao.; **from
one o'clock to three** desde la una
hasta las tres; **from...onwards** a
partir de... ▷ We'll be at home from
seven o'clock onwards. Estaremos en
casa a partir de las siete.

front n parte f delantera ▷ The
switch is at the front of the vacuum
cleaner. El interruptor está en la
parte delantera de la aspiradora.;
the front of the dress el delantero
del vestido; **the front of the
house** la fachada de la casa; **I was
sitting in the front.** (of car) Yo iba

sentado delante.; **at the front of the train** al principio del tren; **in front** delante ▷ **the car in front** el coche de delante; **in front of** delante de ▷ **Laura sits in front of me in class.** Laura se sienta delante de mí en clase.
▶ adj ❶ primero ▷ **the front row** la primera fila

Use **primer** before a masculine singular noun.

❷ delantero ▷ **the front seats of the car** los asientos delanteros del coche; **the front door** la puerta principal

frontier n frontera f

frost n helada f ▷ **There was a frost last night.** Anoche cayó una helada.

frosting n (in US: on cake) glaseado m

frosty adj **It's frosty today.** Hoy ha helado.

frown vb fruncir el ceño

froze, frozen vb see **freeze**

frozen adj congelado

fruit n fruta f; **fruit juice** el zumo de fruta (LatAm el jugo de fruta); **fruit salad** la macedonia (LatAm la ensalada de frutas)

frustrated adj frustrado

fry vb freír

frying pan n sartén f (pl sartenes)

fuel n combustible m ▷ **We've run out of fuel.** Nos hemos quedado sin combustible.

full adj ❶ lleno ▷ **The tank's full.** El depósito está lleno.; **I'm full.** Estoy lleno.; **There was a full moon.** Había luna llena.

❷ completo ▷ **He asked for full information on the job.** Solicitó información completa sobre el trabajo. ▷ **My full name is Ian John Marr.** Mi nombre completo es Ian John Marr.; **at full speed** a toda velocidad

full stop n (punctuation mark) punto m

full-time adj, adv **She's got a full-time job.** Tiene un trabajo de jornada completa.; **She works full-time.** Trabaja la jornada completa.

fully adv (completely) completamente

fumes npl humo m ▷ **exhaust fumes** el humo de los tubos de escape

fun adj divertido ▷ **She's a fun person.** Es una persona divertida.
▶ n **to have fun** divertirse; **It's fun!** ¡Es divertido!; **Have fun!** ¡Que te diviertas!; **for fun** por gusto; **to make fun of somebody** reírse de alguien

funds npl fondos mpl ▷ **to raise funds** recaudar fondos

funeral n funeral m

funfair n ❶ (travelling fair) feria f ❷ (fair on permanent site) parque m de atracciones

funny adj ❶ gracioso ▷ **a funny joke** un chiste gracioso ❸ raro ▷ **There's something funny about him.** Hay algo raro en él.

fur n ❶ piel f; **a fur coat** un abrigo de pieles ❷ pelaje m ▷ **the cat's fur** el pelaje del gato

furious adj furioso

furniture n muebles mpl; **a piece of furniture** un mueble

further adv, adj ❶ más lejos ▷ London is further from here than Paris. Londres está más lejos de aquí que París.; **I can't walk any further.** No puedo andar más.; **How much further is it?** ¿Cuánto queda todavía? ❷ más ▷ Please write to us if you need any further information. No dude en escribirnos si necesita más información.

further education n enseñanza f postescolar

fuse n fusible m ▷ The fuse has blown. Se ha fundido el fusible.

fuss n jaleo m ▷ What's all the fuss about? ¿A qué viene tanto jaleo?; **He's always making a fuss about nothing.** (informal) Siempre monta el número por cualquier tontería.

fussy adj quisquilloso ▷ She is very fussy about her food. Es muy quisquillosa con la comida.

future n futuro m ▷ What are your plans for the future? ¿Qué planes tienes para el futuro?; **in future** de ahora en adelante ▷ Be more careful in future. De ahora en adelante ten más cuidado.

gain vb ganar ▷ What do you hope to gain from this? ¿Qué esperas ganar con esto?; **to gain speed** adquirir velocidad; **to gain weight** engordar

gallery n ❶ (state-owned) museo m de arte ❷ (private) galería f de arte

gamble vb jugarse ▷ He gambled £100 at the casino. Se jugó 100 libras en el casino.

gambling n juego m

game n ❶ juego m ▷ The children were playing a game. Los niños jugaban a un juego. ❷ partido m ▷ a game of football un partido de fútbol; **a game of cards** una partida de cartas; **We have games on Thursdays.** Tenemos deporte los jueves.

gang n ① (of thieves, troublemakers) banda f ② (of friends) pandilla f

gangster n gángster m

gap n ① hueco m ▷ There's a gap in the hedge. Hay un hueco en el seto. ② intervalo m ▷ a gap of four years un intervalo de cuatro años; **gap year** año sabático antes de empezar a estudiar en la universidad

garage n ① (for keeping the car) garaje m ② (for car repairs) taller m

garbage n basura f ▷ the garbage can el cubo de la basura; **That's garbage!** ¡Eso son tonterías!

garden n jardín m (pl jardines)

gardener n jardinero m, jardinera f ▷ He's a gardener. Es jardinero.

gardening n jardinería f ▷ Margaret loves gardening. A Margaret le encanta la jardinería.

garlic n ajo m

garment n prenda f de vestir

gas n ① gas m ▷ a gas cooker una cocina de gas ▷ a gas fire una estufa de gas ▷ a gas leak un escape de gas ② (in US: petrol) gasolina f

gasoline n (in US) gasolina f

gate n ① (made of wood, at airport) puerta f; **Please go to gate seven.** Diríjanse a la puerta siete. ② (made of metal) verja f

gather vb ① reunirse ▷ We gathered around the fireplace. Nos reunimos en torno a la chimenea. ② (objects, information) reunir ▷ We gathered enough firewood to last the night. Reunimos leña suficiente para toda la noche.; **to**

gather speed adquirir velocidad ▷ The train gathered speed. El tren adquirió velocidad.

gave vb see **give**

gay adj gay

GCSE n (= General Certificate of Secondary Education) certificado del último ciclo de la enseñanza secundaria obligatorio
- In Spain, under the reformed educational system, if you leave school at the age of 16, you get a **Título de Graduado en Educación Secundaria**.

gear n ① (of car) marcha f ▷ to change gear cambiar de marcha; **in first gear** en primera ② (equipment) equipo m ▷ camping gear el equipo de acampada ③ (clothes) ropa f ▷ sports gear la ropa de deporte

gear lever n palanca f de cambio

gearshift n (in US) palanca f de cambio

geese npl see **goose**

gel n gel m; **hair gel** el fijador

Gemini n (sign) Géminis m; **I'm Gemini.** Soy géminis.

gender n (of noun) género m

general n general m
▶ adj general; **in general** en general

general election n elecciones fpl generales

general knowledge n cultura f general

generally adv generalmente ▷ I generally go shopping on Saturdays. Generalmente voy de compras los sábados.

generation n generación f (pl generaciones) ▷ the younger generation la nueva generación

generous adj generoso ▷ That's very generous of you. Es muy generoso de tu parte.

genetically-modified adj transgénico

genetics n genética f

Geneva n Ginebra f

genius n genio m ▷ She's a genius. Es un genio.

gentle adj ① (person, voice) dulce ② (wind, touch) suave

gentleman n caballero m

gently adv ① (to say, smile) dulcemente ② (to touch) suavemente

gents n servicio m de caballeros ▷ Can you tell me where the gents is, please? ¿El servicio de caballeros, por favor?; **"gents"** (on sign) "caballeros"

genuine adj ① auténtico ▷ They're genuine diamonds. Son diamantes auténticos. ② sincero ▷ She's a very genuine person. Es una persona muy sincera.

geography n geografía f

gerbil n gerbo m

germ n microbio m

German adj alemán (f alemana) (mpl alemanes)
▸ n ① (person) alemán m, alemana f (mpl alemanes) ▷ the Germans los alemanes ② (language) alemán m ▷ our German teacher nuestro profesor de alemán

German measles n rubéola f ▷ to have German measles tener rubéola

Germany n Alemania f

get vb

> There are several ways of translating **get**. Scan the examples to find one that is similar to what you want to say.

① (have, receive) recibir ▷ I got a letter from him. Recibí una carta de él.; **I got lots of presents.** Me hicieron muchos regalos. ② (obtain) conseguir ▷ He had trouble getting a hotel room. Tuvo dificultades para conseguir una habitación de hotel.; **to get something for somebody** conseguir algo a alguien ▷ The librarian got the book for me. El bibliotecario me consiguió el libro.; **Jackie got good exam results.** Jackie sacó buenas notas en los exámenes. ③ (fetch) ir a buscar ▷ Quick, get help! Rápido, ve a buscar ayuda! ④ (catch, take) coger

> Be very careful with the verb **coger**: in most of Latin America this is an extremely rude word that should be avoided. However, in Spain this verb is common and not rude at all.

▷ They've got the thief. Han cogido al ladrón. (LatAm) Han atrapado al ladrón.) ▷ I'm getting the bus into town. Voy a coger el autobús al centro. (LatAm) Voy a tomar el autobús al centro.) ⑤ (understand) entender ▷ *I don't get the joke. No entiendo el chiste.* ❸ *(arrive)* llegar ▷ *He should get here soon. Debería llegar pronto.*; **to get angry** enfadarse *(LatAm* enojarse*)*; **to get tired** cansarse

> For other phrases with **get** and an adjective, such as "to get old, to get drunk", you should look under the word **old, drunk**, etc.

to get something done mandar hacer algo ▷ *I'm getting my car fixed. He mandado arreglar el coche.*; **I got my hair cut.** Me corté el pelo.; **I'll get it!** (1) *(telephone)* ¡Yo contesto! (2) *(door)* ¡Ya voy yo!

get away vb escapar ▷ *One of the burglars got away. Uno de los ladrones escapó.*

get away with vb **You'll never get away with it.** Esto no te lo van a consentir.

get back vb ❶ volver ▷ *What time did you get back? ¿A qué hora volvisteis?* ❷ recuperar ▷ *He got his money back. Recuperó su dinero.*

get down vb bajar ▷ *Get down from there! ¡Baja de ahí!*

get in vb llegar ▷ *What time did you get in last night? ¿A qué hora llegaste anoche?*

get into vb entrar en ▷ *How did you get into the house? ¿Cómo entraste en la casa?*; **Sharon got into the car.** Sharon subió al coche.; **Get into bed!** ¡Métete en la cama!

get off vb ❶ bajarse de ▷ *Isobel got off the train. Isobel se bajó del tren.* ❸ salir ▷ *He managed to get off early from work yesterday. Logró salir de trabajar pronto ayer.*

get on vb ❶ *(train, bus, bike)* subirse a ▷ *Phyllis got on the bus. Phyllis se subió al autobús.* ❷ llevarse bien ▷ *We got on really well. Nos llevábamos muy bien.* ▷ *He doesn't get on with his parents. No se lleva bien con sus padres.*; **How are you getting on?** ¿Cómo te va?

get out vb ❶ *(leave)* salir ▷ *Get out! ¡Sal!*; **She got out of the car.** Se bajó del coche. ❸ *(take out)* sacar ▷ *She got the map out. Sacó el mapa.*

get over vb ❶ recuperarse de ▷ *It took her a long time to get over the illness. Tardó mucho tiempo en recuperarse de la enfermedad.* ❸ superar ▷ *He managed to get over the problem. Logró superar el problema.*

get round to vb encontrar tiempo para ▷ *I'll get round to it eventually. Ya encontraré tiempo para hacerlo.*

get together vb reunirse ▷ *Could we get together this evening? ¿Podemos reunirnos esta tarde?*

get up vb levantarse ▷ *What time do you get up? ¿A qué hora te levantas?*

ghost n fantasma m

> Although **fantasma** ends in **-a**, it is actually a masculine noun.

giant adj enorme

gift n regalo m; **to have a gift for something** tener dotes para algo ▷ *Dave's got a gift for painting.* Dave tiene dotes para la pintura.

gin n ginebra f

ginger n jengibre m

▸ *adj* **She's got ginger hair.** Es pelirroja.

gipsy n gitano m, gitana f

giraffe n jirafa f

girl n ❶ (young) niña f ▷ *a five-year old girl* una niña de cinco años ❷ (older) chica f ▷ *a sixteen-year old girl* una chica de dieciséis años

girlfriend n ❶ novia f ▷ *Paul's girlfriend is called Janice.* La novia de Paul se llama Janice. ❷ amiga f ▷ *She often went out with her girlfriends.* Solía salir con sus amigas.

give vb dar; **to give something to somebody** dar algo a alguien ▷ *He gave me £10.* Me dio 10 libras.; **to give somebody a present** hacer un regalo a alguien; **to give way** (in car) ceder el paso

give away vb regalar

give back vb devolver ▷ *I gave the book back to him.* Le devolví el libro.

give in vb rendirse ▷ *I give in!* ¡Me rindo!

give up vb darse por vencido ▷ *I couldn't do it, so I gave up.* No podía hacerlo, así que me di por vencido.; **to give oneself up** entregarse ▷ *She gave herself up.* Se entregó.; **to give up doing something** dejar de hacer algo ▷ *He gave up smoking.* Dejó de

fumar.

glad adj contento ▷ *She's glad she's done it.* Está contenta de haberlo hecho.; **I'm glad you're here.** Me alegro de que estés aquí.

> **alegrarse de que** has to be
> followed by a verb in the
> subjunctive.

glamorous adj atractivo

glance vb **to glance at something** echar una mirada a algo ▷ *Peter glanced at his watch.* Peter echó una mirada al reloj.

glass n ❶ (without stem) vaso m ▷ *a glass of milk* un vaso de leche ❷ (with stem) copa f ▷ *a glass of champagne* una copa de champán ❸ (substance) vidrio m ▷ *a glass door* una puerta de vidrio

glasses npl gafas fpl (LatAm anteojos mpl)

glider n planeador m

global adj mundial ▷ *on a global scale* a escala mundial; **a global view** una visión global

globalization n globalización f

global warming n calentamiento m del planeta

globe n globo m terráqueo

gloomy adj oscuro ▷ *He lives in a small gloomy flat.* Vive en un piso pequeño y oscuro.; **She's been feeling very gloomy recently.** Últimamente está muy desanimada.

glorious adj espléndido

glove n guante m

glue n pegamento m

▸ *vb* pegar; **to glue something**

together pegar algo

GM adj = **genetically-modified**; **GM foods** los alimentos transgénicos

go n **to have a go at doing something** probar a hacer algo ▷ He had a go at making a cake. Probó a hacer una tarta.; **Whose go is it?** ¿A quién le toca?; **It's your go.** Te toca a ti.

▶ vb ① **ir** ▷ Where are you going? ¿Adónde vas? ▷ I'm going to the cinema tonight. Voy al cine esta noche.; **to go home** irse a casa; **to go into** entrar en ▷ She went into the kitchen. Entró en la cocina.; **to go for a walk** ir a dar un paseo ② (leave, go away) **irse** ▷ Where's Judy? - She's gone. ¿Dónde está Judy? - Se ha ido. ▷ We went home. Nos fuimos a casa. ③ (work) **funcionar** ▷ My car won't go. El coche no funciona.; **How did the exam go?** ¿Cómo te fue en el examen? ; **I'm going to do it tomorrow.** Lo voy a hacer mañana.

go after vb **perseguir** ▷ Quick, go after them! ¡Rápido, persíguelos!

go away vb **irse** ▷ Go away! ¡Vete!

go back vb **volver** ▷ He's gone back home. Ha vuelto a casa.

go by vb **pasar** ▷ Two policemen went by. Pasaron dos policías.

go down vb ① **bajar** ▷ He went down the stairs. Bajó las escaleras. ▷ The price of computers has gone down. Ha bajado el precio de los ordenadores. ② (deflate)

desinflarse ▷ My airbed's gone down. Mi colchoneta se ha desinflado.; **My brother's gone down with flu.** Mi hermano ha pillado la gripe.

go in vb **entrar** ▷ He knocked on the door and went in. Llamó a la puerta y entró.

go off vb ① (leave) **marcharse** ▷ They went off after lunch. Se marcharon después de comer. ② (explode) **estallar** ▷ The bomb went off at 10 o'clock. La bomba estalló a las 10.; **The gun went off by accident.** El arma se disparó accidentalmente. ③ (sound) **sonar** ▷ My alarm goes off at seven. Mi despertador suena a las siete. ④ (go bad) **echarse a perder** ▷ This milk has gone off. Esta leche se ha echado a perder. ⑤ (go out) **apagarse** ▷ All the lights went off. Se apagaron todas las luces.; **I've gone off that idea.** Ya no me gusta la idea.

go on vb ① (happen) **pasar** ▷ What's going on? ¿Qué pasa? ② (continue) **seguir**; **to go on doing** seguir haciendo ▷ He went on reading. Siguió leyendo. ③ **durar** ▷ The concert went on until 11 o'clock at night. El concierto duró hasta las 11 de la noche.; **to go on at somebody** dar la lata a alguien ▷ They're always going on at me. Están siempre dándome la lata.; **Go on!** ¡Venga! ▷ Go on, tell me what the problem is! ¡Venga, dime cuál es el problema!

a b c d e f g h i j k l m n o p q r s t u v w x y z

go out vb ❶ <u>salir</u> ▷ Are you going out tonight? ¿Vas a salir esta noche? ▷ I went out with Steven last night. Ayer por la noche salí con Steven. ▷ They went out for a meal. Salieron a comer. ❷ <u>apagarse</u> ▷ Suddenly the lights went out. De pronto se apagaron las luces.

go past vb to go past something pasar por delante de algo ▷ He went past the shop. Pasó por delante de la tienda.

go round vb <u>visitar</u> ▷ We want to go round the museum today. Hoy queremos visitar el museo.; **I love going round the shops.** Me encanta ir de tiendas.; **to go round to somebody's house** ir a casa de alguien ▷ We're all going round to Linda's house tonight. Esta noche vamos todos a casa de Linda.; **There's a bug going round.** Hay un virus por ahí rondando.; **Is there enough food to go round?** ¿Hay comida suficiente para todos?

go through vb ❶ <u>atravesar</u> ▷ We went through London to get to Brighton. Atravesamos Londres para llegar a Brighton. ❷ <u>pasar por</u> ▷ I know what you're going through. Sé por lo que estás pasando. ❸ <u>repasar</u> ▷ They went through the plan again. Repasaron de nuevo el plan. ❹ <u>registrar</u> ▷ Someone had gone through her things. Alguien había registrado sus cosas.

go up vb <u>subir</u> ▷ She went up the

stairs. Subió las escaleras. ▷ The price has gone up. El precio ha subido.; **to go up in flames** arder en llamas

go with vb <u>pegar con</u> ▷ Does this blouse go with that skirt? ¿Pega esta blusa con la falda?

goal n ❶ <u>gol</u> m ▷ He scored the first goal. El metió el primer gol. ❷ <u>objetivo</u> m ▷ His goal is to become the world champion. Su objetivo es ser campeón del mundo.

goalkeeper n <u>portero</u> m

goat n <u>cabra</u> f; **goat's cheese** el queso de cabra

god n <u>dios</u> m ▷ I believe in God. Creo en Dios.

goddaughter n <u>ahijada</u> f

godfather n <u>padrino</u> m

godmother n <u>madrina</u> f

godson n <u>ahijado</u> m

goggles npl <u>gafas</u> fpl protectoras (LatAm <u>anteojos</u> mpl protectores)

gold n <u>oro</u> m ▷ a gold necklace un collar de oro

goldfish n <u>pez</u> m de colores (pl peces de colores)

golf n <u>golf</u> m; **a golf club (1)** (stick) un palo de golf **(2)** (place) un club de golf; **a golf course** un campo de golf

gone vb see **go**

good adj ❶ <u>bueno</u>

Use **buen** before a masculine singular noun.

▷ It's a very good film. Es una película muy buena. ▷ a good day un buen día ❸ (kind) <u>amable</u>

▷ *That's very good of you.* Es muy amable de tu parte.; **They were very good to me.** Se portaron muy bien conmigo.; **Have a good journey!** ¡Buen viaje!; **Good!** ¡Bien!; **Good morning!** ¡Buenos días!; **Good afternoon!** ¡Buenas tardes!; **Good evening!** ¡Buenas noches!; **Good night!** ¡Buenas noches!; **I'm feeling really good today.** Hoy me siento realmente bien.; **to be good for somebody** hacer bien a alguien ▷ *Vegetables are good for you.* La verdura te hace bien.; **Jane's very good at maths.** A Jane se le dan muy bien las matemáticas.; **for good** definitivamente ▷ *One day he left for good.* Un día se marchó definitivamente.; **It's no good complaining.** De nada sirve quejarse.

goodbye *excl* ¡adiós!

Good Friday *n* Viernes *m* Santo

good-looking *adj* guapo

goods *npl* productos *mpl* ▷ *They sell a wide range of goods.* Venden una amplia gama de productos.

goose *n* oca *f*

gorgeous *adj* ❶ guapísimo ▷ *She's gorgeous!* ¡Es guapísima! ❷ estupendo ▷ *The weather was gorgeous.* El tiempo fue estupendo.

gorilla *n* gorila *m*

　　Although **gorila** ends in -a, it is actually a masculine noun.

gospel *n* evangelio *m*

gossip *n* ❶ (*rumours*) cotilleo *m* ❸ (*person*) cotilla *mf*

▶ *vb* cotillear (*LatAm* comadrear) ▷ *They were always gossiping.* Siempre estaban cotilleando.

got *vb* **to have got** (*own*) tener ▷ *How many have you got?* ¿Cuántos tienes?; **to have got to do something** tener que hacer algo ▷ *I've got to tell him.* Tengo que decírselo.; *see also* **get**

government *n* gobierno *m*

GP *n* (= *General Practitioner*) médico *m* de cabecera, médica *f* de cabecera

grab *vb* agarrar ▷ *He grabbed my arm.* Me agarró el brazo.

graceful *adj* elegante

grade *n* nota *f* ▷ *He got good grades in his exams.* Sacó buenas notas en los exámenes.

grade school *n* (*in US*) escuela *f* primaria

gradual *adj* gradual

gradually *adv* gradualmente

graduate *vb* licenciarse (*LatAm* recibirse)

graffiti *npl* pintadas *fpl*

grain *n* ❶ grano *m* ▷ *a grain of rice* un grano de arroz ❷ (*wheat, corn etc*) cereales *mpl*

gram *n* gramo *m*

grammar *n* gramática *f*

grammar school *n* colegio selectivo de enseñanza secundaria para alumnos de 11 a 18 años

grammatical *adj* gramatical

gramme *n* gramo *m*

grand *adj* grandioso ▷ *Her house is very grand.* Su casa es grandiosa.

grandchildren *npl* nietos *mpl*

granddad n abuelo m

granddaughter n nieta f

grandfather n abuelo m

grandma n abuela f

grandmother n abuela f

grandpa n abuelo m

grandparents npl abuelos mpl

grandson n nieto m

granny n abuelita f

grape n uva f

grapefruit n pomelo m

graph n gráfico m

grass n ❶ hierba f ▷ The grass is long. La hierba está alta. ❷ (lawn) césped m ▷ "Keep off the grass" "Prohibido pisar el césped"; **to cut the grass** cortar el césped

grasshopper n saltamontes m (pl saltamontes)

grate vb rallar ▷ grated cheese el queso rallado

grateful adj agradecido

grave n tumba f

gravel n grava f

graveyard n cementerio m

gravy n jugo m de carne

grease n ❶ (in hair, on skin) grasa f ❷ (for cars, machines) aceite m

greasy adj ❶ aceitoso ▷ The food was very greasy. La comida estaba muy aceitosa. ❷ graso ▷ He has greasy hair. Tiene el pelo graso.

great adj ❶ estupendo (LatAm chévere) ▷ That's great! ¡Estupendo! ❷ grande

❚ Use **gran** before a singular noun.

▷ a great oak tree un gran roble

Great Britain n Gran Bretaña f

great-grandfather n bisabuelo m

great-grandmother n bisabuela f

Greece n Grecia f

greedy adj ❶ glotón (f glotona) (mpl glotones) ▷ Don't be greedy, you've already had three doughnuts. No seas glotón, ya te has comido tres donuts. ❷ codicioso ▷ She is greedy and selfish. Es codiciosa y egoísta.

Greek adj griego
▶ n ❶ (person) griego m, griega f ▷ The Greeks los griegos ❷ (language) griego m

green adj verde ▷ a green car un coche verde; **a green light** (at traffic lights) un semáforo en verde; **the Green Party** el Partido Verde
▶ n verde m ▷ a dark green un verde oscuro; **greens** (vegetables) la verdura; **the Greens** (party) los verdes

greengrocer's n verdulería f

greenhouse n invernadero m; **the greenhouse effect** el efecto invernadero

greetings npl **Greetings from London!** ¡Saludos desde Londres!; **Season's greetings** Felices Fiestas

greetings card n tarjeta f de felicitación

grew vb see **grow**

grey adj gris ▷ They wore grey suits. Llevaban trajes grises.; **He's going grey.** Le están saliendo canas.; **grey hair** las canas

grid n ① (in road, on map) cuadrícula f ② (of electricity) red f

grief n pena f

grill n ① (of cooker) grill m
○ In Spain the grill is always inside the oven, if there is one at all. They are not as common as they are in Britain.
② (for barbecue) parrilla f; **a mixed grill** una parrillada mixta
▶ vb ① (in cooker) hacer al grill ② (barbecue) asar a la parrilla

grin vb sonreír ampliamente
▷ Dave grinned at me. Dave me sonrió ampliamente.
▶ n amplia sonrisa f

grip vb agarrar

grit n gravilla f

groan vb gemir ▷ He groaned with pain. Gimió de dolor.
▶ n gemido m

grocer n tendero m, tendera f

groceries npl (food) comestibles mpl; **I'll get some groceries.** Traeré algunas provisiones.

grocer's n tienda f de ultramarinos

grocery store n (in US) tienda f de ultramarinos

groom n novio m ▷ the groom and his best man el novio y su padrino de boda

gross adj ① (revolting) horrible; **That's gross!** ¡Qué asco! ② (finance) bruto ▷ gross income ingresos brutos

ground n ① suelo m ▷ The ground's wet. El suelo está húmedo.; **on the ground** en el suelo ▷ We sat on the

ground. Nos sentamos en el suelo. ② campo m (LatAm cancha f) ▷ a football ground un campo de fútbol ③ motivo m ▷ We've got grounds for complaint. Tenemos motivos para quejarnos.

ground coffee n café m molido

ground floor n planta f baja

group n grupo m

grow vb ① crecer ▷ Haven't you grown! ¡Cómo has crecido! ② aumentar ▷ The number of unemployed has grown. Ha aumentado el número de desempleados. ③ cultivar ▷ He grew vegetables in his garden. Cultivaba hortalizas en su jardín.; **He's grown out of his jacket.** La chaqueta se le ha quedado pequeña.; **to grow a beard** dejarse barba ▷ I'm growing a beard. Me estoy dejando barba.; **He grew a moustache.** Se dejó bigote.

grow up vb criarse ▷ I grew up in Rome. Me crié en Roma.; **Oh, grow up!** ¡No seas crío!

growl vb gruñir

grown vb see **grow**

growth n crecimiento m ▷ economic growth crecimiento económico

grudge n **to bear a grudge against somebody** guardar rencor a alguien ▷ He's always had a grudge against me. Siempre me ha guardado rencor.

gruesome adj horroroso

guarantee n garantía f ▷ a five-year guarantee una garantía

de cinco años ▷ *It's still under guarantee.* Todavía tiene garantía.
▶ *vb* garantizar ▷ *I can't guarantee he'll come.* No puedo garantizar que venga.

guard *vb* vigilar ▷ *The police were guarding the entrance.* La policía vigilaba la entrada.
▶ *n* ① (person) guardia *mf* ② (on train) jefe *m* de tren; **a security guard** un guarda jurado

guard dog *n* perro *m* guardián

guess *vb* adivinar ▷ *Can you guess what it is?* A ver si adivinas qué es.; **to guess wrong** equivocarse; **Guess what!** ¿Sabes qué?
▶ *n* suposición *f* (*pl* suposiciones) ▷ *It's just a guess.* Sólo es una suposición.; **Have a guess!** ¡Adivina!

guest *n* ① invitado *m*, invitada *f* ▷ *We have guests staying with us.* Tenemos invitados en casa. ② (in hotel) huésped *mf*

guide *n* ① (book) guía *f* ② (person) guía *mf* ③ (girl guide) exploradora *f*

guidebook *n* guía *f*

guide dog *n* perro *m* lazarillo

guilty *adj* culpable ▷ *He felt guilty about lying to her.* Se sentía culpable por haberle mentido.; **He has a guilty conscience.** Tiene remordimientos de conciencia.

guinea pig *n* cobayo *m* ▷ *She's got a guinea pig.* Tiene un cobayo.

guitar *n* guitarra *f* ▷ *I play the guitar.* Toco la guitarra.

gum *n* (chewing gum) chicle *m*; **a piece of gum** un chicle; **gums** (in mouth) las encías

gun *n* ① (small) pistola *f* ② (rifle) fusil *m*

gunpoint *n* **at gunpoint** a punta de pistola

guy *n* tío *m* (informal) (LatAm tipo *m* informal) ▷ *He's a nice guy.* Es un tío simpático.

gym *n* gimnasio *m* ▷ *I go to the gym every day.* Voy al gimnasio todos los días.; **gym classes** las clases de gimnasia

gymnast *n* gimnasta *mf*

gymnastics *n* gimnasia *f*

gypsy *n* gitano *m*, gitana *f*

h

habit n costumbre f

had vb see **have**

hadn't = **had not**

hail n granizo m
▸ vb granizar

hair n pelo m ▷ She's got long hair.
Tiene el pelo largo.; **to have one's
hair cut** cortarse el pelo; **to brush
one's hair** cepillarse el pelo; **to
wash one's hair** lavarse la cabeza

hairbrush n cepillo m

haircut n corte m de pelo ▷ You
need a haircut. Necesitas un
corte de pelo.; **to have a haircut**
cortarse el pelo

hairdresser n peluquero m,
peluquera f ▷ He's a hairdresser. Es
peluquero.; **at the hairdresser's**
en la peluquería

hair dryer n secador m de pelo

hair gel n fijador m

hairgrip n horquilla f

hair spray n laca f

hairstyle n peinado m

half n ❶ mitad f ▷ half of the
cake la mitad de la tarta; **to cut
something in half** cortar algo
por la mitad; **two and a half** dos y
medio; **half a kilo** medio kilo; **half
an hour** media hora; **half past ten**
las diez y media ❷ (ticket) billete
m para niños ▷ One and two halves,
please. Un billete normal y dos
para niños, por favor.
▸ adj, adv medio ▷ a half chicken
medio pollo

> When you use **medio** before an
> adjective, it does not change.

▷ She was half asleep. Estaba medio
dormida.

half-price adj, adv a mitad de
precio ▷ I bought it half-price. Lo
compré a mitad de precio.

half-term n vacaciones fpl de
mitad de trimestre

half-time n descanso m

halfway adv ❶ a medio camino
▷ Reading is halfway between Oxford
and London. Reading está a medio
camino entre Oxford y Londres.
❷ a la mitad ▷ halfway through the
film a la mitad de la película

hall n ❶ (in house) vestíbulo m
❷ sala f ▷ a lecture hall una sala
de conferencias; **a concert hall**
un auditorio; **a sports hall** un
gimnasio; **village hall** el salón de
actos municipal

Hallowe'en n víspera f de Todos

los Santos

hallway n vestíbulo m

halves npl see **half**

ham n jamón m (pl jamones)
 ● In Spain there are two basic
 kinds of ham in the shops:
 jamón serrano, which is cured
 and similar to Parma ham, and
 jamón de York or **jamón dulce**,
 which is boiled and similar to
 British ham.

hamburger n hamburguesa f

hammer n martillo m

hamster n hámster m

hand n ❶ (of person) mano f
 ▌ Although **mano** ends in -o it is
 actually a feminine noun.

 to give someone a hand echar
 una mano a alguien ▷ Can you give
 me a hand? ¿Me echas una mano?;
 **on the one hand ..., on the other
 hand ...** por un lado ..., por otro ...
 ❷ (of clock) manecilla f
 ▷ vb pasar ▷ He handed me the book.
 Me pasó el libro.

hand in vb entregar ▷ Martin
 handed in his exam paper. Martin
 entregó su examen.

hand out vb repartir ▷ The teacher
 handed out the books. El profesor
 repartió los libros.

handbag n bolso m (LatAm
 cartera f)

handcuffs npl esposas fpl

handkerchief n pañuelo m

handle n ❶ (of door) picaporte
 m ❷ (of cup, briefcase) asa f ❸ (of
 knife, saucepan) mango m
 ▷ vb ❶ encargarse de ▷ Kath

handled the travel arrangements.
Kath se encargó de organizar
el viaje. ❷ manejar ▷ It was a
difficult situation, but he handled it
well. Era una situación difícil, pero
él supo manejarla bien. ❸ tratar
▷ She's good at handling children.
Sabe tratar a los niños.; **"handle
with care"** "frágil"

handlebars npl manillar m

handmade adj hecho a mano (f
 hecha a mano)

handsome adj guapo ▷ My father's
very handsome. Mi padre es muy
guapo.

handwriting n letra f ▷ His
handwriting is terrible. Tiene una
letra horrible.

handy adj ❶ práctico ▷ This knife's
very handy. Este cuchillo es muy
práctico. ❷ a mano ▷ Have you got
a pen handy? ¿Tienes un bolígrafo
a mano?

hang vb ❶ colgar ▷ Mike hung
the painting on the wall. Mike
colgó el cuadro en la pared.
▷ There was a bulb hanging from
the ceiling. Una bombilla colgaba
del techo. ❷ (execute) ahorcar
▷ In the past criminals were hanged.
Antiguamente se ahorcaba a los
criminales.

hang around vb pasar el rato ▷ On
Saturdays we hang around in the
park. Los sábados pasamos el rato
en el parque.

hang on vb esperar ▷ Hang
on a minute please. Espera un
momento, por favor.

hang up vb (clothes, phone) colgar ▷ Don't hang up! ¡No cuelgues! ▷ He hung up on me. Me colgó.

hanger n percha f

hangover n resaca f ▷ I woke up with a hangover. Me desperté con resaca.

happen vb pasar ▷ What happened? ¿Qué pasó?; **As it happens, I do know him.** Da la casualidad de que lo conozco.; **Do you happen to know if she's at home?** ¿Por casualidad sabes si está en casa?

happily adv ❶ alegremente ▷ "Don't worry!", he said happily. "¡No te preocupes!" dijo alegremente. ❷ felizmente ▷ He's happily married. Está felizmente casado.; **And they lived happily ever after.** Y vivieron felices y comieron perdices. ❸ afortunadamente ▷ Happily, everything went well. Afortunadamente todo fue bien.

happiness n felicidad f

happy adj feliz (pl felices) ▷ Janet looks happy. Janet parece feliz.; **to be happy with something** estar contento con algo ▷ I'm very happy with your work. Estoy muy contento con tu trabajo.; **Happy birthday!** ¡Feliz cumpleaños!; **a happy ending** un final feliz

harbour (US **harbor**) n puerto m

hard adj, adv ❶ (not soft) duro ▷ to work hard trabajar duro ❷ (difficult) difícil

hard disk n disco m duro

hardly adv apenas ▷ I hardly know you. Apenas te conozco.; **I've got**

hardly any money. Casi no tengo dinero.; **hardly ever** casi nunca; **hardly anything** casi nada

hard up adj to be hard up estar sin un duro (LatAm estar sin plata) (informal)

harm vb **to harm somebody** hacer daño a alguien ▷ I didn't mean to harm you. No quería hacerte daño.; **to harm something** dañar algo ▷ Chemicals harm the environment. Los productos químicos dañan el medio ambiente.

harmful adj perjudicial ▷ harmful to the environment perjudicial para el medio ambiente

harmless adj inofensivo

harvest n (of fruit, vegetables, cereals) cosecha f

has vb see **have**

hasn't = **has not**

hat n sombrero m

hate vb odiar

hatred n odio m

haunted adj **a haunted house** una casa embrujada

have vb

> Use the verb **haber** to form the perfect tenses.

❶ haber ▷ I've already seen that film. Ya he visto esa película. ▷ If you had phoned me I would have come around. Si me hubieras llamado habría venido.

> If you are using **have** in question tags to confirm a statement use ¿**no?** or ¿**verdad?**.

▷ You've done it, haven't you? Lo has

a
b
c
d
e
f
g
h
i
j
k
l
m
n
o
p
q
r
s
t
u
v
w
x
y
z

hecho, ¿verdad? ▷ They've arrived, haven't they? Ya han llegado, ¿no?

▌ **Have** is not translated when giving simple negative or positive answers to questions.

▷ Have you read that book? - Yes, I have. ¿Has leído el libro? - Sí. ▷ Has he told you? - No, he hasn't. ¿Te lo ha dicho? - No. ❷ **tener** ▷ I have a terrible cold. Tengo un resfriado horrible. ▷ She had a baby last year. Tuvo un niño el año pasado. ▷ Do you have any brothers or sisters? ¿Tienes hermanos?; **to have to do something.** tener que hacer algo. ▷ I have to finish this work. Tengo que terminar este trabajo. ❸ **tomar** ▷ I'll have a coffee. Tomaré un café.; **to have a shower** ducharse; **to have one's hair cut** cortarse el pelo

haven't = **have not**

hay n heno m

hay fever n alergia f al polen

hazelnut n avellana f

he pron él

▌ **he** generally isn't translated unless it is emphatic.

▷ He is very tall. Es muy alto.

▌ Use **él** for emphasis.

▷ He did it but she didn't. Él lo hizo, pero ella no.

head n ❶ cabeza f ▷ He lost his head and started screaming. Perdió la cabeza y empezó a gritar. ❷ (of school) director m, directora f ❸ (leader) jefe m, jefa f ▷ a head of state un jefe de Estado; **Heads or tails? - Heads.** ¿Cara o cruz? - Cara. ▶ vb **to head for** dirigirse a ▷ They headed for the church. Se dirigieron a la iglesia.

headache n dolor m de cabeza ▷ I've got a headache. Tengo dolor de cabeza.

headlight n faro m

headline n titular m

headmaster n director m

headmistress n directora f

headphones npl auriculares mpl

headquarters npl ❶ (of organization) sede f central ❷ (of army) cuartel m general

headteacher n director m, directora f

heal vb curar

health n salud f ▷ She's in good health. Tiene buena salud.

healthy adj sano ▷ a healthy diet una dieta sana

heap n montón m (pl montones)

hear vb oír ▷ We heard the dog bark. Oímos ladrar al perro. ▷ She can't hear very well. No oye bien. ▷ I heard she was ill. Me han dicho que estaba enferma.; **to hear about something** enterarse de algo ▷ I've heard about your new job. Me he enterado de que tienes un nuevo trabajo. ▷ Did you hear the good news? ¿Te has enterado de la buena noticia?; **to hear from somebody** tener noticias de alguien ▷ I haven't heard from him recently. Últimamente no tengo noticias de él.

heart n corazón m (pl corazones); **hearts** (at cards) los corazones ▷ the ace of hearts el as de corazones; **to learn something by heart** aprenderse algo de memoria

heart attack n infarto m

heartbroken adj **to be heartbroken** tener el corazón partido

heat n calor m
▶ vb calentar ▷ Heat gently for five minutes. Caliente a fuego lento durante cinco minutos.

heater n calentador m ▷ a water heater un calentador de agua; **an electric heater** una estufa eléctrica; **Could you put on the heater?** (in car) ¿Puedes poner la calefacción?

heather n brezo m

heating n calefacción f

heaven n cielo m; **to go to heaven** ir al cielo

heavy adj pesado ▷ a heavy load una carga pesada; **This bag's very heavy.** Esta bolsa pesa mucho.; **heavy rain** fuerte lluvia; **he's a heavy drinker** es un bebedor empedernido

he'd = he would; he had

hedge n seto m

hedgehog n erizo m

heel n ① (of shoe) tacón m (pl tacones) ② (of foot) talón m (pl talones)

height n ① (of person) estatura f ② (of object, mountain) altura f

held vb see **hold**

helicopter n helicóptero m

hell n infierno m; **Hell!** ¡Maldita sea!

he'll = he will; he shall

hello excl ① (when you see somebody) ¡hola! ② (on the phone) ¡dígame! (LatAm ¡aló!)

helmet n casco m

help vb ayudar ▷ Can you help me? ¿Puedes ayudarme?; **Help!** ¡Socorro!; **Help yourself!** ¡Sírvete!; **I couldn't help laughing.** No pude evitar reírme.
▶ n ayuda f ▷ Do you need any help? ¿Necesitas ayuda?

helpful adj (book, advice) útil; **You've been very helpful!** ¡Muchas gracias por su ayuda!

hen n gallina f

her adj su (pl sus) ▷ her house su casa ▷ her sisters sus hermanas

███ her is usually translated by the definite article **el/los** or **la/las** when it's clear from the sentence who the possessor is or when referring to clothing or parts of the body.

▷ They stole her car. Le robaron el coche. ▷ She took off her coat. Se quitó el abrigo. ▷ She's washing her hair. Se está lavando la cabeza.
▶ pron ① la

███ Use **la** when **her** is the direct object of the verb in the sentence.

▷ I saw her. La vi. ▷ Look at her! ¡Mírala! ② le

███ Use **le** when **her** means **to her.**

▷ I gave her a book. Le di un libro.

▷ You have to tell her the truth.
Tienes que decirle la verdad. ❸ **se**

▍Use **se** not **le** when **her** is used
　in combination with a direct-
　object pronoun.

▷ Give it to her. Dáselo. ❹ **ella**

▍Use **ella** after prepositions,
　in comparisons, and with the
　verb **to be**.

▷ I'm going with her. Voy con ella.
▷ I'm older than her. Soy mayor
que ella. ▷ It must be her. Debe de
ser ella.

herb n hierba f

here adv aquí ▷ I live here. Vivo
aquí. ▷ Here he is! ¡Aquí está!
▷ Here are the books. Aquí están
los libros.; **Here's your coffee.**
Aquí tienes el café.; **Have you
got my pen? - Here you are.**
¿Tienes mi boli? - Aquí tienes.;
**Here are the papers you asked
for.** Aquí tienes los papeles que
pediste.

hero n héroe m

heroin n heroína f; **a heroin addict**
un heroinómano

heroine n heroína f

hers pron ❶ **el suyo** (pl **los suyos**)
▷ Is this her coat? - No, hers is black.
¿Es éste su abrigo? - No, el suyo
es negro. ❷ **la suya** (pl **las suyas**)
▷ Is this her scarf? - No, hers is red.
¿Es ésta su bufanda? - No, la suya
es roja. ❸ **suyo** m (pl **suyos**) ▷ Is
that car hers? ¿Es suyo ese coche?
❹ **suya** f (pl **suyas**) ▷ Is that wallet
hers? ¿Es suya esa cartera?; **Isobel
is a friend of hers.** Isobel es amiga

suya.

▍Use **de ella** instead of **suyo** if
　you want to avoid confusion
　with "his", "theirs", etc.

▷ Whose is this? - It's hers. ¿De quién
es esto? - Es de ella.

herself pron ❶ (reflexive) **se** ▷ She's
hurt herself. Se ha hecho daño.
❷ (after preposition) **sí misma** ▷ She
talked mainly about herself. Habló
principalmente de sí misma.
❸ (for emphasis) **ella misma** ▷ She
did it herself. Lo hizo ella misma.;
by herself (alone) **sola** ▷ She came
by herself. Vino sola.

he's = he is; he has

hesitate vb dudar ▷ Don't hesitate
to ask. No dudes en preguntar.

heterosexual adj heterosexual

hi excl ¡hola!

hiccup n hipo m ▷ The baby's got
hiccups. El bebé tiene hipo.

hide vb ❶ esconder ▷ Paula hid the
present. Paula escondió el regalo.
❷ esconderse ▷ He hid behind a
bush. Se escondió detrás de un
arbusto.

hide-and-seek n **to play hide-
and-seek** jugar al escondite

hi-fi n equipo m de alta fidelidad

high adj, adv ❶ (building,
mountain) alto ▷ Prices are higher
in Germany. Los precios son
más altos en Alemania.; **How
high is the wall?** ¿Cómo es
de alto el muro? ; **The wall's two
metres high.** El muro tiene dos
metros de altura. ❷ (voice)
agudo ▷ She's got a very high voice.

Tiene la voz muy aguda.; **at high speed** a gran velocidad; **to be high** (*on drugs*) estar colocado (*informal*); **to get high** (*on drugs*) colocarse (*informal*)

higher education n enseñanza f superior

Highers npl (*in Scottish schools*) bachillerato

- Under the reformed Spanish
- Educational System, if students
- stay on at school after the age
- of 16, they can do a two-year
- course - **bachillerato**. In
- order to get in to university,
- they sit an entrance exam - **la**
- **selectividad** - in the subjects
- they have been studying for the
- **bachillerato**.

high-heeled adj **high-heeled shoes** los zapatos de tacón alto

high jump n salto m de altura

high-rise n torre f de pisos

high school n instituto m (*LatAm* liceo m)

hijack vb secuestrar

hijacker n secuestrador m, secuestradora f

hiking n **to go hiking** ir de excursión al campo

hilarious adj graciosísimo

hill n ❶ colina f ▷ *a house at the top of a hill* una casa en lo alto de una colina ❷ cuesta f ▷ *I climbed the hill up to the office.* Subí la cuesta hasta la oficina.

hill-walking n senderismo m
▷ *to go hill-walking* hacer senderismo

him pron ❶ lo
   Use **lo** when **him** is the direct object of the verb in the sentence.
   ▷ *I saw him. Lo vi.* ▷ *Look at him!* ¡Míralo! ❷ le
   Use **le** when **him** means **to him**.
   ▷ *I gave him a book. Le di un libro.* ▷ *You have to tell him the truth.* Tienes que decirle la verdad. ❸ se
   Use **se** not **le** when **him** is used in combination with a direct-object pronoun.
   ▷ *Give it to him. Dáselo.* ❹ él
   Use **él** after prepositions, in comparisons and with the verb **to be**.
   ▷ *I'm going with him.* Voy con él.
   ▷ *I'm older than him.* Soy mayor que él. ▷ *It must be him.* Debe de ser él.

himself pron ❶ (*reflexive*) se ▷ *He's hurt himself.* Se ha hecho daño.
❷ (*after preposition*) sí mismo ▷ *He talked mainly about himself.* Habló principalmente de sí mismo.
❸ (*for emphasis*) él mismo ▷ *He did it himself.* Lo hizo él mismo.; **by himself** (*alone*) solo ▷ *He came by himself.* Vino solo.

Hindu adj hindú (pl hindúes)

hint vb insinuar ▷ *He hinted that I had a good chance of getting the job.* Insinuó que tenía muchas posibilidades de conseguir el trabajo.

hip n cadera f ▷ *She put her hands on her hips.* Se puso las manos en las caderas.

hippo n hipopótamo m

hire vb ❶ alquilar ▷ We hired a car. Alquilamos un coche. ❷ contratar ▷ They hired a lawyer. Contrataron a un abogado.
▶ n alquiler m ▷ car hire el alquiler de coches; **"for hire"** "se alquila"

his adj su (pl sus) ▷ his house su casa
▷ his sisters sus hermanas

his is usually translated by the definite article **el/los** or **la/las** when it's clear from the sentence who the possessor is or when referring to clothing or parts of the body.

▷ They stole his car. Le robaron el coche. ▷ He took off his coat. Se quitó el abrigo. ▷ He's washing his hair. Se está lavando la cabeza.
▶ pron ❶ el suyo (pl los suyos) ▷ Is this his coat? - No, his is black. ¿Es éste su abrigo? - No, el suyo es negro. ❷ la suya (pl las suyas) ▷ Is this his scarf? - No, his is red. ¿Es ésta su bufanda? - No, la suya es roja. ❸ suyo m (pl suyos) ▷ Is that car his? ¿Es suyo ese coche? ❹ suya f (pl suyas) ▷ Is that wallet his? ¿Es suya esa cartera?; **Isobel is a friend of his.** Isobel es amiga suya.

Use **de él** instead of **suyo** if you want to avoid confusion with "hers", "theirs", etc.

▷ Whose is this? - It's his. ¿De quién es esto? - Es de él.

history n historia f

hit vb ❶ pegar ▷ He hit the ball. Le pegó a la bola. ▷ Andrew hit him.

Andrew le pegó. ❷ chocar con
▷ The car hit a road sign. El coche chocó con una señal de tráfico.; **He was hit by a car.** Le pilló un coche.; **to hit the target** dar en el blanco; **to hit it off with somebody** hacer buenas migas con alguien
▶ n éxito m ▷ Kylie's latest hit. El último éxito de Kylie.

hitch n contratiempo m ▷ There's been a slight hitch. Ha habido un pequeño contratiempo.

hitchhike vb hacer autostop

hitchhiker n autostopista mf

hitchhiking n autostop m

HIV n (= human immunodeficiency virus) VIH m

HIV-positive adj seropositivo

hobby n afición f (pl aficiones)

hockey n hockey m ▷ I like playing hockey. Me gusta jugar al hockey.

hold vb ❶ tener ▷ He was holding her in his arms. La tenía entre sus brazos. ❷ sujetar ▷ Hold the ladder. Sujeta la escalera. ❸ contener ▷ This bottle holds one litre. Esta botella contiene un litro.; **to hold a meeting** celebrar una reunión; **Hold the line!** (on telephone) ¡No cuelgue!; **Hold it!** ¡Espera!; **to get hold of something** hacerse con algo

hold on vb ❶ (keep hold) agarrar
▷ The cliff was slippery but he managed to hold on. El acantilado se escurría, pero logró agarrarse.; **to hold on to something** agarrarse a algo ❷ (wait) esperar

▷ Hold on, I'm coming! ¡Espera que ya voy!; **Hold on!** (on telephone) ¡No cuelgue!

hold up vb ❶ levantar ▷ Peter held up his hand. Peter levantó la mano. ❷ retrasar ▷ We were held up by the traffic. Nos retrasamos por culpa del tráfico.; **I was held up at the office.** Me entretuvieron en la oficina. ❸ atracar ▷ to hold up a bank atracar un banco

hold-up n ❶ (at gunpoint) atraco m ▷ A bank clerk was injured in the hold-up. Un empleado del banco resultó herido en el atraco. ❷ (delay) retraso m ▷ No-one explained the reason for the hold-up. Nadie explicó el motivo del retraso. ❸ (traffic) embotellamiento m ▷ a hold-up on the motorway un embotellamiento en la autopista

hole n ❶ (in general) agujero m ▷ a hole in the wall un agujero en la pared ❷ (in the ground, in golf) hoyo m ▷ to dig a hole cavar un hoyo

holiday n ❶ (vacation) vacaciones fpl ▷ the school holidays las vacaciones escolares ▷ to go on holiday irse de vacaciones ▷ to be on holiday estar de vacaciones ❷ (public holiday) día m festivo (LatAm día m feriado) ▷ Next Monday is a holiday. El lunes que viene es día festivo.

Holland n Holanda f

hollow adj hueco

holly n acebo m

holy adj ❶ santo ▷ the Holy Spirit el

Espíritu Santo ❷ sagrado ▷ a holy place un lugar sagrado

home n casa f ▷ at home en casa; **Make yourself at home.** Estás en tu casa.; **an old people's home** una residencia de ancianos ▶ adv ❶ en casa ▷ I'll be home at five o'clock. Estaré en casa a las cinco. ❷ a casa; **to get home** llegar a casa

homeless adj, n sin hogar; **homeless people** los sin techo

home match n partido m en casa

home page n página f principal

homesick adj to be homesick tener morriña

homework n deberes mpl ▷ Have you done your homework? ¿Has hecho los deberes?

homosexual adj homosexual

honest adj ❶ honrado ▷ She's a very honest person. Es una persona muy honrada. ❷ sincero ▷ Tell me your honest opinion. Dame tu sincera opinión.; **To be honest, I don't like the idea.** La verdad es que no me gusta la idea.

honestly adv francamente ▷ I honestly don't know. Francamente no lo sé.

honesty n honradez f

honey n miel f

honeymoon n luna f de miel; **to go on honeymoon** irse de luna de miel

honour (US honor) n honor m

hood n ❶ (on coat) capucha f ❷ (in US: bonnet of car) capó m

hook n ❶ (for hanging clothes)

gancho m ❸ (for hanging paintings) alcayata f ❹ (for fishing) anzuelo m; **to take the phone off the hook** descolgar el teléfono

hooligan n gamberro m, gamberra f

hooray excl ¡hurra!

Hoover® n aspiradora f

hoover vb pasar la aspiradora por ▷ He hoovered the lounge. Pasó la aspiradora por el salón.

hop vb ❶ (animal) brincar ❷ (person) ir a pata coja

hope vb esperar

> Use the subjunctive after **esperar que**.

▷ I hope he comes. Espero que venga.; **I hope so.** Espero que sí.; **I hope not.** Espero que no.
▶ n esperanza f; **to give up hope** perder la esperanza

hopefully adv **Hopefully, he'll make it in time.** Esperemos que llegue a tiempo.

> Use the subjunctive after **esperar que**.

hopeless adj **She's hopeless at maths.** Es una negada para las matemáticas.

horizon n horizonte m

horizontal adj horizontal

horn n ❶ (in car) claxon m ▷ He sounded the horn. Tocó el claxon. ❷ (instrument) trompa f ❸ (of bull) cuerno m (LatAm cacho m)

horoscope n horóscopo m

horrible adj horrible ▷ What a horrible dress! ¡Qué vestido tan horrible!

horrify vb horrorizar

horror n horror m ▷ To my horror I discovered I was locked out. Descubrí con horror que me quedé afuera sin llaves.

horror film n película f de terror

horse n caballo m

horse-racing n carreras fpl de caballos

hose n manguera f

hospital n hospital m ▷ to go into hospital ingresar en el hospital

hospitality n hospitalidad f

host n anfitrión m, anfitriona f (mpl anfitriones)

hostage n rehén m (pl rehenes); **to take somebody hostage** tomar como rehén a alguien

hot adj ❶ caliente ▷ a hot bath un baño caliente ❷ caluroso ▷ a hot country un país caluroso

> When you are talking about a person being hot, you use **tener calor**.

▷ I'm hot. Tengo calor.

> When you talk about the weather being hot, you use **hacer calor**.

▷ It's hot today. Hoy hace calor.
❸ picante ▷ Mexican food's too hot. La comida mejicana es demasiado picante.

hot dog n perrito m caliente

hotel n hotel m

hour n hora f ▷ She always takes hours to get ready. Siempre se tira horas para arreglarse.; **a quarter of an hour** un cuarto de hora; **two and a half hours** dos horas y media; **half an hour** media hora

hourly adj, adv **There are hourly buses.** Hay autobuses cada hora.; **She's paid hourly.** Le pagan por horas.

house n casa f ▷ **at his house** en su casa

housewife n ama f de casa (pl amas de casa) ▷ **She's a housewife.** Es ama de casa.

housework n tareas fpl de la casa

hovercraft n aerodeslizador m

how adv ① cómo ▷ **How are you?** ¿Cómo estás? ② qué ▷ **How strange!** ¡Qué raro!; **He told them how happy he was.** Les dijo lo feliz que era.; **How many?** ¿Cuántos?; **How much?** ¿Cuánto? ▷ **How much is it?** ¿Cuánto es? ▷ **How much sugar do you want?** ¿Cuánto azúcar quieres?; **How old are you?** ¿Cuántos años tienes?; **How far is it to Edinburgh?** ¿Qué distancia hay de aquí a Edimburgo?; **How long have you been here?** ¿Cuánto tiempo llevas aquí?; **How long does it take?** ¿Cuánto se tarda?

▌ Remember the accents on question and exclamation words **cómo**, **qué** and **cuánto**.

however conj sin embargo ▷ **This, however, isn't true.** Esto, sin embargo, no es cierto.

hug vb abrazar ▷ **They hugged each other.** Se abrazaron.
▶ n abrazo m ▷ **to give somebody a hug** dar un abrazo a alguien

huge adj enorme

hum vb tararear

human adj humano ▷ **the human body** el cuerpo humano

human being n ser m humano

humour (US **humor**) n humor m; **to have a sense of humour** tener sentido del humor

hundred num

▌ Use **cien** before nouns or before another number that is being multiplied by a hundred.

a hundred cien ▷ **a hundred people** cien personas

▌ Use **ciento** before a number that is not multiplied but simply added to a hundred.

▷ **a hundred and one** ciento uno

▌ When **hundred** follows another number, use the compound forms, which must agree with the noun.

▷ **three hundred** trescientos
▷ **five hundred people** quinientas personas ▷ **five hundred and one** quinientos uno; **hundreds of people** cientos de personas

hung vb see **hang**

Hungary n Hungría f

hunger n hambre f

▌ Although it's a feminine noun, remember that you use **el** and **un** with **hambre**.

hungry adj **to be hungry** tener hambre ▷ **I'm very hungry.** Tengo mucha hambre.

hunt vb ① cazar ▷ **They hunt foxes.** Cazan zorros.; **to go hunting** ir de caza ② (look for) buscar ▷ **The**

a b c d e f g h i j k l m n o p q r s t u v w x y z

police are hunting the killer. La policía está buscando al asesino.; **to hunt for something** buscar algo ▷ *I've hunted everywhere for that book.* He buscado ese libro por todas partes.

hunting n caza f ▷ *fox-hunting* la caza del zorro

hurricane n huracán m (pl huracanes)

hurry vb ❶ darse prisa (*LatAm* apurarse) ▷ *Hurry up!* ¡Date prisa! (*LatAm* ¡Apúrate!); **Sharon hurried back home.** Sharon volvió a casa a toda prisa.

▶ n **to be in a hurry** tener prisa (*LatAm* tener apuro); **to do something in a hurry** hacer algo a toda prisa; **There's no hurry.** No hay prisa.

hurt vb ❶ hacer daño a ▷ *You're hurting me!* ¡Me haces daño! ▷ *Have you hurt yourself?* ¿Te has hecho daño? ❷ doler ▷ *My leg hurts.* Me duele la pierna.; **Hey! That hurts!** ¡Hey! ¡Que me haces daño! ❸ (*upset*) herir ▷ *I was hurt by what he said.* Me hirió lo que dijo.

▶ adj herido ▷ *Is he badly hurt?* ¿Está herido de gravedad? ▷ *Luckily, nobody got hurt.* Por suerte, nadie salió herido.

husband n marido m

hut n cabaña f

hymn n himno m

hypermarket n hipermercado m

hyphen n guión m (pl guiones)

I pron yo ▷ *Ann and I.* Ann y yo.

▪ I generally isn't translated unless it is emphatic.

▷ *I speak Spanish.* Hablo español.

▪ Use **yo** for emphasis.

▷ *He was frightened but I wasn't.* Él estaba asustado, pero yo no.

ice n hielo m

iceberg n iceberg m (pl icebergs)

ice cream n helado m ▷ *vanilla ice cream* el helado de vainilla

ice cube n cubito m de hielo

ice hockey n hockey m sobre hielo

Iceland n Islandia f

ice rink n pista f de patinaje sobre hielo

ice-skating n patinaje m sobre hielo; **Yesterday we went ice-skating.** Ayer fuimos a patinar sobre hielo.

icing n (on cake) glaseado m; **icing sugar** el azúcar glas

icon n icono m

ICT n (= Information and Communications Technology) informática f

icy adj helado ▷ an icy wind un viento helado ▷ The roads are icy. Las carreteras están heladas.

I'd = I had; I would

idea n idea f ▷ Good idea! ¡Buena idea!

ideal adj ideal

identical adj idéntico

identification n identificación f (pl identificaciones)

identify vb identificar

identity card n carnet m de identidad

idiom n modismo m

idiot n idiota mf

idiotic adj idiota

i.e. abbr es decir

if conj si ▷ If it's fine we'll go swimming. Si hace buen tiempo, iremos a nadar.

> Use **si** with a past subjunctive to translate **if** followed by a past tense when talking about conditions.
> ▷ If you studied harder you would pass your exams. Si estudiaras más aprobarías los exámenes.; **if only** ojalá

> **ojalá** has to be followed by a verb in the subjunctive.
> ▷ If only I had more money! ¡Ojalá tuviera más dinero!; **if not** si no ▷ Are you coming? If not, I'll go with

Mark. ¿Vienes? Si no, iré con Mark.; **if so** si es así ▷ Are you coming? If so, I'll wait. ¿Vienes? Si es así te espero.; **If I were you I would go to Spain.** Yo que tú iría a España.

ignore vb **to ignore something** hacer caso omiso de algo ▷ She ignored my advice. Hizo caso omiso de mi consejo.; **to ignore somebody** ignorar a alguien ▷ She saw me, but she ignored me. Me vió, pero me ignoró completamente.; **Just ignore him!** ¡No le hagas caso!

ill adj enfermo ▷ She was taken ill. Se puso enferma.

I'll = I will

illegal adj ilegal

illness n enfermedad f

illusion n ilusión f (pl ilusiones) ▷ an optical illusion una ilusión óptica; **He was under the illusion that he would win.** Se creía que iba a ganar.

illustration n ilustración f (pl ilustraciones)

I'm = I am

image n imagen f (pl imágenes) ▷ The company has changed its image. La empresa ha cambiado de imagen.

imagination n imaginación f (pl imaginaciones) ▷ She lets her imagination run away with her. Se deja llevar por su imaginación. ▷ It's only your imagination. Son imaginaciones tuyas.

imagine vb imaginarse ▷ You can imagine how I felt! ¡Imagínate

cómo me sentí? ▷ Is he angry? - I
imagine so! ¿Está enfadado? - ¡Me
imagino que sí!

imitate vb imitar

imitation n imitación f (pl
imitaciones); **imitation leather** el
cuero de imitación

immediate adj (decision, answer,
reaction) inmediato

immediately adv
inmediatamente

immigrant n inmigrante mf

immigration n inmigración f (pl
inmigraciones)

impatience n impaciencia f

impatient adj impaciente; **to get
impatient** impacientarse ▷ People
are getting impatient. La gente se
está impacientando.

impatiently adv con impaciencia

import n importación f; **imports**
los productos de importación
▷ vb importar

importance n importancia f

important adj importante

impossible adj imposible

impress vb impresionar ▷ She's
trying to impress you. Está tratando
de impresionarte.

impressed adj impresionado
▷ I'm very impressed! ¡Estoy
impresionado!

impression n impresión f (pl
impresiones) ▷ I was under the
impression that you were going out.
Tenía la impresión de que te ibas.

impressive adj impresionante

improve vb mejorar ▷ The weather
is improving. El tiempo está

mejorando.

improvement n ① (in situation,
design) mejora f; **There's been an
improvement in his French.** Su
francés ha mejorado. ② (in health)
mejoría f

in prep, adv

There are several ways of
translating **in**. Scan the
examples to find one that is
similar to what you want to
say. For other expressions
with **in**, see the verbs **go,
come, get, give,** etc.

① en ▷ In Spain En España
▷ in hospital en el hospital ▷ in
London en Londres ▷ in spring en
primavera ▷ in May en Mayo ▷ in
1996 en mil novecientos noventa
y seis ▷ I did it in three hours. Lo
hice en tres horas. ▷ in French en
francés ▷ in a loud voice en voz alta
② de ▷ the best pupil in the class
el mejor alumno de la clase ▷ at
two o'clock in the afternoon a las
dos de la tarde ▷ the boy in the blue
shirt el muchacho de la camisa
azul ▷ dentro de ▷ I'll see you in
three weeks. Te veré dentro de tres
semanas. ④ por ▷ I always feel
sleepy in the afternoon. Siempre
tengo sueño por la tarde.; **in the
sun** al sol; **in the rain** bajo la
lluvia; **It was written in pencil.**
Estaba escrito a lápiz.; **in here**
aquí dentro ▷ It's hot in here. Aquí
dentro hace calor.; **one person
in ten** una persona de cada diez;
to be in (at home, work) estar ▷ He

wasn't in. No estaba.; **in writing** por escrito

include vb incluir ▷ Service is not included. El servicio no está incluido.

including prep **It will be two hundred pounds, including tax.** Son doscientas libras esterlinas con impuestos incluidos.

income n ingresos mpl ▷ his main source of income su principal fuente de ingresos

income tax n impuesto m sobre la renta

inconvenient adj **It's a bit inconvenient at the moment.** Me viene un poco mal en este momento.

incorrect adj incorrecto

increase n aumento m ▷ an increase in road accidents un aumento de accidentes de tráfico
▶ vb aumentar ▷ They have increased his salary. Le han aumentado el sueldo. ▷ to increase in size aumentar de tamaño

incredible adj increíble

indeed adv realmente ▷ It's very hard indeed. Es realmente difícil.; **Know what I mean? - Indeed I do.** ¿Me comprendes? - Por supuesto que sí.; **Thank you very much indeed!** ¡Muchísimas gracias!

independence n independencia f

independent adj independiente; **an independent school** un colegio privado

index n (in book) índice m alfabético

index finger n dedo m índice

India n India f

Indian adj indio
▶ n indio m, india f ▷ the Indians los indios; **American Indian** el indio americano (la india americana)

indicate vb ❶ indicar ▷ The report indicates that changes are needed. El informe indica que se necesitan cambios. ❷ (when driving) señalizar ▷ He indicated right and turned into the Gran Vía. Señalizó hacia la derecha y torció a la Gran Vía.

indicator n (in car) intermitente m

indigestion n indigestión f (pl indigestiones) ▷ I've got indigestion. Tengo indigestión.

individual adj individual
▶ n individuo m

indoor adj **an indoor swimming pool** una piscina cubierta

indoors adv dentro ▷ They're indoors. Están dentro.; **We'd better go indoors.** Es mejor que entremos.

industrial adj industrial

industrial estate n zona f industrial

industry n industria f ▷ the oil industry la industria petrolífera ▷ I'd like to work in industry. Me gustaría trabajar en la industria.; **the tourist industry** el turismo

inevitable adj inevitable

inexperienced adj inexperto

infant school n colegio m

infection n infección f (pl infecciones) ▷ an ear infection una infección de oído

infectious adj contagioso

infinitive n infinitivo m

inflation n inflación f (pl inflaciones)

influence n influencia f ▷ He's a bad influence on her. Ejerce mala influencia sobre ella.

inform vb informar ▷ Nobody informed me of the change of plan. Nadie me informó del cambio de planes.

informal adj ❶ (meeting, visit) informal ❷ (language) coloquial; **"informal dress"** "no se requiere traje de etiqueta"

information n información f (pl informaciones) ▷ Could you give me some information about trains to Barcelona? ¿Podría darme información sobre trenes a Barcelona?; **a piece of information** un dato

information office n oficina f de información

information technology n informática f

infuriating adj exasperante

ingredient n ingrediente m

inherit vb heredar ▷ She inherited her father's house. Heredó la casa de su padre.

initials npl iniciales fpl

injection n inyección f (pl inyecciones) ▷ The doctor gave me an injection. El médico me puso una inyección.

injure vb herir ▷ He injured his leg. Se hirió la pierna.

injured adj herido

injury n lesión f (pl lesiones)

ink n tinta f

in-laws npl suegros mpl

innocent adj inocente

insane adj loco

inscription n inscripción f (pl inscripciones)

insect n insecto m

insect repellent n loción f anti-insectos (pl lociones anti-insectos)

insert vb introducir ▷ I inserted the coin into the slot. Introduje la moneda en la ranura.

inside n interior m
▶ adv, prep dentro ▷ inside the house dentro de la casa; **Come inside!** ¡Entra!; **Let's go inside, it's starting to rain.** Entremos, está empezando a llover.; **inside out** al revés ▷ He put his jumper on inside out. Se puso el jersey al revés.

insist vb insistir ▷ I didn't want to, but he insisted. Yo no quería, pero él insistió. ▷ He insisted he was innocent. Insistía en que era inocente.; **to insist on doing something** insistir en hacer algo ▷ She insisted on paying. Insistió en pagar.

inspect vb inspeccionar

inspector n inspector m, inspectora f

install vb instalar

instalment n ❶ (of payment) plazo m ▷ to pay in instalments pagar a plazos ❷ (of TV, radio serial) episodio m ❸ (of publication) fascículo m

instance n **for instance** por ejemplo

instant adj inmediato ▷ It was an instant success. Fue un éxito inmediato.; **instant coffee** el café instantáneo

▶ n instante m

instantly adv al instante

instead prep, adv **instead of** en lugar de ▷ We played tennis instead of going swimming. Jugamos al tenis en lugar de ir a nadar. ▷ She went instead of Peter. En lugar de ir Peter, fue ella.; **The pool was closed, so we played tennis instead.** La piscina estaba cerrada, así que jugamos al tenis.

instinct n instinto m

instruct vb **to instruct somebody to do something** ordenar a alguien que haga algo

⏐ **ordenar que** has to be followed by a verb in the subjunctive.

▷ She instructed us to wait outside. Nos ordenó que esperáramos fuera.

instructions npl instrucciones fpl

instructor n instructor m, instructora f ▷ skiing instructor el instructor de esquí ▷ driving instructor el instructor de autoescuela

instrument n instrumento m ▷ Do you play an instrument? ¿Tocas algún instrumento?

insulin n insulina f

insult n insulto m

▶ vb insultar

insurance n seguro m ▷ his car insurance su seguro de automóvil; **an insurance policy** una póliza de seguros

intelligent adj inteligente

intend vb **to intend to do something** tener la intención de hacer algo ▷ I intend to do languages at university. Tengo la intención de estudiar idiomas en la universidad.

intensive adj intensivo

intention n intención f (pl intenciones)

interest n ❶ interés m (pl intereses) ▷ to show an interest in something mostrar interés en algo ❷ afición f (pl aficiones) ▷ My main interest is music. Mi mayor afición es la música.; **It's in your own interest to study hard.** Te conviene estudiar mucho.

▶ vb interesar ▷ It doesn't interest me. No me interesa.; **to be interested in something** estar interesado en algo ▷ I'm very interested in what you're telling me. Estoy muy interesado en lo que me dices.; **Are you interested in politics?** ¿Te interesa la política?

interesting adj interesante

interior n interior m

interior designer n diseñador m de interiores, diseñadora f de interiores

international adj internacional

internet n Internet mf ▷ on the internet en Internet

internet café n cibercafé m
internet user n internauta mf
interpreter n intérprete mf
interrupt vb interrumpir
interruption n interrupción f (pl interrupciones)
interval n intervalo m
interview n entrevista f
▶ vb entrevistar ▷ I was interviewed on the radio. Me entrevistaron en la radio.
interviewer n entrevistador m, entrevistadora f
into prep ❶ a ▷ I'm going into town. Voy a la ciudad. ▷ Translate it into Spanish. Tradúcelo al español. ❷ en ▷ I poured the milk into a cup. Vertí la leche en una taza.; **to walk into a lamppost** tropezar con una farola
introduce vb presentar ▷ He introduced me to his parents. Me presentó a sus padres.
introduction n (in book) introducción f (pl introducciones)
invade vb invadir
invalid n inválido m, inválida f
invent vb inventar
invention n invento m
investigation n investigación f (pl investigaciones)
invisible adj invisible
invitation n invitación f (pl invitaciones)
invite vb invitar ▷ You're invited to a party at Claire's house. Estás invitado a una fiesta en casa de Claire.
involve vb suponer ▷ It involves

a lot of work. Supone mucho trabajo.; **He wasn't involved in the robbery.** No estuvo implicado en el robo.; **She was involved in politics.** Estaba metida en política.; **to be involved with somebody** tener una relación con alguien ▷ She was involved with a married man. Tenía una relación con un hombre casado.; **I don't want to get involved in the argument.** No quiero meterme en la discusión.
Iran n Irán m
Iraq n Iraq m
Ireland n Irlanda f
Irish n (language) irlandés m; **the Irish** (people) los irlandeses
▶ adj irlandés (f irlandesa) (mpl irlandeses)
Irishman n irlandés m (pl irlandeses)
Irishwoman n irlandesa f
iron n ❶ (for clothes) plancha f ❷ (metal) hierro m
▶ vb planchar
ironing n **to do the ironing** planchar; **I hate ironing.** No me gusta nada planchar.
ironing board n tabla f de planchar
irresponsible adj irresponsable ▷ That was irresponsible of him. Eso fue irresponsable por su parte.
irritating adj irritante
is vb see **be**
Islam n Islam m
Islamic adj islámico ▷ Islamic law la

ley islámica

island n isla f

isle n **the Isle of Wight** la Isla de Wight

isn't = **is not**

isolated adj aislado

Israel n Israel m

issue n ❶ tema m

> Although **tema** ends in **-a**, it is actually a masculine noun.

▷ a controversial issue un tema polémico ❷ (magazine) número m ▷ a back issue un número atrasado ▶ vb ❶ hacer público ▷ The minister issued a statement yesterday. El ministro hizo pública una declaración ayer. ❸ (equipment, supplies) proporcionar

IT n (= information technology) informática f

it pron

> When **it** is the subject of a sentence it is practically never translated.

▷ Where's my book? - It's on the table. ¿Dónde está mi libro? - Está sobre la mesa. ▷ It's raining. Está lloviendo. ▷ It's six o'clock. Son las seis. ▷ It's Friday tomorrow. Mañana es viernes. ▷ It's expensive. Es caro. ▷ Who is it? - It's me. ¿Quién es? - Soy yo.

> When **it** is the direct object of the verb in a sentence, use **lo** if it stands for a masculine noun or **la** if it stands for a feminine noun.

▷ There's a croissant left. Do you want it? Queda un croissant. ¿Lo quieres? ▷ It's a good film. Have you seen it? Es una buena película. ¿La has visto?

> Use **le** when **it** is the indirect object of the verb in the sentence.

▷ Give it another coat of paint. Dale otra mano de pintura.

> For general concepts use the word **ello**.

▷ I spoke to him about it. Hablé con él sobre ello. ▷ I'm against it. Estoy en contra de ello.

Italian adj italiano

▶ n ❶ (person) italiano m, italiana f ▷ the Italians los italianos ❷ (language) italiano m

italics npl cursiva f ▷ in italics en cursiva

Italy n Italia f

itch vb picar ▷ It itches. Me pica. ▷ My head is itching. Me pica la cabeza.

itchy adj I've got an itchy nose. Me pica la nariz.

it'd = **it had; it would**

item n ❶ (on list) artículo m ▷ The first item he bought was an alarm clock. El primer artículo que compró fue un despertador. ❷ (on bill) partida f; **an item of news** una noticia; **an item of clothing** una prenda; **a collector's item** una pieza de colección

it'll = **it will**

its adj su (pl sus) ▷ Everything in its place. Cada cosa en su sitio. ▷ It has

its advantages. Tiene sus ventajas.
Its is usually translated by
the definite article **el/los** or
la/las when it's clear from the
sentence who the possessor is
or when referring to clothing
or parts of the body.
▷ *The dog is losing its hair.* El perro
está perdiendo el pelo. ▷ *The bird
was in its cage.* El pájaro estaba
en la jaula.

it's = **it is**; **it has**

itself *pron* (reflexive) <u>se</u> ▷ *The dog
scratched itself.* El perro se rascó.;
**The lesson itself was easy but
the homework was difficult.**
La clase en sí fue fácil, pero les
deberes eran difíciles.

I've = **I have**

j

jack *n* ❶ (*in ordinary pack of cards*)
jota *f* ❷ (*in Spanish pack of cards*)
sota *f*

jacket *n* chaqueta *f*; **jacket
potatoes** las patatas asadas con
piel (*LatAm* las papas asadas con
cáscara)

jail *n* cárcel *f* ▷ *to go to jail* ir a la
cárcel
▶ *vb* **He was jailed for ten years.**
Lo condenaron a diez años de
cárcel.

jam *n* mermelada *f* ▷ *strawberry jam*
la mermelada de fresas; **a traffic
jam** un atasco

jammed *adj* atascado ▷ *The
window's jammed.* La ventana está
atascada.

janitor *n* conserje *mf* ▷ *He's a
janitor.* Es conserje.

January n enero ▷ in January en enero ▷ the January sales las rebajas de enero

Japan n Japón m

Japanese adj japonés (f japonesa) (mpl japoneses)
▶ n ❶ (person) japonés m, japonesa f ▷ the Japanese los japoneses ❷ (language) japonés m

jar n tarro m ▷ a jar of honey un tarro de miel

javelin n jabalina f

jaw n mandíbula f

jazz n jazz m

jealous adj celoso ▷ to be jealous estar celoso

jeans npl vaqueros mpl ▷ a pair of jeans unos vaqueros

Jello® n (in US) gelatina f

jelly n gelatina f

jellyfish n medusa f

jersey n jersey m (pl jerseys)

Jesus n Jesús

Jew n judío m, judía f

jewel n joya f

jeweller (US jeweler) n joyero m, joyera f ▷ She's a jeweller. Es joyera.

jeweller's shop (US jeweler's shop) n joyería f

jewellery (US jewelry) n joyas fpl

Jewish adj judío

jigsaw n rompecabezas m (pl rompecabezas)

job n trabajo m ▷ a part-time job un trabajo de media jornada; You've done a good job. Lo has hecho muy bien.

job centre n oficina f de empleo

jobless adj desempleado

jockey n jockey mf (pl jockeys)

jog vb hacer footing

jogging n footing m ▷ to go jogging hacer footing

join vb hacerse socio de ▷ I'm going to join the ski club. Voy a hacerme socio del club de esquí.; I'll join you later if I can. Yo iré luego si puedo.; If you're going for a walk, do you mind if I join you? Si vais a dar un paseo, ¿os importa que os acompañe?

join in vb He doesn't join in with what we do. No participa en lo que hacemos.; She started singing, and the audience joined in. Empezó a cantar, y el público se unió a ella.

joiner n carpintero m, carpintera f ▷ He's a joiner. Es carpintero.

joint n ❶ articulación f (pl articulaciones) ▷ I've got pains in my joints. Me duelen las articulaciones. ❷ (drugs: informal) porro m; We had a joint of lamb for lunch. Comimos asado de cordero.

joke n ❶ broma f ▷ Don't get upset, it was only a joke. No te enfades, era sólo una broma.; to play a joke on somebody gastarle una broma a alguien ❷ chiste m; to tell a joke contar un chiste
▶ vb bromear; You must be joking! ¡Estás de broma!

jolly adj alegre

Jordan n Jordania f

jotter n bloc m (pl blocs)

journalism n periodismo m

a
b
c
d
e
f
g
h
i
j
k
l
m
n
o
p
q
r
s
t
u
v
w
x
y
z

journalist n periodista mf ▷ I'm a journalist. Soy periodista.

journey n viaje m ▷ to go on a journey hacer un viaje; **The journey to school takes about half an hour.** Se tarda una media hora en ir al colegio.

joy n alegría f

joystick n (for computer games) mando m

judge n juez mf (pl jueces)
▶ vb juzgar

judo n judo m ▷ My favourite sport is judo. Mi deporte favorito es el judo.

jug n jarra f

juggle vb hacer juegos malabares

juice n zumo m ▷ orange juice el zumo de naranja

July n julio m ▷ in July en julio

jumble sale n mercadillo m benéfico

jump vb saltar ▷ They jumped over the wall. Saltaron el muro. ▷ He jumped out of the window. Saltó por la ventana. ▷ He jumped off the roof. Saltó del tejado.; **You made me jump!** ¡Qué susto me has dado!

jumper n jersey m (pl jerseys)

junction n (of roads) cruce m

June n junio m ▷ in June en junio

jungle n selva f

junior school n colegio m

junk n trastos mpl viejos ▷ The attic's full of junk. El desván está lleno de trastos viejos.; **to eat junk food** comer porquerías; **junk shop** la tienda de objetos usados

jury n jurado m

just adv ❶ justo ▷ just in time justo a tiempo ▷ just after Christmas justo después de Navidad ▷ We had just enough money. Teníamos el dinero justo.; **He's just arrived.** Acaba de llegar.; **I did it just now.** Lo acabo de hacer.; **I'm rather busy just now.** Ahora mismo estoy bastante ocupada.; **I'm just coming!** ¡Ya voy!; **just here** aquí mismo ❷ sólo ▷ It's just a suggestion. Es sólo una sugerencia.; **Just a minute!** ¡Un momento!; **just about** casi ▷ It's just about finished. Está casi terminado.

justice n justicia f

k

kangaroo n canguro m

karaoke n karaoke m

karate n kárate m

kebab n pincho m moruno

keen adj entusiasta ▷ a keen supporter un hincha entusiasta; **He doesn't seem very keen.** No parece muy entusiasmado.; **She's a keen student.** Es una alumna aplicada.; **I'm not very keen on maths.** No me gustan mucho las matemáticas.; **He's keen on her.** Ella le gusta.; **to be keen on doing something** tener ganas de hacer algo ▷ I'm not very keen on going. No tengo muchas ganas de ir.

keep vb ① quedarse con ▷ You can keep the watch. Puedes quedarte con el reloj.; **You can keep it.** Puedes quedártelo.

② (remain) mantenerse ▷ to keep fit mantenerse en forma; **Keep still!** ¡Estáte quieto!; **Keep quiet!** ¡Cállate! ③ seguir ▷ Keep straight on. Siga recto.; **I keep forgetting my keys.** Siempre me olvido las llaves.; **"keep out"** "prohibida la entrada"; **"keep off the grass"** "prohibido pisar el césped"

keep on vb continuar ▷ He kept on reading. Continuó leyendo.; **The car keeps on breaking down.** El coche no deja de averiarse.

keep up vb **Matthew walks so fast I can't keep up.** Matthew camina tan rápido que no puedo seguirle el ritmo.

keep-fit n gimnasia f ▷ I go to keep-fit classes. Voy a clases de gimnasia.

kept vb see **keep**

ketchup n salsa f de tomate

kettle n hervidor m

key n llave f

keyboard n teclado m

kick n patada f
▶ vb **to kick somebody** dar una patada a alguien ▷ He kicked me. Me dio una patada.; **He kicked the ball hard.** Le dio un puntapié fuerte al balón.; **to kick off** (in football) hacer el saque inicial

kick-off n saque m inicial ▷ The kick-off is at 10 o'clock. El partido empieza a las diez.

kid n (informal) crío m, cría f; **the kids** los críos
▶ vb bromear ▷ I'm not kidding, it's snowing. No estoy bromeando,

está nevando.; **I'm just kidding.** Es una broma.

kidnap vb secuestrar

kidney n riñón m (pl riñones)

kill vb matar ▷ *She killed her husband.* Mató a su marido.; **to be killed** morir ▷ *He was killed in a car accident.* Murió en un accidente de coche.; **to kill oneself** suicidarse ▷ *He killed himself.* Se suicidó.

killer n (murderer) asesino m, asesina f

kilo n kilo m ▷ *at £5 a kilo* a 5 libras esterlinas el kilo

kilometre (US **kilometer**) n kilómetro m

kilt n falda f escocesa

kind adj amable ▷ *to be kind to somebody* ser amable con alguien; **Thank you for being so kind.** Gracias por su amabilidad.
▶ n tipo m ▷ *It's a kind of sausage.* Es un tipo de salchicha.

kindness n amabilidad f

king n rey m; **the King and Queen** los reyes

kingdom n reino m

kiosk n (stall) quiosco m; **a telephone kiosk** una cabina telefónica

kiss n beso m
▶ vb ❶ besar ▷ *He kissed her passionately.* La besó apasionadamente. ❷ besarse ▷ *They kissed.* Se besaron.

kit n equipo m ▷ *I've forgotten my gym kit.* Me he olvidado el equipo de gimnasia.; **a tool kit** un juego de herramientas; **a sewing kit**

un costurero; **a first-aid kit** un botiquín; **a puncture repair kit** un juego de reparación de pinchazos; **a drum kit** una batería

kitchen n cocina f; **a kitchen knife** un cuchillo de cocina

kite n cometa f

kitten n gatito m, gatita f

kiwi n kiwi m

knee n rodilla f ▷ **to be on one's knees** estar de rodillas

kneel vb arrodillarse

knew vb see **know**

knickers npl bragas fpl (LatAm calzones mpl); **a pair of knickers** unas bragas (LatAm unos calzones)

knife n cuchillo m

knit vb hacer punto (LatAm tejer) ▷ *I like knitting.* Me gusta hacer punto. (LatAm Me gusta tejer.); **She is knitting a jumper.** Está haciendo un jersey a punto.

knives npl see **knife**

knob n ❶ (on door) pomo m ❷ (on radio, TV) dial m

knock vb llamar ▷ *Someone's knocking at the door.* Alguien llama a la puerta.; **to knock somebody down** atropellar a alguien ▷ *She was knocked down by a car.* La atropelló un coche.; **to knock somebody out** (1) (defeat) eliminar a alguien ▷ *They were knocked out early in the tournament.* Fueron eliminados al poco de iniciarse el torneo. (2) (stun) dejar sin sentido a alguien ▷ *They knocked out the watchman.* Dejaron al vigilante sin sentido.

▶ *n* golpe *m*

knot *n* nudo *m* ▷ *to tie a knot in something* hacer un nudo en algo

know *vb*

Use **saber** for knowing facts, **conocer** for knowing people and places.

❶ saber ▷ *Yes, I know.* Sí, ya lo sé. ▷ *I don't know.* No sé. ▷ *I don't know any German.* No sé nada de alemán.; **to know that** saber que ▷ *I didn't know that your Dad was a policeman.* No sabía que tu padre era policía. ❷ conocer ▷ *I know her.* La conozco.; **to know about something (1)** (*be aware of*) estar enterado de algo ▷ *Do you know about the meeting this afternoon?* ¿Estás enterado de la reunión de esta tarde? **(2)** (*be knowledgeable about*) saber de algo ▷ *He knows a lot about cars.* Sabe mucho de coches. ▷ *I don't know much about computers.* No sé mucho de ordenadores.; **to get to know somebody** llegar a conocer a alguien; **How should I know?** ¿Y yo qué sé?; **You never know!** ¡Nunca se sabe!

knowledge *n* conocimiento *m* ▷ *scientific knowledge* el conocimiento científico; **my knowledge of French** mis conocimientos de francés

known *vb see* **know**

Koran *n* Corán *m*

Korea *n* Corea *f*

kosher *adj* kosher

lab *n* laboratorio *m* ▷ *a lab technician* un técnico de laboratorio

label *n* etiqueta *f*

labor *n* (*in US*) **to be in labor** estar de parto; **the labor market** el mercado de trabajo; **labor union** el sindicato

laboratory *n* laboratorio *m*

Labour *n* laboristas *mpl* ▷ *My parents vote Labour.* Mis padres votan a los laboristas.; **the Labour Party** el Partido Laborista

labour *n* **to be in labour** estar de parto

lace *n* ❶ (*of shoe*) cordón *m* (*pl* cordones) ❷ encaje *m* ▷ *a lace collar* un cuello de encaje

lad *n* muchacho *m*

ladder *n* escalera *f*

lady *n* señora *f*; **Ladies and**

gentlemen… Damas y caballeros…; **the ladies'** los servicios de señoras; **a young lady** una señorita

ladybird n mariquita f

lager n cerveza f rubia

laid vb see **lay**

laid-back adj relajado (informal)

lain vb see **lie**

lake n lago m ▷ Lake Michigan el Lago Michigan

lamb n cordero m ▷ a lamb chop una chuleta de cordero

lamp n lámpara f

lamppost n farola f

lampshade n pantalla f

land n tierra f ▷ We have a lot of land. Tenemos mucha tierra.; **a piece of land** un terreno

▶ vb aterrizar ▷ The plane landed at five o'clock. El avión aterrizó a las cinco.

landing n ❶ (of plane) aterrizaje m ❷ (of staircase) rellano m

landlady n ❶ (of rented property) casera f ❷ (of pub) patrona f

landlord n ❶ (of rented property) casero m ❷ (of pub) patrón m (pl patrones)

landscape n paisaje m

lane n ❶ (in country) camino m ▷ a country lane un camino rural ❷ (carriageway) carril m ▷ the outside lane (in the UK) el carril de la derecha

language n idioma m

> Although **idioma** ends in -a, it is actually a masculine noun.
> ▷ Greek is a difficult language. El

griego es un idioma difícil.; **to use bad language** decir palabrotas

language laboratory n laboratorio m de idiomas

lap n vuelta f ▷ I ran 10 laps. Corrí 10 vueltas.; **Andrew was sitting on his mother's lap.** Andrew estaba sentado en el regazo de su madre.

laptop n ordenador m portátil (LatAm computador m portátil)

large adj grande ▷ a large house una casa grande

> Use **gran** before a singular noun.
> ▷ a large number of people un gran número de personas
> Be careful not to translate **large** by largo.

laser n láser m

last adj, adv ❶ pasado ▷ last Friday el viernes pasado ❷ último ▷ the last time la última vez ▷ por última vez ▷ I've lost my bag. - When did you last see it? He perdido el bolso. - ¿Cuándo lo viste por última vez? ❸ en último lugar ▷ the team which finished last el equipo que quedó en último lugar; **He arrived last.** Llegó el último.; **last night** anoche ▷ I couldn't sleep last night. Anoche no pude dormir.; **at last** por fin

▶ vb durar ▷ The concert lasts two hours. El concierto dura dos horas.

lastly adv por último

late adj, adv tarde ▷ I'm often late for school. A menudo llego tarde al colegio. ▷ I went to bed late. Me fui a la cama tarde.; **The flight will**

be one hour late. El vuelo llegará con una hora de retraso.; **in the late afternoon** al final de la tarde; **in late May** a finales de mayo; **the late Mr Philips** el difunto Sr. Philips

lately adv últimamente ▷ I haven't seen him lately. No lo he visto últimamente.

later adv más tarde ▷ I'll do it later. Lo haré más tarde.; **See you later!** ¡Hasta luego!

latest adj último ▷ their latest album su último álbum; **at the latest** como muy tarde ▷ by 10 o'clock at the latest a las 10 como muy tarde

Latin n latín m ▷ I do Latin. Estudio latín.

Latin America n América f Latina

Latin American adj latinoamericano
▶ n latinoamericano m, latinoamericana f

laugh n risa f; **It was a good laugh.** Fue muy divertido.
▶ vb reírse; **to laugh at something** reírse de algo ▷ He laughed at my accent. Se rió de mi acento.; **to laugh at somebody** reírse de alguien ▷ They laughed at her. Se rieron de ella.

launch vb (product, rocket) lanzar

Launderette® n lavandería f automática

Laundromat® n (in US) lavandería f automática

laundry n colada f ▷ She does my laundry. Me hace la colada.

lavatory n servicio m

lavender n lavanda f

law n ❶ ley f ▷ strict laws leyes severas; **It's against the law.** Es ilegal. ❷ derecho m ▷ My sister's studying law. Mi hermana estudia derecho.

lawn n césped m

lawnmower n cortacésped m

lawyer n abogado m, abogada f ▷ My mother's a lawyer. Mi madre es abogada.

lay vb poner ▷ She laid the baby in his cot. Puso al bebé en la cuna. ▷ to lay the table poner la mesa

lay-by n área m de descanso

Although it's a feminine noun, remember that you use **el** and **un** with **área**.

layer n capa f

lazy adj perezoso

lead n

This word has two pronunciations. Make sure you choose the right translation.

❶ (metal) plomo m ▷ a lead pipe una tubería de plomo ❷ (cable) cable m ❸ correa f ▷ Dogs must be kept on a lead. Los perros deben llevarse siempre sujetos con una correa.; **to be in the lead** ir en cabeza
▶ vb llevar ▷ the street that leads to the station la calle que lleva a la estación ▷ It could lead to a civil war. Podría llevar a una guerra civil.; **to lead the way** ir delante

leader n líder mf

lead-free petrol n gasolina f
sin plomo

lead singer n cantante mf
principal

leaf n hoja f

leaflet n folleto m

league n liga f ▷ *They are at the top
of the league.* Están a la cabeza de
la liga.; **the Premier League** la
primera división

leak n ❶ (of gas, chemical) escape m
▷ *a gas leak* un escape de gas ❷ (in
roof) gotera f
▶ vb ❶ (bucket, pipe) tener un
agujero ❷ (roof) tener goteras
❸ (water, gas) salirse

lean vb apoyar ▷ *to lean something
against the wall* apoyar algo contra
la pared; **to lean on something**
apoyarse en algo ▷ *He leant on the
table.* Se apoyó en la mesa.; **to be
leaning against something** estar
apoyado contra algo ▷ *The ladder
was leaning against the wall.* La
escalera estaba apoyada contra la
pared.

lean forward vb inclinarse hacia
adelante

lean out vb asomarse ▷ *She leant
out of the window.* Se asomó a la
ventana.

leap year n año m bisiesto

learn vb aprender ▷ *I'm learning to
ski.* Estoy aprendiendo a esquiar.

learner n **She's a quick learner.**
Aprende con mucha rapidez.

learner driver n conductor m
en prácticas, conductora f en
prácticas

learnt vb see learn

least adj, pron, adv ❶ menor ▷ *I
haven't the least idea.* No tengo la
menor idea. ❷ menos ▷ *the least
expensive hotel* el hotel menos
caro ▷ *It's the least I can do.* Es lo
menos que puedo hacer. ▷ *Maths
is the subject I like the least.* Las
matemáticas es la asignatura
que menos me gusta. ▷ *That's the
least of my worries.* Eso es lo que
menos me preocupa.; **at least**
por lo menos ▷ *It'll cost at least
£200.* Costará por lo menos 200
libras esterlinas.; **There was a
lot of damage but at least
nobody was hurt.** Hubo muchos
daños pero al menos nadie
resultó herido.

leather n cuero m ▷ *a black leather
jacket* una chaqueta de cuero
negra

leave n (from job, army) permiso m
▷ *My brother is on leave for a week.*
Mi hermano está de permiso
durante una semana.
▶ vb ❶ dejar ▷ *Don't leave your
camera in the car.* No dejes la
cámara en el coche. ❷ salir ▷ *The
bus leaves at eight.* El autobús sale
a las ocho. ❸ salir de ▷ *We leave
London at six o'clock.* Salimos de
Londres a las seis. ❹ irse ▷ *They
left yesterday.* Se fueron ayer. ▷ *She
left home when she was sixteen.* Se
fue de casa a los dieciséis años.;
to leave somebody alone dejar
a alguien en paz ▷ *Leave me alone!*
¡Déjame en paz!

leave behind vb dejarse ▷ *I left my umbrella behind in the shop.* Me dejé el paraguas en la tienda.

leave out vb excluir ▷ *Not knowing the language I felt really left out.* Al no saber el idioma me sentía muy excluido.

leaves npl see **leaf**

Lebanon n Líbano m

lecture n ❶ (at university) clase f ❷ (public) conferencia f
▶ vb ❶ dar clases ▷ *She lectures at the technical college.* Da clases en la escuela politécnica. ❷ sermonear ▷ *He's always lecturing us.* Siempre nos está sermoneando.

lecturer n profesor m universitario, profesora f universitaria ▷ *She's a lecturer in German.* Es profesora de alemán en la universidad.

led vb see **lead**

leek n puerro m

left vb see **leave**
▶ adj, adv ❶ izquierdo ▷ *my left hand* mi mano izquierda ❷ a la izquierda ▷ *Turn left at the traffic lights.* Doble a la izquierda al llegar al semáforo.; **I haven't got any money left.** No me queda nada de dinero.; **Is there any ice cream left?** ¿Queda algo de helado?
▶ n izquierda f ▷ *on the left* a la izquierda

left-hand adj **It's on the left-hand side.** Está a la izquierda.

left-handed adj zurdo

left-luggage office n consigna f

leg n pierna f ▷ *She's broken her leg.* Se ha roto la pierna.; **a chicken leg** un muslo de pollo; **a leg of lamb** una pierna de cordero

legal adj legal

leggings n mallas fpl

leisure n tiempo m libre ▷ *What do you do in your leisure time?* ¿Qué haces en tu tiempo libre?

leisure centre n centro m recreativo

lemon n limón m (pl limones)

lemonade n gaseosa f

lend vb prestar ▷ *I can lend you some money.* Te puedo prestar algo de dinero.

length n longitud f; **It's about a metre in length.** Mide aproximadamente un metro de largo.

lens n ❶ (contact lens) lentilla f (LatAm lente m de contacto) ❷ (of spectacles) cristal m ❸ (of camera) objetivo m

Lent n Cuaresma f

lent vb see **lend**

lentil n lenteja f

Leo n (sign) Leo m; **I'm Leo.** Soy leo.

leotard n leotardo m

lesbian n lesbiana f

less adj, pron, adv menos ▷ *It's less than a kilometre from here.* Está a menos de un kilómetro de aquí. ▷ *I've got less than you.* Tengo menos que tú. ▷ *It cost less than we thought.* Costó menos de lo que pensábamos.; **less and less** cada vez menos

lesson n ❶ clase f ▷ an English lesson una clase de inglés ❷ (in textbook) lección f (pl lecciones)

let vb dejar; **to let somebody do something** dejar a alguien hacer algo ▷ Let me have a look. Déjame ver.; **Let me go!** ¡Suéltame!; **to let somebody know something** informar a alguien de algo ▷ We must let him know that we are coming to stay. Tenemos que informarle de que venimos a quedarnos.; **When can you come to dinner? - I'll let you know.** ¿Cuándo puedes venir a cenar? - Ya te lo diré.; **to let in** dejar entrar ▷ They wouldn't let me in because I was under 18. No me dejaron entrar porque tenía menos de 18 años.

> To make suggestions using **let's**, you can ask questions using **por qué no**.

▷ Let's go to the cinema! ¿Por qué no vamos al cine?; **Let's have a break! - Yes, let's.** Vamos a descansar un poco. - ¡Buena idea! ❷ alquilar ▷ "to let" "se alquila"

let down vb defraudar ▷ I won't let you down. No te defraudaré.

letter n ❶ carta f ▷ She wrote me a long letter. Me escribió una carta larga. ❷ letra f ▷ A is the first letter of the alphabet. La "a" es la primera letra del alfabeto.

letterbox n buzón m (pl buzones)

lettuce n lechuga f

leukaemia n leucemia f ▷ He suffers from leukaemia. Tiene leucemia.

level adj llano ▷ a level surface una superficie llana

▶ n nivel m ▷ The level of the river is rising. El nivel del río está subiendo.

level crossing n paso m a nivel

lever n palanca f

liar n mentiroso m, mentirosa f

liberal adj (view, system) liberal; **the Liberal Democrats** los demócratas liberales

Libra n (sign) Libra f; **I'm Libra.** Soy Libra.

librarian n bibliotecario m, bibliotecaria f ▷ I'm a librarian. Soy bibliotecaria.

library n biblioteca f

> Be careful not to translate **library** by librería.

Libya n Libia f

licence n (US license) n permiso m; **a driving licence** un carnet de conducir; **a television licence** licencia que se paga por el uso del televisor (destinada a financiar la BBC)

lick vb lamer

lid n tapa f

lie n mentira f; **to tell a lie** mentir ▷ I know she's lying. Sé que está mintiendo. ▷ You lied to me! ¡Me mentiste! ❷ tumbarse; **He was lying on the sofa.** Estaba tumbado en el sofá.

lie down vb acostarse ▷ Why not go and lie down for a bit? ¿Por qué

no vas a acostarte un rato?; **to be
lying down** estar tendido

lie-in n **to have a lie-in** quedarse
en la cama hasta tarde

lieutenant n teniente mf

life n vida f

lifebelt n salvavidas m (pl
salvavidas)

lifeboat n bote m salvavidas (pl
botes salvavidas)

lifeguard n socorrista mf

life jacket n chaleco m salvavidas
(pl chalecos salvavidas)

lifestyle n estilo m de vida

lift vb levantar ▷ It's too heavy, I can't
lift it. Pesa mucho, no lo puedo
levantar.
▶ n ascensor m ▷ The lift isn't
working. El ascensor no funciona.;
He gave me a lift to the cinema.
Me acercó al cine en coche.;
Would you like a lift? ¿Quieres
que te lleve en coche?

light adj ① (not heavy) ligero ▷ a
light jacket una chaqueta ligera
② (colour) claro ▷ a light blue
sweater un jersey azul claro
▶ n luz f (pl luces) ▷ He switched
on the light. Encendió la luz.; **the
traffic lights** el semáforo; **Have
you got a light?** ¿Tienes fuego?
▶ vb encender

light bulb n bombilla f

lighter n mechero m

lighthouse n faro m

lightning n relámpago m
▷ thunder and lightning truenos y
relámpagos ▷ a flash of lightning
un relámpago

like vb

The most common translation
for **to like** when talking
about things and activities is
gustar. Remember that the
construction is the opposite
of English, with the thing you
like being the subject of the
sentence.

▷ I don't like mustard. No me gusta
la mostaza. ▷ Do you like apples?
¿Te gustan las manzanas? ▷ I like
riding. Me gusta montar a caballo.;
I like him. Me cae bien.; **I'd like...**
quería... ▷ I'd like this blouse in size
10, please. Quería esta blusa en
la talla 10, por favor.; **I'd like an
orange juice, please.** Un zumo de
naranja, por favor.; **I'd like to...** Me
gustaría... ▷ I'd like to go to China.
Me gustaría ir a China.

To ask someone if they would
like something, or like to do
something, use **querer**.

▷ Would you like some coffee?
¿Quieres café? ▷ Would you like to
go for a walk? ¿Quieres ir a dar un
paseo?; **... if you like** ... si quieres
▶ prep como ▷ a city like Paris una
ciudad como París

When asking questions, use
cómo instead of **como**.

▷ What was his house like? ¿Cómo
era su casa?; **What's the weather
like?** ¿Qué tiempo hace?; **It's a bit
like salmon.** Se parece un poco
al salmón.; **It's fine like that.** Así
está bien.; **Do it like this.** Hazlo
así.; **something like that** algo así

likely adj probable ▷ That's not very likely. Es poco probable.

es probable que has to be followed by a verb in the subjunctive.

▷ She's likely to come. Es probable que venga. ▷ She's not likely to come. Es probable que no venga.

lime n (fruit) lima f

limit n límite m ▷ The speed limit is el límite de velocidad

limp vb cojear

line n ❶ (on page) línea f ▷ a straight line una línea recta ❷ (of people) fila f; **railway line** la vía férrea; **Hold the line, please.** No cuelgue, por favor.; **It's a very bad line.** Se oye muy mal.

linen n lino m ▷ a linen jacket una chaqueta de lino

link n ❶ relación f (pl relaciones) ▷ The link between smoking and cancer la relación entre el tabaco y el cáncer; **cultural links** los lazos culturales ❷ (computing) enlace m ▶ vb ❶ (facts) asociar ❷ (towns, terminals) conectar

lion n león m (pl leones)

lip n labio m

lip-read vb leer los labios

lipstick n lápiz m de labios (pl lápices de labios)

liquid n líquido m

liquidizer n licuadora f

Lisbon n Lisboa f

list n lista f ▶ vb ❶ (in writing) hacer una lista de ❷ (verbally) enumerar

listen vb escuchar ▷ Listen to this!

¡Escucha esto! ▷ Listen to me! ¡Escúchame!

lit vb see **light**

liter n (in US) litro m

literature n literatura f

litre n litro m

litter n basura f

litter bin n cubo m de la basura

little adj, pron pequeño ▷ a little girl una niña pequeña; **a little** un poco ▷ How much would you like? - Just a little. ¿Cuánto quiere? - Sólo un poco.; **very little** muy poco ▷ We've got very little time. Tenemos muy poco tiempo.; **little by little** poco a poco

live adj vivo ▷ I'm against tests on live animals. Estoy en contra de los experimentos en animales vivos.; **a live broadcast** una emisión en directo; **a live concert** un concierto en vivo ▶ vb vivir ▷ Where do you live? ¿Dónde vives? ▷ I live in Edinburgh. Vivo en Edimburgo.

live together vb vivir juntos

lively adj (person, personality) alegre

liver n hígado m

lives npl see **life**

living n **to make a living** ganarse la vida; **What does she do for a living?** ¿A qué se dedica?

living room n sala f de estar

lizard n ❶ (small) lagartija f ❷ (big) lagarto m

load n **loads of** un montón de (informal) ▷ They've got loads of money. Tienen un montón de dinero.; **You're talking a load**

of rubbish! ¡Lo que dices es una estupidez!
▶ **vb** cargar ▷ *a trolley loaded with luggage* un carrito cargado de equipaje

loaf n pan m; **a loaf of bread** (1) (French bread) una barra de pan (2) (baked in tin) un pan de molde

loan n préstamo m
▶ **vb** prestar

loaves npl see **loaf**

lobster n langosta f

local adj local ▷ *the local paper* el periódico local; **a local call** una llamada urbana

loch n lago m

lock n cerradura f
▶ **vb** cerrar con llave ▷ *Make sure you lock your door.* No te olvides de cerrar tu puerta con llave.

lock out vb **I was locked out.** (without keys) Me quedé fuera sin llaves.

locker n taquilla f ▷ *left-luggage lockers* las taquillas de consigna; **locker room** el vestuario

lodger n inquilino m, inquilina f

loft n desván m (pl desvanes)

log n leño m

log in vb entrar en el sistema

log off vb salir del sistema

log on vb entrar en el sistema; **to log on to the Net** conectarse a la Red

log out (of computer) vb salir del sistema

logical adj lógico

lollipop n pirulí m (pl pirulís)

London n Londres m

Londoner n londinense mf

loneliness n soledad f

lonely adj solo ▷ *I sometimes feel lonely.* A veces me siento solo.; **a lonely cottage** una casita aislada

long adj, adv largo ▷ *She's got long hair.* Tiene el pelo largo. ▷ *The room is six metres long.* La habitación tiene seis metros de largo.; **a long time** mucho tiempo ▷ *It takes a long time.* Lleva mucho tiempo.; **How long?** (time) ¿Cuánto tiempo? ▷ *How long have you been here?* ¿Cuánto tiempo llevas aquí? ▷ *How long will it take?* ¿Cuánto tiempo llevará?; **How long is the flight?** ¿Cuánto dura el vuelo?; **as long as** siempre que

> **siempre que** has to be followed by a verb in the subjunctive.

▷ *I'll come as long as it's not too expensive.* Iré siempre que no sea demasiado caro.
▶ **vb** **to long to do something** estar deseando hacer algo

longer adv **They're no longer going out together.** Ya no salen juntos.; **I can't stand it any longer.** Ya no lo aguanto más.

long jump n salto m de longitud

loo n wáter m (LatAm baño m)

look n **Have a look at this!** ¡Echale una ojeada a esto!; **I don't like the look of it.** No me gusta nada.
▶ **vb ❶** mirar ▷ *Look!* ¡Mira!; **to look at something** mirar algo ▷ *Look at the picture.* Mira la foto.; **Look out!** ¡Cuidado! **❷** parecer

▷ She looks surprised. Parece sorprendida.; **That cake looks nice.** Ese pastel tiene buena pinta.; **to look like somebody** parecerse a alguien ▷ He looks like his brother. Se parece a su hermano.; **What does she look like?** ¿Cómo es físicamente?

look after vb cuidar ▷ I look after my little sister. Cuido a mi hermana pequeña.

look for vb buscar ▷ I'm looking for my passport. Estoy buscando mi pasaporte.

look forward to vb tener muchas ganas de ▷ I'm looking forward to meeting you. Tengo muchas ganas de conocerte.; **I'm really looking forward to the holidays.** Estoy deseando que lleguen las vacaciones.; **Looking forward to hearing from you...** A la espera de sus noticias...

look round vb ❶ volverse ▷ I called him and he looked round. Lo llamé y se volvió. ❷ mirar ▷ I'm just looking round. Sólo estoy mirando.; **to look round an exhibition** visitar una exposición; **I like looking round the shops.** Me gusta ir a ver tiendas.

look up vb (look for) buscar ▷ If you don't know a word, look it up in the dictionary. Si no conoces una palabra, búscala en el diccionario.

loose adj holgado ▷ a loose shirt una camisa holgada; **a loose screw** un tornillo flojo; **loose change** dinero suelto

lord n (feudal) señor m; **the House of Lords** la Cámara de los Lores; **the Lord** (God) el Señor; **Good Lord!** ¡Dios mío!

lorry n camión m (pl camiones)

lorry driver n camionero m, camionera f ▷ He's a lorry driver. Es camionero.

lose vb perder ▷ I've lost my purse. He perdido el monedero.; **to get lost** perderse ▷ I was afraid of getting lost. Tenía miedo de perderme.

loss n pérdida f

lost vb see **lose**
　▸ adj perdido

lost-and-found n (in US) oficina f de objetos perdidos

lost property office n oficina f de objetos perdidos

lot n **a lot** mucho ▷ She talks a lot. Habla mucho. ▷ Do you like football? - Not a lot. ¿Te gusta el fútbol? - No mucho.; **a lot of** mucho ▷ I drink a lot of coffee. Bebo mucho café. ▷ We saw a lot of interesting things. Vimos muchas cosas interesantes. ▷ He's got lots of friends. Tiene muchos amigos.; **That's the lot.** Eso es todo.

lottery n lotería f ▷ to win the lottery ganar la lotería

loud adj fuerte ▷ The television is too loud. La televisión está muy fuerte.

loudspeaker n altavoz m (pl altavoces)

lounge n sala f de estar

love n amor m; **to be in love** estar enamorado ▷ She's in love with Paul.

Está enamorada de Paul.; **to make love** hacer el amor; **Give Gloria my love.** Dale recuerdos a Gloria de mi parte.; **Love, Rosemary.** Un abrazo, Rosemary.
▶ vb querer ▷ Everybody loves her. Todos la quieren. ▷ I love you. Te quiero.; **I love chocolate.** Me encanta el chocolate.; **Would you like to come? - Yes, I'd love to.** ¿Te gustaría venir? - Sí, me encantaría.

lovely adj ❶ (person) encantador (f encantadora) ▷ She's a lovely person. Es una persona encantadora. ❷ precioso ▷ They've got a lovely house. Tienen una casa preciosa.; **What a lovely surprise!** ¡Qué sorpresa tan agradable! **It's a lovely day.** Hace un tiempo estupendo.; **Is your meal okay? - Yes, it's lovely.** ¿Está bueno? - Sí, buenísimo.; **Have a lovely time!** ¡Que lo paséis bien!

lover n amante mf

low adj, adv bajo ▷ low prices los bajos precios ▷ That plane is flying very low. Ese avión vuela muy bajo.

lower adj inferior

loyalty n lealtad f

loyalty card n tarjeta f de cliente

luck n suerte f ▷ She hasn't had much luck. No ha tenido mucha suerte.; **Bad luck!** ¡Mala suerte!; **Good luck!** ¡Suerte!

luckily adv afortunadamente

lucky adj afortunado ▷ I consider myself lucky. Me considero afortunado.; **to be lucky**

(fortunate) tener suerte ▷ He's lucky, he's got a job. Tiene suerte de tener trabajo.; **That was lucky!** ¡Qué suerte!; **Black cats are lucky in Britain.** En Gran Bretaña los gatos negros traen buena suerte.; **a lucky horseshoe** una herradura de la suerte

luggage n equipaje m

lump n ❶ trozo m ▷ a lump of butter un trozo de mantequilla ❷ (swelling) chichón m (pl chichones) ▷ He's got a lump on his forehead. Tiene un chichón en la frente.

lunch n almuerzo m; **to have lunch** almorzar ▷ We have lunch at half past twelve. Almorzamos a las doce y media.

lung n pulmón m (pl pulmones) ▷ lung cancer el cáncer de pulmón

Luxembourg n Luxemburgo m

luxurious adj lujoso

luxury n lujo m ▷ It was luxury! ¡Era un lujo! ▷ a luxury hotel un hotel de lujo

lying vb see lie

lyrics npl letra f

m

macaroni n macarrones mpl
machine n ❶ máquina f ▷ It's
a complicated machine. Es una
máquina complicada. ❷ (washing
machine) lavadora f
machine gun n ametralladora f
machinery n maquinaria f
mad adj ❶ (crazy) loco ▷ You're
mad! ¡Estás loco! ❷ (angry) furioso
▷ She'll be mad when she finds out. Se
pondrá furiosa cuando se entere.;
He's mad about football. Está
loco por el fútbol.; **She's mad
about horses.** Le encantan los
caballos.
madam n señora f
made vb see **make**
madness n locura f ▷ It's absolute
madness. Es una locura.
magazine n revista f

maggot n gusano m
magic n magia f
▶ adj mágico ▷ a magic wand una
varita mágica; **It was magic!**
(brilliant) ¡Fue fantástico!
magician n mago m, maga f
magnet n imán m (pl imanes)
magnifying glass n lupa f
maid n ❶ (servant) sirvienta f
❷ (in hotel) camarera f; **an old
maid** (spinster) una solterona
maiden name n apellido m de
soltera

● When women marry in Spain
● they don't usually take the
● name of their husband but
● keep their own instead. If the
● couple have children they take
● both their father's and mother's
● surnames.

mail n ❶ correo m; **by mail**
por correo ❷ (letters)
correspondencia f ▷ We receive
a lot of mail. Recibimos mucha
correspondencia.
mailbox n (in US) buzón m (pl
buzones)
mailman n (in US) cartero m
main adj principal ▷ the main
suspect el principal sospechoso
▷ The main thing is to get it finished.
Lo principal es terminarlo.
mainly adv principalmente
main road n carretera f principal
majesty n majestad f; **Your
Majesty** su Majestad
major adj muy importante
▷ a major factor un factor muy
importante; **Drugs are a major**

problem. La droga es un grave problema.; **in C major** en do mayor

Majorca n Mallorca f

majority n mayoría f

make n marca f ▷ *What make is it?* ¿De qué marca es?
▶ vb ❶ hacer ▷ *I'm going to make a cake.* Voy a hacer un pastel. ▷ *I make my bed every morning.* Me hago la cama cada mañana. ▷ *It's well made.* Está bien hecho. ❷ (*prepare*) preparar; **She's making lunch.** Está preparando el almuerzo.; **Two and two make four.** Dos y dos son cuatro. ❸ (*produce*) fabricar ▷ *"made in Spain"* "fabricado en España" ❹ (*earn*) ganar ▷ *He makes a lot of money.* Gana mucho dinero.; **to make somebody do something** hacer a alguien hacer algo ▷ *My mother makes me eat vegetables.* Mi madre me hace comer verduras.; **You'll have to make do with a cheaper car.** Tendrás que conformarte con un coche más barato.; **What time do you make it?** ¿Qué hora tienes?

make up vb ❶ componer ▷ *Women make up thirty per cent of the police force.* Las mujeres componen el treinta por ciento del cuerpo de policía. ❷ inventarse ▷ *He made up the whole story.* Se inventó toda la historia. ❸ hacer las paces ▷ *They had a quarrel, but soon made up.* Riñeron, pero poco después hicieron las paces. ❹ maquillarse

▷ *She spends hours making herself up.* Pasa horas maquillándose.

make-up n maquillaje m; **She put on her make-up.** Se maquilló.

male adj ❶ (*animal, plant*) macho ▷ *a male kitten* un gatito macho ❷ (*person*) varón (pl varones) ▷ *Sex: Male* Sexo: Varón; **Most football players are male.** La mayoría de los futbolistas son hombres.; **a male nurse** un enfermero; **a male chauvinist** un machista
▶ n (*animal*) macho m

mall n centro m comercial

Malta n Malta f

man n hombre m

manage vb ❶ (*get by*) arreglárselas ▷ *We haven't got much money, but we manage.* No tenemos mucho dinero, pero nos las arreglamos. ❷ (*be manager of*) dirigir ▷ *He manages our football team.* Dirige nuestro equipo de fútbol.; **to manage to do something** conseguir hacer algo ▷ *I managed to pass the exam.* Conseguí aprobar el examen.; **Can you manage with that suitcase?** ¿Puedes con la maleta?

management n dirección f

manager n ❶ (*of company, department, performer*) director m, directora f ▷ *I complained to the manager.* Fui a reclamar al director. ❷ (*of restaurant, store*) gerente mf ❸ (*of team*) entrenador m, entrenadora f ▷ *the England manager* el entrenador de la selección inglesa

manageress n (of restaurant, store) gerente f

mango n mango m

maniac n maníaco m, maníaca f; **He drives like a maniac.** Conduce como un loco.

manner n manera f ▷ She was behaving in an odd manner. Se comportaba de una manera extraña.; **He has a confident manner.** Se muestra seguro de sí mismo.

manners npl modales mpl ▷ Her manners are appalling. Tiene muy malos modales.; **good manners** la buena educación; **It's bad manners to speak with your mouth full.** Es de mala educación hablar con la boca llena.

mansion n mansión f (pl mansiones)

mantelpiece n repisa f de la chimenea

manual n manual m

manufacture vb fabricar

manufacturer n fabricante mf

many adj, pron muchos (f muchas) ▷ He hasn't got many friends. No tiene muchos amigos.; **how many?** ¿cuántos? (f ¿cuántas?) ▷ How many hours a week do you work? ¿Cuántas horas trabajas a la semana?; **too many** demasiados (f demasiadas) ▷ Sixteen people? That's too many. ¿Dieciséis personas? Son demasiadas.; **so many** tantos (f tantas) ▷ He told so many lies! ¡Dijo tantas mentiras!

map n ❶ (of country, region)

mapa m

> Although **mapa** ends in **-a**, it is actually a masculine noun.

❷ (of town, city) plano m

marathon n maratón m (pl maratones)

marble n mármol m ▷ a marble statue una estatua de mármol; **a marble** una canica

March n marzo m ▷ in March en marzo ▷ on 9 March el 9 de marzo

march vb desfilar ▷ The troops marched past the King. Las tropas desfilaron delante del Rey.
▶ n marcha f ▷ a peace march una marcha por la paz

mare n yegua f

margarine n margarina f

margin n margen m (pl márgenes) ▷ She wrote a note in the margin. Escribió una nota al margen.

marijuana n marihuana f

mark n ❶ (in exam) nota f ▷ I get good marks for French. Saco buenas notas en francés. ❷ (on skin, clothing) mancha f ▷ You've got a mark on your shirt. Tienes una mancha en la camisa.
▶ vb ❶ corregir ▷ The teacher hasn't marked my homework yet. El maestro no me ha corregido los deberes todavía. ❷ señalar ▷ Mark its position on the map. Señala su posición en el mapa.

market n mercado m

marketing n márketing m

marmalade n mermelada f de naranja

marriage n matrimonio m

married adj casado ▷ They are not married. No están casados.; **a married couple** un matrimonio; **to get married** casarse

marry vb ❶ casarse ▷ They married in June. Se casaron en junio. ❷ casarse con ▷ He wants to marry her. Quiere casarse con ella.; **to get married** casarse ▷ My brother's getting married in March. Mi hermano se casa en marzo.

marvellous (US **marvelous**) adj estupendo ▷ That's a marvellous idea! ¡Es una idea estupenda!

marzipan n mazapán m

mascara n rímel m

masculine adj masculino

mashed potatoes npl puré m de patatas (LatAm puré m de papas)

mask n máscara f

mass n ❶ montón m (pl montones) ▷ a mass of books and papers un montón de libros y papeles ❷ misa f ▷ We go to mass on Sunday. Vamos a misa los domingos.; **the mass media** los medios de comunicación de masas

massage n masaje m

massive adj enorme

master n ❶ (at primary school) maestro m ❷ (at secondary school) profesor m
▶ vb dominar ▷ Students need to master a second language. Los estudiantes tienen que dominar un segundo idioma.

masterpiece n obra f maestra (pl obras maestras)

mat n (doormat) felpudo m; **a table mat** un mantel individual

match n ❶ partido m ▷ a football match un partido de fútbol ❷ cerilla f ▷ a box of matches una caja de cerillas
▶ vb ❶ hacer juego con ▷ The jacket matches the trousers. La chaqueta hace juego con los pantalones. ❷ hacer juego ▷ These colours don't match. Estos colores no hacen juego.

mate n amigo m, amiga f ▷ He always goes on holiday with his mates. Siempre va de vacaciones con sus amigos.

material n ❶ (cloth) tejido m ❷ (information) material m ▷ I'm collecting material for my project. Estoy recogiendo material para mi proyecto.

mathematics n matemáticas fpl

maths n matemáticas fpl

matter n asunto m ▷ It's a matter of life and death. Es un asunto de vida o muerte.; **What's the matter?** ¿Qué pasa?; **as a matter of fact** de hecho
▶ vb importar ▷ I can't give you the money today. - It doesn't matter. No te puedo dar el dinero hoy. - No importa.; **Shall I phone today or tomorrow? - Whenever, it doesn't matter.** ¿Telefoneo hoy o mañana? - Cuando quieras, da igual.; **It matters a lot to me.** Significa mucho para mí.

mattress n colchón m (pl

colchones)

mature adj maduro

maximum n máximo m ▷ a maximum of two years in prison un máximo de dos años de cárcel
▷ adj máximo ▷ The maximum speed is 100 km/h. La velocidad máxima permitida es 100km/h.

May n mayo m ▷ in May en mayo
▷ on 7 May el 7 de mayo; **May Day** el Primero de Mayo

may vb poder ▷ May I smoke? ¿Puedo fumar?
■ **Puede que** has to be followed by a verb in the subjunctive.
▷ I may go. Puede que vaya.
■ **A lo mejor** can also be used but it is a more colloquial alternative.
▷ Are you going to the party? - I don't know, I may. ¿Vas a ir a la fiesta? - No sé, a lo mejor.

maybe adv a lo mejor ▷ Maybe she's at home. A lo mejor está en casa.
▷ Maybe he'll change his mind. A lo mejor cambia de idea.

mayonnaise n mayonesa f

mayor n alcalde m, alcaldesa f

me pron
■ Use **me** to translate **me** when it is the direct object of the verb in the sentence, or when it means **to me**.
▷ me ▷ Look at me! ¡Mírame! ▷ Could you lend me your pen? ¿Me prestas tu bolígrafo?
■ Use **yo** after the verb **to be** and in comparisons.
▷ It's me. Soy yo. ▷ He's older than me. Es mayor que yo.
■ Use **mí** after prepositions.
▷ without me sin mí
■ Remember that **with me** translates as **conmigo**.
▷ He was with me. Estaba conmigo.

meal n comida f; **Enjoy your meal!** ¡Que aproveche!

mean vb ❶ significar ▷ What does "alcalde" mean? ¿Qué significa "alcalde"? ▷ I don't know what it means. No sé lo que significa.
❷ querer decir ▷ That's not what I meant. Eso no es lo que quería decir. ❶ referirse a ▷ Which one did he mean? ¿A cuál se refería?
▷ Do you mean me? ¿Te refieres a mí?; querer hacer algo ▷ I didn't mean to hurt you. No quería hacerte daño.;
Do you really mean it? ¿Lo dices en serio?
▷ adj ❶ (tight-fisted) tacaño
❷ (unkind) mezquino ▷ You're being mean to me. Estás siendo mezquino conmigo.

meaning n significado m

meant vb see **mean**

meanwhile adv mientras tanto

measles n sarampión m ▷ I've got measles. Tengo el sarampión.

measure vb medir

measurement n medida f ▷ What are the measurements of the room? ¿Cuáles son las medidas de la habitación?; **What's your waist measurement?** ¿Cuánto mides de cintura?

meat n carne f

Mecca n La Meca

mechanic n mecánico m, mecánica f ▷ He's a mechanic. Es mecánico.

medal n medalla f

media npl the media los medios de comunicación

medical adj médico ▷ medical treatment el tratamiento médico; **medical insurance** el seguro médico; **to have medical problems** tener problemas de salud; **She's a medical student.** Es una estudiante de medicina.

▶ n He had a medical last week. Se hizo un chequeo la semana pasada.

medicine n ❶ (science) medicina f ▷ I want to study medicine. Quiero estudiar medicina. ❷ (medication) medicamento m ▷ I need some medicine. Necesito un medicamento.

Mediterranean adj mediterráneo

▶ n the Mediterranean el Mediterráneo

medium adj mediano ▷ a man of medium height un hombre de estatura mediana

medium-sized adj a medium-sized town una ciudad de tamaño mediano

meet vb ❶ (by chance) encontrarse con ▷ I met Paul in town. Me encontré con Paul en el centro.; **We met by chance in the supermarket.** Nos encontramos por casualidad

en el supermercado. ❷ (by arrangement) reunirse ▷ The committee met at two o'clock. El comité se reunió a las dos.; **Where shall we meet?** ¿Dónde quedamos? **I'm going to meet my friends at the swimming pool.** He quedado con mis amigos en la piscina.; **I'll meet you at the station.** Te voy a buscar a la estación. ❸ (get to know) conocer ▷ He met Tim at a party. Conoció a Tim en una fiesta.; **Have you met her before?** ¿La conoces?

meeting n ❶ (socially) encuentro m ▷ their first meeting su primer encuentro ❷ (for work) reunión f (pl reuniones) ▷ a business meeting una reunión de trabajo

melon n melón m (pl melones)

melt vb ❶ derretir ▷ Melt 100 grams of butter in a saucepan. Derrita 100 gramos de mantequilla en una sartén. ❷ derretirse ▷ The snow is melting. La nieve se está derritiendo.

member n miembro mf; "members only" "reservado para los socios"; **a Member of Parliament** un diputado (f una diputada)

memorial n a war memorial un monumento a los caídos

memorize vb memorizar

memory n ❶ (also for computer) memoria f ▷ I've got a terrible memory. Tengo una memoria espantosa. ❷ recuerdo m ▷ happy memories los recuerdos felices

men npl see **man**

mend vb arreglar

mental adj mental ▷ mental illness la enfermedad mental; **mental hospital** el hospital psiquiátrico

mention vb mencionar ▷ He didn't mention it to me. No me lo mencionó.; **I mentioned she might come later.** Dije que a lo mejor vendría más tarde.; **Thank you! - Don't mention it!** ¡Gracias! - ¡No hay de qué!

menu n ❶ carta f ▷ Could I have the menu please? ¿Me trae la carta por favor? ❷ (on computer) menú m (pl menús)

meringue n merengue m

merry adj **Merry Christmas!** ¡Feliz Navidad!

merry-go-round n tiovivo m

mess n desorden m; **My hair's a mess, it needs cutting.** Tengo el pelo hecho un desastre; tengo que cortármelo.; **I'll be in a mess if I fail the exam.** Voy a tener problemas si suspendo el examen.

mess about vb **I didn't do much at the weekend, just messed about with some friends.** No hice mucho el fin de semana; estuve ganduleando con unos amigos.; **Stop messing about with my computer!** ¡Deja de toquetear mi ordenador!

mess up vb estropear ▷ You've messed up my cassettes! ¡Me has estropeado los casetes!; **I messed up my chemistry exam.** Metí la pata en el examen de química.

message n mensaje m ▷ a secret message un mensaje secreto; **Would you like to leave him a message?** ¿Quiere dejarle un recado?

messenger n mensajero m, mensajera f

messy adj ❶ (room, person) desordenado ▷ Your room is really messy. Tu habitación está muy desordenada. ❷ (job) sucio; **Her writing is very messy.** Tiene muy mala letra.

met vb see **meet**

metal n metal m

meter n ❶ (for gas, electricity) contador m ❷ (for taxi) taxímetro m ❸ (parking meter) parquímetro m ❹ (in US: unit of measurement) metro m

method n método m

Methodist n metodista m/f ▷ He's a Methodist. Es metodista.

metre n metro m

metric adj métrico

Mexico n Méjico m

mice npl see **mouse**

microchip n microchip m (pl microchips)

microphone n micrófono m

microscope n microscopio m

microwave n microondas m (pl microondas)

midday n mediodía m ▷ at midday al mediodía

middle n medio m ▷ The car was in the middle of the road. El coche estaba en medio de la carretera.; **in the middle of May** a mediados

de mayo; **I woke up in the middle of the morning.** Me desperté a media mañana.; **She was in the middle of her exams.** Estaba en plenos exámenes.
▶ *adj* del medio *inv* ▷ *the middle seat* el asiento del medio

middle-aged *adj* de mediana edad *inv*

middle-class *adj* de clase media *inv*

Middle East *n* **the Middle East** el Oriente Medio

middle name *n* segundo nombre *m*

midge *n* mosquito *m*

midnight *n* medianoche *f* ▷ *at midnight* a medianoche

midwife *n* comadrona *f* ▷ *She's a midwife.* Es comadrona.

might *vb* poder ▷ *The teacher might come at any moment.* El profesor podría venir en cualquier momento.

Puede que has to be followed by a verb in the subjunctive.
▷ *He might come later.* Puede que venga más tarde. ▷ *She might not have understood.* Puede que no haya entendido.

A lo mejor can also be used but it is a more colloquial alternative.
▷ *We might go to Spain next year.* A lo mejor vamos a España el año que viene.

migraine *n* jaqueca *f* ▷ *I've got a migraine.* Tengo jaqueca.

mike *n* micro *m*

mild *adj* suave ▷ *The winters are quite mild.* Los inviernos son bastante suaves.

mile *n* milla *f*
● In Spain distances are expressed in kilometres. A mile is about 1.6 kilometres.
▷ *It's five miles from here.* Está a unas cinco millas de aquí. ▷ *at 50 miles per hour* a 50 millas por hora; **We walked for miles!** ¡Caminamos kilómetros y kilómetros!

military *adj* militar

milk *n* leche *f*
▶ *vb* ordeñar

milk chocolate *n* chocolate *m* con leche

milkman *n* lechero *m*
● In Spain milk is not delivered to people's homes.

milk shake *n* batido *m*

millennium *n* milenio *m*

millimetre (*US* **millimeter**) *n* milímetro *m*

million *n* millón *m* (*pl* millones)
▷ *two million pounds* dos millones de libras esterlinas

millionaire *n* millonario *m*, millonaria *f*

mince *n* carne *f* picada (*LatAm* carne *f* molida)

mind *vb* ● (*look after*) cuidar ▷ *Could you mind the baby this afternoon?* ¿Podrías cuidar al niño esta tarde? ▷ *Could you mind my bags for a few minutes?* ¿Me cuidas las bolsas un momento? ● (*matter*) importar ▷ *Do you*

mind if I open the window? - No, I don't mind. ¿Le importa que abra la ventana? - No, no me importa.; **I don't mind the noise.** No me molesta el ruido.; **Never mind!** **(1)** (don't worry) ¡No te preocupes! **(2)** (it's not important) ¡No importa!; **Mind you don't fall.** Ten cuidado, no te vayas a caer.; **Mind the step!** ¡Cuidado con el escalón!
▶ n **mente** f ▷ What have you got in mind? ¿Qué tienes en mente?; **I haven't made up my mind yet.** No me he decidido todavía.; **He's changed his mind.** Ha cambiado de idea.; **Are you out of your mind?** ¿Estás loco?

mine pron ❶ **el mío** (pl los míos) ▷ Is this your coat? - No, mine is black. ¿Es éste tu abrigo? - No, el mío es negro. ❷ **la mía** (pl las mías) ▷ Is this your scarf? - No, mine is red. ¿Es ésta tu bufanda? - No, la mía es roja. ❸ **mío m** (pl míos) ▷ That car is mine. Ese coche es mío. ❹ **mía** (pl mías) ▷ Sorry, that beer is mine. Disculpa, esa cerveza es mía. ▷ Isabel is a friend of mine. Isabel es amiga mía.
▶ n **mina** f ▷ a coal mine una mina de carbón

miner n minero m, minera f ▷ My father was a miner. Mi padre era minero.

mineral water n agua f mineral

> Although it's a feminine noun, remember that you use **el** and **un** with **agua mineral**.

miniature adj en miniatura

minibus n microbús m (pl microbuses)

Minidisc® n minidisco m

minimum n mínimo m
▶ adj mínimo ▷ The minimum age for driving is 17. La edad mínima para poder conducir es 17 años.

miniskirt n minifalda f

minister n ❶ ministro m, ministra f ▷ the Minister for Education el Ministro de Educación ❷ (of church) pastor m, pastora f

minor adj secundario ▷ a minor problem un problema secundario; **a minor operation** una operación de poca importancia; **in D minor** en re menor

minority n minoría f

mint n ❶ (sweet) caramelo m de menta ❷ (plant) menta f ▷ mint sauce salsa de menta

minus prep menos ▷ sixteen minus three dieciséis menos tres; **I got a B minus for my French.** Me pusieron un notable bajo en francés.; **minus two degrees** dos grados bajo cero

minute n minuto m ▷ Wait a minute! ¡Espera un minuto!
▶ adj minúsculo

miracle n milagro m

mirror n ❶ espejo m ▷ She looked at herself in the mirror. Se miró en el espejo. ❷ (in car) retrovisor m

misbehave vb portarse mal

mischief n She's always up to mischief. Siempre está haciendo travesuras.; **full of mischief** travieso

mischievous adj travieso

miser n avaro m, avara f

miserable adj infeliz (pl infelices)
▷ a miserable life una vida infeliz;
I'm feeling miserable. Me siento
deprimido.; **miserable weather**
un tiempo deprimente

Miss n ❶ señorita f ▷ Miss Peters
wants to see you. La señorita Peters
quiere verte. ❷ (in address) Srta.

miss vb perder ▷ Hurry or you'll
miss the bus. Date prisa o perderás
el autobús.; **It's too good an
opportunity to miss.** Es una
oportunidad demasiado buena
para dejarla pasar.; **He missed the
target.** No dio en el blanco.; **I miss
my family.** Echo de menos a mi
familia.; **You've missed a page.** Te
has saltado una página.

missing adj perdido ▷ the missing
link el eslabón perdido; **to be
missing** faltar ▷ Two members of
the group are missing. Faltan dos
miembros del grupo.; **a missing
person** una persona desaparecida

mist n neblina f

mistake n error m ▷ There must
be some mistake. Debe de haber
algún error.; **a spelling mistake**
una falta de ortografía; **to
make a mistake (1)** (in speaking)
cometer un error ▷ He makes a lot
of mistakes when he speaks English.
Comete muchos errores cuando
habla inglés. **(2)** (get mixed up)
equivocarse ▷ I'm sorry, I made a
mistake. Lo siento, me equivoqué.;
by mistake por error

▶ vb confundir ▷ He mistook me for
my sister. Me confundió con mi
hermana.

mistaken adj **to be mistaken**
estar equivocado

mistletoe n muérdago m

mistook vb see **mistake**

misty adj neblinoso ▷ a misty
morning una mañana neblinosa

misunderstand vb entender
mal ▷ Sorry, I misunderstood you. Lo
siento, te entendí mal.

misunderstanding n
malentendido m

misunderstood vb see
misunderstand

mix n mezcla f ▷ The film is a mix
of science fiction and comedy. La
película es una mezcla de ciencia
ficción y comedia.; **a cake mix** un
preparado para pastel
▶ vb mezclar ▷ Mix the flour with
the sugar. Mezcle la harina con
el azúcar.; **I like mixing with
all sorts of people.** Me gusta
tratar con todo tipo de gente.;
He doesn't mix much. No se
relaciona mucho.

mix up vb confundir ▷ He mixed
up their names. Confundió sus
nombres.; **I'm getting mixed up.**
Me estoy confundiendo.

mixed adj mixto ▷ a mixed salad
una ensalada mixta ▷ a mixed
school un colegio mixto; **I've got
mixed feelings about it.** No sé
qué pensar de ello.

mixer n (for food) batidora f

mixture n mezcla f ▷ a mixture of

spices una mezcla de especias

mix-up n confusión f (pl confusiones)

moan vb quejarse ▷ She's always moaning about something. Siempre se está quejando de algo.

mobile home n caravana f fija (LatAm trailer m)

mobile phone n móvil m

mock vb ridiculizar

▶ adj a **mock exam** un examen de práctica

model n ❶ modelo m ▷ His car is the latest model. Su coche es el último modelo. ❷ maqueta f ▷ a model of the castle una maqueta del castillo ❸ modelo m/f ▷ She's a famous model. Es una modelo famosa.

▶ adj a **model railway** una vía férrea en miniatura; a **model plane** una maqueta de avión; **He's a model pupil.** Es un alumno modelo.

modem n módem m (pl módems)

moderate adj moderado ▷ His views are quite moderate. Tiene opiniones bastante moderadas.; **I do a moderate amount of exercise.** Hago un poco de gimnasia.

modern adj moderno

modernize vb modernizar

moisturizer n crema f hidratante

moldy adj (in US) mohoso

mole n ❶ lunar m ▷ I've got a mole on my back. Tengo un lunar en la espalda. ❷ (animal) topo m

moment n momento m ▷ Just a

moment! ¡Un momento! ▷ at the moment en este momento ▷ any moment now de un momento a otro

monarchy n monarquía f

Monday n lunes m (pl lunes) ▷ I saw her on Monday. La vi el lunes. ▷ every Monday todos los lunes ▷ last Monday el lunes pasado ▷ next Monday el lunes que viene ▷ on Mondays los lunes

money n dinero m ▷ I need to change some money. Tengo que cambiar dinero.

mongrel n perro m mestizo; **My dog's a mongrel.** Mi perro es mestizo.

monitor n (on computer) monitor m

monkey n mono m, mona f

monster n monstruo m

month n mes m ▷ this month este mes ▷ next month el mes que viene ▷ last month el mes pasado

monthly adj mensual

monument n monumento m

mood n humor m ▷ to be in a good mood estar de buen humor ▷ to be in a bad mood estar de mal humor

moody adj (in a bad mood) malhumorado; **to be moody** (temperamental) tener un humor cambiante

moon n luna f ▷ There's a full moon tonight. Esta noche hay luna llena.; **She's over the moon about it.** Está en el séptimo cielo de contenta.

moped n ciclomotor m

moral n moraleja f ▷ the moral

of the story is… la moraleja de la historia es…; **morals** la moral
more *adj, pron, adv* más ▷ *It costs a lot more.* Cuesta mucho más.
▷ *There isn't any more.* Ya no hay más. ▷ *A bit more?* ¿Un poco más?
▷ *Is there any more?* ¿Hay más? ▷ *It'll take a few more days.* Llevará unos cuantos días más.; **more than** más que

> Use **más que** when comparing two things or people and **más de** when talking about quantities.

▷ *He's more intelligent than me.* Es más inteligente que yo. ▷ *more than 20 people* más de 20 personas; **more or less** más o menos; **more than ever** más que nunca; **more and more** cada vez más
morning *n* mañana *f* ▷ *in the morning* por la mañana ▷ *at 7 o'clock in the morning* a las 7 de la mañana ▷ *on Saturday morning* el sábado por la mañana ▷ *tomorrow morning* mañana por la mañana; **the morning papers** los periódicos de la mañana
Morocco *n* Marruecos *m*
mortgage *n* hipoteca *f*
Moscow *n* Moscú *m*
Moslem *n* musulmán *m*, musulmana *f* (*mpl* musulmanes) ▷ *He's a Moslem.* Es musulmán.
mosque *n* mezquita *f*
mosquito *n* mosquito *m*; **a mosquito bite** una picadura de mosquito
most *adj, pron, adv* más ▷ *He's the*

one who talks the most. Es el que más habla. ▷ *the most expensive restaurant* el restaurante más caro; **most of** la mayor parte de ▷ *most of the time* la mayor parte del tiempo; **most of them** la mayoría ▷ *Most of them have cars.* La mayoría tienen coches. ▷ *Most people go out on Friday nights.* La mayoría de la gente sale los viernes por la noche.; **at the most** como mucho ▷ *two hours at the most* dos horas como mucho; **to make the most of something** aprovechar algo al máximo ▷ *He made the most of his holiday.* Aprovechó sus vacaciones al máximo.
moth *n* ❶ mariposa *f* nocturna ❷ (*clothes moth*) polilla *f*
mother *n* madre *f*; **my mother and father** mis padres; **mother tongue** la lengua materna
mother-in-law *n* suegra *f*
Mother's Day *n* Día *m* de la Madre
motivated *adj* **He is highly motivated.** Está muy motivado.
motivation *n* motivación *f* (*pl* motivaciones)
motor *n* motor *m*
motorbike *n* moto *f*

> Although **moto** ends in **-o**, it is actually a feminine noun.

motorboat *n* lancha *f* motora
motorcycle *n* motocicleta *f*
motorcyclist *n* motociclista *mf*
motorist *n* conductor *m*, conductora *f*
motor racing *n* carreras *fpl* de

coches

motorway n autopista f

mouldy adj mohoso

mountain n montaña f ▷ in the mountains en la montaña; **a mountain bike** una bicicleta de montaña

mountaineer n alpinista mf

mountaineering n alpinismo m ▷ I go mountaineering. Hago alpinismo.

mountainous adj montañoso

mouse n (also for computer) ratón m (pl ratones)

mouse mat n alfombrilla f del ratón

mousse n ❶ mousse f ▷ chocolate mousse la mousse de chocolate ❷ (for hair) espuma f

moustache n bigote m ▷ He's got a moustache. Tiene bigote.

mouth n boca f

mouthful n ❶ (of food) bocado m ❷ (of drink) trago m

mouth organ n armónica f

move n ❶ paso m ▷ That was a good move! ¡Ese fue un paso bien dado!; **It's your move.** Te toca jugar. ❷ mudanza f ▷ our move from Oxford to Luton nuestra mudanza de Oxford a Luton; **Get a move on!** ¡Date prisa!
▶ vb ❶ moverse ▷ Don't move! ¡No te muevas! ❷ mover ▷ He can't move his arm. No puede mover el brazo.; **Could you move your stuff please?** ¿Podrías quitar tus cosas de aquí, por favor? ❸ avanzar ▷ The car was moving

very slowly. El coche avanzaba muy lentamente. ❹ conmover ▷ I was very moved by the film. La película me conmovió mucho.; **to move house** mudarse de casa ▷ We're moving in July. Nos mudamos en julio.

move in vb **When are the new tenants moving in?** ¿Cuándo vienen los nuevos inquilinos?

move over vb correrse ▷ Could you move over a bit, please? ¿Te podrías correr un poco, por favor?

movement n movimiento m

movie n película f; **the movies** el cine

moving adj ❶ en movimiento ▷ a moving bus un autobús en movimiento ❷ conmovedor (f conmovedora) ▷ a moving story una historia conmovedora

MP abbr (= Member of Parliament) diputado m, diputada f

MP3 player n reproductor m de MP3

Mr abbr ❶ señor m ▷ Mr Jones wants to see you. El señor Jones quiere verte. ❷ (in address) Sr.

Mrs abbr ❶ señora f ▷ Mrs Philips wants to see you. La señora Philips quiere verte. ❷ (in address) Sra.

Ms abbr ❶ señora f ▷ Ms Brown wants to see you. La señora Brown quiere verte. ❷ (in address) Sra.
- There isn't a direct equivalent
- of **Ms** in Spanish. If you are
- writing to a woman and don't
- know whether she is married,
- use **Señora**.

much adj, pron, adv mucho ▷ I feel much better now. Ahora me siento mucho mejor. ▷ I haven't got much money. No tengo mucho dinero. ▷ Have you got a lot of luggage? - No, not much. ¿Tienes mucho equipaje? - No, no mucho.; **very much** mucho ▷ I enjoyed myself very much. Me divertí mucho.; **Thank you very much.** Muchas gracias.; **how much?** ¿cuánto? ▷ How much time have you got? ¿Cuánto tiempo tienes? ▷ How much is it? ¿Cuánto es?; **too much** demasiado ▷ They give us too much homework. Nos ponen demasiados deberes.; **so much** tanto ▷ I didn't think it would cost so much. No pensé que costaría tanto. ▷ I've never seen so much rain. Nunca había visto tanta lluvia.

mud n barro m

muddle n **to be in a muddle** (books, photos) estar todo revuelto

muddle up vb confundir ▷ He muddles me up with my sister. Me confunde con mi hermana.; **to get muddled up** hacerse un lío (informal) ▷ I'm getting muddled up. Me estoy haciendo un lío.

muddy adj lleno de barro

muesli n muesli m

mug n taza f ▷ Do you want a cup or a mug? ¿Quieres una taza normal o una taza alta?; **a beer mug** una jarra de cerveza
▶ vb atracar ▷ He was mugged in the city centre. Lo atracaron en el centro de la ciudad.

mugging n atraco m

multiple choice test n examen m de tipo test

multiplication n multiplicación f

multiply vb multiplicar ▷ to multiply six by three multiplicar seis por tres

mum n mamá f ▷ my mum mi mamá

mummy n ❶ mamá f ▷ Mummy says I can go. Mamá dice que puedo ir. ❷ (Egyptian) momia f

mumps n paperas fpl ▷ My brother's got mumps. Mi hermano tiene paperas.

murder n asesinato m
▶ vb asesinar ▷ He was murdered. Fue asesinado.

murderer n asesino m, asesina f

muscle n músculo m

museum n museo m

mushroom n champiñón m (pl champiñones)

music n música f

musical adj musical; **I'm not musical.** No tengo aptitudes para la música.
▶ n musical m

musician n músico m, música f ▷ He's a musician. Es músico.

Muslim n musulmán m, musulmana f (mpl musulmanes) ▷ She's a Muslim. Es musulmana.

mussel n mejillón m (pl mejillones)

must vb ❶ (it's necessary) tener que ▷ I must buy some presents. Tengo que comprar unos regalos.; **You mustn't forget to send**

her a card. No te vayas a olvidar de mandarle una tarjeta. ❸ *(I suppose)* deber de ▷ *You must be tired.* Debes de estar cansada.

mustard n mostaza f

mustn't vb = **must not**

my adj mi (pl mis) ▷ *my father* mi padre ▷ *my house* mi casa ▷ *my friends* mis amigos ▷ *my sisters* mis hermanas

> **My** is usually translated by the definite article **el/los** or **la/las** when it's clear from the sentence who the possessor is or when referring to clothing or parts of the body.

▷ *They stole my car.* Me robaron el coche. ▷ *I took off my coat.* Me quité el abrigo. ▷ *I'm washing my hair.* Me estoy lavando la cabeza.

myself pron ❶ *(reflexive)* me ▷ *I've hurt myself.* Me he hecho daño. ❷ *(after preposition)* mí mismo *(f* mí misma*)* ▷ *I talked mainly about myself.* Hablé principalmente de mí mismo.; **a beginner like myself** un principiante como yo ❸ *(for emphasis)* yo mismo *(f* yo misma*)* ▷ *I made it myself.* Lo hice yo misma.; **by myself** solo *(f* sola*)* ▷ *I don't like travelling by myself.* No me gusta viajar solo.

mysterious adj misterioso

mystery n misterio m; **a murder mystery** una novela policíaca

myth n mito m

n

nag vb dar la lata ▷ *She's always nagging me.* Siempre me está dando la lata.

nail n ❶ uña f ▷ *She bites her nails.* Se muerde las uñas. ❷ *(made of metal)* clavo m

nailbrush n cepillo m de uñas

nailfile n lima f para las uñas

nail scissors npl tijeras fpl para las uñas

nail varnish n esmalte m de uñas; **nail varnish remover** el quitaesmaltes

naked adj desnudo

name n nombre m; **What's your name?** ¿Cómo te llamas?

nanny n *(nursemaid)* niñera f

napkin n servilleta f

nappy n pañal m

narrow adj estrecho

nasty adj ❶ malo
Use **mal** before a masculine
singular noun.
▷ Don't be nasty. No seas malo.
❷ desagradable ▷ a nasty smell un
olor desagradable

nation n nación f (pl naciones)

national adj nacional

national anthem n himno m
nacional

nationality n nacionalidad f

national park n parque m
nacional

natural adj natural

naturally adv naturalmente
▷ Naturally, we were very
disappointed. Naturalmente,
estábamos muy decepcionados.

nature n naturaleza f ▷ the
wonders of nature las maravillas
de la naturaleza; **It's not in his
nature to behave like that.**
Comportarse así no es propio
de él.

naughty adj travieso ▷ Naughty
girl! ¡Qué traviesa!

navy n armada f ▷ He's in the navy.
Está en la armada.

navy-blue adj azul marino inv
▷ a navy-blue skirt una falda azul
marino

near adj ❶ cerca ▷ It's fairly near.
Está bastante cerca. ❷ cerca
▷ Where's the nearest service station?
¿Dónde está la gasolinera más
cercana? ❸ in the near future en un
futuro cercano
▶ prep, adv ❶ cerca ▷ Is there a bank
near here? ¿Hay algún banco por

aquí cerca? ❷ cerca de ▷ I live near
Liverpool. Vivo cerca de Liverpool.;
near to cerca de ▷ It's very near
to the school. Está muy cerca del
colegio.

nearby adj cercano ▷ a nearby
village un pueblo cercano
▶ adv cerca ▷ There's a supermarket
nearby. Hay un supermercado
cerca.

nearly adv casi ▷ Dinner's nearly
ready. La cena está casi lista.;
I nearly missed the train. Por poco
pierdo el tren.

neat adj ordenado ▷ My flatmate's
not very neat. Mi compañero de
piso no es muy ordenado.; **He
always looks very neat.** Siempre
está muy pulcro.

necessarily adv not necessarily
no necesariamente

necessary adj necesario

neck n cuello m ▷ a V-neck sweater
un jersey de cuello en pico; **She
had a stiff neck.** Tenía tortícolis.;
the back of your neck la nuca

necklace n collar m

nectarine n nectarina f

need vb necesitar ▷ I need to change
some money. Necesito cambiar
dinero.; **You don't need to go.** No
tienes por qué ir.
▶ n **There's no need to book.** No
hace falta hacer reserva.
  hace falta que has to be
  followed by a verb in the
  subjunctive.
▷ There's no need for you to do that.
No hace falta que hagas eso.

needle n aguja f

negative n (photo) negativo m
▶ adj negativo ▷ He's got a very negative attitude. Tiene una actitud muy negativa.

neglected adj abandonado ▷ The garden is neglected. El jardín está abandonado.

negotiate vb negociar

neighbour (US**neighbor**) n vecino m, vecina f

neighbourhood (US **neighborhood**) n barrio m

neither adj, conj, pron ❶ ninguno de los dos (f ninguna de las dos) ▷ Carrots or peas? - Neither, thanks. ¿Zanahorias o guisantes? - Ninguno de los dos, gracias. ▷ Neither of them is coming. No viene ninguno de los dos. ❷ tampoco ▷ I don't like him. - Neither do I! No me cae bien. - ¡A mí tampoco!; **neither...nor...** ni... ni... ▷ Neither Sarah nor Tamsin is coming to the party. No vienen ni Sarah ni Tamsin a la fiesta.

nephew n sobrino m

nerve n nervio m ▷ That noise really gets on my nerves. Ese ruido me pone los nervios de punta.; **He's got a nerve!** ¡Qué cara tiene!; **I wouldn't have the nerve to do that!** ¡Yo no me atrevería a hacer eso!

nervous adj nervioso ▷ I bite my nails when I'm nervous. Cuando estoy nervioso me muerdo las uñas. ▷ I'm a bit nervous about the exams. Estoy un poco nervioso por los exámenes.

nest n nido m

net n red f ▷ a fishing net una red de pesca

Net n Red f; **to surf the Net** navegar por la Red

netball n especie de baloncesto jugado especialmente por mujeres

Netherlands npl the Netherlands los Países Bajos

network n red f

never adv nunca ▷ Never leave valuables in your car. No dejen nunca objetos de valor en el coche.

> When **nunca** comes before the verb in Spanish it is not necessary to use **no** as well.
> ▷ I never believed him. Yo nunca le creí.; **Never again!** ¡Nunca más!; **Never, ever do that again!** ¡No vuelvas a hacer eso nunca jamás!; **Never mind.** No importa.

new adj nuevo ▷ her new boyfriend su nuevo novio

news n noticia f ▷ That's wonderful news! ¡Qué buena noticia! ▷ good news buenas noticias; **an interesting piece of news** una noticia interesante; **It was nice to have your news.** Me dio alegría saber de ti.; **the news** (on TV) las noticias

newsagent n tienda f de periódicos

newspaper n periódico m

newsreader n ❶ (on TV) presentador m, presentadora f ❷ (on radio) locutor m, locutora f

New Year n Año m Nuevo ▷ to celebrate New Year celebrar el Año Nuevo; **Happy New Year!** ¡Feliz Año Nuevo!; **New Year's Day** el día de Año Nuevo; **New Year's Eve** Nochevieja f (LatAm noche f de Fin de Año); **a New Year's Eve party** una fiesta de Fin de Año

New Zealand n Nueva Zelanda f

New Zealander n neozelandés m, neozelandesa f (mpl neozelandeses)

next adj, adv, prep ❶ próximo ▷ next Saturday el próximo sábado ❷ siguiente ▷ The next day we visited Gerona. Al día siguiente visitamos Gerona. ❸ luego ▷ What did you do next? ¿Qué hiciste luego?; **next to** al lado de ▷ next to the bank al lado del banco; **next door** al lado ▷ They live next door. Viven al lado.; **the next-door neighbours** los vecinos de al lado; **the next room** la habitación de al lado

NHS abbr (= National Health Service) servicio m sanitario de la Seguridad Social

nice adj ❶ (friendly) simpático ▷ Your parents are very nice. Tus padres son muy simpáticos. ❷ (kind) amable ▷ She was always very nice to me. Siempre fue muy amable conmigo. ▷ It was nice of you to remember my birthday. Fue muy amable de tu parte que te acordaras de mi cumpleaños. ❸ (pretty) bonito ▷ That's a nice dress! ¡Qué vestido más bonito!

❹ (good) bueno

Use **buen** before a masculine singular noun.

▷ It's a nice day. Hace buen día. ▷ This paella is very nice. Esta paella está muy buena.; **Have a nice time!** ¡Que te diviertas!

nickname n apodo m

niece n sobrina f

night n noche f ▷ I want a single room for two nights. Quiero una habitación individual para dos noches.; **at night** por la noche; **Good night!** ¡Buenas noches!; **last night** anoche ▷ We went to a party last night. Anoche fuimos a una fiesta.

night club n sala f de fiestas

nightie n camisón m (pl camisones)

nightmare n pesadilla f ▷ to have nightmares tener pesadillas

nightshift n turno m de noche

nil n cero m ▷ We won one-nil. Ganamos uno a cero.

nine num nueve; **She's nine.** Tiene nueve años.

nineteen num diecinueve; **She's nineteen.** Tiene diecinueve años.

nineteenth adj decimonoveno

ninety num noventa ▷ He's ninety. Tiene noventa años.

ninth adj noveno ▷ on the ninth floor en el noveno piso; **on 9th August** el nueve de agosto

no adv, adj no ▷ Are you coming? - No. ¿Vienes? - No. ▷ No thank you. No, gracias. ▷ There's no hot water. No hay agua caliente.; **I've got no**

idea. No tengo ni idea.; **I have no questions.** No tengo ninguna pregunta.; **No way!** ¡Ni hablar!; **"no smoking"** "prohibido fumar"

nobody pron nadie ▷ *There was nobody in the office.* No había nadie en la oficina.

> When **nobody** goes before a verb in English it can be translated by either **nadie ...** or **no ... nadie.**

▷ *Nobody likes him.* No le cae bien a nadie. ▷ *Nobody saw me.* Nadie me vio.

nod vb ① *(in agreement)* asentir con la cabeza ② *(as greeting)* saludar con la cabeza

noise n ruido m; **to make a noise** hacer ruido

noisy adj ruidoso ▷ *the noisiest city in the world* la ciudad más ruidosa del mundo; **It's very noisy here.** Hay mucho ruido aquí.

nominate vb nombrar ▷ *She was nominated for the post.* La nombraron para el cargo.; **He was nominated for an Oscar.** Le nominaron para un Oscar.

none pron

> When **none** refers to something you can count, such as sisters or friends, Spanish uses **ninguno** with a singular verb. When it refers to something you cannot count, such as wine, Spanish uses **nada.**

① ninguno (f ninguna) ▷ *None of my friends wanted to come.* Ninguno

de mis amigos quiso venir. ▷ *There are none left.* No queda ninguno. ② pron ▷ *There's none left.* No queda nada.

nonsense n tonterías fpl ▷ *She talks a lot of nonsense.* Dice muchas tonterías.; **Nonsense!** ¡Tonterías!

non-smoking adj **a non-smoking area** un área reservada para no fumadores

> Although it's a feminine noun, remember that you use **el** and **un** with **área.**

a non-smoking carriage un vagón para no fumadores

non-stop adj, adv ① directo ▷ *a non-stop flight* un vuelo directo; **We flew non-stop.** Tomamos un vuelo directo. ② sin parar ▷ *He talks non-stop.* Habla sin parar.

noodles npl fideos mpl

noon n doce fpl del mediodía; **at noon** a las doce del mediodía

no one pron = **nobody**

nor conj tampoco ▷ *We haven't seen him. - Nor have we.* No lo hemos visto. - Nosotros tampoco.; **neither...nor** ni...ni ▷ *neither the cinema nor the swimming pool* ni el cine ni la piscina

normal adj normal

normally adv ① *(usually)* normalmente ▷ *I normally arrive at nine o'clock.* Normalmente llego a las nueve. ② *(as normal)* con normalidad ▷ *In spite of the strike, airports are working normally.* A pesar de la huelga, los aeropuertos funcionan con normalidad.

north n norte m ▷ *in the north of Spain* en el norte de España
▶ *adj* norte ▷ *North London* el norte de Londres; **the north coast** la costa septentrional
▶ *adv* hacia el norte ▷ *We were travelling north.* Viajábamos hacia el norte.; **north of** al norte de ▷ *It's north of London.* Está al norte de Londres.

North America n América f del Norte

northeast n noreste m; **in the northeast** al noreste

northern *adj* del norte ▷ *Northern Europe* Europa del Norte; **the northern part of the island** la zona norte de la isla

Northern Ireland n Irlanda f del Norte

North Pole n **the North Pole** el Polo Norte

North Sea n **the North Sea** el Mar del Norte

northwest n noroeste m ▷ *in the northwest* al noroeste

Norway n Noruega f

Norwegian *adj* noruego
▶ n ❶ (person) noruego m, noruega f ▷ *the Norwegians* los noruegos ❷ (language) noruego m

nose n nariz f (pl narices)

nosebleed n **I often get nosebleeds.** Me sangra la nariz a menudo.

nosy *adj* fisgón (f fisgona)

not *adv* no ▷ *I'm not sure.* No estoy

seguro. ▷ *Are you coming or not?* ¿Vienes o no?; **Thank you very much. - Not at all.** Muchas gracias. - De nada.

note n ❶ nota f ▷ *I'll drop her a note.* Le dejaré una nota.; **Remember to take notes.** Acuérdate de tomar apuntes.; **to make a note of something** tomar nota de algo ❷ billete m ▷ *a five pound note* un billete de cinco libras

notebook n cuaderno m

notepad n bloc m de notas (pl blocs de notas)

nothing n nada f ▷ *He does nothing.* No hace nada.; **He does nothing but sleep.** No hace nada más que dormir.; **There's nothing to do.** No hay nada que hacer.

> When **nothing** goes before a verb in English it can be translated by either **nada** ... or **no** ... **nada**.

▷ *Nothing frightens him.* Nada lo asusta. ▷ *Nothing will happen.* No pasará nada.

notice n ❶ (physical object) letrero m ▷ *There was a notice outside the house.* Había un letrero fuera de la casa. ❷ (information) aviso m ▷ *There's a notice on the board about the trip.* Hay un aviso en el tablón sobre el viaje.; **a warning notice** un aviso; **He was transferred without notice.** Lo trasladaron sin previo aviso.; **until further notice** hasta nuevo aviso; **Don't take any notice of him!** ¡No le

a
b
c
d
e
f
g
h
i
j
k
l
m
n
o
p
q
r
s
t
u
v
w
x
y
z

hagas caso!

▌ Be careful not to translate **notice** by **noticia**.

▶ vb **to notice something** darse cuenta de algo ▷ *Don't worry. He won't notice the mistake.* No te preocupes. No se dará cuenta del error.

notice board n tablón m de anuncios (pl tablones de anuncios)

nought n cero m

noun n nombre m

novel n novela f

novelist n novelista mf

November n noviembre m ▷ *in November* en noviembre ▷ *on 7th November* el 7 de noviembre

now adv ahora ▷ *What are you doing now?* ¿Qué haces ahora?; **just now** en este momento ▷ *I'm rather busy just now.* En este momento estoy muy ocupado.; **I did it just now.** Lo acabo de hacer.; **It should be ready by now.** Ya debería estar listo.; **from now on** de ahora en adelante; **now and then** de vez en cuando

nowhere adv a ninguna parte ▷ *Where are you going for your holidays? -Nowhere.* ¿Adónde vas en vacaciones? -A ninguna parte.; **nowhere else** a ninguna otra parte ▷ *You can go to the shops but nowhere else.* Puedes ir a las tiendas pero a ninguna otra parte.; **The children were nowhere to be seen.** No se podía ver a los niños por ninguna parte.;

There was nowhere to play. No se podía jugar en ninguna parte.

nuclear adj nuclear ▷ *nuclear power* la energía nuclear

nuisance n fastidio ▷ *It's a nuisance having to clean the car.* Es un fastidio tener que limpiar el coche.; **Sorry to be a nuisance.** Siento molestarle.; **You're a nuisance!** ¡Eres un pesado!

numb adj **numb with cold** helado de frío

number n número m ▷ *They live at number five.* Viven en el número cinco.; *a large number of people* un gran número de gente; **What's your number?** (telephone) ¿Cuál es tu teléfono?

number plate n matrícula f (LatAm placa f)

nun n monja f

nurse n enfermero m, enfermera f; **She's a nurse.** Es enfermera.

nursery n ① (for children) guardería f infantil ② (for plants) vivero m

nursery school n preescolar m (LatAm guardería f)

nut n ① (almond) almendra f ② (peanut) cacahuete m ③ (hazelnut) avellana f ④ (walnut) nuez f (pl nueces); **I don't like nuts.** No me gustan los frutos secos. ⑤ (made of metal) tuerca f

nuts adj **He's nuts.** Está chiflado. (informal)

nylon n nylon

oak n roble m ▷ an oak barrel un barril de roble

oar n remo m

oats npl avena f

obedient adj obediente

obey vb obedecer; **to obey the rules** (in game) atenerse a las reglas del juego

object n objeto m

objection n objeción f (pl objeciones) ▷ There were no objections to the plan. No hubo objeciones al plan.

oboe n oboe m

obsessed adj obsesionado ▷ He's obsessed with trains. Está obsesionado con los trenes.

obsession n obsesión f (pl obsesiones) ▷ Football's an obsession of mine. El fútbol es una obsesión mía.

obvious adj obvio

obviously adv claro ▷ It was obviously impossible. Estaba claro que era imposible.; **Obviously not!** ¡Claro que no!

occasion n ocasión f (pl ocasiones) ▷ a special occasion una ocasión especial; **on several occasions** en varias ocasiones

occasionally adv de vez en cuando

occupation n empleo m

occupy vb ocupar ▷ The toilet was occupied. El lavabo estaba ocupado.

occur vb ocurrir ▷ The accident occurred yesterday. El accidente ocurrió ayer.; **It suddenly occurred to me that...** De repente se me ocurrió que...

ocean n océano m

o'clock adv **at four o'clock** a las cuatro; **It's one o'clock.** Es la una.; **It's five o'clock.** Son las cinco.

October n octubre m ▷ in October en octubre ▷ on 12 October el 12 de octubre

octopus n pulpo m

odd adj **❶** raro ▷ That's odd! ¡Qué raro! **❷** impar ▷ an odd number un número impar; **odd socks** calcetines desparejados

of prep de ▷ a boy of 10 un niño de 10 años ▷ a kilo of oranges un kilo de naranjas ▷ It's made of wood. Es de madera.

　 de + el changes to del.

▷ the wheels of the car las ruedas del

coche; **There were three of us.** Éramos tres.; **a friend of mine** un amigo mío; **That's very kind of you.** Es muy amable de su parte.

off *adj, adv, prep*

> For other expressions with **off**, see the verbs **get**, **take**, **turn** etc.

❶ *(heater, light, TV)* apagado ▷ *All the lights are off.* Todas las luces están apagadas. ❷ *(tap, gas)* cerrado ▷ *Are you sure the tap is off?* ¿Seguro que el grifo está cerrado? ❸ *(milk)* cortado ❹ *(meat)* estropeado; **to be off sick** estar ausente por enfermedad; **a day off** un día libre ▷ *She took a day off work to go to the wedding.* Se tomó un día libre para ir a la boda.; **I've got tomorrow off.** Mañana tengo el día libre.; **She's off school today.** Hoy no ha ido al colegio.; **I must be off now.** Me tengo que ir ahora.; **I'm off.** Me voy.; **The match is off.** El partido se ha suspendido.

offence *(US offense) n (crime)* delito *m*

offer *n* ❶ *(of money, job)* oferta *f* ❷ *(of help)* ofrecimiento *m*; **There was a special offer on tapes.** Las cintas estaban de oferta.

▶ *vb* ofrecer ▷ *He offered me a cigarette.* Me ofreció un cigarrillo.; **He offered to help me.** Se ofreció a ayudarme.

office *n* oficina *f*; **during office hours** en horas de oficina

officer *n (in the army)* oficial *mf*;

police officer el/la agente de policía

official *adj* oficial

off-licence *n* tienda *f* de bebidas alcohólicas

offside *adj* fuera de juego

often *adv* a menudo ▷ *It often rains.* Llueve a menudo.; **How often do you go to the gym?** ¿Cada cuánto vas al gimnasio?

oil *n* ❶ *(for lubrication, cooking)* aceite *m* ❷ *(crude oil)* petróleo *m*; **an oil painting** una pintura al óleo

▶ *vb* engrasar

oil rig *n* plataforma *f* petrolífera

ointment *n* pomada *f*

okay *excl, adv* ❶ *(more formally)* de acuerdo ▷ *Your appointment's at six o'clock. - Okay.* Su cita es a las seis. - De acuerdo. ❷ *(less formally)* vale ▷ *I'll meet you at six o'clock, okay?* Te veré a las seis, ¿vale?; **Are you okay?** ¿Estás bien?; **I'll do it tomorrow, if that's okay with you.** Lo haré mañana, si te parece bien.; **The film was okay.** La película no estuvo mal.

old *adj* ❶ viejo ▷ *an old house* una casa vieja ▷ *an old man* un viejo

> When talking about people it is more polite to use **anciano** instead of **viejo**.

▷ *old people* los ancianos ❷ *(former)* antiguo ▷ *my old English teacher* mi antiguo profesor de inglés; **How old are you?** ¿Cuántos años tienes?; **How old is the baby?** ¿Cuánto tiempo tiene el bebé?; **a twenty-year-old woman**

una mujer de veinte años; **He's
ten years old.** Tiene diez años.;
older adj *my older sister* mi
hermana mayor ▷ *She's two years
older than me.* Es dos años mayor
que yo.; **I'm the oldest in the
family.** Soy el mayor de la familia.

old age pensioner n
pensionista *mf*

old-fashioned adj anticuado ▷ *My
parents are rather old-fashioned.* Mis
padres son bastante anticuados.

olive n aceituna *f*

olive oil n aceite *m* de oliva

Olympic adj olímpico; **the
Olympics** las Olimpiadas

omelette n tortilla *f* francesa

on prep, adv

> There are several ways of
> translating **on**. Scan the
> examples to find one that is
> similar to what you want to
> say. For other expressions
> with **on**, see the verbs **go**, **put**,
> **turn** etc.

❶ en ▷ *on an island* en una isla ▷ *on
the wall* en la pared ▷ *It's on Channel
four.* Lo dan en el Canal cuatro. ▷ *on
TV* en la tele ▷ *on the 2nd floor* en
el segundo piso ▷ *We went on the
train.* Fuimos en tren. ❷ (*on top
of, about*) sobre ▷ *on the table* sobre
la mesa ▷ *a book on Gandhi* un libro
sobre Gandhi

> With days and dates, the
> definite article - **el, los** - is
> used in Spanish instead of a
> preposition.

▷ *on Friday* el viernes ▷ *on Fridays*

los viernes ▷ *on 20 June* el 20 de
junio; **on the left** a la izquierda;
on holiday de vacaciones; **It's
about 10 minutes on foot.** Está
a unos 10 minutos andando.; **She
was on antibiotics for a week.**
Estuvo una semana tomando
antibióticos.; **The coffee is on
the house.** Al café invita la casa.;
The drinks are on me. Invito yo.;
What is he on about? ¿De qué
está hablando?

▶ adj ❶ (*heater, light, TV*)
encendido ▷ *I think I left the light
on.* Me parece que he dejado la luz
encendida. ❷ (*tap, gas*) abierto
▷ *Leave the tap on.* Deja el grifo
abierto. ❸ en marcha ▷ *Is the
dishwasher on?* ¿Está en marcha
el lavavajillas?; **What's on at the
cinema?** ¿Qué echan en el cine?; **Is
the party still on?** ¿Todavía se va
a hacer la fiesta?; **I've got a lot on
this weekend.** Tengo mucho que
hacer este fin de semana.

once adv una vez ▷ *once a week* una
vez a la semana ▷ *once more* una
vez más; **Once upon a time...**
Érase una vez...; **once in a while**
de vez en cuando; **once and for
all** de una vez por todas; **at once**
enseguida

one num, pron uno (f una)

> Use **un** before a masculine
> noun.

▷ *I've got one brother and one
sister.* Tengo un hermano y una
hermana.; **one by one** uno a uno;
one another unos a otros ▷ *They*

all looked at one another. Se miraron todos unos a otros.

oneself pron ❶ (reflexive) se ▷ to wash oneself lavarse ❷ (after preposition, for emphasis) uno mismo (f una misma) ▷ It's quicker to do it oneself. Es más rápido si lo hace uno mismo.

one-way adj a one-way street una calle de sentido único; a one-way ticket un billete de ida

onion n cebolla f

online adj en línea

only adv sólo ▷ We only want to stay for one night. Sólo queremos quedarnos una noche.

▶ adj único ▷ She's an only child. Es hija única. ▷ Monday is the only day I'm free. El lunes es el único día que tengo libre.

▶ conj pero ▷ I'd like the same sweater, only in black. Quería el mismo jersey, pero en negro.

onwards adv en adelante ▷ from July onwards de julio en adelante

open adj abierto ▷ The shop's open on Sunday morning. La tienda está abierta los domingos por la mañana.; **Are you open tomorrow?** ¿Abre mañana?; **in the open air** al aire libre

▶ vb ❶ abrir ▷ What time do the shops open? ¿A qué hora abren las tiendas? ▷ Can I open the window? ¿Puedo abrir la ventana? ❷ abrirse ▷ The door opens automatically. La puerta se abre automáticamente.

opening hours npl horario m de

apertura

opera n ópera f

operate vb (machine) operar; **to operate on someone** operar a alguien

operation n operación f (pl operaciones); **I've never had an operation.** Nunca me han operado.

opinion n opinión f (pl opiniones) ▷ in my opinion en mi opinión; **What's your opinion?** ¿Tú qué opinas?

opinion poll n sondeo m de opinión

opponent n adversario m, adversaria f

opportunity n oportunidad f ▷ I've never had the opportunity to go to Spain. No he tenido nunca la oportunidad de ir a España.

opposed adj **to be opposed to something** oponerse a algo

opposite adj, adv, prep ❶ contrario ▷ It's in the opposite direction. Está en dirección contraria. ❷ opuesto ▷ the opposite sex el sexo opuesto ❸ enfrente ▷ They live opposite. Viven enfrente. ▶ frente a ▷ the girl sitting opposite me la chica sentada frente a mí

opposition n oposición f ▷ There is a lot of opposition to the new law. Hay una fuerte oposición a la nueva ley.

optician n óptico m, óptica f; **He's gone to the optician's.** Ha ido a la óptica.

optimistic adj optimista

option n ❶ opción f (pl opciones)
▷ I've got no option. No tengo otra
opción. ❷ (at school) asignatura
f optativa ▷ I'm doing geology as
my option. Tengo geología como
asignatura optativa.

or conj ❶ o ▷ Would you like tea or
coffee? ¿Quieres té o café?

> Use **u** before words beginning
with "o" or "ho".

▷ six or eight seis u ocho ▷ men or
women mujeres u hombres; **Hurry
up or you'll miss the bus.** Date
prisa, que vas a perder el autobús.
❷ ni ▷ I don't eat meat or fish. No
como carne ni pescado. ▷ She
can't dance or sing. No sabe bailar
ni cantar.

oral adj oral ▷ an oral exam un
examen oral
▶ n examen m oral (pl exámenes
orales) ▷ I've got my Spanish oral
soon. Tengo el examen oral de
español pronto.

orange n naranja f; **orange juice**
el zumo de naranja (LatAm jugo m
de naranja)
▶ adj naranja inv

orchard n huerto m

orchestra n orquesta f

order n ❶ (arrangement) orden m
▷ in alphabetical order por orden
alfabético ❷ (command) orden
f (pl órdenes) ▷ to obey an order
obedecer una orden; **The waiter
took our order.** El camarero tomó
nota de lo que íbamos a comer.; **in
order to** para ▷ He does it in order

to earn money. Lo hace para ganar
dinero.; **"out of order"** "averiado"
▶ vb pedir ▷ We ordered steak
and chips. Pedimos un filete con
patatas fritas.

order about vb dar órdenes a
▷ She was fed up with being ordered
about. Estaba harta de que le
dieran órdenes.

ordinary adj normal y corriente
▷ an ordinary day un día normal y
corriente

organ n (instrument) órgano m

organic adj (fruit, vegetables)
biológico

organization n organización f (pl
organizaciones)

organize vb organizar

original adj original

originally adv al principio

Orkneys npl **the Orkneys** las Islas
Órcadas

ornament n adorno m

orphan n huérfano m, huérfana f

other adj, pron otro (f otra) ▷ on
the other side of the street al otro
lado de la calle; **the other one** el
otro (f la otra) ▷ This one? - No, the
other one. ¿Éste? - No, el otro.; **the
others** los demás (fpl las demás)
▷ The others are going but I'm not.
Los demás van, pero yo no.

otherwise adv, conj ❶ (if not) si no
▷ Note down the number, otherwise
you'll forget it. Apúntate el número,
si no se te olvidará. ❷ (in other
ways) por lo demás ▷ I'm tired, but
otherwise I'm fine. Estoy cansado,
pero por lo demás estoy bien.

ought vb

To translate **ought to** use the conditional tense of **deber**.

▷ I ought to phone my parents. Debería llamar a mis padres.

For **ought to have** use the conditional tense of **deber** plus **haber** or the imperfect of **deber**.

▷ You ought to have warned me. Me deberías haber avisado. ▷ He ought to have known. Debía saberlo.

our adj nuestro ▷ our house nuestra casa

Our is usually translated by the definite article **el/los** or **la/las** when it's clear from the sentence who the possessor is or when referring to clothing or parts of the body.

▷ We took off our coats. Nos quitamos los abrigos. ▷ They stole our car. Nos robaron el coche.

ours pron ❶ el nuestro (pl los nuestros) ▷ Your car is much bigger than ours. Vuestro coche es mucho más grande que el nuestro. ❷ la nuestra (pl las nuestras) ▷ Your house is very different from ours. Vuestra casa es muy distinta a la nuestra. ❸ nuestro m (pl nuestros) ▷ Is this ours? ¿Esto es nuestro? ▷ a friend of ours un amigo nuestro ❹ nuestra f (pl nuestras) ▷ Sorry, that table is ours. Disculpen, esa mesa es nuestra. ▷ Isabel is a close friend of ours. Isabel es muy amiga nuestra.

ourselves pron ❶ (reflexive) nos

▷ We really enjoyed ourselves. Nos divertimos mucho. ❷ (after preposition, for emphasis) nosotros mismos (f nosotras mismas) ▷ Let's not talk about ourselves any more. No hablemos más de nosotros mismos. ▷ We built our garage ourselves. Nos construimos el garaje nosotros mismos.; **by ourselves** solos (f solas) ▷ We prefer to be by ourselves. Preferimos estar solos.

out prep, adv

There are several ways of translating **out**. Scan the examples to find one that is similar to what you want to say. For other expressions with out, see the verbs **go**, **put**, **turn** etc.

fuera ▷ It's cold out. Fuera hace frío.; **She's out.** Ha salido.; **to go out** salir ▷ I'm going out tonight. Voy a salir esta noche.; **to go out with somebody** salir con alguien ▷ I've been going out with him for two months. Llevo dos meses saliendo con él.; **a night out with my friends** una noche por ahí con mis amigos; **"way out"** "salida"; **out of town** fuera de la ciudad ▷ He lives out of town. Vive fuera de la ciudad.; **three kilometres out of town** a tres kilómetros de la ciudad; **to take something out of your pocket** sacar algo del bolsillo; **out of curiosity** por curiosidad; **We're out of milk.** Se nos ha acabado la leche.; **in nine**

cases out of ten en nueve de cada diez casos

▶ adj ❶ (lights, fire) apagado ▷ *All the lights are out.* Todas las luces están apagadas. ❷ (eliminated) eliminado: **That's it, Liverpool are out.** Ya está, Liverpool queda eliminado.; **The film is now out on video.** La película ya ha salido en vídeo.

outdoor adj al aire libre ▷ *an outdoor swimming pool* una piscina al aire libre

outdoors adv al aire libre

outfit n traje m ▷ *a cowboy outfit* un traje de vaquero

outing n excursión f (pl excursiones) ▷ *to go on an outing* ir de excursión

outline n ❶ (summary) esquema m

Although *esquema* ends in **-a**, it is actually a masculine noun.

▷ *This is an outline of the plan.* Aquí tienen un esquema del plan. ❷ (shape) contorno m ▷ *We could see the outline of the mountain.* Veíamos el contorno de la montaña.

outside n, adj ❶ exterior m ▷ *the outside of the house* el exterior de la casa ❷ exterior ▷ *the outside walls* las paredes exteriores

▶ prep, adv ❶ fuera ▷ *It's very cold outside.* Hace mucho frío fuera. ❷ fuera de ▷ *outside the school* fuera del colegio ▷ *outside school hours* fuera del horario escolar

outskirts npl afueras fpl ▷ *on the*

outskirts of town en las afueras de la ciudad

outstanding adj excepcional

oval adj ovalado

oven n horno m

over adj, adv, prep

When something is located over something, use **encima de**. When there is movement over something, use **por encima de**.

❶ encima de ▷ *There's a mirror over the washbasin.* Encima del lavabo hay un espejo. ❷ por encima de ▷ *The ball went over the wall.* La pelota pasó por encima de la pared.; **a bridge over the Thames** un puente sobre el Támesis ❸ más de ▷ *It's over 20 kilos.* Pesa más de 20 kilos.; **The temperature was over 30 degrees.** La temperatura superaba los 30 grados. ❹ durante ▷ *over the holidays* durante las vacaciones ❺ terminado; **I'll be happy when the exams are over.** Estaré feliz cuando se hayan terminado los exámenes.; **over here** aquí; **It's over there.** Está por allí.; **all over Scotland** en toda Escocia; **The shop is over the road.** La tienda está al otro lado de la calle.; **I spilled coffee over my shirt.** Me manché la camisa de café.

overcast adj cubierto ▷ *The sky was overcast.* El cielo estaba cubierto.

overdose n sobredosis f (pl

sobredosis)

overdraft n descubierto m

overseas adv (live, work) en el extranjero ▷ I'd like to work overseas. Me gustaría trabajar en el extranjero.

overtake vb adelantar (LatAm rebasar)

overtime n horas fpl extras ▷ to work overtime trabajar horas extras

overweight adj **to be overweight** tener exceso de peso

owe vb deber ▷ How much do I owe you? ¿Cuánto te debo?

owing to prep debido a ▷ owing to bad weather debido al mal tiempo

owl n búho m

own adj, pron propio ▷ This is my own recipe. Ésta es mi propia receta. ▷ I wish I had a room of my own. Me gustaría tener mi propia habitación.; **on his own** él solo ▷ on our own nosotros solos ▶ vb tener

own up vb confesarse culpable; **to own up to something** confesar algo

owner n propietario m, propietaria f

oxygen n oxígeno m

oyster n ostra f

ozone layer n capa f de ozono

Pacific n **the Pacific** el Pacífico

pacifier n (in US) chupete m

pack vb hacer las maletas (LatAm empacar) ▷ I'll help you pack. Te ayudaré a hacer las maletas.; **I've already packed my case.** Ya he hecho mi maleta.; **Pack it in!** ¡Vale ya!
▶ n paquete m ▷ a pack of cigarettes un paquete de tabaco; **a pack of cards** una baraja

package n paquete m; **a package holiday** unas vacaciones organizadas

packed adj abarrotado ▷ The cinema was packed. El cine estaba abarrotado.

packed lunch n **I take a packed lunch to school.** Me llevo la comida al colegio.

packet n paquete m ▷ *a packet of cigarettes* un paquete de tabaco; **a packet of crisps** una bolsa de patatas fritas

pad n bloc m

paddle vb ❶ (swim) chapotear ❷ remar ▷ *to paddle a canoe* remar en canoa
　▶ n pala f; **to go for a paddle** mojarse los pies

padlock n candado m

page n página f ▷ *on page 13* en la página 13
　▶ vb **to page somebody** llamar a alguien al busca

paid vb see **pay**

pain n dolor m ▷ *a terrible pain* un dolor tremendo ▷ *She's in a lot of pain.* Tiene muchos dolores.; **I've got a pain in my stomach.** Me duele el estómago.; **He's a real pain.** Es un auténtico pelmazo. (informal)

painful adj

> doloroso is used when talking about what causes pain, and dolorido for the person or thing that feels pain.

　❶ doloroso ▷ *a painful injury* una herida dolorosa ❷ dolorido ▷ *Her feet were swollen and painful.* Tenía los pies hinchados y doloridos.; **Is it painful?** ¿Te duele?

painkiller n analgésico m

paint n pintura f
　▶ vb pintar ▷ *to paint something green* pintar algo de verde

paintbrush n ❶ (for an artist) pincel m ❷ (for decorating) brocha f

painter n pintor m, pintora f

painting n ❶ (picture) cuadro m ▷ *a painting by Picasso* un cuadro de Picasso ❷ (activity) pintura f

pair n par m ▷ *a pair of shoes* un par de zapatos; **a pair of scissors** unas tijeras; **a pair of trousers** unos pantalones; **in pairs** por parejas

Pakistan n Paquistán m

Pakistani adj paquistaní (pl paquistaníes)
　▶ n paquistaní mf (pl paquistaníes)

palace n palacio m

pale adj ❶ pálido ▷ *She still looks very pale.* Está todavía muy pálida.; **to turn pale** ponerse pálido ❷ claro ▷ *pale green* verde claro; **pale pink** rosa pálido; **pale blue** azul celeste

Palestine n Palestina f

Palestinian adj palestino
　▶ n palestino m, palestina f

palm n (of hand) palma f; **a palm tree** una palmera

pan n ❶ (saucepan) cacerola f ❷ (frying pan) sartén f (pl sartenes)

pancake n crepe f (LatAm panqueque m)

panic n pánico m
　▶ vb **He panicked as soon as he saw the blood.** Le entró pánico en cuanto vio la sangre.; **Don't panic!** ¡Tranquilo!

panther n pantera f

pantomime n revista f musical navideña

pants npl ❶ (women's underwear)

bragas fpl ❷ (men's underwear)
calzoncillos mpl ❸ (in US)
pantalones mpl

pantyhose npl (in US) medias fpl

paper n ❶ papel m ▷ a paper bag
una bolsa de papel; **a piece of
paper** un papel (LatAm una hoja);
an exam paper un examen
❷ (newspaper) periódico m

paperback n libro m de bolsillo

paper clip n clip m (pl clips)

paper round n **to do a paper
round** repartir los periódicos a
domicilio

parachute n paracaídas m (pl
paracaídas)

parade n desfile m

paradise n paraíso m

paragraph n párrafo m

parallel adj paralelo

paralysed adj paralizado

paramedic n auxiliar m sanitario,
auxiliar f sanitaria

parcel n paquete m

pardon excl **Pardon?** ¿Cómo?

parents npl padres mpl (LatAm
papás mpl)

> Be careful not to translate
> **parents** by **parientes**.

Paris n París m

park n parque m; **a national park**
un parque nacional; **a theme
park** un parque temático; **a car
park** un aparcamiento (LatAm un
estacionamiento)
▶ vb aparcar ▷ Where can I park
my car? ¿Dónde puedo aparcar el
coche?; **"no parking"** "prohibido
aparcar"

parking lot n (in US)
aparcamiento m

parking meter n parquímetro m

parking ticket n multa f de
aparcamiento

parliament n parlamento m; **the
Spanish Parliament** las Cortes

parole n **on parole** en libertad
condicional

parrot n loro m

parsley n perejil m

part n ❶ parte f ▷ The first part
of the play was boring. La primera
parte de la obra fue aburrida.
❷ papel m ▷ She had a small part in
the film. Tenía un pequeño papel
en la película. ❸ pieza f ▷ spare
parts piezas de repuesto; **to take
part in something** participar
en algo ▷ Thousands of people took
part in the demonstration. Miles
de personas participaron en la
manifestación.
▶ vb **to part with something**
desprenderse de algo ▷ I hate to
part with this lamp. Me fastidia
tener que desprenderme de esta
lámpara.

particular adj ❶ (definite)
concreto ▷ I can't remember that
particular film. No recuerdo esa
película concreta. ❷ (special)
especial ▷ He showed a particular
interest in the subject. Mostró un
interés especial en el tema.; **in
particular** en concreto ▷ Are you
looking for anything in particular?
¿Busca algo en concreto? ▷ nothing
in particular nada en concreto

particularly adv especialmente
▷ a particularly boring lecture una
clase especialmente aburrida

partly adv en parte ▷ It was partly
my own fault. En parte fue culpa
mía.

partner n ❶ (in business) socio m,
socia f ❷ (in relationship) pareja f

part-time adj, adv a tiempo
parcial ▷ a part-time job un trabajo
a tiempo parcial ▷ She works part-
time. Trabaja a tiempo parcial.

party n ❶ fiesta f ▷ a birthday
party una fiesta de cumpleaños
❷ partido m ▷ the Conservative
Party el partido conservador
❸ grupo m ▷ a party of tourists un
grupo de turistas

pass n ❶ (in football) pase m ❷ (in
mountains) puerto m ❸ (in exam)
aprobado m; a bus pass un abono
para el autobús
▷ vb ❶ pasar ▷ Could you pass me
the salt, please? ¿Me pasas la sal,
por favor? ▷ The time has passed
quickly. El tiempo ha pasado
rápido. ❷ adelantar ▷ We were
passed by a huge lorry. Nos adelantó
un camión enorme. ❸ pasar por
delante de ▷ I pass his house on my
way to school. Paso por delante de
su casa de camino al colegio.
❹ aprobar ▷ to pass an exam
aprobar un examen

pass out vb desmayarse

passage n ❶ pasaje m ▷ Read the
passage carefully. Lea el pasaje con
atención. ❷ pasillo m ▷ a narrow
passage un estrecho pasillo

passenger n pasajero m,
pasajera f

passion n pasión f (pl pasiones)

passive adj pasivo; a passive
smoker un fumador pasivo

Passover n Pascua f judía

passport n pasaporte m ▷ passport
control el control de pasaportes

password n contraseña f

past adj, adv, prep pasado ▷ This
past year has been very difficult. Este
año pasado ha sido muy difícil.;
**The school is 100 metres past
the traffic lights.** El colegio está
a unos 100 metros pasado el
semáforo.; **to go past** pasar ▷ The
bus went past without stopping. El
autobús pasó sin parar.; **It's half
past ten.** Son las diez y media.;
It's a quarter past nine. Son las
nueve y cuarto.; **It's ten past
eight.** Son las ocho y diez.; **It's
past midnight.** Es pasada la
medianoche.
▷ n pasado m ▷ I try not to think of
the past. Intento no pensar en el
pasado.; **This was common in
the past.** Antiguamente esto era
normal.

pasta n pasta f

pasteurized adj pasteurizado

pastry n ❶ (dough) masa f
❷ (cake) pastel m

patch n ❶ parche m ▷ a patch of
material un parche de tela; **He's
got a bald patch.** Tiene una
calva incipiente.; **They're going
through a bad patch.** Están
pasando una mala racha.

pâté n paté m

path n sendero m

pathetic adj penoso ▷ That was a pathetic excuse. Fue una excusa penosa.

patience n ❶ paciencia f ▷ He hasn't got much patience. No tiene mucha paciencia. ❷ (game) solitario m

patient n paciente m, paciente f ▸ adj paciente

patio n patio m

patrol n patrulla f; **to be on patrol** estar de patrulla

patrol car n coche m patrulla (pl coches patrulla)

pattern n ❶ motivo m ❷ (for sewing) patrón m

pause n pausa f

pavement n acera f

paw n pata f

pay n sueldo m ▷ a pay rise un aumento de sueldo
▸ vb pagar ▷ Can I pay by cheque? ¿Puedo pagar con cheque?; **to pay money into an account** ingresar dinero en una cuenta; **I'll pay you back tomorrow.** Mañana te devuelvo el dinero.; **to pay for something** pagar algo ▷ I paid for my ticket. Pagué el billete.; **I paid £50 for it.** Me costó 50 libras.; **to pay somebody a visit** ir a ver a alguien ▷ Paul paid us a visit last night. Paul vino a vernos anoche.

payment n pago m

payphone n teléfono m público

PC n (= personal computer) PC m

PE n (= physical education) educación f física ▷ We do PE twice a week. Tenemos educación física dos veces a la semana.

pea n guisante m

peace n paz f; **peace talks** negociaciones de la paz; **a peace treaty** un tratado de paz

peaceful adj ❶ (non-violent) pacífico ▷ a peaceful protest una manifestación pacífica ❷ (restful) apacible ▷ a peaceful afternoon una tarde apacible

peach n melocotón m (pl melocotones)

peacock n pavo m real

peak n ❶ (of mountain) cumbre f ❷ (high point) apogeo m ▷ She's at the peak of her career. Está en el apogeo de su carrera profesional.; **in peak season** en temporada alta

peak rate n tarifa f máxima

peanut n cacahuete m (LatAm maní m (pl maníes))

peanut butter n crema f de cacahuete

pear n pera f

pearl n perla f

pebble n guijarro m

peculiar adj raro

pedal n pedal m

pedestrian n peatón m (pl peatones)

pedestrian crossing n paso m de peatones

pee n **to have a pee** hacer pis

peel n piel f
▸ vb pelar ▷ Shall I peel the potatoes? ¿Pelo las patatas?

peg n ❶ (for coats) gancho m ❷ (clothes peg) pinza f ❸ (tent peg) estaca f

pelvis n pelvis f (pl pelvis)

pen n ❶ (ballpoint pen) bolígrafo m ❷ (fountain pen) pluma f ❸ (felt-tip pen) rotulador m

penalty n ❶ pena f ▷ The death penalty la pena de muerte ❷ (in football) penalty m (pl penaltys); **a penalty shoot-out** una tanda de penaltys

pence npl 24 pence 24 peniques

pencil n lápiz m (pl lápices) (LatAm lapicero m); **to write in pencil** escribir a lápiz

pencil case n estuche m

pencil sharpener n sacapuntas m (pl sacapuntas)

penfriend n amigo m por correspondencia, amiga f por correspondencia

penguin n pingüino m

penicillin n penicilina f

penis n pene m

penknife n navaja f

penny n penique m

pension n pensión f (pl pensiones)

pensioner n pensionista mf

people npl ❶ gente f ▷ The people were nice. La gente era simpática. ▷ a lot of people mucha gente ❷ personas fpl ▷ six people seis personas; **People say that...** Dicen que...; **How many people are there in your family?** ¿Cuántos sois en tu familia?; **Spanish people** los españoles

pepper n ❶ pimienta f ▷ Pass the pepper, please. ¿Me pasas la pimienta? ❷ pimiento m (LatAm chile m) ▷ a green pepper un pimiento verde

peppermill n molinillo m de pimienta

peppermint n caramelo m de menta; **peppermint chewing gum** el chicle de menta

per prep por ▷ per person por persona; **per day** al día; **per week** a la semana

per cent adv por ciento ❶ ▷ 50 per cent 50 por ciento

percentage n porcentaje m

percussion n percusión f ▷ I play percussion. Toco la percusión.

perfect adj perfecto ▷ Dave speaks perfect Spanish. Dave habla un español perfecto.

perfectly adv ❶ (very well) perfectamente ▷ You know perfectly well what happened. Sabes perfectamente lo que ocurrió. ❷ (absolutely) completamente ▷ a perfectly normal child un niño completamente normal

perform vb (a play) representar ▷ to perform Hamlet representar Hamlet; **The team performed brilliantly.** El equipo tuvo una brillante actuación.

performance n ❶ espectáculo m ▷ The performance lasts two hours. El espectáculo dura dos horas. ❷ interpretación f (pl interpretaciones) ▷ his performance as Hamlet su interpretación de Hamlet

perfume n perfume m
perhaps adv quizás ▷ Perhaps they were tired. Quizás estaban cansados.

> Use the present subjunctive after **quizás** to refer to the future.

▷ Perhaps he'll come tomorrow. Quizás venga mañana.; **perhaps not** quizás no

period n ❶ periodo m ▷ for a limited period por un periodo limitado ❷ clase f ▷ Each period lasts forty minutes. Cada clase dura cuarenta minutos. ❸ época f ▷ the Victorian period la época victoriana ❹ regla f ▷ I'm having my period. Estoy con la regla.

perm n permanente f ▷ She's got a perm. Lleva permanente.

permanent adj ❶ permanente ▷ a permanent state of tension un estado permanente de tensión ❷ fijo ▷ a permanent job un trabajo fijo

permission n permiso m ▷ Could I have permission to leave early? ¿Tengo permiso para salir antes?

permit n permiso m ▷ a work permit un permiso de trabajo

person n persona f ▷ She's a very nice person. Es muy buena persona.; **in person** en persona

personal adj personal ▷ Those letters are personal. Son cartas personales.; **he's a personal friend of mine** es amigo íntimo mío

personality n personalidad f
personally adv personalmente ▷ Personally I don't agree. Yo personalmente no estoy de acuerdo.; **I don't know him personally.** No lo conozco en persona.; **Don't take it personally.** No te lo tomes como algo personal.

personal stereo n walkman® m
perspiration n transpiración f
persuade vb convencer

> Use the subjunctive after **convencer de que** when translating "to persuade somebody to do something".

▷ She persuaded me to go with her. Me convenció de que fuera con ella.

Peru n Perú m
Peruvian adj peruano
▶ n peruano m, peruana f
pessimistic adj pesimista ▷ Don't be so pessimistic! ¡No seas tan pesimista!

pest n pesado m, pesada f ▷ He's a real pest! ¡Es un pesado!

pester vb dar la lata a ▷ He's always pestering me. Siempre me está dando la lata.

pet n animal m doméstico; **Have you got a pet?** ¿Tenéis algún animal en casa?; **She's the teacher's pet.** Es la enchufada del profesor.

petrol n gasolina f; **unleaded petrol** gasolina sin plomo; **4-star petrol** gasolina súper

petrol station n gasolinera f

pharmacy n farmacia f
  - Pharmacies in Spain are
  - identified by a special green
  - cross outside the shop.

pheasant n faisán m (pl faisanes)

philosophy n filosofía f

phobia n fobia f

phone n teléfono m; **by phone**
por teléfono; **to be on the phone**
(talking) estar al teléfono ▷ She's
on the phone at the moment. Ahora
mismo está al teléfono.; **Can I use
the phone, please?** ¿Puedo hacer
una llamada?
  ▶ vb llamar ▷ I'll phone you
tomorrow. Mañana te llamo.

phone bill n factura f del teléfono

phone book n guía f telefónica

phone box n cabina f telefónica

phone call n llamada f de
teléfono; **to make a phone call**
hacer una llamada

phonecard n tarjeta f telefónica

phone number n número m de
teléfono

photo n foto f

> Although **foto** ends in **-o**, it is
> actually a feminine noun.

to take a photo hacer una foto ▷ I
took a photo of the bride and groom.
Les hice una foto a los novios.

photocopier n fotocopiadora f

photocopy n fotocopia f
  ▶ vb fotocopiar

photograph n fotografía f; **to
take a photograph** hacer una
fotografía ▷ I took a photograph of
the bride and groom. Les hice una
fotografía a los novios.

  ▶ vb fotografiar

photographer n fotógrafo m,
fotógrafa f ▷ She's a photographer.
Es fotógrafa.

photography n fotografía f ▷ My
hobby is photography. Mi hobby es
la fotografía.

phrase n frase f

phrase book n manual m de
conversación

physical adj físico
  ▶ n (in US) reconocimiento m
  médico

physicist n físico m, física f ▷ a
nuclear physicist un físico nuclear

physics n física f ▷ She teaches
physics. Enseña física.

physiotherapist n fisioterapeuta
mf

physiotherapy n fisioterapia f

pianist n pianista mf

piano n piano m ▷ I play the piano.
Toco el piano.

pick n **Take your pick!** ¡Elige el que
quieras!

> Replace **el que** with **la que, los
> que** or **las que** as appropriate
> to agree with the thing or
> things you can take your
> pick of.

  ▶ vb ❶ (choose) elegir ▷ I picked
the biggest piece. Elegí el trozo más
grande. ❷ (for team) seleccionar
▷ I've been picked for the team. Me
han seleccionado para el equipo.
❸ (fruit, flowers) recoger; **to
pick on somebody** meterse con
alguien ▷ She's always picking on
me. Siempre se está metiendo

conmigo.

pick up vb ❶ (from floor, airport, station) recoger ▷ We'll come to the airport to pick you up. Iremos a recogerte al aeropuerto. ❷ (learn) aprender

pickpocket n carterista mf

picnic n picnic m (pl picnics); **to have a picnic** irse de picnic

picture n ❶ (illustration) ilustración f (pl ilustraciones) ❷ (photo) foto f

Although **foto** ends in **-o**, it is actually a feminine noun.

❸ (painting) cuadro m ❹ (portrait) retrato m ❺ (drawing) dibujo m; **to draw a picture of something** dibujar algo; **to paint a picture of something** pintar algo; **the pictures** el cine ▷ Shall we go to the pictures? ¿Vamos al cine?

picture message n mensaje m con foto

pie n ❶ (sweet) tarta f ▷ an apple pie una tarta de manzana ❷ (of meat) pastel m ▷ a meat pie un pastel de carne

piece n ❶ trozo m ▷ a piece of cake un trozo de tarta; **A small piece, please.** Un trocito, por favor. ❷ (individual) pieza f ▷ a 500-piece jigsaw un puzzle de 500 piezas ❸ (of something larger) pedazo f ▷ A piece of plaster fell from the roof. Un pedazo de yeso se cayó del tejado.; **a piece of furniture** un mueble; **a piece of advice** un consejo; **a 10p piece** una moneda de 10 peniques

pier n muelle m

pierced adj **I've got pierced ears.** Tengo los agujeros hechos en las orejas.

pig n cerdo m

pigeon n paloma f

piggyback n **to give somebody a piggyback** llevar a alguien a cuestas

piggy bank n hucha f

pigtail n trenza f

pile n ❶ (untidy heap) montón m (pl montones) ▷ a pile of dirty laundry un montón de ropa sucia ❷ (tidy stack) pila f; **Put your books in a pile on my desk.** Apilad vuestros cuadernos en mi mesa.

pill n píldora f; **to be on the pill** tomar la píldora

pillow n almohada f

pilot n piloto mf ▷ He's a pilot. Es piloto.

pimple n grano m

pin n alfiler m; **pins and needles** el hormigueo ▷ I've got pins and needles. Tengo hormigueo.

PIN n (= personal identification number) número m secreto

pinball n máquina f de bolas; **They're playing pinball.** Juegan a la máquina.

pinch vb ❶ pellizcar ▷ He pinched me! ¡Me ha pellizcado! ❷ birlar (informal) ▷ Who's pinched my pen? ¿Quién me ha birlado el bolígrafo?

pine n pino m ▷ a pine table una mesa de pino

pineapple n piña f

pink adj rosa inv

pint n pinta f
- In Spain measurements are in litres and centilitres. A pint is about 0.6 litres.

to have a pint tomarse una cerveza ▷ He's gone out for a pint. Ha salido a tomarse una cerveza.

pipe n ❶ tubería f ▷ The pipes froze. Se helaron las tuberías. ❷ pipa f ▷ He smokes a pipe. Fuma en pipa.; **the pipes** la gaita ▷ He plays the pipes. Toca la gaita.

pirate n pirata mf

pirated adj pirata inv ▷ a pirated video un vídeo pirata

Pisces n (sign) Piscis m; **I'm Pisces.** Soy piscis.

pistol n pistola f

pitch n ❶ campo m (LatAm cancha f) ▷ a football pitch un campo de fútbol
▶ vb montar ▷ We pitched our tent near the beach. Montamos la tienda cerca de la playa.

pity n ❶ compasión f ▷ They showed no pity. No demostraron ninguna compasión.; **What a pity!** ¡Qué pena!
▶ vb compadecer ▷ I don't hate him, I pity him. No lo odio, lo compadezco.

pizza n pizza f

place n ❶ lugar m ▷ It's a quiet place. Es un lugar tranquilo. ❷ plaza f ▷ Book your place for the trip now. Reserve ya su plaza para el viaje. ❸ (in sports) puesto m ▷ Spain won third place in the games. España consiguió el tercer puesto

en los juegos.; **a parking place** un sitio para aparcar; **to change places** cambiarse de sitio; **to take place** tener lugar ▷ Elections will take place on November 25th. Las elecciones tendrán lugar el 25 de noviembre.; **at your place** en tu casa ▷ Shall we meet at your place? ¿Nos vemos en tu casa?; **Do you want to come round to my place?** ¿Quieres venir a mi casa?
▶ vb colocar ▷ He placed his hand on hers. Colocó su mano sobre la de ella.

plain adj, adv ❶ (not patterned) liso ▷ a plain tie una corbata lisa ❷ (not fancy) sencillo ▷ a plain white blouse una blusa blanca sencilla; **It was plain to see.** Era obvio.
▶ n llanura f

plain chocolate n chocolate m amargo

plait n trenza f ▷ She wears her hair in plaits. Lleva trenzas.

plan n ❶ plan m ▷ What are your plans for the holidays? ¿Qué planes tienes para las vacaciones?; **to make plans** hacer planes; **Everything went according to plan.** Todo fue según lo previsto. ❷ plano m ▷ a plan of the campsite un plano del camping; **my essay plan** el esquema de mi trabajo
▶ vb ❶ (make plans for) planear ▷ We're planning a trip to France. Estamos planeando hacer un viaje a Francia. ❷ (schedule) planificar ▷ Plan your revision carefully. Tienes

a
b
c
d
e
f
g
h
i
j
k
l
m
n
o
p
q
r
s
t
u
v
w
x
y
z

que planificar bien el repaso.;
to plan to do something tener
la intención de hacer algo ▷ *I'm
planning to get a job in the holidays.*
Tengo la intención de encontrar
un trabajo para las vacaciones.

plane n avión m (pl aviones) ▷ *by
plane* en avión

planet n planeta m

> Although **planeta** ends in
> **-a**, it is actually a masculine
> noun.

plant n planta f; **a chemical plant**
una planta química
▶ vb plantar ▷ *We planted fruit trees
and vegetables.* Plantamos árboles
frutales y hortalizas.

plaster n ❶ (for cut) tirita f
❷ (for broken limb) escayola f; **Her
leg's in plaster.** Lleva la pierna
escayolada.

plastic n plástico m ▷ *It's made of
plastic.* Es de plástico.
▶ adj de plástico ▷ *a plastic bag* una
bolsa de plástico

plate n plato m

platform n ❶ andén m (pl
andenes) ❷ (for speaker, performer)
estrado m

play n obra f de teatro; **a play
by Shakespeare** una obra de
Shakespeare; **to put on a play**
montar una obra
▶ vb jugar ▷ *He's playing with
his friends.* Está jugando con sus
amigos. ❷ jugar contra ▷ *Spain
will play Scotland next month.*
España juega contra Escocia el
mes que viene. ❸ jugar a ▷ *Can*

you play pool? ¿Sabes jugar al billar
americano? ❹ tocar ▷ *I play the
guitar.* Toco la guitarra. ❺ poner
▷ *She's always playing that record.*
Siempre está poniendo ese disco.
❻ hacer de ▷ *I would love to play
Cleopatra.* Me encantaría hacer de
Cleopatra.

player n ❶ jugador m, jugadora
f ▷ *a game for four players* un juego
para cuatro jugadores; **a football
player** un futbolista ❷ (musician)
músico m, música f; **a piano
player** un pianista; **a saxophone
player** un saxofonista

playground n ❶ (at school) patio
m de recreo ❷ (in park) columpios
mpl

playgroup n guardería f

playing card n naipe m

playing field n campo m de
deportes (LatAm cancha f de
deportes)

playtime n recreo m

pleasant adj agradable ▷ *We had a
very pleasant evening.* Pasamos una
tarde muy agradable.

please excl por favor ▷ *Two coffees,
please.* Dos cafés, por favor.

> **por favor** is not as common as
> **please** and can be omitted in
> many cases. Spanish speakers
> may show their politeness by
> their intonation, or by using
> **usted**.

Can we have the bill please? ¿Nos
puede traer la cuenta?; **Please
come in.** Pase.; **Would you please
be quiet?** ¿Quieres hacer el favor

de callarte?

pleased adj My mother's not going to be very pleased. A mi madre no le va a hacer mucha gracia.; It's beautiful: she'll be very pleased with it. Es precioso: le va a gustar mucho.; Pleased to meet you! ¡Encantado!

pleasure n placer m ▷ I read for pleasure. Leo por placer.

plenty pron I've got plenty. Tengo de sobra.; That's plenty, thanks. Así está bien, gracias.; plenty of (1) (lots of) mucho ▷ He's got plenty of energy. Tiene mucha energía. (2) (more than enough) de sobra ▷ We've got plenty of time. Tenemos tiempo de sobra.

pliers n alicates mpl

plot n ❶ (of story, play) argumento m ❷ (conspiracy) complot m (pl complots) ▷ a plot against the president un complot contra el presidente ❸ (for vegetables) huerto m
▶ vb conspirar

plough n arado m
▶ vb arar

plug n ❶ (electrical) enchufe m ❷ (for sink) tapón m (pl tapones)

plug in vb enchufar ▷ Is the iron plugged in? ¿Está enchufada la plancha?

plum n ciruela f

plumber n fontanero m, fontanera f ▷ He's a plumber. Es fontanero.

plump adj rechoncho

plural n plural m

plus prep, adj más ▷ 4 plus 3 equals 7.

4 más 3 son 7.; three children plus a dog tres niños y un perro; I got a B plus. Saqué un notable alto.

p.m. abbr at 2 a las dos de la tarde.; at 9 p.m. a las nueve de la noche

Use **de la tarde** if it's light and **de la noche** if it's dark.

pneumonia n pulmonía f

poach vb a poached egg un huevo escalfado

pocket n bolsillo m ▷ He had his hands in his pockets. Tenía las manos en los bolsillos.

pocket money n paga f ▷ How much pocket money do you get? ¿Cuánto te dan de paga?

poem n poema m

Although **poem** ends in -a, it is actually a masculine noun.

poet n poeta m, poetisa f

poetry n poesía f

point n ❶ punto m ▷ They scored five points. Sacaron cinco puntos. ❷ momento m ▷ At that point, we decided to leave. En aquel momento decidimos marcharnos. ❸ (of pencil) punta f ❹ comentario m ▷ He made some interesting points. Hizo algunos comentarios de interés.; They were on the point of finding it. Estaban a punto de encontrarlo.; a point of view un punto de vista; That's a good point! ¡Tiene razón!; That's not the point. No tiene nada que ver.; There's no point. No tiene sentido. ▷ There's no point in waiting. No tiene sentido esperar.;

What's the point? ¿Para qué? ▷ *What's the point of leaving so early?* ¿Para qué salir tan pronto?; **Punctuality isn't my strong point.** La puntualidad no es mi fuerte.; **two point five (2.5)** dos coma cinco (2,5)
▶ *vb* señalar con el dedo ▷ *Don't point!* ¡No señales con el dedo!; **to point at somebody** señalar a alguien con el dedo ▷ *She pointed at Anne.* Señaló a Anne con el dedo.; **to point a gun at somebody** apuntar a alguien con una pistola

point out *vb* ❶ señalar ▷ *The guide pointed out the Alhambra to us.* El guía nos señaló la Alhambra. ❷ indicar ▷ *I should point out that...* Me gustaría indicar que...

pointless *adj* inútil ▷ *It's pointless arguing.* Es inútil discutir.

poison *n* veneno m
▶ *vb* envenenar

poisonous *adj* ❶ (animal, plant) venenoso ❷ (chemical) tóxico ▷ *poisonous gases* gases tóxicos

poke *vb* **He poked me in the eye.** Me metió un dedo en el ojo.

poker *n* póker m ▷ *I play poker.* Juego al póker.

Poland *n* Polonia f

polar bear *n* oso m polar

Pole *n* (person) polaco m, polaca f

pole *n* poste m ▷ *a telegraph pole* un poste de telégrafos; **a tent pole** un mástil de tienda; **a ski pole** un bastón de esquí; **the North Pole** el Polo Norte; **the South Pole** el Polo Sur

police *npl* policía f ▷ *We called the police.* Llamamos a la policía.

police car *n* coche m de policía

policeman *n* policía m (LatAm agente m)

police station *n* comisaría f

policewoman *n* policía f (LatAm agente f)

Polish *adj* polaco
▶ *n* (language) polaco m

polish *n* ❶ (for shoes) betún m ❷ (for furniture) cera f
▶ *vb* (shoes, glass) limpiar; **to polish the furniture** sacar brillo a los muebles

polite *adj* educado ▷ *a polite child* un niño educado; **It's not polite to point.** Es de mala educación señalar con el dedo.

political *adj* político

politician *n* político m, política f

politics *n* política f ▷ *I'm not interested in politics.* No me interesa la política.

polluted *adj* contaminado

pollution *n* contaminación f

polo-necked sweater *n* suéter m de cuello alto

polythene bag *n* bolsa f de plástico

pond *n* ❶ (natural) charca f ❷ (artificial) estanque m

pony *n* poney m

ponytail *n* coleta f ▷ *He's got a ponytail.* Lleva coleta.

pony trekking *n* **to go pony trekking** ir de excursión en poney

poodle *n* caniche m

pool *n* ❶ (pond) estanque m

❷ (swimming pool) piscina f
❸ (game) billar m americano; **a pool table** una mesa de billar; **the pools** las quinielas ▷ I do the pools every week. Juego a las quinielas todas las semanas.

poor adj ❶ pobre

pobre goes after the noun when it means that someone has not got very much money. It goes before the noun when you want to show that you feel sorry for someone.
▷ a poor family una familia pobre
▷ Poor David! ¡Pobre David!; **the poor** los pobres ❸ malo

Use **mal** before a masculine singular noun.
▷ He's a poor actor. Es un mal actor.

pop adj pop inv ▷ pop music la música pop ▷ a pop star una estrella pop ▷ a pop group un grupo de música pop

pop in vb entrar un momento

popcorn n palomitas fpl de maíz

Pope n the Pope el Papa

Although **Papa** ends in **-a**, it is actually a masculine noun.

poppy n amapola f

popular adj popular ▷ Football is the most popular game in this country. El fútbol es el deporte más popular de este país.; **She's a very popular girl.** Es una chica que cae bien a todo el mundo.; **This is a very popular style.** Este estilo está muy de moda.

population n población f (pl poblaciones)

porch n porche m de entrada

pork n carne f de cerdo (LatAm carne f de puerco); **a pork chop** una chuleta de cerdo

porridge n gachas fpl de avena

port n (harbour, town) puerto m

portable adj portátil ▷ a portable TV un televisor portátil

porter n ❶ (in hotel) portero m, portera f ❷ (at station) mozo m de equipajes, moza f de equipajes

portion n ❶ (of food) ración f (pl raciones) ▷ a large portion of chips una ración grande de patatas fritas ❷ (part) porción f (pl porciones) ▷ a small portion of your salary una pequeña porción de tu salario

portrait n retrato m

Portugal n Portugal m

Portuguese adj portugués (f portuguesa) (mpl portugueses)
▶ n (language) portugués m; **the Portuguese** los portugueses

posh adj de lujo ▷ a posh car un coche de lujo

position n posición f (pl posiciones)

positive adj ❶ positivo ▷ a positive attitude una actitud positiva ❷ (sure) seguro ▷ I'm positive. Estoy completamente seguro.

possession n possessions las pertenencias

possibility n posibilidad f ▷ There were several possibilities. Había varias posibilidades.

possible adj posible; **as soon as**

possible lo antes posible

  ■ **es posible que** has to be followed by a verb in the subjunctive.

It's possible that he's gone away. Es posible que se haya ido.

possibly adv tal vez ▷ *Are you coming to the party? - Possibly.* ¿Vas a venir a la fiesta? -Tal vez.; ... **if you possibly can.** ... si es que puedes.; **I can't possibly go.** Me es del todo imposible ir.

post n ❶ correo m ▷ *Has the post arrived yet?* ¿Ha llegado ya el correo?; **by post** por correo; **Is there any post for me?** ¿Tengo alguna carta? ❷ poste m ▷ *The ball hit the post.* El balón dio en el poste.

  ▷ vb mandar por correo ▷ *You could post it.* Puedes mandarlo por correo.; **I've got some cards to post.** Tengo que mandar algunas postales.; **Would you post this letter for me?** ¿Me echas esta carta al correo?

postbox n buzón m (pl buzones)

postcard n postal f

postcode n código m postal

poster n ❶ (public) cartel m ▷ *There are posters all over town.* Hay carteles por toda la ciudad. ❷ (personal) póster m (pl pósters) ▷ *I've got posters on my bedroom walls.* Tengo pósters en las paredes de mi cuarto.

postman n cartero m ▷ *He's a postman.* Es cartero.

post office n oficina f de correos

▷ *Where's the post office, please?* ¿Sabe dónde está la oficina de correos?; **She works for the post office.** Trabaja en correos.

postpone vb aplazar ▷ *The match has been postponed.* El partido ha sido aplazado.

postwoman n cartera f ▷ *She's a postwoman.* Es cartera.

pot n ❶ tarro m (LatAm pote m) ▷ *a pot of jam* un tarro de mermelada; **a pot of paint** un bote de pintura ❷ (teapot) tetera f; **a coffee pot** una cafetera ❸ maría f (informal) ▷ *to smoke pot* fumar maría; **the pots and pans** las cacerolas

potato n patata f (LatAm papa f); **mashed potatoes** el puré de patatas; **a baked potato** una patata asada

pottery n cerámica f

pound n ❶ libra f

  ● In Spain measurements are in grams and kilograms. One pound is about 450 grams.

▷ *a pound of carrots* una libra de zanahorias ❷ libra f esterlina; **20 pounds** 20 libras; **a pound coin** una moneda de una libra

pour vb ❶ echar ▷ *She poured some water into the pan.* Echó un poco de agua en la olla. ❷ llover a cántaros ▷ *It's pouring.* Está lloviendo a cántaros.; **in the pouring rain** bajo una lluvia torrencial

poverty n pobreza f

powder n polvo m; **a fine white powder** un polvillo blanco

power n ① (electrical) corriente f ▷ The power's off. Se ha ido la corriente. ② energía f ▷ nuclear power la energía nuclear ③ poder m ▷ They were in power for 18 years. Estuvieron 18 años en el poder.; **a power point** un enchufe

power cut n apagón m (pl apagones)

powerful adj ① (person, organization, country) poderoso ② (machine, substance) potente

power station n central f eléctrica

practical adj práctico

practically adv prácticamente ▷ It's practically impossible. Es prácticamente imposible.

practice n ① práctica f ▷ You'll get better with practice. Mejorarás con la práctica.; **in practice** en la práctica; **It's normal practice in our school.** Es lo normal en nuestro colegio. ② entrenamiento m ▷ football practice entrenamiento de fútbol; **I'm out of practice.** Estoy desentrenado.; **I've got to do my piano practice.** Tengo que hacer los ejercicios de piano.; **a medical practice** una consulta médica

practise (US practice) vb ① practicar ▷ I practised my Spanish when we were on holiday. Practiqué el español cuando estuvimos de vacaciones. ② (train) entrenarse ▷ The team practises on Thursdays. El equipo se entrena los jueves.

praise vb elogiar ▷ Everyone praises

her cooking. Todo el mundo elogia cómo cocina.

pram n cochecito m de niño

prawn n gamba f

pray vb rezar ▷ to pray for something rezar por algo

prayer n oración f (pl oraciones)

precious adj precioso ▷ a precious stone una piedra preciosa

precise adj preciso ▷ at that precise moment en aquel preciso instante; **to be precise** para ser exacto

precisely adv precisamente ▷ That is precisely what it's meant for. Para eso precisamente está hecho.; **Precisely!** ¡Exactamente! **at 10 a.m. precisely** a las diez en punto de la mañana

predict vb predecir

predictable adj previsible

prefect n monitor m, monitora f

prefer vb preferir ▷ Which would you prefer? ¿Tú cuál prefieres? ▷ I prefer chemistry to maths. Prefiero la química a las matemáticas.

pregnant adj embarazada ▷ She's six months pregnant. Está embarazada de seis meses.

prejudice n prejuicio m ▷ That's just a prejudice. Eso no es más que un prejuicio. ▷ There's a lot of racial prejudice. Hay muchos prejuicios raciales.

prejudiced adj **to be prejudiced against somebody** tener prejuicios contra alguien

premature adj prematuro ▷ a premature baby un bebé prematuro

Premier League n primera f

división

premises npl local m ▷ They're moving to new premises. Se cambian de local.

prep n deberes mpl ▷ history prep los deberes de historia

preparations npl preparativos mpl

prepare vb preparar ▷ He was preparing dinner. Estaba preparando la cena.; **to prepare for something** hacer los preparativos para algo ▷ We're preparing for our holiday. Estamos haciendo los preparativos para las vacaciones.

prepared adj **to be prepared to do something** estar dispuesto a hacer algo ▷ I'm prepared to help you. Estoy dispuesto a ayudarte.

prescribe vb recetar ▷ The doctor prescribed a course of antibiotics for me. El doctor me recetó antibióticos.

prescription n receta f ▷ a prescription for penicillin una receta de penicilina; **on prescription** con receta médica

present adj ❶ presente ▷ He wasn't present at the meeting. No estuvo presente en la reunión. ❷ actual ▷ the present situation la situación actual; **the present tense** el presente
   ▶ n ❶ regalo m; **to give somebody a present** hacer un regalo a alguien ▷ He gave me a lovely present. Me hizo un precioso regalo. ❷ presente m ▷ to live in the present vivir el presente; **at**

present actualmente; **for the present** por el momento; **up to the present** hasta el momento presente
   ▶ vb **to present somebody with something** entregar algo a alguien ▷ The Mayor presented the winner with a medal. El alcalde le entregó una medalla al vencedor.; **He agreed to present the show.** Aceptó presentar el espectáculo.

presenter n presentador m, presentadora f

president n presidente m, presidenta f

press n prensa f ▷ The story appeared in the press last week. La historia salió en la prensa la semana pasada.
   ▶ vb apretar ▷ Don't press too hard! ¡No aprietes muy fuerte!; **He pressed the accelerator.** Pisó el acelerador.

press conference n rueda f de prensa

press-up n flexión f

pressure n presión f (pl presiones); **a pressure group** un grupo de presión; **to be under pressure** estar presionado ▷ She was under pressure from the management. Estaba presionada por la dirección.; **He's been under a lot of pressure recently.** Últimamente ha estado muy agobiado.

presume vb suponer ▷ I presume he'll come. Supongo que vendrá.

pretend vb **to pretend to do**

something fingir hacer algo; **to pretend to be asleep** hacerse el dormido

> Be careful not to translate **to pretend** by **pretender**.

pretty adj, adv ❶ bonito ▷ She wore a pretty dress. Llevaba un vestido bonito. ❷ guapo ▷ She's very pretty. Es muy guapa. ❸ bastante ▷ That film was pretty bad. La película era bastante mala.; **The weather was pretty awful.** Hacía un tiempo horroroso.; **It's pretty much the same.** Es más o menos lo mismo.

prevent vb evitar ▷ to prevent an accident evitar un accidente

> **evitar que** has to be followed by a verb in the subjunctive.
> ▷ I want to prevent this happening again. Quiero evitar que esto se repita.

> **impedir a alguien que** has to be followed by a verb in the subjunctive.
> ▷ to prevent somebody from doing something impedir a alguien que haga algo

previous adj anterior ▷ the previous night la noche anterior; **He has no previous experience.** No tiene experiencia previa.

previously adv antes

price n precio m ▷ What price is this painting? ¿Qué precio tiene este cuadro?; **to go up in price** subir de precio; **to come down in price** bajar de precio

price list n lista f de precios

prick vb pinchar ▷ I've pricked my finger. Me he pinchado un dedo.

pride n orgullo m

priest n sacerdote m

primary school n escuela f primaria

prime minister n primer m ministro, primera f ministra

prince n príncipe m ▷ the Prince of Wales el príncipe de Gales

princess n princesa f ▷ Princess Victoria. La princesa Victoria.

principal adj principal
▶ n director m, directora f

principle n principio m ▷ the basic principles of physics los principios básicos de física; **in principle** en principio; **on principle** por principio

print n ❶ foto f

> Although **foto** ends in -o, it is actually a feminine noun.

▷ colour prints fotos a color ❷ letra f ▷ in small print en letra pequeña ❸ huella f ▷ The policeman took his prints. El policía le tomó las huellas. ❹ grabado m ▷ a framed print un grabado enmarcado

printer n impresora f

printout n copia f impresa

priority n prioridad f ▷ My family takes priority over my work. Mi familia tiene prioridad sobre mi trabajo.

prison n cárcel f ▷ to send somebody to prison for 5 years condenar a alguien a 5 años de cárcel; **in prison** en la cárcel

prisoner n ❶ (in prison) preso m,

a b c d e f g h i j k l m n o p q r s t u v w x y z

presa f ❷ (captive) prisionero m, prisionera f; **to take somebody prisoner** hacer prisionero a alguien

private adj ❶ (not public) privado ▷ private life la vida privada ❷ (for one person only) particular ▷ private lessons clases particulares; **a private bathroom** un baño individual; **"private"** (on envelope) "confidencial"; **in private** en privado

prize n premio m ▷ **to win a prize** ganar un premio

prize-giving n entrega f de premios

prizewinner n premiado m, premiada f

pro n **the pros and cons** los pros y los contras

probable adj probable

probably adv probablemente ▷ He'll probably come tomorrow. Probablemente vendrá mañana.

problem n problema m

> Although **problema** ends in **-a**, it is actually a masculine noun.

▷ the drug problem el problema de la droga; **No problem! (1)** (of course) ¡Por supuesto! ❷ Can you repair it? - No problem! ¿Lo puedes arreglar? - ¡Por supuesto! **(2)** (it doesn't matter) ¡No importa! ▷ I'm sorry about that - No problem! Lo siento - ¡No importa!; **What's the problem?** ¿Qué pasa?

process n proceso m ▷ the peace process el proceso de paz; **We're in the process of painting the kitchen.** Ahora mismo estamos pintando la cocina.

procession n procesión f (pl procesiones)

produce vb ❶ (manufacture, create) producir ❷ (on stage) montar

producer n ❶ (of film, record, TV programme) productor m, productora f ❷ (of play, show) director m, directora f

product n producto m

production n ❶ producción f (pl producciones) ▷ They're increasing production of luxury models. Están aumentando la producción de modelos de lujo. ❷ montaje m ▷ a production of "Hamlet" un montaje de "Hamlet"

profession n profesión f (pl profesiones)

professional n profesional mf ▶ adj profesional ▷ a professional musician un músico profesional

professor n catedrático m, catedrática f

> Be careful not to translate **professor** by the Spanish word **profesor**.

profit n beneficios mpl ▷ **to make a profit** sacar beneficios ▷ a profit of £10,000 unos beneficios de 10.000 libras

profitable adj rentable

program n programa m

> Although **programa** ends in **-a**, it is actually a masculine noun.

▷ a computer program un programa

informático; **a TV program** (in US) un programa de televisión
▶ vb **programar**

programme n **programa** m

> Although **programa** ends in -a, it is actually a masculine noun.

▷ a TV programme un programa de televisión

programmer n **programador** m, **programadora** f ▷ She's a programmer. Es programadora.

progress n **progreso** m ▷ You're making progress! ¡Estás haciendo progresos!

prohibit vb **prohibir** ▷ Smoking is prohibited. Está prohibido fumar.

project n ① (scheme, plan) **proyecto** m ② (at school) **trabajo** m ▷ I'm doing a project on the greenhouse effect. Estoy haciendo un trabajo sobre el efecto invernadero.

projector n **proyector** m

promise n **promesa** f ▷ He made me a promise. Me hizo una promesa.; **That's a promise!** ¡Lo prometo!
▶ vb **prometer** ▷ He didn't do what he promised. No hizo lo que prometió.; **She promised to write.** Prometió que escribiría.; **I'll write, I promise!** ¡Escribiré, lo prometo!

promote vb (employee, team) **ascender** ▷ She was promoted six months later. La ascendieron seis meses después.

promotion n **ascenso** m

prompt adj, adv ① **rápido** ▷ a

prompt reply una rápida respuesta ② **puntual** ▷ He's always very prompt. Siempre es muy puntual.; **at eight o'clock prompt** a las ocho en punto

pronoun n **pronombre** m

pronounce vb **pronunciar** ▷ How do you pronounce that word? ¿Cómo se pronuncia esa palabra?

pronunciation n **pronunciación** f (pl pronunciaciones)

proof n **prueba** f; **I've got proof that he did it.** Tengo pruebas de que lo hizo.

proper adj ① (genuine) **de verdad** ▷ It's difficult to get a proper job. Es difícil conseguir un trabajo de verdad. ② (suitable) **adecuado** ▷ You have to have the proper equipment. Tienes que tener el equipo adecuado.; **If you had come at the proper time...** Si hubieras llegado a tu hora...

properly adv **correctamente** ▷ You're not doing it properly. No lo estás haciendo correctamente.

property n **propiedad** f; **"private property"** "propiedad privada"; **stolen property** objetos robados

propose vb **proponer** ▷ I propose a new plan. Propongo un cambio de planes. ▷ What do you propose to do? ¿Qué te propones hacer?

> **proponer que** has to be followed by a verb in the subjunctive.

▷ He proposed that we stay at home. Propuso que nos quedáramos en casa.; **to propose to somebody**

(for marriage) declararse a alguien
prosecute vb procesar ▷ They
were prosecuted for murder. Les
procesaron por asesinato.
prostitute n prostituta f
protect vb proteger
protection n protección f
protein n proteína f
protest n protesta f; **a protest
march** una manifestación
　▶ vb protestar
Protestant n protestante mf ▷ I'm
a Protestant. Soy protestante.
　▶ adj protestante
protester n manifestante mf
proud adj orgulloso ▷ Her parents
are proud of her. Sus padres están
orgullosos de ella.
prove vb probar ▷ The police
couldn't prove it. La policía no pudo
probarlo.
proverb n proverbio m ▷ a Chinese
proverb un proverbio chino
provide vb proporcionar;
**to provide somebody with
something** proporcionar algo
a alguien ▷ They provided us with
maps. Nos proporcionaron mapas.
provided conj siempre que

> siempre que has to be
followed by a verb in the
subjunctive.

▷ He'll play in the next match
provided he's fit. Jugará el próximo
partido siempre que esté en
condiciones.
prune n ciruela f pasa
PSHE n (= personal, social and
health education) formación social

y sanitaria
psychiatrist n psiquiatra mf
psychological adj psicológico
psychologist n psicólogo m,
　psicóloga f
psychology n psicología f
PTO abbr (= please turn over) sigue
pub n bar m
public n **the public** el público
▷ open to the public abierto al
público; **in public** en público
　▶ adj público; **a public holiday** un
día festivo (LatAm un día feriado);
public opinion la opinión pública;
the public address system la
megafonía; **to be in the public
eye** ser un personaje público
publicity n publicidad f
public school n colegio m privado
public transport n transporte
m público
publish vb publicar
publisher n ❶ (person) editor m,
editora f ❷ (company) editorial f
pudding n postre m ▷ What's for
pudding? ¿Qué hay de postre?; **rice
pudding** el arroz con leche; **black
pudding** la morcilla
puddle n charco m
puff pastry n hojaldre m
pull vb ❶ (to make something move)
tirar ▷ Pull as hard as you can. Tira
con todas tus fuerzas. ❷ (to
tug at something) tirar de (LatAm
jalar) ▷ She pulled my hair. Me tiró
del pelo.; **He pulled the trigger.**
Apretó el gatillo.; **I pulled a
muscle when I was training.** Me
dio un tirón mientras entrenaba.;

You're pulling my leg! ¡Me estás tomando el pelo!; Pull yourself together! ¡Tranquilízate!

pull down vb echar abajo ▷ The old school was pulled down last year. El año pasado echaron abajo la vieja escuela.

pull out vb ❶ (remove) sacar ▷ to pull a tooth out sacar una muela ❷ (car) echarse a un lado ▷ The car pulled out to overtake. El coche se echó a un lado para adelantar. ❸ (from competition) retirarse ▷ She pulled out of the tournament. Se retiró del torneo.

pull through vb recuperarse ▷ They think he'll pull through. Creen que se recuperará.

pull up vb (car) parar ▷ A black car pulled up beside me. Un coche negro paró a mi lado.

pullover n jersey m (pl jerseys)

pulse n pulso m ▷ The nurse took his pulse. La enfermera le tomó el pulso.

pump n ❶ bomba f ▷ a bicycle pump una bomba de bicicleta; a petrol pump un surtidor de gasolina ❷ zapatilla f ▷ She was wearing a black leotard and black pumps. Llevaba malla y zapatillas negras.
▶ vb bombear; to pump up a tyre inflar una rueda

pumpkin n calabaza f

punch n ❶ (blow) puñetazo m ❷ (drink) ponche m
▶ vb dar un puñetazo a ▷ He punched me! ¡Me ha dado un

puñetazo!

punctual adj puntual

punctuation n puntuación f

puncture n pinchazo m ▷ I had a puncture on the motorway. Tuve un pinchazo en la autopista.

punish vb castigar ▷ They were severely punished for their disobedience. Les castigaron severamente por su desobediencia.; to punish somebody for doing something castigar a alguien por haber hecho algo

punishment n castigo m

punk n punki mf; a punk rock band un grupo punk

pupil n alumno m, alumna f

puppet n títere m

puppy n cachorro m

purchase vb adquirir

pure adj puro

purple adj morado

purpose n objetivo m ▷ What is the purpose of these changes? ¿Cuál es el objetivo de estos cambios?; his purpose in life su meta en la vida; It's being used for military purposes. Se está usando con fines militares.; on purpose a propósito ▷ He did it on purpose. Lo hizo a propósito.

purr vb ronronear

purse n ❶ (for money) monedero m ❷ (in US: handbag) bolso m

push n empujón m (pl empujones); to give somebody a push dar un empujón a alguien
▶ vb empujar ▷ Don't push! ¡No

a b c d e f g h i j k l m n o p q r s t u v w x y z

empujes!; **to push a button** pulsar un botón; **to push drugs** pasar droga; **I'm pushed for time today.** Hoy ando fatal de tiempo.; **Push off!** ¡Lárgate!; **Don't push your luck!** ¡No tientes a la suerte!

push around vb dar órdenes a ▷ He likes pushing people around. Le gusta dar órdenes a la gente.

pushchair n silla f de paseo

put vb poner ▷ Where shall I put my things? ¿Dónde pongo mis cosas?; **She's putting the baby to bed.** Está acostando al niño.

put away vb ❶ guardar ▷ Can you put the dishes away, please? ¿Guardas los platos? ❷ (in prison) encerrar ▷ I hope they put him away for a long time. Espero que lo encierren por muchos años.

put back vb ❶ (in place) poner en su sitio ▷ Put it back when you've finished with it. Ponlo en su sitio cuando hayas terminado. ❷ (postpone) aplazar ▷ The meeting has been put back till 2 o'clock. La reunión ha sido aplazada hasta las 2.

put down vb ❶ soltar ▷ I'll put these bags down for a minute. Voy a soltar estas bolsas un momento. ❷ (note) apuntar ▷ I've put down a few ideas. He apuntado algunas ideas.; **to have an animal put down** sacrificar a un animal ▷ We had to have our dog put down. Tuvimos que sacrificar a nuestro perro.; **to put the phone down** colgar

put in vb (install) poner ▷ We're going to get central heating put in. Vamos a poner calefacción central.; **He has put in a lot of work on this project.** Ha dedicado mucho trabajo a este proyecto.; **I've put in for a new job.** He solicitado otro empleo.

put off vb ❶ (light, TV) apagar ▷ Shall I put the light off? ¿Apago la luz? ❷ (delay) aplazar ▷ I keep putting it off. No hago más que aplazarlo. ❸ (distract) distraer ▷ Stop putting me off! ¡Deja ya de distraerme! ❹ (discourage) desanimar ▷ He's not easily put off. No es de los que se desaniman fácilmente.

put on vb ❶ (clothes, lipstick) ponerse ▷ I put my coat on. Me puse el abrigo. ❷ (tape, record) poner ▷ Put on some music. Pon algo de música. ❸ (light, TV) encender ▷ Shall I put the heater on? ¿Enciendo el radiador? ❹ (play, show) representar ▷ We're putting on "Jaws". Estamos representando "Jaws".; **I'll put the potatoes on.** Voy a poner a hacer las patatas.; **to put on weight** engordar ▷ He has put on a lot of weight. Ha engordado mucho.; **She's not ill: she's just putting it on.** No está enferma: es puro teatro.

put out vb apagar ▷ It took them five hours to put out the fire. Tardaron cinco horas en apagar el incendio.; **He's a bit put out that nobody came.** Le sentó mal que no viniera nadie.

put through vb poner (LatAm comunicar) ▷ Can you put me through to the manager? ¿Me pone con el director?

put up vb ❶ (on wall) colgar ▷ The poster's great. I'll put it up on my wall. El póster es genial. Lo colgaré en la pared. ❷ montar ▷ We put up our tent in a field. Montamos la tienda en un prado. ❸ subir ▷ They've put up the price. Han subido el precio.; **My friend will put me up for the night.** Me quedaré a dormir en casa de mi amigo.; **to put one's hand up** levantar la mano ▷ If you have any questions, put your hand up. Quien tenga alguna pregunta que levante la mano.; **to put up with something** aguantar algo ▷ I'm not going to put up with it any longer. No pienso aguantarlo más.; **to put something up for sale** poner algo en venta ▷ They're going to put their house up for sale. Van a poner la casa en venta.

puzzle n rompecabezas m (pl rompecabezas)

puzzled adj perplejo

pyjamas npl pijama m (LatAm piyama m)

> Although **pijama** and **piyama** end in **-a**, they are actually masculine nouns.

▷ my pyjamas mi pijama; **a pair of pyjamas** un pijama

pyramid n pirámide f

Pyrenees npl **the Pyrenees** los Pirineos

qualification n título m ▷ He left school without any qualifications. Dejó la escuela sin sacarse ningún título.

qualified adj ❶ cualificado ▷ a qualified driving instructor un profesor de autoescuela cualificado ❷ titulado ▷ a qualified teacher un profesor titulado; **She was well qualified for the position.** Estaba suficientemente capacitada para el puesto.

qualify vb ❶ sacarse el título (LatAm recibirse) ▷ She qualified as a teacher last year. Se sacó el título de profesora el año pasado. ❷ clasificarse ▷ Our team didn't qualify for the finals. Nuestro equipo no se clasificó para la final.

quality n ❶ calidad f ▷ good-quality paper el papel de calidad ❷ cualidad f ▷ She's got lots of good qualities. Tiene un montón de buenas cualidades.

quantity n cantidad f

quarantine n cuarentena f ▷ in quarantine en cuarentena

quarrel n pelea f; **We had a quarrel.** Nos peleamos.
▶ vb pelearse

quarry n (for stone) cantera f

quarter n cuarto m; **three quarters** tres cuartos; **a quarter of an hour** un cuarto de hora; **a quarter past ten** las diez y cuarto; **a quarter to eleven** las once menos cuarto

quarter-finals npl cuartos mpl de final

quartet n cuarteto m ▷ a string quartet un cuarteto de cuerda

quay n muelle m

queen n ❶ reina f ▷ Queen Elizabeth la reina Isabel ❷ dama f ▷ the queen of hearts la dama de corazones; **the Queen Mother** la reina madre

query n pregunta f
▶ vb poner en duda ▷ No one queried my decision. Nadie puso en duda mi decisión.; **They queried the bill.** Pidieron explicaciones sobre la factura.

question n ❶ pregunta f ▷ Can I ask a question? ¿Puedo hacer una pregunta? ❷ (matter) cuestión f (pl cuestiones) ▷ It's just a question of... Tan sólo es cuestión de...;

It's out of the question. Es imposible.
▶ vb interrogar ▷ He was questioned by the police. Lo interrogó la policía.

question mark n signo m de interrogación

questionnaire n cuestionario m

queue n cola f ▷ People were standing in a queue outside the cinema. La gente hacía cola a las puertas del cine.
▶ vb hacer cola ▷ We had to queue for tickets. Tuvimos que hacer cola para comprar los billetes.

quick adj, adv rápido ▷ Quick, phone the police! ¡Rápido, llama a la policía! ▷ It's quicker by train. Se va más rápido en tren.; **She's a quick learner.** Aprende rápido.; **Be quick!** ¡Date prisa!

quickly adv rápidamente ▷ It was all over very quickly. Se acabó todo muy rápidamente.

quiet adj ❶ (person) callado ▷ You're very quiet today. Estás muy callado hoy. ❷ (engine) silencioso ❸ (place, weekend) tranquilo ▷ a quiet little town un pueblecito tranquilo; **Be quiet!** ¡Cállate!; **Quiet!** ¡Silencio!

quietly adv ❶ en voz baja ▷ She's dead. - He said quietly. Está muerta. - Dijo en voz baja. ❷ sin hacer ruido ▷ He quietly opened the door. Abrió la puerta sin hacer ruido.

quilt n edredón m (pl edredones)

quit vb dejar ▷ I quit my job last week. Dejé mi trabajo la semana pasada. ❷ marcharse ▷ I've been given notice to quit. Me han dado el aviso para que me marche.

quite adv ❶ (rather) bastante ▷ It's quite warm today. Hoy hace bastante calor.; **How was the film? - Quite good.** ¿Qué tal la película? - No está mal. ❷ (completely) totalmente ▷ It's quite different. Es totalmente distinto.; **It's quite clear that this plan won't work.** Está clarísimo que este plan no va a funcionar.; **not quite...** no del todo... ▷ I'm not quite sure. No estoy del todo seguro.; **It's not quite the same.** No es exactamente lo mismo.; **quite a...** todo un ▷ It was quite a shock. Fue todo un susto.; **quite a lot** bastante ▷ quite a lot of money bastante dinero; **There were quite a few people there.** Había bastante gente allí.

quiz n concurso m ▷ a quiz show un programa concurso

quotation n cita f ▷ a quotation from Shakespeare una cita de Shakespeare

quotation marks npl comillas fpl

quote n ❶ cita f ▷ a Shakespeare quote una cita de Shakespeare ❷ presupuesto m ▷ Can you give me a quote for the work? ¿Puede darme un presupuesto por el trabajo?; **quotes** las comillas ▷ in quotes entre comillas
▶ vb citar

r

rabbi n rabino m, rabina f

rabbit n conejo m; **rabbit hutch** la conejera

race n ❶ carrera f; **a cycle race** una carrera ciclista ❷ raza f; **race relations** las relaciones interraciales; **the human race** el género humano
▶ vb ❶ correr ▷ We raced to get there on time. Corrimos para llegar allí a tiempo. ❷ echarle una carrera a; **I'll race you!** ¡Te echo una carrera!

racecourse n hipódromo m

racer n bicicleta f de carreras

racetrack n ❶ (for cars) circuito m ❷ (for cycles) velódromo m

racial adj racial ▷ racial discrimination la discriminación racial

racing car n coche m de carreras

racing driver n piloto mf de carreras

racism n racismo m

racist adj racista
▶ n racista mf > He's a racist. Es racista.

rack n (for luggage) portaequipajes m (pl portaequipajes)

racket n ❶ (for sport) raqueta f
▷ my tennis racket mi raqueta de tenis ❷ (informal: noise) jaleo m
▷ They're making a terrible racket. Están armando muchísimo jaleo.

racquet n raqueta f

radar n radar m

radiation n radiación f

radiator n radiador m

radio n radio f

> Although **radio** ends in -o, it is actually a feminine noun.

on the radio por la radio; **a radio station** una emisora de radio

radioactive adj radiactivo

radish n rábano m

RAF abbr (= Royal Air Force) fuerzas fpl aéreas británicas ▷ He's in the RAF. Está en las fuerzas aéreas británicas.

raffle n rifa f ▷ a raffle ticket una papeleta de rifa

raft n balsa f

rag n trapo m

rage n rabia f ▷ mad with rage loco de rabia; **to be in a rage** estar furioso; **It's all the rage.** Es el último grito.

rail n ❶ (on stairs, bridge, balcony) barandilla f ❷ (for curtains) riel m;

by rail por ferrocarril; **railcard** la tarjeta de descuento para viajes en tren

railroad n (in US) ferrocarril m; **railroad line** la línea ferroviaria; **railroad station** la estación de ferrocarril

railway n ferrocarril m; **railway line** la línea ferroviaria; **railway station** la estación de ferrocarril

rain n lluvia f ▷ in the rain bajo la lluvia
▶ vb llover ▷ It rains a lot here. Aquí llueve mucho.; **It's raining.** Está lloviendo.

rainbow n arco m iris (pl arco iris)

raincoat n impermeable m

rainfall n precipitaciones fpl

rainforest n selva f tropical

rainy adj lluvioso

raise vb ❶ levantar ▷ He raised his hand. Levantó la mano.
❷ mejorar ▷ They want to raise standards in schools. Quieren mejorar el nivel escolar.
❸ aumentar ▷ to raise interest rates aumentar los tipos de interés; **to raise money** recaudar fondos ▷ We're raising money for a new gym. Estamos recaudando fondos para un gimnasio nuevo.

raisin n pasa f

rally n ❶ (of people) concentración f (pl concentraciones) ❷ (driving) rally m (pl rallys) ❸ (in tennis) peloteo m

Ramadan n Ramadán m

rambler n excursionista mf

ramp n rampa f

ran vb see **run**

rang vb see **ring**

range n ❶ (selection, variety) variedad f ▷ There's a wide range of colours. Hay una gran variedad de colores.; **It's out of my price range.** Está fuera de mis posibilidades. ❷ cadena f ▷ a range of mountains una cadena montañosa
▶ vb **to range from...to...** oscilar entre...y... ▷ Temperatures range from 20 to 35 degrees. Las temperaturas oscilan entre los 20 y los 35 grados.; **Tickets range from £2 to £20.** El precio de las entradas va de 2 a 20 libras esterlinas.

rap n rap m

rape n violación f (pl violaciones)
▶ vb violar

rare adj ❶ (unusual) raro ❷ (steak) poco hecho

rash n sarpullido m

rasher n **a rasher of bacon** una loncha de bacon

raspberry n frambuesa f

rat n rata f

rate n ❶ (price) tarifa f ▷ There are reduced rates for students. Hay tarifas reducidas para estudiantes. ❷ (of interest) tipo m ▷ a high rate of interest un tipo de interés elevado

rather adv bastante ▷ I was rather disappointed. Quedé bastante decepcionado.; **rather a lot of** mucho ▷ I've got rather a lot of homework to do. Tengo muchos deberes que hacer.; **I'd rather...** Preferiría... ▷ I'd rather stay in tonight. Preferiría no salir esta noche.

> **preferiría que** has to be followed by a verb in the subjunctive.

▷ I'd rather he didn't come to the party. Preferiría que no viniera a la fiesta.; **rather than...** en lugar de... ▷ We decided to camp, rather than stay at a hotel. Decidimos acampar, en lugar de quedarnos en un hotel.

raw adj (food) crudo; **raw material** la materia prima

razor n maquinilla f de afeitar; **razor blade** la hoja de afeitar

RE abbr (= Religious Education) religión f

reach n **out of reach** fuera del alcance ▷ Keep medicine out of reach of children. Guárdense los medicamentos fuera del alcance de los niños.; **within easy reach of** a poca distancia de ▷ The hotel is within easy reach of the town centre. El hotel está a poca distancia del centro de la ciudad.
▶ vb ❶ (destination, decision) llegar a ▷ We reached the hotel at seven o'clock. Llegamos al hotel a las siete. ❷ (get in touch) ponerse en contacto con ▷ How can I reach you? ¿Cómo puedo ponerme en contacto contigo?

reaction n reacción f (pl reacciones)

reactor n reactor m; **a nuclear**

reactor un reactor nuclear

read vb leer

read out vb (in a loud voice) leer ▷ I was reading it out to the children. Se lo estaba leyendo a los niños.

reading n lectura f ▷ I'll see you in the reading room. Te veo en la sala de lectura.; **I like reading.** Me gusta leer.

ready adj preparado ▷ The meal is ready. La comida está preparada.; **She's nearly ready.** Está casi lista.; **He's always ready to help.** Siempre está dispuesto a ayudar.; **to get ready** prepararse; **to get something ready** preparar algo ▷ He's getting the dinner ready. Está preparando la cena.

real adj ❶ verdadero ▷ the real reason el verdadero motivo ▷ It was a real nightmare. Fue una verdadera pesadilla.; **In real life these things don't happen.** Estas cosas no pasan en la vida real. ❷ auténtico ▷ It's real leather. Es piel auténtica.

realistic adj realista

reality n realidad f

reality TV n telerrealidad f

realize vb **to realize that...** darse cuenta de que... ▷ We realized that something was wrong. Nos dimos cuenta de que algo iba mal.

really adv de verdad ▷ I'm learning German. – Really? Estoy aprendiendo alemán. – ¿De verdad?; **Do you really think so?** ¿Tú crees?; **She's really nice.** Es muy simpática.; **Do you want to**

go? - Not really. ¿Quieres ir? - La verdad es que no.

realtor n (in US) agente m inmobiliario, agente f inmobiliaria

reason n razón f (pl razones) ▷ There's no reason to think that he's dangerous. No hay razón para pensar que es peligroso.; **for security reasons** por motivos de seguridad; **That was the main reason I went.** Fui mayormente por eso.

reasonable adj ❶ razonable ▷ Be reasonable! ¡Sé razonable! ❷ bastante aceptable ▷ He wrote a reasonable essay. Escribió una redacción bastante aceptable.

reasonably adv bastante ▷ The team played reasonably well. El equipo jugó bastante bien.; **reasonably priced accommodation** alojamiento a precios razonables

reassure vb tranquilizar

reassuring adj tranquilizador

rebel n rebelde mf

rebellious adj rebelde

receipt n ❶ (for goods bought) ticket m ❷ (for work done) recibo m

> Be careful not to translate **receipt** by receta.

receive vb recibir

receiver n auricular m; **to pick up the receiver** descolgar

recent adj reciente ▷ recent scientific discoveries los recientes

descubrimientos científicos;
in recent weeks en las últimas
semanas

recently adv últimamente ▷ I
haven't seen him recently. No lo
he visto últimamente.; **until
recently** hasta hace poco

reception n recepción f (pl
recepciones)

receptionist n recepcionista mf
▷ She's a receptionist in a hotel. Es
recepcionista en un hotel.

recipe n receta f

reckon vb creer ▷ What do you
reckon? ¿Tú qué crees?

recognize vb reconocer

recommend vb recomendar
▷ What do you recommend? ¿Qué me
recomienda?

reconsider vb reconsiderar

record n ❶ disco m ❷ récord m
(pl récords) ▷ the world record el
récord mundial; **in record time**
en un tiempo récord; **criminal
record** los antecedentes penales
▷ He's got a criminal record. Tiene
antecedentes penales.; **There
is no record of your booking.**
No tenemos constancia de su
reserva.; **records** los archivos ▷ I'll
check in the records. Miraré en los
archivos.
▶ vb grabar ▷ They've just recorded
their new album. Acaban de grabar
su nuevo álbum.

■ Be careful not to translate **to
record** by **recordar**.

recorded delivery n **to send
something recorded delivery**

enviar algo por correo certificado

recorder n (musical instrument)
flauta f dulce; **cassette recorder** el
cassette; **video recorder** el vídeo

recording n grabación f (pl
grabaciones)

record player n tocadiscos m (pl
tocadiscos)

recover vb recuperarse ▷ He's
recovering from a knee injury. Se
está recuperando de una lesión
de rodilla.

recovery n mejora f; **Best
whishes for a speedy recovery!**
¡Que te mejores pronto!

rectangle n rectángulo m

rectangular adj rectangular

recycle vb reciclar

recycling n reciclaje m

red adj rojo ▷ a red rose una rosa
roja; **Gavin's got red hair.** Gavin
es pelirrojo.; **to go through a red
light** saltarse un semáforo en rojo;
red wine vino tinto

Red Cross n Cruz f Roja

redcurrant n grosella f

redecorate vb ❶ (with paint)
volver a pintar ❷ (with wallpaper)
volver a empapelar

red-haired adj pelirrojo

redo vb rehacer

reduce vb reducir ▷ at a reduced
price a precio reducido; **"reduce
speed now"** "disminuya la
velocidad"

reduction n reducción f (pl
reducciones); **a five per cent
reduction** un descuento del cinco
por ciento; **"huge reductions!"**

"¡grandes rebajas!"

redundant adj **to be made redundant** ser despedido

refer vb **to refer to** referirse a ▷ *What are you referring to?* ¿A qué te refieres?

referee n árbitro m, árbitra f

reference n ❶ referencia f ▷ *He made no reference to the murder.* No hizo referencia al homicidio. ❷ referencias fpl ▷ *Would you please give me a reference?* ¿Me podría facilitar referencias?; **a reference book** un libro de consulta

refill vb volver a llenar ▷ *He refilled my glass.* Volvió a llenarme el vaso.

reflect vb ❶ (image) reflejar ❷ (think) reflexionar

reflection n (image) reflejo m

reflex n reflejo m

reflexive adj reflexivo ▷ *a reflexive verb* un verbo reflexivo

refreshing adj ❶ refrescante ▷ *a refreshing drink* una bebida refrescante ❷ estimulante ▷ *It was a refreshing change.* Fue un cambio estimulante.

refreshments npl refrigerio m

refrigerator n frigorífico m

refuge n refugio m

refugee n refugiado m, refugiada f

refund n reembolso m
▶ vb reembolsar

refuse vb negarse a ▷ *He refused to comment.* Se negó a hacer comentarios.
▶ n basura f; **refuse collection** la

recogida de basuras

regain vb recobrar ▷ *to regain consciousness* recobrar el conocimiento

regard n **with regard to** con respecto a; **Give my regards to Alice.** Dale recuerdos a Alice.; **"with kind regards"** "un cordial saludo"
▶ vb **They regarded it as unfair.** Lo consideraron injusto.; **as regards…** en lo que se refiere a…

regiment n regimiento m

region n región f (pl regiones)

regional adj regional

register n (in hotel) registro m; **to call the register** pasar lista
▶ vb (to enrol) inscribirse; **The car was registered in his wife's name.** El coche estaba matriculado a nombre de su esposa.

registered adj **a registered letter** una carta certificada

registration n número m de matrícula

regret vb arrepentirse ▷ *Try it, you won't regret it!* ¡Pruébalo! ¡No te arrepentirás!; **to regret doing something** arrepentirse de haber hecho algo ▷ *I regret saying that.* Me arrepiento de haber dicho eso.

regular adj ❶ regular ▷ *at regular intervals* a intervalos regulares; **to take regular exercise** hacer ejercicio con regularidad ❷ normal ▷ *a regular portion of fries* una porción normal de patatas fritas

regularly adv con regularidad

regulations npl reglamento m ▷ It's against the regulations. Va en contra del reglamento.; **safety regulations** las normas de seguridad

rehearsal n ensayo m; **dress rehearsal** el ensayo general

rehearse vb ensayar

reindeer n reno m

reins npl riendas fpl

reject vb ❶ (proposal, invitation) rechazar ❸ (idea, advice) desechar; I applied but they rejected me. Presenté una solicitud, pero no me aceptaron.

related adj (connected) relacionado ▷ The two events are not related. Los dos sucesos no están relacionados.; **We're related.** Somos parientes.; **Are you related to her?** ¿Eres pariente suyo?

relation n ❶ pariente mf ▷ He's a distant relation. Es un pariente lejano mío. ❷ relación f (pl relaciones) ▷ It has no relation to reality. No guarda ninguna relación con la realidad.; **in relation to** con relación a

relationship n relación f (pl relaciones) ▷ We have a good relationship. Tenemos una buena relación.; **I'm not in a relationship at the moment.** No tengo relaciones sentimentales con nadie en este momento.

relative n pariente mf

relatively adv relativamente

relax vb relajarse ▷ I relax listening to music. Me relajo escuchando música.; **Relax! Everything's fine.** ¡Tranquilo! No pasa nada.

relaxation n esparcimiento m

relaxed adj relajado

relaxing adj relajante ▷ Having a bath is very relaxing. Darse un baño es muy relajante.; **I find cooking relaxing.** Cocinar me relaja.

release vb ❶ (prisoner) poner en libertad ❷ (report, news) hacer público ❸ (record, video) sacar a la venta

▶ n puesta f en libertad ▷ the release of Nelson Mandela la puesta en libertad de Nelson Mandela; **the band's latest release** el último trabajo del grupo

relevant adj (documents) pertinente.; **That's not relevant.** Eso no viene al caso.; **to be relevant to something** guardar relación con algo ▷ Education should be relevant to real life. La educación debería guardar relación con la vida real.

reliable adj (car, information, person) fiable ▷ He's not very reliable. No es una persona muy fiable.

relief n alivio m ▷ That's a relief! ¡Es un alivio!

relieved adj to be relieved sentir un gran alivio ▷ I was relieved to hear he was better. Sentí un gran alivio al saber que estaba mejor.

a b c d e f g h i j k l m n o p q r s t u v w x y z

religion n religión f (pl religiones)
▷ *What religion are you?* ¿De qué religión eres?

religious adj religioso ▷ *I'm not religious.* No soy religioso.

reluctant adj reacio; **to be reluctant to do something** ser reacio a hacer algo ▷ *They were reluctant to help us.* Eran reacios a ayudarnos.

reluctantly adv de mala gana
▷ *She reluctantly accepted.* Aceptó de mala gana.

rely on vb confiar en ▷ *I'm relying on you.* Confío en ti.

remain vb permanecer ▷ *to remain silent* permanecer callado

remaining adj restante
▷ *the remaining ingredients* los ingredientes restantes

remark n comentario m

remarkable adj extraordinario

remarkably adv extraordinariamente

remember vb ❶ acordarse ▷ *I don't remember.* No me acuerdo. ❷ acordarse de ▷ *I can't remember his name.* No me acuerdo de su nombre. ▷ *I don't remember saying that.* No me acuerdo de haber dicho eso.

> In Spanish you often say **no te olvides - don't forget** - instead of **remember**.

▷ *Remember to write your name on the form.* No te olvides de escribir tu nombre en el impreso.

remind vb recordar ▷ *The scenery here reminds me of Scotland.* Este paisaje me recuerda a Escocia.

> When talking about reminding someone to do something, **recordar a alguien que** has to be followed by a verb in the subjunctive.

▷ *Remind me to speak to Daniel.* Recuérdame que hable con Daniel.

remote adj remoto ▷ *a remote village* un pueblo remoto

remote control n mando m a distancia

remove vb quitar ▷ *Please remove your bag from my seat.* Por favor, quite su bolsa de mi asiento.

renew vb (passport, licence) renovar

renewable adj renovable

renovate vb renovar ▷ *The building's been renovated.* Han renovado el edificio.

rent n alquiler m
▶ vb alquilar ▷ *We rented a car.* Alquilamos un coche.

reorganize vb reorganizar

rep n (= representative) representante mf

repaid vb see **repay**

repair vb reparar ▷ *I got the washing machine repaired.* Me repararon la lavadora.
▶ n reparación f (pl reparaciones)

repay vb (money) devolver; **I don't know how I can ever repay you.** No sé cómo podré devolverle el favor.

repeat vb repetir
▶ n (on TV) reposición f (pl

reposiciones)

repeatedly adv repetidamente

repetitive adj repetitivo

replace vb ❶ sustituir ▷ *Computers have replaced typewriters.* Los ordenadores han sustituido a las máquinas de escribir. ❷ (*batteries*) cambiar

replay n **There will be a replay on Friday.** El partido se volverá a jugar el viernes.
▶ vb ❶ (*match*) volver a jugar ❷ (*tape*) volver a poner

reply n respuesta f
▶ vb responder

report n ❶ (*of event*) informe m ❷ (*news report*) reportaje m ▷ *a report in the paper* un reportaje en el periódico ❸ (*at school*) notas fpl; **I got a good report this term.** He sacado buenas notas este trimestre.
▶ vb ❶ dar parte de ▷ *I reported the theft to the police.* Di parte del robo a la policía. ❷ presentarse ▷ *Report to reception when you arrive.* Preséntese en recepción cuando llegue.; **I'll report back as soon as I hear anything.** En cuanto tenga noticias, te lo haré saber.

reporter n periodista mf

represent vb ❶ (*client, country*) representar a ❷ (*change, achievement*) representar

representative adj representativo

reptile n reptil m

republic n república f

reputation n reputación f (pl reputaciones)

request n petición f (pl peticiones)
▶ vb solicitar

require vb requerir ▷ *Her job requires a lot of patience.* Su trabajo requiere mucha paciencia.

rescue vb rescatar
▶ n rescate m ▷ *a rescue operation* una operación de rescate; **to come to somebody's rescue** ir en auxilio de alguien

research n investigación f (pl investigaciones) ▷ *He's doing research.* Realiza trabajos de investigación.; **She's doing some research in the library.** Está investigando en la biblioteca.

resemblance n parecido m

resent vb **I resent being dependent on her.** Me molesta tener que depender de ella.

reservation n reserva f ▷ *I've got a reservation for two nights.* Tengo una reserva para dos noches.; **I've got reservations about the idea.** Tengo mis reservas al respecto.

reserve n ❶ (*place*) reserva f ▷ *a nature reserve* una reserva natural ❷ (*person*) suplente mf ▷ *I was reserve in the game last Saturday.* Yo era suplente en el partido del sábado.
▶ vb reservar ▷ *I'd like to reserve a table for tomorrow evening.* Quisiera reservar una mesa para mañana por la noche.

reserved adj reservado ▷ *He's quite reserved.* Es bastante reservado.

resident n vecino m, vecina f

▷ local residents los vecinos del lugar

residential adj residencial
▷ a residential area una zona residencial

resign vb dimitir

resist vb resistir

resit vb volver a presentarse a ▷ I'm resitting the exam in December. Me vuelvo a presentar al examen en diciembre.

resolution n propósito m ▷ Have you made any New Year's resolutions? ¿Has hecho algún buen propósito para el Año Nuevo?

resort n centro m turístico ▷ a resort on the Costa del Sol un centro turístico en la Costa del Sol; **a ski resort** una estación de esquí; **as a last resort** como último recurso

resource n recurso m

respect n respeto m; **in some respects** en algunos aspectos
▶ vb respetar

respectable adj ❶ respetable ▷ a respectable family una familia respetable ❷ decente ▷ My marks were quite respectable. Mis notas eran bastante decentes.

responsibility n responsabilidad f

responsible adj responsable
▷ You should be more responsible! ¡Deberías ser más responsable!; **to be responsible for something** ser responsable de algo ▷ He's responsible for booking the tickets. Es responsable de reservar las entradas.; **It's a responsible job.** Es un puesto de responsabilidad.

rest n ❶ descanso m ▷ five minutes' rest cinco minutos de descanso; **to have a rest** descansar ▷ We stopped to have a rest. Nos paramos a descansar. ❷ resto m ▷ the rest of the money el resto del dinero; **the rest of them** los demás ▷ The rest of them went swimming. Los demás fueron a nadar.
▶ vb ❶ descansar ▷ She's resting in her room. Está descansando en su habitación. ▷ He has to rest his knee. Tiene que descansar la rodilla. ❷ apoyar ▷ I rested my bike against the window. Apoyé la bicicleta en la ventana.

restaurant n restaurante m; **restaurant car** el vagón restaurante

restore vb (building, painting) restaurar

restrict vb limitar

rest room n (in US) servicios mpl

result n resultado m ▷ my exam results los resultados de mis exámenes

résumé n (in US) currículum m vitae

retire vb jubilarse

retired adj jubilado ▷ She's retired. Está jubilada.

retirement n since his retirement desde que se jubiló

return n ❶ regreso m ▷ his sudden return home su repentino regreso a casa; **the return journey** el viaje de vuelta ❷ (ticket) billete m de ida y vuelta ▷ A return to Bilbao, please. Un billete de ida y vuelta a Bilbao, por favor.; **in return** a cambio ▷ *She helps me and I help her in return.* Me ayuda y yo la ayudo a cambio.; **in return for** a cambio de; **Many happy returns!** ¡Que cumplas muchos más!

▶ vb ❶ *(go or come back)* volver ▷ *He returned to Spain the following year.* Volvió a España al año siguiente. ❷ *(give back)* devolver

reunion n reunión f (pl reuniones) ▷ *We had a big family reunion at Christmas.* Tuvimos una gran reunión familiar en Navidad.

reuse vb reutilizar

reveal vb revelar

revenge n venganza f ▷ *in revenge* como venganza; **to take revenge** vengarse ▷ *They planned to take revenge on him.* Planearon vengarse de él.

reverse vb *(car)* dar marcha atrás ▷ *He reversed without looking.* Dio marcha atrás sin mirar.; **to reverse the charges** llamar a cobro revertido

▶ adj inverso ▷ *in reverse order* en orden inverso; **in reverse gear** en marcha atrás; **reverse charge call** llamada a cobro revertido

review n ❶ *(of policy, salary)* revisión f (pl revisiones) ❷ *(of subject)* repaso m

revise vb estudiar para un examen ▷ *I haven't started revising yet.* Todavía no he empezado a estudiar para el examen.

revision n **Have you done a lot of revision?** ¿Has estudiado mucho

para el examen?

revolting adj repugnante

revolution n revolución f (pl revoluciones)

reward n recompensa f

rewarding adj gratificante ▷ *a rewarding job* un trabajo gratificante

rewind vb rebobinar ▷ *to rewind a cassette* rebobinar una cinta

rhinoceros n rinoceronte m

rhubarb n ruibarbo m

rhythm n ritmo m

rib n costilla f

ribbon n cinta f

rice n arroz m; **rice pudding** el arroz con leche

rich adj rico; **the rich** los ricos

rid vb **to get rid of** deshacerse de ▷ *I want to get rid of some old clothes.* Quiero deshacerme de algunas ropas viejas.

ridden vb *see* ride

ride n **to go for a ride (1)** *(on horse)* montar a caballo **(2)** *(on bike)* dar un paseo en bicicleta ▷ *We went for a bike ride.* Fuimos a dar un paseo en bicicleta.; **It's a short bus ride to the town centre.** El centro de la ciudad queda cerca en autobús.

▶ vb montar a caballo ▷ *I'm learning to ride.* Estoy aprendiendo a montar a caballo.; **to ride a bike** ir en bicicleta ▷ *Can you ride a bike?* ¿Sabes ir en bicicleta?

rider n ❶ jinete m ▷ *She's a good rider.* Ella monta muy bien a caballo. ❷ *(cyclist)* ciclista mf

ridiculous adj ridículo

riding n (as sport) equitación f
▷ a riding school una escuela de
equitación; **to go riding** montar
a caballo

rifle n rifle m

right adj, adv

There are several ways of
translating **right**. Scan the
examples to find one that
is similar to what you want
to say.

❶ correcto ▷ the right answer la
respuesta correcta **❷** (place,
time, size) adecuado ▷ We're on
the right train. Estamos en el
tren adecuado.; **Is this the right
road for Ávila?** ¿Vamos bien
por aquí para Ávila?; **to be right**
(1) (person) tener razón ▷ You were
right! ¡Tenías razón! **(2)** (statement,
opinion) ser verdad ▷ That's right!
¡Es verdad!; **Do you have the right
time?** ¿Tienes hora? **❸** bien ▷ Am I
pronouncing it right? ¿Lo pronuncio
bien?; **I think you did the right
thing.** Creo que hiciste bien.
❹ (not left) derecho ▷ my right
hand mi mano derecha **❺** (turn,
look) a la derecha ▷ Turn right at
the traffic lights. Cuando llegues
al semáforo dobla a la derecha.;
Right! Let's get started! ¡Bueno!
¡Empecemos!; **I'll do it right away.** Lo
haré enseguida.
▶ n **❶** derecho m ▷ You've got no
right to do that. No tienes derecho
de hacer eso. **❷** derecha f; **on the
right** a la derecha ▷ on the right of

Mr. Yates a la derecha del Sr. Yates

right-hand adj **the right-hand
side** la derecha ▷ It's on the right-
hand side. Está a la derecha.

right-handed adj diestro

ring n **❶** anillo m ▷ a gold ring un
anillo de oro; **a wedding ring** una
alianza **❷** círculo m ▷ to stand in a
ring formar un círculo **❸** (at door)
timbrazo m ▷ After three or four
rings the door was opened. Después
de tres o cuatro timbrazos la
puerta se abrió.; **There was a
ring at the door.** Se oyó el timbre
de la puerta.; **to give somebody
a ring** llamar a alguien por
teléfono; **ring road** la carretera de
circunvalación
▶ vb **❶** llamar ▷ Jo rang this
morning. Jo llamó esta mañana.; **to
ring somebody** llamar a alguien;
to ring back volver a llamar ▷ I'll
ring back later. Volveré a llamar
más tarde.; **to ring up** llamar por
teléfono ▷ sonar ▷ The phone's
ringing. El teléfono está sonando.;
to ring the bell tocar el timbre

ring binder n carpeta f de anillas
(LatAm carpeta f de anillos)

ringtone n tono m de llamada

rinse vb enjuagar

riot n disturbio m

rip vb rasgar ▷ I've ripped my jeans.
Me he rasgado los vaqueros.
▷ My shirt's ripped. Mi camisa está
rasgada.

rip off vb (informal) timar ▷ The
hotel ripped us off. En el hotel nos
timaron.

rip up vb hacer pedazos ▷ He read the note and then ripped it up. Leyó la nota y la hizo pedazos.

ripe adj maduro

rip-off n It's a rip-off! (informal) ¡Es un timo!

rise n ❶ (in prices, temperature) subida f ▷ a sudden rise in temperature una repentina subida de las temperaturas ❷ (pay rise) aumento m
▶ vb ❶ (increase) subir ▷ Prices are rising. Los precios están subiendo. ❷ salir ▷ The sun rises early in June. En junio el sol sale temprano.

risk n riesgo m; **to take risks** correr riesgos; **It's at your own risk.** Es a tu propia cuenta y riesgo.
▶ vb arriesgarse ▷ I wouldn't risk it if I were you. Yo en tu lugar no me arriesgaría.

rival n rival mf
▶ adj ❶ rival ▷ a rival gang una banda rival ❷ competidor (f competidora) ▷ a rival company una empresa competidora

river n río m

road n ❶ carretera f ▷ There's a lot of traffic on the roads. Hay mucho tráfico en las carreteras. ▷ a road accident un accidente de carretera ❷ (street) calle f ▷ They live across the road. Viven al otro lado de la calle.

road map n mapa m de carreteras
Although **mapa** ends in **-a**, it is actually a masculine noun.

road rage n conducta f agresiva al volante

road sign n señal f de tráfico

roadworks npl obras fpl ▷ There are roadworks on the motorway. Hay obras en la autopista.

roast adj asado ▷ roast chicken pollo asado; **roast pork** el asado de cerdo; **roast beef** el rosbif

rob vb ❶ (person) robar; **to rob somebody** robar a alguien ▷ I've been robbed. Me han robado. ❷ (bank) asaltar

robber n ladrón m, ladrona f; **a bank-robber** un asaltante de bancos (f una asaltante de bancos)

robbery n robo m; **a bank robbery** un asalto a un banco; **an armed robbery** un asalto a mano armada

robin n petirrojo m

robot n robot m (pl robots)

rock n ❶ roca f ▷ I sat on a rock. Me senté encima de una roca. ❷ (stone) piedra f ❸ rock m ▷ a rock concert un concierto de rock; **rock and roll** el rock and roll; **a stick of rock** una barra de caramelo

rocket n (spacecraft, firework) cohete m

rocking chair n mecedora f

rocking horse n caballo m de balancín

rod n (for fishing) caña f de pescar

rode vb see **ride**

role n papel m ▷ to play a role hacer un papel

role play n juego m de roles ▷ to do a role play hacer un juego de roles

roll n ❶ rollo m ▷ a toilet roll

un rollo de papel higiénico; **a roll of film** un carrete de fotos ❷ panecillo m ▷ **a cheese roll** un panecillo de queso
▶ vb (ball, bottle) rodar

Rollerblade® n patín m en línea

rollercoaster n montaña f rusa

roller skates npl patines mpl de ruedas

roller-skating n patinaje m sobre ruedas; **to go roller-skating** (sobre ruedas) ir a patinar

Roman adj, n romano ▷ **the Roman empire** el imperio romano; **the Romans** los romanos

Roman Catholic n católico m, católica f ▷ **He's a Roman Catholic.** Es católico.

romance n ❶ (novels) novelas fpl románticas ▷ I read a lot of romance. Leo muchas novelas románticas. ❷ romanticismo m ▷ **the romance of Paris** el romanticismo de París; **a holiday romance** un romance de verano

Romania n Rumanía f

Romanian adj rumano

romantic adj romántico

roof n techo m

roof rack n baca f

room n ❶ habitación f(pl habitaciones) ▷ **She's in her room.** Está en su habitación.; **a single room** una habitación individual; **a double room** una habitación doble ❷ (in school) sala f ▷ **The music room** la sala de música ❸ espacio m ▷ **There's no room for that box. No** hay espacio para esa caja.

root n raíz f(pl raíces)

rope n cuerda f

rose vb see **rise**
▶ n (flower) rosa f

rot vb pudrirse ▷ **As far as I'm concerned he can rot in jail.** Por mí, que se pudra en la cárcel.; **The wood had rotted.** La madera se había podrido.; **Sugar rots your teeth.** El azúcar pica los dientes.

rotten adj podrido ▷ **a rotten apple** una manzana podrida; **rotten weather** un tiempo asqueroso; **That's a rotten thing to do!** ¡Eso está fatal!; **to feel rotten** sentirse fatal

rough adj, adv ❶ áspero ▷ **My hands are rough.** Tengo las manos ásperas. ❷ violento ▷ **Rugby's a rough sport.** El rugby es un deporte violento. ❸ peligroso ▷ **It's a rough area.** Es una zona peligrosa. ❹ agitado ▷ **The sea was rough.** El mar estaba agitado. ❺ aproximado ▷ **I've got a rough idea.** Tengo una idea aproximada.; **to feel rough** sentirse mal; **to sleep rough** dormir en la calle ▷ **A lot of people sleep rough in London.** Mucha gente duerme en la calle en Londres.

roughly adv aproximadamente ▷ **It weighs roughly 20 kilos.** Pesa aproximadamente 20 kilos.

round adj, adv, prep ❶ redondo ▷ **a round table** una mesa redonda ❷ alrededor de ▷ **We were sitting round the table.** Estábamos sentados alrededor de la mesa.;

It's just round the corner. Está a la vuelta de la esquina.; **to go round to somebody's house** ir a casa de alguien; **to have a look round** echar un vistazo ▷ *We had a look round the record section.* Echamos un vistazo a la sección de discos.; **to go round a museum** visitar un museo; **round here** por aquí cerca ▷ *Is there a chemist's round here?* ¿Hay alguna farmacia por aquí cerca?; **all round** por todos lados ▷ *There were vineyards all round.* Había viñedos por todos lados.; **all year round** todo el año; **round about** alrededor de ▷ *It costs round about £100.* Cuesta alrededor de 100 libras esterlinas.; **round about eight o'clock** hacia las ocho

▶ *n* ❶ *(of tournament)* vuelta *f* ❷ *(of boxing match)* round *m* *(pl* rounds*)*; **a round of golf** una vuelta de golf; **a round of drinks** una ronda de bebidas ▷ *He bought them a round of drinks.* Les invitó a una ronda de bebidas.; **I think it's my round.** Creo que me toca pagar.

roundabout *n* ❶ *(at junction)* rotonda *f* ❷ *(at funfair)* tiovivo *m*

rounders *n* juego similar al béisbol

round trip *n* *(in US)* viaje *m* de ida y vuelta; **a round-trip ticket** un billete de ida y vuelta

route *n* itinerario *m* ▷ *We are planning our route.* Estamos planeando el itinerario.; **bus route** el recorrido del autobús

routine *n* rutina *f* ▷ *my daily routine* mi rutina diaria

row

This word has two pronunciations. Make sure you choose the right translation.

n ❶ *(racket)* jaleo *m* ▷ *What's that terrible row?* ¿Qué es ese jaleo tan tremendo? ❷ *(quarrel)* pelea *f*; **to have a row** pelearse ▷ *They've had a row.* Se han peleado. ❸ *(line)* hilera *f* ▷ *a row of houses* una hilera de casas ❹ *(of people, seats)* fila *f* ▷ *in the front row* en primera fila; **five times in a row** cinco veces seguidas

▶ *vb* remar

rowboat *n* *(in US)* barca *f* de remos

rowing *n* remo *m* ▷ *My hobby is rowing.* My hobby es el remo.; **rowing boat** la barca de remos

royal *adj* real ▷ *the royal family* la familia real

rub *vb* ❶ *(stain)* frotar ❷ *(part of body)* restregarse ▷ *Don't rub your eyes.* No te restriegues los ojos.

rub out *vb* borrar

rubber *n* ❶ goma *f* ▷ *rubber soles* suelas de goma ❷ *(eraser)* goma *f* de borrar ▷ *Can I borrow your rubber?* ¿Me prestas la goma?; **a rubber band** una goma elástica

rubbish *n* ❶ basura *f* ▷ *They sell a lot of rubbish at the market.* Venden mucha basura en el mercado.; **That magazine is rubbish!** ¡Esa revista es una porquería! *(informal)* ❷ estupideces *fpl* ▷ *Don't talk*

a b c d e f g h i j k l m n o p q r s t u v w x y z

rubbish! ¡No digas estupideces!; **That's a load of rubbish!** ¡Son puras tonterías!; **rubbish bin** el cubo de la basura; **rubbish dump** el vertedero

▸ *adj* **They're a rubbish team!** ¡Es un equipo que no vale nada!

rucksack *n* mochila *f*

rude *adj* grosero ▷ *He was very rude to me.* Fue muy grosero conmigo.; **It's rude to interrupt.** Es de mala educación interrumpir.; **a rude joke** un chiste verde; **a rude word** una palabrota

rug *n* ❶ (*carpet*) alfombra *f* ❷ (*travelling rug*) manta *f* de viaje

rugby *n* rugby *m* ▷ *He enjoys playing rugby.* Le gusta jugar al rugby.

ruin *n* ruina *f* ▷ *the ruins of the castle* las ruinas del castillo; **in ruins** en ruinas

▸ *vb* ❶ estropear ▷ *It ruined our holiday.* Nos estropeó las vacaciones. ❷ (*financially*) arruinar

rule *n* ❶ regla *f* ▷ *the rules of grammar* las reglas de la gramática; **as a rule** por regla general ❷ norma *f* ▷ *It's against the rules.* Va en contra de las normas.

▸ *vb* gobernar

ruler *n* regla *f*

rum *n* ron *m*

rumour (*US* rumor) *n* rumor *m*

run *n* **to go for a run** salir a correr ▷ *I go for a run every morning.* Salgo a correr todas las mañanas.; **I did a 10-kilometre run.** Corrí 10

kilómetros.; **The criminals are still on the run.** Los delincuentes están todavía en fuga.; **in the long run** a la larga

▸ *vb* ❶ correr; *I ran five kilometres.* Corrí cinco kilómetros.; **to run a marathon** correr un maratón ❷ dirigir ▷ *He runs a large company.* Dirige una gran empresa. ❸ organizar ▷ *They run music courses in the holidays.* Organizan cursos de música en las vacaciones. ❹ (*by car*) llevar ▷ *I can run you to the station.* Te puedo llevar a la estación.; **Don't leave the tap running.** No dejen el grifo abierto. (*LatAm* No dejen la llave abierta.); **to run a bath** llenar la bañera; **The buses stop running at midnight.** Los autobuses dejan de funcionar a medianoche.

run away *vb* huir ▷ *They ran away before the police came.* Huyeron antes de que llegara la policía.

run out *vb* **to run out of something** quedarse sin algo ▷ *We ran out of money.* Nos quedamos sin dinero.; **Time is running out.** Queda poco tiempo.

run over *vb* atropellar; **to get run over** ser atropellado

rung *vb see* **ring**

runner *n* corredor *m*, corredora *f*

runner-up *n* subcampeón *m*, subcampeona *f* (*mpl* subcampeones)

running *n* footing *m* ▷ *Running is my favourite sport.* El footing es mi deporte favorito. ▷ *to go running*

hacer footing

runway n pista f de aterrizaje

rush n prisa f ▷ *I'm in a rush.* Tengo prisa. ▷ *There's no rush. No corre prisa.*; **to do something in a rush** hacer algo deprisa

▶ vb ❶ correr ▷ *Everyone rushed outside.* Todos corrieron hacia fuera. ❷ precipitarse ▷ *There's no need to rush. No hay por qué precipitarse.*

rush hour n hora f punta (*LatAm* hora f pico)

Russia n Rusia f

Russian adj ruso

▶ n ❶ (person) ruso m, rusa f ▷ *the Russians* los rusos ❷ (language) ruso m

rust n óxido m

rusty adj oxidado

rye n centeno m; **rye bread** el pan de centeno

sack n (bag) saco m ▷ *a sack of potatoes* un saco de patatas; **to give somebody the sack** despedir a alguien; **He got the sack.** Lo despidieron.

▶ vb **to sack somebody** despedir a alguien ▷ *He was sacked.* Lo despidieron.

sacred adj (place, object) sagrado

sacrifice n sacrificio m

sad adj triste

saddle n ❶ (for horse) silla f de montar ❷ (on bike) sillín m

saddlebag n ❶ (on bike) cartera f ❷ (for horse) alforja f

safe n caja fuerte (*pl* cajas fuertes)

▶ adj ❶ seguro ▷ *This car isn't safe.* Este coche no es seguro. ❷ a salvo ▷ *You're safe now.* Ya estás a salvo.; **to feel safe** sentirse protegido; **Is the water safe to drink?** ¿Es agua potable?; **Don't worry, it's perfectly safe.** No te preocupes, no tiene el menor peligro.; **safe sex** el sexo sin riesgo

safety n seguridad f; **safety belt** el cinturón de seguridad; **safety pin** el imperdible (LatAm el seguro)

Sagittarius n (sign) Sagitario m; **I'm Sagittarius.** Soy sagitario.

said vb see **say**

sail n vela f
　▶ vb ① (travel) navegar; **to sail around the world** dar la vuelta al mundo navegando ② (leave) zarpar ▷ The boat sails at eight o'clock. El barco zarpa a las ocho.

sailing n (sport) vela f; **to go sailing** hacer vela; **sailing boat** el barco de vela

sailor n marinero m ▷ He's a sailor. Es marinero.

saint n santo m, santa f

> When used before a man's name, the word **Santo** is shortened to **San**, the exceptions being **Santo Tomás** and **Santo Domingo**.
> ▷ Saint John San Juan

sake n **for the sake of the children** por el bien de los niños; **For goodness sake!** ¡Por el amor de Dios!

salad n ensalada f; **salad cream** la mayonesa; **salad dressing** el aliño para la ensalada

salary n sueldo m

sale n ① rebajas fpl ▷ There's a sale on at Harrods. En Harrods están de rebajas. ② venta f ▷ Newspaper sales have fallen. Ha descendido la venta de periódicos.; **on sale** a la venta; **The house is for sale.** La casa está en venta.; **"for sale"** "se vende"

sales assistant n dependiente m, dependienta f

salesman n ① (commercial) representante m ▷ an insurance salesman un representante de seguros ② (sales assistant) dependiente m; **a car salesman** un vendedor de coches

saleswoman n ① (commercial) representante f ▷ an insurance saleswoman una representante de seguros ② (sales assistant) dependienta f

salmon n salmón m (pl salmones)

salon n salón m (pl salones)
▷ beauty salon salón de belleza

salt n sal f

salty adj salado

Salvation Army n Ejército m de Salvación

same adj mismo ▷ the same model el mismo modelo ▷ It's not the same. No es lo mismo.; **They're exactly the same.** Son exactamente iguales.; **The house is still the same.** La casa sigue igual.

sample n muestra f ▷ a free sample una muestra gratuita

sand n arena f

sandal n sandalia f ▷ a pair of

sandals unas sandalias

sand castle n castillo m de arena

sandwich n ❶ (with sliced bread) sandwich m (pl sandwiches) ❷ (with French bread) bocadillo m

sang vb see **sing**

sanitary napkin n (in US) compresa f

sanitary towel n compresa f

sank vb see **sink**

Santa Claus n Papá m Noel

sarcastic adj sarcástico

sardine n sardina f

sat vb see **sit**

satchel n cartera f

satellite n satélite m ▷ by satellite vía satélite; **a satellite dish** una antena parabólica; **satellite television** la televisión vía satélite

satisfactory adj satisfactorio

satisfied adj satisfecho

Saturday n sábado m (pl sábados) ▷ I saw her on Saturday. La vi el sábado. ▷ every Saturday todos los sábados ▷ last Saturday el sábado pasado ▷ next Saturday el sábado que viene ▷ on Saturdays los sábados; **I've got a Saturday job.** Tengo un trabajo los sábados.

sauce n ❶ salsa f ▷ tomato sauce salsa de tomate ❷ crema f ▷ chocolate sauce crema de chocolate

saucepan n cazo m

saucer n platillo m

Saudi Arabia n Arabia f Saudí

sausage n salchicha f; **a sausage roll** un pastelito de salchicha

save vb ❶ (money, time) ahorrar ▷ I've saved £50 already. Ya llevo ahorradas 50 libras. ▷ It saved us time. Nos ahorró tiempo.; **We went in a taxi to save time.** Para ganar tiempo fuimos en taxi. ❷ (person in danger, lives) salvar ❸ (computing) guardar ▷ I saved the file onto a diskette. Guardé el archivo en un disquete.

save up vb ahorrar ▷ I'm saving up for a new bike. Estoy ahorrando para una bici nueva.

savings npl ahorros mpl

savoury adj salado ▷ Is it sweet or savoury? ¿Es dulce o salado?

saw vb see **see**
▶ n sierra f

saxophone n saxofón m (pl saxofones)

say vb decir ▷ to say yes decir que sí ▷ What did he say? ¿Qué dijo él?; **Could you say that again?** ¿Podrías repetir eso?

saying n dicho m

scale n escala f ▷ a large-scale map un mapa a gran escala; **He underestimated the scale of the problem.** Ha subestimado la envergadura del problema.

scales npl ❶ (in kitchen) peso m ❷ (in shop) báscula f ▷ bathroom scales la báscula de baño

scampi npl gambas f rebozadas

scandal n ❶ (outrage) escándalo m ▷ It caused a scandal. Causó escándalo. ❷ (gossip) habladurías fpl ▷ It's just scandal. No son más que habladurías.

Scandinavia n Escandinavia f

Scandinavian adj escandinavo

scar n cicatriz f (pl cicatrices)

scarce adj escaso ▷ scarce resources recursos escasos; **Jobs are scarce.** Escasean los trabajos.

scarcely adv apenas ▷ I scarcely knew him. Apenas lo conocía.

scare n susto m ▷ We got a bit of a scare. Nos pegamos un susto.; **a bomb scare** una amenaza de bomba
  ▶ vb asustar ▷ You scared me! ¡Me has asustado!

scarecrow n espantapájaros m (pl espantapájaros)

scared adj to be scared tener miedo ▷ Are you scared of him? ¿Le tienes miedo?; **I was scared stiff.** Estaba muerto de miedo.

scarf n ❶ (woollen) bufanda f ❷ (light) pañuelo m

scary adj It was really scary. Daba verdadero miedo.; **a scary film** una película de miedo

scene n ❶ escena f ▷ love scenes las escenas de amor ❷ lugar m ▷ at the scene of the crime en el lugar del crimen; **to make a scene** montar el número

scenery n paisaje m

schedule n programa m

Although **programa** ends in -a, it is actually a masculine noun.

  ▷ a production schedule un programa de producción; **There's a tight schedule for** **this project.** Este proyecto tiene un calendario muy justo.; **a busy schedule** una agenda muy apretada; **on schedule** sin retraso; **to be behind schedule** ir con retraso

scheduled flight n vuelo m regular

scheme n plan m ▷ a crazy scheme he dreamed up un plan descabellado que se le ocurrió

scholarship n beca f

school n (for children) colegio m ▷ at school en el colegio ▷ to go to school ir al colegio

schoolbag n bolso m

schoolbook n libro m de texto

schoolboy n colegial m

schoolchildren npl colegiales mpl

schoolgirl n colegiala f

science n ciencia f

science fiction n ciencia f ficción

scientific adj científico

scientist n científico m, científica f

scissors npl tijeras fpl ▷ a pair of scissors unas tijeras

scooter n ❶ (motorcycle) Vespa® f ❷ (child's toy) patinete m

score n (in test, competition) puntuación f (pl puntuaciones) ❷ (in game, match) resultado m ▷ The score was three nil. El resultado fue de tres a cero.; **What's the score?** ¿Cómo van?
  ▶ vb ❶ marcar ▷ to score a goal marcar un gol; **to score a point** anotar un punto; **to score six out of ten** sacar una puntuación de

seis sobre diez ❸ **llevar el tanteo**
▷ Who's going to score? ¿Quién va a
llevar el tanteo?

Scorpio n (sign) Escorpio m; **I'm
Scorpio.** Soy escorpio.

Scot n (person) escocés m,
escocesa f

Scotch tape® n (in US) celo m

Scotland n Escocia f

Scots adj escocés (fescocesa) ▷ a
Scots accent un acento escocés

Scotsman n escocés m (pl
escoceses)

Scotswoman n escocesa f

Scottish adj escocés (fescocesa)
(mpl escoceses) ▷ a Scottish accent
un acento escocés

scout n boy scout m, girl scout f

scrambled eggs npl huevos mpl
revueltos

scrap n trocito m ▷ a scrap of paper
un trocito de papel; **scrap iron** la
chatarra

scrapbook n álbum m de recortes
(pl álbumes de recortes)

scratch vb ❶ (when itchy)
rascarse ▷ Stop scratching! ¡Deja
de rascarte! ❷ (cut) arañar ▷ He
scratched his arm on the bushes.
Se arañó el brazo con las zarzas.
❸ (scrape) rayar ▷ You'll scratch the
worktop with that knife. Vas a rayar
la encimera con ese cuchillo.
▶ n (on skin, floor) arañazo m; **to
start from scratch** partir de cero; **a
scratch card** una tarjeta de
"rasque y gane"

scream n grito m
▶ vb gritar

screen n (television, cinema,
computer) pantalla f

screensaver n salvapantallas m

screw n tornillo m

screwdriver n destornillador m

scribble vb garabatear

scrub vb fregar

sculpture n escultura f

sea n mar m ▷ a house by the sea una
casa junto al mar

> The word **mar** is masculine in
> most cases, but in some set
> expressions it is feminine.

The fishermen put to sea. Los
pescadores se hicieron a la mar.

seafood n marisco m ▷ I don't like
seafood. No me gusta el marisco.;
a seafood restaurant una
marisquería

seagull n gaviota f

seal n (animal) foca f
▶ vb sellar

seaman n marinero m

search vb ❶ buscar ▷ They're
searching for the missing climbers.
Están buscando a los alpinistas
desaparecidos. ❷ registrar
▷ The police searched him for drugs.
La policía lo registró en busca
de drogas.; **They searched
the woods for the little girl.**
Rastrearon el bosque en busca
de la niña.
▶ n ❶ (hunt) búsqueda f; **to
go in search of** ir en busca de
❷ (inspection) registro m

search party n equipo m de
búsqueda

seashore n orilla f del mar ▷ on the

a b c d e f g h i j k l m n o p q r s t u v w x y z

seashore a la orilla del mar

seasick adj **to be seasick** marearse en barco

seaside n playa f

season n estación f (pl estaciones)
▷ *What's your favourite season?*
¿Cuál es tu estación preferida?;
out of season fuera de temporada; **during the holiday season** en la temporada de vacaciones; **a season ticket** un abono

seat n ❶ asiento m ▷ *I was sitting in the back seat.* Yo iba sentada en el asiento trasero.; **Are there any seats left?** ¿Quedan localidades? ❷ escaño m ▷ *to win a seat at the election* conseguir un escaño en las elecciones

seat belt n cinturón m de seguridad (pl cinturones de seguridad)

seaweed n alga f marina

Although it's a feminine noun, remember that you use **el** and **un** with **alga**.

second adj, adv segundo ▷ *the second time* la segunda vez; **to come second** llegar en segundo lugar; **to travel second class** viajar en segunda; **the second of March** el dos de marzo
▷ n segundo m ▷ *It'll only take a second.* Es un segundo nada más.

secondary school n ❶ (*state*) instituto m ❷ (*private*) colegio m

second-class adj, adv (ticket, compartment) de segunda clase;
to travel second-class viajar en

segunda; **second-class postage**
● In Spain there is no first-class
● or second-class postage. If you
● want your mail to arrive fast,
● you must have it sent express
● - **urgente** - from a post office.

secondhand adj de segunda mano

secondly adv en segundo lugar

secret adj secreto
▶ n secreto m ▷ *Can you keep a secret?* ¿Me guardas un secreto?; **in secret** en secreto

secretary n secretario m, secretaria f

secretly adv en secreto

section n sección f (pl secciones)

security n seguridad f; **security guard** el/la guarda jurado

see vb ver ▷ *I can't see.* No veo nada.; **You need to see a doctor.** Tienes que ir a ver a un médico.; **See you!** ¡Hasta luego!; **See you soon!** ¡Hasta pronto!

see to vb encargarse de ▷ *The shower isn't working. Can you see to it please?* La ducha se ha estropeado. ¿Podrías encargarte de eso?

seed n semilla f ▷ *poppy seeds* semillas de amapola; **sunflower seeds** pipas de girasol

seem vb parecer ▷ *She seems tired.* Parece cansada.; **The shop seemed to be closed.** Parecía que la tienda estaba cerrada.; **It seems that...** Parece que... ▷ *It seems you have no alternative.* Parece que no tienes otra opción.; **It seems**

she's getting married. Por lo visto se casa.; **There seems to be a problem.** Parece que hay un problema.

seen vb see **see**

seesaw n balancín m (pl balancines)

seldom adv rara vez

select vb seleccionar

selection n ❶ selección f (pl selecciones) ▷ a selection test una prueba de selección ❷ surtido m ▷ the widest selection on the market el más amplio surtido del mercado

self-catering adj self-catering apartment el apartamento

self-confidence n confianza f en uno mismo ▷ I lost all my self-confidence. Perdí toda la confianza en mí mismo.

self-conscious adj ❶ cohibido ▷ She was really self-conscious at first. Al principio estaba muy cohibida. ❷ acomplejado ▷ She was self-conscious about her height. Estaba acomplejada por su estatura.

self-defence (US self-defense) n defensa f personal ▷ self-defence classes clases de defensa personal; **She killed him in self-defence.** Lo mató en defensa propia.

self-employed adj autónomo ▷ to be self-employed ser autónomo; **the self-employed** los trabajadores autónomos

selfish adj egoísta

self-service adj de autoservicio

sell vb vender ▷ He sold it to me. Me lo vendió.

sell out vb agotarse ▷ The tickets sold out in three hours. Las entradas se agotaron en tres horas.

sell-by date n fecha f de caducidad

Sellotape® n celo m

semi n (house) casa f adosada

semicircle n semicírculo m

semicolon n punto m y coma (pl punto y coma)

semi-detached house n casa f adosada ▷ We live in a semi-detached house. Vivimos en una casa adosada.; **a street of semi-detached houses** una calle de casas pareadas

semi-final n semifinal f

semi-skimmed milk n leche f semidesnatada

send vb mandar ▷ She sent me a birthday card. Me mandó una tarjeta de cumpleaños.

send back vb devolver

send off vb ❶ enviar por correo ▷ We sent off your order yesterday. Le enviamos el pedido por correo ayer. ❷ expulsar ▷ He was sent off. Lo expulsaron.

senior adj, n ❶ (in rank) alto ▷ senior management los altos directivos ❷ (in age) mayor ▷ She's five years my senior. Es cinco años mayor que yo.; **senior school** el instituto de enseñanza secundaria

senior citizen n persona f de la tercera edad

sensational adj sensacional

sense n sentido m ▷ Use your common sense! ¡Usa el sentido común!; **It makes sense.** Tiene sentido.; **sense of smell** olfato; **sense of humour** sentido del humor

sensible adj sensato ▷ Be sensible! ¡Sé sensato!

> Be careful not to translate **sensible** by the Spanish word **sensible**.

sensitive adj sensible

sent vb see **send**

sentence n ❶ oración f (pl oraciones) ▷ What does this sentence mean? ¿Qué significa esta oración? ❷ sentencia f ▷ to pass sentence dictar sentencia ❸ condena f ▷ a sentence of 10 years una condena de 10 años; **the death sentence** la pena de muerte; **He got a life sentence.** Fue condenado a cadena perpetua.

▶ vb **to sentence somebody to life imprisonment** condenar a alguien a cadena perpetua; **to sentence somebody to death** condenar a muerte a alguien

sentimental adj sentimental

separate adj distinto ▷ Men and women have separate exercise rooms. Los hombres y las mujeres tienen salas de ejercicios distintas.; **The children have separate rooms.** Los niños tienen cada uno su habitación.; **I wrote it on a separate sheet.** Lo escribí en

una hoja aparte.; **on separate occasions** en diversas ocasiones

▶ vb ❶ separar ▷ Police moved in to separate the two groups. La policía intervino para separar a los dos grupos. ❷ separarse ▷ Her parents separated last year. Sus padres se separaron el año pasado.

separately adv por separado

separation n separación f (pl separaciones)

September n septiembre m ▷ in September en septiembre ▷ on 23 September el 23 de septiembre

sequel n continuación f (pl continuaciones)

sergeant n ❶ (army) sargento mf ❷ (police) oficial mf de policía

serial n ❶ (on TV, radio) serial m ❷ (in magazine) novela f por entregas

series n serie f

serious adj ❶ serio ▷ You're looking very serious. Estás muy serio. ¿Are you serious? ¿Lo dices en serio? ❷ grave ▷ a serious illness una grave enfermedad

seriously adv ❶ (in earnest) en serio ▷ to take somebody seriously tomar en serio a alguien; **Seriously?** ¿De verdad? ❷ (badly) gravemente ▷ seriously injured gravemente herido

servant n criado m, criada f

serve vb ❶ servir ▷ Dinner is served. La cena está servida.; **It's Agassi's turn to serve.** Al servicio Agassi.; **Are you being served?** ¿Le atienden ya? ❷ cumplir ▷ to

serve a life sentence cumplir cadena perpetua; **to serve time** cumplir condena; **It serves you right.** Te está bien empleado.
▶ *n* servicio *m*

service *vb* (*car, washing machine*) revisar
▶ *n* ❶ servicio *m* ▷ *Service is included.* El servicio está incluido.; **a bus service** una línea de autobús ❷ (*of car, machine*) revisión *f* (*pl* revisiones) ❸ (*at church*) oficio *m* religioso; **the armed services** las fuerzas armadas

service charge *n* servicio *m*
▷ *There's no service charge.* El servicio va incluido.

service station *n* estación *f* de servicio (*pl* estaciones de servicio)

serviette *n* servilleta *f*

session *n* sesión *f* (*pl* sesiones)

set *n* ❶ (*of objects, tools*) juego *m* ▷ *a set of keys* un juego de llaves; **The sofa and chairs are only sold as a set.** El sofá y los sillones no se venden por separado.; **a chess set** un ajedrez; **a train set** un tren eléctrico ❷ (*of ideas, actions*) conjunto *m* ▷ *a set of calculations* un conjunto de cálculos ❸ (*in tennis*) set *m* (*pl* sets) ▷ *She was leading 5-1 in the first set.* Iba ganando 5 a 1 en el primer set.
▶ *vb* ❶ poner ▷ *I set the alarm for seven o'clock.* Puse el despertador a las siete. ❷ establecer ▷ *The world record was set last year.* El récord mundial se estableció el

año pasado. ❸ ponerse ▷ *The sun was setting.* Se estaba poniendo el sol.; **The film is set in Morocco.** La película se desarrolla en Marruecos.; **to set something on fire** prender fuego a algo; **to set sail** zarpar; **to set the table** poner la mesa

set off *vb* salir ▷ *We set off for London at nine o'clock.* Salimos para Londres a las nueve.

set out *vb* salir ▷ *We set out for London at nine o'clock.* Salimos para Londres a las nueve.

settee *n* sofá *m* (*pl* sofás)

settle *vb* ❶ zanjar ▷ *That should settle the problem.* Esto debería zanjar el problema. ❷ pagar ▷ *I'll settle the bill tomorrow.* Mañana pagaré la cuenta.

settle down *vb* calmarse

settle in *vb* adaptarse

seven *num* siete ▷ *She's seven.* Tiene siete años.

seventeen *num* diecisiete ▷ *He's seventeen.* Tiene diecisiete años.

seventeenth *adj* decimoséptimo; **the seventeenth floor** la planta diecisiete; **the seventeenth of April** el diecisiete de abril

seventh *adj* séptimo ▷ *the seventh floor* el séptimo piso; **the seventh of August** el siete de agosto

seventy *num* setenta ▷ *She's seventy.* Tiene setenta años.

several *adj, pron* varios ▷ *several times* varias veces

sew *vb* coser

sewing *n* costura *f* ▷ *I like sewing.*

Me gusta la costura.; **sewing machine** la máquina de coser

sewn vb see **sew**

sex n sexo m ▷ *the opposite sex* el sexo opuesto ▷ **to have sex with somebody** tener relaciones sexuales con alguien; **sex education** la educación sexual

sexism n sexismo m

sexist adj sexista

sexual adj sexual ▷ *sexual discrimination* la discriminación sexual

sexuality n sexualidad f

sexy adj sexy (pl sexy)

shabby adj (person, clothes) andrajoso

shade n ❶ sombra f ▷ *It was 35 degrees in the shade.* Hacía 35 grados a la sombra. ❷ tono m ▷ *a beautiful shade of blue* un tono de azul muy bonito

shadow n sombra f

shake vb ❶ sacudir ▷ *She shook the rug.* Sacudió la alfombra.; "**Shake well before use**" "Agítese bien antes de usarse" ❷ temblar ▷ *He was shaking with cold.* Temblaba de frío.; **Donald shook his head.** Donald negó con la cabeza.; **to shake hands with somebody** dar la mano a alguien ▷ *They shook hands.* Se dieron la mano.

shall vb **Shall I shut the window?** ¿Cierro la ventana?

shallow adj poco profundo

shambles n desastre m ▷ *It's a complete shambles.* Es un desastre total.

shame n vergüenza f ▷ *I'd die of shame!* ¡Me moriría de vergüenza!; **What a shame!** ¡Qué pena!; **It's a shame that…** Es una pena que…

> **es una pena que** has to be followed by a verb in the subjunctive.

▷ *It's a shame he isn't here.* Es una pena que no esté aquí.

shampoo n champú m (pl champús) ▷ *a bottle of shampoo* un bote de champú

shandy n clara f

shape n forma f ▷ *in the shape of a star* en forma de estrella; **to be in good shape** estar en buena forma

share n ❶ (portion) parte f ▷ *He paid his share of the bill.* Pagó su parte de la factura. ❷ (in a company) acción f (pl acciones) ▶ vb compartir ▷ *to share a room with somebody* compartir habitación con alguien

share out vb repartir ▷ *They shared the sweets out among the children.* Repartieron los caramelos entre los niños.

shark n tiburón m (pl tiburones)

sharp adj, adv ❶ afilado ▷ *Be careful, that knife's sharp!* ¡Cuidado con ese cuchillo que está afilado! ❷ (point, spike) puntiagudo ❸ (intelligent) listo ▷ *She's very sharp.* Es muy lista.; **at two o'clock sharp** a las dos en punto

shave vb afeitarse ▷ *He took a bath and shaved.* Se dio un baño y se afeitó.; **to shave one's legs** depilarse las piernas

shaver n **electric shaver** la maquinilla de afeitar eléctrica

shaving cream n crema f de afeitar

shaving foam n espuma f de afeitar

she pron ella

▮ she generally isn't translated unless it's emphatic.
▷ She's very nice. Es muy maja.
▮ Use **ella** for emphasis.
▷ She did it but he didn't. Ella lo hizo, pero él no.

shed n cobertizo m

she'd = **she had**; **she would**

sheep n oveja f

sheepdog n perro m pastor (pl perros pastores)

sheer adj puro ▷ It's sheer greed. Es pura codicia.

sheet n sábana f ▷ to change the sheets cambiar las sábanas; **a sheet of paper** una hoja de papel

shelf n ❶ (on wall, in shop) estante m ❷ (in oven) parrilla f

shell n ❶ (on beach, of tortoise, snail) concha f (LatAm caracol m) ❷ (of egg, nut) cáscara f ❸ (explosive) obús m (pl obuses)

she'll = **she will**

shellfish n marisco m

shelter n refugio m ▷ a bomb shelter un refugio antiaéreo; **to take shelter** refugiarse; **bus shelter** la marquesina de autobús

shelves npl see **shelf**

sherry n jerez m

she's = **she is**; **she has**

Shetland Islands n Islas fpl Shetland

shift n turno m ▷ the night shift el turno de noche ▷ His shift starts at eight o'clock. Su turno empieza a las ocho.; **to do shift work** trabajar por turnos
▶ vb trasladar ▷ I couldn't shift the wardrobe on my own. No podía trasladar el armario yo solo.; **Shift yourself!** (informal) ¡Quita de ahí!

shin n espinilla f

shine vb brillar ▷ The sun was shining. Brillaba el sol.

shiny adj brillante

ship n barco m ▷ by ship en barco

shirt n camisa f

shit excl (rude) ¡Mierda!

shiver vb tiritar ▷ to shiver with cold tiritar de frío

shock n ❶ conmoción f (pl conmociones) ▷ The news came as a shock. La noticia causó conmoción. ❷ calambre m ▷ I got a shock when I touched the switch. Me dio calambre al tocar el interruptor.; **an electric shock** una descarga eléctrica
▶ vb ❶ (upset) horrorizar ▷ They were shocked by the tragedy. Quedaron horrorizados por la tragedia. ❷ (scandalize) escandalizar ▷ Nothing shocks me any more. Ya nada me escandaliza.

shocking adj escandaloso ▷ It's shocking! ¡Es escandaloso!

shoe n zapato m ▷ a pair of shoes un par de zapatos

shoelace n cordón m (pl cordones)

shoe polish n betún m

shoe shop n zapatería f

shone vb see **shine**

shook vb see **shake**

shoot vb ① (fire a shot) disparar
▷ Don't shoot! ¡No disparen!; **to shoot at somebody** disparar contra alguien; **He shot himself with a revolver.** Se pegó un tiro con un revólver.; **He was shot dead by the police.** Murió de un disparo de la policía. ② (execute) fusilar ▷ He was shot at dawn. Lo fusilaron al amanecer. ③ rodar ▷ The film was shot in Prague. La película se rodó en Praga. ④ (in football) chutar

shooting n ① disparos mpl ▷ They heard shooting. Oyeron disparos.; **a shooting** un tiroteo ② caza f ▷ **to go shooting** ir de caza

shop n tienda f ▷ a sports shop una tienda de deportes

shop assistant n dependiente m, dependienta f

shopkeeper n comerciante mf

shoplifting n hurto m en las tiendas

shopping n compra f ▷ Can you get the shopping from the car? ¿Puedes sacar la compra del coche?; **to go shopping (1)** (for food) ir a hacer la compra **(2)** (for pleasure) ir de compras; **I love shopping.** Me encanta ir de compras.; **shopping bag** la bolsa de la compra; **shopping centre** el centro comercial

shop window n escaparate m

shore n orilla f ▷ on the shores of

the lake a orillas del lago; **on shore** en tierra

short adj ① (in length, duration) corto ▷ short hair pelo corto; **a short break** un pequeño descanso; **a short time ago** hace poco ② (in height) bajo ▷ She's quite short. Es bastante baja.; **to be short of something** andar escaso de algo; **at short notice** con poco tiempo de antelación

shortage n escasez f ▷ a water shortage escasez de agua

short cut n atajo m

shortly adv dentro de poco ▷ I'll be there shortly. Estaré allí dentro de poco.; **She arrived shortly after midnight.** Llegó poco después de la medianoche.

shorts npl pantalones mpl cortos ▷ a pair of shorts unos pantalones cortos

short-sighted adj miope

shot vb see **shoot**
▶ n ① (from gun) tiro m ▷ to fire a shot disparar un tiro ② (photo) foto f

⚪ Although **foto** ends in **-o**, it is actually a feminine noun.
▷ a shot of the castle una foto del castillo ③ (injection) inyección f (pl inyecciones)

shotgun n escopeta f

should vb

⚪ When **should** means "ought to", use the conditional tense of **deber**.
deber ▷ You should take more exercise. Deberías hacer más

ejercicio. ▷ *That shouldn't be too hard.* Eso no debería ser muy difícil.

| **tener que** is also a very common way to translate **should**.

▷ *I should have told you before.* Tendría que habértelo dicho antes.

| When **should** means "would", use the conditional tense.

I should go if I were you. Yo que tú, iría.; **I should be so lucky!** ¡Ojalá!

shoulder n hombro m

shouldn't = **should not**

shout vb gritar ▷ *Don't shout!* ¡No grites!
▶ n grito m

shovel n pala f

show n ❶ (in theatre) espectáculo m ❷ (on TV, radio) programa m

| Although **programa** ends in **-a**, it is actually a masculine noun.

fashion show el pase de modelos
▶ vb ❶ enseñar; **to show somebody something** enseñar algo a alguien ▷ *Have I shown you my hat?* ¿Te he enseñado ya mi sombrero? ❷ demostrar ▷ *She showed great courage.* Demostró gran valentía.; **It shows.** Se nota. ▷ *I've never been riding before. - It shows.* Nunca había montado a caballo antes. - Se nota.

show off vb presumir

shower n ❶ ducha f; **to have a shower** ducharse ❷ chubasco

m ▷ *scattered showers* chubascos dispersos

shown vb see **show**

show-off n fantasmón m, fantasmona f (mpl fantasmones)

shrank vb see **shrink**

shriek vb chillar

shrimps npl camarones mpl

shrink vb (clothes, fabric) encogerse

Shrove Tuesday n martes m de carnaval

shrug vb **to shrug one's shoulders** encogerse de hombros

shrunk vb see **shrink**

shuffle vb (cards) barajar

shut vb cerrar ▷ *What time do the shops shut?* ¿A qué hora cierran las tiendas?

shut down vb cerrar ▷ *The cinema shut down last year.* El cine cerró el año pasado.

shut up vb callarse ▷ *Shut up!* ¡Cállate!

shuttlecock n volante m

shy adj tímido

Sicily n Sicilia f

sick adj ❶ enfermo ▷ *She looks after her sick mother.* Cuida de su madre enferma. ❷ de mal gusto ▷ *That's really sick!* ¡Eso es de muy mal gusto! **to be sick** devolver (LatAm arrojar) ▷ *I was sick twice last night.* Anoche devolví dos veces.; **I feel sick.** Tengo ganas de devolver.; **to be sick of something** estar harto de algo ▷ *I'm sick of your jokes.* Estoy harto de tus bromas.

sickness n enfermedad f

side n ❶ (of object, building, car)

lado *m* ▷ *He was driving on the wrong side of the road.* Iba por el lado contrario de la carretera.; **a house on the side of a mountain** una casa en la ladera de una montaña; **We sat side by side.** Nos sentamos uno al lado del otro. ❷ (of pool, bed, road) borde *m* ▷ *The car was abandoned at the side of the road.* El coche estaba abandonado al borde de la carretera.; **by the side of the lake** a la orilla del lago ❸ (of paper, record, tape) cara *f* ▷ *Play side* A. Pon la cara A. ❹ (team) equipo *m* ▷ *He's on my side.* Está en mi equipo.; **I'm on your side.** Yo estoy de tu parte.; **to take somebody's side** ponerse de parte de alguien; **to take sides** tomar partido; **the side entrance** la entrada lateral

sideboard *n* aparador *m*

side-effect *n* efecto *m* secundario

sidewalk *n* (*in US*) acera *f*

sideways *adv* **to look sideways** mirar de reojo; **to move sideways** moverse de lado

sieve *n* ❶ (for liquids) colador *m* ❷ (for solids) criba *f*

sigh *n* suspiro *m*
▷ *vb* suspirar

sight *n* ❶ vista *f* ▷ *I'm losing my sight.* Estoy perdiendo la vista.; **at first sight** a primera vista; **to know somebody by sight** conocer a alguien de vista; **in sight** a la vista ❷ espectáculo *m* ▷ *It was an amazing sight.* Era un espectáculo asombroso.; **Keep**

out of sight! ¡Que no te vean!; **the sights** las atracciones turísticas; **to see the sights of London** hacer turismo por Londres

sightseeing *n* **to go sightseeing** hacer turismo

sign *n* ❶ (notice) letrero *m* ❷ (signal, gesture, indication) señal *f* ▷ *road sign* la señal de tráfico ▷ *She made a sign to the waiter.* Le hizo una señal al camarero. ▷ *There's no sign of improvement.* No hay señales de mejoría. ❸ (star sign) signo *m* ▷ *What sign are you?* ¿De qué signo eres?
▷ *vb* firmar

sign on *vb* apuntarse al paro

signal *n* señal *f*
▷ *vb* **to signal to somebody** hacer señas a alguien

signature *n* firma *f*

significance *n* importancia *f*

significant *adj* significativo

sign language *n* lenguaje *m* por señas

signpost *n* señal *f*

silence *n* silencio *m*

silent *adj* ❶ (place) silencioso ▷ *a silent room* una habitación silenciosa ❷ (person) callado

silk *n* seda *f* ▷ *a silk scarf* un pañuelo de seda

silky *adj* sedoso

silly *adj* tonto

silver *n* plata *f* ▷ *a silver medal* una medalla de plata

similar *adj* parecido; **similar to** parecido a

simple *adj* ❶ sencillo ▷ *It's very*

simple. Es muy sencillo. ❷ simple
▷ He's a bit simple. Es un poco
simple.

simply adv sencillamente

sin n pecado m

since prep, adv, conj ❶ desde
▷ since then desde entonces; I
haven't seen him since. Desde
entonces no lo he vuelto a ver.
❷ desde que ▷ I haven't seen her
since she left. No la he visto desde
que se fue.; It's a few years since
I've seen them. Hace varios años
que no los veo. ❸ como ▷ Since
you're tired, we'll stay at home.
Como estás cansado podemos
quedarnos en casa.

sincere adj sincero

sincerely adv Yours sincerely...
Atentamente...

sing vb cantar

singer n cantante mf

singing n canto m ▷ singing lessons
clases de canto

single adj ❶ individual ▷ a single
room una habitación individual
▷ a single bed una cama individual
❷ soltero ▷ a single mother una
madre soltera ❸ solo ▷ She hadn't
said a single word. No había dicho
una sola palabra.; not a single
thing nada de nada
▶ n ❶ (ticket) billete m de ida
❷ single m ▷ a CD single un single
en CD

single parent n She's a single
parent. Es madre soltera.

singular n singular ▷ in the singular
en singular

sink n ❶ (in the kitchen) fregadero
m ❷ (in the bathroom) lavabo m
▶ vb ❶ hundir ▷ We sank the
enemy's ship. Hundimos el buque
enemigo. ❷ hundirse ▷ The boat
was sinking fast. El barco se hundía
rápidamente.

sir n señor m ▷ Yes sir. Sí, señor.

siren n sirena f

sister n ❶ hermana f ▷ my little
sister mi hermana pequeña
❷ (nurse) enfermera f jefe

sister-in-law n cuñada f

sit vb sentarse ▷ He sat in front of
the TV. Se sentó frente a la tele.;
to be sitting estar sentado ▷ He
was sitting in front of the TV. Estaba
sentado frente a la tele.; to sit an
exam presentarse a un examen

sit down vb sentarse ▷ He sat
down at his desk. Se sentó en su
escritorio.

site n ❶ lugar m ▷ the site of the
accident el lugar del accidente
❷ (campsite) camping m (pl
campings); building site la obra

sitting room n sala f de estar (pl
salas de estar)

situation n situación f (pl
situaciones)

six num seis ▷ He's six. Tiene seis
años.

sixteen num dieciséis ▷ He's
sixteen. Tiene dieciséis años.

sixteenth adj decimosexto;
the sixteenth floor la planta
dieciséis; the sixteenth of
August el dieciséis de agosto

sixth adj sexto ▷ the sixth floor el

sexto piso; **the sixth of August** el seis de agosto

sixty num sesenta ▷ She's sixty. Tiene sesenta años.

size n ❶ (of object, place) tamaño m ▷ plates of various sizes platos de varios tamaños

- Spain uses the European system for clothing and shoe sizes. ❷ (of clothing) talla f ▷ What size do you take? ¿Qué talla usas? ❸ (of shoes) número m; **I take size five.** Calzo un treinta y ocho.

skate vb patinar

skateboard n monopatín m (pl monopatines)

skateboarding n **to go skateboarding** montar en monopatín

skates npl patines mpl

skating n patinaje m; **to go skating** ir a patinar; **skating rink** la pista de patinaje

skeleton n esqueleto m

sketch n boceto m
▷ vb esbozar

ski vb esquiar
▷ n esquí m ▷ a pair of skis unos esquís; **ski boots** las botas de esquí; **ski lift** el telesilla

Although **telesilla** ends in -a, it is actually a masculine noun.

ski pants los pantalones de esquí; **ski pole** el bastón de esquí (pl bastones de esquí); **ski slope** la pista de esquí; **ski suit** el traje de esquí

skid vb patinar

skier n esquiador m, esquiadora f

skiing n esquí m ▷ I love skiing. Me encanta el esquí.; **to go skiing** ir a esquiar; **to go on a skiing holiday** irse de vacaciones a esquiar

skilful adj hábil

skill n habilidad f ▷ It requires a lot of skill. Requiere mucha habilidad.

skilled adj (worker, labour) cualificado

skimmed milk n leche f desnatada

skin n piel f; **skin cancer** el cáncer de piel

skinhead n cabeza mf rapada (pl cabezas rapadas)

skinny adj flaco

skip n contenedor m de basuras
▷ vb saltarse ▷ You should never skip breakfast. No debes saltarte nunca el desayuno.; **to skip school** hacer novillos

skirt n falda f

skive vb (informal) escaquearse; **to skive off school** hacer novillos

skull n ❶ (of corpse) calavera f ❷ (in anatomy) cráneo m

sky n cielo m

skyscraper n rascacielos m (pl rascacielos)

slam vb cerrar de un portazo ▷ She slammed the door. Cerró la puerta de un portazo.; **The door slammed.** La puerta se cerró de un portazo.

slang n argot m

slap n bofetada f
▷ vb dar una bofetada a

slate n teja f de pizarra

sledge n trineo m

sledging n **to go sledging** ir en trineo

sleep n sueño m ▷ lack of sleep falta de sueño; **I need some sleep.** Necesito dormir.; **to go to sleep** dormirse
▶ vb dormir ▷ I couldn't sleep last night. Anoche no podía dormir.

sleep in vb dormir hasta tarde

sleep together vb acostarse juntos

sleep with vb acostarse con

sleeping bag n saco m de dormir

sleeping car n coche m cama (pl coches cama)

sleeping pill n somnífero m

sleepy adj **to feel sleepy** tener sueño

sleet n aguanieve f

Although it's a feminine noun, remember that you use **el** with **aguanieve**.

sleeve n (of shirt, coat) manga f

slept vb see **sleep**

slice n ❶ (of bread) rebanada f ❷ (of cake) trozo m ❸ (of lemon, pineapple) rodaja f ❹ (of ham, cheese) loncha f
▶ vb cortar

slide n ❶ (in playground) tobogán m (pl toboganes) ❷ (photo) diapositiva f ❸ (hair slide) pasador m
▶ vb deslizarse ▷ Tears were sliding down his cheeks. Las lágrimas se deslizaban por sus mejillas.; **She slid the door open.** Corrió la puerta.

slight adj ligero ▷ a slight improvement una ligera mejoría; **a slight problem** un pequeño problema

slightly adv ligeramente ▷ They are slightly more expensive. Son ligeramente más caros.

slim adj delgado
▶ vb adelgazar ▷ I'm trying to slim. Estoy intentando adelgazar.; **I'm slimming.** Estoy a régimen.

sling n cabestrillo m ▷ She had her arm in a sling. Llevaba el brazo en cabestrillo.

slip n ❶ (mistake) desliz m (pl deslices) ❷ (underskirt) combinación f (pl combinaciones); **a slip of paper** un papelito; **a slip of the tongue** un lapsus
▶ vb resbalar ▷ He slipped on the ice. Resbaló en el hielo.

slipper n zapatilla f

slippery adj resbaladizo

slope n ❶ (surface) cuesta f ▷ The street was on a slope. La calle era en cuesta. ❷ (angle) pendiente f ▷ a slope of 10 degrees una pendiente del 10 por ciento

slot n ranura f

slot machine n ❶ (for gambling) máquina f tragaperras (pl máquinas tragaperras) ❷ (vending machine) máquina f expendedora

slow adj, adv lento ▷ to go slow ir lento; **Drive slower!** ¡Conduce más despacio!; **My watch is slow.** Mi reloj se atrasa.

slow down vb reducir la velocidad
▷ *The car slowed down.* El coche redujo la velocidad.

slowly adv lentamente

slug n babosa f

slum n barrio m bajo

smack n cachete m
▶ vb dar un cachete a

small adj pequeño (*LatAm* chico)
▷ *two small children* dos niños pequeños

smart adj ① elegante ▷ *a smart navy blue suit* un elegante traje azul marino ② listo ▷ *He thinks he's smarter than Sarah.* Se cree más listo que Sarah.

smash vb ① romper ▷ *They smashed windows.* Rompieron ventanas. ② romperse ▷ *The glass smashed into tiny pieces.* El vaso se rompió en pedazos.

smashing adj estupendo ▷ *That's a smashing idea.* Me parece una idea estupenda.

smell n olor m ① *a smell of lemon* un olor a limón; **the sense of smell** el olfato
▶ vb oler ▷ *That dog smells!* ¡Cómo huele ese perro! ▷ *I can't smell anything.* No huelo nada.; **I can smell gas.** Me huele a gas.; **to smell of something** oler a algo ▷ *It smells of petrol.* Huele a gasolina.

smelly adj maloliente ▷ *The pub was dirty and smelly.* El pub era sucio y maloliente.; **He's got smelly feet.** Le huelen los pies.

smile n sonrisa f
▶ vb sonreír

smoke n humo m
▶ vb fumar ▷ *I don't smoke.* No fumo. ▷ *to stop smoking* dejar de fumar

smoker n fumador m, fumadora f

smoking n **Smoking is bad for you.** Fumar es malo para la salud.; **"no smoking"** "prohibido fumar"

smooth adj liso ▷ *a smooth surface* una superficie lisa

SMS n (= short message service) SMS m; **an SMS message** un mensaje SMS

smudge n borrón m (*pl* borrones)

smuggle vb **to smuggle in** meter de contrabando; **to smuggle out** sacar de contrabando

smuggler n contrabandista mf

smuggling n contrabando m

snack n **to have a snack** picar algo

snack bar n cafetería f

snail n caracol m

snake n serpiente f

snap vb partirse ▷ *The branch snapped.* La rama se partió.; **to snap one's fingers** chasquear los dedos

snatch vb arrebatar; **to snatch something from somebody** arrebatar algo a alguien ▷ *He snatched the keys from my hand.* Me arrebató las llaves de la mano.; **My bag was snatched.** Me robaron el bolso.

sneak vb **to sneak in** entrar a hurtadillas; **to sneak out** salir a hurtadillas

sneeze vb estornudar

sniff vb ① sorberse la nariz ▷ *Stop*

sniffing! ¡Deja de sorberte la nariz!
❷ olfatear ▷ *The dog sniffed my hand.* El perro me olfateó la mano.;
to sniff glue esnifar pegamento

snob n esnob mf (pl esnobs)

snooker n billar m

snooze n (*informal*) cabezadita f ▷ *to have a snooze* echar una cabezadita

snore vb roncar

snow n nieve f
▷ vb nevar ▷ *It's snowing.* Está nevando.

snowball n bola f de nieve

snowflake n copo m de nieve

snowman n muñeco m de nieve ▷ *to build a snowman* hacer un muñeco de nieve

so conj, adv ❶ (*therefore*) así que ▷ *The shop was closed, so I went home.* La tienda estaba cerrada, así que me fui a casa.; **So what?** ¿Y qué? ❷ (*so that*) para que

para que has to be followed by a verb in the subjunctive.

▷ *He took her upstairs so they wouldn't be overheard.* La subió al piso de arriba para que nadie los oyera. ❸ (*very, as*) tan ▷ *He was talking so fast I couldn't understand.* Hablaba tan rápido que no lo entendía. ▷ *He's like his sister but not so clever.* Es como su hermana pero no tan listo.; **It was so heavy!** ¡Pesaba tanto!; **How's your father? - Not so good.** ¿Cómo está tu padre? - No muy bien.; **so much** tanto ▷ *She's got so much energy.* Tiene tanta energía.; **so**

many tantos ▷ *I've got so many things to do today.* Tengo tantas cosas que hacer hoy.; **That's not so.** No es así. ❹ (*also*) también; **so do I** y yo también ▷ *I work a lot. - So do I.* Trabajo mucho. - Y yo también.; **I love horses. - So do I.** Me encantan los caballos. - A mí también.; **I think so.** Creo que sí.; **... or so ...** o así ▷ *ten or so people* diez personas o así

soak vb ❶ poner en remojo ▷ *Soak the beans for two hours.* Ponga las judías en remojo dos horas. ❷ empapar ▷ *Water had soaked his jacket.* El agua le había empapado la chaqueta.

soaking adj empapado ▷ *By the time we got back we were soaking.* Cuando regresamos estábamos empapados.; **Your shoes are soaking wet.** Tienes los zapatos calados.

soap n jabón m

soap opera n telenovela f

soap powder n detergente m en polvo

sob vb sollozar

sober adj sobrio

soccer n fútbol m ▷ *to play soccer* jugar al fútbol; **soccer player** el/la futbolista

social adj social ▷ *social problems* problemas sociales; **I have a good social life.** Tengo mucha vida social.

socialism n socialismo m

socialist adj, n socialista

social security n seguridad f

social; **to be on social security** cobrar de la seguridad social

social worker n asistente m social, asistenta f social

society n ① sociedad f ▷ a multi-cultural society una sociedad pluricultural ② asociación f (pl asociaciones) ▷ a drama society una asociación de amigos del teatro

sociology n sociología f

sock n calcetín m (pl calcetines) (LatAm media f)

socket n enchufe m

sofa n sofá m (pl sofás)

soft adj ① suave ▷ a soft towel una toalla suave ② blando ▷ The mattress is too soft. El colchón es demasiado blando.; **to be soft on somebody** ser blando con alguien; **soft cheeses** los quesos tiernos; **a soft drink** un refresco; **soft drugs** las drogas blandas; **soft option** la alternativa fácil

software n software m

soggy adj ① (bread, biscuits) revenido ② (salad) pasado

soil n tierra f

solar power n energía f solar

sold vb see **sell**

sold out adj agotado ▷ The tickets are all sold out. Están agotadas todas las entradas.

soldier n soldado m

solicitor n ① (for lawsuits) abogado m, abogada f ② (for wills, property) notario m, notaria f

solid adj sólido ▷ a solid wall un muro sólido; **solid gold** oro

macizo; **for three solid hours** durante tres horas seguidas

solo n solo m ▷ a guitar solo un solo de guitarra

solution n solución f (pl soluciones)

solve vb resolver

some adj, pron

> When **some** refers to something you can't count, it usually isn't translated.

▷ Would you like some bread? ¿Quieres pan? ▷ Would you like some coffee? - No thanks, I've got some. ¿Quiere café? - No gracias, ya tengo.; **I only want some of it.** Sólo quiero un poco.

> When **some** refers to something you can count, use **alguno**, which is shortened to **algún** before a masculine singular noun.

▷ some day algún día ▷ some books algunos libros; **some day next week** un día de la semana que viene; **Some people say that...** Hay gente que dice que...; **some of them** algunos ▷ I only sold some of them. Sólo vendí algunos.

somebody pron alguien ▷ I need somebody to help me. Necesito que me ayude alguien.

somehow adv de alguna manera ▷ I'll do it somehow. De alguna manera lo haré.; **Somehow I don't think he believed me.** Por alguna razón me parece que no me creyó.

someone pron alguien ▷ I need someone to help me. Necesito que me ayude alguien.

something *pron* algo ▷ **something special** algo especial; **It cost £100, or something like that.** Costó 100 libras, o algo así.; **His name is Peter or something.** Se llama Peter o algo por el estilo.

sometime *adv* algún día ▷ **You must come and see us sometime.** Tienes que venir a vernos algún día.; **sometime last month** el mes pasado

sometimes *adv* a veces ▷ *Sometimes I drink beer.* A veces bebo cerveza.

somewhere *adv* en algún sitio ▷ *I left my keys somewhere.* Me he dejado las llaves en algún sitio.; **I'd like to go on holiday, somewhere exotic.** Me gustaría irme de vacaciones, a algún sitio exótico.

son *n* hijo *m*

song *n* canción *f* (*pl* canciones)

son-in-law *n* yerno *m*

soon *adv* pronto ▷ **very soon** muy pronto; **soon afterwards** poco después; **as soon as possible** cuanto antes

sooner *adv* antes ▷ *Can't you come a bit sooner?* ¿No puedes venir un poco antes?; **sooner or later** tarde o temprano; **the sooner the better** cuanto antes mejor

soprano *n* soprano *f*

Although **soprano** ends in -o, it is actually a feminine noun.

sore *adj* **It's sore.** Me duele.; **I have a sore throat.** Me duele la garganta.; **That's a sore point.**

Ése es un tema delicado.
▷ *n* llaga *f*

sorry *adj* **I'm sorry.** Lo siento. ▷ *I'm very sorry.* Lo siento mucho.; **I'm sorry I'm late.** Siento llegar tarde.; **Sorry!** ¡Perdón!; **Sorry?** ¿Cómo?; **I'm sorry about the noise.** Perdón por el ruido.; **You'll be sorry!** ¡Te arrepentirás!; **to feel sorry for somebody** sentir pena por alguien

sort *n* tipo *m* ▷ *What sort of bike have you got?* ¿Qué tipo de bicicleta tienes?; **all sorts of...** todo tipo de...

sort out *vb* **①** ordenar ▷ *Sort out all your books.* Ordena todos tus libros. **②** arreglar ▷ *They have sorted out their problems.* Han arreglado sus problemas.

soul *n* alma *f*

Although it's a feminine noun, remember that you use **el** and **un** with **alma**.

② soul *m* ▷ *a soul singer* una cantante de soul

sound *n* **①** (*noise*) ruido *m* ▷ *the sound of footsteps* el ruido de pasos **②** (*volume*) volumen *m*
▷ *vb* sonar ▷ *That sounds interesting.* Eso suena interesante.; **It sounds as if she's doing well at school.** Parece que le va bien en el colegio.; **That sounds like a good idea.** Eso me parece una buena idea.
▷ *adj* válido ▷ *His reasoning is perfectly sound.* Su argumentación es perfectamente válida.; **Julian gave me some sound advice.**

Julian me dio un buen consejo.;
sound asleep profundamente
dormido

soundtrack n banda f sonora

soup n sopa f

sour adj agrio

south n sur m ▷ *the South of France*
el sur de Francia
　▶ adj del sur ▷ *a south wind* un
viento del sur; **the south coast** la
costa meridional
　▶ adv hacia el sur ▷ *We were*
travelling south. Viajábamos hacia
el sur.; **south of** al sur de ▷ *It's south*
of London. Está al sur de Londres.

South Africa n Sudáfrica f

South America n Sudamérica f

South American adj
sudamericano
　▶ n sudamericano m,
sudamericana f ▷ *South Americans*
los sudamericanos

southeast n sudeste m;
southeast England el sudeste de
Inglaterra

southern adj **Southern England**
el sur de Inglaterra

South Pole n Polo m Sur

southwest n sudoeste m

souvenir n recuerdo m ▷ *souvenir*
shop la tienda de recuerdos

soya n soja f

space n espacio m ▷ *There isn't*
enough space. No hay espacio
suficiente.; **a parking space** un
sitio para aparcar

spacecraft n nave f espacial

spade n pala f; **spades** (*at cards*)
las picas ▷ *the ace of spades* el as

de picas
　█ Be careful not to translate
　spade by **espada**.

spaghetti n espaguetis mpl

Spain n España f

Spaniard n (*person*) español m,
española f

spaniel n perro m de aguas

Spanish adj español
　▶ n español m
　● The official name for the
　　Spanish language in Spain and
　　Latin America is **el castellano**
　　and this is also the term some
　　Spanish speakers prefer to use.
　▷ *Spanish lessons* las clases
de español; **the Spanish** los
españoles

spanner n llave f inglesa

spare adj ❶ de repuesto ▷ *spare*
wheel la rueda de repuesto ❷ de
sobra ▷ *Have you got a spare pencil?*
¿Tienes un lápiz de sobra?; **spare**
part el repuesto; **spare room** el
cuarto de los huéspedes; **spare**
time el tiempo libre
　▶ vb **Can you spare a moment?**
¿Tienes un momento?; **I can't**
spare the time. No tengo
tiempo.; **They've got no money**
to spare. No les sobra el dinero.;
We arrived with time to spare.
Llegamos con tiempo de sobra.
　▶ n **I've lost my key. - Have you**
got a spare? He perdido la llave.
- ¿Tienes una de sobra?

sparkling adj con gas ▷ *sparkling*
water agua con gas; **sparkling**
wine vino espumoso

sparrow n gorrión m (pl gorriones)

spat vb see **spit**

speak vb hablar; **Do you speak English?** ¿Hablas inglés? ▷ She spoke to him about it. Habló de ello con él.; **Could I speak to Alison? - Speaking!** ¿Podría hablar con Alison? - ¡Soy yo!

speaker n ❶ (loudspeaker) altavoz m (pl altavoces) ❷ (at conference) orador m, oradora f; **French speakers** los hablantes de francés

special adj especial

specialist n especialista mf

speciality n especialidad f

specialize vb especializarse ▷ She specialized in Russian. Se especializó en ruso.; **We specialize in skiing equipment.** Estamos especializados en material de esquí.

specially adv especialmente ▷ It can be very cold here, specially in winter. Llega a hacer mucho frío aquí, especialmente en invierno.

species n especie f

specific adj ❶ específico ▷ certain specific issues ciertos temas específicos ❷ concreto ▷ Could you be more specific? ¿Podrías ser más concreto?

specs, spectacles npl gafas fpl (LatAm anteojos mpl)

spectacular adj espectacular

spectator n espectador m, espectadora f

speech n discurso m ▷ to make a speech dar un discurso

speechless adj **I was speechless.** Me quedé sin habla.

speed n velocidad f ▷ at top speed a toda velocidad; **a three-speed bike** una bicicleta de tres marchas

speed up vb acelerar

speedboat n lancha f motora

speeding n exceso m de velocidad ▷ He was fined for speeding. Lo multaron por exceso de velocidad.

speed limit n límite m de velocidad; **to break the speed limit** saltarse el límite de velocidad

spell vb deletrear ▷ Can you spell that please? ¿Me lo deletrea, por favor?; **How do you spell "library"?** ¿Cómo se escribe "library"?; **I can't spell.** Cometo faltas de ortografía.
▶ n hechizo m ▷ to be under somebody's spell estar bajo el hechizo de alguien; **to cast a spell on somebody** hechizar a alguien

spelling n ortografía f ▷ My spelling is terrible. Cometo muchas faltas de ortografía.; **a spelling mistake** una falta de ortografía

spend vb ❶ gastar ▷ They spend enormous amounts of money on advertising. Gastan cantidades enormes de dinero en publicidad. ❷ dedicar ▷ He spends a lot of time and money on his hobbies. Dedica mucho tiempo y dinero a sus aficiones. ❸ pasar ▷ He spent a month in France. Pasó un mes en Francia.

spice n especia f

spicy adj picante

spider n araña f

spill vb You've spilled coffee on your shirt. Se te ha caído café en la camisa.

spinach n espinacas fpl

spine n columna f vertebral

spire n aguja f

spirit n ❶ espíritu m ▷ a youthful spirit un espíritu joven ❷ brío m ▷ They played with great spirit. Jugaron con mucho brío.

spirits npl licores mpl ▷ I don't drink spirits. No bebo licores.; **to be in good spirits** estar de buen ánimo

spiritual adj espiritual

spit vb escupir

spit out vb escupir ▷ I spat it out. Lo escupí.

spite n **in spite of** a pesar de; **out of spite** por despecho

spiteful adj ❶ (person) rencoroso ❷ (action) malintencionado

splash vb salpicar ▷ Don't splash me! ¡No me salpiques!; **He splashed water on his face.** Se echó agua en la cara.
▶ n chapoteo m ▷ I heard a splash. Oí un chapoteo.; **a splash of colour** una mancha de color

splendid adj espléndido

splinter n astilla f

split vb ❶ partir ▷ He split the wood with an axe. Partió la madera con un hacha. ❷ partirse ▷ The ship hit a rock and split in two. El barco chocó con una roca y se partió en dos. ❸ dividir ▷ a decision that will split the party una decisión que dividirá al partido; **They decided to split the profits.** Decidieron repartir los beneficios.

split up vb separarse

spoil vb ❶ estropear ▷ It spoiled our holiday. Nos estropeó las vacaciones. ❷ mimar ▷ Grandparents like to spoil their grandchildren. A los abuelos les encanta mimar a los nietos.

spoiled adj mimado ▷ a spoiled child un niño mimado

spoilsport n aguafiestas mf (pl aguafiestas)

spoke vb see **speak**

spoken vb see **speak**

spokesman n portavoz m (pl portavoces) (LatAm vocero m)

spokeswoman n portavoz f (pl portavoces) (LatAm vocera f)

sponge n esponja f; **sponge bag** la bolsa de aseo; **sponge cake** el bizcocho

sponsor n patrocinador m, patrocinadora f
▶ vb patrocinar ▷ The tournament was sponsored by local firms. El torneo fue patrocinado por empresas locales.

spontaneous adj espontáneo

spooky adj The house is really spooky at night. La casa te pone los pelos de punta de noche.

spoon n cuchara f

spoonful n cucharada f

sport n deporte m; **sports bag** la bolsa de deporte; **sports car** el coche deportivo; **sports jacket** la chaqueta de sport

sportsman n deportista m

sportswear n ropa f de deporte

sportswoman n deportista f

sporty adj deportista ▷ I'm not very sporty. No soy muy deportista.

spot n ❶ mancha f ▷ There's a spot on your shirt. Tienes una mancha en la camisa. ❷ lunar m ▷ a red dress with white spots un vestido rojo con lunares blancos ❸ grano m ▷ He's covered in spots. Está lleno de granos. ❹ sitio m ▷ It's a lovely spot for a picnic. Es un sitio precioso para un picnic.; **on the spot (1)** (immediately) en el acto ▷ They gave her the job on the spot. Le dieron el trabajo en el acto. **(2)** (at the same place) en el mismo sitio ▷ Luckily they were able to mend the car on the spot. Afortunadamente consiguieron arreglar el coche en el mismo sitio.
　▶ vb notar ▷ I spotted a mistake. Noté un error.

spotlight n foco m

spotty adj con granos

sprain vb torcerse ▷ She's sprained her ankle. Se ha torcido el tobillo.
　▶ n torcedura f

spray n (spray can) spray m (pl sprays)
　▶ vb ❶ rociar ▷ She sprayed perfume on my hand. Me roció perfume en la mano. ❷ fumigar ▷ to spray against insects fumigar contra los insectos; **There was graffiti sprayed on the wall.** Había pintadas de spray en la pared.

spread vb ❶ extender ▷ She spread a towel on the sand. Extendió una toalla sobre la arena. ❷ untar ▷ Spread the top of the cake with whipped cream. Unte la parte superior de la tarta con nata montada. ❸ propagarse ▷ The news spread rapidly. La noticia se propagó rápidamente.

spread out vb ❶ dispersarse ▷ The soldiers spread out across the field. Los soldados se dispersaron por el campo. ❷ desplegar ▷ He spread the map out on the table. Desplegó el mapa sobre la mesa.

spring n ❶ primavera f ▷ in spring en primavera ❷ (metal) muelle m ❸ (of water) manantial m; **spring onion** la cebolleta

springtime n primavera f

sprint n carrera f de velocidad; **the women's 100 metres sprint** los cien metros lisos femeninos
　▶ vb correr a toda velocidad ▷ She sprinted for the bus. Corrió a toda velocidad para coger el autobús.

> Be very careful with the verb **coger**: in most of Latin America this is an extremely rude word that should be avoided. However, in Spain this verb is common and not rude at all.

sprouts npl **Brussels sprouts** las coles de Bruselas

spy n espía mf
　▶ vb **to spy on somebody** espiar a alguien

spying n espionaje m

square n ❶ (shape) cuadrado m ❷ (in town) plaza f ▷ the town

square la plaza mayor
▶ *adj* cuadrado ▷ *two square metres* dos metros cuadrados; **It's two metres square.** Mide dos por dos.

squash n (*sport*) squash m; **squash court** la cancha de squash; **squash racket** la raqueta de squash; **orange squash** la naranjada; **lemon squash** la limonada
▶ *vb* aplastar ▷ *You're squashing me.* Me estás aplastando.

squeak *vb* ❶ (*mouse, child*) chillar ❷ (*door, wheel*) chirriar ❸ (*shoes*) crujir

squeeze *vb* ❶ exprimir ▷ *Squeeze two large lemons.* Exprima dos limones grandes. ❷ apretar ▷ *She squeezed my hand.* Me apretó la mano.; **The thieves squeezed through a tiny window.** Los ladrones se colaron por una pequeña ventana.

squirrel n ardilla f

stab *vb* apuñalar

stable n cuadra f
▶ *adj* estable ▷ *a stable relationship* una relación estable

stack n pila f ▷ *There were stacks of books on the table.* Había pilas de libros sobre la mesa.; **They've got stacks of money.** Tienen cantidad de dinero.

stadium n estadio m

staff n ❶ (*in company*) personal m ❷ (*in school*) profesorado m

stage n etapa f ▷ *in stages* por etapas; **at this stage in the negotiations** a estas alturas de las negociaciones ❷ escenario m ▷ *The band came on stage late.* El grupo salió tarde al escenario.; **I always wanted to go on the stage.** Siempre quise dedicarme al teatro.

stain n mancha f
▶ *vb* manchar

stainless steel n acero m inoxidable

stair n escalón m (*pl* escalones)

staircase n escalera f

stairs npl escaleras fpl

stale *adj* (*bread*) duro

stalemate n punto m muerto ▷ *to reach a stalemate* llegar a un punto muerto; **The game ended in stalemate.** (*in chess*) La partida terminó en tablas.

stall n puesto m ▷ *He's got a market stall.* Tiene un puesto en el mercado.; **the stalls** (*in theatre*) la platea

stammer n tartamudeo m; **He's got a stammer.** Es tartamudo.

stamp n sello m (*LatAm* estampilla f) ▷ *My hobby is stamp collecting.* Mi afición es coleccionar sellos.; **stamp album** el álbum de sellos (*pl* álbumes de sellos)
▶ *vb* sellar ▷ *The file was stamped "confidential".* El archivo iba sellado como "confidencial".; **The audience stamped their feet.** El público pateaba.

stand *vb* ❶ estar de pie ▷ *He was standing by the door.* Estaba de pie junto a la puerta.; **What are you standing there for?** ¿Qué haces ahí de pie?; **They all stood when I came in.** Se pusieron de pie cuando entré. ❷ soportar ▷ I can't stand all this noise. No soporto todo este ruido.

stand for vb ❶ significar ▷ "EU" stands for "European Union". "EU" significa "European Union". ❷ consentir ▷ I won't stand for it any more! ¡No pienso consentirlo más!

stand in for vb sustituir

stand out vb destacar

stand up vb ❶ ponerse de pie ▷ I stood up and walked out. Me puse de pie y me fui. ❷ estar de pie ▷ She has to stand up all day. Tiene que estar todo el día de pie.

stand up for vb defender ▷ Stand up for your rights! ¡Defiende tus derechos!

standard adj normal ▷ the standard procedure el procedimiento normal; **standard equipment** el equipamiento de serie
▶ n nivel m ▷ The standard is very high. El nivel es muy alto.; **She's got high standards.** Es muy exigente.; **standard of living** el nivel de vida

Standard Grades npl certificado del último ciclo de la enseñanza secundaria obligatorio
- In Spain, under the reformed educational system, if you leave school at the age of 16, you get a **Título de Graduado en Educación Secundaria**.

stands npl tribuna fsg

stank vb see **stink**

staple n grapa f
▶ adj básico ▷ their staple food su alimento básico

stapler n grapadora f

star n estrella f ▷ a TV star una estrella de televisión; **the stars** el horóscopo
▶ vb to star in a film protagonizar una película; **The film stars Nicole Kidman.** La protagonista de la película es Nicole Kidman.; **...starring Johnny Depp** ...con Johnny Depp

stare vb mirar fijamente ▷ Andy stared at him. Andy lo miraba fijamente.

star sign n signo m del zodíaco ▷ What star sign are you? ¿De qué signo eres?

start n ❶ principio m ▷ at the start of the film al principio de la película ▷ from the start desde el principio ▷ for a start para empezar; **Shall we make a start on the washing-up?** ¿Nos ponemos a fregar los platos? ❷ (of race) salida f
▶ vb ❶ empezar ▷ What time does it start? ¿A qué hora empieza?; **to start doing something** empezar a hacer algo ▷ I started learning Spanish two years ago. Empecé a aprender español hace dos años. ❷ (business, organization, campaign) montar ▷ He wants to start his own business. Quiere montar su propio negocio. ❸ arrancar ▷ He couldn't start the car. No conseguía arrancar

el coche.

start off vb ponerse en camino
▷ We started off first thing in the morning. Nos pusimos en camino pronto por la mañana.

starter n (first course) primer m plato

starve vb morirse de hambre
▷ People are starving. La gente se muere de hambre.; **I'm starving!** ¡Me muero de hambre!

state n estado m ▷ It's an independent state. Es un estado independiente.; **He wasn't in a fit state to drive.** No estaba en condiciones de conducir.; **Tim was in a real state.** Tim estaba de los nervios.; **the States** Estados m Unidos
▶ vb declarar ▷ He stated his intention to resign. Declaró su intención de dimitir.; **Please state your name and address.** Por favor indique su nombre y dirección.

statement n ❶ declaración f (pl declaraciones) ▷ statements by witnesses las declaraciones de testigos ❷ afirmación f (pl afirmaciones) ▷ Andrew now disowns the statement he made. Ahora Andrew desmiente la afirmación que hizo.; **a bank statement** un extracto de cuenta

station n estación f (pl estaciones); **bus station** la estación de autobuses; **police station** la comisaría; **radio station** la emisora de radio

stationer's n papelería f

statue n estatua f

stay n estancia f ▷ my stay in Spain mi estancia en España
▶ vb quedarse ▷ Stay here! ¡Quédate aquí! ▷ I'm going to be staying with friends. Me voy a quedar en casa de unos amigos.; **Where are you staying? In a hotel?** ¿Dónde estás? ¿En un hotel?; **to stay the night** pasar la noche; **We stayed in Belgium for a few days.** Pasamos unos días en Bélgica.

stay in vb quedarse en casa

stay up vb quedarse levantado
▷ We stayed up till midnight. Nos quedamos levantados hasta las doce.

steady adj ❶ fijo ▷ a steady job un trabajo fijo; **a steady boyfriend** un novio formal ❷ firme ▷ a steady hand un pulso firme ❸ constante ▷ a steady pace un ritmo constante; **Steady on!** ¡Calma!

steak n filete m

steal vb robar

steam n vapor m ▷ a steam engine una máquina de vapor

steel n acero m

steep adj empinado

steeple n aguja f

steering wheel n volante m

step n ❶ paso m ▷ He took a step forward. Dio un paso adelante. ❷ peldaño m ▷ She tripped over the step. Tropezó con el peldaño.
▶ vb dar un paso ▷ I tried to step

forward. Traté de dar un paso adelante.; **Step this way, please.** Pase por aquí, por favor.

step back *vb* retroceder

stepbrother *n* hermanastro *m*

stepdaughter *n* hijastra *f*

stepfather *n* padrastro *m*

stepladder *n* escalera *f* de tijera

stepmother *n* madrastra *f*

stepsister *n* hermanastra *f*

stepson *n* hijastro *m*

stereo *n* equipo *m* de música

sterling *adj* **pound sterling** la libra esterlina; **one hundred pounds sterling** cien libras esterlinas

stew *n* estofado *m* (*LatAm* guisado *m*)

steward *n* ❶ (*on plane*) auxiliar *m* de vuelo ❷ (*on ship*) camarero *m*

stewardess *n* ❶ (*on plane*) auxiliar *f* de vuelo ❷ (*on ship*) camarera *f*

stick *n* palo *m*; **a walking stick** un bastón (*pl* unos bastones)
▶ *vb* ❶ pegar ▷ *Stick the stamps on the envelope.* Pegue los sellos en el sobre. ❷ pegarse ▷ *The rice stuck to the pan.* El arroz se pegó a la olla. ❸ meter ▷ *He stuck the letter in his briefcase.* Metió la carta en el maletín.; **I can't stick it any longer.** Ya no lo aguanto más.

stick out *vb* sacar ▷ *The little girl stuck out her tongue.* La niña sacó la lengua.

sticker *n* pegatina *f*

stick insect *n* insecto *m* palo

sticky *adj* ❶ pegajoso ▷ *to have sticky hands* tener las manos

pegajosas ❷ adhesivo ▷ *a sticky label* una etiqueta adhesiva

stiff *adj* rígido; **to have a stiff neck** tener tortícolis; **to feel stiff** estar agarrotado
▶ *adv* **to be bored stiff** estar aburrido como una ostra; **to be frozen stiff** estar tieso de frío; **to be scared stiff** estar muerto de miedo

still *adv* ❶ todavía ▷ *I still haven't finished.* No he terminado todavía. ▷ *Are you still in bed?* ¿Todavía estás en la cama?; **Do you still live in Glasgow?** ¿Sigues viviendo en Glasgow?; **better still** mejor aún ❷ (*even so*) aun así ▷ *She knows I don't like it, but she still does it.* Sabe que no me gusta, pero aun así lo hace. ❸ (*after all*) en fin ▷ *Still, it's the thought that counts.* En fin, la intención es lo que cuenta.
▶ *adj* quieto ▷ *He stood still.* Se quedó quieto.; **Keep still!** ¡No te muevas!

sting *n* picadura *f* ▷ *a bee sting* una picadura de abeja
▶ *vb* picar

stink *vb* apestar ▷ *You stink of garlic!* ¡Apestas a ajo!
▶ *n* tufo *m* ▷ *the stink of beer* el tufo a cerveza

stir *vb* agitar

stitch *vb* coser
▶ *n* ❶ (*in sewing*) puntada *f* ❷ (*in knitting, wound*) punto *m* ▷ *I had five stitches.* Me pusieron cinco puntos.

stock *n* ❶ reserva *f* ▷ *stocks of*

ammunition reservas de munición ❷ **existencias** *fpl* ▷ *the shop's stock* las existencias de la tienda; **Yes, we've got your size in stock.** Sí, nos quedan existencias de su número.; **out of stock** agotado ▷ *I'm sorry, they're both out of stock.* Lo siento, están los dos agotados. ❸ **caldo** *m* ▷ *chicken stock* caldo de pollo

▶ *vb* **vender** ▷ *Do you stock camping stoves?* ¿Venden infiernillos?

stock cube *n* pastilla *f* de caldo

stocking *n* media *f*

stole *vb see* **steal**

stolen *vb see* **steal**

stomach *n* estómago *m*

stomach ache *n* dolor *m* de estómago; **I have a stomach ache.** Me duele el estómago.

stone *n* ❶ **piedra** *f* ▷ *a stone wall* un muro de piedra ❷ **hueso** *m* ▷ *an apricot stone* un hueso de albaricoque

  ● In Spain measurements are in grams and kilograms. One stone is about 6.3 kg.

I weigh eight stone. Peso unos cincuenta kilos.

stood *vb see* **stand**

stool *n* taburete *m*

stop *vb* ❶ **parar** ▷ *The bus doesn't stop there.* El autobús no para allí. ❷ **pararse** ▷ *The music stopped.* Se paró la música.; **This has got to stop!** ¡Esto se tiene que acabar!; **I think the rain's going to stop.** Creo que va a dejar de llover.; **to stop doing something** dejar

de hacer algo ▷ *to stop smoking* dejar de fumar ❸ **acabar con** ▷ *a campaign to stop whaling* una campaña para acabar con la caza de ballenas; **to stop somebody doing something** impedir que alguien haga algo

> **impedir que** has to be followed by a verb in the subjunctive.

▷ *She would have liked to stop us seeing each other.* Le hubiera gustado impedir que nos siguiéramos viendo.; **Stop!** ¡Alto!

▶ *n* **parada** *f* ▷ *a bus stop* una parada de autobús; **This is my stop.** Yo me bajo aquí.

stopwatch *n* cronómetro *m*

store *n* ❶ **tienda** *f* ▷ *a furniture store* una tienda de muebles ❷ **almacén** *m* (*pl* almacenes) ▷ *a grain store* un almacén de grano

▶ *vb* ❶ **guardar** ▷ *They store potatoes in the cellar.* Guardan patatas en el sótano. ❷ **almacenar** ▷ *to store information* almacenar información

storey *n* planta *f* ▷ *a three-storey building* un edificio de tres plantas

storm *n* tormenta *f*

stormy *adj* tormentoso

story *n* ❶ (*tale*) cuento *m* ❷ (*account*) historia *f*

stove *n* ❶ (*in kitchen*) cocina *f* ❷ (*camping stove*) infiernillo *m*

straight *adj* ❶ recto ▷ *a straight line* una línea recta ❷ liso ▷ *straight hair* pelo liso ❸ (*not gay*) heterosexual

▶ adv **He looked straight at me.** Me miró directamente a los ojos.; **straight away** enseguida; **I'll come straight back.** Vuelvo enseguida.; **Keep straight on.** Siga todo recto.

straightforward adj ❶ sencillo ▷ It's very straightforward. Es muy sencillo. ❷ sincero ▷ She's very straightforward. Es muy sincera.

strain n tensión f (pl tensiones); **It was a strain.** Fue muy estresante.
▶ vb **to strain one's eyes** forzar la vista; **I strained my back.** Me dio un tirón en la espalda.; **to strain a muscle** sufrir un tirón muscular

strange adj raro ▷ That's strange! ¡Qué raro!

> **es raro que** has to be followed by a verb in the subjunctive.
> ▷ It's strange that she doesn't talk to us anymore. Es raro que ya no nos hable.

stranger n desconocido m, desconocida f

> Be careful not to translate **stranger** by **extranjero**.
> ▷ Don't talk to strangers. No hables con desconocidos.; **I'm a stranger here.** Yo no soy de aquí.

strangle vb estrangular

strap n ❶ (of bra, dress) tirante m ❷ (of watch, camera, suitcase) correa f ❸ (of bag) asa f

> Although it's a feminine noun, remember that you use **el** and **un** with **asa**.

straw n ❶ paja f ▷ a straw hat un sombrero de paja ❷ pajita f ▷ He was drinking his lemonade through a straw. Se bebía la gaseosa con pajita.; **That's the last straw!** ¡Eso es la gota que colma el vaso!

strawberry n fresa f (LatAm frutilla f)

stray adj extraviado ▷ a stray cat un gato extraviado

stream n riachuelo m

street n calle f

streetcar n (in US) tranvía m

> Although **tranvía** ends in **-a**, it is actually a masculine noun.

streetlamp n farola f

streetwise adj **to be streetwise** sabérselas todas

strength n fuerza f ▷ with all his strength con todas sus fuerzas

stress vb recalcar ▷ I would like to stress that... Me gustaría recalcar que...
▶ n estrés m ▷ She's under a lot of stress. Está pasando mucho estrés.

stretch vb ❶ estirarse ▷ The dog woke up and stretched. El perro se despertó y se estiró.; **I went out to stretch my legs.** Salí a estirar las piernas.; **My jumper stretched after I washed it.** Se me dio de sí el jersey al lavarlo. ❷ tender ▷ They stretched a rope between two trees. Tendieron una cuerda entre dos árboles.

stretcher n camilla f

stretchy adj elástico

strict adj estricto

strike n huelga f; **to be on strike** estar en huelga; **to go on strike** hacer huelga

▶ vb golpear ▷ She struck him across the mouth. Le golpeó en la boca.; **The clock struck three.** El reloj dio las tres.; **to strike a match** encender una cerilla

striker n ❶ (person on strike) huelguista mf ❷ (footballer) delantero m, delantera f

string n cuerda f; **a piece of string** una cuerda

strip vb desnudarse

▶ n tira f; **strip cartoon** la tira cómica (LatAm historieta f)

striped adj a rayas; **a striped skirt** una falda de rayas

stripe n franja f

stroke vb acariciar

▶ n derrame m cerebral ▷ to have a stroke sufrir un derrame cerebral; **a stroke of luck** un golpe de suerte

stroll n paseo m ▷ to go for a stroll ir a dar un paseo

stroller n (in US) silla f de paseo

strong adj fuerte

strongly adv (recommend, advise) encarecidamente ▷ We strongly advise you to... Te aconsejamos encarecidamente que...; **I don't feel strongly about it.** Me da un poco igual.

struck vb see **strike**

struggle vb forcejear ▷ He struggled, but he couldn't escape. Forcejeó, pero no pudo escapar.; **to struggle to do something** **(1)** (fight) luchar por hacer algo ▷ He struggled to get custody of his daughter. Luchó por conseguir la custodia de su hija. **(2)** (have

difficulty) pasar apuros para hacer algo ▷ They struggle to pay their bills. Pasan apuros para pagar las facturas.

▶ n lucha f ▷ a struggle for survival una lucha por la supervivencia; **It was a struggle.** Nos costó mucho.

stubborn adj terco

stuck vb see **stick**

▶ adj atascado ▷ The lid is stuck. La tapadera está atascada.; **to get stuck** quedarse atascado; **We got stuck in a traffic jam.** Nos metimos en un atasco.

stuck-up adj (informal) creído

stud n ❶ (earring) pendiente m ❷ (on football boots) taco m

student n estudiante mf

studio n estudio m ▷ a TV studio un estudio de televisión; **a studio flat** un estudio

study vb estudiar

stuff n cosas fpl ▷ Have you got all your stuff? ¿Tienes todas tus cosas?; **I need some stuff for hay fever.** Me hace falta algo para la alergia al polen.

stuffy adj (room) mal ventilado; **It's stuffy in here.** Hay un ambiente muy cargado aquí.

stumble vb tropezar

stung vb see **sting**

stunk vb see **stink**

stunned adj pasmado ▷ I was stunned. Me quedé pasmado.

stunning adj pasmoso

stunt n (in film) escena f peligrosa

stuntman n especialista m

stupid adj estúpido

stutter vb tartamudear
▶ n tartamudeo m; **He's got a stutter.** Es tartamudo.

style n estilo m

subject n ❶ (topic, theme) tema m
　Although **tema** ends in -**a**, it is actually a masculine noun.
❷ (at school) asignatura f ▷ What's your favourite subject? ¿Cuál es tu asignatura preferida?

submarine n submarino m

subscription n (to paper, magazine) suscripción f (pl suscripciones); **to take out a subscription to** suscribirse a

subsidy n subvención f (pl subvenciones)

substance n sustancia f

substitute n ❶ (replacement) sustituto m, sustituta f ❷ (in football, rugby) suplente mf
▶ vb sustituir ▷ to substitute A for B sustituir a B por A

subtitled adj subtitulado

subtitles npl subtítulos mpl ▷ a Spanish film with English subtitles una película española con subtítulos en inglés

subtle adj sutil

subtract vb restar ▷ to subtract 3 from 5 restar 3 a 5

suburb n barrio m residencial
▷ a London suburb un barrio residencial de Londres; **They live in the suburbs.** Viven en las afueras.

subway n ❶ (underground) metro m ❷ (underpass) paso m subterráneo

succeed vb ❶ tener éxito ▷ to succeed in business tener éxito en los negocios ❷ salir bien ▷ The plan did not succeed. El plan no salió bien.; **to succeed in doing something** lograr hacer algo

success n éxito m
　Be careful not to translate **success** by **suceso**.

successful adj de éxito (LatAm exitoso) ▷ a successful lawyer un abogado de éxito; **a successful attempt** un intento fructífero; **to be successful** tener éxito; **to be successful in doing something** lograr hacer algo

successfully adv con éxito

such adj, adv ❶ tan ▷ such a long journey un viaje tan largo ❷ tal
▷ I wouldn't dream of doing such a thing. No se me ocurriría hacer tal cosa.; **such a lot** tanto ▷ such a lot of work tanto trabajo ▷ such a long time ago hace tanto tiempo; **such as** como; **as such** propiamente dicho ▷ She's not an expert as such, but... No es una experta propiamente dicha, pero...;
There's no such thing as the yeti. El yeti no existe.

such-and-such adj tal ▷ such-and-such a place tal lugar

suck vb chupar; **to suck one's thumb** chuparse el pulgar

sudden adj repentino ▷ a sudden change un cambio repentino; **all of a sudden** de repente

suddenly adv de repente

suede n ante m (LatAm gamuza

f) ▷ **suede jacket** una chaqueta de ante

suffer vb sufrir ▷ *She was really suffering*. Sufría de verdad.; **to suffer from something** padecer de algo ▷ *I suffer from hay fever.* Padezco de alergia al polen.

suffocate vb ahogarse

sugar n azúcar m

suggest vb ❶ sugerir

Use the subjunctive after **sugerir que**.

▷ *She suggested going out for a pizza.* Sugirió que saliéramos a tomar una pizza. ❷ aconsejar

Use the subjunctive after **aconsejar que**.

▷ *I suggested they set off early.* Yo les aconsejé que salieran pronto.; **What are you trying to suggest?** ¿Qué insinúas?

suggestion n sugerencia f ▷ *to make a suggestion* hacer una sugerencia

suicide n suicidio m; **to commit suicide** suicidarse

suit n ❶ (*man's*) traje m
❷ (*woman's*) traje m de chaqueta
▷ vb ❶ venir bien a ▷ *What time would suit you?* ¿Qué hora te vendría bien?; **That suits me fine.** Eso me viene estupendamente.
❷ sentar bien a ▷ *That dress really suits you.* Ese vestido te sienta la mar de bien.; **Suit yourself!** ¡Haz lo que te parezca!

suitable adj ❶ conveniente ▷ *a suitable time* una hora conveniente
❷ apropiado ▷ *suitable clothing*

ropa apropiada

suitcase n maleta f (*LatAm* valija f)

suite n suite f ▷ *a suite at the Paris Hilton* una suite en el Hilton de París; **a bedroom suite** un dormitorio completo; **a three-piece suite** un tresillo

sulk vb estar de mal humor

sultana n pasa f de Esmirna

sum n suma f ▷ *a sum of money* una suma de dinero

sum up vb resumir; **To sum up...** Resumiendo...

summarize vb resumir

summary n resumen m (*pl* resúmenes)

summer n verano m ▷ *summer clothes* ropa de verano ▷ *the summer holidays* las vacaciones de verano

summertime n verano m

summit n cumbre f

sun n sol m ▷ *in the sun* al sol

sunbathe vb tomar el sol

sunblock n crema f solar de protección total

sunburn n quemadura f

sunburnt adj quemado por el sol; **Mind you don't get sunburnt!** ¡Cuidado de no quemarte con el sol!

Sunday n domingo m (*pl* domingos) ▷ *I saw her on Sunday.* La vi el domingo. ▷ *every Sunday* todos los domingos ▷ *last Sunday* el domingo pasado ▷ *next Sunday* el domingo que viene ▷ *on Sundays* los domingos

Sunday school n catequesis f

- The Spanish equivalent of
- **Sunday school** takes place
- during the week after school
- rather than on a Sunday.

sunflower n girasol m

sung vb see **sing**

sunglasses npl gafas fpl de sol

sunk vb see **sink**

sunlight n luz f del sol

sunny adj soleado ▷ a sunny morning una mañana soleada; **It's sunny.** Hace sol.; **a sunny day** un día de sol

sunrise n salida f del sol

sunroof n techo m corredizo

sunscreen n protector m solar

sunset n puesta f del sol

sunshine n sol m ▷ in the sunshine al sol

sunstroke n insolación f (pl insolaciones)

suntan n bronceado m; **to get a suntan** broncearse; **suntan lotion** la crema bronceadora; **suntan oil** el aceite bronceador

super adj estupendo

supermarket n supermercado m

supernatural adj sobrenatural

superstitious adj supersticioso

supervise vb supervisar

supervisor n supervisor m, supervisora f

supper n cena f

supplement n suplemento m

supplies npl provisiones fpl; **medical supplies** material médico

supply vb suministrar; **to supply somebody with something** suministrar algo a alguien ▷ The centre supplied us with all the equipment. El centro nos suministró todo el material.

▶ n suministro m ▷ the water supply el suministro de agua; **a supply of paper** una remesa de papel

supply teacher n profesor m interino, profesora f interina

support vb ❶ (emotionally) apoyar ▷ My mum has always supported me. Mi madre siempre me ha apoyado. ❷ (financially) mantener ▷ She had to support five children on her own. Tenía que mantener a cinco niños ella sola.; **What team do you support?** ¿De qué equipo eres?

> Be careful not to translate **to support** by soportar.

▶ n apoyo m

supporter n ❶ hincha mf ▷ a Liverpool supporter un hincha del Liverpool ❷ partidario m, partidaria f ▷ a supporter of the Labour Party un partidario del partido laborista

suppose vb suponer ▷ I suppose he'll be late. Supongo que llegará tarde. ▷ Suppose you win the lottery... Supón que te toca la lotería...; **I suppose so.** Supongo que sí.; **You're supposed to show your passport.** Tienes que enseñar el pasaporte.; **You're not supposed to smoke in the toilet.** No está permitido fumar en el servicio.; **It's supposed to be the best hotel in the city.** Dicen que es el mejor hotel de la ciudad.

supposing conj **Supposing you won the lottery...** Suponiendo que te tocara la lotería...

> **suponiendo que** has to be followed by a verb in the subjunctive.

sure adj seguro ▷ *Are you sure?* ¿Estás seguro? **Sure!** ¡Claro! **to make sure that...** asegurarse de que... ▷ *I'm going to make sure the door's locked.* Voy a asegurarme de que la puerta está cerrada con llave.

surely adv **Surely you don't believe that?** ¿No te creerás eso, no?

surf n espuma f de las olas
▶ vb (*in sea*) hacer surf; **to surf the Net** navegar por Internet

surface n superficie f

surfboard n tabla f de surf

surfing n surf m ▷ **to go surfing** hacer surf

surgeon n cirujano m, cirujana f

surgery n ① (*room*) consultorio m médico ② (*treatment*) cirugía f

surname n apellido m

surprise n sorpresa f

surprised adj **I was surprised to see him.** Me sorprendió verlo.; **I'm not surprised that ...** No me sorprende que ...

surprising adj sorprendente

surrender vb rendirse

surround vb rodear ▷ **surrounded by trees** rodeado de árboles

surroundings npl entorno m ▷ *a hotel in beautiful surroundings* un

hotel en un hermoso entorno

survey n encuesta f ▷ *They did a survey of a thousand students.* Hicieron una encuesta a mil estudiantes.

survive vb sobrevivir

survivor n superviviente mf
▷ *There were no survivors.* No hubo supervivientes.

suspect vb sospechar
▶ n sospechoso m, sospechosa f

suspend vb ① (*from school*) expulsar temporalmente ② (*from team*) excluir ③ (*from job*) suspender

suspense n ① incertidumbre f ▷ *The suspense was terrible.* La incertidumbre era terrible. ② suspense m ▷ *a film with lots of suspense* una película llena de suspense

suspicious adj ① (*mistrustful*) receloso ▷ *He was suspicious at first.* Al principio estaba receloso. ② (*suspicious-looking*) sospechoso ▷ *a suspicious person* un individuo sospechoso

swallow vb tragar

swam vb see **swim**

swan n cisne m

swap vb cambiar ▷ *to swap A for B* cambiar A por B; **Do you want to swap?** ¿Quieres que cambiemos?

swear vb ① jurar ▷ *to swear allegiance to* jurar fidelidad a ② decir palabrotas ▷ *It's wrong to swear.* No se deben decir palabrotas.

swearword n palabrota f

sweat n sudor m
▶ vb sudar

sweater n jersey m (pl jerseys) (LatAm suéter m)

Swede n (person) sueco m, sueca f

Sweden n Suecia f

Swedish adj, n sueco

sweep vb barrer ▷ To sweep the floor barrer el suelo

sweet n ❶ caramelo m ▷ a bag of sweets una bolsa de caramelos
❷ postre m ▷ Are you going to have a sweet? ¿Vas a tomar postre?
▶ adj ❶ dulce ▷ a sweet wine un vino dulce ❷ amable ▷ That was really sweet of you. Fue muy amable de tu parte.

sweetcorn n maíz m dulce

swept vb see **sweep**

swerve vb girar bruscamente ▷ I swerved to avoid the cyclist. Giré bruscamente para esquivar al ciclista.

swim n to go for a swim ir a nadar
▶ vb nadar ▷ Can you swim? ¿Sabes nadar?; **She swam across the river.** Cruzó el río a nado.

swimmer n nadador m, nadadora f

swimming n natación f
▷ swimming lessons clases de natación; **Do you like swimming?** ¿Te gusta nadar?; **to go swimming** ir a nadar; **swimming cap** el gorro de baño; **swimming costume** el traje de baño; **swimming pool** la piscina; **swimming trunks** el bañador

swimsuit n traje m de baño

swing vb ❶ (on a swing) columpiarse ❷ balancearse ▷ Her bag swung as she walked. El bolso se balanceaba según iba andando.; **He was swinging on a rope.** Se balanceaba colgado de una cuerda. ❸ colgar ▷ A large key swung from his belt. Le colgaba una gran llave del cinturón. ❹ balancear ▷ He was swinging his bag back and forth. Balanceaba la bolsa de un lado al otro.
▶ n columpio m

Swiss adj, n suizo; **the Swiss** los suizos

switch n interruptor m
▶ vb cambiar de ▷ We switched partners. Cambiamos de pareja.

switch off vb (TV, machine, engine) apagar

switch on vb (TV, machine, engine) encender (LatAm prender)

Switzerland n Suiza f

swollen adj hinchado ▷ My ankle is very swollen. Tengo el tobillo muy hinchado.

swop vb see **swap**

sword n espada f

swore vb see **swear**

sworn vb see **swear**

swot n empollón m, empollona f
▶ vb empollar

swum vb see **swim**

swung vb see **swing**

syllabus n programa m de estudios

    ⓘ Although **programa** ends in -a, it is actually a masculine noun.

symbol n símbolo m

sympathetic *adj* comprensivo

Be careful not to translate **sympathetic** by **simpático**.

sympathize *vb* **to sympathize with somebody (1)** (*feel sorry for*) compadecerse de alguien **(2)** (*understand*) comprender a alguien

sympathy *n* **❶** (*sorrow*) compasión *f* **❷** (*understanding*) comprensión *f*

symptom *n* síntoma *m*

Although **síntoma** ends in **-a**, it is actually a masculine noun.

syringe *n* jeringuilla *f*

system *n* sistema *m*

Although **sistema** ends in **-a**, it is actually a masculine noun.

table *n* mesa *f*; **to lay the table** poner la mesa

tablecloth *n* mantel *m*

tablespoon *n* cuchara *f* de servir

tablet *n* pastilla *f*

table tennis *n* tenis *m* de mesa ▷ **to play table tennis** jugar al tenis de mesa

tackle *vb* **to tackle somebody (1)** (*in football*) entrar a alguien **(2)** (*in rugby*) placar a alguien; **to tackle a problem** abordar un problema

tact *n* tacto *m*

tactful *adj* diplomático

tactics *npl* táctica *fsg*

tadpole *n* renacuajo *m*

tag *n* (*label*) etiqueta *f*

tail *n* **❶** (*of horse, bird, fish*) cola *f* **❷** (*of dog, bull, ox*) rabo *m*; **Heads**

or tails? ¿Cara o cruz?

tailor n sastre m ▷ He's a tailor. Es sastre.

take vb ❶ (medicine) tomar ▷ Do you take sugar? ¿Tomas azúcar?; **He took a plate out of the cupboard.** Sacó un plato del armario. ❷ (take with you) llevar ▷ He goes to London every week, but he never takes me. Va a Londres todas las semanas, pero nunca me lleva.; **It takes about one hour.** Se tarda más o menos una hora.; **It won't take long.** No tardará mucho tiempo.; **That takes a lot of courage.** Hace falta mucho valor para eso. ❸ (bear) soportar ▷ He can't take being criticized. No soporta que le critiquen. ❹ (exam, subject at school) hacer ▷ Have you taken your driving test yet? ¿Ya has hecho el examen de conducir? ❺ aceptar ▷ We take credit cards. Aceptamos tarjetas de crédito.

take after vb parecerse a ▷ She takes after her mother. Se parece a su madre.

take apart vb desmontar

take away vb ❶ llevarse ▷ They took away all his belongings. Se llevaron todas sus pertenencias. ❷ quitar ▷ She was afraid her children would be taken away from her. Tenía miedo de que le quitaran a los niños.; **hot meals to take away** platos calientes para llevar

take back vb devolver ▷ I took it back to the shop. Lo devolví a la

tienda.; **I take it all back!** ¡Retiro lo dicho!

take off vb ❶ despegar ▷ The plane took off 20 minutes late. El avión despegó con 20 minutos de retraso. ❷ quitar ▷ Take your coat off. Quítate el abrigo.

take out vb sacar ▷ He opened his wallet and took out some money. Abrió la cartera y sacó dinero.; **He took her out to the theatre.** La invitó al teatro.

take over vb hacerse cargo de ▷ He took over the running of the company last year. Se hizo cargo del control de la empresa el año pasado.; **to take over from somebody (1)** (replace) sustituir a alguien **(2)** (in shift work) relevar a alguien

takeaway n (meal) comida f para llevar

takeoff n (of plane) despegue m

tale n cuento m

talent n talento m ▷ He's got a lot of talent. Tiene mucho talento.; **to have a talent for something** tener talento para algo; **He's got a real talent for languages.** Tiene verdadera facilidad para los idiomas.

talented adj de talento ▷ She's a talented pianist. Es una pianista de talento.

talk n ❶ conversación f (pl conversaciones) ▷ We had a long talk about her problems. Tuvimos una larga conversación acerca de sus problemas.; **I had a talk with**

my Mum about it. Hablé sobre eso con mi madre.; **to give a talk on something** dar una charla sobre algo ▷ *She gave a talk on ancient Egypt.* Dio una charla sobre el antiguo Egipto. ❷ *(gossip)* habladurías fpl ▷ *It's just talk.* Son sólo habladurías.
▷ *vb* hablar ▷ *What did you talk about?* ¿De qué hablasteis?; **to talk to somebody** hablar con alguien; **to talk to oneself** hablar consigo mismo; **to talk something over with somebody** discutir algo con alguien

talkative *adj* hablador (f habladora)

tall *adj* alto; **to be two metres tall** medir dos metros

tame *adj (animal)* domesticado

tampon *n* tampón *m (pl* tampones)

tan *n* bronceado *m;* **to get a tan** broncearse

tangerine *n* mandarina *f*

tank *n* ❶ *(for water, petrol)* depósito *m* ❷ *(on truck)* cisterna *f* ❸ *(military)* tanque *m;* **a fish tank** un acuario

tanker *n* ❶ *(ship)* petrolero *m* ❷ *(truck)* camión *m* cisterna *f (pl* camiones cisterna); **an oil tanker** un petrolero; **a petrol tanker** un camión cisterna

tap *n* ❶ *(for water)* grifo *m (*LatAm llave *f)* ❷ *the hot tap* el grifo de agua caliente ❸ *(gentle knock)* golpecito *m* ▷ *I heard a tap on the window.* Oí un golpecito en la

ventana.; **There was a tap on the door.** Llamaron a la puerta.

tap-dancing *n* claqué *m* ▷ *I do tap-dancing.* Bailo claqué.

tape *vb* grabar ▷ *Did you tape that film last night?* ¿Grabaste la película de anoche?
▷ *n* ❶ *(cassette)* cinta *f* ❷ *(sticky tape)* cinta *f* adhesiva

tape measure *n* cinta *f* métrica

tape recorder *n* ❶ *(large)* casete *m* ❷ *(hand-held)* grabadora *f*

target *n* ❶ *(board)* diana *f* ❷ *(goal)* objetivo *m*

tart *n* tarta *f* ▷ *an apple tart* una tarta de manzana

tartan *adj* escocés (f escocesa) *(mpl* escoceses) ▷ *a tartan scarf* una bufanda escocesa

task *n* tarea *f*

taste *n* ❶ sabor *m* ▷ *It's got a really strange taste.* Tiene un sabor muy extraño. ❷ gusto *m* ▷ *His joke was in bad taste.* Su broma fue de mal gusto.; **Would you like a taste?** ¿Quiere probarlo?
▷ *vb* probar ▷ *Would you like to taste it?* ¿Quiere probarlo?; **to taste of something** saber a algo ▷ *It tastes of fish.* Sabe a pescado.; **You can taste the garlic in it.** Se le nota el sabor a ajo.

tasty *adj* sabroso

tattoo *n* tatuaje *m*

taught *vb see* **teach**

Taurus *n (sign)* Tauro *m;* **I'm Taurus.** Soy tauro.

tax *n* impuesto *m;* **income tax** el impuesto sobre la renta; **I**

pay a lot of tax. Pago muchos impuestos.

taxi n taxi m; **a taxi driver** un/una taxista

taxi rank n parada f de taxis

TB abbr (= tuberculosis) tuberculosis f

tea n ❶ té ▷ Would you like some tea? ¿Te apetece un té?; **a cup of tea** una taza de té ❷ (afternoon tea) merienda f; **to have tea** merendar ▷ We had tea at the Savoy. Merendamos en el Savoy. ❸ (evening meal) cena f; **to have tea** cenar ▷ We're having sausages and beans for tea. Vamos a cenar salchichas con alubias.

tea bag n bolsita f de té

teach vb ❶ enseñar ▷ My sister taught me to swim. Mi hermana me enseñó a nadar. ❷ (subject) dar clases de ▷ She teaches physics. Da clases de física.; **That'll teach you!** ¡Así aprenderás!

teacher n ❶ (in secondary school) profesor m, profesora f ▷ a maths teacher un profesor de matemáticas ▷ She's a teacher. Es profesora. ❷ (in primary school) maestro m, maestra f

team n equipo m ▷ a football team un equipo de fútbol

teapot n tetera f

tear n lágrima f; **She was in tears.** Estaba llorando.
▶vb ❶ romper ▷ Be careful or you'll tear the page. Ten cuidado que vas a romper la página.; **He tore his jacket.** Se rasgó la chaqueta.;

Your shirt is torn. Tu camisa está rota. ❷ romperse ▷ It won't tear, it's very strong. No se rompe, es muy resistente.

tear up vb hacer pedazos ▷ He tore up the letter. Hizo pedazos la carta.

tease vb ❶ atormentar ▷ Stop teasing that poor animal! ¡Deja de atormentar al pobre animal! ❷ tomar el pelo a ▷ He's teasing you. Te está tomando el pelo.; **I was only teasing.** Lo decía en broma.

teaspoon n cucharita f

teatime n (in evening) hora f de cenar ▷ It was nearly teatime. Era casi la hora de cenar.; **Teatime!** ¡A la mesa!

tea towel n paño m de cocina

technical adj técnico; **a technical college** el centro de formación profesional (LatAm la escuela politécnica)

technician n técnico m, técnica f

technological adj tecnológico

technology n tecnología f

teddy bear n osito m de peluche

teenage adj ❶ (boy, girl) adolescente ▷ She has two teenage daughters. Tiene dos hijas adolescentes. ❷ (fashion) para adolescentes ▷ a teenage magazine una revista para adolescentes

teenager n adolescente mf

teens npl She's in her teens. Es adolescente.

tee-shirt n camiseta f

teeth npl see **tooth**

telephone n teléfono m ▷ on the

telephone al teléfono; **a telephone box** una cabina telefónica; **a telephone call** una llamada telefónica; **a telephone directory** una guía telefónica; **a telephone number** un número de teléfono

telescope n telescopio m

television n televisión f ▷ *The match is on television tonight.* Ponen el partido en televisión esta noche.

tell vb decir ▷ *I told him I was going on holiday.* Le dije que me iba de vacaciones.; **to tell somebody to do something** decir a alguien que haga algo

> Use the subjunctive after *decir a alguien que* when translating "to tell somebody to do something".

▷ *He told me to wait a moment.* Me dijo que esperara un momento.; **to tell lies** decir mentiras; **to tell a story** contar un cuento; **I can't tell the difference between them.** No puedo distinguirlos.; **You can tell he's not serious.** Se nota que no se lo toma en serio.

tell off vb regañar

telly n (informal) tele f ▷ *to watch telly* ver la tele

temper n genio m ▷ *He's got a terrible temper.* Tiene muy mal genio.; **to be in a temper** estar de mal humor; **to lose one's temper** perder los estribos

temperature n temperatura f; **to have a temperature** tener fiebre

temple n ❶ (building) templo m

❷ (on head) sien f

temporary adj temporal

temptation n tentación f (pl tentaciones)

tempting adj tentador (f tentadora)

ten num diez ▷ *She's ten.* Tiene diez años.

tend vb **to tend to do something** tener tendencia a hacer algo ▷ *He tends to arrive late.* Tiene tendencia a llegar tarde.

tennis n tenis m ▷ *to play tennis* jugar al tenis; **a tennis ball** una pelota de tenis; **a tennis court** una pista de tenis; **a tennis racket** una raqueta de tenis

tennis player n tenista mf ▷ *He's a tennis player.* Es tenista.

tenor n tenor m

tenpin bowling n bolos mpl ▷ *to go tenpin bowling* jugar a los bolos

tense adj tenso

▶ n tiempo m; **the present tense** el presente; **the future tense** el futuro

tension n tensión f (pl tensiones)

tent n tienda f de campaña

tenth adj décimo ▷ *the tenth floor* el décimo piso; **the tenth of August** el diez de agosto

term n ❶ (at school) trimestre m ▷ *It's nearly the end of term.* Ya casi es final de trimestre. ❷ plazo m ▷ *in the long term* a largo plazo; **to come to terms with something** aceptar algo ▷ *He hasn't yet come to terms with his disability.* Todavía no ha aceptado su invalidez.

terminal adj (illness, patient) terminal
▶ n (of computer) terminal m; **airport terminal** la terminal del aeropuerto; **bus terminal** la terminal de autobuses

terminally adv **to be terminally ill** estar en fase terminal

terrace n ❶ (patio) terraza f ❷ (row of houses) hilera f de casas adosadas; **the terraces** (in stadium) las gradas

terraced adj adosado ▷ a terraced house una casa adosada

terrible adj espantoso ▷ This coffee is terrible. Este café es espantoso.; **I feel terrible.** Me siento fatal.

terrific adj (wonderful) estupendo ▷ That's terrific! ¡Estupendo!; **You look terrific!** (to a girl or woman) ¡Estás guapísima!

terrified adj aterrorizado ▷ I was terrified! ¡Estaba aterrorizado!

terrorism n terrorismo m

terrorist n terrorista mf; **a terrorist attack** un atentado terrorista

test n ❶ prueba f ▷ a spelling test una prueba de ortografía ❷ (on blood, urine) análisis m (pl análisis) ▷ a blood test un análisis de sangre ❸ (driving test) examen m de conducir ▷ He's just passed his test. Acaba de aprobar el examen de conducir.
▶ vb probar; **to test something out** probar algo; **He tested us on the new vocabulary.** Nos hizo una prueba del vocabulario

nuevo.; **She was tested for drugs.** Le hicieron la prueba antidoping.

text n (text message) mensaje m
▶ vb enviar un mensaje a ▷ I'll text you when I get there. Te envío un mensaje cuando llegue.

textbook n libro m de texto ▷ a Spanish textbook un libro de texto de español

text message n mensaje m de texto

Thames n Támesis m

than conj ❶ (in comparisons) que ▷ She's taller than me. Es más alta que yo. ❷ (with numbers) de ▷ more than 10 years más de 10 años

thank vb dar las gracias a ▷ Don't forget to write and thank them. Acuérdate de escribirles y darles las gracias.; **thank you** gracias; **thank you very much** muchas gracias

thanks excl ¡Gracias!; **thanks to** gracias a ▷ Thanks to him, everything went OK. Gracias a él, todo salió bien.

that adj ❶ ese m (f esa) ▷ that man ese hombre ▷ that road esa carretera

> To refer to something more distant, use **aquel** and **aquella**.

❷ aquel m (f aquella) ▷ Look at that car over there! ¡Mira aquel coche! ▷ THAT road there aquella carretera; **that one** ése m (f ésa) ▷ This man? - No, that one. ¿Este hombre? - No, ése. ▷ Do you like this photo? - No, I prefer that one. ¿Te

gusta esta foto? - No, prefiero ésa.
To refer to something more
distant, use **aquél** and **aquélla**.

❸ aquél m (f aquélla) ▷ *That one
over there is cheaper.* Aquél es más
barato. ▷ *Which woman? - That one
over there.* ¿Qué mujer? -Aquélla.

▶ *pron* ❶ ése m (f ésa, neut eso);
Who's that? (who is that man)
¿Quién es ése?; **Who's that?** (who
is that woman) ¿Quién es ésa?;
Who's that? (on the telephone)
¿Con quién hablo? ▷ *That's
impossible.* Eso es imposible.
▷ *What's that?* ¿Qué es eso?

To refer to something more
distant, use **aquél**, **aquélla**
and **aquello**.

❷ aquél m (f aquélla, neut aquello)
▷ *That's my French teacher over there.*
Aquél es mi profesor de francés.
▷ *That's my sister over by the
window.* Aquélla de la ventana es
mi hermana. ▷ *That was a silly thing
to do.* Aquello fue una tontería.; **Is
that you?** ¿Eres tú? ❸ *(in relative
clauses)* que ▷ *the man that saw us* el
hombre que nos vio

After a preposition **that**
becomes **el que**, **la que**, **los
que**, **las que** to agree with
the noun.

▷ *the man that we spoke to* el
hombre con el que hablamos
▷ *the women that she was chatting
to* las mujeres con las que estaba
hablando

▶ *conj* que ▷ *He thought that Henry
was ill.* Creía que Henry estaba

enfermo.

▶ *adv* **It's about that high.** Es más
o menos así de alto.; **It's not that
difficult.** No es tan difícil.

the *def art* ❶ el m (pl los) ▷ *the boy* el
niño ▷ *the cars* los coches

a + **el** changes to **al** and **de** + **el**
changes to **del**.

▷ *They went to the theatre.* Fueron al
teatro. ▷ *the soup of the day* la sopa
del día ❷ la f (pl las) ▷ *the woman* la
mujer ▷ *the chairs* las sillas

theatre (US **theater**) n teatro m

theft n robo m

their *adj* su (pl sus) ▷ *their house* su
casa ▷ *their parents* sus padres

Their is usually translated by
the definite article **el/los** or
la/las when it's clear from the
sentence who the possessor is,
particularly when referring to
clothing or parts of the body.

▷ *They took off their coats.* Se
quitaron los abrigos. ▷ *Someone
stole their car.* Alguien les robó
el coche.

theirs *pron* ❶ el suyo (pl los suyos)
▷ *Is this their car? - No, theirs is red.*
¿Es éste su coche? - No, el suyo es
rojo. ❷ la suya (pl las suyas) ▷ *Is
this their house? - No, theirs is white.*
¿Es ésta su casa? - No, la suya es
blanca.

Use **de ellos** (masculine) or
de ellas (feminine) instead
of **suyo** if you want to be
specific about a masculine or
feminine group.

▷ *It's not our car, it's theirs.* No es

nuestro coche, es suyo. ▷ *Whose is this? - It's theirs.* ¿De quién es esto? - Es de ellos. | **Isobel is a friend of theirs.** Isobel es amiga suya.

them pron ❶ los *m* (flas)

Use **los** or **las** when **them** is the direct object of the verb in the sentence.

▷ *I didn't know them.* No los conocía. ▷ *Look at them!* ¡Míralos! ▷ *I had to give them to her.* Tuve que dárselos. ❷ les

Use **les** when **them** means **to them.**

▷ *I gave them some brochures.* Les di unos folletos. ▷ *You have to tell them the truth.* Tienes que decirles la verdad. ❸ se

Use **se** not **les** when **them** is used in combination with a direct-object pronoun.

▷ *Give it to them.* Dáselo. ❹ ellos *m* (fellas)

Use **ellos** or **ellas** after prepositions, in comparisons, and with the verb **to be.**

▷ *It's for them.* Es para ellos. ▷ *We are older than them.* Somos mayores que ellos. ▷ *It must be them.* Deben de ser ellos.

theme park *n* parque *m* temático

themselves pron ❶ (reflexive) se ▷ *Did they hurt themselves?* ¿Se hicieron daño? ❷ (after preposition) sí mismos (f sí mismas) ▷ *They talked mainly about themselves.* Hablaron sobre todo de sí mismos. ❸ (for emphasis) ellos mismos (f ellas mismas) ▷ *They*

built it themselves. Lo construyeron ellos mismos.; **by themselves** por sí mismos (f por sí mismas) ▷ *The girls did it all by themselves.* Las chicas lo hicieron todo por sí mismas.

then adv, conj ❶ (next) después ▷ *I get dressed. Then I have breakfast.* Me visto. Después desayuno. ❷ (in that case) pues ▷ *My pen's run out. - Use a pencil then!* Se me ha acabado el bolígrafo. - ¡Pues usa un lápiz! ❸ (in those days) en aquella época ▷ *There was no electricity then.* En aquella época no había electricidad.; **now and then** de vez en cuando ▷ *Do you play chess? - Now and then.* ¿Juegas al ajedrez? - De vez en cuando.; **By then it was too late.** Para entonces ya era demasiado tarde.

there adv ahí ▷ *Put it there, on the table.* Ponlo ahí, en la mesa.; **over there** allí; **in there** ahí dentro; **on there** ahí encima; **up there** ahí arriba; **down there** ahí abajo; **There he is!** ¡Ahí está!; **there is** hay ▷ *There's a factory near my house.* Hay una fábrica cerca de mi casa.; **there are** hay ▷ *There are 20 children in my class.* Hay 20 niños en mi clase.; **There has been an accident.** Ha habido un accidente.

therefore adv por lo tanto

there's = **there is**; **there has**

thermometer *n* termómetro *m*

these adj estos *m* (f estas) ▷ *these shoes* estos zapatos ▷ *these houses* estas casas

▶ *pron* **éstos** m (**éstas**) ▷ I want these! ¡Quiero éstos!

they *pron* **ellos** m (**ellas**)

they generally isn't translated unless it's emphatic.

▷ They're fine, thank you. Están bien, gracias.

Use **ellos** or **ellas** as appropriate for emphasis.

▷ We went to the cinema but they didn't. Nosotros fuimos al cine pero ellos no.; **They say that...** Dicen que... ▷ They say that the house is haunted. Dicen que la casa está embrujada.

they'd = **they had**; **they would**

they'll = **they will**

they're = **they are**

they've = **they have**

thick *adj* ❶ (wall, slice) grueso

▷ Give him a thick slice. Dále una rebanada gruesa.; **The walls are one metre thick.** Las paredes tienen un metro de grosor.

❷ (soup) espeso ▷ My soup turned out too thick. La sopa me quedó demasiado espesa. ❸ (informal: stupid) corto

thief *n* ladrón m, ladrona f (mpl ladrones)

thigh *n* muslo m

thin *adj* ❶ fino ▷ a thin slice una rebanada fina ❷ delgado ▷ She's very thin. Está muy delgada.

thing *n* cosa f ▷ Where shall I put my things? ¿Dónde pongo mis cosas?; **How's things?** ¿Qué tal?; **What's that thing called?** ¿Cómo se llama

eso?; **You poor thing!** ¡Pobrecito!; **The best thing would be to leave it.** Lo mejor sería dejarlo.

think *vb* ❶ pensar ▷ What do you think about it? ¿Qué piensas? ▷ What are you thinking about? ¿En qué estás pensando?; **I'll think it over.** Lo pensaré. ❷ creer ▷ I think you're wrong. Creo que estás equivocado.; **I think so.** Creo que sí.; **I don't think so.** Creo que no. ❸ (imaginar) ▷ Think what life would be like without cars. Imagínate cómo sería la vida sin coches.

third *adj, adv* tercero

Use **tercer** before a masculine singular noun.

▷ the third prize el tercer premio ▷ the third time la tercera vez; **the third of March** el tres de marzo ▶ n (fraction) tercio m; **a third of the population** una tercera parte de la población

thirdly *adv* en tercer lugar

Third World *n* Tercer Mundo m

thirst *n* sed f

thirsty *adj* **to be thirsty** tener sed

thirteen *num* trece ▷ I'm thirteen. Tengo trece años.

thirteenth *adj* decimotercero; **the thirteenth floor** la planta trece; **the thirteenth of January** el trece de enero

thirty *num* treinta ▷ He's thirty. Tiene treinta años.

this *adj* este m (festa) ▷ this boy este niño ▷ this road esta carretera; **this one** éste m (festa) ▷ Pass me that pen. - This one? Acércame ese

bolígrafo. - ¿Este?
▶ *pron* éste m (ésta, neut esto)
▷ *This is my office and this is the meeting room.* Éste es mi despacho y ésta es la sala de reuniones.
▷ *What's this?* ¿Qué es esto?; **This is my mother.** (introduction) Te presento a mi madre.; **This is Gavin speaking.** (on the phone) Soy Gavin.

thistle *n* cardo m

thorough *adj* minucioso
▷ *a thorough check* un control minucioso; **She's very thorough.** Es muy meticulosa.

thoroughly *adv* minuciosamente
▷ *I checked the car thoroughly.* Revisé el coche minuciosamente.; **Mix the ingredients thoroughly.** Mézclense bien los ingredientes.; **I thoroughly enjoyed myself.** Me divertí muchísimo.

those *adj* ❶ esos m (esas) ▷ *those shoes* esos zapatos ▷ *those girls* esas chicas

> To refer to something more distant, use **aquellos** and **aquellas.**

❷ aquellos m (aquellas) ▷ *those houses over there* aquellas casas
▶ *pron* ❶ ésos m (ésas) ▷ *I want those!* ¡Quiero ésos!

> To refer to something more distant, use **aquéllos.**

❷ aquéllos m (aquéllas) ▷ *Ask those children. - Those over there?* Pregúntales a esos niños. - ¿A aquéllos?

though *conj, adv* aunque ▷ *Though*

she was tired she stayed up late. Aunque estaba cansada, se quedó levantada hasta muy tarde.; **It's difficult, though, to put into practice.** Pero es difícil llevarlo a la práctica.

thought *vb see* **think**
▶ *n* idea f ▷ *I've just had a thought.* Se me ocurre una idea.; **He kept his thoughts to himself.** No le dijo a nadie lo que pensaba.; **It was a nice thought, thank you.** Fue muy amable de tu parte, gracias.

thoughtful *adj* ❶ (deep in thought) pensativo ▷ *You look thoughtful.* Pareces pensativo. ❷ (considerate) considerado ▷ *She's very thoughtful.* Es muy considerada.

thoughtless *adj* desconsiderado
▷ *She's very thoughtless.* Es muy desconsiderada.; **It was thoughtless of her to mention it.** Fue una falta de consideración por su parte mencionarlo.

thousand *num* **a thousand** mil ▷ *a thousand euros* mil euros; **two thousand pounds** dos mil libras; **thousands of people** miles de personas

thread *n* hilo m

threat *n* amenaza f

threaten *vb* amenazar ▷ *He threatened me.* Me amenazó.; **to threaten to do something** (person) amenazar con hacer algo

three *num* tres ▷ *She's three.* Tiene tres años.

threw *vb see* **throw**

a b c d e f g h i j k l m n o p q r s t u v w x y z

thrilled adj **I was thrilled.** Estaba emocionada.

thriller n ❶ (film) película f de suspense (LatAm película f de misterio) ❷ (novel) novela f de suspense (LatAm novela f de misterio)

thrilling adj emocionante

throat n garganta f ▷ **I have a sore throat.** Me duele la garganta.

through adj, adv, prep ❶ a través de ▷ **to look through a telescope** mirar a través de un telescopio; **The window was dirty and I couldn't see through.** La ventana estaba sucia y no podía ver nada. ❷ por ▷ **The thief got in through the window.** El ladrón entró por la ventana. ▷ **to walk through the woods** pasear por el bosque; **to go through a tunnel** atravesar un túnel; **all through the night** durante toda la noche; **from May through to September** desde mayo hasta septiembre

throughout prep **throughout Britain** en toda Gran Bretaña; **throughout the year** durante todo el año

throw vb tirar ▷ **He threw the ball to me.** Me tiró la pelota.; **to throw a party** dar una fiesta; **That really threw him.** Eso lo desconcertó por completo.

throw away vb ❶ (rubbish) tirar ❷ (chance) desperdiciar

throw out vb ❶ (throw away) tirar ❷ (person) echar ▷ **I threw him out.** Lo eché.

throw up vb devolver

thumb n pulgar m

thumb tack n (in US) chincheta f

thump vb **to thump somebody** pegar un puñetazo a alguien

thunder n truenos mpl

thunderstorm n tormenta f

Thursday n jueves m (pl jueves) ▷ **I saw her on Thursday.** La vi el jueves. ▷ **every Thursday** todos los jueves ▷ **last Thursday** el jueves pasado ▷ **next Thursday** el jueves que viene ▷ **on Thursdays** los jueves

tick n ❶ señal f ▷ **Place a tick in the appropriate box.** Marque con una señal la casilla correspondiente. ❷ tictac m ▷ **The clock has a loud tick.** El reloj tiene un tictac muy fuerte.; **in a tick** en un instante ▶ vb ❶ marcar ▷ **Tick the appropriate box.** Marque la casilla correspondiente. ❷ (clock) hacer tictac

tick off vb ❶ (on form, list) marcar con una señal ▷ **The teacher ticked the names off in the register.** El profesor marcó los nombres de la lista con una señal. ❷ (scold) regañar ▷ **He was ticked off for being late.** Le regañaron por llegar tarde.

ticket n ❶ (for bus, train, tube, plane) billete m (LatAm boleto m) (LatAm for plane only pasaje m) ❷ (for cinema, theatre, concert, museum) entrada f ❸ (for baggage, coat, parking) ticket m (pl tickets); **a parking ticket** (fine) una multa por estacionamiento indebido

ticket inspector n revisor m,

revisora f

ticket office n taquilla f

tickle vb hacer cosquillas a ▷ She enjoyed tickling the baby. Le gustaba hacer cosquillas al niño.

tide n marea f; **high tide** la marea alta; **low tide** la marea baja

tidy adj ordenado ▷ Your room is very tidy. Tu habitación está muy ordenada.
▶ vb (room) ordenar

tidy up vb (toys) recoger ▷ Don't forget to tidy up afterwards. No os olvidéis de recoger las cosas después.

tie n ① (necktie) corbata f ② (in sport) empate m
▶ vb ① (shoelaces, parcel) atar; **to tie a knot in something** hacer un nudo en algo ② empatar ▷ They tied three all. Empataron a tres.

tie up vb ① (person, shoelaces, parcel) atar ② (boat) atracar

tiger n tigre m

tight adj ① (fitting) ceñido ▷ tight jeans vaqueros ceñidos ② (too small) estrecho ▷ This dress is a bit tight. Este vestido es un poco estrecho.

tighten vb ① (rope) tensar ② (screw) apretar

tightly adv (firmly) con fuerza ▷ She held his hand tightly. Le agarró la mano con fuerza.; **tightly closed** fuertemente cerrado

tights npl medias fpl ▷ a pair of tights unas medias

tile n ① (on roof) teja f ② (for wall) azulejo m ③ (for floor) baldosa f

till n caja f
▶ prep, conj ① hasta ▷ I waited till 10 o'clock. Esperé hasta las 10. ▷ till then hasta entonces ② hasta que ▷ We stayed there till the doctor came. Nos quedamos allí hasta que vino el médico.

> **hasta que** has to be followed by a verb in the subjunctive when referring to an event in the future.

▷ Wait till I come back. Espera hasta que yo vuelva.

time n ① hora f ▷ What time is it? ¿Qué hora es? ▷ What time do you get up? ¿A qué hora te levantas? ▷ It was two o'clock, Spanish time. Eran las dos, hora española.; **on time** a la hora ▷ He never arrives on time. Nunca llega a la hora. ② tiempo m ▷ I'm sorry, I haven't got time. Lo siento, no tengo tiempo. ▷ We waited a long time. Esperamos mucho tiempo. ▷ Have you lived here for a long time? ¿Hace mucho tiempo que vives aquí?; **from time to time** de vez en cuando; **in time** a tiempo ▷ We arrived in time for lunch. Llegamos a tiempo para el almuerzo.; **just in time** justo a tiempo ③ momento m ▷ This isn't a good time to ask him. Éste no es buen momento para preguntarle.; **for the time being** por el momento; **in no time** en un momento ▷ It was ready in no time. Estuvo listo en un momento. ④ vez f (pl veces) ▷ this time esta vez ▷ How many times? ¿Cuántas veces?; **at times** a veces; **two at a time** de dos en dos; **in a week's time** dentro de una semana; **Come and see us any time.** Ven a vernos cuando quieras.; **to have a good time** pasarlo bien ▷ Did you have a good time? ¿Lo pasaste bien?; **two times two is four** dos por dos son cuatro

time off n tiempo m libre

timetable n ❶ (for train, bus, school) horario m ❷ (schedule of events) programa m

Although **programa** ends in -a, it is actually a masculine noun.

tin n ❶ (can) lata f ▷ a tin of beans una lata de alubias ❷ (metal) estaño m

tin opener n abrelatas m (pl abrelatas)

tiny adj minúsculo

tip n ❶ (money) propina f ▷ to leave a tip dejar propina ❷ (advice) consejo m ▷ a useful tip un consejo práctico ❸ (end) punta f ▷ It's on the tip of my tongue. Lo tengo en la punta de la lengua.; **a rubbish tip** un vertedero de basuras; **This place is a complete tip!** ¡Esto es una pocilga!
▶ vb dar una propina a ▷ Don't forget to tip the waiter. No te olvides de darle una propina al camarero.

tiptoe n **on tiptoe** de puntillas

tired adj cansado ▷ I'm tired. Estoy cansado.; **to be tired of something** estar harto de algo

tiring adj cansado

tissue n Kleenex® m (pl Kleenex)

title n (of novel, film) título m

to prep ❶ a

a + el changes to **al**.

▷ to go to Portugal ir a Portugal ▷ to go to school ir al colegio ▷ the train to London el tren a Londres; **I've never been to Valencia.** Nunca he estado en Valencia.; **from...to...** de...a... ▷ from nine o'clock to half past three de las nueve a las tres y media ❷ de ▷ It's easy to do. Es fácil de hacer. ▷ the key to the front door la llave de la puerta principal ❸ (up to) hasta ▷ to count to ten contar hasta diez ❹ (in order to) para ▷ I did it to help you. Lo hice para ayudarte. ▷ She's too young to go to school. Es muy pequeña para ir al colegio. **; ready to go** listo para irse ❺ con ▷ to be kind to somebody ser amable con alguien ▷ They were very kind to me. Fueron muy amables conmigo.; **Give it to her!** ¡Dáselo!; **That's what he said to me.** Eso fue lo que me dijo.; **I've got things to do.** Tengo cosas que hacer.; **ten to nine** las nueve menos diez

toad n sapo m

toast n ❶ (bread) pan m tostado; **a piece of toast** una tostada ❷ (speech) brindis m (pl brindis); **to drink a toast to somebody** brindar por alguien

toaster n tostadora f

tobacco n tabaco m

tobacconist's n estanco m (LatAm tabaquería f)

today adv hoy

toddler n niño m pequeño, niña f pequeña

toe n dedo m del pie (pl dedos de los pies) ▷ The dog bit my big toe. El perro me mordió el dedo gordo del pie.

toffee n caramelo m

together adv ❶ juntos ▷ Are they still together? ¿Todavía están juntos? ❷ (at the same time) a la vez ▷ Don't all speak together! ¡No habléis todos a la vez!; **together with** junto con

toilet n ❶ (in public place) servicios mpl ❷ (in house) wáter m

toilet paper n papel m higiénico

toiletries npl artículos mpl de perfumería

toilet roll n rollo m de papel higiénico

told vb see **tell**

toll n (on bridge, motorway) peaje m

tomato n tomate m ▷ tomato soup sopa de tomate

tomorrow adv mañana ▷ tomorrow morning mañana por la mañana ▷ tomorrow night mañana por la noche; **the day after tomorrow** pasado mañana

ton n tonelada f ▷ a ton of coal una tonelada de carbón; **That old bike weighs a ton.** Esa bici vieja pesa una tonelada.

tongue n lengua f; **to stick out one's tongue at somebody** sacar la lengua a alguien

tonic n tónica f; **a gin and tonic** un gin-tonic

tonight adv esta noche ▷ Are you going out tonight? ¿Vas a salir esta noche?

tonsillitis n amigdalitis f ▷ She's got tonsillitis. Tiene amigdalitis.

tonsils npl amígdalas fpl

too adv ❶ (as well) también ▷ My sister came too. Mi hermana también vino. ❷ (excessively) demasiado ▷ The water's too hot. El agua está demasiado caliente.; **too much** demasiado ▷ too much butter demasiada mantequilla ▷ At Christmas we always eat too much. En Navidades siempre comemos demasiado.; **too many** demasiados (f demasiadas) ▷ too many chairs demasiadas sillas; **Too bad!** (what a pity) ¡Qué pena!

took vb see **take**

tool n herramienta f; **a tool box** una caja de herramientas

tooth n diente m

toothache n dolor m de muelas ▷ These pills are good for toothache. Estas pastillas son buenas para el dolor de muelas.; **I've got toothache.** Me duele una muela.

toothbrush n cepillo m de dientes

toothpaste n dentífrico m

top n ❶ parte f de arriba ▷ at the top of the page en la parte de arriba de la página ❷ (of mountain) cima f ❸ (of box, jar) tapa f ❹ (of bottle) tapón m (pl tapones); **a bikini top** la parte de arriba del bikini; **the top of the table** el tablero de la mesa; **on top of the cupboard** encima del armario;

a
b
c
d
e
f
g
h
i
j
k
l
m
n
o
p
q
r
s
t
u
v
w
x
y
z

There's a surcharge on top of that. Hay un recargo, además.; **from top to bottom** de arriba abajo ▷ I searched the house from top to bottom. Busqué en la casa de arriba abajo.

▶ adj ❶ (shelf) de arriba ▷ it's on the top shelf está en la estantería de arriba; **the top layer of skin** la capa superior de la piel; **the top floor** el último piso ❸ eminente ▷ a top surgeon un eminente cirujano; **a top model** una top model; **a top hotel** un hotel de primera; **He always gets top marks in French.** Siempre saca excelentes notas en francés.; **at top speed** a máxima velocidad

topic n tema m

Although **topic** ends in -a, it is actually a masculine noun.

▷ The essay can be on any topic. La redacción puede ser sobre cualquier tema.

torch n (electric) linterna f

tore, torn vb see **tear**

tortoise n tortuga f

torture n tortura f ▷ It was pure torture. Fue una tortura.

▶ vb torturar ▷ Stop torturing that poor animal! ¡Deja de torturar al pobre animal!

total adj ❶ total ▷ The total cost was very high. El coste total fue muy alto.; **the total amount** el total

▶ n total m; **the grand total** la suma total

totally adv totalmente

touch n **to get in touch with**

somebody ponerse en contacto con alguien; **to keep in touch with somebody** mantenerse en contacto con alguien; **Keep in touch!** (1) (write) ¡Escribe de vez en cuando! (2) (phone) ¡Llama de vez en cuando!; **to lose touch** perder el contacto; **to lose touch with somebody** perder el contacto con alguien

▶ vb tocar ▷ Don't touch that! ¡No toques eso!

tough adj ❶ difícil ▷ It was tough, but I managed okay. Fue difícil, pero me las arreglé.; **It's a tough job.** Es un trabajo duro. ❷ duro ▷ The meat is tough. La carne está dura. ❸ resistente ▷ tough leather gloves guantes de cuero resistentes; **He thinks he's a tough guy.** Le gusta hacerse el duro.; **Tough luck!** ¡Mala suerte!

tour n ❶ recorrido m turístico ▷ We went on a tour of the city. Hicimos un recorrido turístico por la ciudad.; **a package tour** un viaje organizado; **a bus tour** un viaje en autobús ❷ (of building, exhibition) visita f ❸ (by band) gira f; **to go on tour** ir de gira

▶ vb **Robbie Williams is touring Europe.** Robbie Williams está haciendo una gira por Europa.

tour guide n guía m turístico, guía f turística

tourism n turismo m

tourist n turista mf; **tourist information office** la oficina de información y turismo

towards prep hacia ▷ He came towards me. Vino hacia mí.

towel n toalla f

tower n torre f

tower block n ❶ (of flats) bloque m de pisos ❷ (of offices) bloque m de oficinas

town n ciudad f ▷ the town centre el centro de la ciudad

town hall n ayuntamiento m

tow truck n (in US) grúa f

toy n juguete m; **a toy shop** una juguetería; **a toy car** un coche de juguete

trace n rastro m ▷ There was no trace of the robbers. No había rastro de los ladrones.
▶ vb ❶ (draw) trazar ❷ (locate) encontrar

tracing paper n papel m de calco

track n ❶ (dirt road) camino m ❷ (railway line) vía f ❸ (in sport) pista f ❹ (song) canción f (pl canciones) ▷ This is my favourite track. Ésta es mi canción preferida. ❺ (trail) huella f ▷ They followed the tracks for miles. Siguieron las huellas durante millas.

track down vb encontrar ▷ The police never tracked down the killer. La policía nunca encontró al asesino.

tracksuit n chándal m (pl chándals)

tractor n tractor m

trade n oficio m ▷ to learn a trade aprender un oficio

trade union n sindicato m

tradition n tradición f (pl tradiciones)

traditional adj tradicional

traffic n tráfico m ▷ There was a lot of traffic. Había mucho tráfico.

traffic circle n (in US) rotonda f

traffic jam n atasco m

traffic lights npl semáforo m

traffic warden n guardia mf de tráfico ▷ I'm a traffic warden. Soy guardia de tráfico.

tragedy n tragedia f

tragic adj trágico

trailer n ❶ (for luggage, boat) remolque m ❷ (of film) tráiler m (pl tráilers)

train n tren m
▶ vb entrenar ▷ to train for a race entrenar para una carrera; **to train as a teacher** estudiar magisterio; **to train an animal to do something** enseñar a un animal a hacer algo

trained adj cualificado (LatAm calificado) ▷ highly trained workers los trabajadores altamente cualificados; **She's a trained nurse.** Es enfermera diplomada.

trainee n (apprentice) aprendiz m, aprendiza f (mpl aprendices) ▷ He's a trainee plumber. Es aprendiz de fontanero.; **She's a trainee teacher.** Es profesora de prácticas.

trainer n ❶ (sports) entrenador m, entrenadora f ❷ (of animals) amaestrador m, amaestradora f

trainers npl zapatillas fpl de deporte

training n ❶ formación f

▷ *a training course* un curso de formación ❷ *(in sport)* entrenamiento *m*; **He strained a muscle in training.** Se hizo un esguince entrenando.

tram *n* tranvía *m*

> Although **tranvía** ends in **-a**, it is actually a masculine noun.

tramp *n* vagabundo *m*, vagabunda *f*

trampoline *n* cama *f* elástica

transfer *n* ❶ transferencia *f* ▷ *a bank transfer* una transferencia bancaria ❷ *(sticker)* calcomanía *f*

translate *vb* traducir ▷ *to translate something into English* traducir algo al inglés

translation *n* traducción *f* (pl traducciones)

translator *n* traductor *m*, traductora *f* ▷ *Anita's a translator.* Anita es traductora.

transparent *adj* transparente

transplant *n* trasplante *m* ▷ *a heart transplant* un trasplante de corazón

transport *n* transporte *m* ▷ *public transport* el transporte público

trap *n* trampa *f*

trash *n (in US)* basura *f*; **the trash can** el cubo de la basura

travel *n* **Air travel is relatively cheap.** Viajar en avión es relativamente barato.

▶ *vb* viajar ▷ *I prefer to travel by train.* Prefiero viajar en tren.; **I'd like to travel round the world.** Me gustaría dar la vuelta al mundo.; **We travelled over 800**

kilometres. Hicimos más de 800 kilómetros.; **News travels fast!** ¡Las noticias vuelan!

travel agency *n* agencia *f* de viajes

travel agent *n* ❶ *(shop)* agencia *f* de viajes ❷ *(person)* agente *f* de viajes

traveller *(US* **traveler)** *n* viajero *m*, viajera *f*

traveller's cheque *(US* **traveler's check)** *n* cheque *m* de viaje (pl cheques de viaje)

travelling *(US* **traveling)** *n* **I love travelling.** Me encanta viajar.

travel sickness *n* mareo *m*

tray *n* bandeja *f*

tread *vb* pisar; **to tread on something** pisar algo ▷ *He trod on her foot.* Le pisó el pie.

treasure *n* tesoro *m*

treat *n* **As a birthday treat, I'll take you out to dinner.** Como es tu cumpleaños, te invito a cenar.; **She bought a special treat for the children.** Les compró algo especial a los niños.; **I'm going to give myself a treat.** Me voy a dar un gusto.

▶ *vb* tratar ▷ *The hostages were well treated.* Los rehenes fueron tratados bien.; **She was treated for a minor head wound.** La atendieron de una leve herida en la cabeza.; **to treat somebody to something** invitar a alguien a algo ▷ *I'll treat you!* ¡Te invito yo!

treatment *n* ❶ *(medical)* tratamiento *m* ▷ *an effective* *treatment for eczema* un tratamiento efectivo contra el eccema ❷ *(of person)* trato *m* ▷ *We don't want any special treatment.* No queremos ningún trato especial.

treble *vb* triplicarse ▷ *The cost of living has trebled.* El coste de la vida se ha triplicado.

tree *n* árbol *m*

tremble *vb* temblar

trend *n* ❶ *(tendency)* tendencia *f* ❷ *(fashion)* moda *f* ▷ *the latest trend* la última moda

trendy *adj* moderno

trial *n (in law)* juicio *m*

triangle *n* triángulo *m*

tribe *n* tribu *f*

trick *n* ❶ broma *f* ▷ *to play a trick on somebody* gastar una broma a alguien ❷ truco *m* ▷ *It's not easy: there's a trick to it.* No es fácil: tiene un truco.
▶ *vb* **to trick somebody** engañar a alguien

tricky *adj (problem)* peliagudo

tricycle *n* triciclo *m*

trip *n* viaje *m* ▷ *to go on a trip* ir de viaje ▷ *Have a good trip!* ¡Buen viaje!; **a day trip** una excursión de un día
▶ *vb (stumble)* tropezarse ▷ *He tripped on the stairs.* Se tropezó en las escaleras.; **to trip up** tropezarse; **to trip somebody up** poner la zancadilla a alguien

triple *adj* triple

triplets *npl* trillizos *mpl (fpl* trillizas)

trivial *adj* insignificante

trod, trodden *vb see* **tread**

trolley *n* carrito *m*

trombone *n* trombón *m (pl* trombones)

troops *npl* tropas *fpl*

trophy *n* trofeo *m*

tropical *adj* tropical

trouble *n* problema *m*

> Although **problema** ends in -a, it is actually a masculine noun.

▷ *The trouble is, it's too expensive.* El problema es que es demasiado caro.; **What's the trouble?** ¿Qué pasa?; **to be in trouble** tener problemas; **stomach trouble** problemas de estómago; **to take a lot of trouble over something** poner mucho cuidado en algo; **Don't worry, it's no trouble.** No te preocupes, no importa.

troublemaker *n* alborotador *m*, alborotadora *f*

trousers *npl* pantalones *mpl* ▷ *a pair of trousers* unos pantalones

trout *n* trucha *f*

truant *n* **to play truant** hacer novillos

truck *n* camión *m (pl* camiones)

truck driver *n* camionero *m*, camionera *f* ▷ *He's a truck driver.* Es camionero.

true *adj (love, courage)* verdadero; **It's true.** Es verdad.; **to come true** hacerse realidad ▷ *I hope my dream will come true.* Espero que mi sueño se haga realidad.

trumpet *n* trompeta *f*

trunk *n* ❶ *(of tree)* tronco *m* ❷ *(of*

elephant) trompa f ❸ *(luggage)* baúl m ❹ *(in US: of car)* maletero m

trunks *npl* **swimming trunks** el traje de baño

trust *n* confianza f ▷ **to have trust in somebody** tener confianza en alguien
▶ *vb* **Don't you trust me?** ¿No tienes confianza en mí?; **Trust me!** ¡Confía en mí!; **I don't trust him.** No me fío de él.

truth *n* verdad f

try *n* intento m ▷ **his third try** su tercer intento; **to give something a try** intentar algo; **It's worth a try.** Vale la pena intentarlo.; **Have a try!** ¡Inténtalo!
▶ *vb* ❶ intentar ▷ **to try to do something** intentar hacer algo; **to try again** volver a intentar ❷ probar ▷ **Would you like to try some?** ¿Quieres probar un poco?

try on *vb (clothes)* probarse

try out *vb (product, machine)* probar

T-shirt *n* camiseta f

tube *n* tubo m; **the Tube** *(underground)* el Metro

tuberculosis *n* tuberculosis f ▷ **He's got tuberculosis.** Tiene tuberculosis.

Tuesday *n* martes m (*pl* martes) ▷ **I saw her on Tuesday.** La vi el martes. ▷ **every Tuesday** todos los martes ▷ **last Tuesday** el martes pasado ▷ **next Tuesday** el martes que viene ▷ **on Tuesdays** los martes

tuition *n* clases fpl ▷ **private tuition** clases particulares

tulip *n* tulipán m (*pl* tulipanes)

tumble dryer *n* secadora f

tummy *n* tripa f (*informal*); **he has a tummy ache** le duele la tripa

tuna *n* atún m (*pl* atunes)

tune *n (melody)* melodía f; **to play in tune** tocar bien

Tunisia *n* Túnez m

tunnel *n* túnel m

Turk *n* turco m, turca f ▷ **the Turks** los turcos

turkey *n* pavo m

Turkey *n* Turquía f

Turkish *adj* turco
▶ *n (language)* turco m

turn *n (bend in road)* curva f; **"no left turn"** "prohibido girar a la izquierda"; **to take turns** turnarse; **It's my turn!** ¡Me toca a mí!
▶ *vb* ❶ girar ▷ **Turn right at the lights.** Gira a la derecha al llegar al semáforo. ❷ *(become)* ponerse ▷ **When he's drunk he turns nasty.** Cuando se emborracha se pone desagradable.; **The weather turned cold.** Empezó a hacer frío.; **to turn into something** convertirse en algo ▷ **The holiday turned into a nightmare.** Las vacaciones se convirtieron en una pesadilla.

turn back *vb* volver hacia atrás ▷ **We turned back.** Volvimos hacia atrás.

turn down *vb* ❶ rechazar ▷ **He turned down the offer.** Rechazó la oferta. ❷ bajar ▷ **Shall I turn the heating down?** ¿Bajo la calefacción?

turn off *vb* ❶ *(light, radio)* apagar

❸ (tap) cerrar ❹ (engine) parar

turn on vb ❶ (light, radio) encender ❷ (tap) abrir ❸ (engine) poner en marcha

turn out vb resultar ▷ It turned out to be a mistake. Resultó ser un error. ▷ It turned out that she was right. Resultó que ella tenía razón.

turn round vb ❶ (car) dar la vuelta ❷ (person) darse la vuelta

turn up vb ❶ (appear) aparecer ▷ She never turned up. No apareció. ❸ (volume, heat) subir ▷ Could you turn up the radio? ¿Puedes subir la radio?

turning n We took the wrong turning. (1) (in the country) Nos equivocamos de carretera. (2) (in the city) Nos equivocamos de bocacalle.

turnip n nabo m

turquoise adj turquesa inv

turtle n tortuga f de mar

tutor n (private teacher) profesor m particular, profesora f particular

tuxedo n (in US) esmoquin m (pl esmóquines)

TV n tele f

tweezers npl pinzas fpl ▷ a pair of tweezers unas pinzas

twelfth adj duodécimo ▷ the twelfth floor el duodécimo piso; **the twelfth of August** el doce de agosto

twelve num doce ▷ She's twelve. Tiene doce años.; **twelve o'clock** las doce

twentieth adj vigésimo; **the twentieth floor** la planta veinte;

the twentieth of May el veinte de mayo

twenty num veinte ▷ He's twenty. Tiene veinte años.

twice adv dos veces ▷ He had to repeat it twice. Tuvo que repetirlo dos veces.; **twice as much** el doble ▷ He gets twice as much pocket money as me. Le dan el doble de paga que a mí.

twin n mellizo m, melliza f ▷ my twin brother mi hermano mellizo; **identical twins** gemelos; **a twin room** una habitación con dos camas

twinned adj hermanado ▷ Nottingham is twinned with Minsk. Nottingham está hermanada con Minsk.

twist vb torcer; **He's twisted his ankle.** Se ha torcido el tobillo.

two num dos ▷ She's two. Tiene dos años.; **The two of them can sing.** Los dos saben cantar.

type n tipo m ▷ What type of camera have you got? ¿Qué tipo de cámara tienes?
▶ vb escribir a máquina ▷ to type a letter escribir una carta a máquina

typewriter n máquina f de escribir

typical adj típico

tyre n neumático m

u

UFO abbr (= Unidentified Flying Object) OVNI m (= el Objeto Volador No Identificado)

ugly adj feo

UK abbr (= United Kingdom) RU m (= el Reino Unido)

ulcer n úlcera f; **a mouth ulcer** una llaga en la boca

Ulster n Ulster m

umbrella n paraguas m (pl paraguas)

umpire n árbitro m, árbitra f

UN abbr (= United Nations) ONU f (= la Organización de las Naciones Unidas)

unable adj **to be unable to do something** no poder hacer algo ▷ Unfortunately, he was unable to come. Desafortunadamente, no ha podido venir.

unanimous adj unánime

unavoidable adj inevitable

unbearable adj insoportable

unbelievable adj increíble

uncertain adj incierto ▷ The future is uncertain. El futuro es incierto.; **to be uncertain about something** no estar seguro de algo; **She was uncertain how to begin.** No sabía muy bien cómo empezar.

uncle n tío m; **my uncle and aunt** mis tíos

uncomfortable adj incómodo

unconscious adj inconsciente

under prep

> When something is located under something, use **debajo de**. When there is movement involved, use **por debajo de**.

❶ debajo de ▷ The cat's under the table. El gato está debajo de la mesa. ▷ The tunnel goes under the Channel. El túnel pasa por debajo del Canal.; **under there** ahí debajo ▷ What's under there? ¿Qué hay ahí debajo? ❷ menos de ▷ under 20 people menos de 20 personas; **children under 10** niños menores de 10 años

underage adj **He's underage.** Es menor de edad.

underground adj (below ground level) subterráneo

▶ adv bajo tierra ▷ Moles live underground. Los topos viven bajo tierra.

▶ n metro m ▷ Is there an underground in Barcelona? ¿Hay

metro en Barcelona?

underline vb subrayar

underneath prep, adv

> When something is located underneath something, use **debajo de**. When there is movement involved, use **por debajo de**.

❶ debajo de ▷ underneath the carpet debajo de la moqueta ▷ I got out of the car and looked underneath. Bajé del coche y miré debajo. ❷ por debajo de ▷ I walked underneath a ladder. Pasé por debajo de una escalera.

underpants npl calzoncillos mpl ▷ a pair of underpants unos calzoncillos

underpass n paso m subterráneo

undershirt n (in US) camiseta f

understand vb entender ▷ Do you understand? ¿Entiendes? ▷ I don't understand the question. No entiendo la pregunta.; **Is that understood?** ¿Está claro?

understanding adj comprensivo ▷ She's very understanding. Es muy comprensiva.

understood vb see **understand**

undertaker n empleado m de una funeraria, empleada f de una funeraria; **the undertaker's** la funeraria

underwater adj, adv ❶ subacuático ▷ underwater photography fotografía subacuática ❷ bajo el agua ▷ This sequence was filmed underwater. Esta secuencia se filmó bajo el

agua.

underwear n ropa f interior

undo vb ❶ (button, blouse) desabrochar ❷ (knot, parcel, shoe laces) desatar ❸ (zip) abrir

undress vb (get undressed) desnudarse ▷ The doctor told me to undress. El médico me dijo que me desnudase.

unemployed adj parado (LatAm desempleado) ▷ He's been unemployed for a year. Lleva parado un año.; **the unemployed** los parados (LatAm los desempleados)

unemployment n desempleo m

unexpected adj inesperado ▷ an unexpected visitor una visita inesperada

unexpectedly adv de improviso

unfair adj injusto ▷ This law is unfair to women. Esta ley es injusta para las mujeres.

unfamiliar adj desconocido ▷ I heard an unfamiliar voice. Oí una voz desconocida.

unfashionable adj pasado de moda

unfit adj I'm unfit at the moment. En este momento no estoy en forma.

unfold vb desplegar ▷ She unfolded the map. Desplegó el mapa.

unforgettable adj inolvidable

unfortunately adv desafortunadamente

unfriendly adj antipático ▷ The waiters are a bit unfriendly. Los camareros son un poco antipáticos.

a b c d e f g h i j k l m n o p q r s t u v w x y z

ungrateful adj desagradecido

unhappy adj infeliz (pl infelices)
▷ He was very unhappy as a child.
De niño fue muy infeliz.; **to look unhappy** parecer triste

unhealthy adj ❶ (food) malo para la salud ❷ (ill) con mala salud ❸ (atmosphere) malsano

uniform n uniforme m; **school uniform** el uniforme de colegio

uninhabited adj ❶ (house) deshabitado ❷ (island) despoblado

union n (trade union) sindicato m

Union Jack n bandera f del Reino Unido

unique adj único

unit n unidad f ▷ a unit of measurement una unidad de medida; **a kitchen unit** un módulo de cocina

United Kingdom n Reino m Unido

United Nations n Naciones fpl Unidas

United States n Estados mpl Unidos

universe n universo m

university n universidad f
▷ She's at university. Está en la universidad. ▷ Lancaster University la Universidad de Lancaster

unleaded petrol n gasolina f sin plomo

unless conj a no ser que

| **a no ser que** has to be followed by a verb in the subjunctive.

▷ I won't come unless you phone me.

No vendré a no ser que me llames.;
Unless I am mistaken, we're lost. Si no me equivoco, estamos perdidos.

unlikely adj poco probable ▷ That's possible, but unlikely. Es posible pero poco probable.

| **es poco probable que** has to be followed by a verb in the subjunctive.

▷ He's unlikely to come. Es poco probable que venga.

unload vb descargar ▷ We unloaded the furniture. Descargamos los muebles.

unlock vb abrir ▷ He unlocked the door of the car. Abrió la puerta del coche.

unlucky adj **to be unlucky (1)** (be unfortunate) tener mala suerte
▷ Did you win? - No, I was unlucky.
¿Ganaste? - No, tuve mala suerte.
(2) (bring bad luck) traer mala suerte ▷ They say thirteen is an unlucky number. Dicen que el número trece trae mala suerte.

unmarried adj soltero ▷ an unmarried mother una madre soltera; **an unmarried couple** una pareja no casada

unnatural adj poco natural

unnecessary adj innecesario

unpack vb deshacer ▷ I unpacked my suitcase. Deshice la maleta.;
I haven't unpacked my clothes yet. Todavía no he sacado la ropa de la maleta.

unpleasant adj desagradable

unplug vb desenchufar

unpopular adj impopular ▷ *It was an unpopular decision.* Fue una decisión impopular.; **She's an unpopular child.** Tiene muy pocos amigos.

unrealistic adj poco realista

unreasonable adj (attitude, person, behaviour) poco razonable

unreliable adj poco fiable ▷ *The car was slow and unreliable.* El coche era lento y poco fiable.; **He's completely unreliable.** Es muy informal.

unroll vb desenrollar

unscrew vb ❶ (screw) destornillar ❷ (lid) desenroscar

unsuccessful adj (attempt) fallido; **to be unsuccessful in doing something** no conseguir hacer algo; **an unsuccessful artist** un artista sin éxito

unsuitable adj (clothes, equipment) inapropiado

untidy adj ❶ (disorganized) desordenado ▷ *Your bedroom is really untidy.* Tu cuarto está muy desordenado. ❷ (writing) descuidado; **She always looks so untidy.** Siempre va tan desaliñada.

untie vb ❶ (knot, parcel) deshacer ❷ (shoelace, animal) desatar

until prep, conj ❶ hasta ▷ *I waited until 10 o'clock.* Esperé hasta las 10.; **until now** hasta ahora ▷ *It's never been a problem until now.* Hasta ahora nunca ha sido un problema.; **until then** hasta entonces ▷ *Until then I'd never been*

to Italy. Hasta entonces no había estado nunca en Italia. ❷ hasta que ▷ *We stayed there until the doctor came.* Nos quedamos allí hasta que vino el médico.

> **hasta que** has to be followed by a verb in the subjunctive when referring to a future event.

▷ *Wait until I come back.* Espera hasta que yo vuelva.

unusual adj ❶ poco común ▷ *an unusual shape* una forma poco común ❷ raro

> **es raro que** has to be followed by a verb in the subjunctive.

▷ *It's unusual to get snow at this time of year.* Es raro que nieve en esta época del año.

unwilling adj **He was unwilling to help me.** No estaba dispuesto a ayudarme.

unwrap vb abrir ▷ *We unwrapped the presents.* Abrimos los regalos.

up prep, adv

> For other expressions with **up**, see the verbs **come**, **put**, **turn** etc.

arriba ▷ *up on the hill* arriba,de la colina ▷ *up there* allí arriba; **up north** en el norte; **They live up the road.** Viven en esta calle, un poco más allá.; **to be up** estar levantado ▷ *He's not up yet.* Todavía no se ha levantado.; **What's up?** ¿Qué hay?; **What's up with her?** ¿Qué le pasa?; **to go up** subir ▷ *The bus went up the hill.* El autobús subió la colina.;

to go up to somebody acercarse a alguien ▷ *She came up to me. Se me acercó.*; **up to** hasta ▷ *up to now* hasta ahora; **It's up to you.** Depende de ti.

uphill *adv* **to go uphill** ir cuesta arriba

upper *adj* superior

upright *adj* (*not stooping*) derecho ▷ *to stand upright* tenerse derecho

upset *n* I had a stomach upset. Tenía mal el estómago.

▶ *adj* disgustado ▷ *She's still a bit upset.* Todavía está un poco disgustada.; **Don't get upset.** No te enfades.; **I had an upset stomach.** Tenía mal el estómago.

▶ *vb* **to upset somebody** disgustar a alguien; **Don't upset yourself.** No te enfades.

upside down *adv* al revés ▷ *The painting was hung upside down.* El cuadro estaba colgado al revés.

upstairs *adv* arriba ▷ *Where's your coat? - It's upstairs.* ¿Dónde está tu abrigo? - Está arriba.; **the people upstairs** los de arriba; **He went upstairs to bed.** Subió para irse a la cama.

up-to-date *adj* ❶ (*car, stereo*) moderno ❷ actualizado ▷ *an up-to-date timetable* un horario actualizado; **to bring somebody up-to-date on something** poner a alguien al corriente de algo; **to bring something up-to-date** actualizar algo

upwards *adv* hacia arriba ▷ *to look upwards* mirar hacia arriba

urgent *adj* urgente

urine *n* orina *f*

US *abbr* (= United States) EEUU *mpl* (= los Estados Unidos)

us *pron* ❶ nos

Use **nos** to translate **us** when it is the direct object of the verb in the sentence, or when it means to **us**.

▷ *They helped us. Nos ayudaron.* ▷ *Look at us!* ¡Míranos! ❷ nosotros (*f* nosotras)

Use **nosotros** or **nosotras** after prepositions, in comparisons, and with the verb to **be**.

▷ *Why don't you come with us?* ¿Por qué no vienes con nosotras? ▷ *They are older than us.* Son mayores que nosotros. ▷ *It's us.* Somos nosotros.

USA *abbr* (= United States of America) EEUU *mpl* (= los Estados Unidos)

use *n* uso *m* ▷ *"directions for use"* "modo de empleo"; **It's no use shouting, she's deaf.** Es inútil gritar, es sorda.; **It's no use, I can't do it.** No hay manera, no puedo hacerlo.; **to make use of something** usar algo

▶ *vb* usar ▷ *Can I use your phone?* ¿Puedo usar tu teléfono?; **I used to go camping as a child.** De pequeño solía ir de acampada.; **I didn't use to like maths, but now I love it.** Antes no me gustaban las matemáticas, pero ahora me encantan.; **to be used to something** estar acostumbrado a algo ▷ He wasn't used to driving on the right. No estaba acostumbrado a conducir por la derecha.

useful adj útil

useless adj inútil ▷ a piece of useless information una información inútil; **You're useless!** ¡Eres un inútil!; **This computer is useless.** Este ordenador no sirve para nada.; **It's useless asking her.** No sirve de nada preguntarle.

user n usuario m, usuaria f

user-friendly adj fácil de usar

usual adj habitual; **as usual** como de costumbre

usually adv normalmente ▷ I usually get to school at about half past eight. Normalmente llego al colegio sobre las ocho y media.

vacancy n ❶ (job) vacante f ❷ (in hotel) habitación f libre; **"no vacancies"** "completo"

vacant adj libre ▷ a vacant seat un asiento libre

vacation n (in US) vacaciones fpl ▷ to be on vacation estar de vacaciones ▷ to take a vacation tomarse unas vacaciones

vaccinate vb vacunar

vacuum vb pasar la aspiradora ▷ to vacuum the hall pasar la aspiradora por el vestíbulo

vacuum cleaner n aspiradora f

vagina n vagina f

vague adj ❶ vago ▷ I've only got a vague idea what he means. Tengo sólo una vaga idea de lo que quiere decir. ❷ distraído ▷ He's getting a bit vague in his old age. Se está poniendo un poco distraído en su vejez.

vain adj vanidoso ▷ *He's so vain!* ¡Es más vanidoso!; **in vain** en vano

Valentine card n tarjeta f del día de los enamorados

Valentine's Day n día m de los enamorados

valid adj válido ▷ *a valid passport* un pasaporte válido; **This ticket is valid for three months.** Este billete tiene una validez de tres meses.

valley n valle m

valuable adj ❶ de valor inv ▷ *a valuable painting* un cuadro de valor ❷ valioso ▷ *valuable help* una valiosa ayuda

value n valor m

van n furgoneta f

vandal n vándalo m

vandalism n vandalismo m

vandalize vb destrozar

vanilla n vainilla f ▷ *a vanilla ice cream* un helado de vainilla

vanish vb desaparecer; **to vanish into thin air** esfumarse

variety n variedad f

various adj varios ▷ *We visited various villages in the area.* Visitamos varias aldeas de la zona.

vary vb variar

vase n jarrón m (pl jarrones)

VAT n IVA m

Although **IVA** ends in **-A**, it is actually a masculine noun.

VCR n (= video cassette recorder) vídeo m

VDU n (= visual display unit) monitor m

veal n carne f de ternera

vegan n vegetariano m estricto, vegetariana f estricta

vegetable n ❶ (to be cooked) verdura f ▷ *vegetable soup* sopa de verduras ❸ (for salads) hortaliza f ▷ *peppers, tomatoes and other vegetables* pimientos, tomates y otras hortalizas

vegetarian n vegetariano m, vegetariana f ▷ *I'm a vegetarian.* Soy vegetariano.

▶ adj **vegetarian lasagne** lasaña vegetariana

vehicle n vehículo m

vein n vena f

velvet n terciopelo m

vending machine n máquina f expendedora

verb n verbo m

verdict n veredicto m

vertical adj vertical

vertigo n vértigo m ▷ *I get vertigo.* Tengo vértigo.

very adv muy ▷ *very tall* muy alto; **It's very cold.** Hace mucho frío.; **not very interesting** no demasiado interesante; **very much** muchísimo; **We were thinking the very same thing.** Estábamos pensando exactamente lo mismo.

▶ adj mismo ▷ *in this very house* en esta misma casa

vest n ❶ (underclothing) camiseta f ❷ (in US: waistcoat) chaleco m

vet n veterinario m, veterinaria f

▷ *She's a vet.* Es veterinaria.

via prep ❶ por ▷ *We drove to Lisbon via Salamanca.* Fuimos a Lisboa por Salamanca. ❷ vía ▷ *a flight via Brussels* un vuelo vía Bruselas

vicar n párroco m

vice n (*tool*) tornillo m de banco

vicious adj ❶ brutal ▷ *a vicious attack* una brutal agresión ❷ feroz ▷ *a vicious dog* un perro feroz; **He was a vicious man.** Era un hombre despiadado.; **a vicious circle** un círculo vicioso

victim n víctima f ▷ *He was the victim of a mugging.* Fue víctima de un atraco.

victory n victoria f

video vb grabar en vídeo (LatAm grabar en video) ▷ *They videoed the whole wedding.* Grabaron en vídeo toda la boda.

▶ n vídeo m (LatAm video m) ▷ *to watch a video* ver un vídeo; **a video camera** una videocámara; **a video cassette** una cinta de vídeo; **a video game** un videojuego; **a video recorder** un vídeo; **a video shop** un videoclub

view n ❶ vista f ▷ *There's an amazing view.* La vista es magnífica. ❷ opinión f (pl opiniones) ▷ *in my view* en mi opinión

viewer n telespectador m, telespectadora f

viewpoint n punto m de vista

vile adj repugnante

villa n chalet m

village n ❶ (*large*) pueblo m

❷ (*small*) aldea f

vine n ❶ (*trailing*) vid f

❸ (*climbing*) parra f

vinegar n vinagre m

vineyard n viñedo m

viola n viola f

violence n violencia f

violent adj violento

violin n violín m (pl violines)

violinist n violinista mf

virgin n virgen f (pl vírgenes) ▷ *to be a virgin* ser virgen

Virgo n (*sign*) Virgo m; **I'm Virgo.** Soy virgo.

virtual reality n realidad f virtual

virus n (*also computing*) virus m (pl virus)

visa n visado m (LatAm visa f)

visible adj visible

visit n visita f ▷ *my last visit to my grandmother* la última visita que le hice a mi abuela; **I saw him on my latest visit to Spain.** Lo vi la última vez que estuve en España.

▶ vb visitar

visitor n ❶ (*tourist*) visitante mf ❷ (*guest*) visita f ▷ *to have a visitor* tener visita

visual adj visual

vital adj vital

vitamin n vitamina f

vivid adj vivo ▷ *vivid colours* colores vivos; **to have a vivid imagination** tener una imaginación desbordante

vocabulary n vocabulario m

vocational adj (*course*) de formación profesional

vodka *n* vodka *m*

> Although **vodka** ends in **-a**, it is actually a masculine noun.

voice *n* voz *f* (*pl* voces)

voice mail *n* buzón *m* de voz

volcano *n* volcán *m* (*pl* volcanes)

volleyball *n* voleibol *m*

volt *n* voltio *m*

volume *n* (sound) volumen *m*;
to turn the volume up subir el volumen

voluntary *adj* voluntario;
to do voluntary work hacer voluntariado

volunteer *n* voluntario *m*, voluntaria *f*
▶ *vb* **to volunteer to do something** ofrecerse a hacer algo

vomit *vb* vomitar

vote *vb* votar ▷ *Who did you vote for?* ¿A quién votaste?
▶ *n* voto *m*

voucher *n* vale *m* ▷ *a gift voucher* un vale de regalo

vowel *n* vocal *f*

vulgar *adj* vulgar

wage *n* paga *f* ▷ *He collected his wages.* Recogió la paga.

waist *n* cintura *f*

waistcoat *n* chaleco *m*

wait *vb* esperar ▷ *I'll wait for you.* Te esperaré. ▷ *Wait a minute!* ¡Espera un momento!; **to keep somebody waiting** hacer esperar a alguien ▷ *They kept us waiting for hours.* Nos hicieron esperar durante horas.; **I can't wait for the holidays.** Estoy deseando que lleguen las vacaciones.; **I can't wait to see him again.** Me muero de ganas de verlo otra vez.

waiter *n* camarero *m*

waiting list *n* lista *f* de espera

waiting room *n* sala *f* de espera

waitress *n* camarera *f*

wake up *vb* despertarse ▷ *I woke*

up at six o'clock. Me desperté a las seis.; **to wake somebody up** despertar a alguien ▷ *Please would you wake me up at seven o'clock?* ¿Podría despertarme a las siete, por favor?

Wales n Gales m ▷ *I'm from Wales.* Soy de Gales.; **the Prince of Wales** el Príncipe de Gales

walk vb ❶ andar ▷ *We walked 10 kilometres.* Anduvimos 10 kilómetros. ❷ *(go on foot)* ir a pie ▷ *Are you walking or going by bus?* ¿Vas a ir a pie o en autobús? ❸ *(for fun)* pasear ▷ *I like walking through the park.* Me gusta pasear por el parque.; **to walk the dog** pasear al perro

▶ n paseo m; **to go for a walk** ir a pasear; **It's 10 minutes' walk from here.** Está a 10 minutos de aquí a pie.

walking n ❶ *(going on foot)* andar m ▷ *Walking is good for your health.* Andar es bueno para la salud. ❷ *(hill walking)* senderismo m

walking stick n bastón m *(pl bastones)*

Walkman® n walkman® m

wall n ❶ *(of room, building)* pared f ❷ *(freestanding)* muro m ❸ *(of castle, city)* muralla f

wallet n cartera f

wallpaper n papel m pintado

walnut n nuez f *(pl nueces)*

wander around vb pasear ▷ *I just wandered around for a while.* Estuve paseando un poco.

want vb querer ▷ *Do you want some*

cake? ¿Quieres un poco de pastel?; **to want to do something** querer hacer algo ▷ *What do you want to do tomorrow?* ¿Qué quieres hacer mañana?; **to want somebody to do something** querer que alguien haga algo ▷ *They want us to wait here.* Quieren que esperemos aquí.

   ▌ **querer que** has to be followed by a verb in the subjunctive.

war n guerra f; **to be at war** estar en guerra

ward n sala f

wardrobe n armario m

warehouse n almacén m *(pl almacenes)*

warm adj ❶ caliente ▷ *warm water* agua caliente ❷ caluroso ▷ *a warm day* un día caluroso ▷ *a warm welcome* una calurosa bienvenida; **warm clothing** ropa de abrigo; **This jumper is very warm.** Este jersey es muy calentito.; **He's a very warm person.** Es una persona muy afectuosa.; **It's warm in here.** Aquí dentro hace calor.; **I'm too warm.** Tengo demasiado calor.

warm up vb ❶ *(for sport)* hacer ejercicios de calentamiento ❷ *(food)* calentar

warn vb advertir ▷ *Well, I warned you!* ¡Ya te lo había advertido!; **to warn somebody to do something** aconsejar a alguien que haga algo

   ▌ Use the subjunctive after **aconsejar a alguien que.**

warning n advertencia f

Warsaw n Varsovia f

wart n verruga f

was vb *see* **be**

wash n **to have a wash** lavarse; **to give something a wash** lavar algo; **The car needs a wash.** Al coche le hace falta un lavado.

▶ vb ❶ lavar ▷ *to wash the car* lavar el coche ❷ *(have a wash)* lavarse ▷ *Every morning I get up, wash and get dressed.* Todas las mañanas me levanto, me lavo y me visto.; **to wash one's hands** lavarse las manos; **to wash up** lavar los platos

washbasin n lavabo m

washcloth n *(in US)* toallita f para lavarse

washing n *(clean laundry)* ropa f lavada; **to do the washing** lavar la ropa; **dirty washing** la ropa para lavar; **Have you got any washing?** ¿Tienes ropa para lavar?

washing machine n lavadora f

washing powder n detergente m

washing-up n **to do the washing-up** lavar los platos

washing-up liquid n lavavajillas m *(pl* lavavajillas*)*

wasn't = **was not**

wasp n avispa f

waste n ❶ desperdicio m ▷ *It's such a waste!* ¡Qué desperdicio!; **It's a waste of time.** Es una pérdida de tiempo. ❷ residuos mpl ▷ *nuclear waste* residuos radioactivos

▶ vb *(food, space, opportunity)* desperdiciar; **to waste time**

perder el tiempo ▷ *There's no time to waste.* No hay tiempo que perder.; **I don't like wasting money.** No me gusta malgastar el dinero.

wastepaper basket n papelera f

watch n reloj m

▶ vb ❶ mirar; **Watch me!** ¡Mírame! ❷ ver ▷ *to watch TV* ver la tele ❸ vigilar ▷ *The police were watching the house.* La policía vigilaba la casa.

watch out vb tener cuidado; **Watch out!** ¡Cuidado!

water n agua f

> Although it is a feminine noun, remember that you use **el** with **agua**.

▶ vb regar ▷ *He was watering his tulips.* Estaba regando los tulipanes.

waterfall n cascada f

watering can n regadera f

watermelon n sandía f

waterproof adj impermeable; **a waterproof watch** un reloj sumergible

water-skiing n esquí m acuático ▷ *to go water-skiing* hacer esquí acuático

water sports npl deportes mpl acuáticos

wave n ola f

▶ vb **to wave to somebody (1)** *(say hello)* saludar a alguien con la mano **(2)** *(say goodbye)* hacer adiós a alguien con la mano

wax n cera f

way n ❶ manera f ▷ *She looked*

at me in a strange way. Me miró de manera extraña.; **This book tells you the right way to do it.** Este libro explica cómo hay que hacerlo.; **You're doing it the wrong way.** Lo estás haciendo mal.; **in a way…** en cierto sentido…; **a way of life** un estilo de vida ❷ (route) camino *m* ▷ *We stopped for lunch on the way.* Paramos a comer en el camino.; **Which way is it?** ¿Por dónde es?; **The supermarket is this way.** El supermercado es por aquí.; **Do you know the way to the hotel?** ¿Sabes cómo llegar al hotel?; **He's on his way.** Está de camino.; **It's a long way.** Está lejos. ▷ *It's a long way from the hotel.* Está lejos del hotel.; **"way in"** "entrada"; **"way out"** "salida"; **by the way…** a propósito…

we *pron* nosotros (*f* nosotras)

　▌ we generally isn't translated unless it's emphatic.
　▷ *We were in a hurry.* Teníamos prisa.

　▌ Use **nosotros** or **nosotras** as appropriate for emphasis.
　▷ *They went but we didn't.* Ellos fueron pero nosotros no.

weak *adj* ❶ débil ❷ (tea, coffee) poco cargado

wealthy *adj* rico

weapon *n* arma *f*

　▌ Although it's a feminine noun, remember that you use **el** and **un** with **arma**.

wear *vb* llevar ▷ *She was wearing*

a hat. Llevaba un sombrero.; **She was wearing black.** Iba vestida de negro.

weather *n* tiempo *m* ▷ *What's the weather like?* ¿Qué tiempo hace?

weather forecast *n* pronóstico *m* del tiempo

Web *n* **the Web** la Web

web browser *n* navegador *m* de Internet

webcam *n* webcam *f*

web page *n* página *f* web

website *n* sitio *m* web

we'd = **we had; we would**

wedding *n* boda *f*; **wedding anniversary** el aniversario de boda; **wedding dress** el vestido de novia

Wednesday *n* miércoles *m* (*pl* miércoles) ▷ *I saw her on Wednesday.* La vi el miércoles. ▷ *every Wednesday* todos los miércoles ▷ *last Wednesday* el miércoles pasado ▷ *next Wednesday* el miércoles que viene ▷ *on Wednesdays* los miércoles

weed *n* hierbajo *m* ▷ *The garden's full of weeds.* El jardín está lleno de hierbajos.

week *n* semana *f* ▷ *in a week's time* dentro de una semana; **a week on Friday** el viernes de la semana que viene; **during the week** durante la semana

weekday *n* día *m* entre semana

　▌ Although **día** ends in **-a**, it is actually a masculine noun.

on weekdays los días entre

semana
weekend n fin m de semana;
next weekend el próximo fin de
semana
weigh vb pesar ▷ How much do you
weigh? ¿Cuánto pesas?; **to weigh**
oneself pesarse
weight n peso m; **to lose weight**
adelgazar; **to put on weight**
engordar
weightlifting n levantamiento
m de pesas
weird adj raro
welcome n bienvenida f ▷ They
gave her a warm welcome. Le
dieron una calurosa bienvenida.;
Welcome! ¡Bienvenido!

If you're addressing a
woman remember to use the
feminine form: **¡Bienvenida!**
If you're addressing more
than one person use the
plural form **¡Bienvenidos!** or
¡Bienvenidas!.

▶ vb **to welcome somebody** dar
la bienvenida a alguien; **Thank**
you! - You're welcome! ¡Gracias!
- ¡De nada!
well adj, adv ❶ bien ▷ You did that
really well. Lo hiciste realmente
bien.; **She's doing really well**
at school. Le va muy bien en el
colegio.; **to be well** estar bien
▷ I'm not very well at the moment.
No estoy muy bien en este
momento.; **Get well soon!** ¡Que
te mejores!; **Well done!** ¡Muy
bien! ❷ bueno ▷ It's enormous!
Well, quite big anyway. ¡Es

enorme! Bueno, digamos que
bastante grande.; **as well**
también ▷ We worked hard, but we
had some fun as well. Trabajamos
mucho, pero también nos
divertimos.; **as well as** además
de ▷ We went to Gerona as well as
Sitges. Fuimos a Gerona, además
de Sitges.
▶ n pozo m
we'll = we will
well-behaved adj **to be well-**
behaved portarse bien
wellingtons npl botas fpl de
agua
well-known adj conocido ▷ a
well-known film star un conocido
actor de cine
well-off adj adinerado
Welsh adj galés (f galesa)
▶ n (language) galés m; **the Welsh**
los galeses
Welshman n galés m (pl galeses)
Welshwoman n galesa f
went vb see **go**
were vb see **be**
we're = we are
weren't = were not
west n oeste m
▶ adj occidental ▷ the west coast
la costa occidental; **the West**
Country el sudoeste de
Inglaterra
▶ adv hacia el oeste ▷ We were
travelling west. Viajábamos hacia
el oeste.; **west of** al oeste de
▷ Stroud is west of Oxford. Stroud
está al oeste de Oxford
western n western m

▶ adj occidental ▷ the western part of the island la parte occidental de la isla; **Western Europe** Europa Occidental

West Indian adj antillano; **She's West Indian.** Es antillana.

▶ n antillano m, antillana f

West Indies npl **the West Indies** las Antillas

wet adj mojado ▷ wet clothes ropa mojada; **to get wet** mojarse; **dripping wet** chorreando; **wet weather** el tiempo lluvioso; **It was wet all week.** Llovió toda la semana.

wetsuit n traje m de buzo

we've = we have

whale n ballena f

what adj, pron ❶ qué

> Use **qué** (with an accent) in direct and indirect questions and exclamations.

▷ What subjects are you studying? ¿Qué asignaturas estudias? ▷ What's it for? ¿Para qué es? ▷ I don't know what to do. No sé qué hacer. ▷ What a mess! ¡Qué desorden!

> Only translate **what is** by **qué es** if asking for a definition or explanation.

▷ What is it? ¿Qué es? ▷ What's a tractor, Daddy? ¿Qué es un tractor, papá? ❷ cuál (pl cuáles)

> Translate **what is** by **cuál es** when not asking for a definition or explanation.

▷ What's her telephone number? ¿Cuál es su número de teléfono?

❸ lo que

> Use **lo que** (no accent) when **what** isn't a question word.

▷ I saw what happened. Vi lo que pasó.; **What? (1)** (what did you say?) ¿Cómo? **(2)** (shocked) ¿Qué?; **What's your name?** ¿Cómo te llamas?

wheat n trigo m

wheel n rueda f; **steering wheel** el volante

wheelchair n silla f de ruedas

when adv cuándo

> Remember the accent on **cuándo** in direct and indirect questions.

▷ When did he go? ¿Cuándo se fue? ▶ conj cuando ▷ She was reading when I came in. Cuando entré ella estaba leyendo.

> **cuando** has to be followed by a verb in the subjunctive when referring to an event in the future.

▷ Call me when you get there. Llámame cuando llegues.

where adv dónde

> Remember the accent on **dónde** in direct and indirect questions.

▷ Where do you live? ¿Dónde vives? ▷ Where are you from? ¿De dónde eres?; **Where are you going?** ¿Adónde vas?

▶ conj donde ▷ a shop where you can buy coffee una tienda donde se puede comprar café

whether conj si ▷ I don't know whether to go or not. No sé si ir o no.

which adj, pron ❶ cuál (pl cuáles)

> Remember the accent on **cuál** and **cuáles** in direct and indirect questions.

▷ Which one would you like? ¿Cuál quieres? ❷ qué

> Use **qué** (with an accent) before nouns.

▷ Which flavour do you want? ¿Qué sabor quieres? ❸ (that) que

▷ It's an illness that causes nerve damage. Es una enfermedad que daña los nervios.

> After a preposition **que** becomes **el que**, **la que**, **los que**, **las que** to agree with the noun.

▷ That's the film which I was telling you about. Ésa es la película de la que te hablaba. ❹ lo cual ▷ The cooker isn't working, which is a nuisance. La cocina no funciona, lo cual es un fastidio.

while conj ❶ mientras ▷ You hold the torch while I look inside. Aguanta la linterna mientras yo miro por dentro. ❷ mientras que ▷ Isobel is very dynamic, while Kay is more laid-back. Isabel es muy dinámica, mientras que Kay es más tranquila.

▶ n a while un rato ▷ after a while después de un rato; a while ago hace un momento ▷ He was here a while ago. Hace un momento estaba aquí.; for a while durante un tiempo ▷ I lived in London for a while. Viví en Londres durante un tiempo.; quite a while mucho

tiempo ▷ I haven't seen him for quite a while. Hace mucho tiempo que no lo veo.

whip n (for horse) fusta f

▶ vb ❶ (animal) fustigar ❷ (person) azotar ❸ (eggs, cream) batir

whipped cream n nata f montada

whiskers npl (of animal) bigotes mpl

whisky n whisky m (pl whiskys)

whisper vb susurrar

whistle n silbato m ▷ The referee blew his whistle. El árbitro tocó el silbato.

▶ vb ❶ (with a whistle) pitar ❷ (with mouth) silbar

white adj blanco ▷ He's got white hair. Tiene el cabello blanco.; white wine el vino blanco; white bread el pan blanco; white coffee el café con leche; a white man un hombre blanco; white people los blancos

whiteboard n pizarra f blanca; an interactive whiteboard una pizarra interactiva

Whitsun n Pentecostés m

who pron ❶ quién (pl quiénes)

> Remember the accent on **quién** and **quiénes** in direct and indirect questions.

▷ Who said that? ¿Quién dijo eso? ▷ Who is it? ¿Quién es? ▷ We don't know who broke the window. No sabemos quién rompió la ventana. ❷ que ▷ the people who know us las personas que nos conocen

After a preposition **que** becomes **el que**, **la que**, **los que**, **las que** to agree with the noun.

▷ *the women who she was chatting with* las mujeres con las que estaba hablando

Note that **a** + **el que** becomes **al que**.

▷ *the boy who I gave it to* el chico al que se lo di

whole adj entero ▷ *two whole days* dos días enteros; **the whole afternoon** toda la tarde; **the whole world** todo el mundo ▷ n **The whole of Wales was affected.** Todo Gales se vio afectado.; **on the whole** en general

wholemeal adj integral ▷ *wholemeal bread* pan integral

wholewheat adj (*in US*) integral

whom pron ❶ quién (pl quiénes)

Remember the accent on **quién** and **quiénes** in direct and indirect questions.

▷ *With whom did you go?* ¿Con quién fuiste? ❷ (*when not a question*) quien ▷ *the man whom I saw* el hombre a quien vi

whose adj ❶ (*in questions*) de quién (pl de quiénes)

Remember the accent on **quién** and **quiénes** in direct and indirect questions.

▷ *Whose books are these?* ¿De quiénes son estos libros? ❷ (*relative*) cuyo ▷ *the girl*

whose picture was in the paper la muchacha cuya foto venía en el periódico

▶ pron de quién (pl de quiénes)

Remember the accent on **quién** and **quiénes** in direct and indirect questions.

▷ *Whose is this?* ¿De quién es esto?

why adv por qué

Remember to write **por qué** as two words with an accent on **qué** when translating **why**.

▷ *Why did you do that?* ¿Por qué hiciste eso?; **Why not?** ¿Por qué no?; **That's why he did it.** Por eso lo hizo.

wicked adj ❶ (*evil*) malvado ❷ (*really great*) sensacional

wide adj, adv ancho ▷ *a wide road* una carretera ancha ▷ *How wide is it?* - *It's five metres wide.* ¿Cómo es de ancho? - Tiene cinco metros de ancho.; **wide open** abierto de par en par ▷ *The door was wide open.* La puerta estaba abierta de par en par.; **wide awake** completamente despierto

widow n viuda f ▷ *She's a widow.* Es viuda.

widower n viudo m ▷ *He's a widower.* Es viudo.

width n anchura f

wife n esposa f

wig n peluca f

wild adj ❶ salvaje ▷ *a wild animal* un animal salvaje ❷ silvestre ▷ *wild flowers* flores silvestres ❸ loco ▷ *She's a bit wild.* Es un poco loca.

ENGLISH > SPANISH

wildlife n flora f y fauna

will n (document) testamento m
▶ vb

 will can often be translated by the present tense, as in the following examples.
▷ Come on, I'll help you. Venga, te ayudo. ▷ Will you help me? ¿Me ayudas?

 Use **voy a**, **va a**, etc + the infinitive to talk about plans and intentions.
▷ What will you do? ¿Qué vas a hacer?

 Use the future tense when guessing what will happen or when making a supposition.
▷ It won't take long. No llevará mucho tiempo. ▷ We'll probably go out later. Seguramente saldremos luego.

 Use **querer** for "to be willing" in emphatic requests, and invitations.
▷ Tom won't help me. Tom no me quiere ayudar. ▷ Will you be quiet! ¿Te quieres callar? ▷ Will you have some tea? ¿Quieres tomar un té?

willing adj **to be willing to do something** estar dispuesto a hacer algo

win vb ganar ▷ Did you win? ¿Ganaste? ▷ to win a prize ganar un premio
▶ n victoria f

wind n (rope, wire) enrollar
▶ n viento m; **a wind instrument** un instrumento de viento; **wind power** la energía eólica

window n ❶ (of building) ventana f ❷ (in car, train) ventanilla f; **a shop window** un escaparate ❸ (window pane) cristal m (LatAm vidrio m) ▷ to break a window romper un cristal

windscreen n parabrisas m (pl parabrisas)

windscreen wiper n limpiaparabrisas m (pl limpiaparabrisas)

windshield n (in US) parabrisas m (pl parabrisas)

windshield wiper n (in US) limpiaparabrisas m (pl limpiaparabrisas)

windsurfing n windsurf m; **to go windsurfing** hacer windsurf

windy adj **a windy day** un día de viento; **It's windy.** Hace viento.

wine n vino m ▷ white wine el vino blanco ▷ red wine el vino tinto; **a wine bar** un bar especializado en vinos; **a wine glass** una copa de vino; **the wine list** la carta de vinos

wing n ala f

 Although it's a feminine noun, remember that you use **el** and **un** with **ala**.

wink vb guiñar el ojo; **to wink at somebody** guiñar el ojo a alguien

winner n ganador m, ganadora f

winning adj vencedor (f vencedora) ▷ the winning team el equipo vencedor; **the winning goal** el gol de la victoria

winter n invierno m

wipe vb limpiar; **to wipe one's feet**

limpiarse los zapatos; **to wipe one's nose** limpiarse la nariz;
Did you wipe up that water you spilled? ¿Recogiste el agua que derramaste?

wire n alambre m; **copper wire** el hilo de cobre; **the telephone wire** el cable del teléfono

wisdom tooth n muela f del juicio

wise adj sabio

wish vb **to wish for something** desear algo ▷ **What more could you wish for?** ¿Qué más podrías desear?; **to wish to do something** desear hacer algo ▷ **I wish to make a complaint.** Deseo hacer una reclamación.; **I wish you were here!** ¡Ojalá estuvieras aquí!; **I wish you'd told me!** ¡Me lo podrías haber dicho!; **to wish somebody happy birthday** desear a alguien un feliz cumpleaños
▶ n deseo m ▷ **to make a wish** pedir un deseo; **"best wishes"** (on birthday card) "felicidades"; **"with best wishes, Kathy"** "un abrazo, Kathy"

wit n ingenio m

witch n bruja f

with prep ❶ con ▷ **He walks with a stick.** Camina con un bastón.; **Come with me.** Ven conmigo. ❷ de ▷ **a woman with blue eyes** una mujer de ojos azules ▷ **Fill the jug with water.** Llena la jarra de agua.; **We stayed with friends.** Nos quedamos en casa de unos amigos.

within prep dentro de ▷ **I want it back within three days.** Quiero que me lo devuelvas dentro de tres días.; **The police arrived within minutes.** La policía llegó a los pocos minutos.; **The shops are within easy reach.** Las tiendas están cerca.

without prep sin ▷ **without a coat** sin abrigo ▷ **without speaking** sin hablar

witness n testigo mf ▷ **There were no witnesses.** No había testigos.

witty adj ingenioso

wives npl see **wife**

wizard n brujo m

woken up vb see **wake up**

woke up vb see **wake up**

wolf n lobo m

woman n mujer f; **a woman doctor** una doctora

won vb see **win**

wonder vb preguntarse ▷ **I wonder why she said that.** Me pregunto por qué dijo eso.; **I wonder where Caroline is.** ¿Dónde estará Caroline?

wonderful adj maravilloso

won't = **will not**

wood n ❶ madera f ▷ **It's made of wood. Es de madera.** ❷ (for fire) leña f ❸ bosque m ▷ **We went for a walk in the wood.** Fuimos a pasear por el bosque.

wooden adj de madera ▷ **a wooden chair** una silla de madera

woodwork n carpintería f

wool n lana f ▷ **It's made of wool.**

a b c d e f g h i j k l m n o p q r s t u v w x y z

Es de lana.

word n palabra f; **What's the word for "shop" in Spanish?** ¿Cómo se dice "shop" en español?; **in other words** en otras palabras; **to have a word with somebody** hablar con alguien ▷ *Can I have a word with you?* ¿Puedo hablar contigo?; **the words** (lyrics) la letra

word processing n procesamiento m de textos

word processor n procesador m de textos

wore vb see **wear**

work n trabajo m ▷ *She's looking for work.* Está buscando trabajo.; **It's hard work.** Es duro.; **at work** en el trabajo ▷ *He's at work until five o'clock.* Está en el trabajo hasta las cinco.; **He's off work today.** Hoy tiene el día libre.; **to be out of work** estar sin trabajo

▶ vb ❶ trabajar ▷ *She works in a shop.* Trabaja en una tienda. ❷ funcionar ▷ *The heating isn't working.* La calefacción no funciona.

work out vb ❶ (exercise) hacer ejercicio ▷ *I work out twice a week.* Hago ejercicio dos veces a la semana. ❷ (turn out) salir ▷ *I hope it will work out well.* Espero que salga bien. ❸ (calculate) calcular ▷ *I worked it out in my head.* Lo calculé en mi cabeza. ❹ (understand) entender ▷ *I just couldn't work it out.* No lograba entenderlo.; **It works out at £10 each.** Sale a 10 libras esterlinas

por persona.

worker n trabajador m, trabajadora f; **She's a good worker.** Trabaja bien.

work experience n **I'm going to do my work experience in a factory.** Voy a hacer las prácticas en una fábrica.

working-class adj de clase obrera ▷ *a working-class family* una familia de clase obrera

workman n obrero m

worksheet n hoja f de ejercicios

workshop n taller m ▷ *a drama workshop* un taller de teatro

workstation n terminal f de trabajo

world n mundo m; **the world champion** el campeón mundial; **the World Cup** la Copa del Mundo

worm n gusano m

worn vb see **wear**

▶ adj gastado ▷ *The carpet is a bit worn.* La moqueta está un poco gastada.; **worn out** agotado ▷ *We were worn out after the long walk.* Estábamos agotados después de andar tanto.

worried adj preocupado ▷ *to be worried about something* estar preocupado por algo

worry vb preocuparse; **Don't worry!** ¡No te preocupes!

worse adj, adv peor ▷ *It was even worse than mine.* Era incluso peor que el mío.

worst adj peor ▷ *the worst student in the class* el peor alumno de la clase; **Maths is my worst subject.**

Las matemáticas es la asignatura que peor se me da.

▶ n **The worst of it is that...** Lo peor es que...; **at worst** en el peor de los casos; **if the worst comes to the worst** en el peor de los casos

worth adj **to be worth** valer ▷ It's worth a lot of money. Vale mucho dinero.; **It's worth it.** (worthwhile) Vale la pena.

would vb

The conditional is often used to translate **would** + verb.

▷ I said I would do it. Dije que lo haría. ▷ If you asked him he'd do it. Si se lo pidieras, lo haría. ▷ If you had asked him he would have done it. Si se lo hubieras pedido, lo habría hecho.

When **would you** is used to make requests, translate using **poder** in the present.

▷ Would you close the door please? ¿Puedes cerrar la puerta, por favor?; **I'd like ...** (1) (it would be good) Me gustaría ... ▷ I'd like to go to China. Me gustaría ir a China. (2) (can I have) Quería ... ▷ I'd like three tickets please. Quería tres entradas.; **Would you like a biscuit?** ¿Quieres una galleta?

Use the subjunctive after **querer que**.

▷ Would you like me to iron your jeans? ¿Quieres que te planche los pantalones?; **Would you like to go to the cinema?** ¿Quieres ir al cine?

wouldn't = **would not**

wound vb see **wind**

▶ vb **herir** ▷ He was wounded in the leg. Fue herido en la pierna.

▶ n **herida** f

wrap vb **envolver** ▷ She's wrapping her Christmas presents. Está envolviendo los regalos de Navidad.

wrapping paper n **papel** m de regalo

wreck n **cacharro** m ▷ That car is a wreck! ¡Ese coche es un cacharro!; **After the exams I was a complete wreck.** Después de los exámenes estaba hecho polvo.

▶ vb ❶ **destruir** ▷ The explosion wrecked the whole house. La explosión destruyó toda la casa. ❷ (car) **destrozar** ❸ **echar por tierra** ▷ The bad weather wrecked our plans. El mal tiempo echó por tierra nuestros planes.

wrestler n **luchador** m, **luchadora** f

wrestling n **lucha** f **libre**

wrinkled adj **arrugado**

wrist n **muñeca** f

write vb **escribir** ▷ to write a letter escribir una carta

write down vb **anotar** ▷ Can you write it down for me, please? ¿Me lo puedes anotar, por favor?

writer n **escritor** m, **escritora** f

writing n **letra** f ▷ I can't read your writing. No entiendo tu letra.; **in writing** por escrito

written vb see **write**

wrong adj, adv ❶ **incorrecto**
▷ the wrong answer la respuesta

a
b
c
d
e
f
g
h
i
j
k
l
m
n
o
p
q
r
s
t
u
v
w
x
y
z

incorrecta; **You've got the wrong number.** Se ha equivocado de número. ❷ mal ▷ *You've done it wrong.* Lo has hecho mal.; **to go wrong** (*plan*) ir mal; **to be wrong** estar equivocado ▷ *You're wrong about that.* En eso estás equivocado.; **What's wrong?** ¿Qué pasa? ▷ *What's wrong with her?* ¿Qué le pasa?

wrote *vb see* **write**

Xmas *n* (= *Christmas*) Navidad *f*
X-ray *vb* hacer una radiografía de ▷ *They X-rayed my arm.* Me hicieron una radiografía del brazo. ▶ *n* radiografía *f* ▷ *I had an X-ray taken.* Me hicieron una radiografía.

y

yacht n yate m

yawn vb bostezar

year n año m ▷ last year el año pasado; **to be 15 years old** tener 15 años; **an eight-year-old child** un niño de ocho años; **I'm in Year 8.** Estoy en segundo de secundaria.

yell vb gritar

yellow adj amarillo

yes adv sí ▷ Do you like it? - Yes. ¿Te gusta? - Sí

yesterday adv ayer ▷ yesterday morning ayer por la mañana

yet adv todavía ▷ Have you eaten? - Not yet. ¿Ya has comido? - Todavía no. ▷ It's not finished yet. Todavía no está terminado.; **Have you finished yet?** ¿Has terminado ya?

yoghurt n yogur m

yolk n yema f

you pron

> There are formal and informal ways of saying **you** in Spanish. As you look down the entry, choose the informal options if talking to people your own age or that you know well. Otherwise use the formal options. Note that subject pronouns are used less in Spanish - for emphasis and in comparisons.

❶ (informal: 1 person) tú ▷ What do YOU think about it? ¿Y tú qué piensas? ▷ She's younger than you. Es más joven que tú.; **You don't understand me.** No me entiendes. ❷ (informal: 2 or more people) vosotros mpl, vosotras fpl ▷ You've got kids but we haven't. Vosotros tenéis hijos pero nosotros no. ▷ They're younger than you. Son más jóvenes que vosotros. ▷ I'd like to speak to you. (ie all female) Quiero hablar con vosotras.; **How are you?** ¿Qué tal estáis? ❸ (formal: 1 person) usted ▷ They're younger than you. Son más jóvenes que usted. ▷ This is for you. Esto es para usted.; **How are you?** ¿Cómo está? ❹ (formal: 2 or more people) ustedes

> **ustedes** is always used in Latin America instead of **vosotros**.

▷ They're younger than you. Son más jóvenes que ustedes. ▷ This is for you. Esto es para ustedes.; **How** are you? ¿Cómo están?

When **you** means "one" or "people" in general, the impersonal **se** is often used.

▷ I doubt it, but you never know. Lo dudo, pero nunca se sabe.

When **you** is the object of the sentence, you have to use different forms from the ones above. See translations 5 to 10 below.

⑤ (informal: 1 person) te ▷ I love you. Te quiero. ▷ Shall I give it to you? ¿Te lo doy?; **This is for you.** Esto es para ti.; **Can I go with you?** ¿Puedo ir contigo? **⑥** (informal: 2 or more people:) os ▷ I saw you. Os vi.; **I gave them to you.** Os los di. **⑦** (formal: 1 person - direct object) lo msg, la fsg ▷ May I help you? ¿Puedo ayudarlo? ▷ I saw you, Mrs Jones. La vi, señora Jones. **⑧** (formal: 1 person - indirect object) le

Change **le** to **se** before another object pronoun.

▷ I gave you the keys. Le di las llaves.; **I gave them to you.** Se las di. **⑨** (formal: 2 or more people - direct object) los mpl, las fpl ▷ May I help you? ¿Puedo ayudarlos? **⑩** (formal: 2 or more people - indirect object) les

Change **les** to **se** before another object pronoun.

▷ I gave you the keys. Les di las llaves.; **I gave them to you.** Se las di.

young adj joven (pl jóvenes); **young people** los jóvenes; **He's younger than me.** Es menor que

yo.; **my youngest brother** mi hermano pequeño

your adj

Use **tu** and **vuestro/vuestra** etc with people your own age or that you know well, and **su/sus** otherwise.

① (informal: 1 person) tu (pl tus)

Remember there's no accent on **tu** meaning "your".

▷ your house tu casa ▷ your books tus libros **②** (informal: 2 or more people) vuestro

Remember to make **vuestro** agree with the person or thing it describes.

▷ your dog vuestro perro ▷ These are your keys. Éstas son vuestras llaves. **③** (formal) su (pl sus)

Use **su** when talking to **one** person or to a **group** of people. **su** is used in Latin America instead of **vuestro**.

▷ Can I see your passport, sir? ¿Me enseña su pasaporte, señor? ▷ your uncle and aunt sus tíos

Use **el**, **la**, **los**, **las** as appropriate with parts of the body and to translate **your** referring to people in general.

▷ Have you washed your hair? ¿Te has lavado el pelo?; **It's bad for your health.** Es malo para la salud.

yours pron

Use **tuyo/tuya** etc and **vuestro/vuestra** etc with people your own age or that you know well, and **su/sus** otherwise.

① (informal: 1 person) tuyo
Remember to make **tuyo**
agree with the person or thing
it describes.
▷ Is that box yours? ¿Ésa caja es
tuya?
　Add the definite article when
　yours means "your one" or
　"your ones".
I've lost my pen. Can I use yours?
He perdido el bolígrafo. ¿Puedo
usar el tuyo?; **These are my keys
and those are yours.** Éstas son
mis llaves y ésas son las tuyas.
② (informal: 2 or more people)
vuestro
Remember to make **vuestro**
agree with the person or thing
it describes.
▷ That's yours. Eso es vuestro.
　Add the definite article when
　yours means "your one" or
　"your ones".
**These are my keys and those are
yours.** Éstas son mis llaves y ésas
son las vuestras. **③** (formal) suyo
Use **suyo** in more formal
situations with **one** person
or a **group** of people, and
remember to make it agree
with the person or thing it
describes. **suyo** is always used
instead of **vuestro** in Latin
America.
▷ That's yours. Eso es suyo.
　Add the definite article when
　yours means "your one" or
　"your ones".
I've lost my pen. Can I use yours?

He perdido el bolígrafo. ¿Puedo
usar el suyo?; **These are my keys
and those are yours.** Éstas son
mis llaves y ésas son las suyas.;
Yours sincerely... Le saluda
atentamente...

yourself pron
Use **te, tú mismo** and **ti
mismo** when you are talking
to someone of your own age
or that you know well and **se**
and **usted mismo** otherwise.
① (reflexive) te ▷ Have you hurt
yourself? ¿Te has hecho daño?
② (for emphasis) tú mismo (f tú
misma) ▷ Do it yourself! ¡Hazlo tú
mismo! **③** (after a preposition)
ti mismo (f ti misma) ▷ You did
it for yourself. Lo hiciste para ti
mismo. **④** (reflexive) se ▷ Have you
hurt yourself? ¿Se ha hecho daño?
⑤ (after a preposition, for emphasis)
usted mismo (f usted misma)
▷ You did it for yourself. Lo hizo
para usted mismo. ▷ Do it yourself!
¡Hágalo usted mismo!

yourselves pron
In Spain use **os** and **vosotros
mismos** when talking to
people your own age or that
you know well, and **se** or
ustedes mismos otherwise.
In Latin America **se** and
ustedes mismos replace both
os and **vosotros mismos**.
① (reflexive) os ▷ Did you enjoy
yourselves? ¿Os divertisteis?
② (after a preposition, for
emphasis) vosotros mismos (f

vosotras mismas) ▷ *Did you make it yourselves?* ¿Lo habéis hecho vosotros mismos? ❸ *(reflexive)* se ▷ *Did you enjoy yourselves?* ¿Se divirtieron? ❹ *(after a preposition, for emphasis)* ustedes mismos *(f* ustedes mismas) ▷ *Did you make it yourselves?* ¿Lo han hecho ustedes mismos?

youth club *n* club *m* juvenil *(pl* clubs juveniles)

youth hostel *n* albergue *m* juvenil

Yugoslavia *n* Yugoslavia *f* ▷ *in the former Yugoslavia* en la antigua Yugoslavia

zany *adj* estrafalario

zebra *n* cebra *f*

zebra crossing *n* paso *m* de cebra

zero *n* cero *m*

zip *n* cremallera *f*

zip code *n* *(in US)* código *m* postal

zipper *n* *(in US)* cremallera *f*

zodiac *n* zodíaco *m* ▷ *the signs of the zodiac* los signos del zodíaco

zone *n* zona *f*

zoo *n* zoo *m*

zoom lens *n* zoom *m*

zucchini *n* *(in US)* calabacín *m* *(pl* calabacines)

VERB TABLES

Introduction

The following section contains 59 tables of Spanish verbs (some regular and some irregular) in alphabetical order. Each table shows the following tenses and forms: **Present, Preterite, Future, Present Subjunctive, Imperfect, Conditional, Imperative, Past Participle** and **Gerund**. At the bottom of each table are several examples to help you see how the verb is used.

On the Spanish side of the dictionary, Spanish verbs are followed by a number (e.g. **hablar** [26] *vb* <u>to speak</u>). This number corresponds to a page number in the verb tables where the pattern the verb follows is shown. When you come across **cambiar** [26] *vb* <u>to change</u>, for example, you will know that **cambiar** follows the same pattern as that of **hablar** shown in verb table 26.

The regular verbs shown in these tables are:

hablar (regular **–ar** verb, verb table 26)
comer (regular **–er** verb, verb table 9)
vivir (regular **–ir** verb, verb table 59)
lavarse (regular **–ar** reflexive verb, verb table 30)

Some Spanish verbs are regular except for their past participles.

Escribir (to write) and **abrir** (to open) follow the pattern for **vivir** in verb table 59 except that the past participle for **escribir** is **escrito** and that of **abrir** is **abierto**. **Imprimir** (to print) also follows the pattern for **vivir** but can either have the regular past participle **imprimido** or the irregular one **impreso**.

Romper (to break) follows the pattern for **comer** in verb table 9 except that it has the irregular past participle **roto**.

Table
2

actuar *to act*

PRESENT		PRESENT SUBJUNCTIVE	
(yo)	actúo	(yo)	actúe
(tú)	actúas	(tú)	actúes
(él/ella/usted)	actúa	(él/ella/usted)	actúe
(nosotros/as)	actuamos	(nosotros/as)	actuemos
(vosotros/as)	actuáis	(vosotros/as)	actuéis
(ellos/ellas/ustedes)	actúan	(ellos/ellas/ustedes)	actúen

PRETERITE		IMPERFECT	
(yo)	actué	(yo)	actuaba
(tú)	actuaste	(tú)	actuabas
(él/ella/usted)	actuó	(él/ella/usted)	actuaba
(nosotros/as)	actuamos	(nosotros/as)	actuábamos
(vosotros/as)	actuasteis	(vosotros/as)	actuabais
(ellos/ellas/ustedes)	actuaron	(ellos/ellas/ustedes)	actuaban

FUTURE		CONDITIONAL	
(yo)	actuaré	(yo)	actuaría
(tú)	actuarás	(tú)	actuarías
(él/ella/usted)	actuará	(él/ella/usted)	actuaría
(nosotros/as)	actuaremos	(nosotros/as)	actuaríamos
(vosotros/as)	actuaréis	(vosotros/as)	actuaríais
(ellos/ellas/ustedes)	actuarán	(ellos/ellas/ustedes)	actuarían

IMPERATIVE
actúa / actuad

PAST PARTICIPLE
actuado

GERUND
actuando

--------- EXAMPLE PHRASES ---------

Actúa de una forma muy rara.
Actuó en varias películas.
¿Quién **actuará** en su próxima
  película?

He's acting very strangely.
He was in several films.
Who will be in his next film?

PRESENT

(yo)	adquiero
(tú)	adquieres
(él/ella/usted)	adquiere
(nosotros/as)	adquirimos
(vosotros/as)	adquirís
(ellos/ellas/ustedes)	adquieren

PRESENT SUBJUNCTIVE

(yo)	adquiera
(tú)	adquieras
(él/ella/usted)	adquiera
(nosotros/as)	adquiramos
(vosotros/as)	adquiráis
(ellos/ellas/ustedes)	adquieran

PERFECT

(yo)	adquirí
(tú)	adquiriste
(él/ella/usted)	adquirió
(nosotros/as)	adquirimos
(vosotros/as)	adquiristeis
(ellos/ellas/ustedes)	adquirieron

IMPERFECT

(yo)	adquiría
(tú)	adquirías
(él/ella/usted)	adquiría
(nosotros/as)	adquiríamos
(vosotros/as)	adquiríais
(ellos/ellas/ustedes)	adquirían

FUTURE

(yo)	adquiriré
(tú)	adquirirás
(él/ella/usted)	adquirirá
(nosotros/as)	adquiriremos
(vosotros/as)	adquiriréis
(ellos/ellas/ustedes)	adquirirán

CONDITIONAL

(yo)	adquiriría
(tú)	adquirirías
(él/ella/usted)	adquiriría
(nosotros/as)	adquiriríamos
(vosotros/as)	adquiriríais
(ellos/ellas/ustedes)	adquirirían

IMPERATIVE

adquiere / adquirid

GERUND

adquiriendo

PAST PARTICIPLE

adquirido

--- EXAMPLE PHRASES ---

Hemos adquirido una colección de sellos.

We've bought a stamp collection.

Al final **adquirirán** los derechos de publicación.

They will get the publishing rights in the end.

¿Lo **adquirirías** por ese precio?

Would you buy it for that price?

Table
4

almorzar *to have lunch*

PRESENT

(yo)	almuerzo
(tú)	almuerzas
(él/ella/usted)	almuerza
(nosotros/as)	almorzamos
(vosotros/as)	almorzáis
(ellos/ellas/ustedes)	almuerzan

PRESENT SUBJUNCTIVE

(yo)	almuerce
(tú)	almuerces
(él/ella/usted)	almuerce
(nosotros/as)	almorcemos
(vosotros/as)	almorcéis
(ellos/ellas/ustedes)	almuercen

PRETERITE

(yo)	almorcé
(tú)	almorzaste
(él/ella/usted)	almorzó
(nosotros/as)	almorzamos
(vosotros/as)	almorzasteis
(ellos/ellas/ustedes)	almorzaron

IMPERFECT

(yo)	almorzaba
(tú)	almorzabas
(él/ella/usted)	almorzaba
(nosotros/as)	almorzábamos
(vosotros/as)	almorzabais
(ellos/ellas/ustedes)	almorzaban

FUTURE

(yo)	almorzaré
(tú)	almorzarás
(él/ella/usted)	almorzará
(nosotros/as)	almorzaremos
(vosotros/as)	almorzaréis
(ellos/ellas/ustedes)	almorzarán

CONDITIONAL

(yo)	almorzaría
(tú)	almorzarías
(él/ella/usted)	almorzaría
(nosotros/as)	almorzaríamos
(vosotros/as)	almorzaríais
(ellos/ellas/ustedes)	almorzarían

IMPERATIVE

almuerza / almorzad

PAST PARTICIPLE

almorzado

GERUND

almorzando

EXAMPLE PHRASES

¿A qué hora **almuerzas**?

Almorcé en un bar.

Mañana **almorzaremos** todos juntos.

What time do you have lunch?

I had lunch in a bar.

We'll all have lunch together tomorrow.

PRESENT

(yo)	ando
(tú)	andas
(él/ella/usted)	anda
(nosotros/as)	andamos
(vosotros/as)	andáis
(ellos/ellas/ustedes)	andan

PRESENT SUBJUNCTIVE

(yo)	ande
(tú)	andes
(él/ella/usted)	ande
(nosotros/as)	andemos
(vosotros/as)	andéis
(ellos/ellas/ustedes)	anden

PRETERITE

(yo)	anduve
(tú)	anduviste
(él/ella/usted)	anduvo
(nosotros/as)	anduvimos
(vosotros/as)	anduvisteis
(ellos/ellas/ustedes)	anduvieron

IMPERFECT

(yo)	andaba
(tú)	andabas
(él/ella/usted)	andaba
(nosotros/as)	andábamos
(vosotros/as)	andabais
(ellos/ellas/ustedes)	andaban

FUTURE

(yo)	andaré
(tú)	andarás
(él/ella/usted)	andará
(nosotros/as)	andaremos
(vosotros/as)	andaréis
(ellos/ellas/ustedes)	andarán

CONDITIONAL

(yo)	andaría
(tú)	andarías
(él/ella/usted)	andaría
(nosotros/as)	andaríamos
(vosotros/as)	andaríais
(ellos/ellas/ustedes)	andarían

IMPERATIVE

anda / andad

PAST PARTICIPLE

andado

GERUND

andando

--- EXAMPLE PHRASES ---

Voy andando al trabajo todos los días.

I walk to work every day.

Anduvimos al menos 10 km.

We walked at least 10 km.

No sé por dónde **andará**.

I don't know where he will be.

Table
6

caer *to fall*

PRESENT

(yo)	caigo
(tú)	caes
(él/ella/usted)	cae
(nosotros/as)	caemos
(vosotros/as)	caéis
(ellos/ellas/ustedes)	caen

PRESENT SUBJUNCTIVE

(yo)	caiga
(tú)	caigas
(él/ella/usted)	caiga
(nosotros/as)	caigamos
(vosotros/as)	caigáis
(ellos/ellas/ustedes)	caigan

PRETERITE

(yo)	caí
(tú)	caíste
(él/ella/usted)	cayó
(nosotros/as)	caímos
(vosotros/as)	caísteis
(ellos/ellas/ustedes)	cayeron

IMPERFECT

(yo)	caía
(tú)	caías
(él/ella/usted)	caía
(nosotros/as)	caíamos
(vosotros/as)	caíais
(ellos/ellas/ustedes)	caían

FUTURE

(yo)	caeré
(tú)	caerás
(él/ella/usted)	caerá
(nosotros/as)	caeremos
(vosotros/as)	caeréis
(ellos/ellas/ustedes)	caerán

CONDITIONAL

(yo)	caería
(tú)	caerías
(él/ella/usted)	caería
(nosotros/as)	caeríamos
(vosotros/as)	caeríais
(ellos/ellas/ustedes)	caerían

IMPERATIVE

cae / caed

PAST PARTICIPLE

caído

GERUND

cayendo

EXAMPLE PHRASES

Me **caí** por las escaleras.	I fell down the stairs.
Ese edificio **se está cayendo**.	That building is falling down.
Se me ha caído un guante.	I've dropped one of my gloves.

PRESENT

(yo)	cuezo
(tú)	cueces
(él/ella/usted)	cuece
(nosotros/as)	cocemos
(vosotros/as)	cocéis
(ellos/ellas/ustedes)	cuecen

PRESENT SUBJUNCTIVE

(yo)	cueza
(tú)	cuezas
(él/ella/usted)	cueza
(nosotros/as)	cozamos
(vosotros/as)	cozáis
(ellos/ellas/ustedes)	cuezan

PRETERITE

(yo)	cocí
(tú)	cociste
(él/ella/usted)	coció
(nosotros/as)	cocimos
(vosotros/as)	cocisteis
(ellos/ellas/ustedes)	cocieron

IMPERFECT

(yo)	cocía
(tú)	cocías
(él/ella/usted)	cocía
(nosotros/as)	cocíamos
(vosotros/as)	cocíais
(ellos/ellas/ustedes)	cocían

FUTURE

(yo)	coceré
(tú)	cocerás
(él/ella/usted)	cocerá
(nosotros/as)	coceremos
(vosotros/as)	coceréis
(ellos/ellas/ustedes)	cocerán

CONDITIONAL

(yo)	cocería
(tú)	cocerías
(él/ella/usted)	cocería
(nosotros/as)	coceríamos
(vosotros/as)	coceríais
(ellos/ellas/ustedes)	cocerían

IMPERATIVE
cuece / coced

PAST PARTICIPLE
cocido

GERUND
cociendo

--- EXAMPLE PHRASES ---

Cuécelo a fuego lento.
Aquí nos **estamos cociendo**.
No lo **cuezas** demasiado.

Cook it over a gentle heat.
It's boiling in here.
Don't overcook it.

Table
8

coger *to take, to catch*

PRESENT

(yo)	cojo
(tú)	coges
(él/ella/usted)	coge
(nosotros/as)	cogemos
(vosotros/as)	cogéis
(ellos/ellas/ustedes)	cogen

PRESENT SUBJUNCTIVE

(yo)	coja
(tú)	cojas
(él/ella/usted)	coja
(nosotros/as)	cojamos
(vosotros/as)	cojáis
(ellos/ellas/ustedes)	cojan

PRETERITE

(yo)	cogí
(tú)	cogiste
(él/ella/usted)	cogió
(nosotros/as)	cogimos
(vosotros/as)	cogisteis
(ellos/ellas/ustedes)	cogieron

IMPERFECT

(yo)	cogía
(tú)	cogías
(él/ella/usted)	cogía
(nosotros/as)	cogíamos
(vosotros/as)	cogíais
(ellos/ellas/ustedes)	cogían

FUTURE

(yo)	cogeré
(tú)	cogerás
(él/ella/usted)	cogerá
(nosotros/as)	cogeremos
(vosotros/as)	cogeréis
(ellos/ellas/ustedes)	cogerán

CONDITIONAL

(yo)	cogería
(tú)	cogerías
(él/ella/usted)	cogería
(nosotros/as)	cogeríamos
(vosotros/as)	cogeríais
(ellos/ellas/ustedes)	cogerían

IMPERATIVE

coge / coged

PAST PARTICIPLE

cogido

GERUND

cogiendo

EXAMPLE PHRASES

La **cogí** entre mis brazos.
Estuvimos cogiendo setas.
¿Por qué no **coges** el tren de las seis?

I took her in my arms.
We were picking mushrooms.
Why don't you get the six o'clock train?

PRESENT

(yo)	como
(tú)	comes
(él/ella/usted)	come
(nosotros/as)	comemos
(vosotros/as)	coméis
(ellos/ellas/ustedes)	comen

PRESENT SUBJUNCTIVE

(yo)	coma
(tú)	comas
(él/ella/usted)	coma
(nosotros/as)	comamos
(vosotros/as)	comáis
(ellos/ellas/ustedes)	coman

PRETERITE

(yo)	comí
(tú)	comiste
(él/ella/usted)	comió
(nosotros/as)	comimos
(vosotros/as)	comisteis
(ellos/ellas/ustedes)	comieron

IMPERFECT

(yo)	comía
(tú)	comías
(él/ella/usted)	comía
(nosotros/as)	comíamos
(vosotros/as)	comíais
(ellos/ellas/ustedes)	comían

FUTURE

(yo)	comeré
(tú)	comerás
(él/ella/usted)	comerá
(nosotros/as)	comeremos
(vosotros/as)	comeréis
(ellos/ellas/ustedes)	comerán

CONDITIONAL

(yo)	comería
(tú)	comerías
(él/ella/usted)	comería
(nosotros/as)	comeríamos
(vosotros/as)	comeríais
(ellos/ellas/ustedes)	comerían

IMPERATIVE

come / comed

GERUND

comiendo

PAST PARTICIPLE

comido

=========== EXAMPLE PHRASES ===========

No **come** carne.
No **comas** tan deprisa.
Se ha comido todo.

He doesn't eat meat.
Don't eat so fast.
He's eaten it all.

Table
10

conducir *to drive*

PRESENT

(yo)	conduzco
(tú)	conduces
(él/ella/usted)	conduce
(nosotros/as)	conducimos
(vosotros/as)	conducís
(ellos/ellas/ustedes)	conducen

PRESENT SUBJUNCTIVE

(yo)	conduzca
(tú)	conduzcas
(él/ella/usted)	conduzca
(nosotros/as)	conduzcamos
(vosotros/as)	conduzcáis
(ellos/ellas/ustedes)	conduzcan

PRETERITE

(yo)	conduje
(tú)	condujiste
(él/ella/usted)	condujo
(nosotros/as)	condujimos
(vosotros/as)	condujisteis
(ellos/ellas/ustedes)	condujeron

IMPERFECT

(yo)	conducía
(tú)	conducías
(él/ella/usted)	conducía
(nosotros/as)	conducíamos
(vosotros/as)	conducíais
(ellos/ellas/ustedes)	conducían

FUTURE

(yo)	conduciré
(tú)	conducirás
(él/ella/usted)	conducirá
(nosotros/as)	conduciremos
(vosotros/as)	conduciréis
(ellos/ellas/ustedes)	conducirán

CONDITIONAL

(yo)	conduciría
(tú)	conducirías
(él/ella/usted)	conduciría
(nosotros/as)	conduciríamos
(vosotros/as)	conduciríais
(ellos/ellas/ustedes)	conducirían

IMPERATIVE

conduce / conducid

PAST PARTICIPLE

conducido

GERUND

conduciendo

--- EXAMPLE PHRASES ---

Conduces muy bien.
¿**Condujiste** tú?
Él los **conducirá** a la mesa.

You are a really good driver.
Was it you driving?
He'll show you to your table.

PRESENT

(yo)	construyo
(tú)	construyes
(él/ella/usted)	construye
(nosotros/as)	construimos
(vosotros/as)	construís
(ellos/ellas/ustedes)	construyen

PRESENT SUBJUNCTIVE

(yo)	construya
(tú)	construyas
(él/ella/usted)	construya
(nosotros/as)	construyamos
(vosotros/as)	construyáis
(ellos/ellas/ustedes)	construyan

PRETERITE

(yo)	construí
(tú)	construiste
(él/ella/usted)	construyó
(nosotros/as)	construimos
(vosotros/as)	construisteis
(ellos/ellas/ustedes)	construyeron

IMPERFECT

(yo)	construía
(tú)	construías
(él/ella/usted)	construía
(nosotros/as)	construíamos
(vosotros/as)	construíais
(ellos/ellas/ustedes)	construían

FUTURE

(yo)	construiré
(tú)	construirás
(él/ella/usted)	construirá
(nosotros/as)	construiremos
(vosotros/as)	construiréis
(ellos/ellas/ustedes)	construirán

CONDITIONAL

(yo)	construiría
(tú)	construirías
(él/ella/usted)	construiría
(nosotros/as)	construiríamos
(vosotros/as)	construiríais
(ellos/ellas/ustedes)	construirían

IMPERATIVE

construye / construid

PAST PARTICIPLE

construido

GERUND

construyendo

=============== EXAMPLE PHRASES ===============

Están construyendo una escuela.

Yo solo **construí** el puzzle.

Aquí **construirán** una autopista.

They are building a new school.

I did the jigsaw puzzle on my own.

They're going to build a new motorway here.

Table
12

contar to tell, to count

PRESENT

(yo)	cuento
(tú)	cuentas
(él/ella/usted)	cuenta
(nosotros/as)	contamos
(vosotros/as)	contáis
(ellos/ellas/ustedes)	cuentan

PRESENT SUBJUNCTIVE

(yo)	cuente
(tú)	cuentes
(él/ella/usted)	cuente
(nosotros/as)	contemos
(vosotros/as)	contéis
(ellos/ellas/ustedes)	cuenten

PRETERITE

(yo)	conté
(tú)	contaste
(él/ella/usted)	contó
(nosotros/as)	contamos
(vosotros/as)	contasteis
(ellos/ellas/ustedes)	contaron

IMPERFECT

(yo)	contaba
(tú)	contabas
(él/ella/usted)	contaba
(nosotros/as)	contábamos
(vosotros/as)	contabais
(ellos/ellas/ustedes)	contaban

FUTURE

(yo)	contaré
(tú)	contarás
(él/ella/usted)	contará
(nosotros/as)	contaremos
(vosotros/as)	contaréis
(ellos/ellas/ustedes)	contarán

CONDITIONAL

(yo)	contaría
(tú)	contarías
(él/ella/usted)	contaría
(nosotros/as)	contaríamos
(vosotros/as)	contaríais
(ellos/ellas/ustedes)	contarían

IMPERATIVE
cuenta / contad

PAST PARTICIPLE
contado

GERUND
contando

--- EXAMPLE PHRASES ---

Venga, **cuéntamelo**.
Nos **contó** un secreto.
Prométeme que no se lo
contarás a nadie.

Come on, tell me.
He told us a secret.
Promise you won't tell anyone.

PRESENT

(yo)	crezco
(tú)	creces
(él/ella/usted)	crece
(nosotros/as)	crecemos
(vosotros/as)	crecéis
(ellos/ellas/ustedes)	crecen

PRESENT SUBJUNCTIVE

(yo)	crezca
(tú)	crezcas
(él/ella/usted)	crezca
(nosotros/as)	crezcamos
(vosotros/as)	crezcáis
(ellos/ellas/ustedes)	crezcan

PRETERITE

(yo)	crecí
(tú)	creciste
(él/ella/usted)	creció
(nosotros/as)	crecimos
(vosotros/as)	crecisteis
(ellos/ellas/ustedes)	crecieron

IMPERFECT

(yo)	crecía
(tú)	crecías
(él/ella/usted)	crecía
(nosotros/as)	crecíamos
(vosotros/as)	crecíais
(ellos/ellas/ustedes)	crecían

FUTURE

(yo)	creceré
(tú)	crecerás
(él/ella/usted)	crecerá
(nosotros/as)	creceremos
(vosotros/as)	creceréis
(ellos/ellas/ustedes)	crecerán

CONDITIONAL

(yo)	crecería
(tú)	crecerías
(él/ella/usted)	crecería
(nosotros/as)	creceríamos
(vosotros/as)	creceríais
(ellos/ellas/ustedes)	crecerían

IMPERATIVE
crece / creced

PAST PARTICIPLE
crecido

GERUND
creciendo

––––––––––––––– EXAMPLE PHRASES –––––––––––––––

Esas plantas **crecen** en Chile.	*Those plants grow in Chile.*
Crecimos juntos.	*We grew up together.*
Cuando **crezca**, ya verás.	*You'll see, when he grows up.*

Table
14

cruzar *to cross*

PRESENT

(yo)	cruzo
(tú)	cruzas
(él/ella/usted)	cruza
(nosotros/as)	cruzamos
(vosotros/as)	cruzáis
(ellos/ellas/ustedes)	cruzan

PRESENT SUBJUNCTIVE

(yo)	cruce
(tú)	cruces
(él/ella/usted)	cruce
(nosotros/as)	crucemos
(vosotros/as)	crucéis
(ellos/ellas/ustedes)	crucen

PRETERITE

(yo)	crucé
(tú)	cruzaste
(él/ella/usted)	cruzó
(nosotros/as)	cruzamos
(vosotros/as)	cruzasteis
(ellos/ellas/ustedes)	cruzaron

IMPERFECT

(yo)	cruzaba
(tú)	cruzabas
(él/ella/usted)	cruzaba
(nosotros/as)	cruzábamos
(vosotros/as)	cruzabais
(ellos/ellas/ustedes)	cruzaban

FUTURE

(yo)	cruzaré
(tú)	cruzarás
(él/ella/usted)	cruzará
(nosotros/as)	cruzaremos
(vosotros/as)	cruzaréis
(ellos/ellas/ustedes)	cruzarán

CONDITIONAL

(yo)	cruzaría
(tú)	cruzarías
(él/ella/usted)	cruzaría
(nosotros/as)	cruzaríamos
(vosotros/as)	cruzaríais
(ellos/ellas/ustedes)	cruzarían

IMPERATIVE

cruza / cruzad

PAST PARTICIPLE

cruzado

GERUND

cruzando

——————— EXAMPLE PHRASES ———————

No **cruces** la calle con el
semáforo en rojo.
Cruzaron la carretera.
Hace tiempo que no **me cruzo**
con él.

Don't cross the road when the
signal's at red.
They crossed the road.
I haven't seen him for a long time.

PRESENT

(yo)	doy
(tú)	das
(él/ella/usted)	da
(nosotros/as)	damos
(vosotros/as)	dais
(ellos/ellas/ustedes)	dan

PRESENT SUBJUNCTIVE

(yo)	dé
(tú)	des
(él/ella/usted)	dé
(nosotros/as)	demos
(vosotros/as)	deis
(ellos/ellas/ustedes)	den

PRETERITE

(yo)	di
(tú)	diste
(él/ella/usted)	dio
(nosotros/as)	dimos
(vosotros/as)	disteis
(ellos/ellas/ustedes)	dieron

IMPERFECT

(yo)	daba
(tú)	dabas
(él/ella/usted)	daba
(nosotros/as)	dábamos
(vosotros/as)	dabais
(ellos/ellas/ustedes)	daban

FUTURE

(yo)	daré
(tú)	darás
(él/ella/usted)	dará
(nosotros/as)	daremos
(vosotros/as)	daréis
(ellos/ellas/ustedes)	darán

CONDITIONAL

(yo)	daría
(tú)	darías
(él/ella/usted)	daría
(nosotros/as)	daríamos
(vosotros/as)	daríais
(ellos/ellas/ustedes)	darían

IMPERATIVE

da / dad

PAST PARTICIPLE

dado

GERUND

dando

——————— EXAMPLE PHRASES ———————

Me **da** miedo la oscuridad.
I'm scared of the dark.

Nos **dieron** un par de entradas gratis.
They gave us a couple of free tickets.

Te **daré** el número de mi móvil.
I'll give you my mobile phone number.

Table
16

decir *to say, to tell*

PRESENT

(yo)	digo
(tú)	dices
(él/ella/usted)	dice
(nosotros/as)	decimos
(vosotros/as)	decís
(ellos/ellas/ustedes)	dicen

PRESENT SUBJUNCTIVE

(yo)	diga
(tú)	digas
(él/ella/usted)	diga
(nosotros/as)	digamos
(vosotros/as)	digáis
(ellos/ellas/ustedes)	digan

PRETERITE

(yo)	dije
(tú)	dijiste
(él/ella/usted)	dijo
(nosotros/as)	dijimos
(vosotros/as)	dijisteis
(ellos/ellas/ustedes)	dijeron

IMPERFECT

(yo)	decía
(tú)	decías
(él/ella/usted)	decía
(nosotros/as)	decíamos
(vosotros/as)	decíais
(ellos/ellas/ustedes)	decían

FUTURE

(yo)	diré
(tú)	dirás
(él/ella/usted)	dirá
(nosotros/as)	diremos
(vosotros/as)	diréis
(ellos/ellas/ustedes)	dirán

CONDITIONAL

(yo)	diría
(tú)	dirías
(él/ella/usted)	diría
(nosotros/as)	diríamos
(vosotros/as)	diríais
(ellos/ellas/ustedes)	dirían

IMPERATIVE

di / decid

PAST PARTICIPLE

dicho

GERUND

diciendo

EXAMPLE PHRASES

Pero ¿qué **dices**? *What are you saying?*
Me lo **dijo** ayer. *He told me yesterday.*
¿Te **ha dicho** lo de la boda? *Has he told you about the wedding?*

PRESENT

(yo)	dirijo
(tú)	diriges
(él/ella/usted)	dirige
(nosotros/as)	dirigimos
(vosotros/as)	dirigís
(ellos/ellas/ustedes)	dirigen

PRESENT SUBJUNCTIVE

(yo)	dirija
(tú)	dirijas
(él/ella/usted)	dirija
(nosotros/as)	dirijamos
(vosotros/as)	dirijáis
(ellos/ellas/ustedes)	dirijan

PRETERITE

(yo)	dirigí
(tú)	dirigiste
(él/ella/usted)	dirigió
(nosotros/as)	dirigimos
(vosotros/as)	dirigisteis
(ellos/ellas/ustedes)	dirigieron

IMPERFECT

(yo)	dirigía
(tú)	dirigías
(él/ella/usted)	dirigía
(nosotros/as)	dirigíamos
(vosotros/as)	dirigíais
(ellos/ellas/ustedes)	dirigían

FUTURE

(yo)	dirigiré
(tú)	dirigirás
(él/ella/usted)	dirigirá
(nosotros/as)	dirigiremos
(vosotros/as)	dirigiréis
(ellos/ellas/ustedes)	dirigirán

CONDITIONAL

(yo)	dirigiría
(tú)	dirigirías
(él/ella/usted)	dirigiría
(nosotros/as)	dirigiríamos
(vosotros/as)	dirigiríais
(ellos/ellas/ustedes)	dirigirían

IMPERATIVE

dirige / dirigid

PAST PARTICIPLE

dirigido

GERUND

dirigiendo

--- EXAMPLE PHRASES ---

Dirijo esta empresa desde hace dos años.
Hace días que no me **dirige** la palabra.
Se dirigía a la parada del autobús.

I've been running this company for two years.
He hasn't spoken to me for days.
He was making his way to the bus stop.

Table
18

dormir *to sleep*

PRESENT

(yo)	duermo
(tú)	duermes
(él/ella/usted)	duerme
(nosotros/as)	dormimos
(vosotros/as)	dormís
(ellos/ellas/ustedes)	duermen

PRESENT SUBJUNCTIVE

(yo)	duerma
(tú)	duermas
(él/ella/usted)	duerma
(nosotros/as)	durmamos
(vosotros/as)	durmáis
(ellos/ellas/ustedes)	duerman

PRETERITE

(yo)	dormí
(tú)	dormiste
(él/ella/usted)	durmió
(nosotros/as)	dormimos
(vosotros/as)	dormisteis
(ellos/ellas/ustedes)	durmieron

IMPERFECT

(yo)	dormía
(tú)	dormías
(él/ella/usted)	dormía
(nosotros/as)	dormíamos
(vosotros/as)	dormíais
(ellos/ellas/ustedes)	dormían

FUTURE

(yo)	dormiré
(tú)	dormirás
(él/ella/usted)	dormirá
(nosotros/as)	dormiremos
(vosotros/as)	dormiréis
(ellos/ellas/ustedes)	dormirán

CONDITIONAL

(yo)	dormiría
(tú)	dormirías
(él/ella/usted)	dormiría
(nosotros/as)	dormiríamos
(vosotros/as)	dormiríais
(ellos/ellas/ustedes)	dormirían

IMPERATIVE
duerme / dormid

PAST PARTICIPLE
dormido

GERUND
durmiendo

EXAMPLE PHRASES

No **duermo** muy bien. — *I don't sleep very well.*
Nos dormimos en el cine. — *We fell asleep at the cinema.*
Durmió durante doce horas. — *He slept for twelve hours.*

PRESENT

(yo)	elijo
(tú)	eliges
(él/ella/usted)	elige
(nosotros/as)	elegimos
(vosotros/as)	elegís
(ellos/ellas/ustedes)	eligen

PRESENT SUBJUNCTIVE

(yo)	elija
(tú)	elijas
(él/ella/usted)	elija
(nosotros/as)	elijamos
(vosotros/as)	elijáis
(ellos/ellas/ustedes)	elijan

PRETERITE

(yo)	elegí
(tú)	elegiste
(él/ella/usted)	eligió
(nosotros/as)	elegimos
(vosotros/as)	elegisteis
(ellos/ellas/ustedes)	eligieron

IMPERFECT

(yo)	elegía
(tú)	elegías
(él/ella/usted)	elegía
(nosotros/as)	elegíamos
(vosotros/as)	elegíais
(ellos/ellas/ustedes)	elegían

FUTURE

(yo)	elegiré
(tú)	elegirás
(él/ella/usted)	elegirá
(nosotros/as)	elegiremos
(vosotros/as)	elegiréis
(ellos/ellas/ustedes)	elegirán

CONDITIONAL

(yo)	elegiría
(tú)	elegirías
(él/ella/usted)	elegiría
(nosotros/as)	elegiríamos
(vosotros/as)	elegiríais
(ellos/ellas/ustedes)	elegirían

IMPERATIVE

elige / elegid

PAST PARTICIPLE

elegido

GERUND

eligiendo

--- EXAMPLE PHRASES ---

Nosotros no **elegimos** a nuestros padres, ni ellos nos **eligen** a nosotros.

We don't choose our parents and neither do they choose us.

Creo que **ha elegido** bien.

I think he's made a good choice.

No lo **eligieron** ellos.

They didn't choose it.

Table
20

empezar *to start, to begin*

PRESENT

(yo)	empiezo
(tú)	empiezas
(él/ella/usted)	empieza
(nosotros/as)	empezamos
(vosotros/as)	empezáis
(ellos/ellas/ustedes)	empiezan

PRESENT SUBJUNCTIVE

(yo)	empiece
(tú)	empieces
(él/ella/usted)	empiece
(nosotros/as)	empecemos
(vosotros/as)	empecéis
(ellos/ellas/ustedes)	empiecen

PRETERITE

(yo)	empecé
(tú)	empezaste
(él/ella/usted)	empezó
(nosotros/as)	empezamos
(vosotros/as)	empezasteis
(ellos/ellas/ustedes)	empezaron

IMPERFECT

(yo)	empezaba
(tú)	empezabas
(él/ella/usted)	empezaba
(nosotros/as)	empezábamos
(vosotros/as)	empezabais
(ellos/ellas/ustedes)	empezaban

FUTURE

(yo)	empezaré
(tú)	empezarás
(él/ella/usted)	empezará
(nosotros/as)	empezaremos
(vosotros/as)	empezaréis
(ellos/ellas/ustedes)	empezarán

CONDITIONAL

(yo)	empezaría
(tú)	empezarías
(él/ella/usted)	empezaría
(nosotros/as)	empezaríamos
(vosotros/as)	empezaríais
(ellos/ellas/ustedes)	empezarían

IMPERATIVE

empieza / empezad

PAST PARTICIPLE

empezado

GERUND

empezando

EXAMPLE PHRASES

Empieza por aquí.

¿Cuándo **empiezas** a trabajar en el sitio nuevo?

La semana que viene **empezaremos** un curso nuevo.

Start here.

When do you start work at the new place?

We'll start a new course next week.

PRESENT

(yo)	entiendo
(tú)	entiendes
(él/ella/usted)	entiende
(nosotros/as)	entendemos
(vosotros/as)	entendéis
(ellos/ellas/ustedes)	entienden

PRESENT SUBJUNCTIVE

(yo)	entienda
(tú)	entiendas
(él/ella/usted)	entienda
(nosotros/as)	entendamos
(vosotros/as)	entendáis
(ellos/ellas/ustedes)	entiendan

PRETERITE

(yo)	entendí
(tú)	entendiste
(él/ella/usted)	entendió
(nosotros/as)	entendimos
(vosotros/as)	entendisteis
(ellos/ellas/ustedes)	entendieron

IMPERFECT

(yo)	entendía
(tú)	entendías
(él/ella/usted)	entendía
(nosotros/as)	entendíamos
(vosotros/as)	entendíais
(ellos/ellas/ustedes)	entendían

FUTURE

(yo)	entenderé
(tú)	entenderás
(él/ella/usted)	entenderá
(nosotros/as)	entenderemos
(vosotros/as)	entenderéis
(ellos/ellas/ustedes)	entenderán

CONDITIONAL

(yo)	entendería
(tú)	entenderías
(él/ella/usted)	entendería
(nosotros/as)	entenderíamos
(vosotros/as)	entenderíais
(ellos/ellas/ustedes)	entenderían

IMPERATIVE

entiende / entended

PAST PARTICIPLE

entendido

GERUND

entendiendo

--- EXAMPLE PHRASES ---

No lo **entiendo**.
¿**Entendiste** lo que dijo?
Con el tiempo lo **entenderás**.

I don't understand.
Did you understand what she said?
You'll understand one day.

Table
22

enviar _to send_

PRESENT

(yo)	envío
(tú)	envías
(él/ella/usted)	envía
(nosotros/as)	enviamos
(vosotros/as)	enviáis
(ellos/ellas/ustedes)	envían

PRESENT SUBJUNCTIVE

(yo)	envíe
(tú)	envíes
(él/ella/usted)	envíe
(nosotros/as)	enviemos
(vosotros/as)	enviéis
(ellos/ellas/ustedes)	envíen

PRETERITE

(yo)	envié
(tú)	enviaste
(él/ella/usted)	envió
(nosotros/as)	enviamos
(vosotros/as)	enviasteis
(ellos/ellas/ustedes)	enviaron

IMPERFECT

(yo)	enviaba
(tú)	enviabas
(él/ella/usted)	enviaba
(nosotros/as)	enviábamos
(vosotros/as)	enviabais
(ellos/ellas/ustedes)	enviaban

FUTURE

(yo)	enviaré
(tú)	enviarás
(él/ella/usted)	enviará
(nosotros/as)	enviaremos
(vosotros/as)	enviaréis
(ellos/ellas/ustedes)	enviarán

CONDITIONAL

(yo)	enviaría
(tú)	enviarías
(él/ella/usted)	enviaría
(nosotros/as)	enviaríamos
(vosotros/as)	enviaríais
(ellos/ellas/ustedes)	enviarían

IMPERATIVE
envía / enviad

PAST PARTICIPLE
enviado

GERUND
enviando

--- EXAMPLE PHRASES ---

Envíe todos sus datos personales. _Send all your personal details._
La han **enviado** a Guatemala. _They've sent her to Guatemala._
Nos **enviarán** más información. _They'll send us further information._

PRESENT

(yo)	estoy
(tú)	estás
(él/ella/usted)	está
(nosotros/as)	estamos
(vosotros/as)	estáis
(ellos/ellas/ustedes)	están

PRESENT SUBJUNCTIVE

(yo)	esté
(tú)	estés
(él/ella/usted)	esté
(nosotros/as)	estemos
(vosotros/as)	estéis
(ellos/ellas/ustedes)	estén

PRETERITE

(yo)	estuve
(tú)	estuviste
(él/ella/usted)	estuvo
(nosotros/as)	estuvimos
(vosotros/as)	estuvisteis
(ellos/ellas/ustedes)	estuvieron

IMPERFECT

(yo)	estaba
(tú)	estabas
(él/ella/usted)	estaba
(nosotros/as)	estábamos
(vosotros/as)	estabais
(ellos/ellas/ustedes)	estaban

FUTURE

(yo)	estaré
(tú)	estarás
(él/ella/usted)	estará
(nosotros/as)	estaremos
(vosotros/as)	estaréis
(ellos/ellas/ustedes)	estarán

CONDITIONAL

(yo)	estaría
(tú)	estarías
(él/ella/usted)	estaría
(nosotros/as)	estaríamos
(vosotros/as)	estaríais
(ellos/ellas/ustedes)	estarían

IMPERATIVE

está / estad

PAST PARTICIPLE

estado

GERUND

estando

--- EXAMPLE PHRASES ---

Estoy cansado.
Estuvimos en casa de mis padres.
¿A qué hora **estarás** en casa?

I'm tired.
We went to my parents' house.
What time will you be home?

Table
24

freír *to fry*

PRESENT

(yo)	frío
(tú)	fríes
(él/ella/usted)	fríe
(nosotros/as)	freímos
(vosotros/as)	freís
(ellos/ellas/ustedes)	fríen

PRESENT SUBJUNCTIVE

(yo)	fría
(tú)	frías
(él/ella/usted)	fría
(nosotros/as)	friamos
(vosotros/as)	friais
(ellos/ellas/ustedes)	frían

PRETERITE

(yo)	freí
(tú)	freíste
(él/ella/usted)	frio
(nosotros/as)	freímos
(vosotros/as)	freísteis
(ellos/ellas/ustedes)	frieron

IMPERFECT

(yo)	freía
(tú)	freías
(él/ella/usted)	freía
(nosotros/as)	freíamos
(vosotros/as)	freíais
(ellos/ellas/ustedes)	freían

FUTURE

(yo)	freiré
(tú)	freirás
(él/ella/usted)	freirá
(nosotros/as)	freiremos
(vosotros/as)	freiréis
(ellos/ellas/ustedes)	freirán

CONDITIONAL

(yo)	freiría
(tú)	freirías
(él/ella/usted)	freiría
(nosotros/as)	freiríamos
(vosotros/as)	freiríais
(ellos/ellas/ustedes)	freirían

IMPERATIVE

fríe / freíd

PAST PARTICIPLE

frito

GERUND

friendo

EXAMPLE PHRASES

Fríelo en esta sartén.
He frito el pescado.
Nos freíamos de calor.

Fry it in this pan.
I've fried the fish.
We were roasting in the heat.

PRESENT

(yo)	he
(tú)	has
(él/ella/usted)	ha
(nosotros/as)	hemos
(vosotros/as)	habéis
(ellos/ellas/ustedes)	han

PRESENT SUBJUNCTIVE

(yo)	haya
(tú)	hayas
(él/ella/usted)	haya
(nosotros/as)	hayamos
(vosotros/as)	hayáis
(ellos/ellas/ustedes)	hayan

PRETERITE

(yo)	hube
(tú)	hubiste
(él/ella/usted)	hubo
(nosotros/as)	hubimos
(vosotros/as)	hubisteis
(ellos/ellas/ustedes)	hubieron

IMPERFECT

(yo)	había
(tú)	habías
(él/ella/usted)	había
(nosotros/as)	habíamos
(vosotros/as)	habíais
(ellos/ellas/ustedes)	habían

FUTURE

(yo)	habré
(tú)	habrás
(él/ella/usted)	habrá
(nosotros/as)	habremos
(vosotros/as)	habréis
(ellos/ellas/ustedes)	habrán

CONDITIONAL

(yo)	habría
(tú)	habrías
(él/ella/usted)	habría
(nosotros/as)	habríamos
(vosotros/as)	habríais
(ellos/ellas/ustedes)	habrían

IMPERATIVE
not used

PAST PARTICIPLE
habido

GERUND
habiendo

──────── EXAMPLE PHRASES ────────

¿**Has visto** eso?
Ya **hemos ido** a ver esa película.
Eso nunca **había pasado** antes.

Did you see that?
We've already been to see that film.
That had never happened before.

Table
26

hablar *to speak, to talk*

PRESENT

(yo)	hablo
(tú)	hablas
(él/ella/usted)	habla
(nosotros/as)	hablamos
(vosotros/as)	habláis
(ellos/ellas/ustedes)	hablan

PRESENT SUBJUNCTIVE

(yo)	hable
(tú)	hables
(él/ella/usted)	hable
(nosotros/as)	hablemos
(vosotros/as)	habléis
(ellos/ellas/ustedes)	hablen

PRETERITE

(yo)	hablé
(tú)	hablaste
(él/ella/usted)	habló
(nosotros/as)	hablamos
(vosotros/as)	hablasteis
(ellos/ellas/ustedes)	hablaron

IMPERFECT

(yo)	hablaba
(tú)	hablabas
(él/ella/usted)	hablaba
(nosotros/as)	hablábamos
(vosotros/as)	hablabais
(ellos/ellas/ustedes)	hablaban

FUTURE

(yo)	hablaré
(tú)	hablarás
(él/ella/usted)	hablará
(nosotros/as)	hablaremos
(vosotros/as)	hablaréis
(ellos/ellas/ustedes)	hablarán

CONDITIONAL

(yo)	hablaría
(tú)	hablarías
(él/ella/usted)	hablaría
(nosotros/as)	hablaríamos
(vosotros/as)	hablaríais
(ellos/ellas/ustedes)	hablarían

IMPERATIVE

habla / hablad

PAST PARTICIPLE

hablado

GERUND

hablando

EXAMPLE PHRASES

Hoy **he hablado** con mi hermana.	I've spoken to my sister today.
No **hables** tan alto.	Don't talk so loud.
No **se hablan**.	They don't talk to each other.

PRESENT

(yo)	hago
(tú)	haces
(él/ella/usted)	hace
(nosotros/as)	hacemos
(vosotros/as)	hacéis
(ellos/ellas/ustedes)	hacen

PRESENT SUBJUNCTIVE

(yo)	haga
(tú)	hagas
(él/ella/usted)	haga
(nosotros/as)	hagamos
(vosotros/as)	hagáis
(ellos/ellas/ustedes)	hagan

PRETERITE

(yo)	hice
(tú)	hiciste
(él/ella/usted)	hizo
(nosotros/as)	hicimos
(vosotros/as)	hicisteis
(ellos/ellas/ustedes)	hicieron

IMPERFECT

(yo)	hacía
(tú)	hacías
(él/ella/usted)	hacía
(nosotros/as)	hacíamos
(vosotros/as)	hacíais
(ellos/ellas/ustedes)	hacían

FUTURE

(yo)	haré
(tú)	harás
(él/ella/usted)	hará
(nosotros/as)	haremos
(vosotros/as)	haréis
(ellos/ellas/ustedes)	harán

CONDITIONAL

(yo)	haría
(tú)	harías
(él/ella/usted)	haría
(nosotros/as)	haríamos
(vosotros/as)	haríais
(ellos/ellas/ustedes)	harían

IMPERATIVE

haz / haced

PAST PARTICIPLE

hecho

GERUND

haciendo

--- EXAMPLE PHRASES ---

Lo **haré** yo mismo.	*I'll do it myself.*
¿Quién **hizo** eso?	*Who did that?*
Quieres que **haga** las camas?	*Do you want me to make the beds?*

Table
28

ir *to go*

PRESENT

(yo)	voy
(tú)	vas
(él/ella/usted)	va
(nosotros/as)	vamos
(vosotros/as)	vais
(ellos/ellas/ustedes)	van

PRESENT SUBJUNCTIVE

(yo)	vaya
(tú)	vayas
(él/ella/usted)	vaya
(nosotros/as)	vayamos
(vosotros/as)	vayáis
(ellos/ellas/ustedes)	vayan

PRETERITE

(yo)	fui
(tú)	fuiste
(él/ella/usted)	fue
(nosotros/as)	fuimos
(vosotros/as)	fuisteis
(ellos/ellas/ustedes)	fueron

IMPERFECT

(yo)	iba
(tú)	ibas
(él/ella/usted)	iba
(nosotros/as)	íbamos
(vosotros/as)	ibais
(ellos/ellas/ustedes)	iban

FUTURE

(yo)	iré
(tú)	irás
(él/ella/usted)	irá
(nosotros/as)	iremos
(vosotros/as)	iréis
(ellos/ellas/ustedes)	irán

CONDITIONAL

(yo)	iría
(tú)	irías
(él/ella/usted)	iría
(nosotros/as)	iríamos
(vosotros/as)	iríais
(ellos/ellas/ustedes)	irían

IMPERATIVE

ve / id

PAST PARTICIPLE

ido

GERUND

yendo

--- EXAMPLE PHRASES ---

¿**Vamos** a comer al campo?
El domingo **iré** a Edimburgo.
Yo no **voy** con ellos.

Shall we have a picnic in the country?
I'll go to Edinburgh on Sunday.
I'm not going with them.

PRESENT

(yo)	juego
(tú)	juegas
(él/ella/usted)	juega
(nosotros/as)	jugamos
(vosotros/as)	jugáis
(ellos/ellas/ustedes)	juegan

PRESENT SUBJUNCTIVE

(yo)	juegue
(tú)	juegues
(él/ella/usted)	juegue
(nosotros/as)	juguemos
(vosotros/as)	juguéis
(ellos/ellas/ustedes)	jueguen

PRETERITE

(yo)	jugué
(tú)	jugaste
(él/ella/usted)	jugó
(nosotros/as)	jugamos
(vosotros/as)	jugasteis
(ellos/ellas/ustedes)	jugaron

IMPERFECT

(yo)	jugaba
(tú)	jugabas
(él/ella/usted)	jugaba
(nosotros/as)	jugábamos
(vosotros/as)	jugabais
(ellos/ellas/ustedes)	jugaban

FUTURE

(yo)	jugaré
(tú)	jugarás
(él/ella/usted)	jugará
(nosotros/as)	jugaremos
(vosotros/as)	jugaréis
(ellos/ellas/ustedes)	jugarán

CONDITIONAL

(yo)	jugaría
(tú)	jugarías
(él/ella/usted)	jugaría
(nosotros/as)	jugaríamos
(vosotros/as)	jugaríais
(ellos/ellas/ustedes)	jugarían

IMPERATIVE

juega / jugad

GERUND

jugando

PAST PARTICIPLE

jugado

———————————— EXAMPLE PHRASES ————————————

Juego al fútbol todos los domingos.

I play football every Sunday.

Están jugando en el jardín.

They're playing in the garden.

Jugarán contra el Real Madrid.

They'll play Real Madrid.

Table
30

lavarse *to wash oneself*

PRESENT

(yo)	me lavo
(tú)	te lavas
(él/ella/usted)	se lava
(nosotros/as)	nos lavamos
(vosotros/as)	os laváis
(ellos/ellas/ustedes)	se lavan

PRESENT SUBJUNCTIVE

(yo)	me lave
(tú)	te laves
(él/ella/usted)	se lave
(nosotros/as)	nos lavemos
(vosotros/as)	os lavéis
(ellos/ellas/ustedes)	se laven

PRETERITE

(yo)	me lavé
(tú)	te lavaste
(él/ella/usted)	se lavó
(nosotros/as)	nos lavamos
(vosotros/as)	os lavasteis
(ellos/ellas/ustedes)	se lavaron

IMPERFECT

(yo)	me lavaba
(tú)	te lavabas
(él/ella/usted)	se lavaba
(nosotros/as)	nos lavábamos
(vosotros/as)	os lavabais
(ellos/ellas/ustedes)	se lavaban

FUTURE

(yo)	me lavaré
(tú)	te lavarás
(él/ella/usted)	se lavará
(nosotros/as)	nos lavaremos
(vosotros/as)	os lavaréis
(ellos/ellas/ustedes)	se lavarán

CONDITIONAL

(yo)	me lavaría
(tú)	te lavarías
(él/ella/usted)	se lavaría
(nosotros/as)	nos lavaríamos
(vosotros/as)	os lavaríais
(ellos/ellas/ustedes)	se lavarían

IMPERATIVE
lávate / lavaos

PAST PARTICIPLE
lavado

GERUND
lavándose

EXAMPLE PHRASES

Se lava todos los días.   *He washes every day.*
Ayer **me lavé** el pelo.   *I washed my hair yesterday.*
Nos lavaremos con agua fría. *We'll wash in cold water.*

PRESENT

(yo)	leo
(tú)	lees
(él/ella/usted)	lee
(nosotros/as)	leemos
(vosotros/as)	leéis
(ellos/ellas/ustedes)	leen

PRESENT SUBJUNCTIVE

(yo)	lea
(tú)	leas
(él/ella/usted)	lea
(nosotros/as)	leamos
(vosotros/as)	leáis
(ellos/ellas/ustedes)	lean

PRETERITE

(yo)	leí
(tú)	leíste
(él/ella/usted)	leyó
(nosotros/as)	leímos
(vosotros/as)	leísteis
(ellos/ellas/ustedes)	leyeron

IMPERFECT

(yo)	leía
(tú)	leías
(él/ella/usted)	leía
(nosotros/as)	leíamos
(vosotros/as)	leíais
(ellos/ellas/ustedes)	leían

FUTURE

(yo)	leeré
(tú)	leerás
(él/ella/usted)	leerá
(nosotros/as)	leeremos
(vosotros/as)	leeréis
(ellos/ellas/ustedes)	leerán

CONDITIONAL

(yo)	leería
(tú)	leerías
(él/ella/usted)	leería
(nosotros/as)	leeríamos
(vosotros/as)	leeríais
(ellos/ellas/ustedes)	leerían

IMPERATIVE

lee / leed

PAST PARTICIPLE

leído

GERUND

leyendo

— EXAMPLE PHRASES —

Hace mucho tiempo que no **leo**.	*I haven't read anything for ages.*
¿**Has leído** esta novela?	*Have you read this novel?*
Lo **leí** hace tiempo.	*I read it a while ago.*

Table
32

llover *to rain*

PRESENT		PRESENT SUBJUNCTIVE	
	llueve		llueva

PRETERITE		IMPERFECT	
	llovió		llovía

FUTURE		CONDITIONAL	
	lloverá		llovería

IMPERATIVE	PAST PARTICIPLE	
not used		llovido

GERUND
lloviendo

--- EXAMPLE PHRASES ---

Está lloviendo.	*It's raining.*
Llovió sin parar.	*It rained non-stop.*
Hace semanas que no **llueve**.	*It hasn't rained for weeks.*

PRESENT

(yo)	muero
(tú)	mueres
(él/ella/usted)	muere
(nosotros/as)	morimos
(vosotros/as)	morís
(ellos/ellas/ustedes)	mueren

PRESENT SUBJUNCTIVE

(yo)	muera
(tú)	mueras
(él/ella/usted)	muera
(nosotros/as)	muramos
(vosotros/as)	muráis
(ellos/ellas/ustedes)	mueran

PRETERITE

(yo)	morí
(tú)	moriste
(él/ella/usted)	murió
(nosotros/as)	morimos
(vosotros/as)	moristeis
(ellos/ellas/ustedes)	murieron

IMPERFECT

(yo)	moría
(tú)	morías
(él/ella/usted)	moría
(nosotros/as)	moríamos
(vosotros/as)	moríais
(ellos/ellas/ustedes)	morían

FUTURE

(yo)	moriré
(tú)	morirás
(él/ella/usted)	morirá
(nosotros/as)	moriremos
(vosotros/as)	moriréis
(ellos/ellas/ustedes)	morirán

CONDITIONAL

(yo)	moriría
(tú)	morirías
(él/ella/usted)	moriría
(nosotros/as)	moriríamos
(vosotros/as)	moriríais
(ellos/ellas/ustedes)	morirían

IMPERATIVE

muere / morid

PAST PARTICIPLE

muerto

GERUND

muriendo

EXAMPLE PHRASES

Murió a las cinco de la madrugada.
Cuando **me muera**...
Se le **ha muerto** el gato.

He died at five in the morning.
When I die...
His cat has died.

Table
34

mover *to move*

PRESENT		PRESENT SUBJUNCTIVE	
(yo)	muevo	(yo)	mueva
(tú)	mueves	(tú)	muevas
(él/ella/usted)	mueve	(él/ella/usted)	mueva
(nosotros/as)	movemos	(nosotros/as)	movamos
(vosotros/as)	movéis	(vosotros/as)	mováis
(ellos/ellas/ustedes)	mueven	(ellos/ellas/ustedes)	muevan

PRETERITE		IMPERFECT	
(yo)	moví	(yo)	movía
(tú)	moviste	(tú)	movías
(él/ella/usted)	movió	(él/ella/usted)	movía
(nosotros/as)	movimos	(nosotros/as)	movíamos
(vosotros/as)	movisteis	(vosotros/as)	movíais
(ellos/ellas/ustedes)	movieron	(ellos/ellas/ustedes)	movían

FUTURE		CONDITIONAL	
(yo)	moveré	(yo)	movería
(tú)	moverás	(tú)	moverías
(él/ella/usted)	moverá	(él/ella/usted)	movería
(nosotros/as)	moveremos	(nosotros/as)	moveríamos
(vosotros/as)	moveréis	(vosotros/as)	moveríais
(ellos/ellas/ustedes)	moverán	(ellos/ellas/ustedes)	moverían

IMPERATIVE
mueve / moved

PAST PARTICIPLE
movido

GERUND
moviendo

————————— EXAMPLE PHRASES —————————

Mueve la mesa hacia la derecha. *Move the table over to the right.*
Se está moviendo. *It's moving.*
No **se movieron** de casa. *They didn't leave the house.*

PRESENT

(yo)	niego
(tú)	niegas
(él/ella/usted)	niega
(nosotros/as)	negamos
(vosotros/as)	negáis
(ellos/ellas/ustedes)	niegan

PRESENT SUBJUNCTIVE

(yo)	niegue
(tú)	niegues
(él/ella/usted)	niegue
(nosotros/as)	neguemos
(vosotros/as)	neguéis
(ellos/ellas/ustedes)	nieguen

PRETERITE

(yo)	negué
(tú)	negaste
(él/ella/usted)	negó
(nosotros/as)	negamos
(vosotros/as)	negasteis
(ellos/ellas/ustedes)	negaron

IMPERFECT

(yo)	negaba
(tú)	negabas
(él/ella/usted)	negaba
(nosotros/as)	negábamos
(vosotros/as)	negabais
(ellos/ellas/ustedes)	negaban

FUTURE

(yo)	negaré
(tú)	negarás
(él/ella/usted)	negará
(nosotros/as)	negaremos
(vosotros/as)	negaréis
(ellos/ellas/ustedes)	negarán

CONDITIONAL

(yo)	negaría
(tú)	negarías
(él/ella/usted)	negaría
(nosotros/as)	negaríamos
(vosotros/as)	negaríais
(ellos/ellas/ustedes)	negarían

IMPERATIVE

niega / negad

PAST PARTICIPLE

negado

GERUND

negando

--- EXAMPLE PHRASES ---

No lo **niegues**.
Se negó a venir con nosotros.
No me **negarás** que es barato.

Don't deny it.
She refused to come with us.
You can't say it's not cheap.

Table
36

oír _to hear_

PRESENT		PRESENT SUBJUNCTIVE	
(yo)	oigo	(yo)	oiga
(tú)	oyes	(tú)	oigas
(él/ella/usted)	oye	(él/ella/usted)	oiga
(nosotros/as)	oímos	(nosotros/as)	oigamos
(vosotros/as)	oís	(vosotros/as)	oigáis
(ellos/ellas/ustedes)	oyen	(ellos/ellas/ustedes)	oigan

PRETERITE		IMPERFECT	
(yo)	oí	(yo)	oía
(tú)	oíste	(tú)	oías
(él/ella/usted)	oyó	(él/ella/usted)	oía
(nosotros/as)	oímos	(nosotros/as)	oíamos
(vosotros/as)	oísteis	(vosotros/as)	oíais
(ellos/ellas/ustedes)	oyeron	(ellos/ellas/ustedes)	oían

FUTURE		CONDITIONAL	
(yo)	oiré	(yo)	oiría
(tú)	oirás	(tú)	oirías
(él/ella/usted)	oirá	(él/ella/usted)	oiría
(nosotros/as)	oiremos	(nosotros/as)	oiríamos
(vosotros/as)	oiréis	(vosotros/as)	oiríais
(ellos/ellas/ustedes)	oirán	(ellos/ellas/ustedes)	oirían

IMPERATIVE
oye / oíd

GERUND
oyendo

PAST PARTICIPLE
oído

--------- EXAMPLE PHRASES ---------

No **oigo** nada.

Si no **oyes** bien, ve al médico.

¿Has **oído** eso?

I can't hear anything.

If you can't hear properly, go and see the doctor.

Did you hear that?

PRESENT

(yo)	huelo
(tú)	hueles
(él/ella/usted)	huele
(nosotros/as)	olemos
(vosotros/as)	oléis
(ellos/ellas/ustedes)	huelen

PRESENT SUBJUNCTIVE

(yo)	huela
(tú)	huelas
(él/ella/usted)	huela
(nosotros/as)	olamos
(vosotros/as)	oláis
(ellos/ellas/ustedes)	huelan

PRETERITE

(yo)	olí
(tú)	oliste
(él/ella/usted)	olió
(nosotros/as)	olimos
(vosotros/as)	olisteis
(ellos/ellas/ustedes)	olieron

IMPERFECT

(yo)	olía
(tú)	olías
(él/ella/usted)	olía
(nosotros/as)	olíamos
(vosotros/as)	olíais
(ellos/ellas/ustedes)	olían

FUTURE

(yo)	oleré
(tú)	olerás
(él/ella/usted)	olerá
(nosotros/as)	oleremos
(vosotros/as)	oleréis
(ellos/ellas/ustedes)	olerán

CONDITIONAL

(yo)	olería
(tú)	olerías
(él/ella/usted)	olería
(nosotros/as)	oleríamos
(vosotros/as)	oleríais
(ellos/ellas/ustedes)	olerían

IMPERATIVE

huele / oled

PAST PARTICIPLE

olido

GERUND

oliendo

─────── EXAMPLE PHRASES ───────

Huele a pescado.	It smells of fish.
Olía muy bien.	It smelled really nice.
Con esto ya no **olerá**.	This will take the smell away.

Table
38

pagar *to pay*

PRESENT

(yo)	pago
(tú)	pagas
(él/ella/usted)	paga
(nosotros/as)	pagamos
(vosotros/as)	pagáis
(ellos/ellas/ustedes)	pagan

PRESENT SUBJUNCTIVE

(yo)	pague
(tú)	pagues
(él/ella/usted)	pague
(nosotros/as)	paguemos
(vosotros/as)	paguéis
(ellos/ellas/ustedes)	paguen

PRETERITE

(yo)	pagué
(tú)	pagaste
(él/ella/usted)	pagó
(nosotros/as)	pagamos
(vosotros/as)	pagasteis
(ellos/ellas/ustedes)	pagaron

IMPERFECT

(yo)	pagaba
(tú)	pagabas
(él/ella/usted)	pagaba
(nosotros/as)	pagábamos
(vosotros/as)	pagabais
(ellos/ellas/ustedes)	pagaban

FUTURE

(yo)	pagaré
(tú)	pagarás
(él/ella/usted)	pagará
(nosotros/as)	pagaremos
(vosotros/as)	pagaréis
(ellos/ellas/ustedes)	pagarán

CONDITIONAL

(yo)	pagaría
(tú)	pagarías
(él/ella/usted)	pagaría
(nosotros/as)	pagaríamos
(vosotros/as)	pagaríais
(ellos/ellas/ustedes)	pagarían

IMPERATIVE

paga / pagad

PAST PARTICIPLE

pagado

GERUND

pagando

--------- EXAMPLE PHRASES ---------

¿Cuánto te **pagan** al mes? *How much do they pay you a month?*
Lo **pagué** en efectivo. *I paid for it in cash.*
Yo te **pagaré** la entrada. *I'll pay for your ticket.*

PRESENT

(yo)	pido
(tú)	pides
(él/ella/usted)	pide
(nosotros/as)	pedimos
(vosotros/as)	pedís
(ellos/ellas/ustedes)	piden

PRESENT SUBJUNCTIVE

(yo)	pida
(tú)	pidas
(él/ella/usted)	pida
(nosotros/as)	pidamos
(vosotros/as)	pidáis
(ellos/ellas/ustedes)	pidan

PRETERITE

(yo)	pedí
(tú)	pediste
(él/ella/usted)	pidió
(nosotros/as)	pedimos
(vosotros/as)	pedisteis
(ellos/ellas/ustedes)	pidieron

IMPERFECT

(yo)	pedía
(tú)	pedías
(él/ella/usted)	pedía
(nosotros/as)	pedíamos
(vosotros/as)	pedíais
(ellos/ellas/ustedes)	pedían

FUTURE

(yo)	pediré
(tú)	pedirás
(él/ella/usted)	pedirá
(nosotros/as)	pediremos
(vosotros/as)	pediréis
(ellos/ellas/ustedes)	pedirán

CONDITIONAL

(yo)	pediría
(tú)	pedirías
(él/ella/usted)	pediría
(nosotros/as)	pediríamos
(vosotros/as)	pediríais
(ellos/ellas/ustedes)	pedirían

IMPERATIVE

pide / pedid

PAST PARTICIPLE

pedido

GERUND

pidiendo

──────── EXAMPLE PHRASES ────────

No nos **pidieron** el pasaporte.
Hemos pedido dos cervezas.
Pídele el teléfono.

They didn't ask us for our passports.
We've ordered two beers.
Ask her for her telephone number.

Table
40

pensar *to think*

PRESENT

(yo)	pienso
(tú)	piensas
(él/ella/usted)	piensa
(nosotros/as)	pensamos
(vosotros/as)	pensáis
(ellos/ellas/ustedes)	piensan

PRESENT SUBJUNCTIVE

(yo)	piense
(tú)	pienses
(él/ella/usted)	piense
(nosotros/as)	pensemos
(vosotros/as)	penséis
(ellos/ellas/ustedes)	piensen

PRETERITE

(yo)	pensé
(tú)	pensaste
(él/ella/usted)	pensó
(nosotros/as)	pensamos
(vosotros/as)	pensasteis
(ellos/ellas/ustedes)	pensaron

IMPERFECT

(yo)	pensaba
(tú)	pensabas
(él/ella/usted)	pensaba
(nosotros/as)	pensábamos
(vosotros/as)	pensabais
(ellos/ellas/ustedes)	pensaban

FUTURE

(yo)	pensaré
(tú)	pensarás
(él/ella/usted)	pensará
(nosotros/as)	pensaremos
(vosotros/as)	pensaréis
(ellos/ellas/ustedes)	pensarán

CONDITIONAL

(yo)	pensaría
(tú)	pensarías
(él/ella/usted)	pensaría
(nosotros/as)	pensaríamos
(vosotros/as)	pensaríais
(ellos/ellas/ustedes)	pensarían

IMPERATIVE

piensa / pensad

PAST PARTICIPLE

pensado

GERUND

pensando

———————————— EXAMPLE PHRASES ————————————

No lo **pienses** más.

Está pensando en comprarse un piso.

Pensaba que vendrías.

Don't think any more about it.

He's thinking of buying a flat.

I thought you'd come.

PRESENT

(yo)	puedo
(tú)	puedes
(él/ella/usted)	puede
(nosotros/as)	podemos
(vosotros/as)	podéis
(ellos/ellas/ustedes)	pueden

PRESENT SUBJUNCTIVE

(yo)	pueda
(tú)	puedas
(él/ella/usted)	pueda
(nosotros/as)	podamos
(vosotros/as)	podáis
(ellos/ellas/ustedes)	puedan

PRETERITE

(yo)	pude
(tú)	pudiste
(él/ella/usted)	pudo
(nosotros/as)	pudimos
(vosotros/as)	pudisteis
(ellos/ellas/ustedes)	pudieron

IMPERFECT

(yo)	podía
(tú)	podías
(él/ella/usted)	podía
(nosotros/as)	podíamos
(vosotros/as)	podíais
(ellos/ellas/ustedes)	podían

FUTURE

(yo)	podré
(tú)	podrás
(él/ella/usted)	podrá
(nosotros/as)	podremos
(vosotros/as)	podréis
(ellos/ellas/ustedes)	podrán

CONDITIONAL

(yo)	podría
(tú)	podrías
(él/ella/usted)	podría
(nosotros/as)	podríamos
(vosotros/as)	podríais
(ellos/ellas/ustedes)	podrían

IMPERATIVE
puede / poded

PAST PARTICIPLE
podido

GERUND
pudiendo

--- EXAMPLE PHRASES ---

¿**Puedo** entrar? — Can I come in?
Puedes venir cuando quieras. — You can come when you like.
¿**Podrías** ayudarme? — Could you help me?

Table
42

poner *to put*

PRESENT

(yo)	pongo
(tú)	pones
(él/ella/usted)	pone
(nosotros/as)	ponemos
(vosotros/as)	ponéis
(ellos/ellas/ustedes)	ponen

PRESENT SUBJUNCTIVE

(yo)	ponga
(tú)	pongas
(él/ella/usted)	ponga
(nosotros/as)	pongamos
(vosotros/as)	pongáis
(ellos/ellas/ustedes)	pongan

PRETERITE

(yo)	puse
(tú)	pusiste
(él/ella/usted)	puso
(nosotros/as)	pusimos
(vosotros/as)	pusisteis
(ellos/ellas/ustedes)	pusieron

IMPERFECT

(yo)	ponía
(tú)	ponías
(él/ella/usted)	ponía
(nosotros/as)	poníamos
(vosotros/as)	poníais
(ellos/ellas/ustedes)	ponían

FUTURE

(yo)	pondré
(tú)	pondrás
(él/ella/usted)	pondrá
(nosotros/as)	pondremos
(vosotros/as)	pondréis
(ellos/ellas/ustedes)	pondrán

CONDITIONAL

(yo)	pondría
(tú)	pondrías
(él/ella/usted)	pondría
(nosotros/as)	pondríamos
(vosotros/as)	pondríais
(ellos/ellas/ustedes)	pondrían

IMPERATIVE

pon / poned

PAST PARTICIPLE

puesto

GERUND

poniendo

--- EXAMPLE PHRASES ---

Ponlo ahí encima.
Lo **pondré** aquí.
Todos **nos pusimos** de acuerdo.

Put it on there.
I'll put it here.
We all agreed.

PRESENT

(yo)	prohíbo
(tú)	prohíbes
(él/ella/usted)	prohíbe
(nosotros/as)	prohibimos
(vosotros/as)	prohibís
(ellos/ellas/ustedes)	prohíben

PRESENT SUBJUNCTIVE

(yo)	prohíba
(tú)	prohíbas
(él/ella/usted)	prohíba
(nosotros/as)	prohibamos
(vosotros/as)	prohibáis
(ellos/ellas/ustedes)	prohíban

PRETERITE

(yo)	prohibí
(tú)	prohibiste
(él/ella/usted)	prohibió
(nosotros/as)	prohibimos
(vosotros/as)	prohibisteis
(ellos/ellas/ustedes)	prohibieron

IMPERFECT

(yo)	prohibía
(tú)	prohibías
(él/ella/usted)	prohibía
(nosotros/as)	prohibíamos
(vosotros/as)	prohibíais
(ellos/ellas/ustedes)	prohibían

FUTURE

(yo)	prohibiré
(tú)	prohibirás
(él/ella/usted)	prohibirá
(nosotros/as)	prohibiremos
(vosotros/as)	prohibiréis
(ellos/ellas/ustedes)	prohibirán

CONDITIONAL

(yo)	prohibiría
(tú)	prohibirías
(él/ella/usted)	prohibiría
(nosotros/as)	prohibiríamos
(vosotros/as)	prohibiríais
(ellos/ellas/ustedes)	prohibirían

IMPERATIVE

prohíbe / prohibid

PAST PARTICIPLE

prohibido

GERUND

prohibiendo

--- EXAMPLE PHRASES ---

Le **prohibieron** la entrada en el bingo.
Han prohibido el acceso a la prensa.
Te **prohíbo** que me hables así.

She was not allowed into the bingo hall.
The press have been banned.
I won't have you talking to me like that!

Table
44

querer *to want*

PRESENT		PRESENT SUBJUNCTIVE	
(yo)	quiero	(yo)	quiera
(tú)	quieres	(tú)	quieras
(él/ella/usted)	quiere	(él/ella/usted)	quiera
(nosotros/as)	queremos	(nosotros/as)	queramos
(vosotros/as)	queréis	(vosotros/as)	queráis
(ellos/ellas/ustedes)	quieren	(ellos/ellas/ustedes)	quieran

PRETERITE		IMPERFECT	
(yo)	quise	(yo)	quería
(tú)	quisiste	(tú)	querías
(él/ella/usted)	quiso	(él/ella/usted)	quería
(nosotros/as)	quisimos	(nosotros/as)	queríamos
(vosotros/as)	quisisteis	(vosotros/as)	queríais
(ellos/ellas/ustedes)	quisieron	(ellos/ellas/ustedes)	querían

FUTURE		CONDITIONAL	
(yo)	querré	(yo)	querría
(tú)	querrás	(tú)	querrías
(él/ella/usted)	querrá	(él/ella/usted)	querría
(nosotros/as)	querremos	(nosotros/as)	querríamos
(vosotros/as)	querréis	(vosotros/as)	querríais
(ellos/ellas/ustedes)	querrán	(ellos/ellas/ustedes)	querrían

IMPERATIVE
quiere / quered

PAST PARTICIPLE
querido

GERUND
queriendo

———————————— EXAMPLE PHRASES ————————————

Te **quiero**.
Quisiera preguntar una cosa.
No **quería** decírmelo.

I love you.
I'd like to ask something.
She didn't want to tell me.

PRESENT

(yo)	río
(tú)	ríes
(él/ella/usted)	ríe
(nosotros/as)	reímos
(vosotros/as)	reís
(ellos/ellas/ustedes)	ríen

PRESENT SUBJUNCTIVE

(yo)	ría
(tú)	rías
(él/ella/usted)	ría
(nosotros/as)	riamos
(vosotros/as)	riais
(ellos/ellas/ustedes)	rían

PRETERITE

(yo)	reí
(tú)	reíste
(él/ella/usted)	rio
(nosotros/as)	reímos
(vosotros/as)	reísteis
(ellos/ellas/ustedes)	rieron

IMPERFECT

(yo)	reía
(tú)	reías
(él/ella/usted)	reía
(nosotros/as)	reíamos
(vosotros/as)	reíais
(ellos/ellas/ustedes)	reían

FUTURE

(yo)	reiré
(tú)	reirás
(él/ella/usted)	reirá
(nosotros/as)	reiremos
(vosotros/as)	reiréis
(ellos/ellas/ustedes)	reirán

CONDITIONAL

(yo)	reiría
(tú)	reirías
(él/ella/usted)	reiría
(nosotros/as)	reiríamos
(vosotros/as)	reiríais
(ellos/ellas/ustedes)	reirían

IMPERATIVE

ríe / reíd

GERUND

riendo

PAST PARTICIPLE

reído

=========== EXAMPLE PHRASES ===========

No **te rías** de mí.
Si **ríes** mucho te saldrán arrugas.
Se ríe de cualquier cosa.

Don't laugh at me.
If you laugh too much you'll get lines.
She laughs at anything.

Table
46

reñir *to tell off*

PRESENT

(yo)	riño
(tú)	riñes
(él/ella/usted)	riñe
(nosotros/as)	reñimos
(vosotros/as)	reñís
(ellos/ellas/ustedes)	riñen

PRESENT SUBJUNCTIVE

(yo)	riña
(tú)	riñas
(él/ella/usted)	riña
(nosotros/as)	riñamos
(vosotros/as)	riñáis
(ellos/ellas/ustedes)	riñan

PRETERITE

(yo)	reñí
(tú)	reñiste
(él/ella/usted)	riñó
(nosotros/as)	reñimos
(vosotros/as)	reñisteis
(ellos/ellas/ustedes)	riñeron

IMPERFECT

(yo)	reñía
(tú)	reñías
(él/ella/usted)	reñía
(nosotros/as)	reñíamos
(vosotros/as)	reñíais
(ellos/ellas/ustedes)	reñían

FUTURE

(yo)	reñiré
(tú)	reñirás
(él/ella/usted)	reñirá
(nosotros/as)	reñiremos
(vosotros/as)	reñiréis
(ellos/ellas/ustedes)	reñirán

CONDITIONAL

(yo)	reñiría
(tú)	reñirías
(él/ella/usted)	reñiría
(nosotros/as)	reñiríamos
(vosotros/as)	reñiríais
(ellos/ellas/ustedes)	reñirían

IMPERATIVE

riñe / reñid

PAST PARTICIPLE

reñido

GERUND

riñendo

--- EXAMPLE PHRASES ---

Les **riñó** por llegar tarde a casa.

She told them off for getting home late.

Nos **reñía** sin motivo.

She used to tell us off for no reason.

PRESENT

(yo) reúno
(tú) reúnes
(él/ella/usted) reúne
(nosotros/as) reunimos
(vosotros/as) reunís
(ellos/ellas/ustedes) reúnen

PRESENT SUBJUNCTIVE

(yo) reúna
(tú) reúnas
(él/ella/usted) reúna
(nosotros/as) reunamos
(vosotros/as) reunáis
(ellos/ellas/ustedes) reúnan

PRETERITE

(yo) reuní
(tú) reuniste
(él/ella/usted) reunió
(nosotros/as) reunimos
(vosotros/as) reunisteis
(ellos/ellas/ustedes) reunieron

IMPERFECT

(yo) reunía
(tú) reunías
(él/ella/usted) reunía
(nosotros/as) reuníamos
(vosotros/as) reuníais
(ellos/ellas/ustedes) reunían

FUTURE

(yo) reuniré
(tú) reunirás
(él/ella/usted) reunirá
(nosotros/as) reuniremos
(vosotros/as) reuniréis
(ellos/ellas/ustedes) reunirán

CONDITIONAL

(yo) reuniría
(tú) reunirías
(él/ella/usted) reuniría
(nosotros/as) reuniríamos
(vosotros/as) reuniríais
(ellos/ellas/ustedes) reunirían

IMPERATIVE

reúne / reunid

PAST PARTICIPLE

reunido

GERUND

reuniendo

——————— EXAMPLE PHRASES ———————

Han **reunido** suficientes pruebas. *They have gathered enough evidence.*

No **reúne** las condiciones necesarias. *He doesn't meet the necessary requirements.*

Se reunían una vez por semana. *They used to meet once a week.*

Table
48

saber *to know*

PRESENT

(yo)	sé
(tú)	sabes
(él/ella/usted)	sabe
(nosotros/as)	sabemos
(vosotros/as)	sabéis
(ellos/ellas/ustedes)	saben

PRESENT SUBJUNCTIVE

(yo)	sepa
(tú)	sepas
(él/ella/usted)	sepa
(nosotros/as)	sepamos
(vosotros/as)	sepáis
(ellos/ellas/ustedes)	sepan

PRETERITE

(yo)	supe
(tú)	supiste
(él/ella/usted)	supo
(nosotros/as)	supimos
(vosotros/as)	supisteis
(ellos/ellas/ustedes)	supieron

IMPERFECT

(yo)	sabía
(tú)	sabías
(él/ella/usted)	sabía
(nosotros/as)	sabíamos
(vosotros/as)	sabíais
(ellos/ellas/ustedes)	sabían

FUTURE

(yo)	sabré
(tú)	sabrás
(él/ella/usted)	sabrá
(nosotros/as)	sabremos
(vosotros/as)	sabréis
(ellos/ellas/ustedes)	sabrán

CONDITIONAL

(yo)	sabría
(tú)	sabrías
(él/ella/usted)	sabría
(nosotros/as)	sabríamos
(vosotros/as)	sabríais
(ellos/ellas/ustedes)	sabrían

IMPERATIVE
sabe / sabed

GERUND
sabiendo

PAST PARTICIPLE

sabido

--- EXAMPLE PHRASES ---

No lo **sé**.	I don't know.
¿**Sabes** una cosa?	Do you know what?
Pensaba que lo **sabías**.	I thought you knew.

PRESENT

(yo)	saco
(tú)	sacas
(él/ella/usted)	saca
(nosotros/as)	sacamos
(vosotros/as)	sacáis
(ellos/ellas/ustedes)	sacan

PRESENT SUBJUNCTIVE

(yo)	saque
(tú)	saques
(él/ella/usted)	saque
(nosotros/as)	saquemos
(vosotros/as)	saquéis
(ellos/ellas/ustedes)	saquen

PRETERITE

(yo)	saqué
(tú)	sacaste
(él/ella/usted)	sacó
(nosotros/as)	sacamos
(vosotros/as)	sacasteis
(ellos/ellas/ustedes)	sacaron

IMPERFECT

(yo)	sacaba
(tú)	sacabas
(él/ella/usted)	sacaba
(nosotros/as)	sacábamos
(vosotros/as)	sacabais
(ellos/ellas/ustedes)	sacaban

FUTURE

(yo)	sacaré
(tú)	sacarás
(él/ella/usted)	sacará
(nosotros/as)	sacaremos
(vosotros/as)	sacaréis
(ellos/ellas/ustedes)	sacarán

CONDITIONAL

(yo)	sacaría
(tú)	sacarías
(él/ella/usted)	sacaría
(nosotros/as)	sacaríamos
(vosotros/as)	sacaríais
(ellos/ellas/ustedes)	sacarían

IMPERATIVE

saca / sacad

PAST PARTICIPLE

sacado

GERUND

sacando

=============== EXAMPLE PHRASES ===============

Ya **he sacado** las entradas.
Saqué un 7 en el examen.
No **saques** la cabeza por la
ventanilla.

I've already bought the tickets.
I got 7 points in the exam.
Don't lean out of the window.

Table
50

salir   _to come out, to go out_

PRESENT

(yo)	salgo
(tú)	sales
(él/ella/usted)	sale
(nosotros/as)	salimos
(vosotros/as)	salís
(ellos/ellas/ustedes)	salen

PRESENT SUBJUNCTIVE

(yo)	salga
(tú)	salgas
(él/ella/usted)	salga
(nosotros/as)	salgamos
(vosotros/as)	salgáis
(ellos/ellas/ustedes)	salgan

PRETERITE

(yo)	salí
(tú)	saliste
(él/ella/usted)	salió
(nosotros/as)	salimos
(vosotros/as)	salisteis
(ellos/ellas/ustedes)	salieron

IMPERFECT

(yo)	salía
(tú)	salías
(él/ella/usted)	salía
(nosotros/as)	salíamos
(vosotros/as)	salíais
(ellos/ellas/ustedes)	salían

FUTURE

(yo)	saldré
(tú)	saldrás
(él/ella/usted)	saldrá
(nosotros/as)	saldremos
(vosotros/as)	saldréis
(ellos/ellas/ustedes)	saldrán

CONDITIONAL

(yo)	saldría
(tú)	saldrías
(él/ella/usted)	saldría
(nosotros/as)	saldríamos
(vosotros/as)	saldríais
(ellos/ellas/ustedes)	saldrían

IMPERATIVE
sal / salid

PAST PARTICIPLE
salido

GERUND
saliendo

———————————— EXAMPLE PHRASES ————————————

Hace tiempo que no **salimos**.

Por favor, **salgan** por la puerta de atrás.

Salió un par de veces con nosotros.

We haven't been out for a while.

Please leave via the back door.

He went out with us a couple of times.

PRESENT

(yo)	sigo
(tú)	sigues
(él/ella/usted)	sigue
(nosotros/as)	seguimos
(vosotros/as)	seguís
(ellos/ellas/ustedes)	siguen

PRESENT SUBJUNCTIVE

(yo)	siga
(tú)	sigas
(él/ella/usted)	siga
(nosotros/as)	sigamos
(vosotros/as)	sigáis
(ellos/ellas/ustedes)	sigan

PRETERITE

(yo)	seguí
(tú)	seguiste
(él/ella/usted)	siguió
(nosotros/as)	seguimos
(vosotros/as)	seguisteis
(ellos/ellas/ustedes)	siguieron

IMPERFECT

(yo)	seguía
(tú)	seguías
(él/ella/usted)	seguía
(nosotros/as)	seguíamos
(vosotros/as)	seguíais
(ellos/ellas/ustedes)	seguían

FUTURE

(yo)	seguiré
(tú)	seguirás
(él/ella/usted)	seguirá
(nosotros/as)	seguiremos
(vosotros/as)	seguiréis
(ellos/ellas/ustedes)	seguirán

CONDITIONAL

(yo)	seguiría
(tú)	seguirías
(él/ella/usted)	seguiría
(nosotros/as)	seguiríamos
(vosotros/as)	seguiríais
(ellos/ellas/ustedes)	seguirían

IMPERATIVE

sigue / seguid

GERUND

siguiendo

PAST PARTICIPLE

seguido

--- EXAMPLE PHRASES ---

Siga por esta calle hasta el final.

Go on till you get to the end of the street.

Nos seguiremos viendo.

We will go on seeing each other.

Nos **siguió** todo el camino.

He followed us all the way.

Table
52

sentir *to feel*

PRESENT		PRESENT SUBJUNCTIVE	
(yo)	siento	(yo)	sienta
(tú)	sientes	(tú)	sientas
(él/ella/usted)	siente	(él/ella/usted)	sienta
(nosotros/as)	sentimos	(nosotros/as)	sintamos
(vosotros/as)	sentís	(vosotros/as)	sintáis
(ellos/ellas/ustedes)	sienten	(ellos/ellas/ustedes)	sientan

PRETERITE		IMPERFECT	
(yo)	sentí	(yo)	sentía
(tú)	sentiste	(tú)	sentías
(él/ella/usted)	sintió	(él/ella/usted)	sentía
(nosotros/as)	sentimos	(nosotros/as)	sentíamos
(vosotros/as)	sentisteis	(vosotros/as)	sentíais
(ellos/ellas/ustedes)	sintieron	(ellos/ellas/ustedes)	sentían

FUTURE		CONDITIONAL	
(yo)	sentiré	(yo)	sentiría
(tú)	sentirás	(tú)	sentirías
(él/ella/usted)	sentirá	(él/ella/usted)	sentiría
(nosotros/as)	sentiremos	(nosotros/as)	sentiríamos
(vosotros/as)	sentiréis	(vosotros/as)	sentiríais
(ellos/ellas/ustedes)	sentirán	(ellos/ellas/ustedes)	sentirían

IMPERATIVE

siente / sentid

PAST PARTICIPLE

sentido

GERUND

sintiendo

--- EXAMPLE PHRASES ---

Siento mucho lo que pasó.

I'm really sorry about what happened.

Sentí un pinchazo en la pierna.
No creo que lo **sienta**.

I felt a sharp pain in my leg.
I don't think she's sorry.

PRESENT

(yo)	soy
(tú)	eres
(él/ella/usted)	es
(nosotros/as)	somos
(vosotros/as)	sois
(ellos/ellas/ustedes)	son

PRESENT SUBJUNCTIVE

(yo)	sea
(tú)	seas
(él/ella/usted)	sea
(nosotros/as)	seamos
(vosotros/as)	seáis
(ellos/ellas/ustedes)	sean

PRETERITE

(yo)	fui
(tú)	fuiste
(él/ella/usted)	fue
(nosotros/as)	fuimos
(vosotros/as)	fuisteis
(ellos/ellas/ustedes)	fueron

IMPERFECT

(yo)	era
(tú)	eras
(él/ella/usted)	era
(nosotros/as)	éramos
(vosotros/as)	erais
(ellos/ellas/ustedes)	eran

FUTURE

(yo)	seré
(tú)	serás
(él/ella/usted)	será
(nosotros/as)	seremos
(vosotros/as)	seréis
(ellos/ellas/ustedes)	serán

CONDITIONAL

(yo)	sería
(tú)	serías
(él/ella/usted)	sería
(nosotros/as)	seríamos
(vosotros/as)	seríais
(ellos/ellas/ustedes)	serían

IMPERATIVE

sé / sed

PAST PARTICIPLE

sido

GERUND

siendo

————————— EXAMPLE PHRASES —————————

Soy español.
¿**Fuiste** tú el que llamó?
Era de noche.

I'm Spanish.
Was it you who phoned?
It was dark.

Table
54

tener *to have*

PRESENT		PRESENT SUBJUNCTIVE	
(yo)	tengo	(yo)	tenga
(tú)	tienes	(tú)	tengas
(él/ella/usted)	tiene	(él/ella/usted)	tenga
(nosotros/as)	tenemos	(nosotros/as)	tengamos
(vosotros/as)	tenéis	(vosotros/as)	tengáis
(ellos/ellas/ustedes)	tienen	(ellos/ellas/ustedes)	tengan

PRETERITE		IMPERFECT	
(yo)	tuve	(yo)	tenía
(tú)	tuviste	(tú)	tenías
(él/ella/usted)	tuvo	(él/ella/usted)	tenía
(nosotros/as)	tuvimos	(nosotros/as)	teníamos
(vosotros/as)	tuvisteis	(vosotros/as)	teníais
(ellos/ellas/ustedes)	tuvieron	(ellos/ellas/ustedes)	tenían

FUTURE		CONDITIONAL	
(yo)	tendré	(yo)	tendría
(tú)	tendrás	(tú)	tendrías
(él/ella/usted)	tendrá	(él/ella/usted)	tendría
(nosotros/as)	tendremos	(nosotros/as)	tendríamos
(vosotros/as)	tendréis	(vosotros/as)	tendríais
(ellos/ellas/ustedes)	tendrán	(ellos/ellas/ustedes)	tendrían

IMPERATIVE
ten / tened

PAST PARTICIPLE
tenido

GERUND
teniendo

================ EXAMPLE PHRASES ================

Tengo sed.
No **tenía** suficiente dinero.
Tuvimos que irnos.

I'm thirsty.
She didn't have enough money.
We had to leave.

PRESENT

(yo)	traigo
(tú)	traes
(él/ella/usted)	trae
(nosotros/as)	traemos
(vosotros/as)	traéis
(ellos/ellas/ustedes)	traen

PRESENT SUBJUNCTIVE

(yo)	traiga
(tú)	traigas
(él/ella/usted)	traiga
(nosotros/as)	traigamos
(vosotros/as)	traigáis
(ellos/ellas/ustedes)	traigan

PRETERITE

(yo)	traje
(tú)	trajiste
(él/ella/usted)	trajo
(nosotros/as)	trajimos
(vosotros/as)	trajisteis
(ellos/ellas/ustedes)	trajeron

IMPERFECT

(yo)	traía
(tú)	traías
(él/ella/usted)	traía
(nosotros/as)	traíamos
(vosotros/as)	traíais
(ellos/ellas/ustedes)	traían

FUTURE

(yo)	traeré
(tú)	traerás
(él/ella/usted)	traerá
(nosotros/as)	traeremos
(vosotros/as)	traeréis
(ellos/ellas/ustedes)	traerán

CONDITIONAL

(yo)	traería
(tú)	traerías
(él/ella/usted)	traería
(nosotros/as)	traeríamos
(vosotros/as)	traeríais
(ellos/ellas/ustedes)	traerían

IMPERATIVE

trae / traed

PAST PARTICIPLE

traído

GERUND

trayendo

──────── EXAMPLE PHRASES ────────

¿**Has traído** lo que te pedí?
No **trajo** el dinero.
Trae eso.

Have you brought what I asked?
He didn't bring the money.
Give that here.

Table
56

valer *to be worth*

PRESENT		PRESENT SUBJUNCTIVE	
(yo)	valgo	(yo)	valga
(tú)	vales	(tú)	valgas
(él/ella/usted)	vale	(él/ella/usted)	valga
(nosotros/as)	valemos	(nosotros/as)	valgamos
(vosotros/as)	valéis	(vosotros/as)	valgáis
(ellos/ellas/ustedes)	valen	(ellos/ellas/ustedes)	valgan

PRETERITE		IMPERFECT	
(yo)	valí	(yo)	valía
(tú)	valiste	(tú)	valías
(él/ella/usted)	valió	(él/ella/usted)	valía
(nosotros/as)	valimos	(nosotros/as)	valíamos
(vosotros/as)	valisteis	(vosotros/as)	valíais
(ellos/ellas/ustedes)	valieron	(ellos/ellas/ustedes)	valían

FUTURE		CONDITIONAL	
(yo)	valdré	(yo)	valdría
(tú)	valdrás	(tú)	valdrías
(él/ella/usted)	valdrá	(él/ella/usted)	valdría
(nosotros/as)	valdremos	(nosotros/as)	valdríamos
(vosotros/as)	valdréis	(vosotros/as)	valdríais
(ellos/ellas/ustedes)	valdrán	(ellos/ellas/ustedes)	valdrían

IMPERATIVE
vale / valed

PAST PARTICIPLE
valido

GERUND
valiendo

EXAMPLE PHRASES

¿Cuánto **vale** eso?	How much is that?
No **valía** la pena.	It wasn't worth it.
Valga lo que **valga**, lo compro.	I'll buy it, no matter how much it costs.

PRESENT

(yo)	vengo
(tú)	vienes
(él/ella/usted)	viene
(nosotros/as)	venimos
(vosotros/as)	venís
(ellos/ellas/ustedes)	vienen

PRESENT SUBJUNCTIVE

(yo)	venga
(tú)	vengas
(él/ella/usted)	venga
(nosotros/as)	vengamos
(vosotros/as)	vengáis
(ellos/ellas/ustedes)	vengan

PRETERITE

(yo)	vine
(tú)	viniste
(él/ella/usted)	vino
(nosotros/as)	vinimos
(vosotros/as)	vinisteis
(ellos/ellas/ustedes)	vinieron

IMPERFECT

(yo)	venía
(tú)	venías
(él/ella/usted)	venía
(nosotros/as)	veníamos
(vosotros/as)	veníais
(ellos/ellas/ustedes)	venían

FUTURE

(yo)	vendré
(tú)	vendrás
(él/ella/usted)	vendrá
(nosotros/as)	vendremos
(vosotros/as)	vendréis
(ellos/ellas/ustedes)	vendrán

CONDITIONAL

(yo)	vendría
(tú)	vendrías
(él/ella/usted)	vendría
(nosotros/as)	vendríamos
(vosotros/as)	vendríais
(ellos/ellas/ustedes)	vendrían

IMPERATIVE
ven / venid

GERUND
viniendo

PAST PARTICIPLE
venido

—— EXAMPLE PHRASES ——

Vengo andando desde la playa.

I've walked all the way from the beach.

¿**Vendrás** conmigo al cine?
Prefiero que no **venga**.

Will you come to see a film with me?
I'd rather he didn't come.

Table
58

ver *to see*

PRESENT

(yo)	veo
(tú)	ves
(él/ella/usted)	ve
(nosotros/as)	vemos
(vosotros/as)	veis
(ellos/ellas/ustedes)	ven

PRESENT SUBJUNCTIVE

(yo)	vea
(tú)	veas
(él/ella/usted)	vea
(nosotros/as)	veamos
(vosotros/as)	veáis
(ellos/ellas/ustedes)	vean

PRETERITE

(yo)	vi
(tú)	viste
(él/ella/usted)	vio
(nosotros/as)	vimos
(vosotros/as)	visteis
(ellos/ellas/ustedes)	vieron

IMPERFECT

(yo)	veía
(tú)	veías
(él/ella/usted)	veía
(nosotros/as)	veíamos
(vosotros/as)	veíais
(ellos/ellas/ustedes)	veían

FUTURE

(yo)	veré
(tú)	verás
(él/ella/usted)	verá
(nosotros/as)	veremos
(vosotros/as)	veréis
(ellos/ellas/ustedes)	verán

CONDITIONAL

(yo)	vería
(tú)	verías
(él/ella/usted)	vería
(nosotros/as)	veríamos
(vosotros/as)	veríais
(ellos/ellas/ustedes)	verían

IMPERATIVE

ve / ved

PAST PARTICIPLE

visto

GERUND

viendo

=========== EXAMPLE PHRASES ===========

No **veo** muy bien.
Los **veía** a todos desde la ventana.
¿**Viste** lo que pasó?

I can't see very well.
I could see them all from the window.
Did you see what happened?

PRESENT

(yo)	vivo
(tú)	vives
(él/ella/usted)	vive
(nosotros/as)	vivimos
(vosotros/as)	vivís
(ellos/ellas/ustedes)	viven

PRESENT SUBJUNCTIVE

(yo)	viva
(tú)	vivas
(él/ella/usted)	viva
(nosotros/as)	vivamos
(vosotros/as)	viváis
(ellos/ellas/ustedes)	vivan

PRETERITE

(yo)	viví
(tú)	viviste
(él/ella/usted)	vivió
(nosotros/as)	vivimos
(vosotros/as)	vivisteis
(ellos/ellas/ustedes)	vivieron

IMPERFECT

(yo)	vivía
(tú)	vivías
(él/ella/usted)	vivía
(nosotros/as)	vivíamos
(vosotros/as)	vivíais
(ellos/ellas/ustedes)	vivían

FUTURE

(yo)	viviré
(tú)	vivirás
(él/ella/usted)	vivirá
(nosotros/as)	viviremos
(vosotros/as)	viviréis
(ellos/ellas/ustedes)	vivirán

CONDITIONAL

(yo)	viviría
(tú)	vivirías
(él/ella/usted)	viviría
(nosotros/as)	viviríamos
(vosotros/as)	viviríais
(ellos/ellas/ustedes)	vivirían

IMPERATIVE

vive / vivid

PAST PARTICIPLE

vivido

GERUND

viviendo

─────── EXAMPLE PHRASES ───────

Vivo en Valencia.
Vivieron juntos dos años.
Hemos vivido momentos difíciles.

I live in Valencia.
They lived together for two years.
We've had some difficult times.

Table
60

volver *to return*

PRESENT		PRESENT SUBJUNCTIVE	
(yo)	vuelvo	(yo)	vuelva
(tú)	vuelves	(tú)	vuelvas
(él/ella/usted)	vuelve	(él/ella/usted)	vuelva
(nosotros/as)	volvemos	(nosotros/as)	volvamos
(vosotros/as)	volvéis	(vosotros/as)	volváis
(ellos/ellas/ustedes)	vuelven	(ellos/ellas/ustedes)	vuelvan

PRETERITE		IMPERFECT	
(yo)	volví	(yo)	volvía
(tú)	volviste	(tú)	volvías
(él/ella/usted)	volvió	(él/ella/usted)	volvía
(nosotros/as)	volvimos	(nosotros/as)	volvíamos
(vosotros/as)	volvisteis	(vosotros/as)	volvíais
(ellos/ellas/ustedes)	volvieron	(ellos/ellas/ustedes)	volvían

FUTURE		CONDITIONAL	
(yo)	volveré	(yo)	volvería
(tú)	volverás	(tú)	volverías
(él/ella/usted)	volverá	(él/ella/usted)	volvería
(nosotros/as)	volveremos	(nosotros/as)	volveríamos
(vosotros/as)	volveréis	(vosotros/as)	volveríais
(ellos/ellas/ustedes)	volverán	(ellos/ellas/ustedes)	volverían

IMPERATIVE
vuelve / volved

PAST PARTICIPLE
vuelto

GERUND
volviendo

--- EXAMPLE PHRASES ---

Mi padre **vuelve** mañana.
No **vuelvas** por aquí.
Ha vuelto a casa.

My father's coming back tomorrow.
Don't come back here.
He's gone back home.